In Hell With Eyes Wide Open

The Saga Continues…

Jean Pauley

The Jean Ellen Novel Series™
Volume II

Copyright © 2009, 2010, 2011 Jean Pauley
All rights reserved.

ISBN: 978-0-9848100-0-0 (paperback)

The Jean Ellen Novel Series™
CreateSpace, a DBA of *On-Demand Publishing, LLC.*
4900 Lacross Rd.
North Charleston, SC, 29406, USA
"IN HELL WITH EYES WIDE OPEN" 2nd Edition, 1st print--paperback, September 2013.

Reproduction or translation of any part of this work beyond that permitted by Section 107 and 108 of the United States Copyright Act without the permission of the copyright owner is unlawful.

This book is sold subject to the condition that it shall not, by way of trade or otherwise, be lent, resold, hired out, or otherwise circulated without the publisher's and author's prior consent in any form of binding or cover other than that in which it is published and without a similar condition including this condition being imposed on the subsequent purchaser.

Legal Disclaimers:
Certain characters in this work are actual people, and some are inventions, and certain events portrayed did take place; however, this is partly a work of fiction. This riveting tale is educational and is a dark comedy characterized by morbid and grimly satiric humor. This story possesses gloomy and disturbing elements. Most, but not all characters, names, incidents, organizations, and dialogues, in the novel series, either are the products of the author's imagination, or are used fictitiously. This book is not intended to provide legal advice and is for informational purposes only. The information in this book may not be suitable for all consumer situations, and contains adult content. For legal advice, consult an attorney.

The views expressed in this work are solely those of the author and do not necessarily reflect the views of the publisher, and the publisher hereby disclaims any responsibility for them.

CONTENTS

	TITLE PAGE	i
	COPYRIGHT	ii
	LEGAL DISCLAIMERS	iii
	CONTENTS	iv-v
	ABOUT THE AUTHOR	vi-vii
	MORE BOOKS BY AUTHOR	viii
	DEDICATION	ix
	VOLUME II AND WARNING	x
1	IT'S JUST A DREAM	1
2	THE JURY TRIAL, 1998	61
3	THE DECEPTION REVEALED	66
4	A LEAP OF FAITH	113
5	UNEQUALLY YOKED	169
6	WHAT'S LOVE GOT TO DO WITH IT?	206

CONTENTS

7	ULTIMATUM	271
8	BREAKING THE CAMEL'S BACK	300
9	THE BETRAYAL	394
10	A FREE PASS OUT OF JAIL	436
11	CHECK MATE	497
12	LEVELING THE PLAYING FIELD	574
13	MAKING A DEAL WITH THE DEVIL	644
14	THE UNIMAGINABLE	687
15	THE ESCAPE	758

ABOUT AUTHOR

Photo by Anne-Marie Pauley

Jean Pauley, author of *Heading For Heartbreak*, her debut novel of her bestseller book series, currently lives in the USA, and pens more psychological-comedic dramas. After twelve years of Catholic school, the author attended University of Houston, Rice University, and University of Arkansas in Little Rock, Arkansas, to name just a few corridors she walked, but graduated in 1999 *cum laud* with a BA in English Literature and a Minor in Behavioral Sciences from Grand Canyon University, a small, private Baptist university in Phoenix, Arizona. Jean Pauley aspires to give back hope to the walking dead. Her award-winning character development leaves her reader salivating for more understanding of the human condition. For three decades, the author has consistently attended seminars at Landmark Education Corporation, which sells paradigm shifts globally. Jean Pauley is a lifetime student in the development of individual transformation, effectiveness, and communication. Her writing reflects the ideas, insights, and distinctions, based on Landmark Education Corporation's technology, but her writing reflects her deep understanding of both the carnal man *and* the spirit man. Her creative energy flows because she connects with the only source of life—the Living God of the Holy Bible and His Son, our Lord, Jesus Christ. This author makes the distinction in her storytelling between the carnal man, whose mind disconnects from his soul, and the spirit man, who connects to something greater than his flesh. What moves, motivates, and inspires the carnal man, is completely different from what moves, motivates, and inspires the spirit man, wherein the Holy Bible is the spirit man's instruction.

MORE BOOKS BY AUTHOR

E-BOOKS and PAPERBACKS now available for sale. Go to www.jeanpauley.com to purchase.

The Jean Ellen Novel Series™ publications include books by Jean Pauley:

Volume I.
HEADING FOR HEARTBREAK
A true tale that launches from a present day child custody trial and tethers to the past decades--a staggering journey of risk, loss, and revelation! Learn how a woman beat scumbag lawyers and bought-off family law judges against all odds.

Volume II.
IN HELL WITH EYES WIDE OPEN
The Saga Continues...

Volume III.
THE PRETENSE, The Closing Argument.
Released 2014.

Volume IV.
FUN IN ORLANDO. A New Chapter.
Release date to be announced.

Dedicated to Will Reece,
Why would a man give me anything unless God had placed an anointing for favor and increase upon my life?
Thank you, beautiful man.

JEAN PAULEY

VOLUME II

FOR MATURE EYES ONLY

WARNING: DO NOT READ, STORE, OR LEAVE THIS HARDBACK, OR PAPERBACK, IN EXTREME HEAT; I.E., POOLSIDE, BEACH, OR SAUNA. THE GLUE IN THE BOOK BINDING/SPINE WILL MELT IN EXTREME TEMPERATURES AND PAGES WILL BECOME LOOSE. READ AND STORE IN A COOL AND DRY PLACE.

JEAN PAULEY

1
IT'S JUST A DREAM

The saga continues...

SEPTEMBER 1988, ONE MONTH BEFORE RICH AND FAMOUS. I drag out of my king-size bed, after a short, mid-day nap, and slip into my pink and white leather boat shoes. My pregnancy makes me feel constantly tired. I consider my new reality, and though still determined to reach my business goal, I have fallen out of my comfort zone. I am in this harsh and ill-fitting place, which demands of me complete faith in God. I had been teetering on the edge of the diving board for the past two years, all the while, wanting to jump off, but not having the courage to make the leap. God put me into this distressing and thorny place—he pushed me off the diving board. My argument that I did not know how to swim was irrelevant. I had begged God to reveal himself to me when I was a young girl on my knees and staring up at the huge crucifix that hung over the alter in our Catholic church. My comfort zone had become a crutch, especially over the last two years, and I had fallen into a place of perversion with the need to lie to preserve what felt familiar. I was a creator of deceits while possessing a crippling fear of the unknown. I had bought the lie. I had led a secret life for two years and had become the great manipulator.

The two-year long debate over whether to move up to Indiana to be with my loving husband, Leonardo, or to stay in Texas for my children, was now over. My indecisiveness dissipated and relief lingered inside of discomfort. This unfamiliar place, with so many unknown variables, frightened me. I was pregnant with Seth's child, his first child, and my third child. I had just enrolled Bella into morning kindergarten. I was running an apparel design, manufacturing, and wholesale business with my unemployed boyfriend, and there was no income of any sort coming into our business. Our funds were quickly depleting. Setting aside the quickly vanishing $10,000 Bank of America loan I took out, without Seth's knowledge, and Seth's $10,000 bodily injury settlement check that we were quickly spending up, too, we had had no income since April, five months earlier.

For the past five months, Seth and I employed two full-time seamstresses, at minimum wage, and paid cheap rent on a commercial building. We had bought food and gas for my van with my credit card. Verna, my lead seamstress, and Gladys's numerous replacements--women who often lied about their sewing skills—all worked for us, from 8-5 pm, Monday through Friday, and they were producing a magnificent 150-piece line of resort wear that I had designed. Seth and I were betting the bank that we would win big orders at the two apparel markets with this flashy spring and summer line.

I heard sewing machine hammers stitching non-stop in the bank lobby, as I brushed out my long, dark brown hair in the back room, where Seth, Bella, and I had been sleeping since moving out of the apartment complex five months earlier. I was walking on a tight rope these days while trying to balance personal well-being and financial well-being. I often prayed that I would have no, unexpected, financial outlays that would burn down my smooth-operating garment factory.

I had maxed out all of my credit cards over the last sixty days and no longer could make the monthly payments on the current debt, nor could I pay the amount due each month to Bank of America on the $10,000 business loan. Creditors had begun ringing my phone non-stop harassing me for payments. I did not even want to think about Leonardo having the van repossessed, the only vehicle Seth and I had available to us, but I was certain my husband had no intention of paying off any vehicle that this unholy union was driving.

I was not excited about my apparel business anymore; on the contrary, I wanted to run away from this wretched reality. I did not want to cope with the stress of deadlines and having no money. I did not want to dwell in this grievous place another day, which raced me toward either, an outcome of poverty—my punishment for having fallen for the lie, or toward a financial reward, unexpected, but the result of God having mercy on me. I felt conflicted over what I could expect in the end. My fears haunted me over my sins, yet I remained hopeful, and kept the faith, that I would have success regardless of what I felt was due me. I recalled as a teenager sitting in the Catholic pew with my parents and siblings during Sunday mass and reading the Penitential Act, part of an hour-long rite that I had become numb to and recited without earnestness.

***

Priest: "Lord, we have sinned against you, Lord have mercy on us."

We, the congregation, responded, "For we have sinned against you. Lord, have mercy."

The priest shouted, "Lord, show us your mercy and love."

The congregation bellowed, "And grant us your salvation."

***

At the time, I considered the ritual to reconcile with God empty and meaningless. These days, prayer was all I had, and I often begged, "Lord, have mercy on me, for I am not worthy to receive you, but only say the word, and I shall be healed."

And while my business had transformed from once being a symbol of my courage and faith, in myself, I now perceived my fledgling business as a result of me being only about myself and having had no relationship with our Lord. On the other hand, I was thrilled about having another child, and worried at the same time that something could be wrong with this child—a punishment of some form for my infidelity and other grievous sin, too hard for me to bear. I had not seen an obstetrician and diligently prayed for my unborn, doubting God had my best in mind. I could not pay my current debts, much less could I afford costly insurance to cover a hospital stay, or expensive doctor visits. I asked God every day to preserve my child in perfect form, and God gave me the insight that I carried a boy.

I had another good reason to worry about this pregnancy, too. My first child, Joseph, was in intensive care for three weeks after his birth with medical bills and surgery costs that mounted up to more than $80,000. Joseph had been born with a birth defect. Ropes of intestine hung outside his abdomen, a condition that happens when something goes awry during organ development between the sixth and tenth week after conception. My son was one in five-thousand babies born with this condition called Gastroschisis, meaning "belly cleft" in Greek. The intestines meet the amniotic fluid and a hard film develops around the intestine, which can hinder the newborn's intestinal function, sometimes for months; and, even worse, sometimes the blood does not reach the twisted intestines and that portion of the intestine dies. Joseph did not have any complications. The doctors stuffed him back together, stitched his abdominal wall closed, and after three weeks, my one-month premature baby ate heartily and was not colicky. I could see, in hindsight, that God's word was good when he instructed that if we pray in numbers, he would answer prayers. Everyone in the family was praying for my firstborn eight years ago.

I wondered who prayed for me in this desperate hour. My mother was not talking to me, nor was my father talking to me. Leonardo would not give me the time of day, anymore, either. My most loyal friends thought I had gone insane and stopped calling me, too. I secretly agreed with their choice to be uninvolved with Seth and me. I had gone completely stupid in their eyes. Even Todd, my first husband, who had driven me away via his alcoholism, now acted arrogant around me and rendered to me looks as if he pitied me! His new attitude toward me stemmed out of the fact that I was no longer a threat to the man who drank himself into a stupor every night. I was no longer in a position to take Todd back to court, over custody of our son, now that Leonardo and I split up.

I paid my employee, Verna, every week, to sew up my beautiful clothes. I confided in the sixty-something year old, and the heavy-set woman was kind to me. I was grateful for my loyal employee and friend; otherwise, without Verna's support, my self-doubts might have been too heavy for me to carry this load, and believe I had what it took to pull off this apparel business.

I knew that I would have a boy with Seth; but, unlike my previous pregnancy with Bella, when the doctor performed a sonogram, and proved the sex of the baby, I had only my intuition to tell me that I would have another son. Was my intuition my soul speaking to my spirit man?

I speculated whether the sonograms caused my firstborn to have the birth defect. I read that a new study suggested exposure to ultrasound affects fetal brain development, but that researchers say the findings in mice should not discourage pregnant women from having ultrasound scans for medical reasons. I did not trust the agenda of the medical profession. We were their lab rats while we afforded the industry to make billions off our participation. The article stated the effects of ultrasound in human brain development are not yet determined, but there are disorders thought to be the result of misplacement of brain cells during the development. These disorders range from mental retardation and childhood epilepsy, to developmental dyslexia, autism spectrum disorders, and schizophrenia. I prayed that my son would not have any of these disorders.

I felt unsure about every aspect of my life. I was learning to disregard my feelings and lean on God. I was waiting on God to give me the answers, but I did not really believe he would talk to me. I struggled to believe God cared anything about me. I was thankful to have another chance to have another child, because, in my mind, this child allowed me to redeem myself. I could and would be a better mother. I had yet to forgive myself over having aborted my unborn child. I had something to prove as a human being made in the image of God. My selfishness had caused me to carry a brutal memory that cost me, at times, a good night of sleep. I was certain that my extreme selfishness was the path to eternal damnation during those sleepless nights. I believed that, in the future, a day would come when alien space ships would descend halfway down the firmament and hover over the world's population. I would not ascend, and be admitted on board, because I would not make the frequency connection with a higher being. I would not ascend to the next dimension, with other light beings and loving souls, because of my greatest sin. My low-light frequency would not plug into their space craft, or plug into their higher minds, and allow them to beam me up to go anywhere better. I would stay on this planet of low light, low-frequency idiots, who were all selfish like me! I imagined what a society of only that mind-set would look like, and wondered how many more lifetimes I would elect to go around these same mountains because I could not see past my emotions and feelings.

Seth, on the other hand, sounded ecstatic about his new life, and frequently boasted the future arrival of his child with me and some of his family members--his mother, Wilma; his teenage brother, Frank; and Demelza, his neurotic sister, who was divorced once, and had two daughters who were Bella's age. All were local family members who Seth, Bella, and I frequently encountered while at his mother's apartment taking showers for the lack of us having our own shower in the bank building where we had been living for the past five months.

Runi, his best friend, who fortunately for me, lived a million miles away in Springfield, Missouri, heard Seth's excitement, daily, over his new-founded apparel empire and unborn child. I did not trust Seth to be who he said he was for me--a straight man in love with me. And while I doubted his words to be sincere, I also believed that Seth wanted this family, too, regardless of whether he was in love with me, or not, or whether he was gay, bi-, or straight. I concluded that Seth wanted to create the loving family unit that he did not have while growing up with an extreme alcoholic and abusive father and a raging, co-dependent mother, who together, as a married couple, had created four children and lived at poverty level in a singlewide most of their lives in Paducah, Kentucky. Perhaps Seth, like me, believed that having a family would provide him an opportunity to prove to himself, that he could do it better than his own parents could as parents and spouses.

My boyfriend telephoned his so-called *brother*, Runi, frequently--sometimes twice a day. If I were privy to their long-distant conversations, and most of the time I was in the room when they talked on the phone, I found myself hanging on to every word Seth spoke, and analyzing each phrase and laugh for homosexual innuendoes. I heard every *"I love you, man!"* that came out of Seth's mouth, as a threat to our relationship. Seth told Runi in every conversation, repeatedly, how much he loved him, and I found his words to his man friend odd. Seth seldom expressed his passion for me. My concept of *them against me* began to take form and erode at my ability to trust Seth.

The apparel markets in Dallas and Chicago were next month; each show was one week long, and both show weeks were back-to-back. All the fabric had finally arrived from the Garment District in New York City, and steady Verna, and a different seamstress we had to hire every week, sewed up my line of resort wear. I had been right about finding good talent--a qualified seamstress was hard to come by. I was sorry to have lost Gladys who, at one point, had been my lead seamstress and best talent.

One new employee had lied to me during her interview about her skill level and told me that she was a professional seamstress, and I did not learn the truth until after she ruined a good portion of my silk taffeta that cost me fifty-dollars a yard. I also got that, no matter how awful an employee, I had no heart to fire anybody--maybe because my former employer fired me, just before I married Todd. I had taken the rejection very hard, so I asked Seth to do the dirty deed—after all, he had appointed himself Vice-President, and me President, as I had learned in a telephone conversation he had with Runi. Seth had no problem carrying out my order to fire anybody. Verna, thereafter, ensured that the new hire created each piece with professional perfection, in a cheap muslin fabric, before anybody chopped into the final textile. I was suspicious that my former employee, Gladys, had told Verna, the day Gladys quit me, to leave me, too, and to go work with her at her mother's alteration shop. I prayed my employee, Verna, would not walk out on me before we got to the markets.

I woke up from my nap feeling thirsty and wanted a Diet Coke. I walked through the lobby and informed the girls, who were sewing, that I was taking a stroll down the street and would return shortly. I headed out the front door of our shop, and down Main

Street, while slowly breathing in the cool, fall air before entering into the hardware store, two doors down. Just inside the entrance was a soda pop machine, but I needed change. I looked around for the storeowner, but, instead, spotted an extravagant model train set. I walked over to appreciate, what obviously took years to build, and what reflected to be, bygone days. I heard a voice from behind me say "Good afternoon."

I turned to see an elderly man, in his late sixties, who I presumed to be the storeowner. I looked up at the tall man and smiled back. "I am fascinated with your choo choo."

He chuckled. "That set reflects the Halcyon Days when Lionel was at its peak in the early 1950's. I'll turn it on for you." He then walked over to a switchboard, at the end of the thirty-foot table, and attempted to entertain me, but a technical issue delayed the fun.

I studied the man while he fiddled with his toy. He wore dungarees and a gold T-shirt sporting the town's high school football team; a burgundy logo of a mean-looking bulldog was on his backside. I heard success and turned my attention from the bald gent to see noisy locomotive engines, with tooting whistles, hauling freight cars while rolling down the winding tracks, with blinking railroad lights, and moving barrier gates at street intersections. "I love it! My children have to see this train set."

"Oh, by all means, bring them over. How old are they?"

"My daughter is five and my son is seven."

"I have grandkids that age and older. I have a grown son and daughter, too--both are married. My son has no kids, but my daughter has the boy and three girls."

"Lucky you--family is the heart of creation."

"It certainly is," he acknowledged with a nod. "The problem with today's world is that too many men do not take on what is their responsibility--and to be fair, women, too. It is the father who is the spiritual head, the priest, and the teacher of the family; but, I guess, all this flies in the face of the *politically correct* feminist teachings."

"I agree."

"Do you really?"

I nodded yeah, but I quietly re-evaluated my beliefs and confirmed that I had little respect for most of the men *in my life*. I was examining their core values.

"Scripture is the instruction book," he continued, "and we are told that fathers are not to exasperate their children, but, instead, are to bring them up in the training and instruction of the Lord-- Ephesians 6:4."

I smiled, and thought about my own father, and how I had run away from his oppressive control, only to find myself married too young, and living with another control freak--an alcoholic in the making.

"Do you read the Bible?" He asked me.

"Uh…not lately." I felt I stood in the midst of a *should have* moment and was embarrassed to not own the knowledge found in the Bible. My childhood did not include us reading the Bible together, or individually, but for me, not having read Scripture was now like not having ever read *The Three Little Pigs*. Where had I been all my life-- behind closed doors?

"Too many feminist teachings of our day have encouraged divorce, too," he reiterated. "Sons need their fathers, too. Jesus worked in a carpenter shop with his father. In the Talmud, it is said that he who does *not* teach his son a trade is considered as having taught him thievery."

"What is the Talmud?"

"It's the rabbinic law."

"Oh." I saw that I had not weaved spiritual knowledge into my life. I gazed back down at the train set, and considered that Seth had gone to Bible College, and earned a Bachelor of Arts Degree in Bible Studies—he knew God's Word, and yet, he had no convictions regarding right and wrong. He had both parents at home while growing up, like me. His father was an alcoholic. My father was *the son* of an alcoholic, and my mother told me that children of alcoholics have the same personality as the alcoholic parent, but without the alcohol. I concluded the alcoholic personality to be insecure, with a need to control, in order to avoid feeling any more pain. My first husband was an alcoholic; and in spite of all Todd's drinking efforts, to avoid feeling whatever thoughts he wanted to suppress, I caused him to feel great pain by my act of unfaithfulness, and proved to him that his life was not, at all, under his control. Seth described his father as an acute and mean alcoholic, and I questioned whether an alcoholic father at home was like having no father at home; and then, I questioned my firstborn's home life with his alcoholic father and became instantly concerned that Todd was teaching our son to control his feelings with alcohol, too.

I felt depressed over my economic situation while I attempted to embrace my pregnant and grim reality without using drugs or alcohol; and, so far, my sobriety was an enlightening experience—I had committed to not allowing my circumstances to control my thoughts, a practice not yet automatic. I felt wrong about leaving my son in his current situation, but I could not rescue Joseph because I did not have lawyer fees. A custody fight would be expensive. I switched gears to avoid more feelings of unworthiness and said to the old man, "I gave my son a train set recently for Christmas, but it didn't hold his attention very long—I think he and his father got rid of my gift. My kids like these video games more. They have the Nintendo Super Mario Brothers' video games. They are obsessed with these games! I'm thinking there should be more in life than playing video games every time they have a free moment. I'm regretting having ever bought the first video game."

He nodded and looked unhappy over my words. "My grandkids sit in front of those video games night and day, too! I don't like them, either. Trains reflected old America. They were the heart of our economy back in the day. I guess these kids don't relate. Did you know that the Lionel Train Company actually had its own television show?"

"No, I didn't know that," I answered while not wanting to tell him I wasn't conscious until recently.

"I'm older than dirt," he said, and then let out a long breath as if missing the old days. "TV mesmerized America and the public's interest in toy trains waned. This train-maker here was the father and son railroad of Joshua Lionel Cowen and Lawrence Cowen. The company ended in 1959 when they sold their interest in Lionel to a distant relative. The founders of Lionel were an immigrant family that arrived in New York after the Civil War--around 1865.

"1865--that was a long time ago. I think people had a stronger work ethic back then, too. Kids worked in the fields. They didn't sit in front of TV or video games all day."

"True! Americans had to rebuild their country after the Civil War."

Leonardo and I once owned an antebellum in Evansville, Indiana, built in 1865, too—the same year the Civil War ended. I missed my sweet husband, and all the ease, and goodness, he brought into my life. I again advanced the topic beyond my sad thoughts of losing my second husband whom I had loved in some odd way. "This train set is a collector's piece," I expressed as I walked around a densely populated city with dozens of buildings, including a church with a towering white steeple, a hardware store with a light in the front window, a pharmacy with a soda fountain, and many homes like my former mansion on the Ohio River. I focused on an animated switch tower, and then on a culver unloader which grabbed metal pipes. There was even an animated sawmill with whirring blades, but my eyes kept darting back to the church with the towering steeple. I felt overwhelmed by my life. I wanted to cry, but refused to break down in front of my neighbor. I held back my tears and lost myself in the perfect little town. There were people dressed in clothing and top hats from another era, and green-tunneled mountains, shaggy trees, images of lakes and working drawbridges with flashing red lights. I had run away from Evansville, Indiana, in fear of what now intrigued me—a small town in the middle of nowhere. "I was born in the wrong era," I admitted. "I wish I had been born in a gentle era like this one."

"You're a young thing. The fifties was a good decade, when people still talked about morals, and when Joe DiMaggio was the star of the New York Yankees." He lit up, "That was my baseball team!"

I could not relate to any team but to Joseph's little league team, and then that thought led me to the time when Todd disparaged my already crippled image to all the parents on our son's team. I was the parent who did not have custody of my child. I already felt as if I were branded with the Puritanical scarlet letter A, required to be worn by adulterers, but Todd's most recent manipulative act was more humiliation than I could bear. He had no right to bring up the details of our demise to all the parents of Joseph's entire team while they ate dinner one night, as a group, at a baseball camp that he purposely did not invite me to attend that weekend. I felt Todd further robbed me of what dignity I had left. I did not want to show my face around the baseball field anymore. I held back my tears of despair. "DiMaggio married Marilyn Monroe," I said while attempting to move past my disheartening story.

The old man lit up at the very mention of the actress. "Monroe had three marriages--first to James Dougherty, then to Joe DiMaggio, and lastly, to Arthur Miller. It was also widely rumored that she had had an affair with President John F. Kennedy, his brother Senator Robert Kennedy, or both. Marlon Brando, in his autobiography *Songs My Mother Taught Me*, also claimed that he had had a relationship with her."

"Busy woman," I quipped while relating to Marilyn's search for happiness. She was the most beautiful and sexy woman in Hollywood, and every man wanted her, yet she was so miserable that she committed suicide. I related to her dysfunctional life, to her extreme unhappiness, but I would never kill myself. I would not exit at the bottom—no way.

I was still thinking about my son, his baseball team, and Todd's mean act, when he told the little league gang that I was an unfaithful wife and got pregnant with another man's child while still married to him. My ex-husband had managed to alienate me from my son's life by disparaging my character to all the parents on the little league team, and I suspected, to anyone else who would listen to the victim's story. I felt angry while I picked up a disabled flatbed train car with an airplane mounted on top with words painted on the side of its cargo--*Beechcraft Bonanza*. I sat the piece down and examined another military--looking flatbed.

"That piece in your hand was what Lionel introduced about the time you were born," the storeowner added. "They called that car the *Atomic Energy Commission*. That is a rocket launcher car. There was a cold war going on here in America."

"I remember. I'm glad the wars are finally over," I inputted while I sat his collectible down and noted I had little regard for war or for war memorabilia. "All I remember, on the six o'clock news, while growing up, were body sacks coming back from Vietnam." I shrugged off grim memories of chronic warring that lasted the first eighteen years of my life. I rubbed my swollen belly while silently praying that my children would never experience war.

"The railroads were literally America's engines of progress. The Golden Spike meeting of the Union Pacific and Central Pacific lines, in 1869, unified the continent, and signaled the birth of a world power; but when the 60's arrived, the railroads scrapped passenger lines, and Americans started driving to the suburbs and flying cross-country. That decade saw the demise of New York's Pennsylvania Station, and the retirement of the Twentieth Century Limited, and the passing of the founder of the Lionel Company. The railroad was no longer our cultural icon."

"You're very interesting," I said while I looked at my watch and saw that it was nearly noon. "I have to go pick up my daughter from school. She's in half-day kindergarten."

"Do your kids go to La Porte Elementary?"

I felt uncomfortable telling people about having split up my kids in a divorce. What a mistake, I had been a fool. "Yes, they do." I lied and quickly changed the topic to avoid telling him that I had given up my firstborn when I did not have to, because I had suffered from guilt, and worse, I had left him with an alcoholic. I felt I was falling apart at every seam. Everything about my life was wrong! I managed to hold it together, in front of the stranger while adhering to a strict code to not make him feel uncomfortable with a show of my weakness, but I needed to quickly escape before I fell apart. "Before I forget, I came in here to buy a Diet Coke. Do you have change for a dollar?"

"Certainly!" He trotted behind his counter and gave me silver out of his cash register drawer. "God bless you. Come see me again."

I smiled and felt somebody cared about me while I exchanged a paper bill for his coins. My eyes welled up. Up until that moment, I felt the whole world rejected me--my two children, my parents, my relatives, my best employee--Gladys, my ex-husband--Todd, and my current husband--Leonardo. Even my current boyfriend was wrong-- Seth did not love me. "God bless you, too," I whispered to the wise man from another era, while I wiped a tear off my cheek. "Thank you for the change and for the history lesson."

"You're welcome," he smiled. "Are you okay?"

"Yeah, I am," I nodded while keeping a stiff upper lip. "I'm just tired, very tired, and very thirsty." I walked over to the door and dropped coins into his machine, but I knew Diet Coke was not what I needed to quench my thirst. I needed something more satisfying in my life. I waved goodbye and hurried toward my red van parked behind our building. I first flew into my shop to see if Seth had come home yet, but the girls had not seen him. He did not have a vehicle, so he had to be nearby, or at least within walking distance. Maybe he went down to *Angel's Diner*. I exited the rear door of my sewing shop, jumped back into my red cargo van, and headed toward Bella's elementary school. I wondered if Seth was being faithful to me, and recalled the day Bella told me that she saw Seth and David kissing in Florida.

***

Seth had entered into my apartment a few hours after Bella shocked me with what she had witnessed in the Clearwater, Florida hotel; but, before Seth came home, and painted any pictures for me in his defense, I had already drawn my own conclusions about him and the hotel bartender. I knew that David was angry that I showed up at his hotel, unwilling to continue a romantic relationship with him, and the fact that I had brought my handsome neighbor with me was a double slap in David's pretty GQ model's face. I had also thwarted any continued play with my handsome neighbor with the sloping brow, sculpted face, and deep-set green eyes, when I told Seth that he and I were *not* going to carry on sexually after we left Key West because I was reuniting with the bartender to continue the relationship we had started a few weeks earlier. I felt Seth and I had seduced each other in Key West for reasons that had nothing to do with love. I did not trust Seth's motives, either. I figured my neighbor was jealous of David, and had bragged to the bartender about our fling in Key West, too. I had changed my mind about David while I was in Key West with Seth. I did not trust the bartender's motives either, and thought of him as the hotel gigolo. I speculated, too, that when I left the Clearwater hotel that night, with my surprise visitor from Switzerland, that David may have set up Seth to lose, with David's attitude being that if he was going to lose me, then Seth would lose me, too--you know, male ego running amuck. David may have kissed Seth knowing that Bella was awake and watching them, which would explain why David warned me the following morning to be more cautious about who I left Bella with overnight. If David's act meant that braggadocios Seth would lose me, then perhaps David felt the unveiling of his secret was worth the sacrifice, while knowing that Bella would tell me what she had seen that night in their room. If so, David's plan worked. Seth being gay, and me being pregnant with his child, completed freaked me out.

After Bella let the cat out of the bag, I treated Seth indifferently when he walked into my apartment several hours later, but he did *not* notice my change in attitude because he was determined to find his sunglasses.

"I've misplaced my shades. Have you seen them, Jean?" He asked while turning up sofa cushions in my living room.

"No, I haven't. What do they look like?" I impatiently answered while I stood there with my arms folded and on the defensive.

"They are gold wire with rose-colored lenses."

"I find that ironic, Seth, that it is *you* and *not me* who wear the rose-colored glasses! The table has certainly turned on me!"

"Where's Bella?" He asked.

Obviously, my last statement flew right over his head. "She's two doors down, at Daddy's apartment."

"I bet your daughter took my sunglasses," he said while storming into her bedroom.

I stood in the living room and considered the choices I had available to me. I could throw out the unemployed liar with no car, or

I could look the other way, and keep my plan in place. My thoughts were distracted when Seth came marching out of Bella's bedroom with a twisted pair of gold-rim sunglasses and yelling at me. "Look at what I found in the bottom of her closet! Look what she did to my glasses!"

"I'm sorry," I said with absolutely no sympathy. "Why would she do that to your glasses?"

"Because she doesn't like me."

"And why not, Seth?" I challenged.

"Why would I know?" He snipped. "Maybe she's just a spoiled brat who is angry that mama has a new boyfriend?"

"Or maybe she doesn't like you because she thinks you're a bad person!"

"What?" He indignantly prompted.

"A liar is a bad person, right?"

"What are you saying?" He snarled.

"Bella saw you kissing David."

He laughed as if ridiculous. "She saw what?"

"She saw you and David kissing in that hotel room that night I was at Cliff's beach house."

"She's lying."

"I don't think so, Seth."

"She's lying," he repeated.

"She's never been around that kind of behavior. Bella wouldn't even know men kissed, had she not seen you and David kissing that night. I assume you are bi-sexual?"

"That's absurd."

"Are you?"

"No! I am not bi-sexual!"

"Are you gay, Seth?"

"Are you, Jean?"

"No, Seth, I am not gay. And no one is saying anything to the contrary about my sexual orientation, either."

"Bella is lying. She's just angry that I pushed Leonardo out of the picture."

"Ooooh!" I exhorted while recalling that day in my lawyer's office. "It makes sense to me now. I get why you wanted to tell my lawyer that horrible lie about Leonardo."

"What lie?"

"What lie? You told my father's friend, Attorney Hoppas, that Leonardo was a homosexual. Why, Seth? Why did you say that about my husband?"

"I just thought it would help you."

"Help *you*, you mean. You told that lie to that lawyer so that when I eventually found out the truth about you, you would have a defense."

"What the hell are you talking about?"

"I got your number, Seth. If I had supported your lie, and had told my dad's friend that Leonardo was gay, then later, down the road, when I found you out to be a homo, or a bi-, all the same to me, then you would defend yourself, and plant the seed of doubt in everyone's mind, by telling them that I call everyone, that I'm about to divorce, *gay*. You were setting me up!"

"Oh, you are crazy, Jean." He sneered.

"No, I am not!—But you are seriously evil, Seth."

The slight, dark-haired, thirty-two year old male laughed.

"What is so funny?" I felt exasperated while Seth remained silent. I continued putting the pieces together. "David asked me the morning after you two drank a bottle of *Jack*, why I would just go off and leave my daughter with strange men. What a fool I was! I told him that I trusted you. He warned me about you and said I didn't really know you."

"He was just jealous because you and I had been together in Key West."

***

I snapped out of the memory of that argument I had with Seth while I became aware that I would never trust him. The father of my third child was a chronic liar; and ironically, while I admitted that I, too, had been a great liar for years while married to Leonardo, I now saw that I had manifested a mirror image of myself in the form of

Seth. I could not turn back the hands of time, either. Fate had a hold on my life. I suddenly felt stuck in hell with eyes wide open. I had no choices anymore.

I drove up to the front of the La Porte Elementary School and saw my beautiful kindergartner standing there with her teacher and classmates, waiting for me to pick her up. I recognized that God blessed me with wholesome when He gave me my first two children, and I wanted this next child, more than anything in the world. I considered who I was and felt confused. Why did I suffer now from an identity crisis?

I recalled a childhood Biblical story often read to me from the pulpit. Eve had told the serpent, "We may eat the fruit of the tree of the garden, but of the fruit of the tree, which is in the midst of the garden, God has said, 'You shall not eat it, nor shall you touch it, lest you die.'" Then the serpent said to the woman, "You will *not* surely die. For God knows that in the day you eat of it, your eyes will be opened; and you will be like God, knowing good and evil." I never thought much about the story until now. Eve did not know who she was when the serpent tempted her; and the serpent lied to her when he told her that *if* she ate the forbidden fruit, *then* her eyes would be open, and she would be like God. In that moment, when Eve took the bait, Eve did not know that she was already like God and that her eyes were already open—she suffered an identity crisis, too. In the Book of Genesis, God said, "Let US make man in OUR image, according to OUR likeness…so God created man in His own image." I was beginning to see the Light.

WEEKS LATER and I found myself on the phone begging a nineteen-year old, hung-over, college coed, to be her word. "I don't have money," I begged Stephanie, "but I'll make you my spokes model when I make the big time."

"Oh, I don't know," she moaned. "I was up too late last night. I look like shit."

"I know you drank too much, but you could never take a bad picture."

"My boyfriend is here with me, right now. We don't have a car."

"I'll pick you up, p-l-e-a-s-e, Stephanie."

"I don't know," she groaned again. "I'm still in bed."

"You have to do this for me," I begged the daughter of my best friend, Charley. "I designed these clothes for women like you and me. I can't use one of these short, stacked hoodwinks. I need your 5'10" self. You won't regret it, p-l-e-a-s-e, do this for me."

"Okay," she acquiesced, "but you have to pick me up."

"Not a problem."

"And I'm going to bring my boyfriend with me today," she added.

"No problem—maybe we'll use him, too. Tell him to wear shorts."

"He's very good looking."

"I wouldn't expect anything different from you, Steph."

"What time will you be here?"

I looked at my clock and it was nearly 10:00 a.m. "How far is Sam Houston State from me?"

"From where you are to Huntsville is about a one-hour and forty-minute drive."

I looked at the clock again. "Okay. Seth and I will leave now. We'll be there before noon."

"Okay. We're going back to sleep."

"Be ready when I get there."

"Okay," she said as if my demand was taxing on her.

I hung up the phone and looked at my boyfriend. "That was like pulling wisdom teeth. Last night was Homecoming."

"I'll grab the keys to the van," Seth offered. "What do we need to take with us?"

"All these rack of clothes," I said while I scanned the bank lobby. "And shoes and accessories--I'll put it all together. We'll drop Bella at Todd's before we head north. I'll call our photographers, before we leave for Huntsville, and let them know what time to meet us at the hotel in Galveston. I'll tell them to meet us in the lobby of the San Louis Hotel on the seawall. We'll walk across the street and shoot on the beach first, before the sun goes down. I want sand dunes in the pictures."

"How long is the drive from the university to Galveston?" He asked me.

"What do you think? Two hours?"

"About that," he answered. "Tell the team to meet us at 2:00 p.m. We don't want to wait on them to make an hour drive from Clear Lake City."

"That's not going to leave us a lot of time to shoot before the sun goes down."

"Eight posters is the objective, right?" Seth reminded.

"Right, we'll just shoot until we can't shoot. I paid the photographers $1200 up front. We'll get our money's worth."

"And what will the posters cost us?"

"She said to blow up a photograph to poster-size will be $250 each."

"So we'll need to shell out another $2,000?" He appeared concerned over the cost.

I nodded no while not wanting to disclose that I had already paid the photographers in full with the last of the $10,000 loan I borrowed from the bank.

"How much more do we have to come up with?"

"They gave me a discount. The $1200 covers everything." I lied to preserve the day.

"Good," Seth said as he rolled a rack of our collection toward the back door. We parked our van behind the building. "We better hurry," he urged.

I picked up the phone and dialed Todd to let him know that I would drop Bella at his apartment, before we did an all-day photo shoot in Galveston, Texas. He agreed to keep his daughter for the day, and then I scrambled to collect my own personal shoes and accessories for Charley's oldest child to wear that day.

THE PHOTO SHOOT. We first shot on the isolated beach. We posed Stephanie, along with her boyfriend, in the dunes. All he wore was only a pair of short shorts with our emphasis placed on the beautiful, tall blonde woman wearing my pink and gold sarong resort wear. Her boyfriend's strong physique and handsome face added to the intrigue of our photos, but he paled in comparison to Miss Texas runner-up. After many shots, in many outfits, in the dunes, we then headed toward the water where a blue and white catamaran floated curiously up to shore. The owners, three, young, college-age boys, were more than happy to allow Stephanie to climb onboard their boat. We shot her standing next to the mast wearing a long, slinky, halter-top dress in a polyester print called blue sharks tooth. She wore an over-sized brim straw hat and no shoes. Her boyfriend did not get on the boat, and the owners obliged us when we asked them to step off their boat. The hotel across the street was happy to host *Jean Wynn, the American Designer* and her entourage that included her assistant, two photographers, and two models. Seth, my assistant, and the creator of large tales, told the desk clerk and hotel manager that we were doing a shoot for a glossy, Texas magazine, which would feature our clothes and their five-star hotel. The hotel allowed us to take over the grand lobby that evening. We shot pictures of Stephanie grabbing onto a Mayan face carved out of a large, smooth stone that sat on a pedestal on the granite floor. She wore my turquoise and yellow backless jumpsuit in another picture, with a blue and goldenrod Macaw Parrot perched on her arm. A staff member from behind the front desk took the huge bird out of a cage in the lobby upon our request to accessorize. We shot leggy pictures of the blonde siren wearing a sexy, sand color, trench coat dress while she held open the elevator doors off the lobby with a come-hither look. We then headed out to the back of the hotel, to the pool area. We shot her wearing a long, slinky, swimsuit cover-up as she stepped into a natural form pool just as the sun set. We shot from early afternoon until dark. We did a sunset shoot capturing silhouettes of palm trees. Spotlights, which normally shone on palm tree bases at dark, now reflected off Stephanie and my resort wear collection. My model stood in the center of an arched bridge over the hotel's pool, an ideal prop for my metallic-colored silk taffeta garments.

A WEEK LATER. While the husband and wife photography team developed my pictures, I drove Seth and my two young children--Bella and Joseph--over to a sprawling, vacant, one-story, waterfront home in Nassau Bay, not far from the Johnson Space Center entrance. The 570-acre community of Nassau Bay, established in the early sixties, and originally called home by the astronauts, remained to be a well-maintained residential area, with its own parks and yacht club. I had been eyeing this community since I was a child. The waterfront homes had originally sold from $20,000 to $30,000 in 1963; and now, twenty-five years later, the cost to me would be $650,000 for the same home on the water.

My parents drove us four kids to Clear Lake City every summer to swim and play in a park owned by my father's employer. The paper mill had bought acreage off NASA Rd. 1 during the sixties; and I loved nothing more, than diving into the park's pool, with my sister and two brothers, on a Sunday afternoon, and then running down to the edge of the salty lake, under the piney thicket, and watching the speedboats bounce off the water. I remember riding in the back of my father's four-door sedan, sitting beside my three siblings and gawking at the beautiful two-story brick homes with immaculate green yards and wishing we lived in the neighborhood near the park, instead of us having to commute twenty miles from southeast Houston. Fortunately, for my own pride, my father drove a fairly new, Chevrolet Bel Air, which he bragged he paid only the factory price of $2,508.00; and, while we cruised through fancy neighborhoods for aerospace and chemical engineers, we did not look like we lived on the poor side of the tracks. I would ask my parents why we did not live in one of these fine, two-story houses, and my mother would answer that the homes were too expensive in Clear Lake Forest for an accountant who worked at a paper mill. I questioned why my father did not get a better paying job. After all, he was a college graduate. Why did he work the same poor paying job his entire life?

I pulled up to a home in a cul-de-sac, on the water, in Nassau Bay, with Seth and my two children. I pointed to the *For Sale* sign.

"This is the house I have my eyes set on. I love the three sets of double doors at the top of the steps."

Seth nodded. "Wow, Jean, quite an impressive home."

"This place is my motivation and my goal. It's vacant."

"Mommy, are you going to buy that house?" Bella asked.

I turned and looked into the back of the van at my two young children who stood behind me and peered out the front window, too. "If I sell a lot of clothes and make enough money, then that's my plan."

"Oh!" five year Bella exclaimed. "I like this house better than the Indiana house."

"Me too," I agreed while I recalled the three-story antebellum Leonardo bought me in hopes that I would move up there permanently. "This house is three miles from where you live, Joseph."

He smiled and then exclaimed, "This house has a swimming pool, Mommy!" My eight-year old son read that fact from the signpost of information.

"Yes," I answered, "and a lake and a boat house, too."

Seth opened his door. "Let's walk around to the back. I want to see this spread."

"Me, too," Joseph inputted as he walked in between the two captain chairs and jumped out Seth's front door. Bella exited through my driver's side door.

We walked around the side of the house to find mature palm trees planted along the waterfront, and an empty boathouse made of wood with a wood shingle roof to match the estate. The backside of the sprawling estate was floor to ceiling windows, and we all peered into the magnificent house while imagining what it would be like to live like royalty. I secretly wished for the life I once had with Leonardo. Seth, Bella, and I had been living in the bank for months now, and, by our standards, we considered a bathing facility a luxury.

"Look at the shower, Jean!" Seth said as we peered into a bathroom of granite walls, floor, and gold fixtures.

"Wow, a shower for six. What would that be like?"

"And three shower heads! I could get use to this lifestyle," Seth added with excitement and then turned to look at me. "Do you think that we'll get a lot of orders next week?"

I shrugged, "I don't know. I hope so." I turned and walked out onto the pool deck, and then stepped up onto the diving board. "I'm counting on a huge amount of orders. If not, then we're in trouble, Seth. We're just about out of money." I laid down on the diving board and looked into the deep end of the pool while Seth sat down on the edge of the pool nearby me and dangled his feet in the water.

"Do you *really* think we will sell a lot of clothes, Jean?"

"I like our product line, don't you?" I asked with doubt.

He nodded, "Yeah, our clothes are great."

"They are, aren't they? I doubted my opinion. "Some of those three hundred buyers, that I sent invitations to, should come to our showroom, although I have not one RSVP. I firmly believe though, that if they see what I'm selling, they will order."

"I hope you're right, Jean."

I hoped I was right, too, and prayed that the buyers would just drop in. I watched Bella and Joseph chase each other near the lake. They laughed and seemed so carefree while I tried to consider a single reason for why we would not have enough orders, after next week, to pull ourselves out of this bleak-looking hole.

My son ran up to me and interrupted my consideration. "Are you going to buy a boat for the boat house, Mommy?"

I smiled. "First, we have to buy the house, son, then the furniture, and then the boat."

"Buy a motor boat, Mom, not a sailboat. Sailboats are too slow," Joseph offered.

I smiled at my son while I speculated over how long Leonardo would allow me and Seth to drive the van while neither one of us made payments on the vehicle? Surely, my estranged husband had no grace in his heart for either one of us; and, it was just a matter of time, before the repo man showed up at the door of the old bank building that we called home. "I like speed boats, too, Joseph." I said while I shrugged off the looming transportation problem and kept my confidence up. In my mind's eye, I could see me at the upcoming markets, talking to buyers, writing up orders. I would go to a lender, after the two shows, with all my orders, and get a short-term loan, so that we could manufacturer our product and deliver orders just before spring. My expectations seemed reasonable, though I doubted I could get another loan, since I had stopped making payments on the $10,000 loan that I had borrowed from my bank after Leonardo called it quits. My clothing designs were pretty, and I could produce them in mass quantity with a loan. I could take my orders over the border of Mexico and get them sewn up cheaper. I would figure out how to pay for production after I got the apparel orders. As long as I had the orders, I would be fine. I laid there on the diving board while looking into the deep and absorbing my future and wondering how God felt about my plans. Would he help me? I figured I was not in God's good grace, either, and did not want to look too close at that relationship.

Later that evening while back home at the bank building off Main Street in La Porte, Texas, I answered my ringing phone. "Hello."

"Jean Ellen, this is your mother."

Her voice always cracked when she was nervous. "I know your voice, Mom."

"Are you okay?"

"I'm hanging on," I answered while feeling hurt that she had not spoken to me in months.

"I'm just stunned, Jean Ellen--just sick! I cannot believe that you left that sweet husband of yours for--"

I interrupted. "I'm pregnant, Mom."

"Your father and I heard that from Leonardo. You broke that sweet man's heart."

"Oh, boo hoo! You didn't get his wedding invitation, Mom?" I chided.

"Your father and I are so upset with you. You don't have enough sense to come out of the rain."

"I don't want to hear it!" I snapped. "Life is what it is, now, Mom. I'm having a child with Seth."

"That man sucked you up like a vacuum. He's trash and he's going to spit you out as fast as you--"

"I'm not going to listen to this!" I said before slamming the phone down on the woman. I was so sad and angry to have lost my mother's support. I wanted to cry, but couldn't feel anything but anger. She had not once, set foot in my La Porte bank, to see my 150-piece spring line of women's resort wear. I had learned, early in life, not to expect emotional support from the German stoic I called Dad; however, my sweet mother had always encouraged me to live large, until recently. I recalled dropping in on my parents with Leonardo one evening, and that after my husband told my father about his great job offer in Indiana, and then disclosed to him that I did not want to leave Houston and my six-year old son, that my father responded, "Take the job, Leonardo. Move up to Indiana. She'll follow you." I threw Dad an angry look that evening, shook my head in disappointment, and then walked out of their living room to find my mother.

Seth had watched me battle my mother over the phone and then hang up on her. "What's up?" He asked.

"My mother is angry that I divorced Leonardo. She doesn't care that I'm pregnant. She hates you."

He laughed. "She'll come around, Jean."

"I won't hold my breath. You know," I angrily blasted, "I ran away from home to get away from that control freak I call my father. Now, she's angry with me for leaving Leonardo because she was hoping to move into the upstairs apartment in our Indiana home and leave the control freak for good. I mistakenly married a drunk the first time, and my parents thought I should stay miserably married to Todd, that I had no further choices, after they protested our wedding. Moreover, when I left Todd, against their wishes, they supported him getting custody of our son. Now, my son is growing up with an alcoholic! Had my parents ever supported me, even once in my life, I would *not* have been torn between my second husband and my first-born child over the last two years. My father advised Leonardo to go to Indiana and take that job regardless of my feelings about not wanting to move away from my son, and here I am! I'm the bad guy!"

"Forget about them. You don't need them."

"No, I don't!" I fumed, but I really did not believe Seth's words. I did need my parents' support, but I did not feel that I ever had their support a day in my life.

THE APPAREL MARKET. OCTOBER 1988. Finally, my day of reckoning had arrived. Seth backed into the unloading docks of the Dallas Market Center, the heart of the World Trade Center, Trade Mart, and International Apparel Mart and Market Hall. Other regional wholesalers also unloaded their vans of showroom décor, furniture, clothing racks, and hundreds of boxes of apparel, and everything else needed, to set up, from scratch, a glitzy eye-catching store. I pulled out a map of the 1.8 million square foot facility to get our bearings. "I'm so excited, Seth. I created this possibility out of nothing! I caused this dream to come to fruition. This act makes me like a god, right?" I smiled while waiting for a remark.

Seth chuckled, "Firstly, *we* created this dream."

I smiled and repeated, "We" while I considered that Leonardo and I, together, spent $70,000 on my business, and Seth invested $10,000—his settlement check from his car wreck.

"And let's hope *we* have the luck of Calvin Klein today!"

"Luck?" I asked.

"You told me that a buyer, from a big department store chain, got off the wrong floor and saw Klein's designs, and then placed a $50,000 order."

"Yep," I confirmed with a nod, "he got a $50,000 order from a retailing giant, Bonwit Teller, which changed the life of the ingenious designer. I don't believe in luck, or accident."

"Why not?"

"Luck is man-made, and yuck is luck gone bad. Events occur when they do, because they are caused by prior events, and those events were caused to occur when they did by events yet more prior, and so on, and so on, all the way back to the beginning of time." I waited for his response.

Seth chuckled just before throwing my red van into park and getting out. I hastily jumped out, too, while Seth continued to talk to me over the hood of our red van. "The ancients call that belief of yours *fate*--the sequence of causes which form the entire history of the world."

"I call it *what goes around comes around*--both the good and the bad cause a sequence of events."

"So do you believe that we have choice?" Seth inquired of me.

"Yes and no."

"You chose to create this company, didn't you?"

"Did I?"

"Yes, you did," he answered.

"Maybe God chose to give me the idea to create it?"

"Then you're a puppet with options set by God?"

"Maybe I am a puppet."

Seth chuckled. "So why bother to aim at anything at all, if you are just God's puppet?"

I shrugged without an answer. I did not know the answer.

Seth continued, "So, you believe, that if a certain event has been fated to occur for all time, why worry about trying to bring A about, if B is fated? B will happen whatever you do?"

I looked at Seth and smiled. "No, B will not necessarily happen, even if Plan B might have been part of God's purpose for my life. I believe a person can screw up the original plan once set in motion by God."

Seth nodded as if he considered the validity of my answer.

I considered the man I still loved in Switzerland, and how I ended our relationship. Cliff had my heart from day one. Perhaps the man I met in Florida was fated to be more than a summer romance. Had I never met Todd Wynn, then I would have never gone to the hotel in Clearwater, Florida the first time. In addition, had I not ever gone to that hotel where I would eventually spend many summers thereafter, with various other men, I would have never met Cliff. In addition, what if I had just been faithful to Leonardo, moved to Indiana, and trusted that God would make everything okay with my two children and me? Or, better yet, what if I had remained faithful to my first husband and not divorced Todd? Perhaps Todd would be sober today.

I continued to share my considerations with Seth. "If all I had to do was make the right choice, based on God's Word, then I would be heading toward my destiny, right?"

Seth shrugged, "I don't know."

"You're the Bible college graduate! Why don't you know?"

He laughed. "I need a smoke," he said while he took out a pack of cigarettes from his shirt pocket and lit one up.

"Perhaps when my parents had protested my first marriage to Todd, and I did not honor thy parents, as God commands us, I jumped onto the wrong path? I wonder, how do I get back on track, or better, how would I know I am on the right path, if I ever get there?"

"You can't start over, you can start again. All you have is just today. Yesterday doesn't exist and tomorrow may never come."

I considered Seth's words while I watched him climb up onto the dock and pull a large, flatbed cart, on wheels, down the ramp, to the back of the van. He opened the back doors of our vehicle while I considered my next words. "It's true that yesterday is gone and over, but today was created out of yesterday. Did I make the right choices yesterday?" I cringed at my answer while I helped Seth lift a rattan couch out of the back of my red van.

"Too late, if you didn't," he shot back while we positioned the sofa onto a large cart on wheels.

I tittered while I considered the magnitude of his statement. I did not make choices based on obeying God's Word. I worried about everything these days, especially my future. I shrugged off my anxiety and stayed in the moment. "We'll have to make many trips down here," I said while referring to all the heavy furniture we would have to haul up to our showroom. "Let's leave this sofa here for now and check in. We need the keys to the showroom, and I don't want to cart this sofa any further than I have to."

"Are you sure?" Seth asked as if believing our sofa might disappear.

"Lock up the van," I said while I pulled my soft, black leather brief case out of the back. "These are business people here, not thieves, and they don't care about our couch."

Seth did as I instructed, and then we walked through the nearby, heavy steel doors and started following signs down a long, underground tunnel that led us to *Convention Center Showroom Management*. Once we passed through another set of heavy, steel doors, and went up another flight, via escalator, we found ourselves inside a crowded maze. We passed through thick, noisy crowds and passed what felt like miles, and miles, of glass-front showrooms, hundreds of sample stores with beautiful décor, lights, and furnishings, highlighting beautiful apparel. I was impressed with most presentations, but sure that these vendors had nothing on me. I planned to hang my huge, black, *Plexiglas* sign, with illuminated, white neon script, spelling *Jean Wynn, an American Designer*, smack dab in the center of my showroom. *Who I was* would be the first thing buyers saw when they walked through my showroom doors. I had numerous round racks and square racks--enough clothing racks to hang all one hundred and fifty pieces of my colorful resort wear collection. I had handpicked my glass-front showroom, and had reserved my space months ago, in the Women's Wear Section, of this huge apparel market, that management defined as a *spring and summer apparel show*. Buyers, who bought their women's wear for all the Macy's and Dillard's department stores, and other anchor stores, at the malls, across this quadrant of America, shopped here this week; and those, who owned clothing boutiques, that sold only women's apparel purchased their inventory here this week, too. I was quite optimistic about the event while I walked with Seth toward the management's office of the convention center, to pick up the keys to my front door. I reserved my showroom in an area of the convention center, for those like myself, who wanted a showroom just for this particular exhibition--an area called the Temporary Showrooms for Women's Wear. Seth and I walked through the high rent, permanent, showroom area called *Group III* on our way up to Management's Office. I studied the high-end showrooms while I dreamed of one day being one of these fashion designers. These exquisite showrooms were where brokers for the top apparel manufacturers like Calvin Klein, Liz Claiborne, Bill Blass, and Yves Saint Laurent sold their designs. I read a sign in the hallway advertising *District One Five Lounge* on the top floor, claiming to have a panoramic view of downtown Dallas. I was watching a couple of beautiful, young models sauntering around in clothes with paper hangtags still on them, when Seth spoke to me, "You ought to walk around wearing our designs, too."

"That's a good idea. I'll change into one of our outfits after we get set up." I laughed, "I'll be known as the pregnant model wearing resort wear! That's funny!"

Seth laughed. "You show a little, but being different is the whole point here."

"True."

He continued, "After seeing the energy the vendors put into setting up each one of these showrooms, I can see we have a lot of work to do before tomorrow. We need to buy some colorful crepe paper for starters. The way it looks to me, everyone set up days ago."

"I didn't think to ask when we could come in and set up. I assumed we had one day, but I guess that assumption was crazy thinking on my part."

"Even if we had a week to set up, Jean, we don't have an extra day in hotel charges. We're doing the best we can, with our limited funds. We don't need more than a day to set up our showroom."

"What *I needed* was a financial consultant to help me price our stuff," I said while feeling irritated with my assistant. "You told me you were a financial consultant. Didn't you tell a bunch of rich Jews how they should invest their money?"

"Yes, I did," he smiled without any further explanation.

I questioned why he didn't run with the ball months ago, and continued to complain. "I did not figure in our operating costs, prepaid expenses, current liabilities, or projected revenue goals! This operation was too big for me. I needed help, Seth, and I didn't have the money to hire a CPA to hammer out the bottom line. *We* got too involved in the manufacturing end of this business and completely ignored the cost factor."

"Don't worry about it now, Jean. We'll sell our clothes cheap, and figure out how to manufacture our orders even cheaper after we get the orders."

"I guess," I said while feeling dismal about the situation. Seth approached a pretty blonde in our path. "Excuse me, Miss, which way to Management's Office?"

The woman pointed down the long corridor; "Walk through the food section, and stay straight on course, and when you get to the elevator banks, then go up to the third floor."

"Thank you," Seth said as she walked away. "This place is huge!" He commented.

"Imagine how many buyers we might see tomorrow. Look at the crowd here, already!" I said as we entered into the food section. Hundreds of vendors sat at small, four-chair, round tables, and all of them were dressed to the hilt. Seth and I kept walking toward the elevator banks while we eyed the tables of food that we could not afford to eat.

"I find this crowd intimidating, Seth."

"Why?"

"Every designer, that is anybody, is represented here! Why would anybody want to buy my clothes? I'm nobody!"

Seth took my hand and led me through the eatery. "This business is all illusion. Don't stop believing in your fantasy."

"You're right," I acknowledged while feeling unsure about my creation. I would not express another moment of doubt to Seth. I did not want my thoughts to be reason for my demise. Why did I consider that my thoughts, alone, were the key to my success, or to my demise? How did God's Word factor into this equation?

We stepped into the elevator, headed up to the third floor, and found direction to Management's Office for Temporary Showrooms.

We walked down another long corridor and spotted the office, stepped through a heavy wooden door, and found a couple of blonde, slim, beauty queens, in their twenties, sitting behind two desks. We smiled, greeted one another, and then I pulled out of my soft, leather briefcase, a copy of my showroom reservation. I gave my paperwork to the most interested woman, who sat nearest the door. She pulled a chart off her desk and looked for my reserved showroom number on a maze of showrooms.

"Someone else moved into that room," she said nonchalantly.

"Who?" My stomach tightened.

"An importer has it. I'm sorry."

"I'm sorry? You erred! I reserved this room last July. I paid you nearly $900 for that showroom that you have given to *the importer*. You're telling me that someone else has my room?"

"Yes, I'm sorry."

"Well, that's not acceptable!" I firmly rejected while believing I could not be any angrier.

"I'll give you another room, but I don't have many left, anymore."

"Not my problem, either!" I yelled.

"I suggest you take this matter up with the man who has your room. Maybe he'll move out."

"Again, not my job to relocate him! I sent out three-hundred invitations, to buyers across America, to see my collection in *that* showroom; and now, you want to give me another showroom? Where?"

"I'm sorry ma'am for this situation. I know you're upset."

"Upset? I just want the room I booked and paid for!"

"I can give you a refund."

"A refund!" I looked at Seth. "Unbelievable!"

"Seth shook his head in disbelief and stepped into the brisk conversation. "We ought to sue you. Just give us what you have available."

The woman nodded, and Seth turned to me. "We'll get the room that she has available right now, and then tell whoever is in our space to move out and go there."

"What other options do we have?" I asked.

The woman gave us keys and a map to our new location. I studied the map and saw that where we were to initially be located, and where we landed, were miles and miles apart from each other, and, in fact, not even on the same floor. I silently fell apart. How would my three hundred invited buyers find me now? I did not know what we would do, if the group, who had our showroom, did not move out.

Seth and I angrily left Management's Office and walked up to the doors of our original showroom and peered in. What we saw was horrid--a fabulous showroom, which obviously took a week to assemble. There were wall racks covered with beautiful, colorful, clothes, and the leasee had painted all the showroom walls black. Bright spotlights shone down from the ceiling and onto the wall displays, which featured wool sweaters in color groupings of teal, fuchsia, gold, purple, and red. Seth and I looked at each other in despair.

"He's never going to move out!" I lamented while I stared at a well-dressed Middle Eastern man inside my showroom. "That damn management group gave this *snake in the grass* our showroom with their blessings! That thief ruined our chance for success! I will sue him!"

"We'll sue management!" Seth supported.

"We'll sue everybody!" I spewed.

"I'm going to try to persuade him, Jean," Seth said as he barged straight up to the Middle Eastern male standing just inside the showroom door. I followed Seth and then quietly stood beside him.

"Excuse me, sir. My name is Seth Zherneboh, and this is Jean Wynn. Jean is a designer with a collection here this week."

"Pleased to meet you both," the stranger said rather friendly. I nodded and shot him a friendly smile.

"I hate to break this news to you, sir, but you're in our designer's showroom!" Seth said to the male wearing expensive Italian wear slacks and a dress shirt. "Ms. Wynn here reserved this showroom, four months ago, and we would like you to leave immediately. We will exchange rooms with you."

I did not believe Seth was the least bit persuasive.

"This is *my* showroom! I reserved months ago, too." The dark-skinned man refuted, while folding his arms across his crisp, white, long sleeve shirt and appearing defensive.

I could see that he was sure not to budge.

"Can you prove you booked this room, months ago?" Seth requested.

"No."

"Well, I can prove we booked this room a long time ago. You take this other room," Seth insisted while pointing to the map he held in his hand. "Management said you have our room, and you should trade with us."

The man chuckled. "I spent a week setting up. This market begins tomorrow. I reserved this room. You go now. I will not trade. I will not move."

My eyes met with Seth. "Forget it, Seth."

"I don't want to forget it! This is clearly not his showroom," he firmly spouted.

"It is *my* showroom," the man declared. "Go, or else I will call Security."

"Good," Seth said. "Call Security!"

"Come on, Seth," I urged and gently tugged on his arm to pull him away, before a brawl began, and the convention center kicked us out all together.

"I will sue you, asshole!" Seth yelled before walking out of what was once our store.

We left spitting nails and headed toward the new location. And, as we went from elevator to another floor and crossed over the food court again, I became clear that my destiny was not in favor of me winning, and dread burst forth. Perhaps I would never see the first of the three hundred invited buyers! "Some persuasion skills you have, Seth! I know I could have done better!" I angrily spewed as we found ourselves walking down one endless hallway, and then down another, until we came upon an endless corridor where pink and blue plastic flags hung from the hallway ceiling as far as the eye could see. In the center of this mile-long tunnel of endless ceiling flags, we found our new showroom.

"*You* had an opportunity to put him out, too," Seth defended.

"That thief was going nowhere!" I argued while I watched my business partner unlock an empty glass-front space ready for our creative expression.

"I gave him something to think about when I told him that I'm going to sue him; and if this week does not pan out for us, we might consider suing someone."

"I *will* sue Management if I don't make a million dollars this week," I affirmed.

We stepped inside the empty box with three white walls and one glass wall and doorway off the hallway. Seth flipped on the lights. The space was big enough to park two cars inside. We smiled at each other. "Anything is possible," I said to Seth. "I'm sorry I got angry at you. None of this stuff is your fault."

"You're right, it's not my fault. We have to work with what we have now, and we better get busy."

"Let's move," I added while realizing we did not bring enough décor. We headed back down to the unloading docks and emptied out our van onto rolling carts.

After working on the showroom all night, and making a trip to the local Wal-Mart for colorful crepe paper, Scotch tape, ceiling hooks, and chains, we turned the blank canvas into a beautiful tropical paradise. The eight framed posters of my tall blonde model sat on top of the shelves on three walls. The young, slender woman, who posed against beach dunes, and on a fabricated rock waterfall, at the San Luis Hotel, in Galveston, Texas, featured my favorite resort pieces in poster-size frames. My signature logo appeared at the bottom of each poster advertising me to be the designer. I hung the same apparel shown in the posters directly below the affiliated advertising. I hung colorful windsocks of parrots from the ceiling, placed an artificial palm tree in the center of the room under my white neon signature sign, and positioned a rattan sofa in tropical print nearby the palm tree and between carrousels of tropical prints. I had a small, dark, antique "order" desk, with 1780 Sheraton-styled legs, in the center of the room, under my white neon signature logo sign, and I set a blue leather, Queen Ann style chair, behind the table. Seth and I would fill out purchase orders on stationary carrying my logo--*Jean Wynn, An American Designer*. I had a black leather portfolio, sitting on top of my elegant desk and showcasing my entire sample collection. I planned to open up the catalogue and show to all prospects that walked into my store. The beautiful Stephanie modeled each piece, in print. Six garment racks were strategically placed inside the room, and an array of beautiful colors in rainbow hues hung throughout the store--fantasy wear I had created, and Verna, and my other seamstresses, had sewn. Each piece had a stitched-in white satin label with my scripted logo of my name, along with size and care instructions printed in black ink on the reverse side. A black and white glossy cardstock hangtag with my signature logo, and price, and style number was pinned into every garment in the store, too. I had to admit I was appreciating the professionalism my showroom exalted when a stylish and friendly woman in her mid-forties sashayed into our room and greeted us. "Hello! I'm your neighbor across the hallway."

Seth and I both acknowledged her and introduced ourselves with a handshake.

"I love your collection," she said to me as she thumbed through a rack of my designs. "I have heard your name before," she queried.

I chuckled and replied, "I did a runway show once at the Houston airport."

"Maybe I was passing through the airport and saw you?" She answered while I watched her closely examine the quality of a garment.

"The fashion show was on a delayed plane that sat on the tarmac."

"Oh, then I didn't see your show. Your work is very polished," she said while she inspected a garment.

"Thank you," I humbly responded. I saw that Seth took great pride in her words.

"You ought to be hanging your beautiful collection in the Women's Wear section, not here in Infant Wear," she advised.

I looked at Seth with a dropped jaw and saw he heard what I had heard, too.

"Infant Wear?" I asked as if to confirm my nightmare.

She nodded yes.

"You've got to be kidding!" I exalted.

"No, all these stores down this hallway, and over some, are

baby merchandise. That's why the hallway ceiling is decorated with pink and blue flags."

"No way!" Seth screeched. "I'm going to sue those bastards! I can't believe this crap!"

I fell into the nearby sofa and shook my head in disbelief while I stared up at the ceiling. Not only were my three hundred invited buyers not ever going to find me in this matrix, but also no one who walked down this hallway would have any interest in buying Women's Wear! Only buyers in need of infant wear would ever venture our way.

"Seth, go right away to management and demand another show room!"

"I certainly will," he said as he raced out the door.

I looked at my neighbor, "What are you selling?"

"Women's caftans."

"In the baby section?"

"I had no choice. A friend, who sells infant wear, invited me into her showroom. I figured pregnant women like to wear caftans."

"Good point."

She continued, "My friend and I got here a week ago. This show is billed as *spring and summer wear,* but I hear through the grapevine, that those who shop this particular market are buyers who want Christmas inventory and immediate delivery."

I could not believe what I was hearing! My nightmare kept unraveling. What else did I *not* know? I calculated that Christmas was less than two months away. "Christmas inventory?"

"Yes, like wool sweaters, knit skirts, coats, lined slacks--you know, the kind of apparel that you receive at Christmas when snow is on the ground."

"Seth and I saw snow on the ground when we arrived," I said with regret while in disbelief.

"Oh yeah, it snows in Dallas at times. We're having a very cold winter here."

"I feel like throwing up," I admitted to the woman while internalizing my reality. I was stuck in baby hell with tropical resort wear no one wanted to buy right now.

"There is a bathroom down the hallway. I'll watch your showroom, if you would like me to."

"Thank you," I said as I raced out the door and down the hallway under the pink and blue flags. I had suspicion that what I had was a bad case of morning sickness on top of a great amount of stress.

Thirty minutes later when I returned to our showroom, Seth had already returned and sat alone looking despondent. "There are no more showrooms, Jean. This is it."

I stared at Seth. "We have a week here. We'll find the buyers and bring them in. We have no choice but to work with what we have to work with."

I walked alone around the market for the rest of the week, looking into glass-front stores and watching business transactions between brokers and buyers. On this day, I wore a knee-length bright yellow summer dress I had designed. I knew I should saunter like the 5'9" model I could appear to be; but, instead, I moved awkwardly through *Group III* and felt more like a shunned child with a belly swelling out of a stomach peek hole. I once considered the dress sexy, but on me, I felt out of place in the land of wintry garments. I questioned the outcome of the event. I summed up my unhappiness and the reason for my business failure, with a conclusion that I walked outside of God's world. No miracles were coming my way due to my disobedience of God's Word. The tourist, who lived in a beachfront hotel, for weeks at a time, over the past two years, experienced more nothing. Was I experiencing God's wrath? I hung my head low, in humiliation, as I exited the land of my dream--*Group III*. And then, as if needing to confirm what I already suspected, I ventured over to the land of temporary showrooms, on the fourth floor, and stood just outside the door of my original showroom, #4A78. I watched a stream of buyers enter and exit with purchase orders in hand. I wondered if the shop owner who managed the showroom felt guilty gaining at my expense. I had wanted so much more than the unexpected unfolding, and I questioned my grim reality. I wanted to know God and his world of blessings because my circumstances were obviously *not* God's blessings. I wanted to be on the path God had designed for me.

Since my arrival to Dallas, I worried about how Seth and I would recover from this crash. We had not a single sale, the first six days of the seven-day event, and I had *no answer* for what the future entailed. As long as I had held on to hope, like I had over the past months, I noticed I had unusual stamina; but now, my fear of the unknown depleted my energy, and I felt depressed and without any answers. My hope dissipated due to my circumstances. I understood, as I sadly walked away from my original showroom, that if I chose to succumb to my fears, then, obviously, I had no faith in God saving this day, or any day. I swore my circumstances would never be reason for me to stop believing in God's power to turn my life around, for the better. No circumstances, no matter how dire, were going to send me into a place of resignation and permanent depression. I certainly had no ability to turn this mess around. I was without answers; and for the lack of answers, I now begged God for a miracle.

I questioned what I had mistakenly believed in so strongly that brought me to this place of disaster? Obviously, I had misunderstood something in my act of creation. Perhaps I needed to stop centering my life around my wants, and my desires, and start believing in a loving God that wanted me to depend on him. What did it really matter what I wanted in my life because God would have the final say anyway. Perhaps, I just needed to understand the rulebook and learn how to submit and follow directions.

I considered my favorite sport, football, when I considered what I had experienced at the Convention Center over the week. An interception is a move in the game and involves a player throwing a pass, and the opposition player cuts off the pass and usually gains possession of the ball for his team. I assumed God was working for the betterment of his team when he intercepted the ball in my game; and I, the player on the other team, who had possession and control of the ball, ultimately came short of the goal. I wondered what God had in mind for my life if not this plan I had in mind?

As I walked through the hallways of the mall, feeling disconnected from everything I mistakenly believed I once controlled;

I became conscious that I could choose to listen to any voice in my head, as if choosing a radio frequency. Perhaps these grim circumstances were a test for me, a woman who had been so self-centered for so long that she would hurt her loving husband and terminate her child because the child was inconvenient. The sad truth hit me hard. I murmured, "Please, forgive me, Lord, for I am unworthy of your blessings, give me patience, wisdom, and compassion." In that moment, I promised God that I would embrace any circumstances that came toward me from that day forward; and no matter how hard the situation might prove to be before me, I would keep the faith that He had not given me anything I could not handle. I would be a beacon of light and be still enough to hear His voice.

After strolling around the Dallas Market Center and feeling invisible, for most of a week, I came to the conclusion that I lacked confidence to walk up to strangers and ask them to come see my collection of women's resort wear in Infant Wear. I strongly suspected that Seth and I would have more of the same regarding poor sales, if we drove fifteen hours north and set up my $830 reserved showroom at The Apparel Center in Chicago. The odds of the Chicago exhibit hall giving my paid-for-in-full showroom away to another vendor, too, were one in a million, but the fact that Illinois temperatures currently included ice and snow made me fear taking any further risks with my spring/summer line. Regional buyers here in Dallas were ordering wool sweaters and scarves with immediately delivery for their Christmas store shelves, and I reasoned the same was true for the week of November 5, 1988 in the chilly and bleak Windy City. I would be trafficking resort wear to a bunch of hard nipples who considered only their survival against extreme temperatures for the next several months.

I headed down the long hallway of baby pink and baby blue flags and entered into our showroom. Seth sat alone behind the antique desk looking at *Women's Wear Daily*. "Reading anything interesting?"

Seth held up the rag for my view. "Did you know this fashion-industry trade journal is considered the bible of fashion?"

"I did know that! Thus, the reason for why you are reading my subscription." I said without a lot of enthusiasm while bummed out over not having any buyers come into our store all week.

"Yeah, this journal came out in 1955, and *WWD* reporters were assigned to sit in the last row of seats of the 1955 couture shows--a sign of the newspaper's low stature; but since then, this paper has risen to prominence. Listen to what this says," Seth instructed and then read, "*The Chief of Publications, John Fairchild, actually turned his newspaper's attention to the social scene of fashion designers and their clients, and helped manufacture a cult of celebrity around designers. When a designer's statements or works offended Fairchild, he would retaliate, sometimes banning any reference to the designers in his newspapers, sometimes for years at a stretch. The newspaper sparred with Givenchy, Balenciaga, Perry Ellis, Yves Saint Laurent, Giorgio Armani, Oscar de la Renta, among others.*'"

Seth looked up from the article. "Fairchild has a lot of power if he alienates those designers. We need to get our clothing line advertised in here. Every store buyer in America reads this publication to see what's hot and what's in. Look at these one-page ads! This designer here has three one-page ads back-to-back!"

"That's my dream, Seth." I stepped up closer to the desk and flipped through what my boyfriend pointed out and viewed the impressive ads myself while without a clue as to how we could afford to market our line.

"I think we should skip the Chicago show and sell door-to-door directly to beach front boutiques in Florida."

"Really?" Seth looked interested in my latest proposition.

"Yeah, there is no point in us putting ourselves in this same situation up there in Chicago where it's even colder."

Our conversation was interrupted when someone walk into our store. I looked toward the front door and spotted a middle-aged, Latino man, of average build, and of great confidence, with a pretty, slender, Caucasian woman, in her late thirties. They were dressed elegantly, in fine business attire, and both adorned with heavy gold jewelry. They stood beside each other smiling, and she stood beside a rack of my clothing designs, and began to pull out various pieces of my collection for her inspection while he introduced themselves. I remained fixed in place, and did not walk up to either one of them, to sell them on my line, but, on the contrary, judged them in a few seconds to be designers looking for new ideas. I stood there with my arms folded across my chest, feeling annoyed while watching the statuesque female inspect the workmanship of a hemline. She looked up at me and smiled, "Are you Jean Wynn?"

"Yes," I said while feeling irked. I was upset because I had no sales that week, and now they threatened to steal my designs!

"You remind me of a little unknown designer that I discovered back in the 70's. Her name was *Adrienne Vittadini*."

I shrugged while not familiar with the name.

"Vittadini just opened up a boutique in Beverly Hills this year. You have a special quality about your work like she does." The woman said as she continued to examine one design after another.

I instantly let my guard down. "Thank you."

She looked up at me. "I am Gabrielle Baker and this is my husband, Alfredo Suarez."

"Pleased to meet you. I am Jean Wynn, and this is my business partner, Seth Zherneboh."

The couple nodded with pleasure.

"Where do you manufacture your line?" The Latin male asked me.

I did not know how to answer his question when Seth suddenly piped in. "We run a sweat shop just outside of Houston."

I then interrupted Seth before he elaborated any further with false details that would give them a sense that we had our act together. "I intend to find a cheaper way to produce my clothes in mass quantity. I recently wrote the General Consulate's Office of Mexico and asked that they give me the names of Mexican businesses. I need clothing manufacturers, textile suppliers, and shipping partners right now."

"What do you project to make in total sales this year?" She asked.

I felt embarrassed by the question and skipped over the truth. "I don't have a business plan yet," I said while realizing I had shed light on our true ignorance about the whole game.

The woman looked at her partner and smiled, and then continued, "A formal business plan is of little interest to us, or to any investor at this stage of your business gestation. A business plan really does not mean much when you're talking about manufacturing businesses. As an investor, I will want to see a project plan. You cannot, and I stress, *cannot* devise a business plan without a project plan; so, if you've got a business plan but no project plan, then all of your money, time and effort was wasted."

"I don't," I confirmed.

"Good!" She exclaimed. "It is much better to walk through the elements of a project plan, filling in all the blanks that you can before developing a business plan."

I smiled. I was actually on the right track while having felt distressed over the past months with considerations like I had not done enough, and that I needed to run a TV commercial and develop a nation-wide sales force. I continued, "The group senior vice president of Horizon Media on Third Avenue in New York City wrote me a letter and informed me that they could help me with planning and placing media, but that their billings were in excess of one hundred million dollars. I can't write a check to get this ball rolling." I giggled while I watched them chuckle; and then, I continued to share my vision. "Horizon Media also works closely with a number of advertising agencies who have extensive experience in fashion. I could not, and still cannot, imagine how I would ever afford $100 million dollars for TV commercials. And, on the scale of another grandiose idea, I schemed to invite buyers, across America, to a weekend of fun at an oceanfront resort in Puerto Vallarta, Mexico. They would watch a night-time fashion show, on a moon-lit pool deck, dance to a semi-famous band, get drunk on free libations, eat from a wonderful seafood buffet, and then give me large orders for their stores, out of their sense of obligation to the designer, who put on the generous event."

The couple chuckled again, and the Latino male spouted, "I like the way you think, Ms. Wynn."

"Me, too," his wife added. The businesswoman continued to talk to me while giving little attention to Seth. "Any kind of sales projections for stylized consumer products like yours is unmitigated fiction. You can never know how much you are going to sell--consumers are fickle."

The woman's handsome husband with brown skin and jet-black hair reiterated, "We like what we see here, Miss Wynn, and we can consult with you about your manufacturing needs, too. We work with a manufacturer in Italy. We have textile suppliers there. Perhaps you can come to Italy?"

"Perhaps I can," I answered while stunned by the unexpected invitation. I instantly thought of my Switzerland love, Cliff. He was part of the Italian textile world, too, and, in fact, had told me on the phone, one morning, that he was leaving on a train that same morning for an appointment with an apparel manufacturer in Italy. What was the relationship between Cliff Hubert and this couple? The idea of my Switzerland love networking behind the scenes for me was an interesting thought; and, this couple finding me, in this maze of baby merchandise, was odd at best. Was Cliff watching me from afar? I had to appease my curiosity. "I don't understand how you found me here in the middle of the Infant Wear Section in this huge apparel mart?"

The couple again glanced at each other as if determining who would speak first, and then she continued, "We were walking through and spotted your beautiful showroom."

I nodded. "Do you sell Infant Wear?"

"No," she answered and then coyly glanced at her husband again.

Why did I feel this meeting was no accident? Had God placed an anointing for favor and increase upon my life? Had God seared me upon Cliff's heart? After all, earlier that year, in the spring of 1988, before I was pregnant, I had shared with the man, who lived in Switzerland, the details of my apparel business efforts. I also knew Cliff saw me walking into troubled waters before I did, that day he kissed me goodbye forever on that hotel pool deck, and left me to contend with David and Seth by my own choosing. How I wished I had my beautiful European back. How I wish I could turn back the hands of time and undo many things.

The woman executive continued, "We carry only eight lines of women's apparel in our permanent showroom in *Group III* including Adrienne Vittadini's collection."

The woman's husband interrupted his wife while he pulled out a business card from his suit jacket, handed it to my partner, and continued to talk to me. "We would like very much for both of you to come to our showroom today and see what we could offer you. We have buyers from all the big department stores in America coming in this week to buy Adrienne Vittadini and our other lines, too. We run one-page ads for our designers in *WWD* every month."

Seth lit up. "I was just perusing through our latest copy of *WWD!*"

"Then," the businessman said to Seth, "if you have this month's copy, you will see that *Baker & Suarez* bought five one-page ads for Vittadini, and on each of those pages is our *Group III* address here at the Market Center with telephone number for buyers to make appointments."

Seth and I both nodded, and I felt as if a dream was coming true.

"My wife and I believe you might fit into our showroom very nicely. We are looking for one more collection."

My heart leaped in excitement, and I looked at Seth who appeared as thrilled as I did; and without any hesitation, my partner leaped at the Latino man's offer.

"Yes, Jean and I would very much like to see what *Baker & Suarez* have going on. We'll find a lull in our busy schedule later this afternoon and come to your fashion house of exquisite designers."

"Very well, thank you, sir," Mr. Suarez said while eagerly shaking Seth's extended hand, and then, turning his attention back to me. "We are part of *Group III* on the second floor. As my wife already said, we have a permanent showroom year-round here at The Market Center which gives our designers exposure to more than 200,000 buyers at our fifty-plus markets held each year."

"I look forward to seeing your showroom," I added just before we bid our adieus and the couple exited our store.

"Wow, how did that happen, Jean?" Seth marveled.

"I have no clue," I answered. I was dumbfounded and considered whether Cliff was behind them finding us in the midst of Infant Wear? Did my lover still want me to come to Italy via them?

A WEEK LATER. I glanced over at the driver and watched Seth stare down the Florida coastal highway and smoke his twentieth cigarette for the day as we headed back toward Madeira Beach, Florida. I felt a flutter in my belly and realized my baby's first kick. "Our baby is stretching!" I declared with great excitement while I rubbed my belly. "Feel him!"

Seth reached over and laid his hand on my ballooning self. I watched his eyes pop when our baby moved again. "We're really having a baby!"

"Are you ready to be a daddy?"

"I can hardly wait! It's like a dream come true, Jean."

I smiled. "I'm tired, Seth. Let's go back to our motel."

"I'm tired, too. It's been a long day."

"Stop at that convenience store we went to yesterday, and let's get some dinner to take back with us."

"Alright, I have to make sure mama keeps up her strength."

"I'll have more strength when I take off these damn shoes. I can't wear four-inch heels all day long, anymore. My feet and my back are killing me! I really should not be wearing high heels at all while pregnant because when I walk on my toes I force the baby to press up against my lower spine," I said as I thumbed through the notes in my lap.

"Did you know high heels have been around for about 6000 years?" Seth asked. "In fact, illustrations of spiky heels have been uncovered in Egyptian tombs dating back to 4000 BC."

"Didn't know that, Seth."

"Didn't either, until I got into my Master's program and studied ancient history."

"I figured these shoes were derived from something misogynistic," I said as I flipped through notes we had collected over the days in Florida. "We have six appointments tomorrow--our first is at 10:00 a.m."

"Six appointments, at a minimum of one thousand dollars per order--"

"—is six thousand dollars a day!" I summed. "And if we stay out here on the road for the next six weeks, then it's possible we could go home with $250,000 worth of orders."

"Is that realistic, Jean?"

"Yes, if we burn the rubber all day every day and get the appointments like we did today and earlier this week. Since we left Dallas, one week ago, we have $35,000 in orders. In addition, we wasted a lot of time in Mississippi and Alabama. Florida boutiques are proving to be profitable."

Imagine what we could have done had we established a nation-wide sales force," Seth pitched.

"Live and learn," I retorted while clear I blundered when I expected Seth to handle that part of my business since day one.

Seth pulled up into the convenience store parking lot and headed toward the front of the store in my red van. "How are we going to manufacturer these orders?" Seth asked while he turned off the vehicle.

"I'm not clear *where* yet, but I'm sure we can get a loan from a bank, to do whatever we have to do, to get these clothes sewn up and delivered on time. Alfredo Suarez and his wife will guide us into the right direction."

"We're on our way!" Seth gleefully confirmed as I got out on my side of the van. "The Dallas show was not a complete loss after all," I offered while feeling giddy about our future, too, and smoothing down my knee-length black skirt. "I think it's very possible that we could hang this same spring and summer line in the *Baker and Suarez Group III* showroom in January."

"You think so?" Seth challenged.

"Yeah, that's a spring/summer show. *Baker and Suarez* liked us. And the buyers will definitely be there in January shopping for spring and summer stock," I said as I walked up to Seth.

Seth smiled at me and began loudly singing a Billy Joel tune while he led us toward the store.

"♫*Don't go changing to try and please me,
You never let me down before…mmm*♫
♫*And don't imagine you're too familiar,
And, I don't see you any more…*♫"

I smiled and followed the showboat that sported dark business slacks and a white dress shirt up to the front door. I felt my boyfriend was happy about his life with me. I also found Seth's ability to unabashedly sing loudly, wherever we went, humorous, as was the case now, and yesterday, too, when we had entered into this same establishment about this same time of evening. Seth liked all eyes on him.

My lead singer held the front door open for me, and I walked past the slight man with the dark, wavy hair and entered into the cold A/C. I noticed a line of customers waiting to checkout and two cashiers staring at us when we entered. Seth, once fired from a band as their lead singer, while on a road trip, sang to the entire room:

"♫*I would not leave you in times of trouble,
We never could have come this far…mmm*♫
♫ *I took the good times, I'll take the bad times
I'll take you, Jean, just the way you are…*♫ "

I felt life was as good as good gets, now that we were getting sales from beachside boutiques; and even my suspicions about my boyfriend's sexuality no longer mattered to me. I preferred to believe Seth when he told me that he was not gay. I was living my dream and no longer on that uncommitted fence that I had been on for two years, which made me feel emotionally torn between a man and a child. I was certain now I was on my way to being the next great American designer, and with a child on the way to boot. I had reason to be happy!

Seth and I parted ways, and I headed down the bottle aisle of mustard and mayonnaise looking for something low fat to eat from a jar. My boyfriend had quit singing while he hunted for something to eat, too. We had checked into a motel a block away, earlier that week;

and each evening, after a day of calling on beachfront boutiques, or hotel gift shops, we would walk into this same store and get food and drinks. Our cash flow was next to nothing, and reserved for extreme emergency, and we were living off the only good credit card I had in my possession—a credit card that my estranged husband, Leonardo, had yet to cancel. Strangely, I was still an authorized user of a credit card he paid on each month. I picked up a can of Hormel Chili and was reading the label for its fat content when a strange male's voice broke through my concentration. "Ms. Wynn?"

I turned to see who was talking to me and found a short, middle-aged man standing before me, wearing a plaid, long-sleeve shirt with pearl snaps, tight-fitting Wranglers, and round-toe boots. He wore a sad-looking face.

"Yes?" I kindly answered.

He then flashed, in front of my face, a flipped open wallet and began talking. I leaned toward the black leather billfold and studied a silver star. He was with the Pinellas County Sheriff's Department.

"I'm Detective Landers, and I need you to step outside with me," he said with no show of expression.

"What?" I said as if he were joking.

"I'm an undercover detective, and I am requesting you step outside, ma'am."

"Is this a joke?" I stepped back and saw, by his expression, that the cowboy was dead serious.

"This is no joke, ma'am."

I looked around and saw that the officer was by himself. I spotted Seth on the other side of the convenience store staring into the refrigerator.

"Please step outside, ma'am."

"Okay," I politely submitted while I sat the can of chili down, on the nearby shelf, and led the stout man back through the glass front door. I noticed the two store clerks, who stood side-by-side each other behind the cashier's counter, closely watching our encounter, as I exited the building, with the cop following behind me. Once I stepped outside, I flipped around and faced the officer who held a look of great authority, but before he could speak, I shot back from an even greater place of authority, "What's this about, sir?"

"The two store clerks inside reported you as having passed off a stolen credit card, ma'am."

"No sir! Not true!" I folded my arms across my chest. "I haven't even used my credit card in there yet."

"Do you have a Shell Oil credit card?"

I hesitated. "Yes, but it is not stolen."

"Where do you work?"

"I work for myself," I answered while understanding I was now defending myself and already feeling indicted.

"And what do you do?" He dryly questioned as if any show of compassion would kill his sense of authority.

"I design, manufacture and wholesale women's apparel," I answered while feeling incensed by the entire situation.

"And how long have you been doing it?"

"How long have I been *doing it?* I chuckled at my own twisted interpretation. "It feels like I've been *doing it* all my life, but this is really my first time." I purposely ran my eyes down the squatty man's pudgy body. "How long have you been *doing it?*"

"Don't break my balls," he slammed back.

"You're not married, are you?"

His expression shifted to appear more personal and challenged. "Is that your husband in there?" He pointed to inside the store.

"No, he's my sales associate. My husband lives in Indiana."

"Are you and your sales associate living together?"

"No," I lied.

"Do you live in Indiana, too?"

"No, I live in Houston."

"Is your sales associate also your boyfriend?"

"Yes."

"How long have you been divorced from the man in Indiana?"

"Our divorce is not final yet."

"And when is your baby due?"

I looked down at my swollen belly and then back up at the cop who gave me a look of disdain. I knew instantly what was up his crawl with me. "Look, officer. I'm doing business here in Florida, not running a stolen credit card ring. I've spent five months developing a line of clothes; and now, I'm selling my apparel line to beachfront stores down the coastline."

"With your boyfriend?" He stood with his hands on his gun belt and one finger on his gun's trigger.

"With my sales associate." I assumed by his stance that he had a personal issue with me.

"Please hand over your purse, ma'am."

I obliged and pulled my purse off my shoulder. He took my purse and sat it on the ground. I then watched him unclip handcuffs off his left hip. He then walked around to my backside and cuffed me.

"Oh shit, she really hurt you!" I rebuked. "I get it! I'm being punished for doing business with my sales associate."

"It's just precautionary, ma'am, while I interrogate you." He tightened the cuffs around my wrist and then stepped back in front of me.

"Oh, right! Pregnant businesswoman in tight-fitting skirt and stilettos is going to take off running!"

He did not respond, but picked up my purse again off the ground and pulled out my wallet.

"You never answered my question, officer. You're not married are you?"

"No, I'm not," he said while he flipped through my wallet's contents.

"Ha! I could have won that bet! Where are you from?"

"New York State," he blurted. He threw my purse back on the ground and held my wallet under his armpit while he took out a writing pad from his pocket and wrote something.

"I bet you could not get any respect in New York from anybody--not from the wife, nor from the employer. So then, you figured you would move to this sleepy beach town and take your anger out on unsuspecting women?"

His expression soured, and I knew I hit home on some level. He put his notepad back into his front shirt pocket and then walked behind me one more time and tightened my cuffs even tighter.

"Ouch, that hurts!" I blasted.

He stepped in front of me again, smiled, and then slipped his foot in between my heels and forced me to spread my legs. "Please do what I need you to do--spread your legs!" He ordered before getting on his radio and asking dispatch to send a female officer to the scene.

I assumed I was going to jail as I tried to spread my legs as wide apart as my short black skirt would allow. I baited, "Your former wife, or was it girlfriend? She wouldn't do what you ordered, would she? I bet you fought with her over your need to control her. And I bet you even handcuffed her to the bed at night to keep her at home!"

"Have you been here before?" He angrily shouted.

"Yes, I have been in this place before. I had cuffs put on me in the past, but not by a real cop." I winked.

"Well, now you have!" He said with a smirk and began searching through my wallet again. "Have you been to this store before today?"

"Oh, have I been to *this store* before! Yes, I have been here before, too! Yesterday, and maybe the day before, if my memory serves me well."

"Who was your last long-term employer?"

"I worked for an oil company, but that was years and years ago. What's that got to do with the price of rice?"

"What oil company?"

"I worked for Shell, Conoco, and Marathon. I worked for all of them."

He examined all my defunct credit cards and pulled out my only good credit card--a Shell credit card. "Who is Leonardo Vinci?"

"My estranged husband."

"What is the name of your sales associate?"

"Seth Zherneboh."

I wondered if Seth had stolen something from this convenience store. I recalled the days before, when Seth and I had shopped here, but I only remembered him kissing me while standing in line to check out. I did not believe Seth was a thief. "I am still using my husband's credit card with his permission."

"Stay here," the cop ordered while he walked over to the patrol car that just arrived.

I spotted Seth coming out of the store. He did not step off the front porch and walk toward me, but kept his distance and yelled from where he stood, "What's going on here, Jean?"

"I don't have a clue. I think I'm being arrested."

Seth and I both looked at the undercover cop, who leaned over into a cop car and talked to a female officer in uniform, sitting behind the steering wheel.

The male cop left the woman officer and walked back up to me while I watched her park her patrol car and get out. "Ma'am, I'm asking that you listen to me carefully. Probable cause exists here for me to arrest you. I have reasonable suspicion, and there are enough facts and circumstances to lead me to believe you have committed a crime here."

"I have not!" I said with complete indignation.

"I have to protect these businesses, and it's their word against yours, so I am arresting you. You have the right to remain silent. You have the right to retain counsel, and you should know that anything you say might and could be held against you--"

Seth walked up closer and interrupted, "Hey, why are you arresting her, officer?"

"Sir, she is being arrested for using a stolen credit card yesterday in the store."

"We did not use a stolen credit card yesterday, or ever!"

The cop pulled out a gun and pointed it at Seth, "Put your hands in the air, sir!"

"Whoa!" Seth said while he raised his arms. "No need for a gun, Mr. Police Officer."

"Sir, you are under arrest for being an accomplice in this crime. The amount you two charged was over fifty dollars, and therefore, you have both committed a felony."

The female officer walked up behind Seth, took him by the wrist, and slapped on handcuffs.

The male officer dropped his gun and continued, "Sir, you have the right to remain--"

Seth shouted over the officer, who read him his Miranda Rights, "What the hell is going on here, Jean?"

I shrugged and angrily spewed, "It's a nightmare. I guess this asshole here doesn't have anything better to do with his life."

The female officer walked over to me. "I suggest you watch your mouth, ma'am. Come with me and get in my car," she ordered as she led me to her official vehicle, opened the back seat door, and waited while I slid into the back. She then slammed the door shut and walked away. The interior of the car was silent while I watched Seth and the two police officers talk in the parking lot. The male officer then took Seth's arm and led him over to his squad car. Seth got into the back seat, and the officer shut the door on him. The uniformed man then opened his driver's door, sat down, and got on his radio.

I sat there with great confusion and noticed there were no handles on the door. I peered back out the window and watched the cop drive away with Seth. What had we done? How did this event fit into the scheme of my life as an up-and-coming fashion designer? Was this arrest more punishment for me breaking God's commandments? Did God curse my life because I had killed my unborn child and committed adultery?

I walked down the hallway of the Madeira Beach substation on a yellow striped line with my wrists handcuffed behind my back. The arresting male officer led me from my holding cell, to a small room, with only a desk and two hardback chairs, wherein, he removed my handcuffs and then chained my wrist to the leg of a metal chair. He pulled up the other matching chair, straddled the seat while facing its backside and me, and then began interrogating me. He held my large black leather purse in front of me while he removed its contents and asked me questions.

"Admit you are involved in a credit card scam."

"No!" I could hear Seth in the nearby distance singing a tune by Billy Joel called *Vienna*. He sang lyrics with a message telling someone to slow down because you can't be everything you want to be before your time. I assumed Seth was trying to tell me something. "What are you going to do with my boyfriend?"

"He's in a holding cell around the corner, and we're taking him to Tampa along with you. He'll be admitted into the men's unit, and you'll be booked into the women's unit." The cop pulled out numerous sales receipts strewn throughout the contents of my purse, and examined each expenditure.

"I left the Dallas Apparel Market and hit the road a week ago to make money. You've made a huge mistake. And you have really pissed me off with this arrest! Why would I invest the kind of money, that I did over the last year, to develop my line of apparel, and then use a stolen credit card for a fifty-five dollar purchase? How ridiculous! I spent tens of thousands of dollars on employee salaries. I paid rent for a commercial property, for utilities, for expensive fabrics, for showroom leases at the apparel markets in Dallas and Chicago, and for an assortment of endless expenses to include invitations for buyers! Why would I make that kind of investment, and then turn around and use a stolen credit card for a small purchase, you idiot!" I fumed. "You're hurting me financially, and I'm going to sue you for this bullshit!"

"I'll give you a contact number for a lawyer," he razzed.

I took a breath and watched the officer go through my bulging wallet. He examined pictures of Joseph and Bella.

"Who are these kids?"

"Mine!"

"You're a busy woman." The man unfolded and read a personal note I still carried around from my second husband. He then looked up at me. "Who is Leonardo?"

"I already told you--my soon-to-be ex-husband."

"Seems like a nice guy." The officer then opened up my day planner and studied the pages of notes regarding my apparel business and sales appointments. He examined all my credit cards again, too. "Well, since you will not admit to any connection to a credit card theft ring, I guess it won't matter if I cut up these credit cards."

"It will matter!" I angrily yelled. "I don't have any cash to continue my sales trip! I'm living on credit!"

"Not anymore," he said while he put the cards into his shirt pocket. "You know, lady, you don't make sense. You say you are a manufacturer, designer, and wholesaler, and you just left a showroom in Dallas, a week ago, with a line of clothes you are now wholesaling here in Florida. That sounds like a woman who doesn't have a problem with finances to me. You admitted to having employees. You could afford a payroll."

"Yep!" I quipped without any need to catch him up on my financial plight. In a way, I had felt using my estranged husband's credit card was like using a stolen credit card, but I reasoned had Leonardo not wanted me to use his card, he would have closed the account, like he had done with the other credit cards. Leonardo was a good man.

"I don't believe you don't have any cash, ma'am."

"You didn't find any cash in my wallet did you?"

He nodded no. "And not finding cash in your purse doesn't mean you don't have cash stashed back at your motel, or in your ATM account." He smiled, stood up, pulled my credit cards out of his shirt pocket, and walked over toward the desk. "You're being charged with using a stolen credit card. I don't have a choice but to destroy all your credit cards." He pulled a pair of scissors out of a drawer and began cutting up each card, and smiled at me as if he took delight in his destructive act. "I guess you'll have to go to the bank and make a withdrawal if you need to buy something--that is, when you get out of here, whenever that might be," he harangued. "My guess is that you could be in here for a *v-e-r-y* long time. I'm pretty sure you won't be finishing up any sales tour *this* year."

I shook my head in disbelief over this ever unfolding nightmare I called my apparel business. I could not believe the officer destroyed my only good credit card when I had only forty dollars cash to my name.

"Now," he continued, "You're allowed to make one phone call."

"Give me the damn phone!" I said with great fury. "You've ruined my life!"

"The only person you can blame is yourself," the cop quipped.

"Is that right?" I challenged. "We'll see about that."

TWO HOURS LATER, at the inner-city Tampa Corrections Facility, I stood inside a jail cell with the phone's receiver next to my ear and listened to the operator talk to the party I had dialed. I studied eight other women wearing the same drab blue jail uniform I wore while I listened to the operator make my first phone call from behind bars. "This is the Tampa Corrections Facility calling. You have a call from" and then the machine paused and then instructed me to say my name.

"Jean Wynn," I announced over my end.

The operator continued, "If you are willing to accept this call, please press the pound sign."

There was a lull; and then, I heard the party I called respond, "Hello."

"Dad!" I hollered while remembering he was hard of hearing. "I'm in jail, and I need your help getting out. It's all a great misunderstanding. They charged me with using a stolen credit card. I didn't do it! I had nothing to do with any crime. Seth and I were just selling my clothes door-to-door, when this cop walked up to me at this convenience store and arrested me. I need your help getting out of here! They charged me with a felony, and I can't afford a lawyer."

There was a lull, and I understood my father was trying to internalize what I had just said to him before he replied.

"I will have nothing to do with you and Seth, Jean Ellen. This is not my problem. You'll have to do this one without me. You're on your own." He hung up the phone.

I listened to the phone disconnect and felt stunned by his rejection. I sat down on my nearby cot trying to sort out what had happened to my life, and then began to uncontrollably cry over my reality.

A long night slipped slowly by me, and the next day, I became part of an early morning cattle call which included a group of us female inmates being relocated to some court-room like setting within the Tampa Corrections Facility. A jailer brought Seth into the courtroom, too, with a group of male prisoners, and they sat on the opposite side of the courtroom. We locked eyes, but neither smiled at the other. I eventually found myself standing in front of a camera in this room full of prisoners, who all waited their turn to go before the judge. I could see on a TV screen a judge, in a black robe, who sat at a bench in some far away courtroom, and he could see this jailbird through a monitor on his bench.

"How do you plead?" He asked me.

"Not guilty."

"And how do you plan to make bail?"

"I don't! I'm not spending a dime on this crap! I was falsely arrested!"

"Okay, Miss Wynn, the court will release you on your own recognizance. An officer of the court will meet with you later today, at the jail, to draw up your paperwork. You're dismissed."

I noticed a police officer signaling me to walk out of the room. I was led back to my jail cell; and nearly twelve hours later, I finally met with an officer of the court who had me sign ROR papers—Released on Recognizance. The jail then released me, with court-ordered instruction to immediately return to Texas, and to call them, every Wednesday, until the case went to trial. If I did not call every week, then the court would have me put back in jail.

Two nights had passed since the arrest. I waited at the front of the Tampa Corrections Facility for Seth while realizing I did not know where my van was any longer. The jail released Seth, within an hour, after me.

We greeted each other without a kiss or hug. Sleep deprivation consumed both of us, and I felt short tempered. "Now what?" I asked. "Where's the van?"

Seth pulled out a document in the handful of documents he received upon his exit from jail. "The Tampa Police Department Impound Lot has our van. We have to go to this address--110 South 34th Street."

I peered down at the piece of paper and did not recognize the street name. "Where is that street?"

"They said the lot is about four miles from here."

"And how are we going to get there?" I pleaded while already knowing the answer.

"We don't have any choice, but to walk, Jean."

I considered the four mile walk in heels, and the thought was excruciating considering I had no sleep the night before, and my back was killing me from my pregnancy. "And how much will getting our van out of impound cost us?"

Seth looked down at his paper. "Wrecker fee and storage fee for two days will be about $300."

"And what money will we use to get our van back?"

"Your charge card," Seth answered.

"I don't have any plastic anymore, Seth. The cop who arrested us destroyed my only good credit card."

"Shit!" He angrily exploded. "Can you call your father?"

"I did. He hung up on me. He wants nothing to do with us."

"Call your mother, Seth."

"Shit," he groaned. "What was I thinking?" He blasted as if suddenly out of his mind. "Ma was right about all of this!"

"What do you mean?"

"I mean," he yelled, "I am an idiot to have ever gone along, for one second, with this cockeyed, harebrained business scheme of yours!"

I heard his lack of loyalty, and my anger flashed. He was betraying me. I refuted his position. "Yesterday, before we walked into that store, you thought we had both oars in the water. Now, due to a set of circumstances, outside of our control, you want to jump ship and insult my intelligence?"

"Yeah, I do! I spent the $10,000 bodily injury settlement check I got from my car wreck on this insanity."

"You weren't injured!" I spewed. "You probably caused the car wreck on purpose!"

"What was I thinking?" He sounded agitated. "I could have bought myself some transportation; but now, I'm driving a van that will soon vanish, too! How ludicrous of me to think, for one day, we would be anything, but a failure! Oh, you deceived me, bitch! I don't want anything ever to do with this ill-conceived apparel business, ever again! Do you understand me?"

"My business is not ill-conceived, and I am *not* a bitch! Do you understand me? And, you're not going to tell me which way is up, or call me those kind of insulting names!"

"You're insane, bitch!"

I shook my head while ready to pounce.

"Oh right," he continued, "we're going to buy a sprawling house on the water after this sales season! Now, what are we going to do? Are you going to become a brain surgeon now? We don't even have enough money, for gas, to drive back to Texas! Moreover, what do we do now that we're both broke and unemployed, Jean? Did you consider that scenario as a possibility?"

"Well, maybe you will have to stop depending on my husband's money and credit card, Seth, and get a job!"

"Oh, shit!" he screamed. "I can't believe I'm in this trap!"

"Trap? You think you are in a trap, Seth? The hell with you! I can't believe I'm having your baby!"

"I can't believe you are, either!" I spewed while remembering how often he sang Billy Joel's lyrics to me, "♪*I would not leave you in times of trouble*♪... ." Why did I ever believe the first word he sang to me?

2
THE JURY TRIAL, 1998

TEN YEARS LATER. While I recall those days, in the late 80's, when I had more ambition than good sense, I can see now, how my karma found me and kicked me in the butt. For reason I clearly understand now, my ignorance, not God, cut short my blessings. My dream to buy a half-million dollar home on the water and to be a successful fashion designer was not in His plan. Hindsight is 20/20 and wisdom came with a great price. If anything could go wrong those weeks before, during, and after the apparel markets, it did. One minute, I'm doing a runway fashion show on a delayed flight with Marvin the Harlem Globetrotter, an event that creates a buzz about this Texas designer from Houston to Manhattan Island of New York City; and, the next moment, my number one seamstress quits me only weeks before my sample line fabric arrives because she judges Seth and me to be immoral. I take Seth with me, to Florida, to buy fabric for my next season, and we miss the entire textile convention in Miami because my seamstress plotted with my husband to give me the wrong dates. The textile suppliers delay the fabric shipment I need to produce the showroom sample line for the Dallas and Chicago markets, until the last moment; and, when my fabric finally arrives, I am rushed and short on professional seamstresses. I manage to produce a beautiful, 150-piece sample line for the two shows under a tight deadline; and then, when I arrive in Dallas, I discover a thief stole my reserved showroom. My three-hundred invited buyers cannot locate this Texas designer because management has buried me deep inside Infant Wear. Very few buyers wander into our showroom over the course of the seven days, but an important Group III broker, at the Dallas Apparel Mart, somehow finds me, and invites me to hang my line in his impressive showroom in the next upcoming show. I am suddenly excited about my business again, and hopeful that I will be the next household name in the world of fashion design. I forfeit my paid-for-in-full Chicago showroom for the following week, and, instead, hit the ocean front boutiques along the Gulf Coast and sell my clothes; and, just as the sales start racking up in Florida, the police arrest me and I find myself standing behind bars in the Tampa Bay Correctional Facility and facing a felony charge. The police cut up all my charge cards, which includes destroying the only good charge card I still have available for buying gas and food; and, if that hardship was not enough reason for me to end my sales season, the court then orders me to return to Houston immediately. I do not pass go. I do not collect $200 more dollars. My sales season is suddenly over.

I obviously paid no attention to spiritual law, until that disastrous moment, when the convenience store arrested me. Seth and I were setup and framed. I had been right to suspect, before the arrest, that I might suffer in some way for my past sins. Now I knew, for certain, that I had created all of this mess by my own doings. Today, I am wiser, but the lesson had been costly.

I believe we are all composites of vibrating molecules; some of us vibrate at higher frequencies, and some of us vibrate at lower frequencies. I attracted Seth and other people, into my life, who stopped and prevented my success. Back in those days, I vibrated at a lower frequency than the frequency of love. I was a member of a world, which evolved around ego, a heavier frequency than the world of love. Today, because of my painful mistakes, I understand I cannot afford to not understand Scripture, nor allow myself to fall to a lower place of vibration.

Apostle Paul wrote in 1 Thessalonians 4:15-16: *For this, we say to you by the word of the Lord, that we, who are alive and remain until the coming of the Lord, shall not go before those who are asleep. For the Lord himself shall descend from heaven with a shout, with the voice of the archangel, and with the trump of God, and the dead in Christ shall rise first. Then we, who are alive and remain, shall be caught up together with them in the clouds, to meet the Lord in the air, so shall we ever be with the Lord.*

Today, I believe God's people, both alive and dead, will ascend one day because they vibrate at His frequency—the frequency of integrity and love. His people will be able to rapture into God's kingdom because they obey his laws and are of his essence.

I was a liar back then, in the 80's; and as a result, I was married three times, lost custody of my firstborn, had an abortion, and my apparel business crashed and burned. I now sit here, in this courtroom, ten years later, dealing with yesterday's world, and though I no longer resonate there, I am still paying the price for my sins.

I have hope that this jury will see past their allegations, and that I will win permanent custody of my two young sons. I believe God's word will prevail in this courtroom because John 1:4-5 cites

"...because in Him IS life, and the life IS the light of men. And the light shines in darkness, and the darkness comprehend it not."

These corrupt liars, to include my husband, and his lawyers, and their lying witnesses, cannot see my guiding light; however, I believe God picked this jury for me, and that they do see my light. They see with a third eye. I vibrate from a place of love now. I connect to God's frequency, a higher and lighter frequency called love; and, I believe this jury will connect to my frequency.

Jesus said in John 13:33-36: *"Let not your heart be troubled, ye believe in God, believe also in me. In my Father's house are many mansions: If it were not so, I would have told you. I go to prepare a place for you. And, if I go and prepare a place for you, I will come again, and receive you unto myself, that where I am, there ye may be also."*

Seth's lawyer walked away from the witness stand, and over to the bench, where he and my lawyer then had a sidebar with the judge.

Seth's attorney walked back over to the witness box and continued asking me questions. "Is it true that you and your current husband, Seth, who was just your neighbor at the time I am referring to, went to Florida together while you were still married to your second husband, Leonardo?"

"Yes," I answered and then peered at the jury while suspecting they thought the worst of me. "Seth was not working when I met him. He was living at his mother's apartment with her and his teenage brother. They shared a two-bedroom apartment behind my apartment. Seth volunteered to help me in my apparel business. I asked him to go with me to Miami for a textile convention."

"And isn't it true that, after you and Seth left the textile convention in Miami, you drove up to Clearwater, Florida with him so that you could reunite with an old boyfriend, who was the bartender at the hotel where you and Seth stayed when you got to Clearwater?"

"I admit I did. I was acting single. My marriage to Leonardo was over for the most part—we had not talked in months. I didn't want to move to Indiana and have his children because I had two children already in Texas. I wanted to stay in Texas and continue to live next door to my son."

"And next door to your son's father, too, right?"

I ignored his insinuation. "The debate over whether I should move to Indiana, or stay in Texas, made me crazy." I turned toward the jury and pleaded for their mercy. "If you've never been emotionally torn, then you won't understand my actions."

"Ms. Wynn, are you telling the jurists you were emotionally torn between various men that you were sleeping with while married to your second husband?"

My lawyer jumped to his feet, "Objection, leading the witness."

"Sustained," the judge answered.

"Ms. Wynn, were you torn between various men that you were sleeping with while married to your second husband?"

I wiped the tears from my eyes. They harshly judged me for my past. The lawyer stereotyped me while he tried to convince this jury that I am an immoral and unstable woman. These lawyers held me accountable for my past. They unfairly evaluated me, with not all the facts taken into consideration, such as the fact that I had transformed into one of the Light. "As I said," I continued to explain, "that two-year long debate made me crazy. The debate between a six-year old, freckled face, little boy, and a loving husband, whom I adored, too, split me down the middle. I lost myself in distractions, in an effort to not feel sadness anymore. I was my own worst enemy back in those days, and I will say this--" I paused and connected to the jury. "I got what I deserved for wallowing in confusion, for too long, and for not having any conviction. I ended up with this husband."

Seth's attorney flipped around toward the judge and yelled, "Objection! The statement is not offered for the truth of the matter asserted, but for another purpose!"

"Overruled," answered the judge.

I swore to myself, in that very moment, I would never practice family law, or sit on a bench. If I were to act in a legal capacity, then I would become an advocate for family law reform. I would also stop judging, or stereotyping, or pegging, or evaluating other peoples' lives. What did any of us really understand if we have not walked in another person's shoes? What did this jury really know about me?

3
THE DECEPTION REVEALED

A DECADE EARLIER, NOVEMBER 1988. I patiently stood in my Houston apartment and listened to the fabric broker explain their service while waiting to hear the bottom line—could I, or could I not, order only the amount of fabric I needed to produce $35,000 of orders I had in hand? The woman continued, "We are a wholesale textile manufacturer—I'll have to check our inventory for that particular fabric. We work differently than a jobber."

"What's a jobber?"

"When garment manufacturers finish cutting and sewing, they invariably end up with surplus fabric. The garment manufacturer places orders for their fabrics many months in advance of production. The manufacturers simply cannot accurately estimate their textile needs because they make their estimates prior to sales. Their textile estimates can be over, or under, what they actually need—usually, they come under. Manufacturers sell their surplus fabric to intermediaries called fabric jobbers. These jobbers typically make large purchases—often they buy the manufacturer's entire fabric surplus. The jobber is willing to make this kind of purchase, even though it is likely to include some fabric that is not very desirable, because he is buying it for a fraction of the original wholesale fabric prices."

"I see. So you manufacture the actual textile?"

"Yes—our fabrics cost more than jobbers' fabrics. We actually do the weaving and finishing."

I learned a day too late I was paying premium price for my fabric. "Do you have the blue and orange sharks tooth in your inventory?" I asked.

"That fabric is gone."

"But you could make it again, right?"

"We can usually do another run, but only for customers wishing to purchase large quantities of 1000 yards, or more, of an item. The average lead-time is four weeks. How many yards do you need?"

"I need 1200 yards of the blue sharks tooth print, and 1200 yards of the orange sharks tooth—the fabric is rayon. Over half of my total orders were the pieces made up in this fabric."

"I see. I'm checking my computer, and I'm not showing availability—a designer bought the exclusivity right."

"But you sold me sample yardage. I assumed when I bought sample yardage from you, and then made up my showroom designs in this fabric, I would then have the opportunity to order more of the same fabric to meet my customers' needs."

"Yes, that is a common assumption; however, if a designer comes to us and is willing to buy up front all the fabric she needs for her entire season, and requests exclusivity rights, too, we will make that agreement with her for the right price."

"And how much does it take to get exclusivity on a particular fabric?"

"Oh, it depends—in this case, the designer locked in the sharks tooth for $200,000."

I did the math in my head—had I sold at least 1,000 garments in each of the fifty states, then I would have sold 50,000 garments total. Each garment required one yard of fabric, which meant I would have to buy 50,000 yards of fabric; and at $4 per yard, I would have to spend $200,000 to lock in the blue and orange rayon, too. My head spun—I could not believe that these textile suppliers had not told me about this risk upfront, before I spent money on sample yardage? I realized, too, that having an established sales force across the USA was mandatory to justify locking in a fabric upfront, and securing exclusivity. "Thank you, ma'am, for your help. Let me digest what you've told me, and I'll get back with you."

"Thank you," the woman said just before I hung up my end.
I sat down on the nearby couch and stared at a framed poster on my living room wall. Charley's daughter, Stephanie, modeled my best

selling design in the blue sharks tooth print, which I had just discovered I no longer had a right to purchase. Stephanie sported a blue bra top that tied in the front; and over the bra-top, she wore a matching three-quarters length button-less vest with capped sleeves that exposed a long slinky waistline, and belly button, over a low-slung matching wrap short, also with center tie. The matching three-piece ensemble required no buttons, no zippers, and very little fabric. I felt frustrated and angry over all the roadblocks. Everything had been a bust from the word go! I held $35,000 worth of orders in my hands, and I could not get off the ground. The convenience store had me falsely arrested, and my entire sales season went up in smoke. The Florida court had ordered me to immediately return to Houston. The court had ordered me to call the court every week, and warned me, that if I did not call them, as ordered, then they would come to my home, arrest me, and hold me in jail until my trial. I replayed the memory of being handcuffed to a chair in a small interrogation room at a substation and watching a cop cut up my only good credit card. Little did the Pyg realize he had ruined my entire sales effort with that one destructive act! I had no way to continue my road sales trip when I got out of jail. I was furious over how the arresting officer, and the court, treated me, and I believed I had the right to sue someone! I would find a Florida lawyer and sue for the injustice I encountered. I picked up the Tampa Bay Yellow Pages I had taken from our last motel room and flipped to Attorneys. I scanned the pages and immediately began making phone calls and talking to secretaries.

A WEEK LATER. "I have a felony," I clarified for the man who gave me back hope. A Coral Gables lawyer, who had mailed me his curriculum vitae, which highlighted that he specialized in false arrests, and had won numerous awards in excess of $1,000,000, had returned my call that day. "The store clerks alleged I used a stolen credit card. I did no such thing; nor would I ever! I have spent a total of $70,000 on my apparel business, and I have put all that I have into this spring and summer line. All my money, energy, heart, and belief went into the development of this spring and summer line so I could get to the Dallas Apparel Mart and to the Chicago Apparel Center and make sales. Why, I ask you, would I leave the Dallas Apparel Mart, hit the road, and use a stolen credit card to purchase $55 worth of items at a convenience store?"

"I don't know."

"I wouldn't! I have enough money for a hot dog!"

The lawyer laughed. "Ms. Wynn, I must counsel you on where you stand right at the moment. You have a problem. A felony is a crime with a possible penalty of a year to life in prison; and a felony conviction will cause you the loss of your civil rights such as voting, the ability to own a weapon, or to drive, as is the case with DUI felonies."

"I didn't do anything wrong, but be at the wrong place at the wrong time!"

"I understand, Ms. Wynn. The law protects citizens wrongfully deprived of their liberty. If the police did not have *probable cause* to arrest you, then you can sue for false imprisonment. That's what we will have to discover first—if the cop had *probable cause*."

"They had no *probable cause*—I was just in the store with my sales partner, Seth, buying some food. We had gone in there the evening before, too, but we passed off no stolen credit card either time. The cop did not find any stolen credit card on my person, or on Seth's, nor did the cop have any proof we passed off any stolen credit card. I want to sue these creeps for ruining my sales season!" I blasted. "I paid employees for four months to produce my samples so I could take my designs on the road! I bought fabric, haberdashery. I paid rent, utilities, and I want justice for this false arrest which put me in the hole!"

"Your case is interesting. The police have *probable cause* when there are enough facts to lead a reasonable person to conclude you are committing, or have committed a crime. *Probable cause* is a considerably higher standard than the mere *suspicion* an officer needs in order to stop you briefly, to investigate possible criminal activity. The belief must be based on objective facts and circumstances, and not on the personal opinions and suspicions of law enforcement."

"The arresting officer hated me."

"Why is that?"

"I had a bad attitude toward him when he started harassing me—I told the cop that I would have *won* a bet that he was *not* married. I think he was angry because his wife left him for *her* sales associate, and he was taking it out on me."

"I see—well then, maybe he did make it personal. Let's hope so, but determining whether an officer had cause to arrest you requires two analytically distinct steps—first, the court must ascertain when the arrest occurred, and what the arresting officer knew then; and second, the court decides whether the officer's knowledge, at the time of arrest, constituted adequate knowledge of the felony. If the officer believes a felony has been committed, then he makes the arrest, and then contacts the prosecuting attorney."

"What happens next?"

"First, there will be a preliminary hearing held before a judge. The defense may cross-examine and present witnesses. If the judge believes there was a crime committed, the case proceeds. The prosecuting attorney brings the defendant before a judge, and the court arraigns the defendant, if probable cause exists. He is told of the charges and enters a plea."

"We are not guilty of anything!"

"I'm certain you are not. The defense then sees the state's evidence through a process known as discovery. Therefore, at this time, Ms. Wynn, we have to exercise patience. First, before we can sue anyone, we have to get the state to drop the felony charges."

"Will they do that?"

"I don't know at this point—I must see the discovery first."

"And when we discover their charges are bogus, then we can sue them?"

"Once the felony charges are dropped, then we will sue."

"Who will we sue?"

"Most likely, we'll sue the convenience store for both punitive and compensatory damages. Malice is when a defendant knowingly gives a false statement to the police. We will have to determine if the store clerks were malicious. False arrest and detention resulting in post-traumatic distress disorder has been reason for courts to make large awards. I had a case similar to this one—the court found the officer liable; and the court awarded plaintiff compensatory damages for emotional distress, mental anguish, and loss of liberty on the false arrest claim. In an action for false arrest, the court awards the plaintiff punitive damages, in addition to compensatory damages. At no time, did the officer have any evidence that the couple took anything, or that either one of them took anything. The couple was held without *probable cause* and statements were libelous."

"That's exactly what we have here!"

"I believe so, too, Ms. Wynn. Compensatory damages are what plaintiff sustained as a proximate result of the malicious prosecution, and consists of injury, or loss to reputation, or character, time spent in jail, humiliation, physical or mental suffering, distress, embarrassment, nervous shock, impairment of social and business standing, loss of earnings, and attorney fees. Do you feel you have suffered any of these?"

"I have been dealing with all of that stuff—I'm broke, pregnant, and my family believes Seth and I are Bonnie and Clyde!"

The lawyer laughed. "I feel you have a strong case here. My partner and I will handle this case for you on contingency, and we have won over a million dollars for each client that has come to us with just this type of case. We get paid 33-1/3% of whatever we win for you, and I must warn you this case could take years before it settles or goes to court."

"How many years?"

"Three, five—I don't know. In Florida, a plaintiff must first demonstrate a reasonable basis for recovery of punitive damages. Then plaintiff must prove intentional conduct or gross negligence by clean and convincing proof. We will have to subpoena the store witnesses—all this takes time, and money, which is why we request 33-1/3% of any award."

"I understand."

"My partner and I will take this case on contingency, meaning you don't pay us until we get an award from the court. If we don't get an award, then you don't owe us anything."

"That sounds ideal!"

"Okay, well then, if you have no more questions, then I'll get off here and have my secretary draft a retainer agreement for your signature. I'll drop the retainer agreement in the mail today; and when you get the documents, please sign the original, immediately, and return to me, and then we'll begin working on your case."

"Okay. Thank you so much, Mr. Haggard."

"Call me Andrew."

"I will need both you and Seth to sign the retainer agreement, since both of you are suing."

WINTER 1989. The sun had not risen yet each morning when Seth and I headed down the stairs of our two-bedroom apartment to jump into my red van and to drive my very pregnant self to the nearby bus stop. My boyfriend would sit behind the steering wheel and wait with me in the warm van until the city bus came rolling up; at which time, I would then jump out of the cozy capsule and into the December cold and wave good bye. A temp agency placed me in a full-time typist position for the Hermann Hospital Board of Trustees, which required I take a sixteen-mile bus ride to the Houston Medical Center, a complex of sixty-two medical buildings. Monday through Friday, I would get off the bus on Fannin Street and walk a few blocks to the first high-rise ever built outside of the downtown district, and built to entice doctors to move to the new Medical Center area. I would make my way up to the top of a 1948 early modernism building via elevator, and sit at a desk with a view of the city from the fifteenth floor and transcribe a backlog of months of notes of the trustees' weekly meetings. My pay was $10.00 per hour, which averaged $1,720.00 a month; and after only a few weeks of service, I had an offer to come back full-time, after I gave birth. Although I found typing from a Dictaphone all day long completely boring, I was grateful to have the job and did not decline nor accept the post-delivery job offer. I would have to give some thought to leaving my newborn to a stranger all day.

Seth landed a sales position at one of the anchor stores at the mall across the street from our apartment—he earned minimum wage of $3.35 per hour plus commission selling furniture and appliances. For the time being while I worked, too, we had no financial difficulties paying for our rent, utilities, and food. The temp job offered no medical benefits; and the very fact that I worked in a high-rise of doctor clinics, and still had not had my first visit to an OB/GYN, due to a lack of funds, was a sad commentary about my life, and about this country.

Dorothy and Ron were a newly married couple and my new friends, introduced to me by my boyfriend—Seth had known Dorothy for years. I can best describe Dorothy as a haggard-looking blonde with fading classic features and large droopy breasts, and Ron as a tall, slender, below average-looking blonde male whom Dorothy apparently snagged into matrimony to help her with the bills and her three kids from previous marriages. Ron was a fully employed machinist and simpleton, and Dorothy worked nights as a cocktail waitress at a topless bar. She had been inspired by my apparel adventure, and hence, began designing her own line of G-strings for the dancers where she worked and for every other strip bar in Houston. I heard that imitation was the sincerest form of flattery, but my intuition told me the woman was trying to get Seth's attention.

Frequently, for the lack of money, Seth and I ventured out on a Saturday night to visit our friends. Dorothy and Ron's apartment represented oppression of some sort to me, and I would instantly become stumped how this family or any family could live in such a vortex of garbage. The public domain as I called their family room was cluttered with old worn chairs and broken end tables and outdated lamps, and a depressing oil on canvas painted by Dorothy with too much black hung on the wall. Her painting looked like a Rorschach ink blot. A tired-looking sewing machine permanently sat open at one end of the room, hundreds of little pieces of fabric scraps littered the thread-barren carpet, and piles of unused fabric pieces sat on top of everything. Dirty cereal bowls and Taco Bell wrappings added to the room's clutter, along with a smelly litter box for some mysterious cat that I never saw, and an old TV with rabbit ears sat across from a couch that I guessed came from Good Will. Dirty dishes piled high on top the kitchen counters, and the garbage, in the kitchen can, consistently overflowed onto the floor with beer bottles spilling out. The Linoleum floor in the kitchen, and in the hallway, curled up at the seams; and if one ventured toward the back of the apartment, to find a bathroom, or to check on a child, two more neglected, but large bedrooms, were discovered, each mishandled with huge amounts of clothing and shoes tossed everywhere, and suggesting peril if entered.

Seth and I would take Bella with us; and my six-year old daughter would play video games with Dorothy's two pre-pubescence daughters and son, in the back bedroom, while Dorothy, Seth, Ron, and I would visit all evening in the front room. I reminded my young daughter, each time, before we went to their apartment that she was not to go outside and play because the apartment community was an amalgamation of meager people with pointless direction.

Alcoholic drinks steadily flowed all night for all non-pregnant types, as well as did an array of discussions usually spurted out between puffs on cigarettes. I informed my audience, "The former Governor of Texas, Mark White, heads up the Board of Trustees for this private hospital. He mostly talks about the hospital's expenses, and its biggest and most costly problem--the overflow of indigent patients, from Ben Taub's emergency room, who land at our door. Ben Taub is a Trauma Center, and eighty percent of all admissions come through the emergency center; and although they have 650 beds, that situation is insufficient."

"Well," Dorothy asked, "can't their emergency room patients go to St. Luke's Hospital or to Methodist Hospital or to M.D. Anderson or to Texas Children's Hospital?"

Seth jumped into the conversation. "These private hospitals are liable for anything that happens to a critical patient if they turn away someone on the basis of having no insurance. A few years ago when I lived with Ma back in Clear Lake City, a woman was near death from a drug overdose, and when she was admitted to Humana Clear Lake Hospital, after discovering the woman was uninsured, the hospital discharged her the next day to Ben Taub against the advice of the receiving physician there at Humana. In the ambulance, the woman's heart and lungs failed, and she died two days later which prompted the first lawsuit against a Texas hospital under so-called anti-dumping laws."

I added to my boyfriend's thoughts, "There will be two charity hospitals in the city soon—the Lyndon B. Johnson General Hospital will open sometime this year. It's not located in the Medical Center, but is on the north side of the city. This new hospital should alleviate some of Ben Taub's patient overflow problems, too. I will have my baby at LBJ."

Dorothy looked at Seth. "Would you please take her in for a checkup—I can't believe she hasn't seen a doctor yet!"

Seth threw his hands up defensively without an answer and looked at me.

"I haven't had a free day in months," I added. "If I don't go to work, I don't get paid."

"No excuse," Dorothy slammed back. "You're delicate, and you and baby need to be checked."

"I agree." I shook my head and wiped a tear away while I felt anxious about the well-being of my unborn.

Ron glanced over at me and saw my distress. "Seth, you need to get a part-time job—your little mama needs to take some time out for herself and baby."

"I don't need another job!" Seth retorted. "What I need is a job that pays better. I'm working for minimum wage plus commission, and every time I walk onto the sales floor, to work my shift, there are four other sales people competing with me. I'm not making any money over there at the mall."

"What are you going to do when Jean quits working?" Dorothy asked.

"I've been looking—went on an interview a couple of days ago for a group down in the Galleria area that sells life insurance."

"I didn't know that," I said to Seth while sounding disappointed with his unwillingness to share his life with me.

Seth turned his attention away from Dorothy. "I didn't want to say anything unless I got the job first, but it looks good for me. The company is an independent fee-only and fee-based financial advisory focusing on financial planning and the management of assets. The upside of this company, that I'm considering working for, is that no insurance company, bank, or brokerage firm owns this company, and the company is free from any outside influence. They are strong in investment management, financial planning, estate planning, retirement planning, and tax planning—I can pitch any product to a client."

I looked over at Ron who was smiling; Ron then blurted, "Hey Seth—I know a couple that needs some health insurance." He pointed to me.

"I wish I could afford health insurance!" Seth barked.

"I've got a part-time sales position open, Seth." Dorothy offered and then looked over at me with a grin. "I don't know if you've heard this story, Jean."

"What story?" I asked.

"Seth might get mad at me for telling this story!" Dorothy giggled and then looked at Seth. He shrugged, as if without a clue. She turned her attention back to me. "Seth has gone out with me to the strip bars and helped me sell my G-strings."

I looked at Seth feeling hurt that he had no further interest in my apparel business, but that he was now helping Dorothy sell her dancer costumes. "I haven't heard this story, either, Seth," I said to my boyfriend and then looked back at Dorothy to tell me more.

Seth remained cool.

Dorothy continued, "Men are generally not allowed in the back of the strip bars where the dancers dress for stage; unless of course, they are gay. So, Seth follows me, into the dressing rooms, and prances around like a queen in front of all these naked women. Funniest thing you've ever seen, Jean. The dancers love him, and he sells lots of G-strings for me!"

I snickered, but I was not amused with the fact that my boyfriend was hanging with Dorothy when I was not around, and entertaining naked women with his flaming act. I locked eyes with Seth in disappointment, and he knew I had his number now. "I bet he's a natural!" I sarcastically expressed to Dorothy.

Everyone laughed but me.

LATER THAT SAME NIGHT. I felt fat and unattractive while I laid there in the dark next to my boyfriend in my king-size bed. Earlier that evening, Dorothy heightened my fears, when she disclosed to me that Seth was hanging out with her, behind my back. I had never felt that Seth loved me from the start. First, there were my suspicions about him kissing David, then my suspicions grew about his relationship with Runi, his so-called *brother*; and now, I had my suspicions about Seth and Dorothy.

Perhaps I was just an insecure pregnant woman, but I had never forgotten the words Seth had told me at the beginning of our relationship when I asked him what he had told Runi about me before leaving on the Florida trip. He admitted, "I told him [Runi] that I had to do what I had to do!" Seth admitted to me that night while we sat on the mopeds and talked on the beach in Key West, that *he had to do what he had to do*...[to get out of mama's apartment, and hopefully, to get ahead financially, too, by jumping on my bandwagon called the next great American designer.] I did not hear a man claim he loved me, but, instead, I heard Seth tell Runi that he was willing to take a big risk, with me, strictly out of financial necessity; and heart had nothing to do with any of his decisions. I felt Seth had seduced his way into my life under false pretense.

I snapped out of that grim memory. The father of my next child needed to hold me. I was trembling with insecurity. I scooted toward his side of the bed, reached over, and wrapped my arm over his chest.

He stirred, "Are you okay, Jean?"

"No, I need to feel closer to you. Please hold me."

He rose up on his elbows and leaned over to turn on the lamp beside the bed, and with a stern look on his face he said, "Look! Let's get something straight," he said with great irritation. "Do *not* come on to me anymore! I am *not* attracted to pregnant women!"

His words were cutting and said deliberately to strike at my self-worth. "Pregnant *women?* How dare you attempt to tear me down while I already feel fat and unattractive while I carry *our* child?" I sat up in the bed and held my belly while I detested the fact that this vicious man was the father of my next child. "This is my third child, Seth, but you should know that you are the first bastard in my life. And while I have come to understand, that what you find attractive, and unattractive, is simply a reflection of your degenerate mind—your constant, irascible nature proves you are consumed with fear, and I am acquitted, and held at no fault for your weak mind! And, frankly, Seth, your need to push me away, tonight, shows you up to be nothing more than an insensitive asshole! Your mean words will not make me feel anything more!"

Seth stood up. "I don't need to listen to your mindless crap all night long, Jean." He put on a pair of jeans and T-shirt and then exited out of the bedroom and walked down the hallway toward the living room. I heard the front door open and slam shut, and I prayed he would come back before the baby was born.

The following morning, I woke with a feeling of dread while I worked out the worst-case scenario in my head. I found myself alone in bed at this late morning hour. I threw on my robe and headed down the hallway, stopped and peered into my daughter's bedroom and saw she was still asleep on this Sunday morning. Once in the living area, I found relief to see Seth on the other side of the breakfast bar standing over the stove and staring into a pot.

As was the case most mornings for this 180-pound pregnant woman, I was hungry. I squeezed past Seth without saying the first word to him, and he did not speak to me. I opened an overhead cabinet and pulled out a loaf of bread and a jar of peanut butter, then opened the refrigerator and grabbed the grape jelly and began making myself a sandwich. When I finished the construction project, I poured myself a tall glass of milk and emptied out the gallon jug. I threw the plastic milk carton in the nearby trashcan, took my food and drink to the coffee table in the living room, and sat down on the sofa in front of a TV news show. I had no regard for high calorie foods, fats, or carbs, for the first time in my life, and it showed. I no longer had my svelte figure and enjoyed every bite of every meal, but I wondered if I was not stuffing down my feelings.

I had barely taken a bite into my sandwich when I heard Seth angrily scream, "Mother fucker! I can't believe you drank the last of the goddamn milk!"

His inappropriate outburst startled me, and I assumed he was still angry. "I'm sorry—I didn't know you needed any milk. I always drink milk with my peanut butter to avoid choking."

"Shit, I was making oatmeal!" He continued to yell, "Goddamn it!"

"I didn't know you were cooking oatmeal—"

"You saw I was boiling water."

"I wasn't paying any attention to what you were doing. There is a store across the street, Seth—go buy some milk!"

"You find money for milk, bitch!" He screamed again while he headed toward me and then turned toward the front door. He stopped in the threshold and let out a long loud scream of frustration which ended with the expletive "Fuck!" accompanied by one hard strike at the wall with his fist.

I could not believe what I had just witnessed. I stood up for a closer look and saw he had left a hole in the sheet rock. "Are you a total nutcase? I have never seen such insane behavior a day in my life! I cannot believe you knocked a hole in the wall. You are off the chain, Seth. You are not going to act like a white trash renter if you live with me!"

He grabbed his face and fell into the nearby leather chair as if having a mental break down. He sprung up, turned toward the door again, as if to exit, but stopped and put his fist through yet another wall and screamed, "Fuck you!"

"Stop destroying the walls!" I yelled. I remained standing behind the coffee table and was ready to take him on if he tried to put another hole in the walls. He gave me a look to kill and then walked toward the back of the apartment. I followed him. "You are out of your mind, Seth. The real problem is *not* that I drank the last of the milk! The real problem is that--"

Bella peered out her door and looked upset. I stopped following Seth and told my daughter to stay in her bedroom. Just as I entered into our master bedroom, I saw Seth pull my *Jean Wynn*, white neon sign off the wall. "Stop!" I screamed as I watched him smash it into the floor.

"You're the fucking problem, bitch!" He yelled.

"I can't believe you are this crazy!" I said while I searched the room for something of his that he valued. I swung open the closet door, and there, on the floor, stashed in the back corner, was an Early American, pot-bellied lamp, with a fluted top, and made entirely of milk glass painted with gold and deep pink roses on both sections of the lamp, and trimmed with a gold filigree metal. I picked up the fragile piece while I heard Seth scream at me from the other side of the room, "Don't do it! My mother gave me that lamp as a gift!" He bellowed.

His plea did not move me, and without a bit of hesitation, I smashed his sentimental possession into the floor and watched his mother's gift break into a million pieces. "Is that how you like to play?" I yelled back. "My ex-husband gave me that expensive signature sign you smashed into the floor, asshole!" Tears ran down my face.

Seth rushed across the room and toward me. "You fucking bitch!" He pushed me as hard as he could into the back of the closet. I tripped and fell backward into the closet wall. Instantly, I felt an excruciating pain in my swollen belly and screamed out in agony. I cried while I rubbed my big belly and stayed put until I felt the baby move. "I can't believe you would hurt our baby!" I screamed.

Seth appeared to have no remorse and immediately left our bedroom. I remained on the floor in the closet surrounded by broken glass, and fell apart over my reality. I heard the front door slam shut, just as Bella found me in the closet crying.

"Are you alright, Mommy?"

"No, Bella—I made the biggest mistake in my life hooking up with him," I said from the corner of the closet.

"We need to leave him, Mommy."

"I have nowhere to go, Bella—my parents want nothing to do with me since I left Leonardo—I have no job or money right now." I picked myself up and stepped around the glass. "Did he leave the apartment?"

Bella nodded yes. "Your foot is bleeding, Mommy."

"I'm okay," I said as I stepped outside of the closet and wiped the tears off my face. "I'll make this situation work out for us, Bella—it won't always be like this between Seth and me. Seth is freaking out because he is afraid."

"You need to leave him—he's mean."

"He's mean because he thinks I ruined his life."

"He has ruined *our* life, Mom!"

"Seth told me his father was a mean drunk, and that his mother always fought with his father over his chronic drinking—that fighting between his parents was all he knew for the first eighteen years of his life. There were money issues, too—the family didn't have enough money, either."

"So Seth doesn't want a family?"

"Something like that, Bella—but, he'll see, after the baby is born, that everything is different with us."

THE WINTER rolled by slowly, and I gave birth, on a Saturday, at 3:30 p.m., at the brand new, charity hospital, Lyndon B. Johnson Hospital; and as I expected, I had a baby boy who was healthy—thank you, God. My son was striking in appearance with brown eyes and sparse dark hair. I was instantly fascinated with this child, and intuitively, I knew he came into the world for a great purpose. I took my baby boy home on the second day after his entrance into the world, and soon thereafter, began searching the library to understand more about this little stranger. I learned that Louis XV, of Versailles, the King of France, was born on this day in 1715, and that there were at least eighteen composers born on Harper's birthday between 1710 and 1989: Ernst Eichner, Jean-Francois Le Sueur, Johann Nepomuk Poissi, Friedrich Fesca, Ignacy Feliks Dobrzynski, Robert Fuchs, Gustav Hollaender, and Richard Wurz. I was to know that this child would soon prefer the grand, the beautiful, and the noble, so said an astrological chart depicting a unique picture, at the time, my son was born, and at the place, he was born. My son's emotions would tend to rule his thought processes, and he, like me, was born with his moon being in Sagittarius, which meant we were both idealists. I recalled a conversation I had with Leonardo on the balcony of a penthouse, six years earlier—I struggled then with many disappointments. In an attempt to comfort me, Leonardo told me that Hamlet and I were both idealists; and he said that the Shakespearean character and I saw ourselves as evolving, and for that reason, Leonardo found me fascinating. He said I had the soul of a poet, and warned me that I was too sensitive, delicate, and complex to endure the cruel pressures of a cruel world, and recommended I learn to stand strong. I prayed my son's childhood at home would be kind to his idealistic nature, and that he, like the composers, would be able to hear the music of life. I called my son Harper, of English origin, and one, who plays the harp, the instrument of angels, which links heaven and earth. The sonorous sounds of the harp are healing to the body, mind, and spirit; and, I prayed unhappy parents would not shake my son, and that his God-given talent to hear life's music would blossom.

My boyfriend quit selling furniture at the mall shortly before I gave birth to our son. Seth got the position in uptown Houston with Rick Moore Security Financial Group, the independent fee-only and fee-based financial advisory company that focused on financial planning and the management of assets. They were strong in investment management, financial planning, estate planning, retirement planning, and tax planning; and Seth believed he could sell affiliated products to Johnny Lunch-Bucket. Every morning, the thirty-five year old donned a suit and tie, jumped into my red van, and drove twenty-five minutes into the Galleria area and left me alone without a vehicle. He took pride that his employer gave him an office with a window and a base pay of $400 per week, which was to last no longer than a three-month probationary period; and before he could sell anything to anybody, he first had to study, test, and get licensure. Seth explained to me that once he became a licensee and had his Series 6, 63, 65, and 66 licenses—only then could he sell the affiliated products; and when I asked what all those licenses were for, my boyfriend further explained he needed the licenses to act as an *investment advisor*. And unless Seth had a Series 7, he could not act as a *stockbroker*. A Series 7 license would allow Seth to enter the securities industry to sell any type of securities, but he first had to take the Series 7 examination—formally known as the General Securities Representative Examination. Individuals who pass the Series 7 are eligible to register with all self-regulatory organizations to trade.

I could not imagine how he could advise anybody on their financial health, considering we had eviction notices on our door every month, since I had quit working for the board of trustees at the hospital.

SIX MONTHS LATER. As Seth and I previously agreed to do back in the days when we were minus one child and scooted around on mopeds in Key West with high hopes of becoming wealthy, our family of four drove up to Springfield, Missouri from Houston to visit the "inner circle" as Seth tagged his clan of male friends. I looked forward to meeting Runi's wife, too. I had heard from Seth that she was a good Christian woman. Our eleven hour drive north was made easy with a seven-month old bottomless pit due to the fact that I breast fed, and for the sacrifice of my youthful breasts, Harper was a healthy and content baby who seldom cried.

Once in Springfield, a mid-size town with a population of 260,923, we then found our way into a traditional neighborhood development and pulled up to the front of a circa 1940's, quaint, two-story, stick build painted white, with a gray asphalt hipped roof, and front and side dormers with gables. A large oak tree hung over the long, single-car driveway, the grass was tall, and a multitude of overgrown bushes grew up around the side of the house and around the front and side-porch railings. Three older model cars sat in the driveway in front of my new, red van. Seth and I smiled at each other while he turned off the engine. We sprung open the driver's side and passenger doors to prepare to unload children and cargo just as I spotted the smiling homeowners exiting the front door to greet us. Strange arms flung wide open and hugged me while I hung on to my baby boy and Seth introduced me to the couple who appeared to be in their early- to late-thirties. My boyfriend introduced Bella as his daughter, and then took our son from me and set Harper into his best friend's arms and announced, "Harper, meet your Uncle Runi! And Uncle Runi, this little man here is Harper--my most prized creation, and the latest addition to our family!"

Joyce said to me, "Your baby is beautiful, Jean."

"Thank you," I returned while I watched Runi interact with my child. He smiled and held the baby tight. The man with black shoulder length curly hair looked into the boy's brown eyes and then looked down to Bella. "Is this a pretty good baby brother?"

Bella smiled, "I like him a lot!"

Joyce retorted, "You're no longer the baby anymore, Bella. What do you think about that?"

"That's okay," the six-year old answered. "I'm still my mom's only daughter!"

"That's pretty special!" Joyce declared while I agreed, too.

Runi ogled over the baby boy in his arms, and then gave Seth the smile and the nod while I wondered why he and Joyce had no children of their own after a decade of marriage?

"What do you think about my son, Uncle Runi?" Seth prompted.

"You did well, brother!" Runi answered.

The couple invited us into their home wherein the six of us walked through the front door and found one of Joyce's three children sitting on the couch and watching TV. Gabe immediately stood up and his mother introduced us. The nineteen-year old looked like his mother--an extremely handsome man with shaggy, dark hair, and brown eyes. He was polite and well spoken like his mama, too. We all joined Gabe in the living room for the next hour for conversation and coffee. I learned the young man still lived at home, worked construction, and played a guitar in a band. Joyce's two older children, both daughters, were married with their own children and living elsewhere in Springfield; and Joyce took delight in talking about her daughters and her grandchildren. Runi's wife was a natural-born beauty of American Indian heritage with long wavy coal black hair, high cheekbones, brown eyes, and a dimple in her squared chin. I quickly bonded with this extroverted and short woman, who had a history of hard times and bad marriages. As the evening passed, she invited me to join her on a shopping trip; and the two of us headed to the grocery store to buy food for dinner. I also suspected she wanted some alone time with me.

"Runi is rather pleasant," I admitted to her while in the car she drove to the store. "So these two *brothers* are inseparable, huh?" I was anxious to get her take on Runi and Seth.

"I met Seth the same time I began dating Runi--twelve, thirteen years ago."

"I find Runi to be a bit reserved and mysterious."

Joyce chuckled and rolled her eyes. "Once he gets to know you, then he opens up. Runi was dictating to me, today, before you guys arrived, *what* I was to talk about, or *not* talk about with you."

"Oh!" I was surprised to hear he coached her.

"Seems Seth made you out to be quite *upper-class*," she continued.

"What?"

"You know—high society."

"Oh, that's not me!"

"No, it's not. You're down to earth, Jean—you are not at all, what they painted you out to be. I was expecting some snobby, city girl to walk into my house."

"I don't know why Seth keeps describing me like that—he told me in the past I acted like part of the bourgeoisie."

"What exactly does he mean by that?"

"He says he loves that I'm bourgeoisie. I didn't know exactly what that term meant until I looked it up not too long ago. He is saying I belong to the social class that owns the means of production in a capitalist society." I did not tell this woman that I felt Seth had hooked up with me for one reason, that he was betting the bank that I would make a lot of money at the apparel markets.

"Runi told me you were high society."

"I'm not high society—I grew up in a lower middle-class neighborhood which is a ghetto now. And in truth, I haven't ventured too far from there—Seth and I have been on the verge of an eviction every month since I quit working to have Harper."

"That's hard," Joyce consoled. "Seth has never met a woman like you, Jean. Seth is a small town boy, comes from a blue collar background—never had a pot to pee in; and you, Jean, are this fashion designer, and--"

"Not anymore."

"I know, but you have been around some. Seth is lucky to have you."

"I think so, too," I sarcastically retorted.

Joyce looked over at me and smiled. "Maybe you have figured him out by now?"

"Enough to know that I've probably made one of the biggest mistakes in my life," I grimly admitted. "I would like to know more about the father of my son. Is he truly a psycho? Or am I just an insecure and paranoid woman, as he often calls me?"

"You're not that!" She angrily blasted. "You want more? I'll tell you what I know—for starters, I don't trust him or Runi. I have never considered Seth anything but a bad influence on my marriage."

"What do I have on my hands, Joyce?" I groaned.

"I've seen enough, Jean. When Seth was old enough to know better, and out of college, he was taking young girls to bed."

"Young girls?"

"Young as in fourteen years old—if that old," Joyce clarified. "He had no sense of right, or wrong, way back then."

I could not believe what I was hearing about the father of my last child and despondently shook my head. "I've seen enough, too, and I know he's got the morals of an alley cat. I guess I got what I deserved for my past ways."

"You don't deserve to be treated badly."

"We're fighting over money—we don't have enough," I confided. "And I can't stop thinking…well, never mind." I stopped in mid-sentence because I did not want to tell her everything I had discovered about him.

"Jean, you can trust me—I think we'll be friends forever."

I looked at Joyce and held back the tears, but I refused to tell her that I thought he was in love with her husband. "He hangs on to this job that doesn't pay but $400 a week. I don't understand why he doesn't move on."

"Because, Jean, Seth is arrogant—he thinks he's too good to work like everybody else. His arrogance has been consistent over the years I've known him."

"I knew he was fighting with his mother over money when I first met him—I should have run for the hills then. One afternoon, I walked up to their apartment—they lived in the apartment right behind mine. The front door was wide open—they didn't notice me while I stood there, in the threshold, watching them fight. He was in her face, and they were shouting at each other—I was embarrassed. I had never heard anyone talk to his or her parent like that, or vice versa. The way they were talking to each other, using all this obscenity—I had never heard anything like it in my life. She was mad at him because he wanted to borrow money from her that day."

"He has a younger brother, too, right?"

"Yeah, and he's only sixteen years old. Seth's mother was paying the rent, and utilities, for their two-bedroom apartment, and Seth was sharing a bedroom with his teenage brother and not working. And there was another day, when I walked around to the backside of our apartment building. I saw Seth sitting on his mother's porch, smoking dope out of a toilet paper cylinder while his Nissan was being repossessed right there in front of him."

Joyce shook her head in disapproval. "He has a history of unemployment, Jean. He was once married to a registered nurse."

"I know—Debbie."

"She had a good job at the hospital and put him through his master's program; and then, he got a job at a convenience store after he finished school, and that's where he met Runi."

"What happened to that marriage?" I asked.

"I don't know exactly, but I'm sure she had her fill of him and walked away."

"I've been very upset with everything, Joyce. I don't know how we're going to get out of this financial hole, either. I keep thinking something is going to break for Seth—but he's not sold a single client on anything since he started that job. I think his potential clients get a bad vibe from him and feel they can't trust him with their money."

"Probably—a person can't hide their true nature. Seth is a liar. All I can say to you, Jean, is pray—there is power in prayer."

"I do all the time—I don't have any other choice."

"I don't understand you, Jean. Why Seth? I mean you are beautiful, smart—you're running your own business. Why did you hook up with Seth?"

"You sound like my mother—she said he sucked me up like a vacuum. She and my father won't have anything to do with me. They haven't even met their sixth grandchild, Harper."

"Do they live near you?"

"Yes, they're twenty minutes away." I shook my head as if I didn't know the answer for my dilemma, but I knew why I had ended up with Seth—I had been a liar for so many years while married to Leonardo; and now, I was stuck in a relationship with a man I considered a con. "I feel like I've woken up in hell with my eyes wide open, Joyce."

"I don't understand."

"It's one thing to be in hell with your eyes closed, but it's another thing to wake up and find yourself in hell with your eyes wide open."

When Joyce and I arrived back at the house with groceries to start cooking dinner, we discovered Seth, and his so-called *brother*, Runi, had left to take a tour of the ever-growing town, and had left word with Joyce's son, Gabe, that they would be back at 6:00 p.m. in time for dinner. Joyce and I cooked pot roast, green beans, potatoes, and corn bread, and set a table for five—Gabe had informed us that he would not be present for dinner because he had band rehearsal.

About two hours later, around 6:00 p.m., Seth and Runi walked into the house with a new face I had not met before this moment. His name was Aiden Cooper; and he was of remarkable beauty with long, straight, golden hair, tanned and flawless skin, high cheekbones, and symmetrical lips alluding to great sensuality. Aiden had a prominent squared chin and strong jaw line, and his eyes of the deepest blue sparkled come-hither. I was attracted to this mythical creature--a man with perfectly proportioned features, a wide chest and arms of brawn, but I kept my thoughts to myself and wondered if he found me attractive? Not once did I ever catch him looking at me on the sly. I found his disinterest in me odd because since I had turned twenty years old, all men looked at me.

I felt the dinner conversation passed a bit awkwardly. I sat and listened to Seth, Runi, and Aiden dominate the table talk with silly banter. I waited to hear something interesting. The immaturity of the triptych, which ranged in age from thirty-two years to thirty-five, bewildered me. They acted as if they were stoned. Seth had a master's degree; Runi had been working on his master's degree for nearly five years; and, as for Aiden, I didn't know how far up the evolutionary ladder he had evolved, but assumed he had not lived too many life times.

Seth sat back in his chair, cleared his throat, and composed himself as if about to say something profound while some at the table waited with baited breath to hear him speak—I was not one of them. "So tell me, Aiden, since our first and only year together, at Southwest Missouri State, have you gained any more wisdom in your old age?"

"It's so simple to be wise," Aiden replied. "Just think of something stupid to say and then don't say it."

The table laughed.

I looked to Joyce, rolled my eyes, and said to her, "A lot of beautiful people are stupid. There's a tremendous amount of idiots who look so good—it's frightening."

Joyce laughed and held her tea glass up high. "Amen, sister!"

Runi sternly looked at his wife, "Oh, little Miss Sunshine is joining forces against us."

"We're just teasing you guys," I defended. "Anyway, I just called all the men at this table good looking! Why would you get upset?"

"Sure you did!" Seth retorted. "Though I would agree, we are a handsome trio."

The other two males cheered on Seth with "I agree," and "Here's to beautiful people!"

Aiden then blurted, "A day without sunshine is like, you know--night."

Runi and Seth fell apart over Aiden's funny, and I concluded they were stoned.

"Being stupid has its own reward, doesn't it, neighbor?" Joyce asked Aiden.

Runi defended their neighbor, "And look who *you* married, Joyce!"

Joyce blasted, "Had you only warned me, Runi, while we dated, that I was your prize for being stupid!"

"I'm confused now," Aiden admitted. "Who is stupid—us or them?"

Runi and Seth chuckled.

I softened any hurt feelings by answering Aiden. "Seth says we're all stupid—that in the realm of all existence, human beings are probably the least evolved. He says it's the aliens we should fear—not one another."

Runi elbowed Seth in the ribcage, "Hey bro, that's a bit arrogant. I'll have you know, I'm evolved!"

Seth winked at Runi.

"You're both arrogant!" Joyce snapped. She then looked my way and said, "Seth use to hold court back in the day. He would sit on a chair, and everyone else sat down on the floor at his feet, and he'd go on for hours."

Seth laughed and nudged Runi, "I remember those meetings!" Seth said to me, "We were a bunch of college guys, and we had fascinating conversations that lasted for hours, and listened to really great music. We created the kind of social atmosphere in which we could relax." Seth chuckled, "I would wax elegantly for hours and hours and hours--"

"--and for hours, and hours, and hours," Runi emphasized.

"All drug induced, I suspect," I scoffed.

Joyce laughed, "Of course!"

I looked at Seth, "I've got a question, Seth. If aliens are looking for intelligent life, then why would you fear an alien?"

Everyone laughed.

"Good one!" Joyce cheered on.

Seth stood up and loudly belched. "Good dinner, girls."

"Oh Seth," I grumbled at his lack of table manners and looked at Joyce. "His mother did not raise him right."

"Excuse me, one and all," Seth interrupted me. "China honors the tradition that the belch is a complement. Also, in China, and in Japan, eating very loudly, and slurping your food, is considered a sign of respect to the host or hostess to show how much you are enjoying the food."

"Personally, I think it's gross when you eat like that!" I replied.

"Me, too," Joyce supported. "And this is America—not a tribal world."

Seth laughed. "Forgive my barbarism; my complements go to the cooks. Men! How about a little one-on-one tonight?"

"Let's do it," Runi affirmed and then stood up. "I'll get the ball."

"You girls want a little court action?" Seth dutifully asked his friend's wife and me.

I nodded no.

Joyce hissed, "You might get a little court action one day, Seth, but not this evening. Go do your *one-on-one* without us—that's what you prefer anyway."

Seth guffawed at Joyce's remark. "You haven't changed a bit in the ten years I've known you!"

"Neither have you, Seth!" Joyce barked back in a friendly tone.

I remained sitting at the table and watched the three men get up and leave through the side door with their basketball. I heard my van start up and back out of the driveway; and then, Joyce got up, too, and invited me to join her with coffee in their newly remodeled basement. "I rented a movie for us."

"Let me make a bowl of rice cereal for Harper before we go down there."

"Bella," Joyce asked my daughter. "My grandkids have *The Game Boy*—it's set up on the TV in the living room. Would you like to play it up here, or watch a movie with us?"

Bella blurted *"Game Boy!"* just as Gabe walked through the front door and greeted us.

"How was your band rehearsal?" I asked.

"Cool, but our drummer quit at the end of the night," he said nonchalantly.

"What's up Steve's butt now?" Joyce asked her youngest.

"The dude wants to get paid for last weekend, but the club owner didn't pay anybody. Steve thinks we got paid cash under the table, and that we're not sharing with him, so he says he's going straight to Gino and ask him about the money. We sent him with our blessings, and told him to bring our pile, too!" Gabe chuckled, "Like that will happen!"

"File a complaint against Gino for violation of basic labor standards—for non-payment of wages." Joyce suggested.

"Where do I go to do that, Mom?"

"I'm not sure, call the Labor Board."

"Right on," he said.

"Would you play Nintendo with Bella, Gabe?" Joyce asked.

"Yeah, sure!" He said with great enthusiasm. "Let's play, Bella! Are you any good?"

Bella smarted back, "I beat my big brother a lot!"

"Oh good! You can try to beat me then—I'm pretty good!"

"I bet I can beat you easy!"

Joyce and I laughed and then headed downstairs to watch a movie. She had rented *The Color Purple*; and although the movie was released four years earlier, in 1985, neither one of us had seen the Steven Spielberg adaptation to Alice Walker's novel.

The movie was long—154 minutes; and when it ended, I hesitated to talk about some of the subjects that hit too close to home for my comfort. Joyce, on the other hand, went straight for the jugular.

"I'm always amazed with Hollywood's agenda to normalize homosexuality," she said. "I always thought of homosexuality as a perversion. Did you notice the bisexual relationship between Celie and the female jazz singer was normalized—what was her name?"

"Shug Avery."

"Yeah, that's it. Shug tells Celie initially, *You sure is ugly*; and then, she and Celie have a lesbian relationship. The movie portrays their homosexual relationship as a simple fact, with no value judgment! Did you catch that?"

"Yeah, I did," I answered while wondering if *judgment* was the very thing we attached to support our fears?

Joyce continued her rant, "Romans 1: 26 says 'Men committed indecent acts with other men, and received in themselves the due penalty for their *perversion*'—it does not say for their *normalcy!* Homosexuality is a perversion--an aberrant sexual practice."

I was reticent to embark upon a conversation that had been dominating my thoughts since Florida. I watched Joyce get up off the couch and turn off the video player that sat on top of the TV. She walked over to the basement windows that were high on the wall and looked outside while I remained sitting on the couch breastfeeding Harper.

"I see Seth and Runi are here—they're sitting in the van out there in the driveway."

I nodded and spoke to Harper, "What do you think Daddy is doing out there?"

"What do *you* think they are doing out there, Jean?" Joyce questioned me.

I looked up. "Talking, I guess."

"I have to be honest with you, Jean—you deserve to know what I know. It only took me ten years to finally figure out that I have been a fool."

"What do you mean?"

"Runi and Seth are gay."

Joyce confirmed my worst fear, and my stomach churned—I really did have a child with a gay man. Oh, my God! I was right--Seth cared nothing about me. He had never loved me—he loved Runi. They tricked me into having *their* child! I wanted to be wrong. "How do you know Runi is gay?"

"It's obvious—and I don't know why I never saw it before now."

"Saw what?"

"I went to a New Year's party with Runi. He's been friends with Mitt for years, but I've never gone to Mitt's house for any reason, until I went to this party last New Year's. Everyone at the party was gay—except for me. Straight men don't hang out with gay men, unless we are living in New York or LA. This is Springfield, Missouri for God's sake!"

"I don't think so, either—my second husband, Leonardo, did not tell his guy friends he loved them every time he spoke with one of them on the phone. Seth tells Runi that he loves him two, or three times, in every phone call—that's weird."

"They're in love with each other, Jean—they just never came out of the closet. Runi's parents are too conservative—Seth's mother is a churchgoer, too, and you and I are their covers."

"Is *inner circle* code for their boy club?" I asked Joyce.

"Absolutely, Jean—the term *inner circle* evolved out of the 1960's gay theatre. Gay actors defined themselves as *insiders* of their own secret world—in the big world, others considered them *outsiders*. The gay members of the theatre circle embraced the club-like characteristic of their gay world. Much was below the radar back then, and the inner circle shared the secret life of being gay."

"So if I understand then—their club-like gay organization neutralized any moral indignation?"

"The *inner circle* is a solvent of morality!"

"My daughter told me that she saw Seth kissing the bartender in Florida—Seth denied it, and said my daughter was just upset with him because he came between me and Leonardo."

"And this bartender was a guy?"

"Yes, a guy I dated briefly last summer when I was in Florida with Cheryl, one of my best friends."

"You should worry about getting AIDS."

"I do now—I worry all the time."

"I have accumulated years of strange occurrences that now make sense to me, Jean; and now that I know Runi is gay, the details all fit together."

"I have details, too, that make sense to me now, too. Here's a story for you. Seth and his brother, Taylor, got into a huge fight, about a year before I met Seth. The fight ended their business relationship. They once shared an insurance office together. And, what I deduced from Seth was that his brother walked into their office, one night, very late, and found Seth with someone—I assume it was a man. Because if not, then why would Taylor violently protest over Seth being with a woman?"

"He wouldn't."

"No, he wouldn't—after all, Seth was single at the time. And, did his brother *ever* protest that night! Taylor took the *Zherneboh* sign, which hung over the front door of their insurance office, and broke it in half—he slammed the sign over the desk top and broke the sign into two pieces, and told Seth that as far as he was concerned, his oldest brother had died that night."

"I'm surprised Seth told you that much, Jean."

"Seth still hangs on to that broken sign. I asked him what happened to his sign, and he told me that story—I guess he believes that I will remain in the dark forever, and never put the pieces together. And, from what I have seen, Taylor appears to really hate his oldest sibling. Taylor and his wife, and their three daughters, have never come over to meet me, or Seth's firstborn child—and they live twenty minutes away."

"It's a good thing you are not legally married to Seth—you're not equally yoked. And, I hope you understand why I put you, and your children, in the upstairs bedroom, and Seth down here, to sleep tonight. Please, don't take it personal, but I'm trying to be an example of what I preach to my son."

"I do understand—I respect your values."

"I know it might seem crazy to you that I insist you and Seth not sleep together under my roof—"

"No apology needed; and yeah, while Seth and I have been living together for over a year, and we have a child together, I really don't want to sleep with Seth tonight."

"You are not married in the eyes of God."

"And I don't want to marry him!" I angrily spouted. "It won't hurt me to not sleep with Seth for a night or two…or even for the rest of my life."

Seth and Runi came downstairs and interrupted us, and I held my bitterness inside. Neither one of them had a clue what Joyce and I discussed; nor did Seth understand I now knew his game. The bastard would never take my son away and partner with Uncle Runi.

Seth called for my attention. "Jean! Runi wants to go to bed, and you and I are invited to Aiden's house for a social engagement tonight."

"Oh, we are?" I said with contempt. I looked at Joyce for her reaction.

Joyce interrupted, "Go ahead—I'm tired, too. Runi and I got up quite early this morning. I'll keep an eye on your children."

"The baby is asleep."

"Put him in my grandkid's playpen for the night—it's upstairs in your bedroom, Jean."

"He should sleep for the rest of the night now that I have filled his belly up with cereal and milk."

"Don't worry about him, or Bella, right now—they're in good company."

An hour later, I found myself in Aiden's dilapidated 800 square foot rental, not far from Joyce and Runi's home. I sat on the couch next to Seth, and Aiden sat directly across from us on another sofa. A tall glass bong sat on the coffee table between us, and I watched Aiden pack the water pipe with weed. He then placed the bong up to his mouth and inhaled while he torched the weed bowl with his lighter. He choked on what he inhaled, but managed to hold the smoke inside his lungs while he passed the pipe over to Seth. We took turns hitting the bong. The room seemed to float while I gazed at Aiden and fantasized he was Narcissus, the handsome mortal lad who captured the heart of all the maidens, but wanted none of them— I assumed Aiden was gay, too. Narcissus had bent over a pool for a drink and had fallen in love with his own reflection; and after watching Aiden all evening act as if I did not exist, I summed he was a narcissistic homosexual, too. Echo, the fairest nymph, who tried to capture Narcissus' heart, angered the Greek goddess Hera, who then turned against Echo in rage. Hera condemned Echo to never use her tongue again, except to repeat what others told her. Similar, the marijuana had tied my tongue. I had no ability to initiate any conversation with Seth's old college friend. I was still upset over what Joyce had revealed to me, earlier that night, in the basement, and I was currently bored with the dingy conversation shared between the two stoners. I was barely staying awake when the ground suddenly shook.

"Why would you want that, Seth?" Aiden pointed toward me, "--when you can have this?" He pointed to himself.

Seth laughed and said nothing in response.

"Excuse me?" I interrupted while shocked by what I just heard.

Aiden kept his eyes fixed on Seth and ignored me. "Indecision and nervousness are not attractive traits in you, man!"

I looked to Seth for a reaction, but he remained cool and dared not look my way. "The art of seduction," Seth said to Aiden, "has a lot more to do with social skills, than with naked physical attraction—it's not the ten pounds I find unattractive, but the inner fear, man."

Was Seth talking about me? Did I hear him just say to Aiden that I was fat or fearful? I asked Seth with great indignation, "What are you talking about?"

Aiden interrupted me. "And she is—"

Seth stopped Aiden in mid-sentence. "She is fearless--the composition of everything I need at this time. I am not like you, Aiden. I identify myself as straight up and right on. I'm married with children now!"

Their exchange dumbfounded me. Was Seth covering his tracks now?

Aiden arrogantly continued, "So, do you believe it will be easier in the long-term now that friends and wife have met?"

"What are you asking, Aiden?" I fearfully asked.

Aiden glanced at me and then looked at Seth. "Why don't you take her home—she looks tired?"

"Want to go home, lil' mama?" Seth sweetly asked me. I trembled and bitterly whispered, "Get me out of here."

We drove a few blocks and arrived back at Joyce and Runi's house. No words were exchanged between Seth and me in the van, or while we let ourselves into their home through the side door. I was upset with everything I had heard that evening, but I did not want to start fighting with Seth, who in turn would just deny all allegations I would make against his character. Everyone was asleep when we entered into the dark house and made our way through the kitchen and down the stairs into the basement.

"Now, you are aware, Jean," Seth whispered as he removed the sofa cushions, "that Joyce does not want us sleeping together under her roof."

I watched the man unfold the sleeper sofa. "I know that, Seth." I whispered back while feeling terrified. "I just...." I stopped in mid-thought and felt a need to cling on to an ideal, to an apparition who had vanished before my very eyes. I had been deceived and had fallen in love with my own self-delusion. Seth had never been a man of honorable character. "I don't want to sleep upstairs. I want to sleep with you—I'm scared."

Joyce had left sheets, a blanket, and a pillow on the floor next to the couch. I watched Seth open up the foldout couch and make up his bed. "Jean, the dope has made you paranoid. Go upstairs with the baby," he kindly said as he crawled on top the mattress. "I'm very tired. I'll see you tomorrow morning." He clicked off the table lamp next to the sofa.

I stood frozen next to the bed while Seth pulled the blanket over his head and went to sleep. I felt as if I was watching my child sink to the bottom of a deep pool. I forced myself to walk away, from his bed, and head up the basement stairs while guided by only a dim light that shone from above. I made my way to the other guest room, on the second floor, and crawled into the designated bed, with all my clothes on, while terrified by what the *the inner circle* revealed to me. I cuddled with my daughter, who was in the bed next to me asleep.

THE FOLLOWING MORNING, Harper beckoned for me to wake up. I sat up in bed and saw Bella remained asleep. The clock on the nightstand read 6:00 a.m., and the sun had barely risen. I slipped out of the bed and picked up a wet baby, who was thrilled to see me. Harper reminded me what was important—him. I changed his diaper, and then headed downstairs with him, to prepare a bowl of cereal, and found Joyce in the kitchen alone, sitting at the table with a cup of coffee.

"Oh, there's that cute boy—give me that baby!" She ordered.

I handed her Harper and then prepared his breakfast. "Would you like to feed him?" I asked while pouring rice into a bowl.

"I would indeed!"

"Thank you. I'll take a shower, if you don't mind, while you feed him."

She spoke directly to the baby, "Mommy has to take a shower, and you and I are going to get to know each other, baby Harper!" She looked up smiling at me. "Use the shower in the basement—there are fresh towels in the bathroom cabinet."

"Okay." I exited the kitchen for my luggage in my bedroom, pulled out clean clothes, and then headed downstairs for the basement bathroom. I noticed Seth was gone and made note to self to ask Joyce, when I got out of the shower, where Seth had disappeared to that morning.

I stepped into the warm shower with the weight of my sad world on my shoulders. I wrangled with my disturbing situation, and had no answers as to how I would manage to take care of a six-year old little girl, and a newborn infant, without Seth's help. I dried myself off and dressed while anxious to share with Joyce what I had experienced at Aiden's house the night before. Perhaps she could give me some good advice. As I exited the bathroom, I saw Seth tiptoeing down the basement stairs—he looked like a deer caught in headlights when he spotted me coming out of the bathroom.

"Where have you been?" I politely asked.

"I was at Aiden's house."

"Aiden's house?" I had assumed he and Runi had been out to breakfast. "When did you go there?"

"I left last night after you went to bed."

A WEEK LATER, on a Saturday afternoon, and after many hours of defensive, and fruitless, shouting matches, over what was said and heard the previous weekend, in Springfield, Missouri, Seth and I laid down our swords, for the day, and strolled through the local mall window shopping with our two children. We had no money to spend on anything, but the family outing was a nice diversion from our grim reality. I had been housebound all week due to Seth driving my van to his appointments each day, and leaving me at home with young children and no vehicle. I tolerated Seth, and secretly understood I was co-dependent on a man I considered a great con man. I was willing to give him the benefit of the doubt, too, when he defended the homosexual allegations and said that, for me, to conceive of him as gay was absurd! He stated that everything I alleged about him was hearsay and that there was not a single ounce of truth, or evidence, supporting any of the charges that I made against his character. He was right—I had never seen him with another man. I wanted to believe everything Seth said to me in his defense; and, I wanted, more than anything, to have the perfect little family, that I believed was possible to have with Seth and our children, that I eventually began doubting what I had concluded about him, and found some relief from my anguish. Perhaps Seth was right; maybe I was paranoid and insecure. And what if I did stop judging him in this unkind light?

I pushed Harper in the baby stroller toward Macy's, and Bella walked on one side of me, and Seth on the other side, when I spotted a stocky, black guy, in his mid-thirties, sashaying over to us with a great, toothy smile.

"Oh shit," Seth moaned under his breath.

I looked over at Seth and noticed discomfort written across his face as the man drew near. I glanced back over at the approaching stranger, and upon closer inspection, I immediately noticed effeminate ways.

The burly, but well-dressed man, wearing navy-blue Dockers, and a perfectly pressed, faded-blue denim, long-sleeve, sport shirt, gold wristwatch, and expensive, leather loafers, stopped right in front of us. He extended to Seth a weak hand, along with kind words. "Oh, if it's not my lovely brother, Seth Zherneboh! I haven't seen you in ages. How are you?"

"Long time no see!" Seth mumbled.

"And speaking of *brother*, I saw your brother the other day over at the grocery store."

"Oh you did," Seth regretfully replied while he computed I was hanging on to every word of this flamboyant-speaking black man with dancing hand gestures.

"Yes, I did—what's his name?" He queried.

Seth reluctantly submitted, "Taylor?"

"Yeah, Taylor—that's the name!" The stranger nodded while standing with one hand on his hip, and the other hand held out in a weak-wristed fashion. "Taylor told me that you died from AIDS. That's odd, right?"

My mouth fell agape while I heard Seth laugh off his brother's lie.

"No such luck," Seth refuted. "My brother has got some anger issues—never got over me breaking out on my own and terminating our partnership—if you know what I mean."

"Oh, certainly I do!" The man obliged. "You two ran that insurance office together--not too long ago, either, right?"

Seth nodded, "It's been a while."

"I remember that story. Well, any-who, that mentality is so senseless, friend, but what can we do?—It's just one of those things life delivers to us. I always say one shouldn't do business with family anyhow anyway."

"Never do business with family," Seth assented.

"What are you doing now, Seth?"

"I'm an investment advisor." Seth then looked away from all of us as if preoccupied by something *out there*.

"Are you doing well?"

He turned his attention toward the black man. "I'm rolling—I have a corner office up in the sky in the Galleria area--with a view of the city, to boot!"

I noted how Seth avoided the truth while the friendly stranger gave my two children and me a quick once over—"And who are these beautiful people, Seth?"

Seth turned his attention back to the group and quickly introduced us without any enthusiasm, "This is my girlfriend, Jean, and her daughter, Bella, and this is my son—Harper."

"Oh!—you had a baby!" He said to Seth.

"Pleased to meet you," I responded with an extended hand. "I didn't catch your name?"

The man reached out and braised my hand. "My name is Renee, and it is a pleasure."

"And how do you know Seth" I inquired.

"Oh, he and I go way back to the days when—"

"Seth interrupted, "I'm sorry, but we are trying to catch a movie here and—"

"Oh, I'm sorry—of course you are!" Renee patronized. "Well, Seth, whatever you are doing, it's all looking good, darling. What a surprise—you have a baby!"

"Yeah," Seth said as he began walking away from his problem.

"Take care now, loves!" Renee said while he swooshed away.

Bella and I giggled; and then, the kids and I caught up with Seth who was determined to get away from the incriminating. The stranger's sudden appearance in our life completely unraveled Seth, as revealed by his strained facial expression. "So" I chided, "You know all the gay guys in the mall, too!" I gave Seth an inauthentic smile.

Seth ignored me.

"And what movie did we plan on seeing, Seth? Homophobia, Part Two!"

"Don't start with me, Jean."

LATER THAT SAME EVENING, Seth and I and the kids, once again, ventured to the wrong side of the tracks. I did not have any reason to argue with Seth that day over what I had witnessed at the mall. There was nothing to argue about anymore. Apparently, the black man knew Seth in the Biblical sense, and had I vocalized any supporting data I had recently gathered to support my theory about my counterfeit boyfriend, Seth would have simply called my suspicions more homophobic conjecture.

We parked our red van in a littered parking lot of the apartment complex and walked up to Dorothy and Ron's apartment. Seth knocked on the door; and while I stood on their dirty front porch, with him and the kids, gazing at a wet stringy mop standing on handle-end against the door frame, I questioned why an over-stuffed bag of smelly garbage, which sat next to my feet, had not found its way to the dumpster? Dorothy swung open the door, from the other side, and greeted us. I detected uneasiness in her demeanor.

"Come in, everybody!" She asked me, "How are you?"

"I'm fine, thank you." Clearly, she was upset about something.

We all exchanged polite greets and hugs while Ron walked into the room and joined us.

Ron acknowledged Seth.

"Hey Ron," Seth returned with an embrace.

"How's mama?" Ron asked me while he rendered a hug for me, too.

"I'm good."

Dorothy continued, "I cleaned up my house today because I knew you guys were coming over tonight."

I wondered what corner of the room she cleaned. "Oh, you don't have to go out of your way for us, Dorothy!" I retorted while I looked for a safe spot to set my baby down.

"You can just lay a blanket down on the floor for Harper right there, in front of the couch, Jean." Dorothy moved the coffee table out of the way.

"Thank you," I said while I handed Seth our son and began unpacking my baby's diaper bag. "You look very pretty tonight, Dorothy."

"I really tried tonight to pull it together, but I'm not feeling very pretty tonight."

"What's the matter," I asked as I watched Seth and Ron disappear into the kitchen.

Ron turned and interrupted, "Would you girls like a beer?"

"Wait!" Dorothy intercepted. "Before we start drinking, would you like to go to the grocery store with me, Jean? We need some soft drinks for the kids."

"Sure—" I looked over at Seth, "Please watch Harper while I go to the store with Dorothy." I saw Bella and Dorothy's two girls dart down the hallway toward the back while giggling.

"No problem," Seth assured.

I walked with Dorothy to her car parked under a nearby carport.

"How is your clothing line doing?"

"Oh," she groaned, "I've had very little repeat business."

"I guess a dancer only needs so many G-strings."

"That's the bottom line."

I chuckled at her pun. "What else do we need from the store other than Coke?" I asked while I got into her clunker.

"I needed to get you alone, Jean," she spewed. "I am so mad at Seth!"

I hesitated to speak while I considered that nothing she would say to me, at this point, would shock me. "Join the club," I batted back.

"You need to know something, Jean."

"Probably not."

"Really, you do."

"Okay—shoot me."

"He's coming over here, to my apartment, during his lunch hour, and hitting on me." She stopped and waited for my reaction.

"He really is a maggot, isn't he?" I calmly stated while feeling angry again.

"I told him off. My Lord, he's just had a child with you! I respect you, and I would not want you to think, for a minute, that I was trying to steal the father of your son away. I told him that he should stay with you and be a good father to his child."

"You can have him, Dorothy!"

"I don't want him!" She jeered as she pulled out of the parking lot of the apartment complex.

I shook my head over the latest revelation that Seth was a lying two-timer who could not be trusted around our own friends.

"There is something else I think you should know, too."

"There's more?" I groaned.

"My marriage is on shaky ground."

"I guess Seth knows that?"

"Yes, he does—which does not mean he's entitled to come on to me."

"I understand."

"Ron is the problem. He was living with a man before I met him—I'm not his cup of tea."

"And this man was who?"

"He was Ron's partner for years," she said while we drove down the busy Houston boulevard.

"Oh," I said while once again getting sick to my stomach. "But you married him? Why?"

She shook her head, "Mistake."

We pulled up to the convenience store. "Let's get a couple of Cokes, Jean—so they don't think we left to talk about them."

"I don't care what *they* think anymore."

"Me, either," she agreed.

"Do you think Seth and Ron are lovers, Dorothy?"

"I wouldn't put it past my husband," she said while we both got out of the car and went inside the store. "He can't seem to narrow his focus, either."

A few minutes later, we arrived back to the apartment to find the kids still in the back bedroom playing Nintendo, and the men outside, on the back porch, smoking cigarettes. I saw that Harper was asleep on the floor, in front of the couch, as I walked past him to set the bag of Cokes in the kitchen. I was angry at the constant flow of negative energy that had been coming at me for weeks now. What more could I learn about Seth? He was a chronic liar and an unfaithful bi-sexual who could not earn a dollar. I looked outside the kitchen window, saw Seth talking to his good ol' buddy, and imagined them in each other's arms. I seethed at the con job he did on my life, while I took the liters of Coke out of the plastic bag and set one bottle on the counter. I stepped into the threshold of the opened back door with the other liter. I vigorously shook the bottle, and just as I approached my boyfriend, who conversed with Ron and ignored me as usual, I twisted off the cap and aimed the spewing bottle of soda right at Seth.

"Hey, what the hell are you doing, Jean?!!!" Seth hollered while Ron laughed.

I sat the empty bottle down and growled under my breath, "I want to go home now!"

DAYS LATER. I looked down at the baby, who sat in his infant seat, on the floor, next to my library chair, while I wrote the last note for the day. I had a spiral notebook full of industry notes after only a month of library visits. "Listen carefully, Harper. I think I have finally mapped out how this business flows," I said to the infant who smiled at every word I spoke directly to him. "I will develop two lines of clothes every year—a spring/summer line and a fall/winter line. I will begin in March, of every year, my spring/summer collection. First, I will go to Paris to view spring collections every March. Then I, acting as a *shopper stylist*, will research the Paris market and bring back information on competitive lines. I'll get information like upcoming trends, and that season's colors and fabrics. I then will make a prediction on coming trends and create designs for my spring/summer line. In May, I sketch my spring line, execute the first patterns, and sew up all my designs in muslin. I have June and July to complete these tasks. Then, by August, I begin my fabric design stage, and I have--" I stopped to count the months. "I have only August and September to design my fabric. In addition, in August, I have to go to Paris, again, to view the fall collections; and in September, I must predict and design my fall collection. In October, I must print and order my spring/summer fabric, and I have no more than six months for fabric production and shipping. In addition, in October, I must execute patterns and sew up muslin samples for the fall collection. In January, I have to begin the fabric design stage for the fall collection. By February 1, one month before I receive my designer fabrics for the spring/summer collection, I must have completed my sample line, made up in muslin fabric. I must have my fall/winter fabric printed and ordered no later than March 1; and again, I have six months for fabric production and shipping. I get my spring/summer fabric the following month, in March, delivered to me; and then, the final sewing of all spring/summer sample lines, needed for each sales representative, in each of the fifty states, begins in April, and the sewing is completed by June 30—that's three months to complete all the sample lines. Also, in April, I plan for May's photo shoot of the spring/summer line. In May, I do the spring/summer photo shoot; and in May, I plan an August weekend, at a Mexican resort, for all the most important buyers, across America, to come see the spring/summer line. In addition, in May, I have to telephone buyers regarding their itineraries—that is a very hectic month. In June, I have to have all print work completed before July first—this includes the portfolios, brochures, garment tags, etc. for the spring/summer line. I need the invitations to the Mexican resort printed, too. The entire Mexican resort event has to be planned in June, too—another very hectic month. In July, I finalize my fall/winter muslin sample line. Then, in July, I price and deliver all my spring/summer sample lines to the sales force; and I mail out all the invitations to the Mexican resort spring/summer showing. In August, I receive all my fall/winter fabric and the sewing of all sample lines begins. In addition, by August 1, the sales force begins selling the spring/summer line; and the sales force has through October 30 to meet sales quotas. I also have a spring/summer premiere showing for buyers at the Mexican resort in August. Moreover, in August, I have market invitations for the October shows printed up, too, for the spring/summer line. In September, the samples for the fall/winter collection are to be completed by October 1 for the October photo shoot." I looked at my baby and took a deep breath. "Mama's done a lot of research. Hurry and grow up, Harper—I need a smart man on my team."

    My baby laughed and kicked as if he understood my predicament.

    "I'm not finished yet, Harper—I have a few more pages to go over with you. In October, I'm once again at the Dallas Apparel Mart to show my spring collection; and this time, I'm hanging in Group III in the fabulous showroom of Alfredo Suarez and Gabrielle Baker—not in the infant aisle!" I reconsidered what I had just said to my son. "No offense, Harper."

My baby giggled.

"After Dallas, then it is directly to Chicago. I'll get my Group III people to connect me up there, in Chicago, with some major apparel broker. Then, in November, I manufacture all my spring/summer orders and complete no later than January 15. And, in October, I have to do all the print work and invitations for my fall/winter line. Also, in November, I must prepare for the next upcoming apparel markets in January, and have market invitations sent out to buyers for the January shows, which feature my spring/summer line." I looked at my baby again. "Next time I do this business, I'll have it right, and I will have lots and lots of orders."

Harper kicked in joy.

"I love you, baby. You're so supportive of me—I'm almost finished telling you about my month-to-month business operation. In December, I deliver all my fall/winter sample lines to the sales force, and they have through March to meet their sales quotas. In January, I ship all my spring/summers orders from the manufacturer, which is located in Mexico. I will have a warehouse in Texas that will receive all my clothes from Mexico and distribute the clothing to all the stores across America, no later than February 15. Of course, I'm taking orders for this same spring/summer line at the January show, and I manufacture those orders in Mexico, too, and ship out to Texas warehouse, no later than mid-February. When the clothes arrive at my Texas warehouse, we inspect and ship the orders to my customers, no later than March 1. Customers will receive a bill along with their spring/summer order; and then, I get paid! In March, I show my fall/winter line at the Dallas and Chicago apparel markets." I stopped. "Whew!" I looked at my baby and saw he listened intently. "The whole process to develop and sell a spring/summer line takes two years. If I were to begin in 1993, then I will collect monies from buyers in March '95—two years later."

I looked at little Harper. "How else will we escape this impoverished life if I don't try again?" I picked up my baby, and we strolled home just in time to meet Bella at the bus stop.

LATER THAT DAY. Seth arrived home from work, after dark, and found me sitting at his old, electric, Sears typewriter, at the dining table, with an infant laying on top a bed pillow at my feet. I inconspicuously pulled out the paper in the typewriter and slid the paper, and a business card, under the nearby placemat on the table—I did not want Seth to discover I was writing Cliff a letter.

Bella lay on her belly on the floor, in front of the TV, watching late evening sitcoms. Once the summer passed, and the new school year began, that September 1989, I had to focus only on Harper, and myself, during the day while Bella attended first grade full time. The school bus picked up Bella, every weekday morning, and brought her back home eight hours later. For 7 a.m. until 2:30 p.m., I was alone in our apartment with Harper with no car. Since my baby boy was only days old, I often put him in his stroller; and I would push him for miles to the nearest library, and there we would stay for most of the day reading books. Sometimes I read children's books to Harper, and sometimes I read adult books aloud to myself while Harper sat at my feet and listened, too. I read everything I could find about the fashion industry and told my child what I dreamed while I sat at the library all day and constructed a business plan for my next business start-up.

Seth looked afflicted when he walked through the front door, that night, and found me sitting at his old, electric, Sears typewriter, at the dining table. He said hello to Bella and me, and then walked past the little girl on the floor, without any show of affection, and then past me, without a kiss, while heading toward the back of the apartment.

I looked down at Harper, who looked up and grinned at me. "He's looking for you—just wait and see. You come first."

Seth came back down the hallway and spotted Harper on the floor. "There's my son!" He leaned into me and gave me a kiss before picking up our son. "What has my son been doing all day?"

Harper smiled at his father while I detected marijuana on Seth's person.

"We went to the library, again, today. What did *you do* today, Seth?" I asked.

Bella turned from the TV and watched Seth hold her baby brother. "I want to go to the library, Mama."

"I'll take you this weekend when I have the van, Bella. You have some books to take back, too, don't you?"

Bella shook her head, "I read all of them."

"Go find them, right now, and stack them up on this table."

Bella jumped up and headed off to her bedroom. A few minutes later, she came back into the room with her three books and laid them down in front of me.

"Now, go take a bath," I instructed. "You have school tomorrow, and it is getting late."

Seth took the baby into the master bedroom, and I followed them. "How was your day," I asked in the threshold while still curious where he smoked a reefer during business hours.

"It was alright," he answered while he laid Harper down in the center of the king-size bed and then pulled off his tie, suit jacket, white dress shirt, and suit slacks. He laid his clothes across a chair, and then lay on the bed, wearing only silk boxers, and cuddled his baby boy.

I lay down beside them, too. "Did you have a lot of appointments today?"

He chuckled. "Funny story. I was driving along the 610 Loop this morning, and this young girl, twenty-two, blonde, and actually pretty sexy, motioned at me to pull over."

"Why?"

"Well, I didn't know why—so I pulled over."

"You pulled over on the freeway?"

"No, I took the first exit, and she followed me."

"And what did she want, as if I don't know."

Seth laughed, and I caught sight of movement in his crotch, and instantly, but silently, balked at his act of unfaithfulness.

"She rolled up beside my car and rolled down her window." He shook his head as if he had no idea she was picking him up. "I rolled down my window and said hello, and she grinned and wanted to know if I was married."

"And what did you tell the slut, who picks men up on the freeway?"

"I told her that I liked her 300ZX."

"Of course—that is your dream car, Seth," I said with animosity. "How did you answer her question?"

"I told her that I was single."

"You're not single!" I spouted.

"Well, technically we're not married Jean."

"Screw you, Seth. Did you tell the slut that you once had a 300ZX, but that because you are a loser, the bank repossessed your car?"

He laughed. "No, I didn't."

"I guess your honesty just goes where convenient!"

"Look, Jean, I took advantage of this morning's situation and asked her if she was interested in a healthcare plan, and she said her roommate might be—so I followed her over to her apartment and met her roommate."

"You did what?" My anger flashed.

"Oh, what the hell, Jean! Take a pill."

"I don't take pills!"

"I'll take any opportunity that I can get—if it means business."

"What the hell are you about?" I resounded. "We have a baby, Seth, and we are broke. I've been waiting for you to close the first deal, since you started with this company, and you haven't closed *anything ever*. Nobody wants to pay *you* to act as his or her *investment advisor!* You've been with Moore Security for over three months, and you have earned nothing but your weekly base pay. Four hundred dollars a week is not enough money for us to live on, Seth—and now you are picking up women on the freeway and smoking dope with them? I bet you didn't even go to the office today."

Seth laughed. "Sure I did!"

"I smelled the marijuana on you when you walked through the door tonight. Are you trying to piss me off? —because, if you are, it's working!" I angrily jumped up off the bed and walked out of the bedroom infuriated with the irresponsible creep. I headed directly to the dining table and took the letter I was writing Cliff out from underneath the placemat. I looked around to find a better hiding place and placed my sentiments under the kitchen rug in front of the sink. I then picked up the eviction notice off the kitchen counter and took it to Seth. "Here is what the front office left taped to our door today. We have twenty-four hours to pay the rent! I need last week's check to pay the rent by the deadline."

"I don't have one. There are no more weekly checks."

"What do you mean?"

"My ninety-day probation period is over. Rick says if I want to stay with the company, I work on commission only."

I stood there stumped for answers. "There is no more money?"

"Nope."

"What are we supposed to do, Seth?"

"I guess we'll have to sell something to pay the rent this month."

"Sell what?" I asked.

"We don't have to have an eight-chair teak wood table and matching buffet."

I shook my head in disbelief at how far I had sunk. "We don't have any food, either, Seth. And the phone bill is due this week, too, or they will disconnect the phone."

"I'll ask Ma to help us," he angrily shot back.

"You're going to have to get a better paying job, Seth. For Pete's sake, you have a master's degree, and the economy is strong."

"I'm talking to a couple of clients—something should break soon."

"And if you don't close these clients, then what? How do we pay our bills four weeks from now? Are you going to ask Ma again?"

"Leave me alone, Jean—I'm tired."

"From what, Seth? A ménage a trois?"

THE NEXT DAY, I finished writing Cliff's letter using the electric typewriter, and I searched for his business card for the mailing address. I remembered I had forgotten to move his card out from under the placemat the night before when I placed the unfinished letter I wrote under the kitchen rug. I picked up the placemat but did not see his card. I searched under all eight placemats; and then, I looked under the teakwood table and eight chairs; and then, I searched the floor of the entire living area! I even looked under the kitchen rug—I could not find Cliff's business card anywhere. I suspected someone else had found the evidence of where my heart was stationed between last night and that very moment, and Seth—well, I knew he would never own up to the theft, and Cliff, well, he would never learn of my fate or the love I still held for him.

I heard the doorbell ring and went to the front door. I swung the door open and saw two women standing in front of me.

"Are you the lady selling the eight chair dining table?"

"Yes I am."

4
A LEAP OF FAITH

JULY 1990. A knock on the front door woke me up from a deep sleep. I peered at the clock beside my bed and was surprised to see it was mid-afternoon. I heard the knock again and sat up to get my bearings. I was not expecting any visitor. Twenty-month old Harper lay asleep beside me on the king-size bed while I slipped on my shower thongs and headed toward the front door of our two-bedroom Houston apartment.

I swung the door wide open, and there stood one of my best friends.

"Charley!"

"Hey, Jean!" She stood there smiling. "Surprise!"

"I'd say! What are you doing way over here on this side of town?"

"Checking up on you—I tried to call, but your phone is disconnected." She walked into my near-empty living room carrying two, brown paper bags full of groceries. "I brought you and Bella some good nutrition—you need to get food stamps and eat better, especially now that you are eating for two again."

"Thank you," I said while I grabbed the bags that she handed to me. In that moment, I struggled again with a sense of failure as a woman who once had her act together. "Thank you, again."

"You're welcome." Charley dug into her shoulder-strap purse and pulled out some cash—"Take this, too."

"Oh, no, I can't." I supplemented my feelings of failure with inauthenticity as if *not* taking the much-needed money would help my pride diminish.

"Please, I insist. We want you to have it—get your telephone turned back on."

"Okay, if you insist." I said as I took the roll of twenties. My ego made her loving act of generosity all about how poorly I looked in that moment. "But Bob doesn't have a job, right now--you two are being unreasonable. Thank you so much. I'll pay you back."

"You're welcome. And don't worry about paying us back."

I sat the bags of groceries down on top of one of the few pieces of furniture in the living room—a cheap, Formica top table, with banged up chrome legs, that Seth and I had bought at a junk store, since we had sold my teak wood table and eight chairs with matching buffet for rent money. I gave Charley a welcome hug. "How is Bob doing?"

"Not good. He sits around and smokes like a freight train—coughs all day long, and he complains all the time about everything—he is the walking dead. I'm thinking about giving him back his engagement ring—I made a huge mistake moving in with him, like *you* have done with Seth."

"I did," I confirmed while I considered whether to turn my

telephone back on a priority now—our lack of food was a bigger problem. "You don't want to marry Bob anymore?"

"No, that phase passed—I want somebody with some life left in his bones."

I chuckled.

"Enough about me, are you okay?" She peered at my swollen belly.

"Yeah, I am," I lied as I walked the bags of groceries over to the kitchen counter and began to put them up while I considered how long Seth and I had financially struggled with having no money—the months had turned into years, and the conditions were getting worse and worse. I set a gallon of milk inside my refrigerator and then pulled out of the gift bag a quart of orange juice and butter. Charley ventured over, peered into my refrigerator, and saw I had only a single bunch of green wilted onions on the shelves.

"I can't believe you're having another child with him!" She scolded while she peered at the lack of contents.

"This baby is my surprise package from Heaven," I calmly answered and smiled. "I have no choice but to embrace my unexpected situation—I could never have another abortion. I love this child!"

Charley shook her head in disapproval—you should have your tubes tied after you have this baby. I did after I had my fourth child."

"I should, but I don't know if I can afford that procedure. We don't have any health insurance."

My friend turned her attention from the empty refrigerator shelves to again studying my near-empty living room. "How can you live this way even one day—especially while knowing where you come from? You have no phone, no food—all your beautiful furniture and household possessions are gone. You have no health insurance—he has *your* vehicle every day! You are threatened with an eviction every month."

"I've had to sell everything to pay the rent each month—even my washer and dryer."

"What's wrong with that man?"

JEAN PAULEY

"He's not earning any money—not even a weekly base pay any more."

The fact that Seth put my children and me into this hard place called poverty caused Charley outrage, as evidenced by her facial expression. "You need to find a food pantry, Jean, and get on welfare—food stamps."

"Where would I find a food pantry?"

"I'm not sure, but call your local churches—they know where you can get free food. Then, you can get on the government dole, too—call The Texas Department of State Health Services and get on the welfare system. They have a program called WIC for women and their babies—you can get free milk and cheese."

"I don't know about any of this stuff," I said as I wiped the tears away from my cheeks. "I've never had any experience with food stamps—I've never even known anyone on food stamps, or on welfare, or who went to food pantries."

"You can get free medical checkups, too, for yourself and your babies. Where is Harper?"

"He's in my bed sleeping—come see him!" I wiped the tears off my cheeks.

We walked into the adjacent bedroom. Charley ogled over my sleeping baby boy. "He's so big," she whispered. "He looks like Seth."

"He's pretty like his daddy. He likes to exercise with Mommy, too. I lay on the floor with my legs up in the air—I put him on top of my feet, and he thinks he's flying. He's got the cutest giggle."

She smiled. "What are you going to do for money after you have this next baby?"

"I don't know—daycare is too expensive for two babies. Seth and I are both eager to resolve this Florida situation."

"That legal case could go on for years."

"I know—"

"And you don't have anything else to sell from what I see."

"I know, I don't. I've hawked everything—even my diamonds and oil paintings, but I can only take one day at a time."

"You ought to take back your van—it's *your* van! Why are you letting Seth drive it?"

"So he can work!"

"But he's *not* working, Jean—there is no money coming in. Maybe you ought to just leave him, right now, before you get any further into this sad situation."

"I don't have anywhere to go, Charley. In addition, if someone was to hire this pregnant woman, and I *was* to go to work, then I wouldn't make any money after I paid daycare each week for two babies. I don't have a college degree—at the most I've ever made in my life was ten dollars an hour."

"You don't need a college degree; you've got great experience under your belt."

I shook my head in disagreement while my fear of taking care of three children all by myself kicked into reality. "I haven't held a paying job in six years, since I last worked for the oil companies, except for the short stint I did at the hospital, before Harper was born."

"They offered you a job, right?"

"Yes, the board of trustees said I could come back after the baby was born."

"Maybe that job is still available?"

"Probably not, it's been too long."

"You could get a secretarial job."

"I don't know. Computer technology has changed so drastically since I last worked for the oil companies—nobody will hire me anymore."

"Don't underestimate yourself, Jean—you have a lot to offer. Bob and I don't have any room in his small condo for extra persons, and I'm about to take my daughter and walk out, too; otherwise, I'd have you and your kids move in with us, and help you get back on your feet."

"That's all right—I'm staying in this situation for now. I'll figure out something once I have this baby."

"I sure hope you do. Don't wait on that Florida lawsuit, that might be years down the road before you ever see one dime."

"I don't want Harper to wake up yet," I said while I led my friend out of the master bedroom and back into the living room.

Charley walked over to a small card table with Seth's electric typewriter sitting on top and a folding chair in front. "I know you can get a job after the baby is born. You've done some amazing things over the years—anybody would hire you, Jean. Don't let Seth tell you otherwise."

"He tries to break me down emotionally. He's insulting and angry that I've put him into the position of responsibility. He says my conversation is *good for the length of one cocktail at a bar.* He talks like he's superior to me, because he has a master's degree and I don't have any kind of college degree."

"He might have a college degree, but don't forget he jumped into your business for the lack of having anything going on."

"And he wants nothing else to do with my *silly* business, as he calls my apparel business."

"He's a loser, and I don't like him, Jean—I never have."

"I don't like him, either, Charley—he tricked me. He calls himself *a piece of shit* when he argues with me—I always agree with him."

Charley snickered. "He hates himself, Jean."

"I think he does, too." I quietly considered how I could ever work full-time, take care of two babies, and a little girl, all by myself. I stared over at my typewriter and wished that Cliff's business card had not mysteriously disappeared—I was certain that had the Swiss received my heart-felt letter, I would have heard from him. "I started writing these days," I confessed. "I'm writing down all my feelings—it helps me get past my sadness and anger. And I sleep a lot, too."

"You're probably depressed."

"I don't think so. I'm just six-weeks pregnant," I answered while considering the validity of her statement. "Or maybe I am depressed, and maybe I just don't own up to that fact, but Harper is my delight—I love this baby, and I love being at home with him during the day. And Bella, she's amazing, too. These kids of mine are everything important to me these days. I still believe, too, I can start up this apparel business again, and this time, I can, and will do it better. But I don't know if I will ever be able to go at that speed again, now that I will have two babies and a little girl."

"Your children's well-being is dependent upon you, Jean. And your well-being is dependent upon you never giving up on your dream."

"When I ran my apparel business—I didn't have enough time for Bella, and I regret that I neglected her. Now, I'll have three kids soon."

"We women make sacrifices. You're all they have; and you're going to have to figure out how to provide for them one way, or another, but mark my words, Jean—Seth won't be around in the long run—he's waiting on that pending lawsuit to payout, and then he *will* leave you and the kids. Seth is only about Seth."

Her words were hard to hear, but I knew what she said was probably true. "He's waiting on a couple of lawsuits—"

"He is?"

I nodded yes. "He's involved in some kind of class-action lawsuit involving an apartment complex and a pesticide company. Seth, and his mother, and younger brother, lived together in this apartment complex, before they moved into the apartment complex where you and I once lived; and the pesticide company exposed the residents, at that apartment complex, to a very harmful chemical called chlordane. A landscaping company sprayed chlordane on the grounds. Some of the residents got very sick—the chemical came through the a/c vents. It leached into the pool."

"That would explain a lot," Charley quipped. "Seth acts like a man who doesn't think straight."

"He's crazy. One minute he's yelling and screaming; and the next, he's on cloud nine, as if we don't have a care in the world, and we have an eviction notice on our front door!"

"He sounds like he's bi-polar," my friend suggested.

"Or high—I think he's smoking pot when he is supposedly hard at work every day."

"That would explain his irresponsible behavior and mood swings. I don't think he's working at all, Jean."

I shrugged. "I don't know what he is doing behind my back,

really. But, on a better note, the other day, some strange man came to my front door, out of the blue, and handed me two hundred dollars cash, and a ham, too—Seth and I were thrilled about getting that cash, but before midnight, Harper had fallen into the table leg and cracked open his head. He needed some stitches, and Seth and I rushed him down to the emergency room. The hospital charged us two hundred dollars right there on the spot—I couldn't believe we spent all the money we had at the ER. And Seth, after he gave the hospital the cash, his personality changed into that of a monster."

"You should have just walked out of the hospital and told them to bill you!"

"I didn't know we could do that, at the time," I admitted to my friend while realizing I did not know how to be poor. "And my cousin's son died in a car crash, recently--"

"Oh, I'm sorry."

"Thank you. He was a teenage driver, and his death, and his mother's loss, both moved me—I can't imagine losing one of my children. I could not move out of the state to be with Leonardo because I could not leave Joseph. I couldn't send my condolences because I don't have a telephone. I couldn't drive to the funeral and be supportive because I didn't have the gas money. I couldn't even afford to buy a sympathy card; and truthfully, my plight embarrasses me. I don't want to be around my highbrow family. I feel they would look at my life and judge me in the worst light. For Pete's sake, Seth and I walk around the grocery store, in the evenings, looking for free food samples just so we can eat. I *am* crazy to find myself in this horrible situation after I had been given everything by Leonardo—I had a man who adored me."

"You're *not* crazy. You're strong, Jean, and you'll find a way out of this mess. Why don't you call your parents?"

"They won't talk to me. They've turned their backs on me—my mother says I don't have enough sense to get out of the rain. My father has always been non-supportive. He took back the money he saved for me for college, and told me that I wasn't smart enough to go to college, when I was a senior in high school. Look at my life now—obviously, he was right!"

"Don't believe his cruel words—your father's words were abusive, like Seth's words are abusive. You are an amazing mother and fashion designer, Jean."

"Thank you," I said. "I am amazed by what I've done, and I will not let my horrid circumstances kill my belief in myself. I did *not* wind up in this place because I am stupid! Or did I, Charley?"

"No, you did not," Charley comforted.

"My father never came around once to see my apparel business when I was operating out of the bank building in La Porte. I feel like he never wanted me to be successful."

"I think your father was the first man who emotionally broke you down."

"I watched him control my mother—I hated him for how he treated her."

"What does your father do for work?"

"He is a bean counter—he went to college. And the same company employs him since he graduated from University of Houston. He sits in a cubicle, all day, and once, in thirty years, his company promoted him to a low-paying, supervisory position in the same accounting department. I don't know what makes him stay? I'd be brain dead, if I were him."

"I think your father is threatened by you."

"Why?"

"Because, if you fly higher than him, then he will have to question his own lack of courage to take a risk in his own life."

"I think he's threatened in more ways than one—I believe he feels that any independence I might gain, might motivate my mother to leave him, and their unhappy marriage would come to an end. So, he sets the ground rules, which dictate to my mother that they are, now, to turn their backs on their firstborn--me. They protested my first marriage to Todd; and then, they protested my divorce from the chronic alcoholic because I had a child—let's, by all means, raise a child in the home where the parents are fighting every night over alcoholism!" I felt exasperated over their logic. "Then my father tells Leonardo to move to Indiana, and my father was completely clear at the time, that I did not want to leave my first-born son in Texas.

Now, they turn their backs on me! I'm weary of these fearful men, who want to control me, and now, I'm with Seth, another one--a misogamist, fear-based, drug user."

"Well, at least you recognize you are drawn to men like your daddy. But, nevertheless, you're going to end up out on the streets homeless, if you don't do something to help yourself and your kids—you can't depend on the current control freak to make your life successful."

"I know, I know;" I said with tears streaming down my face, "but I'm really scared."

Charley reached over and gave me a hug. "Just take one day at a time."

I hugged her back, and then pulled back, with a great determination to escape this fear I felt, caused by my circumstances. "I won't be like them! I've been thinking—I'm going back to school after this baby is born—the government will give me money for tuition, books, and living expenses. I learned about that opportunity from Seth's sister—she's divorced, raising two daughters, and finishing her psychology degree. Now that's a woman who seems to have multiple personalities, and she's going to counsel people!"

Charley chuckled. "I'm sure Seth comes from a long line of crazy people."

"I would like to know the answer to that question."

"Going back to school is great, if you can figure out how to do that without Seth in your life. And I think you can find a subsidized daycare program, too, for women like yourself who return to school."

"I'm determined to improve my situation, Charley."

SEVERAL MONTHS LATER. Seth took the weekday off, from his nonpaying job, to pick up his so-called *brother*, Runi, at the Houston Intercontinental Airport. My boyfriend's previous confession describing his *brotherly* relationship with Runi as *being one of the same loin, but not of the same mother* now made sense to me after connecting the dots. Runi's wife, Joyce, would be joining us Saturday evening because she had to work the day Runi arrived here from

Springfield, Missouri. Seth left me, his four-month pregnant girlfriend alone, again, with the two children, and took my red cargo van to pick up his best friend that early Friday morning. I expected the guys would be back within an hour, since we lived only twenty minutes away from the biggest airport in Houston; but six hours passed before they arrived back home. The sun was setting, and I was hungry and irritated with Seth when they both entered through the front door of our bare apartment.

"Finally, you show up. Not even a phone call, Seth? Runi, why don't you teach him the rules of consideration?" I said with a smile, so as not to make a bad first impression.

Runi stood in the threshold and smiled. "Hi Jean--" he said before Seth interrupted.

"I took my brother, here, on a tour of our grand city."

"There is no food in the house, Seth. I have nothing to cook for dinner." I watched Seth briskly walked through the room toward the bathroom.

"Well, that won't do little mama," Seth gently replied, with a kind smile while he darted into the water closet with one hand grabbing his crotch. "Excuse me while I drain the lizard."

I shot a smile at Runi, though I felt irritated over Seth's lack of concern that the kids and I had nothing to eat all day, and over my boyfriend's inability to call me, once, in six hours. I walked up to Runi with a smile and hug, "Welcome to our home."

"Thank you," he kindly replied.

My gesture was pretense, at best, that his presence was my pleasure, but my mother raised me to be a gracious hostess, and a people pleaser. On the contrary, Runi's temporary occupation in my home disturbed my psychic because Seth and I had had way too many arguments over my presumption that Runi was his lover. A steady inquisition, on my part, had existed between Seth and me ever since our trip to Springfield, Missouri. I felt Seth had been a liar from the beginning of our relationship, and had entrapped me with two more children. I resented Seth, more each day, due to the prevailing issue that I found myself, and my children, in a place of poverty, with no car, and stuck with a man, who was neither in love with me, nor supportive of my dream to rebuild my fashion business again. And, to add fuel to my growing dissatisfaction with him, Seth had deflected my allegations about his sexual orientation, and infidelities, by calling his contender, me, *a paranoid nutcase* when I tried to appease my doubts.

I noticed our guest and Seth both looked disheveled when they first walked into the apartment. Their eyes appeared glazed over as if they were high. "Where did you guys go all day?" I politely asked Runi. "I've been expecting you two to walk through the door since early this morning."

Runi was about to answer when Seth exited the bathroom while zipping up his trousers and blurted, "I took Runi up to my office and introduced him to my boss."

"I needed my van, Seth." He knew I was displeased with his game in which he had led me to believe, early that morning, he would be right back with our weekend guest. "I showed my brother my office with the window view."

"Some view he's got there," Runi meekly added.

"Oh! Were you impressed with his *window view?*" I sarcastically asked Runi.

Runi grinned and looked as if not sure what I meant. "He's got a cool setup over there."

"And what was your impression of boss man?" I asked Runi out of a constant curiosity I had maintained, for months, about Seth's employer, who, for some strange reason, kept a non-productive employee in an expensive corner office, with a view of uptown Houston.

"Rick seems alright," the slight man with long, dark, curly hair answered.

I was sure hell would freeze over, before Runi would ever open up to me on any level, which enforced for me, again, how much I looked forward to seeing Joyce the following day. I would dig and find out whether she and Runi were heading for divorce court, or not, and if they were, then I would assume Seth would probably divorce me shortly thereafter, too. I suspected when I had this last child, Seth would eventually try to take custody of his two children and raise them with his boyfriend, whom he had already introduced to my children as

Uncle Runi. "So how is Joyce doing?"

"She's okay," Runi answered without any show of emotion.

"Good," I nodded while confirming, again, that Runi was not giving me any details about anything. "Now what time will her plane arrive tomorrow?"

"I think about 6:00 p.m." Runi answered.

"She's great. I can't wait to see her! We have to catch up!" I noted Runi's expression suddenly appeared a bit stressed.

Seth interrupted, "How about a non-alcoholic strawberry daiquiri, Jean?"

"I'd like one; but first, let's discuss dinner. Have you guys eaten yet?"

"Yeah," Seth answered, "We had a late lunch at the Galleria."

"Yeah, that was quite a meal, bro!" Runi said while rubbing his belly. "I'm still full!"

Seth obviously played big shot that day and had spent what little money we had in our possession at a restaurant. Any meal in the ritzy Galleria area was easily forty dollars for two people. "Seth!" I blurted, "I need some money—please. I'm going to *Buenos Taco* and pick up some dinner for me and the kids." I stuck my hand out and waited for Seth, or his brother, to pull a wallet out of a back trouser pocket while aware that had Runi not been there, there would have been no discussion of buying anything other than another carton of eggs, or a bag of pintos, or a can of tuna.

Seth handed me a twenty as if we had more than two of those notes in the bank. "Thank you! And, I will spend it all in one place! Keep an eye on Harper. Bella is at the neighbors." I then walked out the door without asking either of them if they would like something to eat.

I walked down the stairs and stepped into my red cargo van; and as I jerked out of the parking space to back out, a glass pipe rolled up between the captain chairs from the back of the van. I leaned over and picked up the clear glass tube, which appeared to be drug paraphernalia. There was a small screen inside the slender cylinder and placed near its end. I smelled the instrument and did not detect marijuana, and I did not believe Seth and Runi used the pipe to smoke cannabis. I held on to the suspicious appliance while I drove, and when I got to the Mexican restaurant, I took my find inside with me. I spotted a table of four teenage boys and walked up to them.

"Excuse me, gentlemen." I said while I laid the item in question down on their table. "Do any of you know what this glass pipe is used for?

They stared at the clear tube with a milky white residue and then looked at each other, as if considering whether they should answer me or not.

One of them blurted, "Lady, that's a crack pipe!"

"Are you sure?"

The dark-haired male picked up the contraption and examined the device. "Yep," he said while he passed the tool to his friends.

The next young male, who inspected the apparatus, added for my further understanding, "You put the crack at the end, light, and then inhale."

"I see." I concluded the substance they smoked caused the glazed-over look in Seth and Runi's eyes. "What exactly is crack?" I asked them.

"It's a form of cocaine."

"So it's a white powder?"

"No, it's a rock—it's been converted from the white powder."

"I see."

"And from what I hear," the same boy continued, "crack is pretty intense and makes its users paranoid."

"*Paranoid*, huh?" That word inflamed me because I had been called paranoid by Seth, one too many times.

The table nodded in agreement. A third teenager added, "It's called the Devil drug because it leads to severe dependence, like PCP does."

"I see," I said while taking the pipe from the lad and concluding Seth was most likely leaving every day, in my van, to go off and smoke crack, which explained why he had not closed any business deals with any clients since he started with the investment firm, and why he always called me *paranoid*.

I ordered my tacos, and then returned to the apartment and hid the crack pipe in my bedroom closet. I kept my knowledge to myself that Seth used crack and planned to further question Joyce about Runi's drug habits when I met up with her the following day—I would ask his wife, of ten years, if she knew whether or not Runi smoked crack, and if he could have brought the substance with him from Missouri.

I fed my two children Mexican food and then put them to bed for the evening. The sun had gone down, and Seth and Runi were still interested in making daiquiris for us three, and watching a movie they had rented from the video store. I lay my pregnant self on the floor, in front of the TV, in the living room, and peered into the kitchen while waiting on my drink, and on them to start the movie—I was happy to have adult company for a change.

Runi and Seth stood beside each other in front of the pass-through bar in the kitchen while they ran the noisy blender and prepared the drinks. I could not watch their efforts from my position on the floor, but I could see them from the shoulders up. Every smile, and every glance, they exchanged between themselves, exacerbated how I felt about Seth and his boyfriend.

"What's taking you guys so long with that drink?" I grumbled.

Seth came waltzing out of the kitchen and gleefully handed me a tall glass of their non-alcoholic strawberry concoction. "This drink will be worth every minute you had to wait, Jean!"

I sat up off the floor and took the glass. "Thank you!"

"Suck it down, baby!" Seth said playfully.

I took a sip. "This is very good!"

Seth walked back into the kitchen and spouted, "Houston, we have a lift off!"

Runi chuckled.

Seth began wiping off the kitchen counters and throwing trash into the kitchen garbage. "Give me a minute everybody. Let me rid of the messy evidence of our sweet brew; and then, we'll all settle down for some Bond action."

I did not particularly care for James Bond movies; but tonight, I was more interested in studying my competition, and watching how the two men interacted with one another. I quickly drank down the strawberry drink; and within minutes, I suddenly felt my eyes rolling into the back of my head. "I feel like I'm going to pass out!" I said to the men while surprised by the onset of an unexpected sleepy state.

"Are the lights dimming?" Seth asked me and then turned to Runi and spouted, "Pregnant women sleep all the time."

"But I napped all day, and I want to stay up and watch this movie with you guys."

Runi smiled, "You can watch the DVD tomorrow, if you can't keep your eyes open."

"I guess so," I answered while I yawned and felt I could not fight off sleep. I had barely laid my head down on a pillow on the floor when I went unconscious.

My passing out the night before was the last thing I remembered when I woke up in the dark and strangely found myself in my bed. I did not recall walking to my bedroom, crawling into bed, or Seth putting me into bed; and I questioned how I had gotten there. The clock on the nightstand illuminated 6:00 a.m., and I was startled that I had slept ten hours!

I felt rested and leaped out of bed to get my bearings. I had a need to check on Harper and Bella, and to find out where Seth was at this early morning hour. After waking up in Springfield, Missouri, and seeing Seth sneak back into Joyce and Runi's basement, after being at Aiden Cooper's house all night, I now suspected Seth and Runi had managed to find time to be together last night while I slept. I walked through the dark bedroom and swung open the door. The living room and kitchen was quiet. I walked across the living room and peered into my children's room where I saw them both in their beds asleep. There was no sign of Seth or Runi anywhere in the apartment. When I walked back through the living room, I noticed the couch had been moved, out of the corner, and sat about three feet away from the wall. I walked up closer and studied the arrangement. Why had they moved the couch? Moreover, why had I passed out as I had the night before? My mind raced with my suspicions and *paranoia,* as Seth often labeled my conclusions about him, and quickly, I summed up what happened the night before—they had drugged my non-alcoholic daiquiri with sleeping pills. I knew their motive. They pulled the couch out, from a tight corner, because they had used the over-sized, cushioned arm of the couch for sex. One of them leaned over the side of the wide arm to brace himself for penetration. I speculated as to who was the receiver? A sickening feeling came over me, and I ran to the bathroom and puked. I had not experienced any previous morning sickness to date, and I figured my reality had played havoc on my stomach that morning—that, or the sleeping pills. I was angry Seth had no regard for my unborn child—I did not even drink coffee while I was pregnant! I would store up my evidence against the unfaithful, drug using manipulator, and when Joyce flew in later that evening, I would tell her what I had on both of them.

  I had managed to rinse my mouth, after vomiting over the commode, when I heard Seth and Runi walk into the apartment. I walked out of the bedroom, and into the living room, and gave them a disgusted look and angry attitude.

  "Well, good morning!" Runi gleefully said to me while not acknowledging the obvious—the unhappiness I intentionally directed toward both of them.

  I forced a smile at the deviates.

  Seth added to the pretense and cheerfully said, "We just had a wonderful breakfast."

  I just glared at Seth and bit my tongue.

  Runi yawned. "Hey, bro, I think I'm going to take myself to bed and sleep for a few hours."

  I knew then, they had been up all night long.

  "Yeah, that's a good idea," Seth responded. "Think I'll hit the sack myself."

  "Did you guys sleep at all last night?"

  "Not much," Runi answered.

  "You can get some good shuteye in our bed," Seth offered.

"You don't mind, do you, Jean?"

"No, both of you should go to sleep, and don't *worry* about anything."

Seth tittered, "What *would* we worry about, Jean?"

I shot back a phony chuckle and answered, "You *should* worry your enemy will sneak up on you when you least expect it—like when you're asleep, Seth."

They both laughed at my threat, and Seth retorted, "I *should worry*, Jean. I should worry about your crazy thoughts."

I knew Seth knew me well enough to read between the lines. The creep knew I knew they had drugged me. "Be careful you don't make me truly crazy, Seth," I solemnly warned.

Seth laughed while Runi backed off and remained silent. Seth looked at Runi and smarted off, "See bro, I told you, she's paranoid."

"Go to hell, Seth!" I snapped while I again heard he was building a case against me. "Give me *my* van key!"

Seth complied with my demand. "Don't use up all the gas," he ordered as I walked out the front door.

Later that Saturday evening, Runi, Seth, and I, and the two kids—Bella and Harper--met Joyce at the airport. We picked her up just outside baggage. I jumped out of the captain's chair when Seth stopped the van at the curb and greeted my new friend with a hug while her husband and Seth hustled her luggage inside the vehicle.

"How was your flight?" I asked while I noted the men on the other side of the van.

"Oh, it was interesting," she answered as if amused. "I'll have to tell you more, later, Jean." Her eyes darted toward the other side of the van, as if what she had to say was for my ears only. "So how's mama doing?"

"As good as one can expect a pregnant woman to be!"

"You're looking healthy."

"I've gained nearly thirty pounds already! I feel so unattractive."

Joyce chuckled, "You're pregnant,—you're with child. You are beautiful!"

"Seth doesn't find--" I whispered while using air quotes formed in the air with my fingers, "'pregnant *women* attractive.'"

Joyce's mouth gaped while in disbelief over his stonyhearted words just as Seth walked up to give his friend's wife a hug. "Good to see you, Joyce!"

"You, too, Seth," she said while embracing him and sounding indifferent. She looked over Seth's shoulder at me and rolled her eyes while still disturbed by my disclosure. She turned from Seth and toward her husband. "So how are you, Runi?" She coolly asked while she followed him to the van.

"I'm good, Joyce," he politely answered while he took the shoulder strap bag she handed him and set inside the van.

I could feel their mutual aloofness toward each other while I watched Joyce climbed up behind Runi, through the sliding door on the side of the van, and sit down beside him on the bench seat. I stepped into the front passenger seat and watched Seth get in behind the steering wheel.

Joyce leaned over Runi and grinned at the young girl sitting on the other side of him. "It's nice to see you again, Bella."

"Thank you—you, too," she answered with a smile.

Seth shifted gear and drove away from the crowded passenger pickup area.

"Where to now, brother?" Runi asked the driver.

"I'm taking all of us to see the Christmas lights in the Uptown District. We'll hang out at the Williams Water Wall for a while."

Joyce smiled with an approving nod, and I added for her knowledge, "The wall is sixty feet high and water cascades down over it; and at night, the water wall is illuminated by lights—it's really beautiful. The wall is situated at the end of a lovely little park, and there are usually musicians."

"That sounds wonderful," she said and then looked at my daughter. "How is school going, Bella?"

My daughter smiled. "It's okay—I'm out for the holidays."

"She could make better grades," I said to Joyce.

"What grade are you in, Bella?"

"First," she answered and then referred to her baby brother on the floor between the captain chairs. "My brother has eighteen teeth now."

Joyce reached over to stroke the baby's leg. Harper was strapped down in a car seat on the floor between the captain chairs.

"He's a cute little boy—how old is he now, Bella?"

"He's a year and..." She looked to me for the answer.

"Harper is twenty months," I finished.

"I'm hungry, mama." Bella advised.

"Me, too," Joyce added for my daughter's consideration. "I left the store today and raced to the airport. Find a good restaurant, Seth, Jean. Runi and I are taking you all out—our Christmas gift to you from us."

"You don't have to do that, Joyce!" I said.

"Nonsense! You're showing us all this hospitality—it's the least we can do."

"Well, that's generous of you both," Seth interrupted.

"It is, isn't it?" Runi teased his friend back.

AFTER DINNER, the six of us drove around the Galleria area. We slowly toured around Memorial Park. Seth informed our guests, "This is one of the largest urban parks in the United Sates."

"I didn't know that, Seth," I said. I turned to Joyce in the back seat, "This park has three miles of running trails—I use to run here, when I lived over here, on this side of town, with Leonardo. I will run like a fanatic after the baby is born—it's the only way to lose this weight."

"You were so skinny when I saw you in Springfield the first time, and Harper was only seven or eight months old."

"I always gain sixty pounds, or more, while pregnant—this is the fourth time, and I've taken off every pound, each time, by running like a fanatic—it takes about two months of running every day, and of course, I always quit eating, too. I consume about five hundred calories a day, until I lose the weight."

"You are disciplined, Jean." Joyce confirmed.

"When it comes to my body, I have always been very

conscientious."

Seth interrupted, "This is Memorial Park, and it was once the site of Camp Logan, a World War I U.S. Army training camp, which is why it's called Memorial Park."

"I didn't know you knew so much about this city park, Seth?" I added with great curiosity.

"Runi!" Seth excitedly pointed, "That building over there is the public bathroom I was telling you about."

I flipped my attention to the back seat to see Runi's expression and caught him nodding, as if relating to some story Seth had told him in the past. Joyce and I made eye contact.

"And *why* is that bathroom so important, Seth?" Joyce inquired with obvious sarcasm.

Runi and Seth laughed.

"It's not a funny question, guys!" She angrily retorted. "There are many park amenities here from what I see. You don't point out the golf course, or the volleyball courts, or the picnic areas—instead, you point out the men's room!"

"Oh, Joyce—don't start your crap," her husband warned.

"I didn't start anything, Runi." Joyce looked at me and rolled her eyes, and we both knew that we knew.

The sun set as we left the Memorial Park area, and the six of us cruised down busy streets with elaborate holiday decorations in Uptown Houston. Not too far away, in the same vicinity of the Galleria, we eventually found ourselves sitting under a full moon at the park adjacent to the Williams Water Wall. Joyce and I sat on the grass with Harper while Bella threw a Frisbee with Seth and Runi in front of the roaring water wall. I had finally found some alone time with Joyce and had opened up with her about the weekend discoveries.

"What you need to understand, Jean, is that they have their secret signals. Ironically, I sat next to a man, on the plane, on the way down here, and he told me that he was a counselor. And, when I asked him whom he counseled, he said he counseled gay men! I asked many questions as you could imagine. Did you know gay men cruise for sex in public restrooms--like the public bathroom Seth pointed out at the park this evening? In addition, foot tapping in a stall is a signal for soliciting sex. Cruisers are not sex offenders. Psychologists classify them as deeply, deeply closeted. There is a lot of self-hatred and shame among the closet gays, because they can't allow themselves to come to terms with their sexuality."

"Seth seems so split in personality," I whispered.

"Runi and Seth have heard, since childhood, that to be homosexual is wrong in the eyes of God. Homosexual men, who are out of the closet and openly gay, rarely engage in this cruising behavior because they have no need, or desire, to have sex in a public bathroom."

"That makes sense to me."

"It does to me, too, Jean. And I doubt Runi brought the crack with him on the plane—I don't think he would risk being caught with the drugs," Joyce added while looking perplexed. "I didn't know my husband smoked crack, until you told me about finding the pipe yesterday—I knew he got high, but I've never witnessed him doing anything other than smoking weed."

"Same here—I've never seen Seth do anything, but drink, or smoke marijuana."

"How is your marriage progressing?" I asked.

"I'm angry. Runi has no respect for me. I'm going to sell the house and start a divorce proceeding soon."

"Don't sell your house, Joyce—kick him to the curb."

"We've been married a long time, but he might go quietly if I threaten to tell his parents what I know about their baby boy."

"He will go quietly—like you said, these guys want to be in the closet for whatever reason."

"What about your situation, Jean?"

"Seth is not in love with me—never has been, and we fight all the time. Bella is unhappy and acting out in school. I get a phone call from her first grade teacher almost every week—my daughter doesn't care if the teacher puts her desk out into the hallway!"

"You need to leave him, Jean—for the sake of your children."

I considered telling her about the guys doping me up the night before with sleeping pills, but decided to not say a word—what if what I suspected was just my paranoia? "I assume when you and Runi get a divorce, and after I have Seth's second child, then Seth will divorce me—I hope he stays until I have this child."

"He will, but I'm worried. Seth might try to take your kids, Jean. I think Seth could be dangerous—he might try to disappear with your kids. And he and Runi might finally come out of the closet and be an openly gay couple raising two children."

The thought frightened me while I angrily shook my head at that grim possibility. "He will never take my children away from me—I'll kill him first."

"You need to start stacking up evidence against Seth for when the day comes and he wants to fight you for custody of your two children. Fortunately, for me, I don't have children with Runi—thank God! We don't have anything to fight over except an old house."

"I have a crack pipe now."

"And I'll testify for you, Jean, when that day comes. I'll tell the court what I know about Seth's character."

"Thank you—I hope I'm wrong about Seth, and that I never have to go to court and fight for custody of my babies."

"Don't let your guard down, Jean—Seth's behavior these days stems out of his drug use. If he is a chronic crack user, then he's your problem, and a big problem. My children experimented with drugs when they were younger, and I'm knowledgeable about the worst street drugs—crack, PCP, Meth. Crack cocaine causes a euphoric, overconfident behavior, and magnifies the ego. Crack users also experience high impulsivity, an overload of energy, and delusions and hallucinations, marked by illogical thought and disjointed cognition. In addition, if Seth is doing PCP, then he will often act dishonestly, to the point of delusion, and experience high levels of anger toward you. PCP users can also begin to experience psychotic breaks and schizophrenic behavior. And Meth users become aggressive, impulsive, and selfish—anxiety and agitation alternates with avoidance and depression."

"I see all those behaviors in him," I admitted. "Seth sits on top of the vanity in the bathroom looking in the mirror for hours, and he pinches black heads on his face and chest and arms until they are raw and big sores."

"Yeah, he's on drugs."

Our weekend guests returned to Springfield, Missouri; and soon, thereafter, I had further proof that Seth not only continued to do his drugs during the day while away from home, but also that he had a partner in crime. The two men walked into the apartment, one late evening at dark, and greeted me. Both smelled of reefer and their eyes were glassy. The unexpected guest caught me off guard. I hit the last key stroke of my journal page, before yanking the paper out of the typewriter for privacy. I had started writing a diary, a month earlier, to sort through my feelings regarding this hard time in my life, where I felt alone and destitute. I began grasping for words of strength, and discovered I was forming a personality for myself based on a higher vibration.

I set my writing face down on the table and picked up Harper who sat next to me playing with his blocks. "Hi," I said to Seth as he walked into the front door.

"Hello, Jean. I want you to meet a co-worker of mine—this gentleman is Abbott."

I stood up, walked over to the man, and shook the hand of a pot-bellied, average looking male in his early thirties with thick, mousy brown hair.

Seth continued, "And this is my son, Harper, and my daughter, Bella."

The man shook the baby's small hand, then turned to the little girl on the couch, in front of the TV, and said hello.

Bella returned a quick hello.

"Co-worker, huh? Well, I hope you have more success than Seth has incurred." I asked our smiling guest who looked directly into my eyes.

"Not much more," he chuckled. "I've been focusing on retirement planning since the beginning of my employment there; but lately, my financial advisory skills are not closing anything."

"And why is that?" I asked.

The stranger chuckled and threw his arms up without an answer.

"Don't feel alone in your failure. Seth runs a close race to Willy Loman, the ailing salesman in *Death of a Salesman.*"

"I don't know that character," Abbott admitted while Seth chuckled without a response simply because he did not know whom I was talking about, either.

I looked at Seth, "He's not a character in the Bible. Willy Loman immersed himself in flashbacks. His mind was constantly tormented by the hopes and dreams he had years ago. In addition, his solution was to complain about them, and expect the future to change, as a result. Willy blamed everyone but himself for his failure. He told his wife that people didn't seem to take to him." I looked at Abbott, "That's what Seth tells me when I ask him why he doesn't close any of his clients—it's not his fault, either. People in general just don't like Seth."

Both men roared, and then Seth looked at his friend and said, "Jean believes my clients get a bad vibe from me--that they think I'm an asshole."

"You are!" His co-worker fired back and laughed.

I joined him in his glee. "See, we have group consensus!" I declared with a nod.

Seth laughed, "I'm being ganged up against."

I cut into their fun time. "How long have you worked for Rick?"

"About a year-and-a-half," Abbott answered.

"That's a long time to not be making very much money," I added.

Seth interrupted, "Have you been working there as long as me?"

"Yeah, Seth, you were working for Rick before he hired me." Abbott turned to me, "I didn't really get to know Seth until only recently."

"Lucky you," I drolly snapped. "Are you married?" I asked while still wanting to get to the bottom of what this man actually brought home each month. Seth had been telling me that, with time, his pursuits would grow loyal clients, but I knew Seth to be a liar, and suspected Abbott believed Seth actually brought home some form of a commission check each month.

"No, I'm not married, but I live with my girlfriend."

"What's the difference?" I asked.

"I would think less costly in the end."

I chuckled and assumed this man earned an income, if he was worried about splitting up the pie—I, on the other hand, had no pie. "What does your girlfriend do?"

"She's a buyer for a sports store."

Seth interrupted, "Yeah, Jean, we're going to meet them for dinner this weekend."

"Oh, we are?" I answered while surprised and wondering how we could afford another night out, right after spending borrowed money on Runi and Joyce's recent visit to Houston.

"Our treat," Abbott announced. "My girlfriend's sister will come over and watch your two children, if that is okay?"

I nodded while still questioning who would pay the babysitter. "You and…"

"Beth."

"You and Beth are very sweet. I look forward to meeting your girlfriend." I considered that if I got to know Beth, the buyer for a sports store, then perhaps Beth could hook me up with a job, after I had the baby. "So Abbott, do you intend to continue to work for Rick much longer?"

"No, I need to move on. I haven't sold anything in the last three months."

There was my answer! Abbott had been there for as long as Seth, but not until recently, when he began hanging around with my drug-using boyfriend, for the last several months, did his sales become nil.

THE FOLLOWING DAY, I sat down at my typewriter again. I had not slept much, the night before, because I was hammering out an idea, which I now implemented into reality. I slid a blank piece of paper into the machine and began writing:

IN HELL WITH EYES WIDE OPEN

Dear Rick:
I send this letter anonymously, but I am concerned about <u>our financial</u> well-being in the short-term, and long-term. Given all the data, information, and past experiences, about how personalities affect sales performance, does it not make sense for you to understand what makes successful sales people tick? Recent studies prove that personality traits give managers a leg up in hiring sales people who can meet and exceed expectations. However, not everyone with the "right" personality becomes successful. Why? Because personality is not a case of you have it or you don't. Personality traits provide a recipe for success, but other factors determine whether these traits will be turned on, or just lie dormant.

It is fact that you and I suffer income loss because <u>some of your employees</u> do <u>drugs during work hours</u>, which explains why they are non-producers month after month. I beg, please fire these drug-using, non-producers, so that <u>we may both</u> flourish financially. I know that one of your employees sold you a bill of goods on his experience, and on his positive outlook toward people, and on his practical and pragmatic approach to decision making, and as well, on his attitude toward teamwork and attention to details—blah, blah, blah. You, however, ignored his low-assertiveness, and his low tolerance for frustration, and your employee now does drugs to compensate for his feelings of inferiority.

I stopped typing and picked up my reference book that I checked out of the library, *The Big 5 Personality Traits*. I borrowed excerpts from this book to compose this particular letter. I scanned the book for a sweet closing. I felt underhanded about sending the anonymous letter, but excited, too, about being a cause in the matter. Seth did not know when to get off a dead horse; and I now pushed him into a new direction, so that we would not be evicted at the end of the month—we had nothing else to sell.

WINTER. I sat my very pregnant self in my near-empty living room trying to get comfortable on the couch while watching TV. Finances and the well-being of my unborn child caused me endless distress in the wee hours of the early mornings. I lifted myself up, out of the couch, and waddled over to the front door of our apartment. I stood and looked into my living area. My eyes scanned the long, white walls of the rectangular-shaped jail cell, which trapped me for too long. The cheap beige carpet was hard, and the padding too thin for me to lie on the floor comfortably. My apartment was a blank canvass with no sign of décor or creativity. I turned up the small TV and then walked into my children's bedroom to check on both of them. My daughter and son slept soundly. I walked into the kitchen feeling hungry. There was more than usual in the refrigerator these days, as Seth and I had found a food pantry just down the street, about three miles from our apartment. I had an unlimited supply of expensive pastries past their expirations dates; and, as a result of eating a steady diet of stale cakes and strudels, I had gained another ten pounds in just a few, short weeks. I chose not to eat at this late hour, closed the refrigerator door, and walked out of the kitchen feeling bored. I sat back down on the sofa while committing to lose all this pregnancy fat by running daily before my unborn child was one month old.

I stared at the TV and the evangelist words caught my attention. I turned up the volume. "What will God's people do on the new earth? Well, my sisters and brothers, the Lord says in Isaiah 65: 21-25, *'And they shall build houses and inhabit them. And, they shall plant vineyards and eat the fruit of them. They shall not build and another inhabit. They shall not plant and another eat. For as the days of a tree are the days of my people, my elect shall long enjoy the work of their hands. They shall not labor in vain nor bring forth in trouble, for they are the seed of the blessed of the Lord, and their offspring with them. And, it shall come to pass, that before they call, I will answer. And while they are speaking, I will hear.'"

His Word comforted me, and I listened for more clarity. "And in Malachi 3:2-12, *'And I will come near you for judgment; and I will be a swift witness against the sorcerers, adulterers, perjurers, and against those who exploit wage earners, the widow, the fatherless, and those who turn aside the stranger from his right, and do not fear me,' said the Lord of hosts."*

I felt guilt and unworthiness, again, for my past sins, and feared I would not enter into God's kingdom. The minister continued to read from his Bible:

"For I am the Lord. I do not change; therefore, you are not consumed

sons of Jacob. Even from the days of your fathers, you have gone away from my ordinances and have not kept them. Return to me, and I will return to you,' says the Lord of hosts.
    But you ask, 'Wherein shall we return?'
    The Lord says, 'Will a man rob God? Yet, you have robbed me.'
    And you ask, 'Wherein have we robbed thee?'
    'In tithes and offerings,' says the Lord. 'You are cursed with a curse, for you have robbed me, even this whole nation. Bring all the tithes into the storehouse, that there may be meat in my house, and prove me now herewith,' says the Lord of hosts—'if I will not open for you the windows of heaven, and pour you out a blessing, that there shall not be room enough to receive it. I will rebuke the devourer for your sakes, and he shall not destroy the fruits of your ground, neither shall your vine cast her fruit before the time in the field. And all nations shall call you blessed, for you shall be a delightsome land,' said the Lord of hosts."

    I considered God's Word and knew I had not given anything back to the Lord when I had riches; and now, I was without God's blessings—I had been a taker and not a giver. I had been unappreciative of everything God had blessed me with in the past, and now, I had nothing.

    The evangelist continued, "In Genesis 28:20, we read: *"And Jacob vowed a vow, saying 'if God will be with me, and will keep me in his way that I go, and will give me bread to eat, and raiment to put on, so that I come again to my father's house in peace, then shall the Lord be my God! And this stone, which I have set for a pillar, shall be God's house; and of all that thou shall give me, I will surely give the tenth to Thee!'"*

    I struggled to get up off the couch, and then waddled back into the kitchen and grabbed the checkbook off the kitchen counter. I scanned the ledger and saw that Seth and I had a total of one hundred and twenty dollars in our joint checking account. I believed, without a doubt, the Lord had heard my frequent prayers over the last years, but until I acted, and gave out of faith in God's Word, my last dime, God would not bless me.

    The preacher's words continued to cut through my considerations. *"With men this is impossible; but with God, all things are possible."*

    In that instant, I heard God instruct me to act out of faith. I began writing a check for the preacher's ministry. I filled out the amount to be one hundred dollars while I prayed, "Forgive me Lord for all my transgressions. I promise to walk in faith from this day forward."

The man on TV continued to preach. "King David broke God's commandments—thou shall not kill; that shall not commit adultery. David had Uriah, Bathsheba's husband, killed on the front line of battle so that David could have Uriah's wife for himself. Uriah's wife carried David's child; and after Uriah died, David admitted he had sinned against the Lord. And the Lord forgave David, but because David had treated God and the Word of God with brazen contempt, the Lord told David that the child Bathsheba would bear for him would die."

I turned down the TV not wanting to hear anymore of his scary words. Seth and I had broken the commandments of the Lord, too; and for our acts of disobedience, we now had no blessings and a lot of suffering. "Please, God," I begged, "Protect my innocent children—don't let any man take my children away from me. Protect them from accident, disease, and evil." I pulled a blank envelope out of a box of envelopes I found on my kitchen counter and addressed the donation to the address I saw flash on TV—I would give one hundred dollars to the ministry as an act of faith and obedience.

Suddenly, the clanging of metal echoed from outside just as I sealed the envelope closed. I trotted toward the front door, fearing the worst at this early a.m. hour. I stepped out my front door, and into the night air, and looked toward the parking lot. I saw a tow truck and its driver hooking up my red van. Alas, Leonardo was taking back the vehicle. I raced back into the apartment and ran down the hallway to wake up my boyfriend. "Seth! Get up fast! The van is being repossessed!"

"Oh shit!" Seth cried while leaping out of bed and throwing on jeans, a T-shirt, and then slipping into his loafers before racing out of our apartment. I followed Seth through the front door and stopped on the balcony to watch him race down the stairs and toward the repo man. I witnessed a losing argument and wondered why Leonardo had allowed us to drive the van for as long as we had, considering Seth and

I had never made the first payment. Leonardo and I had been divorced for over two years. While I watch, from our balcony, our only vehicle disappear into the night, I saw my boyfriend with his back to me, frozen at the parking lot curb. He turned and walked back toward our apartment, cursing life while he climbed the stairs.

"How will you get to your appointments now?" I asked.

He shrugged.

"I don't know, either."

"Call your friend, Cheryl," he blasted. "Ask her if she will give me a ride to work tomorrow."

"I'm not calling her at this hour."

"Okay—when the sun rises. She works in the Galleria area, too, and she sits in an office all day. She doesn't need her car."

"Gee, Seth—that's asking a lot from her."

"She's your friend, right?"

"Yeah," I shrugged while aware she despised my low-life boyfriend. "She thinks you ruined my life. What makes you think she will help you out?"

"Do I have any other options here?" He angrily growled.

"Why don't you call one of your family members, or inner-circle friends?"

Seth ignored my question.

"And where's Runi when you need him?" I seethed while I knew Cheryl would give Seth a ride in the morning because she cared about me.

THE SUN ROSE, and Cheryl was on her way over from her apartment to pick up Seth and take him to work. Seth would have to take the discussion to an audacious level later that morning and ask Cheryl to use her car while she sat in her office every day from 8-5. Seth came into the living area dressed in a white, long-sleeve business shirt, red tie, and gray slacks. I sat at the typewriter writing down my feelings when he entered into the room. I had tried to sort out my feelings for weeks now, but one feeling dominated—stress.

"Why don't you ask your mother to help you out, Seth, and leave my best friend out of this grim situation *you* created? Your mother is the reason you are dysfunctional anyway."

"Fuck you, Jean. And I've already asked her for too much financial help."

"But she *always helps* which is why you can't stand on your own two feet," I shot back.

"I can't pay Ma back the money I've already borrowed for rent," he angrily snapped. "Why don't you call *our* lawyer today and see where we stand on this Florida lawsuit?"

"Okay, but we're not even close to negotiating any kind of settlement—we still have to get the felony charges thrown out first. Make sure Cheryl has insurance on her car—if not, you might have to buy a short-term policy."

"Yeah, right," he snarled.

"I'm serious. Her car is old and paid for, and she doesn't make very much money—that's why she works a part-time job in the evenings. She's trying to get ahead. If you wreck her car, and there is no insurance, then you will seriously mess up her life. And you have to fill up her gas tank, too."

"You think, Jean?" He sarcastically asked while he flipped open the front door and then lit a cigarette in the threshold while waiting for her to show up.

"Before she gets here, I want to give you something to mail for me…for us." I got up from behind the typewriter and picked up the envelope I had addressed to the minister in Irving, Texas. I handed Seth the stamped envelope.

He examined what I handed him, and his mouth fell open. "The Benny Hinn Ministries?"

"Yes, the Benny Hinn Ministries. The power of God is great for those who believe in God. And I do—and we need a miracle, Seth."

"And this is a donation?"

"Yes. If we give out of faith, then we shall get God's blessings."

"How much money is in here?" He continued to shake his head in non-belief.

"I wrote him a check for one hundred dollars."

"You wrote a check for one hundred dollars? Are you insane?" He lambasted and then ripped my enveloped into a million pieces before dropping the paper shreds on the floor just in front of him. "You'll fall for anything, Jean."

I agreed with Seth--I had fallen for his lie. "God says we should give money to support his ministry, and we are to trust He will take care of us for being faithful and obedient. What do we have to lose?"

"A hundred dollars! You've been duped, Jean. Don't waste *my* money, what little I have, on such foolishness." He heard a car engine roll up and looked out the door. "Cheryl's here," he said before he slammed the door shut and leaped down the stairs toward her car.

I walked over to where he had been standing and picked up the shredded check and envelope and mumbled, "You're the fool, Seth."

LATER THAT DAY I called Andrew Haggard, our Coral Gables attorney, who was working on our false arrest case on contingency, and because he was working on contingency without any upfront pay, I had no leverage to make him move any faster on the case. He reassured me, after my plea to hurry, that he was just as interested in wrapping up this million-dollar case as we were. "We're at the pre-trial phase in this criminal lawsuit--the discovery phase--in which each party, through the law of civil procedure, can request documents, and other evidence, from other parties. We can compel the production of evidence by using subpoenas, or by taking depositions, or by getting interrogatories, or by making requests for admissions."

"I see."

"Most civil cases are settled after discovery because by that time, both sides are often in agreement about the relative strength and weaknesses of each side's case, and this awareness often results in a settlement which eliminates the expense and risks of a trial—but, we're still dealing with the criminal allegation."

"What if the other side doesn't cooperate?"

"They will cooperate. Florida law requires that probable

cause exist before arresting a person. If there is no probable cause for an arrest, then the arresting agency, and the police officer, may be subject to an action for false arrest and false imprisonment. Within fifteen days, after service of the Notice of Discovery, the prosecutor shall serve a written discovery exhibit, which shall disclose to the defendant, and permit the defendant to inspect, copy, test, and photograph the following information and material within the state's possession or control."

"Has the state served us a written discovery exhibit yet?"

"Not yet, but, I will file a motion and get a list of eye witnesses, investigating officers, and any other witnesses, known by the prosecutor, to have any material information that tends to negate the guilt of the defendant as to the offense charged."

"I see, and then what?"

"Then I'll be able to tell you something, after I see the discovery, like whether, or not, they arrested you without probable cause, and if I can prove that to be the case, then the state will drop the felony charge, and when they do that, then we will go after the convenience store as plaintiffs."

"And how long will that lawsuit take?"

"In a civil matter, defendants, such as a convenience store, typically have greater resources than plaintiffs; and, accordingly, defendants can impose costs on parties like you, who deserve compensation, by dragging out the litigation process, as opposed to offering a fair settlement."

"This case sounds like years and years of legal battles."

"I don't know how long we might have to fight, maybe two or three years, but sometimes these cases settle out of court sooner."

WEEKS LATER, Seth came walking through the door. "What a damn day! Can you believe that bitch has the nerve to tell me that I need to give her money to replace her transmission?"

"Is Cheryl's transmission going out?"

"Yeah, it's slipping."

"Well, you have been driving her car for a month while she's at the office, and you have put a lot of miles on her vehicle."

"She's on drugs!" Seth huffed.

"She is?" I was surprised.

"She admitted to me that she takes ecstasy. In addition, she's telling me that she won't allow me to use her car anymore, if I don't have four hundred dollars to fix her transmission. Her old car had high mileage when I started driving it a month ago."

"We don't have four hundred dollars, Seth."

"I know—and get this. On top of her crazy expectations, Rick called me into his office, this evening, just before I left, and he asserted I used drugs, which reasoned out for him why I consistently fail to perform month after month."

I remained calm while I got that his boss had read my anonymous letter. "Why does Rick suddenly believe you do drugs?"

"I don't know why, Jean, but I told my boss I would take a piss test for him right there on the spot."

"You did?"

"Yeah, I told him I would take a piss test right there!" Seth chuckled. "He said it wasn't necessary."

"What if he had taken you up on your offer?"

"But he didn't;" Seth answered, "and I switched the direction of the conversation, and told him that I had three clients that I strongly felt I would close before the end of the month."

"Is that true, Seth?"

"No," he said. "Not even one, but it took the heat off me regarding his suspicions about me getting high."

"So you're not fired then?"

"No," he said as he walked away down the hall toward our bedroom, pulling off his jacket.

I could not believe Rick had not fired Seth on the spot. Perhaps Seth's employer did not have the courage to fire anyone. I felt disappointed by the unfolding of events.

The following night, Seth walked in from work, with Cheryl following right behind him. I could tell by the expression on her face, when she walked into my apartment, she was the bearer of bad news. "Hi Jean," she said with great indignation. She expressed upset.

"Hey Cheryl," I said while I got up from behind my typewriter. "You're just in time to take a walk with me—I've been cooped up here all day."

"Well, I've been stuck in my office all day, too, and we haven't talked in a long while."

We greeted each other with a hug. I looked at Seth over Cheryl's shoulder and knew something bad had occurred between the two of them that evening. I held the front door open and followed my Florida companion outside, and we headed down the stairs, and then down the street.

"I really appreciate you letting Seth borrow your car for the last month."

"I can't do it any longer, Jean."

"I know."

"He's abusing me. He picks me up late, from my office, stoned every evening—he's high as a kite. He talks like a jerk, too. I have a part-time job. I've been late three times, in the last two weeks, due to Seth's lack of consideration— one more time, and my company fires me. I've told Seth to not be late, but he doesn't respect my wishes. He was late tonight—fortunately, I didn't have to work tonight. I need a new transmission, and he doesn't feel he should contribute to the repair of anything. He's on crack, Jean."

"I know that, too. He says you're on ecstasy, Cheryl."

"I've never used ecstasy. You know me. I only smoke weed, and I do not smoke when I have to work day and night."

"I know how you are—I've vacationed with you back in the good old days."

Cheryl shook her head, "I can't believe you lost Leonardo over that liar. Did you know, Seth offered me some rock?"

I shook my head no.

"I told him that I didn't smoke rock, and he called *me* a liar! And he called me more unbecoming names tonight, when I pressed him for money—I mean, he's using up my gas and expecting me to pay for the gas he uses up every week."

"You need to walk away, Cheryl. I don't care if Seth loses that job, or not—I hoped his employer would fire him a month ago.

He hasn't closed a single deal, and except for the $400-a-week base pay, he received the first three months he worked there, I haven't seen a dime. I don't understand why his boss keeps him there."

"Maybe he's screwing his boss?"

I considered the possibility.

"He's using you, Jean. He doesn't care anything about you—he's staying with you for the lawsuit settlement. Why did you make Seth part of that Florida lawsuit?"

"My marriage to Leonardo was over at the time—I was pregnant with Harper. My apparel business had gone down in flames. I wanted Seth to stay and help me out."

"Some help he's been!" Cheryl sneered. "Is it true that he graduated from a Bible College?"

"Yeah," I nodded. "He's got a Bachelor of Arts in Bible Studies."

"He's a Bible thumper, huh?" She shook her head. "I've never met one that I liked. Seth makes a mockery out of Christianity. Please forgive me, Jean—I feel like you may never speak to me again, after tonight, but I cannot, and will not, help that son-ov'a-bitch one more day."

"I understand—no hard feelings."

"I hate pulling out like this, especially while you are so far along."

"That's okay, Cheryl. If he can't get to his appointments and his boss fires him, then we'll be better off! I have faith in a better day."

THE WEEK PASSED, and Seth had managed to get to work, every day, and have a vehicle, to boot. My thirty-six year old boyfriend had somehow managed to convince his aging mother, Wilma, to loan him enough money to rent a car for a month. I was certain Seth had, once again, convinced Ma to loan him more money, because he had told the woman the same lie that he had told his boss after the threat of a piss test, that he had some profitable deals in the works that were about to pop. Harper's grandmother was a working secretary who earned ten dollars an hour and worked forty hours a week, which justified her short fuse and volatile temper when Seth asked to borrow money from her. She was divorced, for the second time, and had been single for years, due to her own pit-bull personality, which the few, strong men that she dated, could not tolerate very long, before they walked away. She had managed to take half of her second husband's retirement plan in the divorce settlement, which amounted to a measly $80,000, and raise Seth's youngest sibling, Frank, by herself. She told me about both her husbands--Seth's drunken father, Seth senior, and about Frank's adopted father, Bernard. When Seth was only eighteen years old, and still in high school, Seth's abusive and alcoholic father had gone out on a fishing boat with his girlfriend during his legal separation from Wilma. He had drunk too much that day, fell off the small boat, and drowned. I considered the possibility that if Seth's father was as abusive as the family described him to be, then maybe the girlfriend pushed the drunk over the side of the boat. I met the kind and gentle second husband, Bernard, and thought the world of his character—he was a good man, through and through, but because Bernard was *boring*, Wilma divorced the meek steelworker, who had provided her, and her fatherless, fifth child, Frank, a beautiful new home, and good life, for twelve years. Bernard came around to visit his adopted son the first year I came into the family, and I could clearly see the sixty-something year old was heartbroken over the loss of his wife and child. Wilma, however, demonstrated no compassion, or regret, over having hurt the elderly man who appeared lost, and whom she had devastated financially just as he approached his retirement years. The story told to me, by my mother-in-law, was that she had a one-night stand with a used car salesman of Philippine descent, sixteen years earlier, shortly before she met Bernard; and, as a result, of that single date, she gave birth to her fifth child, a pretty, slant-eyed, little boy named Frank. Wilma and I seemed to have that particular scenario in common with one of our children, but Seth's mother was an insecure woman who seemed to resent my very existence from day one. I never understood why she disliked me so much. I gave her an adorable grandson, but I concluded a couple of reasons might have been in play. One reason may have been that I was the pretty, and much younger woman, who came around her house with her firstborn child, and who, unwittingly, stole attention from her younger boyfriends—I threatened the cougar. The second reason, my mother-in-law may have disliked me from the start was because I had simply taken her son away from her. She had gotten Seth back, once already, from Debbie, his first wife. I often thought that I had done Wilma a favor, as time passed. I summed the situation I inherited, but no matter how much money the strapped woman loaned her needy son, she appeared to have a chip on her shoulder toward me—perhaps because I was pregnant, again, and did not work. My suspicions grew regarding my relationship with my mother-in-law; and I questioned whether Seth played on the frustrated woman's sympathies, and told her lies about me, so that she would float him monthly loans, or support him when he finally divorced me and tried to take my children away? After all, Seth lied to everyone else, why would he not lie to his mother.

TWO WEEKS LATER and Seth came storming into the apartment one night. "Well, that's it! I got the boot today!" He spewed. "Fucking asshole—I was so close to closing a deal."

"I'm sorry," I said with complete glee—finally Rick had seen through Seth's lies. "Just remember, when one window closes another window opens up."

Seth rolled his eyes at me.

"Why did Rick fire you?" I asked as if I did not know the answer.

"For the obvious reason—I did not meet my quota."

"Quota?" I guffawed while clear Seth had never closed a single deal in a year-and-a-half. "Well, now you can find a job that actually *pays you* for your efforts."

"Yeah, you think, Jean?" He angrily shouted. "How the hell am I going to find a job when I don't have a vehicle? I had to turn in my rental today. Ma just dropped me off and told me that she won't pay for a rental anymore."

"I guess you'll have to find a job within walking distance;" I spewed, "...but, the point is to bring home money. You took our situation to the extreme. We are so far under. Just look around, Seth!

We don't have anything anymore. You allowed us to sell our washer and dryer because you refused to get a paying job!"

"Why don't you get a job, Jean?"

"Don't talk foolishly—you know why. But, *I will* get a good paying job after this last baby is born." I could see by the look on Seth's face that my words threatened him.

"Oh right—like who is going to hire you?"

"You're mean. You're so threatened I will leave you, if I get a job."

"That would be great if you'd leave, Jean!"

"Obviously, you're not thinking straight—I'm taking the kids with me, if I go."

"And how are you going to support yourself and three children?"

"Just fine, because I'm going to take you to court and you will pay me child support for the two extra children you brought into my life."

His angry face turned downward.

"In fact, I think I'll go back to school, Seth! After the baby is born, I'm going to enroll into the university—maybe that route is not as threatening for you as me getting a job?"

"And how do you think you will afford that adventure?"

"Just like your sister does—I'll take out student loans."

"And you think what, that I'm going to sit around here and babysit?"

"No, Seth—you're a big boy. I would expect you will get a *paying* job, and we'll put our children in daycare." Again, he appeared threatened by my plan to return to school. "What's the matter, Seth— are you afraid you might have to pay me child support, if *you* get a paying job?"

He snarled, "And what makes you think a court would give you custody of the kids? Without me, you don't have any economically viable opportunities!"

I shook my head in anger at his audacity to pigeonhole me as some unemployable high school graduate. Joyce's words echoed in my head: *I'm worried Seth might try to take your kids, Jean. I think Seth could be dangerous*—*he might try to disappear with your kids. And he and Runi might finally come out of the closet and be an openly gay couple raising two children.* I was talking to a man who had no interest in my success. "You actually believe I have no economically viable opportunities? Those very words are why I am going back to college, and because you, Seth, think so little of me *is exactly why* I'm going back to college." I grinned while I trumped his attempted blow to my belief system.

"And how do you plan on getting to school without a car?" He asked smugly.

"There is always the public transit system, if I must. I know you want nothing to do with my personal success, Seth, nor will you have anything to do with another apparel business startup because that, too, may lead to my success; but I don't really need you. I intend to get my bachelor's degree and raise these three kids while I do so. Eventually, I'll jump into a graduate program; and for my thesis, I will pull together a collective of ambitious graduate students, and we will create a successful business, wherein we design, manufacture, and wholesale women's apparel. I've been working on the five-year CEO operational schedule since Harper was born, and next time, I will have an established nation-wide sales force—no thanks to you. I'm serious about my dream and my life."

"I want nothing to do with your silly apparel business!"

"Save your insulting, non-supportive words; I have no need for you in my apparel business. What are you good for anyway? You deceived me, Seth, when you told me you wanted to work that apparel business with me—one failure and you quit? You're a quitter."

"Your thinking is crazy. Who do you think you are?"

"I think I'm entitled to make my dreams come true—that's *who* I think I am!"

"Oh yeah, sure, sure, sure--you're going to be the next Donna Karan of New York City! And I'm going to be a brain surgeon. I might have fallen for your crap once, but I'm no fool! Don't think I will spend a dime on your stupid start-up. I'm not a fool like Daddy Warbucks."

"Oh, right!—you are referring to Leonardo. You think he was a fool? He believed in me and supported me. *I was the fool* to ever think you could be exceptional like he was. You're a loser, Seth—as you have proven to be since my apparel business crashed! You would rather *play safe* and *try* to sell furniture, for minimum wage, and make so little income that you could not pay the rent each month; and if that gig were not bad enough, then you would rather work for Rick, for a year-and-a-half, make zero sales, and zero income, than work a low paying job for us. You don't believe in yourself, and how could I expect you to believe in me? We crashed, Seth, but what you don't understand, and what Leonardo *did* understand, was that winners always fail, but they get back up on their feet when all the odds are against them, and they don't stop until they get what they set out to get."

"And what's that you're going to get? Fame and fortune, Jean?" He mocked.

"Actually, yeah."

He snickered as if I talked crazy. "I can't believe you would even consider the idea of starting up the apparel business again—we have no money."

"Well, like I said, I don't expect you to think like a winner. Losers stop short."

"Jean, are you taking your medication?"

"Screw you, Seth—I'm the only sound person here. You're the one who takes drugs."

ABOUT A WEEK LATER, Seth donned his red *power tie* as he described the article, and his worn-out, gray suit, long overdue for the cleaners, and set out on foot to find a job somewhere along FM 1960, a nearby busy Houston boulevard with miles of small office complexes and retail strip centers. Four hours later, he excitedly returned to our apartment with a paying job that he would begin the next day.

A week later, and the first day he had off from his new sales job, Seth sat among the four of us at our cheap dining table in our bare and near empty apartment. He rocked his chrome and vinyl chair back and crossed his legs on top the table while he talked to his mother and her younger boyfriend, CJ. I sat between Seth and his mother. I held a squirmy toddler who lunged for Wilma. "Do you want to go to Granny?" I asked while looking at her to see if she was receptive to taking him.

Seth's mother smiled and reached for Harper.

I sat back and watched Granny interact with her tenth grandchild, before turning my attention back to Seth who appeared to me to be more relaxed now that he could provide an income for his family. He had barely been on the job, but just knowing that he had his first paycheck coming in another week was a great relief for both of us.

"Would anyone like more coffee?" I asked the gang.

"Thank you," Seth responded and pushed his empty cup toward me. "Ma? CJ?"

"I'll take another cup." CJ answered. "Thank you."

His mother held the frisky boy tightly and replied, "No, thank you—I've had about all the caffeine I can handle in one evening."

Seth continued holding court while I poured coffee for the men. I nonchalantly studied Wilma's new boyfriend. CJ was a sexy, rugged, dark-haired man, who appeared to be in his early- to mid-forties. I summed the man, with twinkling green eyes, thick black brows, a sloping forehead, and silky black hair, to be about ten years younger than Wilma. His claim to fame, and to her heart, according to my mother-in-law, was that he occasionally performed as an Elvis Presley impersonator, strummed a guitar, and sang professionally. CJ rode his Harley Davidson on the weekends, too, often with Wilma on the back, that is when he was not working for his parents' fabrication shop that happened to be located in the exact area of town where I had once dreamed of living—Nassau Bay. Had my apparel business not crashed and burned, I would have bought the waterfront home in Nassau Bay; and now, coincidentally, Wilma's boyfriend would one day inherit a multimillion-dollar business in Nassau Bay from his parents, and most likely, CJ would be able to afford my waterfront home. I sat the coffee pot back into the kitchen, sat down, and wondered if Wilma knew how lucky she was to have CJ? I turned my attention from our handsome guest, who was closer to my age than to his girlfriend's age, and back to the braggadocios man called my boyfriend, who described a day at his new office.

"...This woman sits in front of my desk the other day; and on a scale of one to ten, one being the least appealing in the looks department, she's a minus something—a truly unattractive individual. And she tells me that she wants to model. I don't even want to begin my sales pitch on her, because I'm thinking this woman has to be a set-up, and if I try to sell her six-hundred dollars of headshots, then the Houston Chronicle, or Marvin Zindler from Eye Witness News, will appear, pointing cameras at me for trying to scam her. She says she wants to do commercials, and she needs some headshots, so I consider the commission, and throw her my pitch anyway. I begin telling her that she's an exceptional woman, that newsprint and media need all types of characters, and the next thing you know—she signs up. Two days later, she is sitting in front of my desk with her daughter, and I've got mama writing another six-hundred dollar check." Seth laughed. "What can I do? My boss loves me—I'm the number one salesman."

"You've been there *a week*, Seth," I reminded while disgusted with his job already.

CJ laughed at my crack on my arrogant boyfriend. "Now, let me understand how your business works?" CJ asked Seth. "This woman and her daughter buy $1200 worth of photos from you, and you do what for them?"

Seth wiggled in his chair and then removed his feet from the top of the table, as if a bit uncomfortable with CJ's question. "Well, we give opportunities for those who bought headshots from us, to come in and audition for important clients. Someone like Macy's might need to do a photo shoot of their new spring lines for an ad in the Houston Chronicle—they come to us, and we provide them models."

"I see," CJ nodded. "And how often do you have clients come in looking for ugly models?"

"Not ever, really," Seth laughed. "—but, periodically we do a cattle call. We announce upcoming auditions to all our members."

"So you primarily sell photos?"

Seth nodded yes. "And from what I've seen, Pete's got

thousands and thousands of headshots in storage. I have to laugh at some of these people—everyone wants to be a star."

"I don't think it's right, Seth," I said, "—that you sell a pipe dream, to unsuspecting fools, and then throw their expensive pictures, that never get seen again, into a closet."

"Hey, I'm selling headshots—what they do with their headshots is up to them."

"You promise them lots of opportunities to model when they write you those six-hundred dollar checks for photos," I added for clarity. "Few ever see a paying gig."

Seth did not react to the knowledge he had given me.

"What's the name of your business?" Wilma asked.

"*The Talent House*," I answered for Seth.

"How many employees work there, son?"

"Well, Ma, there's the owner—Pete; and then, there's Chad and me. All three of us do the same thing—we sell a dream."

"You sell over-priced pictures," I corrected.

"Well, at least you have a job that pays the bills, Seth," Wilma defended. She smiled at me and then looked at her boyfriend and blurted, "CJ! Tell Seth the good news."

CJ turned his attention to Seth, and then to me. "I've got a great car deal for you two."

"I can't afford any car just yet," Seth snapped.

"Son! Stop and listen," his mother interrupted. "There's more. Your brother and I got a letter in the mail today, from the lawyers who are working on the chlordane suit. And, as you know, the case was scheduled to go to trial, but the apartment complex executed a settlement agreement with the chlordane plaintiffs."

"How many plaintiffs were there?" I asked her.

"Three hundred," she answered.

"The court found that the apartment complex was negligent, and the apartment complex awarded three residents over $3 million dollars—those were the three most affected by the chlordane exposure. And, according to this letter, the other 297 plaintiffs had to sue the insurance companies because the apartment complex did not have any more money to pay the plaintiffs. So what our lawyers are telling us, now, is that they have settled with the insurance companies."

"Oh yeah!" Seth declared while digesting along with me that we were about to come into some money.

"So now the lawyers have broken down the settlement payoffs based on how sick each plaintiff was found to be, and we fall into the least sick category of the plaintiffs."

"How sick are you?" I asked the youthful-looking, blond woman with blue eyes.

"We're not sick according to our blood work—"

Seth interrupted, "No, Ma—that's not completely true. They found minute traces of chlordane in my blood."

"And what symptoms have you experienced, Seth?" I inquired.

"The doctor, who was categorizing all of us plaintiffs, told me that depression, headaches, dizziness, vision problems, irritability, and muscle twitches are some of the milder symptoms—so, I told him that I suffered all those symptoms."

CJ laughed, "And you get seven thousand dollars and not one million."

"What do you suffer for a million dollars?" I asked Seth.

"Live cancer," he answered.

"Well, I don't think we were exposed to anything," his mother reiterated; "but, we were living there at that apartment complex when the landscaping company sprayed chlordane all over the place, so we made ourselves part of the class action civil lawsuit."

"So, how much, Ma?"

"Like CJ just said--seven thousand dollars."

"I'll take it!" Seth exclaimed.

CJ interrupted, "So now that you have money to buy a car, I've got a nice used 1987 Chevrolet Corsica sitting out there at the fabrication shop that we can't depreciate any more. It's in good shape, 4-door, low mileage, automatic—we used the car as a fleet car. The car drives great."

"I'm interested," Seth coaxed.

"What color is the car?" I asked CJ.

"Emerald Blue," CJ answered.

Wilma added, "And you know where the car's been—so you won't be taken by a dealership and end up with a lemon."

"We'll take the car!" Seth said.

I was thrilled. Life was feeling better now that Seth had a job, and we were getting a car and some cash.

WINTER'S END and my surprise package from heaven had yet to arrive. Seth and I, and my three children, Joseph, Bella, and Harper drove two hours south of Houston, to CJ's newly purchased river house, which sat on the banks of the Colorado River, one of fourteen rivers in Texas. I had weekend visitation with Joseph and knew that my eleven-year old son would enjoy playing on the river with his eight-year old sister, and six cousins, who entered into our lives by association with Seth's family.

The house had a boat dock with a lift, and the river rendered easy access to the Gulf of Mexico, or to an intercostal channel. The structure was eighteen years old, but in great condition, and over 3,000 square feet; and I thought the dwelling magnificent, and much more than a *fishing lodge*, as CJ had called his place.

The weekend plans sounded fun. His mother told Seth and I, that both his sisters, and their six children, would be there, too. Demelza, who had once lived near us in Clear Lake City, a city annexed by Houston, had two daughters about the same age as my daughter, Bella. Patricia, the second oldest child of Wilma's four children, had two girls and two boys about the same ages as my two oldest children, Bella and Joseph. Patricia and her four children had driven to Texas from Florida days earlier. Seth's mother, Wilma, of course, would be there, too, as this fishing lodge belonged to her boyfriend, CJ, who had recently requested she quit her secretarial job in Houston and move in with him down there. My mother-in-law was seriously considering his offer, but conflicted too, because she and CJ fought often over the demands she made on him—for example, Seth's mother insisted the biker/musician/fabrication shop owner not wear his favorite Harley Davidson T-shirts. I felt that request was like asking Santa to not where his black boots. Wilma had a zero batting average with men, so far, and I suspected she was too insecure to depend on another man.

The lot size was large. The house sat back from the river, and in between the wood-framed home, painted dark red, and the old and rickety boat dock, was a wide carport where the biker parked his pickup truck and motorcycle. A wooden bench swing hung from two chains off the carport's side so one could sit and watch the boats pass on the brown river. The river was narrow, and a couple of old, two-story rustic homes, with lots of windows, and natural woods with no paint, sat directly across the way.

The sun had gone down our first day there; and everyone came in off the river, bathed, and then ate. The nine children hid out in the back of the house with Granny while five adults sat around a large table in the living area and played cards. Wilma delighted in spending some alone time with her nine grandchildren, especially Patricia's four kids whom she seldom saw during the year. CJ, and Wilma's two daughters--Demelza and Patricia--and Seth, Wilma's first-born child, and I, played poker that evening.

CJ took a drag off his cigarette and snuffed out the butt. "I fold, and I'm calling it quits, too," he said as he sat his hand face down on the table.

"Me, too," I followed. "I have no more money to lose."

Patricia, whom I considered the definition of a 70's hippie in all aspects of her being, and who had long ago toured the country singing with a group called *Up with People*, added for everyone's consideration, "I should quit, too, and give Mom a break." She was referring to the fact that Wilma had gone into the back of the house, hours ago, to read books and play with her grandchildren.

"Oh, don't worry about Ma!" Demelza sassed. "She'll come out when she's tired."

I studied the two women at the table. Patricia was divorced, had custody of her four children, was a night shift data processor at a bank in Pensacola, and peaceful. She was conscious of others' needs. She had beautiful classic features and wore no makeup. Demelza, the other sister, was pretty, but not extraordinary like big sister. She, too, was divorced with custody of two daughters, and was Wilma's third child. I had gotten to know Demelza, during the days when I first met Seth, and when I had maintained two apartments in Clear Lake City, and I liked Seth's oldest sister Patricia more—she was authentic and kind.

Early on, I summed Demelza to be an extremely insecure woman, too—the apple didn't fall far from the apple tree. I knew she raged like her mother when life got bumpy—screaming was her way when anyone upset her. Early in our relationship, I had smoked a joint one morning, before Seth and I had a child together, and then answered our phone, to hear his sister on the other end. She talked to me about the date she had gone on the night before; and though I was stoned, Demelza's scattered thoughts seemed amplified that morning, and I summed her to have multiple personalities. Unlike her older sister, Patricia, who had a calming effect on people, and a peaceful nature, Demelza lacked focus, and circumstances defined her well-being—I found her spirit unsettling.

Demelza noticed me staring at her. "So Jean, will you start your apparel business back up?" She smirked while already knowing the answer.

"No, that's not possible right now, with Harper being so young, and another one due any day."

Demelza smiled and turned to CJ. "When I first met Jean, just after my brother here introduced his girlfriend to me as a fashion designer, I was a bit hard on her." Demelza laughed.

I chuckled along with Demelza and said what I thought, "That's what jealousy does."

"No!" She screamed, as if not even a possibility. "I'm sorry if I offended you, Jean."

"No, not really," I curtly answered while watching the fat, thirty-five year old, single mother squirm over what I meant by no, not really. I did not like her—she was mean.

She laughed and defended her rude behavior to CJ and her sister. "At that time, I was writing my thesis for my master's program; and I was temporarily caught up in the feminists' movements, and was a supporter for equality in the workplace. I just thought women should avoid anything that might reduce them to mere sexual objects."

"Heels are sexy," I supported. "And they are also symbols of female power. When I tower over a man in my heels, he's the one reduced to smallness."

"Well, yeah, Jean--you're what? Six feet tall? You're an Amazon!"

"Thank you," I said while I rolled my eyes at CJ. "Yeah, so I guess not *all thinking* fits *all people*." The table laughed. I turned my attention back to Seth's sister. "I can see how, if you wore flats, Demelza, some would assume you *are not* a go-getter." I watched her smile fade while she considered I had reduced her to a theme of a common blend, and that she might have to eat her words and wear heels to stand out in a crowd.

She quickly defended, "High heels thrust out the buttocks and arch the back into a natural mammalian courting pose. Lordosis is what we call the copulatory pose. Rats, sheep, dogs, all do it--and it's a natural, sexy posture, that men immediately see as sexual readiness."

"Oh, why do you worry?" I asked her in a mocking manner, indicating that no man was interested in her--not really.

The table laughed at my delicate jab while I smiled at Demelza. I had enough of the fat, college mum's smug attitude toward me because I had mistakenly bred with her loser brother.

Demelza switched focus and found a new victim--her oldest sibling. "I still think you should be a manager for K-Mart, Seth. What are you currently doing now? Ma told me you are working with models," she baited, and then turned to me, a fat pregnant woman, for my reaction, as if I might be jealous.

I remained stoned face.

"For now, I am." He paused and then blurted, "I think I might apply to law school."

I was surprised, and thrilled, to hear Seth say he wanted to be a lawyer. "That's great, Seth!" I exclaimed. "When did you decide that?" I questioned Seth's motive. Was this a tactical move on his part to keep me out of school?

"Just now," he answered.

Demelza added, "You should be good in the practice of law,

brother--considering all the lawyers you've had to hire, in your lifetime, for all your troubles."

Everyone glared at the unkind creature, with an unkempt appearance and bad smell, and from that point forward, no one acknowledged little sister again when she said anything.

"I think *you* should go to law school, Jean," CJ added.

Seth curiously looked at the dark man with the sloping forehead. "Why do you make such an off-the-cuff remark, CJ?"

CJ took a drag off his cigarette and hesitated before answering Seth. "Why not?" The man with tattoos on each arm refuted. "Jean's a smart lady. You already have a degree or two, Seth."

"I do," Seth answered with great pride. "I have a BA in Bible Studies, a BA in Computer Science, a MA in Ancient Near Eastern History, and soon a JD--a Jurist Doctorate. Jean cannot go to law school without first getting her undergrad degree."

"Maybe it's her turn?" CJ challenged and then looked at me.

I agreed--it was my turn. I felt angry over Seth's continual lack of support and shot back, "Seth, you don't have a BA in computer anything. When you got your BA in Bible Studies in the mid-70's, did you learn FORTRAN?"

Seth nodded, "I know a little."

"I bet! I took FORTRAN in community college. Leonardo tried to help me do my FORTRAN homework, at the computer lab, at the Shell refinery, years after you already got your bachelor degree." I slammed back, "Bill Gates wrote the first computer language for personal computers in 1975. You were one year into college, right? Taking freshman basics, right?"

"Okay, Jean. I surrender. I'll admit that I'm short a few hours of having a degree in computer science."

"Then you don't have a degree in computers!" I had grown impatient with Seth's constant lies he told to impress others.

CJ added, "Apple Computers were not even mass marketed until 1977--until then, no one even knew what a personal computer was."

"And fourteen years later, I still don't!" I said. "I have an electric Sears typewriter with hammerheads sitting on my table at home."

"Well, you need to get up to speed!" CJ joked. "There are now a hundred million computers in use worldwide."

"I have lost ground," I sadly admitted to CJ while I affirmed to myself poverty sucked. "I want to go back to school and *get up to speed*, and finish my bachelor's degree, but I can't leave a newborn, and Harper's too young. Bella needs extra help in school, too. All my children need me to be available, right now, and if law school calls Seth, then that sounds good to me! I would love to be married to a successful, rich attorney."

"Married?" Demelza asked as if surprised.

I ignored her and turned to my boyfriend, "You already married me in the shower, remember?"

Seth laughed, and I looked at CJ as if Seth was crazy.

Seth turned to CJ to explain, "Yeah, when Jean and I first got together, I suggested we marry each other in the shower."

"Why wouldn't you just marry her for real?" CJ asked.

"Well, there was a problem--she wasn't divorced yet."

"That sounds so bad, Seth!" I looked at CJ. "I made some bad choices. I'm embarrassed by my life, sometimes."

"Feeling embarrassed is a good sign," CJ comforted. "Some of us refuse to hear God's words and have to learn our lessons the hard way."

"Back then, I thought God's Word was one's opinion. I think differently today, CJ."

CJ chuckled. "A lot of us learn the hard way. I ride with the *Tribe of Judah*, an evangelistic ministry reaching the outlaw biker world. I belong to the Houston Chapter."

"What's your role with them?" I asked.

"I spread God's Word. And, I have a small window of opportunity to preach at biker rallies. I serve breakfast and coffee, and the word of God, to hung-over bikers."

"That sounds like fun!" I said.

"I really like bringing people to the Lord. And I see some crazy things, x-rated things," CJ smiled. "Like when I was at Sturgis last August, I saw this biker dude eating at the Y--right there in broad daylight while I preached!"

"Oh my!" I exclaimed while Seth laughed.

"Too many drugs involved!" CJ continued. "We put these loud speakers in the back of pick-up trucks and blast everyone out of their comas at 6:00 a.m. with the Word straight from the good book." CJ laughed. "You and Seth, and your kids, ought to get involved in a church."

I looked at Seth, and he shrugged as if he considered the possibility. "I'd like to," I told CJ. "I want my children to have a strong spiritual foundation for when times get tough in their lives. I was raised like that, and I believe I'm heading back to my roots."

"Find a good church community. Hey, get married in that church," CJ encouraged and then shrugged, "Why not?"

I chuckled. "Showers don't count?"

CJ threw his hands up, as if he was without the obvious answer.

"This guy here," I said to CJ while pointing to Seth, "...didn't want me to tell anybody that we got married in the shower, and I agreed. I insisted we never mention it, but Runi called that night, and Seth told him we exchanged marital vows."

"Are you *really* married to this clown?" CJ asked me.

"No," I clarified. I assumed Seth wanted to legally bind me to him, so that he would have a bigger stake in having legal custody of our children, or in our apparel business lawsuit settlement. There was only *one man* who had my heart the night I took a shower with Seth. I noticed CJ appeared disturbed. I questioned what Seth's mother had been telling her boyfriend about us. Was it something about Seth's character that rocked CJ? Perhaps CJ suspected Seth was a drug addict, like I did. I pried, "Does it surprise you, CJ, that Seth wants to become a lawyer?"

"Not at all, but it does surprise me that *you* would marry him!" He grinned and knocked a strong fist into Seth's bicep as if to soften his blow.

Seth rubbed his upper arm and gave CJ a go-to-hell-look.

"Sissy boy," CJ teased.

"I'll admit that I'm not the bad-ass biker you claim to be, CJ. I consider myself more of a Renaissance man--educated."

"A Renaissance sissy is what you are!" CJ shot back.

I laughed and defended my boyfriend. "Hey, Seth is cultivated--all 145 pounds of him on a sunny day. He works hard for those Popeye bulges, too. I'll legally marry stud muffin, if he's going to become a lawyer."

"Now, old boy," Seth chided, "Why would it surprise you that she would marry me? Like you said, Jean's a smart lady."

"I'm joking, man," CJ sincerely said to Seth. "I wish you the best of luck, Seth. Law school will be demanding for a man with a wife and three kids."

"I'm up for the challenge," Seth retorted.

"What's the challenge?" I asked while considering Seth would have to quit using drugs.

"I haven't had to study in over ten years. I don't know if I have the discipline."

"Law school is expensive, too," I considered. "Where do you expect to get $50,000 for tuition?"

Patricia asked, "Can you borrow the money?"

"I don't know," Seth said to the woman dressed in a caftan and wearing her long, straight, golden brown hair halfway down her back. "Maybe I can get a student loan," he answered his sister. "I first went to college on Dad's social security, and then took out a student loan for my master's program. Maybe I can borrow more money."

I recalled a recent argument when I informed Seth that I was returning to school, after our second child was born, to earn my bachelor's degree. At the time, he found delight in telling me that we had no money for my tuition, or books, or for that matter, did we have a car for me to drive to school every day.

Patricia continued, "I'm thinking about going back myself and getting a nursing degree."

"Good idea," Seth said. "You've got to take care of yourself, sister. You've got four kids, and from what I hear, a boyfriend that may, or may not be around in the long run."

"I know," she groaned while I quietly angered over Seth's hypocrisy. He was supportive for his younger sister, but not with me. His duplicity was self-defeating. I questioned why he would not want his wife educated and capable of making big bucks. There was only one answer--Seth did not intend to make me his wife for the long term. Runi's wife had been right--he was planning to leave me. I was not the person Seth wanted to share his life with, and I needed to work on my own career, so that one day, I could adequately take care of my three children by myself.

Seth looked at me. "I think I'll just take the LSAT, right away, and go from there."

I looked to CJ and watched him mull over the family's plans.

"That's a good idea, man," CJ said to Seth. "Take the law school exam, because it takes a while for your scores to come back. That's a hard exam from what I hear."

"Law school is very competitive," Seth acknowledged. "I might have to take the exam a couple of times. I need a high score; and once I get the score I need, then I can apply to law schools. And, by the time I get an acceptance from a law school, Jean and I might be way down the road, and have a settlement from Florida."

"And when do you expect to settle with the convenience store?" CJ asked me.

I shrugged. "Your guess is as good as mine, CJ! We might have to go to trial."

Seth began to explain, "As you probably heard from Ma, the felony charges for the theft were dropped by the State of Florida, not too long ago; and now, Jean and I have a civil action against the convenience store. Our lawyers tell us that it's possible that we'll settle out of court and not go to trial. They talk settlement numbers in the millions."

"But they first are going to depose the store clerks," I added for CJ and Patricia's knowledge while still ignoring Demelza.

DAYS LATER. The more I considered Seth going to law school, the more I liked the idea of being married to a lawyer and raising our three young children together. I firmly believed Seth and I could set our differences to the side, and make our marriage work for the sake of our children. We were not legally *married*, but what we had going on was definitely the makings of a marriage, as far as I was concerned, and I had a heart for my family. I did not believe there was anything so pressing, in either one of our lives, or more important than what Seth and I had created together--a family with children--that we could not make our relationship work. I did not believe even Runi could compete with what I brought to the table. I also believed our lack of money had always been our downfall those first four years; but now, after much struggle, and since Seth had taken a paying job, the emotional stress on our lives and relationship clearly diminished. I firmly believed we would be happier with time.

Once Seth expressed his desire, to go to law school, to me, I did not hesitate searching the library for LSAT study guides while Seth was at work. I did not find what he needed at the library, so I purchased the expensive books. *The Talent House,* where Seth worked, was located around the corner, and across the street, from our apartment complex; and when I needed the car, I could simply drop Seth off at work, or he could walk to work. I drove to the bookstore, at the mall, and found three study guides that would help my boyfriend pass the LSAT. I spent a week's grocery money on the study guides. I felt the sacrifice worthy, and that we could eat beans and cornbread, until the next paycheck. I was excited about setting Seth up to win as a partner and provider.

"I got you something, Seth!" I said with great enthusiasm to the man who walked through the front door wearing dress slacks, a white long-sleeve shirt, and tie.

"What did you get me, baby?"

"I bought you three amazing study guides that will help you pass your law school exam!"

Seth walked over to the dining table, and I handed him one book at a time. "This paperback is one of the bestselling study guides. It includes two complete, released exams, and detailed explanations that tell you how to identify quickly the type of question asked and how to go about answering the question."

Seth flipped through the book. "Thank you, Jean."

"And this book here--" I said with great excitement while handing the second one to Seth, "Well, I was told this book is what people read for last minute cram sessions. And this third book goes over all five sections of the LSAT, and includes practice tests with answers." I randomly flipped open the book and read a test question to Seth. *"Estelle states: When I went fishing the other day, every fish that I caught was a salmon, and every salmon I saw I caught. Of the following statements listed below, which conclusion can we draw from the observations of Estelle?*

A. Salmon was the only fish that Estelle saw while she was fishing.
B. While Estelle was fishing no other fish was caught by her.
C. In the area that Estelle fished, there were no other fish.
D. All of the fish that Estelle saw she caught.
E. Estelle did not see any other fish while she was fishing."

I looked up. "And the answer is?"

"B?" He answered.

"You're right! That's awesome! You're going to do just fine on the exam."

Seth smiled and began picking up the books. "I guess tonight is as good as any night to start studying. I'll take these books back here to our bedroom," he said as he headed down the hallway.

"I'll keep the kids out of your hair tonight." I had hope about our future.

5
UNEQUALLY YOKED

A WEEK THEREAFTER, our new friends, and frequent visitors, the boys from *The Talent House*, once again, came over for the evening. Pete, the owner, and Chad, the other salesman, in the three-person company, both liked to hang out at our apartment and get high, and sometimes their girlfriends accompanied them.

On this particular Friday eve, Chad brought over his steady girlfriend, Jenn, a silly, twenty-one year old winch, who actually believed this tall play actor, with tight, blond curls, blue eyes, and a sloping brow to be about her best interest. I personally had never met a more insincere man than Chad, other than my current boyfriend. The sloping brow characteristic both Chad and Seth had in common made me consider whether these charlatans evolved from some kind of reptilian-like origin. Did aliens with venom, long-ago, inseminate humans? Were these men children of the snake?

Chad, a high school graduate, with no further plans for higher education, had placed a small diamond ring on the naïve and vulnerable vixen's finger; and she bought, completely, his sham. Jenn was smitten and in love with this over-indulgent, smooth-talking boy from a wealthy family. I, however, knew Chad to be an unscrupulous alley cat; and I knew, after having had talked to him when Jenn was not around, that he had no conviction for doing what was right. His only interest was in himself. I suspected this nineteen-year-old boy was role modeling after the thirty-six year old egomaniac, and father of Harper and my unborn. I was certain Seth had been mentoring his impressionable co-worker on the art of dirty pool. Pete, their boss and owner of *The Talent House*, on the other hand, possessed a sincere attribute.

They sat around my living room for hours that night drinking, smoking pot supplied by both Seth's co-workers, and chatting. I did not partake in any of the drugs because I was pregnant. Jenn sat in my great old wooden rocker, sucking down her vodka, and chain-smoking her cigarettes. Seth and I sat on the old Goodwill sofa across from her, and Pete and Chad were sitting beside Jenn on a couple of folding chairs we used at the dining table. The night was late, and the kids were asleep.

I smiled at Pete while I sized him up. Pete Stickler was a stocky, 5'8", confident German, who wore high-end department store cologne, along with a manicured scruff--a five o'clock shadow he maintained with a beard trimmer. The thirty-something year old dressed like a million dollar man and always with a flair for the expensive, sharp, and crisp. His champagne taste reflected a cultivated image not taught to him by his blue-collar father, and included pricey cigars, cognac, good weed, a convertible muscle car, and beautiful women—he often touted he had the good life. Pete had spent years living near his American-born mother and stepfather in Italy, and working as a bricklayer alongside his mother's husband. He had brought back with him, to America, a European flare. He recently separated from his former live-in American girlfriend, who had given him a daughter, a beautiful child, now two-years old, whom Pete kept every other weekend while proving to be a responsible daddy.

Seth dominated the conversation with his newfound enthusiasm for his life. "I think it's International Law that interests me most," My boyfriend confirmed to himself and to the group.

"So catch me up here, Seth." Pete requested. "What does an international lawyer do?"

"It's a niche market in law; I guess you could say we're a small group of elite individuals, who actually litigate cases before the World Court and arbitrational tribunals. International lawyers make quite a good living out of that kind of opportunity. I will work for the national governments. Every country, whether large or small, have legal advisory offices; and there are careers to be made here, and everywhere."

"So you would be working with foreign policy, huh?" Chad asked.

Seth nodded, and the boy continued, "My dad does business overseas—foreign policy definitely makes or breaks him."

"I'll litigate governmental efforts to bring countries together," Seth nodded.

"That's a scary thought," Pete jabbed.

Seth laughed.

"No man, I'm kidding." Pete softened. "I really hate to lose you, Seth."

"I'm not going anywhere for a while, boss man."

"I hope you remember me, when you get to be a big dog," Chad pleaded. "I'll work for you under the table, if you know what I mean." He winked.

Seth laughed.

I interrupted the flow between the loyalists while wondering if Chad's meaning was literal, or just offensive to the IRS. I added, "The world is becoming smaller every day because of computers. I see a wide-open field of opportunity in International Law, too. I'm happy about this direction you're taking, Seth!" I smiled at my boyfriend while hoping my words mattered.

Pete broke in and said to Seth, "She's happy, man. You finally scored with her."

"She likes that money," Seth spouted.

"Who doesn't?" Pete snapped back, in my defense, and then looked at me.

I shrugged while appearing as if I did not connect with Seth.

Pete continued, "And speaking of a smaller world," he began while he glanced at me and then back at Seth, "...the Freemasons intend to bring about a New World Order—they're creating one government, a world without borders. Your timing is good to become an International Lawyer. Your services will be in great demand, Seth."

Pete looked over at me, "The Masons *will* make the world a lot smaller. Their plan has been in the works for a long time. Over a century ago, Pope Leo XIII said the Masons ultimate purpose was to overthrow the whole religious and political order of the world which *the Christian* teaching has produced."

"Hold that thought, Pete!" I got my pregnant self up off the couch and walked into the kitchen, grabbed a recent newspaper off the counter, and then returned to our guests. "This article was written a couple of weeks ago, and quotes our current president, George Herbert Walker Bush, as having said, '*We have before us, the opportunity to forge for ourselves, and for future generations, a new world order, a world where the rule of law, not the rule of the jungle, governs the conduct of nations. When we are successful--and we will be--we have a real chance at this new world order, an order in which a credible United Nations can use its peacekeeping role to fulfill the promise and vision of the UN's founders.*'" I stopped reading and looked up at Pete, and then at Seth, "What does he mean when he refers to the law of the jungles?"

Pete answered, "The Law of the Jungle is an expression that

means 'every man for himself', 'anything goes', 'might makes right'--"

Seth injected, "'survival of the strongest', 'survival of the fittest', 'kill or be killed', 'dog eat dog' and 'eat or be eaten.'"

They laughed, and I continued to inquire of them. "So the rule of law is better than the law of the jungle?"

"Not necessarily," Seth answered. "The rule of law is an exceedingly elusive notion. *What is* the rule of law, is the very question."

"Well, if the law is elusive, then that's the role of the Supreme Court to answer, right?" I questioned.

"Yes," Seth nodded.

"What if the Supreme Court is dirty?" Pete questioned.

I considered his statement, and Pete continued, "First you have to understand who is really at the root of the movement to throw out Christianity."

"S-a-t-a-n?" Seth mocked.

"Well, yes," Pete corrected. "According to history, after Pope Leo had finished celebrating Mass in the Vatican Chapel, attended by a few Cardinals and members of the Vatican staff, he suddenly stopped at the foot of the altar. He stood there for about ten minutes, as if in a trance, his face ashen white. Then, Pope Leo went immediately from the Chapel to his office, and composed the prayer to St. Michael, and then instructed his churches that they recite the prayer after all masses everywhere. When asked what had happened, he explained that, as he was about to leave the foot of the altar, he suddenly heard voices--two voices, one kind and gentle, the other guttural and harsh. They seemed to come from near the tabernacle. As he listened, the Pope heard the guttural voice, the voice of Satan in his pride, boasting to our Lord, 'I can destroy your Church.'

The gentle voice of the Lord replied, 'You can? Then go ahead and do so.'

And Satan said, 'To do so, I need more time, and more power.'

And our Lord asked, 'How much time do you need? And how much power do you need?'

Satan responded, '75 to 100 years, and a greater power over those who will give themselves over to my service.'

And our Lord said, 'You have the time; you will have the power. Do with them what you will.'"

Pete finished, paused, and then added, "Ultimately God has authority over Satan, which is why Satan must request of our Lord more time."

Seth laughed, "That's a cute lil' story, Pete. What? Are you Catholic now?"

"No, I'm not Catholic! I am a Christian. History supports what the Freemasons are really about, if you look closer and connect the dots. Our Lord gave Satan another 100 years, his hundred years was up in 1984—seven years ago."

"Uh huh, *history*." Seth nodded and spewed as if irritated, "I'm not connecting the dots. I say *propaganda, conspiracy theory*. Brother, common sense would tell you that when applying faith to logic, there is no rationality. That pope story is part of the shadowy elite's crackpot myths."

"You're a skeptic, Seth," Pete defended.

"I am! And I don't wear any tinfoil hat. If you just twist the supporting evidence to meet your agenda, you can make any story believable. That's my talent, and why I'll make a good lawyer."

"Eck," I interrupted and asserted, "An honest person assumes they are hearing the truth. Why would a pope lie?"

Seth laughed, "Are you kidding? You're naïve, Jean."

I sneered at Seth while Pete continued, "I find it interesting that so many U.S. Presidents have been Freemasons: George Washington, James Monroe, Andrew Jackson, James Polk, James Buchanan, Andrew Johnson, James Garfield, William McKinley, Theodore Roosevelt, Howard Taft, Warren Harding, Franklin D. Roosevelt, Harry Truman, and Gerald Ford. Membership in the Society of Freemasons was very common, about the time of the Revolution, and among America's forefathers, our founding fathers."

"I heard our current president is a Freemason, too," I added.

"Correction," Pete spouted. "George Herbert Walker Bush is a member of the Skull and Bones secret society, or commonly called

The Order. The Skull and Bones Society, at Yale, recruits fifteen seniors each year; and, as of this year, there are about 2,300 total members. While they are students at Yale, members are referred to as Knights; but, after they graduate, and go out into the world, they are known as Patriots, and they work in careers that are geared to fulfilling the purpose of The Order. They are assured positions that facilitate their efforts and are given the big money."

"What order?" I asked.

"The one world order—controlled by the Illuminists," Pete answered. "The Skull and Bones secret society believes *might is right* if you have the power. Their goals are to acquire the power, and to keep the power. This powerful organization is comprised of 10,000 of them at the top of the pyramid, and 6 million at the bottom of the pyramid—they own the biggest corporations and banks in the world. And they would like to get rid of at least one-third of the world's five billion people population, because these welfare recipients and non-productive types are a heavy burden, and are taxing their monetary system."

My eyes were opening more and more each day. "I'm assuming The Skull and Bones Society is a sect of the Freemasons?" I looked to Pete for an answer.

"Did they not make one of their own our latest President of the USA?" Pete pitched for our consideration. "These secret societies occupy offices everywhere in our government. They're active in Congress; they're in the White House; they sit on the benches in courtrooms; they're even Supreme Court Justices forming our laws—which is why I said we were in a dangerous position to allow the Supreme Court to have the final say about anything. Their plan is bigger than most understand. Did you know, that if you're on a jury, and the defendant is a Mason, and he makes the Grand Hailing sign, a secret sign that identifies one Mason to another, you must be sure *not* to make the Mason guilty, for that would disgrace their Order. The Masons obey orders, protect criminal activities, lie if necessary, and are free to commit adultery with anyone, other than another Mason's wife or relative. And the Freemasons claim their Order is a moral one. And the average citizen continues to believe the Masons teach its members good values—that they are Christians."

"That sounds like a group I want to join!" Seth declared and then chuckled.

I rendered Seth a disapproving look.

"We elect presidents who belong to this Order," Pete said as if disturbed.

"It's the *Who's Who Club*," Seth chided. "I'd like some of that protected power."

Chad quipped, "Seth, I think you have little man syndrome!" The nineteen-year old was referring to the fact that Seth was only 5'9" and 145 pounds when wet.

"But you like my big dick, Chad!" Seth slammed back.

"You think his dick is big, Chad?" I added while bothered by another homosexual innuendo. "If that is the case, Chad, you do *way* too many drugs!"

The guys laughed off my opinion while I quietly suffered another blow to my already-altered reality of who Seth really was in character.

My boyfriend's boss moved the conversation back to a more neutral topic. "Freemasons believe mankind's problem is that he has not been allowed free exercise of his reason by a God who restricts man with a series of do's and don'ts."

"I believe that, too!" Seth contributed.

Pete continued, "You don't believe in our Heavenly Father of the Bible, Seth?"

"Sure I do, brother, but there is no right or wrong--it's one man's opinion against another's."

"And you have a degree in Bible Studies?" Pete challenged.

"All the more impressive, right?" Seth challenged.

"So to murder is not wrong?" I questioned.

"Who says it's wrong?" Seth nonchalantly shrugged.

"God!" I answered while clear on that subject after much self-inflicted torment.

Seth snickered as if what I said was ignorant.

Pete continued, "The Masons believe God is a figment of man's mind."

Seth inserted, "They are right, he doesn't exist. That so-called God in the Bible is a debunked myth."

Pete considered Seth's words, "So if God doesn't exist, what mankind calls religion is then fiction?"

"Yes," Seth affirmed.

Pete shook his head, and I saw he did not agree with Seth's beliefs, either; and then, he summed, "You'll make an excellent International Lawyer, working in various world-wide advisory offices on how to implement the Mason's plan for one world order."

"I think so, too," Seth affirmed to Pete. "That's why I want to join them," he said before lowering his voice into a deep sinister sound, "I want what they have--power."

"You sound like Satan," I chided.

"I am Satan," he replied again in a sinister way.

I turned to Pete and angrily quipped, "He's proud to be a creep."

"Oh come on! We are it!" Seth exclaimed as if losing patience for my stand. "Moral values are relative to human experience. Humans are the measure of all things—all intrinsic moral values are based on human desires and interests."

"So you're a Humanist, Seth?" Pete asked.

"Call me what you want. Humans, rather than some divine being, decide what is morally valuable. Human beings, not God, create values; in other words, humans make decisions, and values are established. And, as man develops, his collective consciousness constitutes the necessary God of whom we speak."

I listened carefully to Seth and guessed he had shifted his views because the Word of God conflicted with his lifestyle choice. I assumed, since Seth had indeed graduated from a Christian Bible college fourteen years earlier, that he once believed his current lifestyle choice was a sin in the eyes of our heavenly Father.

Pete scoffed at Seth's position and continued, "The Masons believe man does not need religion, either; and when religion disappears, man can use his mind to solve problems."

"So the Masons want to destroy all religions?" I asked Pete for clarification.

"More correctly, the Masons want to destroy most of mankind—to kill them, or to enslave them. The Masons want to undo everything the Christian Church has produced. The Masons want to eradicate the world of Christianity. The Masons believe if man is taught to give no credence to the God of the living Bible, then man will use *his mind* to solve problems."

"What does man use now, if not his mind?" Seth sarcastically questioned us.

"His faith in the Word," I answered.

"Amen, Jean," Pete toasted.

I turned to Seth, "What is man's reference point when he has a problem to solve, and all he can consider *in his mind* is the anger he feels, that is so great, that the only solution he can come up with is to take his gun out of his safe and murder?"

"Exactly, Jean," Pete said. "He is god, therefore, he makes convenient rules that serve whatever his purpose. The Masons also want to take the right to private property away from everyone, and the right to an orderly government."

"They don't like order?" I asked.

"*Orderly* doesn't mean what you think it means. They plan to have regulators and lenders preemptively engineer the methodic restructuring of a nation's public debt--also called 'orderly default' or 'controlled default'—they have to break down the current situation in order to implement one world-wide monetary system."

"I don't see how they could take our property away--owning property is our Constitutional right," Seth reminded. "Your theory sounds foolish."

Pete shrugged, "I don't know, either, but, eventually, there will be a global restructuring, and a global constitution, too."

I strongly believed what Pete revealed had merit. "So if the Freemasons now occupy Congress, the Supreme Court, the White House, and control the financial markets, then I must believe they certainly can manipulate the world to create one world order."

I questioned how they would create a world with no Christians? I had a strong need to bring Seth to his knees for his own well-being, as well as for the well-being of our family. "If we do not have the Word of God for our soul's enlightenment, nor own the *faith* that stems from that Word--a faith that connects our mind with our spirit man, sparks us like a key to an ignition, and allows us to live with the power of the Holy Spirit, dwelling within us--then all we have is carnal struggle. We miss the greater God-given purpose of our life. And, I know, too, if we don't hold the belief that the power of Christ's blood washed us of our sins—that actual *power* that awakens us to the spirit man that we were born to be, when we finally believe God's Word to be true, then we sadly have no hope of anything greater than a constant struggle. This carnal world *is not it!* If God's Word dictating to us a standard of perfection is *not* relevant, then we've made ourselves the god authority; and there is no higher moral absolute or accountability."

"I am the absolute," Seth said.

"No you're not, Seth," I slammed back. "You have no true *power* if you are not filled with the Holy Spirit. If you do not personally know God, the Father, *and* His Son, Jesus Christ, then the Holy Spirit does not come to you--not to mention, you have no eternal life, so says Jesus. You once learned this truth in Bible College."

Seth scoffed, "You've got to be kidding, Jean! Christians maybe make up one-third of the world's religions. Are you telling me that the Buddhists, Hindu, Jews, Muslims, the tribal orders, and non-religious will all suffer perdition because they don't think like you?"

I shrugged without a response while I struggled with my answer—my conclusion was harsh.

"*Your* god does not love!" Seth slung back at me.

Pete interrupted, "Seth, Adolf Hitler murdered fifty million people during World War II, and he wasn't wrong doing so because he considered himself the absolute, too. He felt the end justified the means--he was creating the Third Reich."

"Hitler's god does not love!" I threw back at Seth. "You do know Hitler served a god, right?" I looked at Seth for an answer.

"I don't know, Jean."

I continued, "Here's a clue--Hitler did not serve my God.

Seth rolled his eyes and looked uncomfortable.

I continued, "Our Heavenly Father endowed us with inalienable rights--life, liberty, and property--and our American government was created to protect those rights in this country. No other bulwark exists to safeguard the natural rights of human beings except our Heavenly Father's sanction. Remove the loving God, and you also remove all claims to liberty, rights, meaning, and purpose."

Pete seemed to want to diffuse the intense argument between me and my boyfriend, and with his Italian accent, our new friend asked with a shrug, "What can we really do about any of this coming trouble?"

"Keep the faith and pray, Pete," I answered, "because God said if my people, which are called by my name, shall humble themselves, and pray, and seek my face, and turn from their wicked ways, then *will I hear them* from heaven, and *will I forgive their sin*, and *I will heal their land.*"

Seth laughed. "Jean's got Jesus."

"Hey, Seth, that's a good thing." Pete advised.

"Seth has bought into the great lie," I sneered.

Seth rolled his eyes again, "And Jean has the truth! Hallelujah!"

I did not respond while I watched Seth mock me. I struggled for the right words and then popped with a rebuttal. "There are three families of faith, but only one family has the truth."

Seth snickered and sarcastically challenged, "Only three families of faith?"

"Hear me out. One family of faith is eastern philosophy, held by those who practice Buddhism, Hinduism, and the New Age Movement. These believers believe there is a god—that is g-o-d with a small *g*. And, these believers see that we live in an evil world of illusion; therefore, we must master *detachment* and *freedom from individualism*. They believe in reincarnation. The second family of faith is the secular view held by atheists, agnostics, materialists, and naturalist—their beliefs center on science, chance. They believe all creation is by chance, and their views embrace Darwin and his theory of evolution, and as well, they buy into the big bang theory. These believers believe we must fight to survive—the survival of the fittest—

and, they believe the universe is meaningless, and we create our own meaning. And then, there is a third family of faith--Christianity and Judaism. We Christians believe, we have the power to be the individuals we were born to be, because the Holy Spirit of Jesus Christ will guide us in our faith, and through Jesus Christ, we possess all that God our Heavenly Father possesses. We walk in faith that God's Word is true. We act accordingly and obey His commandments, and we believe God will fulfill his promises, and we shall have life now and for eternity."

"Wow, Jean," Pete declared, "I thought Seth was the religious expert here?"

"He is," I meekly confirmed. I smiled and watched Pete nod as if I had turned on a light for him.

"So which group does the Freemasonry Religion belong?" Pete asked me.

"Luciferian—any belief that is not Christian or Judaism is a mystical sect created out of Lucifer's great lie. The hardship of my own life opened my eyes recently. In the Garden of Eden, Eve told the serpent, 'We may eat the fruit of the trees of the garden, but of the fruit of the tree, which is in the midst of the garden, God has said, 'You shall not eat it, nor shall you touch it, lest you die.' Then the serpent argued and said to the woman, 'You will *not* surely die. For God knows that in the day you eat of it, your eyes will be opened and you *will be like God*, knowing good and evil.' Eve did not know who she was when the serpent tempted her, and the serpent lied to her when he told her that *if* she ate the forbidden fruit, *then* her eyes would be open and *she would be like God*. In that moment, when Eve took the bait, Eve did not know she was *already* like God, and that her eyes were *already* open."

"Wow," Pete nodded, "I never heard that paradise story from that perspective."

"Lucifer knows that about you, too. And those inside the pyramid, pictured on your currency, know that about you, too, and *they* want to make slaves out of everyone outside the pyramid—*they* don't want you to know the truth. *They* author identity confusion. They *do not* want you to know who you are because the truth will set you free.

Your real identity is that you are like Jesus right now—not in the next world, but right now."

"Hmm," Pete said while mulling over my words. I figured he was connecting the dots to his alleged and so-called conspiracy theory.

I continued, "Jesus was tempted like Eve. In Matthew 4:4, the devil showed up in Jesus' life, showed Jesus all the kingdoms of the world, and their glory, and then said to Jesus, 'All these things I will give you, if you will fall down and worship me.' Jesus did not have identity confusion and replied, 'Away with you, Satan. For it is written, you shall worship the Lord your God, and Him only you shall serve.'"

Pete stood up from the dining chair and walked over toward Seth and me. He stopped in front of us, with a burning fat stogie in one hand, and in the other, held a highball glass filled with a golden elixir, and while impersonating Marlon Brando, he said, "I'm going to lighten up the mood here, though this exchange has been enlightening."

I giggled at his impression of the Italian godfather.

"...I spent my whole life trying not to be careless," he continued. "Women and children can be careless. But not men--"

We laughed.

Pete continued his obviously, well-rehearsed, Godfather movie dialogue. "--Someday, and that day may never come, I'll call upon you to do a service for me, but until that day, accept this justice as a gift on my daughter's wedding day."

Pete smiled and took a swig of his cognac and then continued his theatrics. "I never wanted this for you. I work my whole life--I don't apologize--to take care of my family, and I refused to be a fool, dancing on the string held by all those big shots. I don't apologize--that's my life, but, I thought when it was your time, you would be the one to hold the string."

"Bravo," I said and then clapped, "You're a natural born actor!"

I noticed Seth got quiet, and I questioned where he got stuck—perhaps, after a childhood of watching his mother rage over his mean father's alcoholism, he was angry with God? I figured he felt his boss and I had teamed up together against him, and he felt threatened that his boss and I had more in common than he did with either one of us. I had stolen Seth's coveted lime light that night, but, if I was effective, I prayed my words affected him for the better.

"Italy was a good experience—maybe I'll go back one day," Pete shot back in his natural voice.

Chad passed a joint over to Pete, and I watched Pete take a drag.

"Good job, Godfather," Chad said as he drunkenly stumbled toward my kitchen. "Hey, does anybody want another drink?" He slurred without turning around.

I noticed Chad's girlfriend was on the verge of passing out as she rocked slumped over sideways in my rocking chair. "I think you should take Jenn home, Chad."

Chad walked back out of the kitchen and up to the young woman who appeared to be phasing out in the rocking chair. "You okay, baby?"

Jenn smiled up at him, lunged toward him, and then passed out in his crotch.

"Lay her down, over here on the couch, Chad," I instructed.

Chad lifted up the lightweight and carried her over to the couch. Seth and I got up from the couch and made room for Jenn to lie down.

"You overdosed tonight, baby," he said to his girlfriend.

"What did she overdose on tonight, because I didn't see her drink that much?" I looked at everyone for an answer.

"Oh, she did drink a lot." Chad clarified. "And she did more than just drink and smoke pot."

"What more?" I asked while looking at everyone for an answer, but all I got in response was a feeling that nobody would admit to the truth.

Seth studied his friends. "I think everyone should stay the night--nobody is in condition to drive home."

I nodded in agreement while wondering if an unconscious person would pee on my sofa.

"We'll stay," Chad offered.

"I'm alright, friends—I'm walking home," Pete said. "I'll see you guys tomorrow," he said as he walked out the front door.

Everyone bid his or her adieus to the man we knew lived only a few blocks away.

SPRING 1991. The days slipped away quickly while I watched the baby inside me grow bigger and bigger as evidenced by my ballooning belly. Harper, two-years old, also sprouted every day in the arenas of intelligence and height. I talked constantly to my children about the little brother they would soon have in their lives; and Bella, who would be eight years old, shortly after my fourth child's birth, was excited about having another sibling. She was Mama's helper and had been good with Harper. I was not sure if Harper would accept a younger brother, but he was an easy and content child of few words. I had recently weaned my son off the breast, and considered that my youngest son may soon feel he had to compete with another person for Mama's attention. And each time I had another child, I worried that Joseph, my oldest child, felt he did not belong to this family, because he lived under Todd's roof.

I gained so much weight from eating too much watermelon that the doctor at the charity clinic tested me for gestational diabetes. Seth drove Harper and me, in our emerald blue Corsica to the LBJ Hospital, one early morning, where our unborn baby and I tested healthy and summed fat without complication. The clinic performed an ultrasound, too, and told me that I was entering the 39th week and having a baby girl. I waddled out to the waiting room where I found Seth filling out law school applications while Harper climbed the chairs in the waiting room.

I walked up to Seth and Harper. "They told me I'm carrying a girl--no way! I know this baby is a boy, as surely as I know I breathe oxygen."

He looked up from his work. "Really, they said we're having a girl?"

"Yes."

"Great," Seth exclaimed as if what I knew did not matter.

"I won't be bothered to consider girl names," I said to my

boyfriend. "This child is a boy, and he's my gift to Harper. It's perfect that these two brothers will be so close in age."

"Our gift to Harper."

"Yes, *our* gift." I confirmed.

"Is everything alright with you and the baby?" Seth asked.

"No problems. I took a test called the oral glucose tolerance test, and we're both fine. I am thirty-nine weeks pregnant and could go as long as forty-two weeks."

"So sometime soon we're having a baby?"

"Yep, any day."

"Great news. Now, what do we do from here, Jean?"

"We're done. Let's go home!" I picked up my twenty-five pound toddler and pain surged through my lower back. "You're getting too heavy for Mama to pick up!"

"Let me take him, Jean." Seth offered.

"Thank you," I said while Seth grabbed our toddler from my arms.

"I want to stop and mail these law school applications."

"Can I read what you wrote?" I asked. "Who knows, maybe one day, I'll want to follow in your footsteps."

Seth looked at me as if surprised I would ever consider being a lawyer. "Jean, for now, you focus on being a good mother to our children, and let me take care of the rest," he said while handing me his papers.

I considered I did not trust Seth enough to put my life into his hands while I stared at his handwriting. My grim thoughts forced me to re-read twice what I was staring at so that I could internalize its content. I objected and looked up in question. "You were never the Assistant Precinct Chairman for Precinct #105 for the Republican Party from 1985 until 1988."

Seth just grinned and offered no explanation.

"That's a lie, Seth!"

"Who is going to know the difference?"

"Leonardo held the Assistant Precinct Chairman position. You never did anything with any political party." I looked back down at his application and continued to read, "And you're claiming to be an elected official for the Chester City MUD No. 1, and you represented tax payers on the water board approving utility districts operational expenditures? Again, another Leonardo accomplishment! He was the Treasurer for the Municipal Utility District when we lived in Houston! How can you in good conscience lie like this, Seth?"

"I need to show some kind of past experience in politics."

"You do?"

He nodded yes.

I looked back down at his application and continued to read aloud. "NASA Area Little League volunteer coach for my daughter's seven-year old slow pitch team in 1990?" I looked up and shook my head in disbelief at his audacity. "You never coached her team. We took her and watched from the bleachers."

"I have to get into law school. Do you think they are going to check this shit out?"

"What happens if they do, Seth? What happens if they check on the MUD, or on the Republican Party affiliation, and they discover that you lied on your law school application?"

He snickered. "Then I would get disbarred. They are not going to check on those details."

"You sure are confident. Are you a pathological liar, Seth?"

"Don't start with your virtuous, holier-than-thou crap."

"You lie to me, to your boss, to your mother, on your law school application. Isn't there anything you feel proud of in your life?"

"You won't care that I told these silly lies after I get accepted into law school."

"I don't like lies or liars, Seth, and how can I ever trust you? And your lies will come back to haunt you."

"Remind me to lose sleep," he retorted. "Look, don't get in my way. I have a meeting coming up with the dean of South Texas College of Law."

I was surprised to hear about that opportunity. "Where is that law school?"

"Downtown Houston, about fifteen miles away."

"And why are you talking to the dean?"

"I'll do whatever I have to do, to win a seat. I see my future like this: I'm thirty-six years old with a wife and three kids. I am meeting with the dean of South Texas College of Law tomorrow. I made an appointment with him because I intend to become a real person to him, and not be just a name on an application. I'm going to plead with this man to let me in. I think he will appreciate my place in life, and all my experience, and I intend to ask him to make an exception for my admittance into his law school. I don't want us to have to move anywhere. Houston is good. We have family and friends here--our support system is here. I have a gut feeling this person will recommend me for admission after he meets me. I'm not a kid--I'm a grown man needing a break. I know I can do the work--I have a master's degree! I've written a thesis and proven I can do the work."

"How was your second LSAT score?"

"Good enough, but still not that great."

I took a breath. "I wish you the best, Seth." I wondered then how the lies he told would eventually complicate his life.

"I'm giving one hundred and ten percent, Jean. I intend to get into law school. I want you to be proud of me. Are you, Jean?"

"I am," I said to a man who I saw as desperate. Chronic alcoholism and abuse tormented Seth throughout his childhood that he had learned, at an early age, to invent stories to cover up the dysfunction at home. Perhaps, when he became a lawyer, he could finally feel proud of himself. And perhaps he would be a great lawyer, since he was a great liar.

MARCH 1991. I pushed Harper in his baby stroller across our apartment complex toward the mailboxes. I felt like I was about to give birth any day now. My baby had not moved for the last three days, and I knew that to be a sign I was close to giving birth to my fourth child. I unlocked the mailbox and pulled out what was mostly advertisements and junk mail; and while I stood over the nearby garbage can, tossing the presorted standard postmarks, I came upon a first class letter addressed to Seth from the South Texas College of

Law. We had received several rejection letters, from other law schools, but this law school was the school that we hoped would accept Seth. I anxiously opened the envelope while hoping Seth's meeting with the dean of the law school had paid off. I began to read:

> Dear Seth: The South Texas College of Law is pleased to inform you that we have accepted your application for the Spring Semester 1992. Please remit a $100 seat deposit to this office by April 1991 to reserve you place. This non-refundable deposit will be applied to your tuition at registration. Failure to remit the seat deposit could result in forfeiture of your place. Please also provide official transcripts from all college and universities attended to this office prior to registration. LSAT/LSDAS does not send official transcripts. Registration materials will be sent to you by the Registrar's Office later. Congratulations on your admission. Regina Smith, Director of Admissions.

I was thrilled and could barely contain myself. I turned to my baby in the stroller and began an outpouring of great excitement. "Harper! Daddy is going to law school! Yippee!" I danced in front of my son, and he smiled. "Let's go tell him right away! I can hardly wait to see his reaction!" I hurriedly pushed my son toward the street, and then headed to Seth's office, not but half-a-mile away. Harper and I rolled up to the office building, walked into the lobby area, and then got on the elevator to head up to *The Talent House* on the third floor. I stood inside the elevator while feeling so elated about my life with Seth, when the elevator stopped on the second floor. The doors opened, and no one stood on the other side. I could see that the entire, unoccupied floor was nothing but studs, missing sheetrock and bare concrete floors. Electrical wires dangled from the unfinished ceiling. Suddenly, I heard people talking, and to my surprise, Seth and a beautiful, twenty-something year old woman walked into the elevator area to get on board.

"Hi Seth," I said while exposing all my hurt in sound and look.

"Jean, Harper!" He ignored my obvious reaction and turned to the twenty-five year old woman as if there was no problem. "This is my girlfriend, Jean, and my son, Harper."

The woman acted as if she was not guilty of anything, either. "Hello, Jean," she said coolly and then took my baby's hand, "Hi, beautiful baby."

Harper smiled.

"And who are you?" I indignantly asked her while I took my son's hand out of her grasp by backing the stroller away from her and into the back of the elevator. The couple stepped completely inside the elevator and the doors closed. We moved up to the next floor while I waited for words that would prove me wrong.

"Oh, I'm sorry--I'm Naomi. I'm a model for *The Talent House*. I just signed on with the agency--"

Seth interrupted, "Pete's talking about renting this floor space and expanding. I was just giving Naomi a tour."

"Oh, right," I said rather impatiently while silently crying on the inside. I was not about to waste my breath questioning either one of them regarding the obvious. I was about to give Seth another child any day now, and he was screwing a model on an unoccupied floor.

The elevator opened up on the third floor, and Naomi quickly got off in Pete's lobby and flashed Seth a smile over her shoulder as she quickly walked away. I remained inside the elevator.

"What are you doing up here, Jean?" Seth asked as if all was okay.

"I came up here to give you this letter," I said while I angrily flung the envelope at him. "I see my timing was impeccable!"

I watched him pick up the envelope off the floor. He glanced at the sender's address on the envelope, and without any reaction toward my anger over me busting him with another woman on an isolated floor, or over the possibility of a law school granting him admission, Seth calmly pulled out the letter and silently read. He looked up with a smile and let out a gleeful shrill. "Wow, I did it! I got in!" His mouth gaped while he re-read the letter. He looked back up at me in pure delight. "Can you believe it, Jean? I'm going to law school!"

"I guess Naomi will be impressed with you even more, now."

"Stop it! Jean, don't ruin my moment with your paranoid stuff."

"Don't ruin *your* moment?" I angrily asked. "How about you *not ruining* my life!"

He looked over his shoulder to see if anyone from the office was nearby and then spouted under his breath, "What you saw on the second floor was not what you think."

"Seth, don't underestimate my intelligence. Pete is not expanding his business; he's barely hanging on. I know you well. You let women pick you up on the freeway, right? That's what you told me. You went back to the whore's apartment; and you spent the day with her, and her roommate, and then you come home and get a hard-on while you relive the memory telling your girlfriend about your day. I don't forget anything, especially, that you've always been a dog with fleas."

Seth did not react, but, instead, looked back down at his letter and then back up at me. "This is great news! I'm going to law school!" Seth squatted down in front of Harper and kissed his baby's forehead. "Daddy's going to be a lawyer!"

He stood back up and tried to kiss me, but I pushed him away. "Harper and I are not getting off this elevator." I pushed the ground-floor button while wanting to escape my life. I felt humiliated by the man I was giving children to.

"Okay, then, I'll see you this evening," he said with a smile as the doors tried to shut on him. He knew I had busted him with the model, but it would be a cold day in hell before he would cop to the truth.

"I would assume we'll see you this evening," I spewed while holding the doors open, "…unless you have a date with her on your casting couch."

"Jean, I'll be home at 6:00 p.m.," he calmly reassured me. "Bye Harper, Daddy loves you." He threw his son a kiss and then backed away to watch the doors close.

The doors began to shut again, but I tapped the button on the wall, once more, to have one last say, "You won't be happy until you mess us up, Seth."

"You're delusional, Jean. You look for evidence to hang me, and you find it!"

"I don't have to look too hard, Seth," I said and then flipped him the bird just before the elevator doors shut for good.

He constantly defended his lack of character, and I knew that I now doubted myself. Was I truly paranoid? I was a 205-pound, insecure, pregnant woman, with no job, and having children with a snake in the grass--of course, I doubted myself! This man had told me, when I was pregnant with Harper, that he did not find pregnant *women* attractive after I came on to him one night in bed. He was a heartless bastard.

A WEEK LATER. I gave birth to my fourth child at the same charity hospital, the Lyndon B. Johnson Hospital where Harper had been born two years earlier. Doren, a healthy baby boy weighing in at almost ten pounds was born with brown eyes, a chubby face, and fine blonde hair. I was delighted with my fat baby and felt blessed with another son who would be close in age to Harper. Seth was thrilled with his second son, too.

As I laid there in my hospital bed that evening, I watched Daddy hold his new baby boy while I quietly prayed that we, as a couple, would be happier with each other now that I had given Seth two sons and would soon get my thin body back. Life was turning up, and I preferred to see the good. We had a current income that paid our bills, a running car, three healthy children, and a hopeful future in law.

Seth stood beside my hospital bed with our second child in his arms. He put the baby into my arms and then blurted, "I'm going to leave you now."

My heart sank.

"I've been in here with you for the last twelve hours. I need to get some dinner and take a break from this place. And I want to share the good news, and gloat about my new, baby boy. You know, pass out some cigars. All that breathing was hard work for me," he chuckled.

I did not smile, but felt the struggle to draw him closer to me never ended. "I understand. You should go have some dinner."

"I'm going to look up Dorothy and Ron tonight since Ma's

got our kids. I haven't seen them in ages. You don't mind, do you, if I get out, and have some fun for a couple of hours?"

I shrugged with a poor attitude while aware he knew better than to ask me if I minded. I felt crushed. "Please do not leave me alone," I begged.

"I'm so proud of you, Jean," he said while he gave me a peck on the lips and pretended to not understand me not wanting *him* to go anywhere near those so-called *friends*.

"Are you proud of me, really?" I asked while looking into my son's eyes and wanting *not* to care about Seth anymore.

"I am! I'll be back, get some rest." He kissed me goodbye on the cheek, then gave our son a kiss on the forehead, and then proceeded to walk out of the hospital room.

I had no clue, until that moment, Seth was still associating with those despicable characters, and he had been completely unabashed about telling me where he was going that night, as if our hours of arguments over my insecurities regarding both Dorothy and Ron had never registered with him. How insensitive he was to leave me alone on this night that our second child came into the world!

I laid there in the bed, feeling less than special, and wondering whom Seth would screw that night. I had not seen the couple since Dorothy had told me that Seth was coming over to her apartment, during his lunch hour, and hitting on her while Ron was at work. So now that I was out of the picture, I did not know if Dorothy was still married to Ron, or not, and if not, then Seth was probably having sex with the topless barmaid that night. If she was still married to her bi-sexual husband, Ron, then Seth was probably taking Ron to Motel 6 to celebrate, and probably to celebrate the simple fact that I was away for a night.

I lay in the hospital room alone all that night, holding my son whom I named Doren and reading a book on the zodiac signs that I got from the library. Doren meant *gift*. I had often referred to my unborn child as *my surprise package from heaven*. My gift was born under the sun in Pisces. Doren's kind and sympathetic nature trumped over all other personality traits. He would be compatible with the Cancer sign, which coincidentally was his brother, Harper's sign; and I took delight in knowing these two brothers would be best friends. Doren would possess great charm and have a carefree approach, yet he would be brave and prefer a lot of independence. I prayed his carefree nature would sustain him in a home of tumult. I learned the Pisces sign does well in the performing arts, especially in theatre, and made note to enroll my son into acting classes when he matured. Doren would crave fairytale endings, and be more in love with the idea of love, than being in love itself, and I wondered why? Was the trauma of his parents' eventual divorce reason he would not be capable of authentic love? Did God know my future and send me children equipped to handle broken hearts? Or would Seth's character negatively affect both my sons' character? I prayed my sons would grow up and have hearts for God.

    A WEEK LATER our family of five went to dinner; and as we went through the Mexican buffet, a female employee, in her forties, donning a traditional Mexican folk wear dress, and serving the enchiladas, recognized my boyfriend. "Hi, Seth!" She smiled as if elated to see him.

    "Hi, how are ya?" Seth politely responded.

    I knew Seth could not remember her name because he always used a person's name when greeting someone.

    "Well, actually, I'm bothered by something, Seth." She drizzled cheese onto his enchiladas. "I spent a lot of money on those pictures, for me and for my daughter, and we haven't received one single phone call, from your agency, since that day we were in your office. I have called the agency numerous times, but I cannot get anyone to return my phone calls. I'm beginning to think I wasted twelve-hundred dollars."

    "I'll tell Pete to call you when I go into the office on Monday," Seth said to her just before he slid his tray to the end of the order counter.

    The woman turned her attention to me, "You must be Seth's wife?"

    I nodded while I watched Seth nonchalantly escape the upset woman. "Hi, I'm Jean, and these are our children, Bella, Harper, and

Doren."

"I'm sorry to sound like I'm complaining," she continued, "but I make $4.25 an hour working here, and I have to work two jobs to make ends meet. And when Seth told my daughter, and me, that we would get opportunities to work, well, we believed him."

"I understand," I replied while I looked at Seth for help and wondered how he, in good consciousness, could take this very plain Jane's money and tell her that he could get her modeling jobs?"

The costumed woman continued, "I feel like we were exploited and used just so he could make his commission."

"I'm sorry," I said while feeling guilty by association.

Seth piped in from afar, "Jean, there's people waiting, move down the line."

"I'm sorry," I said to the woman again. "I'll talk to him."

When Seth and I got away from the woman's hearing range, I whispered to him while we walked over to our table, "I'm embarrassed to be with you!"

"It's a job, Jean. I did not force that woman to write those checks."

"No, you did not, but you misled her to believe her twelve-hundred dollar investment would buy her, and her daughter, opportunity to make more money as models. She believed she would have the ability to give up one of her low-paying jobs."

"Yeah, right, that hag is a model."

I shook my head, "What you committed is business fraud."

"No, not fraud!" He whispered. "She bought head shots and got something for her money."

"She and her daughter could have spent a lot less on photos had they gone to the Sears Photography Department. She believed you were going to place her, and her daughter, in modeling jobs, but that was a deception that you created to get her money. That's called business fraud, and she could sue you."

"No, what I did was sell her on a dream, and that is called *good salesmanship;* and that exceptional talent of mine creates, for us, an income to afford our expenses."

I shook my head, and once again, realized I slept with a man who had no integrity.

"When we get back home today, I want to give Brian Flannigan a call; he's one of the inner-circle."

"He's an inner-circle member, too?" I resounded while disgruntle with everything about him. "How many are there?"

"Well, there is Brian, Max, Stan, and George. I haven't seen any of the guys since Max's wedding ten years ago."

"You failed to mention Runi."

"I met Runi at a convenience store where we both worked. I was married to Deb, living in Springfield, Missouri, and working on my master's program at the time I met Runi. The guys from Centroidal Bible College had all graduated by then and gone their own way."

"Is Brian married?" I asked while wondering if the entire inner-circle all hid behind wives?

"Yeah, I think so. He's living up in Ohio and working somewhere; I don't remember where he said he was working last time we talked. I'm thinking I'd like to get my securities license and generate some income as an investment advisor. Brian might have a connection that could help me put this plan all together."

"I see."

"I'd have to renew my licenses. I'll need a Series 6 and Series 63 again. I'll have to take the qualifying exams, but if I could land a big corporate account, and be the managing broker of record, then we would have some income coming in while I'm in law school."

"That plan sounds legitimate. Who will you work for?"

"I found this company called *Inroad Investments and Securities*."

"Who are they?"

"*Inroad* offers investment advice to clients; and as their broker, I would tailor fit for my client, a financial planning report to meet the company's goals. I would include a full range of investment alternatives and strategies. I would provide that kind of information, analysis, and advice. In general, I would assist my client with their retirement plans, profit-sharing plans, 401k plans, and IRA's, including retirement rollovers."

"Do you know how to do all that?"

"Yeah," he smiled. "That's why I take classes and have to pass tests before I'm given licensure."

"Will you have time for law school, if you get a big account that you have to manage?"

"Oh yeah, once I put everything in play, then it's on auto-pilot."

"Auto-pilot, huh?"

"And I pass go and collect a commission."

"I would think there are supervisory procedures designed to achieve compliance, and that you would be paid a commission to stay on top of your account?"

"Of course, there are procedures, Jean."

I nodded and wondered if Seth truly understood his responsibility as an investment advisor?

We ate our Mexican buffet and returned to our apartment. I took the three kids out to play while Seth made his phone call to Brian Flannigan, but the kids and I had barely gotten to the swing set when I realized I had to return to the apartment and change Doren's diaper. I asked Bella to watch her little brother Harper while I went upstairs for a few minutes with the baby. I came into the apartment quietly, without Seth hearing me; he was in the back bedroom on the phone, and I could hear him talking to his old college friend.

"How long have you been married?" He asked. He paused. "Thirteen years is a long time." He paused. "No, Debbie and I were divorced after five years; and then, I left Missouri and headed out to Texas to work the insurance business with my brother." He paused. "No, he and I had a falling out and split up. I went out on my own. I've been with Jean for four years now. She and I have two sons-- Harper, two-years old, and Doren, brand new. Jean has an eight-year old daughter and an eleven-year old son, too, from a previous marriage." Seth paused to listen to his friend; and then, I heard Seth lower his voice. "Does your wife have any idea, you know, about that time when we--" He paused.

I grabbed a diaper out of the children's bedroom, then walked into the master bedroom, and saw that by the look on Seth's face, I had surprised him. I acted as if I heard nothing and laid the baby down on our bed to change his diaper.

Seth moved the conversation along. "So hombre, my wife just stepped in here with our beautiful new addition, my second son, Doren." He paused and then laughed.

I considered his term, *wife*. Since when?

"Family *is* great. Seth paused. "Okay, get back with me on that situation. When are you having your board meeting?" He paused. "Okay, then we'll talk after your meeting tomorrow. I really could use this opportunity, Brian. I'll owe you one, if you can break it open for me." Seth paused. "Okay, take care, bro."

Seth hung up the phone and clapped his hands together while pleased with his effort. "There's definitely an opportunity to be had here," he said to me. "Brian is the Chief Financial Officer for this Fortune 500 company called *Bike World*. They are operating in Ohio. They make sports equipment, too, and Brian thinks the CEO could be persuaded to do something with their employees' pension fund."

"How many employees does the company have?"

"About 200 employees and a $25 million dollar pension fund."

"That's a lot of money to manage, Seth."

"Yeah, if I close this deal, I'll get a commission in the range of $100,000 a year for as long as *Bike World*'s employees' pension is in the care of my brokerage, *Inroad Investments and Securities*."

"A hundred thousand dollars a year would be an amazing income."

"I know. Can you imagine?"

"Yes," I answered while recalling the lifestyle of freedom I shared with Leonardo.

"Brian is going to broach the subject at Monday's board meeting and will let me know what the company wants to do. He said his company would most likely look at other opportunities, too, other than just what I bring to the table."

"Of course."

"But the point is, I'm on the inside now. They'll take a look at what I offer them through *Inroad Investments and Securities*--it's a great company."

"Congratulations."

"Thanks."

"So is Brian still married?"

"Yeah, he is married, and to the same woman for the last thirteen years. He has a couple of kids."

"I guess she then doesn't have any idea?"

"Any idea about what?" He asked as if confused.

"You know, Seth, about *that time*." I winked and then picked up the baby. "I hope you make lots of money," I said to the liar.

Seth laughed. "Jean, you are so paranoid."

"I really am at this point, Seth," I said as I walked out of the room to return to the park. "I don't know which way is up!" I sarcastically spouted to myself once outside of his hearing range.

FIVE MONTHS LATER, AUGUST 1991, and to our great surprise, our Coral Gables, Florida lawyer had us on the phone while he was negotiating an out-of-court settlement with the convenience store. Weeks earlier, our lawyer, and his partner, had deposed the two convenience store clerks who had us arrested for theft by credit card. Our lawyers accidentally discovered, minutes after the deposition, when they went to pay one of the store clerks for her time, she, by her own admission, had been anxiously waiting all morning for the twenty-five dollar payment from the lawyers so she could leave the deposition and go buy beer. She was a chronic alcoholic and had not had a drink all day. And when the two lawyers heard her admission, to needing to buy beer that day, they then questioned her further about her drinking habits while having not understood, during either of the depositions, that both of the clerks were chronic alcoholics. The female clerk admitted to the lawyers that she drank before she went to work on that day in question, and, in fact, testified she and the other store clerk had both been drinking all morning, before they went to work and had us arrested at the store for theft by credit card. The lawyer told us what she had told them that day after the deposition:

"You see, the other clerk is married; but he and I were having an affair at that time, and when his old lady left for work, I joined him at his house. We got our buzz on there, before we went to our job at the convenience store."

"How much do you usually drink before you go to work?"

"Usually we drink up about half a case."

"You two, together, drink half a case of beer, before you go to work?" My lawyer asked again.

"Yep."

"And how many beers are in a case?"

"Twenty-four beers."

"So you and your lover--"

"My former co-worker, please! We ain't on speaking terms no more."

"Okay, your former co-worker."

"Do you still work with him at the store?"

"Nope. I couldn't stay there."

"Why not?"

"Well...the truth is, I got fired for not showing up for work one day. It was too hard to be around my ex- after we broke up. His wife read him the right act, and he acted like he didn't know my name anymore."

"Does your former co-worker still work for the convenience store?"

"Nope, he got fired, too. He lies, not sure why he got fired."

"I see. And did you and your co-worker drink half a case of beer every morning, when you both worked for the convenience store?"

"Yeah, most mornings, that is, if his old lady went to work. She went to work most mornings; then, I'd go to his house."

"So you two drink twelve beers every day before you go to work. Is that correct?"

"Yeah, I guess."

"Would you say you drink six beers, and your co-worker drinks six beers?"

She nodded, "Sometimes more."

"And when did you two start your shift on the day in question?"

"Oh, about 11:00 a.m. we went into work."

"And when did you stop drinking that morning?"

"About 10:30 that morning."

"And why did you think my clients had used a stolen credit card?"

"Well, we got a phone call from the TRW people. They were mad at us 'cause they said that they warned us on the TRW machine, that a credit card we were swiping was stolen, but that we accepted the stolen credit card anyway."

"Who are the TRW people?" The lawyer asked.

"They process the credit card when we swipe the card at the time of purchase. TRW give us an instant verification. The TRW people said the credit card was stolen, but we didn't notice that warning."

"TRW told you that my client's credit card was stolen?"

"Well, no, not exactly. We didn't figure out that we had even taken a stolen credit card until later, when TRW called. We didn't know for sure who gave us that stolen credit card, but we guessed it was your clients' card because we saw them in the store the day we took that bad card. We get into big trouble, with corporate, when we accept a stolen credit card, after the swipe machine warns us not to accept it, so we were just fixin' the problem. We were covering our asses."

"I understand. And why did you accept a stolen credit card at the time of a purchase?"

The woman shrugged, "I'd have to say it was an oversight--didn't mean to."

"Would you agree that had you *not been drinking* before you began your shift, you may have noticed the TRW swipe machine warning you that you were being given a stolen credit card by a customer?"

"Probably," she agreed.

"So based on the fact that you needed to pin someone to a

stolen credit card you accepted the day before, you then had my clients arrested the following day, simply because you had seen them in the store the day before?"

"Yeah, we were making an educated guess, but he looked a bit shifty to us, too."

"When you say he, you mean my client?"

"Uh huh..."

That testimony was all that my lawyer and his partner needed to prove the convenience store had no probable cause to arrest us. We sought malicious and compensatory damages; and based on the probability, that a jury would greatly sympathize with us, the defendants--the convenience store owner, was more than willing to settle out of court with us, and did so immediately after the depositions. Therefore, nearly three years later, after the crash and burn of my Florida sales trip, and of my *Jean Wynn, An American Designer* dream, the insurance company for the convenience store finally awarded Seth and me a check for $300,000, after attorney fees. There was justice, and life just got grander!

SIX WEEKS LATER, OCTOBER 1991, Seth got his licenses to act as an investment advisor in the state of Texas; and *Inroad Investment and Securities* permitted him to be their sales representative. Seth's deal with Brian Flannigan, a member of his *inner-circle* network from Centroidal Bible College, and now, the Chief Financial Officer for *Bike World,* also came to fruition. *Inroad Investment and Securities* crowned Seth their *broker of record* for the $25 million dollar deal he put together with *Bike World.* As a result of his effort with his friend from his college days, to join these two companies, Seth earned a quarterly commission of $25,000, for an undefined amount of years, or until Brian's company chose to place its employees' pension fund with another brokerage house.

Seth, for the second time in his life, became a licensed investment advisor. And like the first time when he wore the professional title *investment advisor,* Seth was required to have a series of licenses, to include Series 5, 6, and 63, before he could close this mega deal with *Inroad Investment and Securities* and *Bike World*. The Series 6 license is the National Association of Securities Dealers minimum required license for an individual to sell mutual funds and variable annuities and is generally used at insurance companies and banks. Full service brokerage firms typically require that their reps hold a Series 7 license because that allows them to provide individual stocks and other securities in addition to mutual funds and variable annuities. The Series 63 is the license that most states require that covers administration, security regulations, brokerage operations, and business practices.

Seth had taken qualifying exams for each one of those licenses, *except* for the stockbroker's Series 7 license, and had passed the rigorous testing. I was quite impressed with my boyfriend's first deal that I had ever known him to close; and now, after having first watched him get into law school, and close a big deal, too, in which he would earn an annual $100,000 commission, I was beginning to believe in him again. I forgave him for the ineptitude he demonstrated our first three years together, when an eviction threatened us every month, and we had no money for anything. I was right, to ever believe, Seth was intelligent enough to do whatever he set out to do.

Seth read the letter to me that he had received from *Bike World*: *"Dear Mr. Zherneboh: Inroad Investment and Securities has approved you to conduct business on a limited basis as a Series 6 licensed individual. You may sell only investment company products until you become registered as a General Securities Representative."* Seth looked up at me. "I'm going to have to study and take one more exam and get my Series 7 license."

"Do whatever you have to do to not lose this account, Seth."

"I'm going to have to pay a fee, too, according to this letter, to *Inroad Investments and Securities*."

"How much?"

"$608.50"

"We can squeeze out the money from your next two paychecks from *The Talent House*."

"I have to pay this fee immediately. I can't wait. Have you heard from our lawyer yet, as to when the insurance company will be cutting that $300,000 settlement check?"

"I called Andrew today, and he said we should get the check this week or next week."

"Wow! Let's go house hunting, baby! Call up a Realtor."

"Okay." I smiled while I got the picture that we had no more money problems; in fact, we were wealthy!

SIX WEEKS LATER--MOVING DAY. I had packed boxes for a week and felt like a little girl on Christmas Eve waiting for Santa. We had close of escrow ten days after we made a cash offer on the property. We had looked at numerous huge homes with four or five bedrooms, and agreed we loved The Woodlands, Texas home, due to the large wooded cul-de-sac lot. The Woodlands was a master planned community and had sixty miles of hike and bike trails and dozens of forested parks scattered throughout the various villages with playground equipment and pools. The Woodlands, Texas had the George Mitchell 1700-acre Nature Preserve and had won an award for sensitivity to natural and created environments. There were three 18-hole golf courses to include the Jack Nicklaus signature golf course and a country club. The Woodlands even boasted the Cynthia Woods Mitchell Pavilion where famous rock bands, symphonies, and ballets performed. In general, this community, built in the forest, and north of Houston, was the ideal place to raise a family.

We bought a 3,500 square foot, two-story custom home of modern architecture. The contemporary home had four bedrooms and three baths, an aluminum roof, and floor-to-ceiling windows in every room downstairs rendering a view of a thick forest unobstructed by any type of fence. My kitchen was a chef's dream with a cook's island, and Seth and I had ordered *Sears Best* in kitchen appliances and had the delivery scheduled the same day we would move in. Today was that day, and I had driven over to our new house with the children and was unloading a few boxes while I waited on Seth, Chad, and Pete to arrive from our apartment with the last of our belongings. The sun sank and still no show of the men folk. I grew impatient and was wondering where they were when I heard noise in the driveway. They walked into the house talking and laughing with beers in their hands. I could smell the marijuana on their persons.

I looked out the front window and did not see a truck in the driveway. "Where have you guys been all day?" I impatiently asked.

"We're celebrating, baby!" Seth declared.

"Come out here onto the patio and join us, Jean." Chad said as he followed Seth out the back door off the living area.

"Where is my stuff?" I demanded to know. I walked outside to speak to Seth. "The sun is going down, and you guys have been gone all day. This was our moving day, Seth. I wanted to get everything out of the apartment today."

"Well, I don't think that is going to happen due to some technical difficulties we encountered earlier in the day."

"What the hell are you talking about?"

Pete interrupted, "I'm sorry, Jean—but, we had to run by Chad's place, and we lost track of time."

"You lost track of time!" I could not believe what I was hearing from these idiots. "This was the most exciting day of my life, and you guys got sidetracked? What sidetracked you, Seth? Your drugs?" I wondered, too, if there were other women involved in their delay.

Seth shrugged, "That's how the dominoes fall sometimes, baby."

His nonchalant excuse outraged me. "Where is the truck that you were borrowing, Seth?"

"I couldn't get the truck."

"And why not?" I looked at Chad for an answer.

Seth continued, "Because by the time we got to Chad's friend's house, he and his truck were gone."

"You guys are such losers!" I stood there shaking my head in disgust. "You're unbelievable, Seth."

Seth chuckled and handed me a joint. "Take a drag, Jean. It will be all right. We'll get the furniture tomorrow."

I wanted nothing to do with their partying. "No, it won't be alright, Seth, because I will have to rent a U-Haul tomorrow! And you will have to move the stuff by yourself tomorrow, because these two guys will be busy at work, and I have three children to handle and cannot help you! We had to be out of the apartment by today! That's how I arranged everything!" I spewed. "I just wish I could count on you to be your word, Seth!" I stepped back into my empty house and slammed the door on the guys to make my point.

Pete came in to see me and to smooth things over. "I'm sorry, Jean," he gently said. "I know you were really excited about moving into your house today."

"I sure was!"

"Chad was the problem today. He made promises that he couldn't deliver. He dragged us all over kingdom come."

"You know, Pete, I appreciate your effort to make excuses for Seth and Chad, but I am really disappointed. Seth was to head up this show, not Chad. I don't even have a bed to sleep on tonight. And I think the drugs are getting in the way of common sense around here. I don't want you guys smoking dope in my house, nor on my patio. My kids are young and impressionable, and I want to be a good example for them. And, as for Seth, well, he has to put the drugs down, because he is starting law school, in the spring, only a few months away. He won't be able to handle law school, if he's doing drugs and high all the time." I heard the kitchen door open and in walked Seth, and the twenty-two year old idiot, and Seth's biggest fan, Chad.

"Would you like a beer, Pete?" Seth asked as he headed toward the refrigerator. "Well, look at this--my new side-by-side." I like this black. When did the refrigerator come?" He asked me.

Today, while you guys were out playing around. Sears delivered all the appliances. Check out the trash compactor and the washer and dryer, too."

Seth inspected the black compactor installed in the lower cabinet near the sink, and then walked into the adjacent utility room to view the white washer and dryer and came back out smiling. "I'm on top of the world, guys!" He gloated. "It's like I died and went to heaven. I've got everything a man could ask for—new kitchen appliances, the best money can buy from Sears; a beautiful wife--"

I snapped, "We're not married, Seth."

"Sure we are! You married me in the shower!"

I rolled my eyes while still feeling angry about my furniture not arriving.

Seth continued, "And I've two beautiful sons, a beautiful daughter, and a beautiful custom home in The Woodlands, Texas, and paid-in-full to boot! And money in the bank to buy whatever I need for this magnificent dream that I'm living. Baby!" Seth looked at me, "Do you want your own car?"

"Yes," I said while feeling the least he could do for me was consider my need for transportation—after all, my apparel business lawsuit brought the house and all of its furnishings.

"You've got one coming!" He looked at his buddies, "I have an income of $100,000 year! And I'm going to law school. What more can a man ask for?"

Pete looked at me. "I'd say you are *a very lucky* man, Seth."

"Thank you, Pete," I injected while acknowledging Pete knew who and what mattered.

I listened to Seth boast to his macho friends and knew he did indeed have everything--he had the American dream. I was beginning to let my guard down, again, in recent days, and to believe he truly loved our children, and me, and that he did not need anything more than what he had achieved with me; and for the first time in a long time, I did not feel threatened by Runi, or any other man or woman. I often prayed though, always with these words, "Thank you, God, for your gifts. None of this would be possible without you, and don't let Seth continue to be an idiot. Make him love us."

6
WHAT'S LOVE GOT TO DO WITH IT?

January 1992. Seth started his spring semester at South Texas College of Law; and every weekday morning that first week, he enthusiastically jumped out of bed with an alarm, and within thirty minutes, ran out the door with a pile of legal textbooks. He fervently told me about the exhilaration he felt sitting among future lawyers of

America while listening to his law professors; and although I felt envious of his opportunity, I was very happy for Seth and an advocate for his success. His success was our success.

When he arrived home after law school, he took a two-hour break in the afternoons from his legal studies to do whatever he felt like doing to relax; and then, he would hit the books for the rest of the evening. And during the second week of his semester, I noticed he was not in the upstairs guest room, studying after that early afternoon break; instead, he was outside working in his yard until late at night.

I was certainly proud of him and told our young sons and daughter how excited I was for Daddy because he was studying to be a lawyer. I explained to Bella that after Seth passed the Texas State Bar exam, he would then have many doors open for him. He was setting the standard for our children and their children, and role modeling for his sons and stepdaughter a behavior worthy of emulating.

Half-way through his third week of classes, something happened to Seth's commitment level. I began to worry our dream might be fading, when I saw him come in from outside, one afternoon, after having taken his two-hour break, and, instead of him slipping away upstairs to study, he sat on the vanity in the downstairs master bathroom in front of the mirror, for hours, and picked on his blackheads, whiteheads, and whisker growth. I had seen this neurotic behavior in past years, and had hoped Seth had put his need to wreak havoc on his body to rest with his new preoccupation called law school. When I saw him perched up on the marble counter top, that afternoon, picking at his face, I did not think much about his action, until I saw him hours later, when he walked into the kitchen--I was shocked! His fingernails gouged out his face, chest, and arms. "My God! What have you done to yourself?"

"I was squeezing pimples," he said and then snickered. "I do that when I'm stressed."

Or high as a kite, I thought to myself. "What are you stressed about?"

"I've got to talk to you about something."

"Talk," I said while suspecting the drugs, he did behind my back, when he was in the yard, was the culprit, and reason for the self-

mutilation.
"What would you say if I told you that I did not want to continue with law school?"
"Why?"
"That is exactly *my* point, Jean. *Why?*"
"I thought you were in law school because you want to be an International Lawyer. You took great effort to get into law school, Seth! You took the LSAT twice! Law school is a great opportunity few have, and I think you're lucky to be where you are, right now. I would love to be in your shoes. You have a paid-for home, me, your children, and a sizable income that affords you to go to school for the next three years, without any worry about finances!"
He shook his head in disagreement while I watched him consider I did not approve of him quitting school.
"I'm just not in the mindset to study."
"I don't get it, Seth? You've had since spring of 1990, when you first sprung it on us that you wanted to go to law school. You've had a year and four months to get into the *right* mindset."
"I told you that studying would be a challenge for me."
"I figured the only challenge for you was to pass the LSAT with a high enough score so you could get into law school, and you did that! I thought the easy part was studying your class notes!"
"It's not easy to study around here!"
"That is not true, Seth. You have that spare bedroom upstairs to use; and the kids and I hang out down here, when you're up there, and we're not loud. You're making excuses for dropping out because you're afraid of failing. You knew law school was competitive when you went in, and now you are just running scared."
"Na, you don't understand. I can't focus!"
"You procrastinate and are intentionally sabotaging your success. I've watched you, every evening, for the last two weeks, screw around with things that don't matter. You'll spend hours arranging your rock collection on the bookshelf in the den. You spend hours arranging knickknacks on those stupid shelves, when you should be upstairs studying. You go out and hunt for moss, after school, to carpet the dirt between the stepping-stones; and you don't

come in until midnight, and then you're too tired to study. And you spend hours talking on the phone, out there in the garage, to your *boyfriend*, instead of being upstairs and studying. I pick up the phone and I hear you talking to Runi."

"So I talk to Runi, big deal!" He angrily blasted.

"So what happened, Seth? You earned a Master's degree; how can law school be that difficult?" I was not letting him divert me with a conversation called your boyfriend *is* a big deal to me, asshole! "Did you fall so far behind in your classes, that you now feel you have to quit?"

"No, they're not too far ahead, that I can't catch up."

"I thought you would have stayed on top of things. I guess your drugs got in the way."

"You're delusional, Jean. I don't do drugs," he defended.

"You didn't even give law school a chance, before you quit trying. I don't understand. Three weeks and you're already done? I felt your passion, when you talked about becoming a lawyer. I heard you tell Pete, and Chad, that you wanted to litigate cases before the World Court and arbitrational tribunals. I was impressed, for a few minutes. We were all impressed! And you--you seemed the most impressed with you. You were excited about the possibility of being able to work for national governments anywhere in the world!"

"I want to be with my children, work in the yard, and not stress over whether, or not, I have to study every day."

"You only studied that first week, Seth. What about our future?"

"You're paranoid, Jean. You worry too much."

"Wrong again. Do you care at all about your kids' future?"

"I do care about my children's future, Jean. Trust me on that one. I haven't let you down; we have a $100,000 a year income coming in here because of my abilities. What makes you think I can't produce like that again?"

I shrugged while feeling greatly disappointed in the man, and wondering how many *inner-circle* friends he had that were Chief Financial Officers in Fortune 500 companies?

"I'm going to quit law school."

"Well, if you do quit school, then I'm going to take a class in the mornings over at Rice University."

"What kind of class?"

"A writing class, Seth. I got a catalogue for Rice University's summer and fall semester in the mail, the other day, and I saw the school offered a series of novel writing classes. There are ten levels of these writing classes, one class per level; and each class is only three weeks long."

"How is it *you* can get into an Ivy League school like that?"

"The writing course is part of their Continuing Education curriculum. The classes are non-accredited and cheaper. Mostly retirees and people who just want to learn how to write and not worry about term papers or taking tests, take these courses."

"That sounds like fun!" Seth snickered. "So you want to be a novelist now, huh?"

"Yeah, well, I want to write, and I think I could get better if I got some writing instruction. I like the idea of attending Southern Ivy and going to a school in a league with Duke and Tulane. You know Leonardo went to Tulane. Did you remember to add that school to your repertoire of achievements on your law school application?"

Seth shot me a go-to-hell look while I grinned over my last slam. I suspected the law school said something to him, and to his classmates, about the applications they submitted, and I suspected Seth got scared, and wanted to quit, before they threw him out for lying. Maybe a professor told him the law school would do a background check and verify all applications before anyone took the Texas State Bar exam?

I made my point and switched gears. I had already spent too much of my energy supporting the loser, when the emphasis should have always been on *my* success. "The writing class is every Tuesday and Thursday morning, for two hours, and is three weeks long."

"Jean, just sign up," he impatiently said while sounding as if acquiescing to second place made him angry. Perhaps his lie did force him out of school. I figured he had to be real pissed at himself for putting himself in a no-win place.

I smiled while appreciating that *my time* had come by default.

I wondered if he supported me because he cared about my happiness, or whether he supported me because the classes were non-accredited and would not apply toward any degree. "Thanks for your support, Seth."

"You can use a break from the kids."

"Wow, thank you." I wondered if he had fallen in love with me while I was busy decorating, cooking, cleaning, and caring for our children; or had he fallen in love with me because I had bought him his LSAT books and supported his efforts to get into law school? I hoped he had a sense of appreciation for me; but maybe he just felt like a quitter and a disappointment to me, and supported me with an agenda that I would forgive him and continue to love him if he allowed me to go to school.

LATER THAT SUMMER. My three-week novel writing class began that June, and I loved driving into the city and attending lecturers at the prestigious university. My Middle Eastern professor, who was as wide as he was short, moved and inspired me. Venkatesh Kulkarni wore a three-piece white polyester suit and white shirt. The writing teacher had very thick, and very black hair, in the style of Albert Einstein, and the high-spirited and animated man entertained our small group of fifteen writers every morning for two hours with his life stories. I was enthralled with the possibility of being a professional writer, and went out after class one day, and bought myself a *Brother Word Processor WP-80* for $299 on sale at Wal-Mart. I would write, and be able to edit on a 5" x 9" green screen, and I could store my writing on a 3-1/2" double-density floppy disk with a 280k format. I bought a small desk, too, and set up a writing corner in the downstairs master bedroom; and in between cooking dinner, and changing diapers, I began writing my first novel.

The professor did not grade anything we wrote, but he assigned various homework projects that we would volunteer to read to our classmates at the next meeting. I found the thought of sharing with total strangers intimidating and lacked the courage to expose my secrets. I wrote morbid, morose, and macabre compositions, and I used symbols to define my feelings about a woman who lived with Satan's incarnate. One day the professor requested we turn in our homework before anyone read their piece; and then, he read my one-page exercise to the class and summed that the writer, who he kept anonymous, expressed peril, and seemed to be pleading for help. He had unmasked his most self-conscious student, and I felt naked.

One particular morning in class, all the courageous, but me, got up, one-by-one, and read their creations from behind the front center podium. I sat quietly in my desk, as usual, analyzing each student's work, and silently grading each paper, either as poorly written, mediocre, or great. After six students read their compositions to us, a thin, passive male, of Mediterranean origin, volunteered to read his paper from behind the podium. The fair-skinned, thirty-year old, began to read slowly, and was well into the first half of his story, when I realized I had not understood a single word he had spoken. I looked around the room and wondered if I was the only person who heard gibberish? I saw everyone politely sitting in their desks and staring at him as if they clearly understood what he read. I turned my attention back to the source of garble and continued to listen, but I heard nothing audible that I could translate into meaning; and then, I considered the thought that everyone else was being polite and understood nothing, either; and with that consideration, a half-laugh slipped out of my mouth. All heads, except the reader's, turned to my direction, and I could not help but smile. I looked down and tried to keep my amusement at bay, but I found the situation funnier and funnier while I watched my classmates politely turn their attention back to the reader who had no clue. Another laugh burst forth from my funny perspective, and that was the end of my ability to maintain my polite composure. My classmates, one-by-one followed in suit; and the hilarity grew for they all now connected to my unspoken humor; and while we intermittently battled our convulsion of chuckles, the guy at the podium never looked up, but continued to read his very long account, as if deeply lost in his words. That morning class was especially enjoyable.

STILL SUMMER 1992. I drove my nine-year old daughter, and myself, across the city for Theatre Under the Stars' Humphrey School of Musical Theatre, or commonly known as TUTS. I had first called this school, when I carried Bella in my womb, wanting to know when I could enroll her into her first class. Management told me then that she would have to be at least four years old; but, when Bella was four, I was too involved in my apparel business to notice, and when she was five, six, seven and eight, I was too poor. Now, I could finally afford such a privilege for my beautiful daughter.

I had enjoyed Broadway hits produced by students of this school every summer as a child. My mother and father would take us four kids to see the performances on the big stage with orchestra pits in the Hermann Park Miller Outdoor Theatre as part of our cultural enrichment. Mom would stand in line early in the morning at the amphitheatre's box office and get six free tickets for that evening's performance; and now, my daughter would have an opportunity to sing and dance in major Broadway productions due to her training and connection to this performance school.

An outstanding professional faculty, who inspired and trained my daughter and other seven-, eight-, and nine-year olds in vocal technique and choreography, conducted the song and dance instruction, and I felt the summer camp a superb and thrilling forum for musical theatre training for my future star.

"Stop, Bella!" I shouted at the nine-year old sitting in the passenger seat beside me.

The pretty brunette with long, wavy hair, looked at me with irritation, and I knew she knew where this moment was going. My stopping her in mid-song and begging her to sing above a whisper had been a redundant drill over the last three weeks. "I can't hear you, Bella! You *have* to sing louder."

"Okay!" She shouted with no patience for my demand. She angrily picked up her sheet music off her lap and begrudgingly began to sing again, "♪Hooray for Hollywood, that screwy, bally hooey Hollywood. Where--♪"

"Stop!" I sternly ordered and then glanced at her from behind the steering wheel while shaking my head in disapproval and wondering if she was still hard of hearing. After numerous ear infections, before the age of two years, Bella had suffered significant hearing loss in both ears. Leonardo and I had her in the hospital at eighteen months to have a tube inserted into a small, surgical opening in each eardrum, to allow air to enter the middle ear, and to allow fluid to flow out of the middle ear through the tube into the ear canal. "I still can't hear you, Bella! You're not any louder."

"I'm singing louder, Mom!"

"No, you're not!" I insisted. "Sing as if you are center stage and there are five hundred people in front of you. Nobody can hear a performer who barely sings over a whisper! And you should have your lyrics memorized at this point! Why don't you?"

She shrugged as if she didn't care anymore while her big brown eyes welled up.

"You've been in your song and dance class for three weeks now, and your school performance is next week."

"I almost have the words memorized," she said timidly.

"Almost? You can't bring sheet music with you on stage. If you're going to be a singer, you have to memorize lyrics and sing loud! Your audience will not be able to hear you, Bella, if you don't sing louder! Now, start over--from the top!"

Bella wiped the tears off her cheek and began singing in a soft, wavering voice as if on the verge of crying. "♪*Hooray for Hollywood, that screwy, bally hooey Hollywood. Where any office boy or young mechanic--*♪"

"Stop! Why can't you raise your voice?" I badgered. "And why do you cry?"

"I don't like you shouting at me."

I felt exasperated. "Okay," I said while lowering my tone of voice. "I see this inability of yours to simply sing loud, all boils down to motivation. I will give you one hundred dollars tonight, if you will learn all the words and sing loudly--"

"One hundred dollars!" She excitedly interrupted.

"Yes, one hundred dollars," I nodded, "*If* you sing loud, and I mean *loud*, and *if* you know the words to this song when I take you home today from class. That means, while you are in class today, you memorize the words you sing, and when we drive home together, I can hear you sing all the words, without a copy of your lyrics in front of you! In addition, you will belt out the words for me. Is that a deal?"

She smiled and quickly nodded in an agreement while she wiped her wet cheeks off.

"Do you know what *belt out* means, Bella?"

"Loud," she snapped as if irked by the silly question.

"Let me demonstrate for you *belt out*. This is *how* I want you to sing if you want me to give you one hundred dollars. I then belted, "♪ *Hooray for Hollywood, that screwy, bally hooey Hollywood--where any office boy or young mechanic can be a panic with just a looking pan!* ♪ "

Bella started laughing, "Stop! You need singing lessons, Mom!"

I laughed. "Really? Maybe I do, but do you understand now what it means to *belt out*?"

"To hurt somebody's ears?" She questioned and then giggled.

"Funny!" Maybe you should be a comedian, too. I grinned. "You're very quick-witted, Bella. I like that about you."

"I'm just teasing you, Mom. You sing okay. Actually, you've been singing so long to us that you're really not that bad anymore."

"Thanks, I think."

"I know what it means to sing loud, okay?"

"Then do it!"

"I will for one hundred dollars," she smiled. "After class, I will *belt out* this song for you on the way home for one hundred dollars, and I'll sing loud and know all the words."

I looked at her and smiled while wondering what I might be doing now had one of my parents forced me out of my shyness?

STILL SUMMER 1992. An hour before the marriage ceremony was to begin, and before the Justice of the Peace and numerous relatives were to arrive, I scrambled to complete all preparations one needs for an afternoon party. I had already showered and put on my makeup, but had refused to don white until the last minute, after I had already bathed and dressed my babies for their parents' wedding. Doren, now eighteen months old, and Harper, four years old, wore their little man suits with bow ties. Bella, nine years old, had dressed herself in a pink floral dress of cotton sateen and wore black patent shoes; and Joseph, now twelve years old, wore black slacks and a white, long-sleeve shirt. I sincerely felt the marriage would create a stronger bond between me and Seth and our children.

I had ordered a small, three-tier, white, wedding cake with pineapple filling from the local bakery, and Seth had left to pick up the focus piece while I set appetizers out on the kitchen table. The occasion was to be a small affair, and no friends were invited--only family members. After all, I considered, Seth and I had already been living together nearly four years and had two biological children. I expected the worse of circumstances were behind us and felt being a happy family a priority and a feasible possibility.

An unfamiliar female arrived at my front door before any guest arrived. She smiled when I opened the door. "I'm Sandra Sombrio, the Justice of the Peace."

I greeted the professionally dressed woman with a handshake. "Hi, I'm Jean Wynn, the bride."

"Pleased to meet you, Jean."

"You, too. Please, come in," I said while motioning for her to step inside my home. "Let's go into the kitchen."

"Your place is beautiful," she said while she followed me through my brightly colored front parlor.

"Thank you," I replied while we stepped inside my turquoise and floral designer kitchen. I watched her set her things down on the butcher-block island. She unzipped her garment bag and pulled out a black robe.

"I'm almost ready," I said while I watched her slip on her vestment. "I have to get dressed, and Seth, the groom--he's already dressed. He'll be here in a few minutes."

"All I need is seventy-five dollars;" she said, "and when your fiancé gets here, I just want to run over a few things with both of you before we start."

"No, problem," I replied while she handed me a document.

"You both need to sign the marriage certificate and then mail it to the Montgomery County Clerk's Office with proof of ID after the ceremony."

"Okay," I said, just as Seth walked into the house through the glass kitchen door holding a shallow box with a three-tier white cake inside it. I introduced Seth to our Justice of the Peace, Sandra Sombrio, while he sat the cake down on top of the kitchen table. They shook hands while I peered at my wedding cake and saw half the icing was on the side of the box. "Oh no," I groaned. "Weren't you careful, Seth?"

"I saw the icing on the cake box, when they handed me the cake!"

"And you paid for this disaster anyway?"

"Yeah, I figured it was too late to do anything different."

"Take the cake back! I won't pay two-hundred dollars for this mess!"

"You don't want a cake today?"

"I really don't," I answered while realizing I had thrown this ceremony together too fast. I had raced into this legal bond, as if I might change my mind had I any time to reconsider what I was about to do with Seth. "I have enough food for everyone to eat; no one will miss the wedding cake."

"Okay," he acquiesced. "I'll take the cake back."

"Before you leave, real quick, let me talk to you," Justice Sombrio said to Seth. "All you two have to do is follow along today-- repeat after me when I instruct you to. Do you have a best man or maid of honor?"

"No," I answered.

"I need witness signatures."

"No problem," Seth said. "My brother will stand as my best man."

"My sister will stand, too," I added. "She can't be a maid or maiden of honor because she's married, but she'll stand as a matron of honor."

I heard guests in the living room. "Seth, hurry and return that cake." I then looked at Sandra, "Please, help yourself to anything on the table; there's wine in the refrigerator, too. I have to get dressed now, before everybody gets here."

"Please, do what you have to do," she kindly insisted.

I walked back into the living area, heading toward my bedroom, and saw that Seth's mother and youngest sibling had arrived together. I greeted the woman, who wore a short, white dress, and I wondered if she was competing with me? Surely, at her age, she knew better, when she dressed. "How are you, Wilma?"

"Well, I don't know. Is this dress okay for me to wear, Jean?"

"I'm wearing a short, white dress," I patiently answered while not appreciating her game.

"I'm sorry, but, I thought you would wear a long, white dress today."

"I'd look like a fool in a fantasy gown!" I turned my attention to Seth's baby brother and greeted him with a warm hug despite my irritation with the woman. "How are you, Frank?"

The handsome college boy smiled sweetly. "I'm fine," he nodded. "How are you?"

"I'm great! Haven't you heard? I'm getting married today to your brother!" He and Wilma giggled. I heard commotion coming through the front door, and I wanted to race into my bedroom, and not let anyone see me before I dressed. My youngest brother, Jerry and his wife, and their four, stair-step boys, with lots of energy, entered upon the scene. I walked over to the couple without speaking another word to Seth's mother and baby brother. I was hugging my brother and sister-in-law, Kim, and their young kids, when my father and other brother, Henry, came through the front door just behind them.

I stepped over to my father and expressed my delight that he showed up. He had refused to have anything to do with the planning of my first marriage to Todd because I had married outside of the Roman Catholic church; and when I had moved in with Leonardo, he never once came to our home, even after we married. "Where's Mom?" I asked Dad while aware my mother despised husband number three. I recalled Mom's angry words to me that day on the phone, nearly four years earlier. She had told me that *Seth had sucked me up like a vacuum, and that he was trash, and that he was going to spit me out as fast as*--, well, I did not know how she ended that sentence, because I had hung up on the angry woman in mid-sentence. I actually did not know *how fast* Seth was going to spit me out, but *when* had always been the twenty million dollar question.

"Your mother sends her love, but she's not feeling well today." My father said while staring at the woman in the black judge's robe, and at Seth's mother, who both stood together talking to each other in the center of the living room.

Although, I knew my mother begrudged Seth's place in this family, and blamed him for the downfall of my second marriage to Leonardo, I believed my father to be authentic when he revealed Mom did not feel well. My father was a man who told no lies, ever. "What's the matter with her?"

"She's had a pain in the abdomen, on the right side, for a long while, and complains of nausea and appetite loss."

My brother interrupted, "And she complains of mental fuzziness, too. She'll sleep eight hours, and then tell us that she feels like she's near exhaustion."

"I think she's depressed," my father added. "She's got a doctor's appointment this next week."

"I'm sorry to hear she's not feeling well, but, I'm certainly glad she's going to see a doctor."

"Me, too," my father said. "She has been complaining a lot these days about different things. I'm happy she's getting checked out, too, so that she can get some answers, and I don't have to listen to her complain anymore," he chuckled.

I smiled just because he thought he was funny, but I had never heard my father say, one day in his life, until just now, that he wished anyone would go to the doctor. My father was always tight with his money, and felt seeking medical care required one to be on their deathbed. He had instilled the fourth-day rule: If you were still sick after three days, and an aspirin did not help you with your fever, then go to the doctor on the fourth day, or maybe not.

I turned to my brother. "How are you, Henry?"

The tall and gaunt, twenty-nine year old bachelor, who still lived at home, nodded thoughtfully. "I'm good," he said as if considering his life's circumstances. "Who is the woman in the black robe over there?"

"Oh that's the Justice of the Peace who came to marry us today. You guys are just going to stand around the living room while she does her thing. Seth and I will be in the center of the circle standing in front of her."

Henry nodded, as if digesting my non-Catholic scenario, when my only sister, and her husband, and three children, came walking through the front door. I beamed when I saw them. I greeted Holly with a hug and whispered, "Can you believe I'm going through with this?"

She hugged me back and whispered, "No, I can't; don't do it."

"No?" I sincerely asked as I stepped back and looked her in the eyes. She peered over at her 6'5" lanky husband, and I looked to see what she saw. Don was talking to my two brothers, Jerry and Henry.

"Marry him if you want," she shrugged and then said under her breath. "I just had the ride from hell with my husband. We fought the whole way over here."

"About what?" I asked my 5'9" slender sister, who was only ten months younger than I was. Strangers often told my sister and me that we looked alike when we were young girls, but as we grew older, our personalities made us look as different as night and day. I found Holly to be emotionally disconnected and inauthentic—personality traits that stemmed out of being fearful. I suspected she had manifested a mirror image of herself when she met her husband. She and Don had commonalities, or familiarities, that drew them together--both were blind to the fact that they each possessed fear of intimacy and were incapable of being seen as less than perfect.

"I don't want to say right now, this is your wedding day. We'll talk about *him* another day."

"Okay," I said. "Try to relax. Go get a glass of wine in the kitchen."

"Now?"

"Yeah, this event is very informal, and FYI, you're standing in as a witness for me."

"Again?" She laughed. "I do need a glass a wine," Holly spouted as she headed toward the kitchen.

My sister's husband, Don, walked up to me. "How is the bride?"

"I'm smiling, right?" I said to the slender giant who was a few days older than I was.

"Never quit trying to be happy. Where's the groom?" The dark haired conservative asked as he peered around the room.

"Seth went to return the wedding cake and get our money back," I answered just as my fiancé walked up on me. "There's my groom! Did you get a refund?"

"Yeah, I did," he answered and then spoke to his brother-in-law. "How are you doing, Don?"

"Good, Seth. Are you ready to legalize your bliss?"

"I'm binding those legal ties," he answered and then chuckled. "I feel like I've been married for years."

I interrupted them, "Excuse us for a moment, Don. I have to get dressed, and I need to talk to my fiancé." I motioned my boyfriend to follow me to the back of the house. We walked into our bedroom, and I closed the door. "Your mother is a real card. Did you notice she is wearing a short, *white* dress?"

"I'll say something to her."

"She knew better—what, do you think she brought a change of clothes? What's her deal with me?"

"She doesn't have anything against you, Jean."

"Uh huh," I said in non-belief. "I'm going to slip into *my white* dress now."

"Okay," he smiled. "I'll see you in the front," he said and then walked out.

"Hey, wait a minute, Seth?"

He stopped and turned back.

"Is your sister Demelza, or your brother, Jeff, coming today?"

"I'll ask Ma."

Minutes later, I came out of the back of the house, in the traditional white, knee-length dress, worn in the middle of the afternoon by a woman, who was marrying for the third time, and already had four children. I spent hours looking for the perfect dress in the mall; and for only seventy dollars, I found an elegant, sleeveless rayon/silk dress with a scooped neckline and eight gold and pearl buttons that ran down the center of the bodice. Seth and I were both 5'9", and I did not want to tower over him today so I also bought white strappy flats. I saw that my mother-in-law now wore an ugly, faded green house frock that looked like it was ready for the Goodwill bin. I noted to self that I had been right about her all along--she had a need to upset me. Did she want to marry Seth today? The longer I had been around the fifty-six year old blonde, the more I understood she competed with me for her son's attention. I guessed that today, she needed to push my buttons.

Seth walked up to me, "I talked to Ma."

I whispered, "I see she was considerate enough to bring some casual clothing. She really went out of her way."

"Come on, Jean. Lighten up." Seth replied. "Neither Demelza, nor Jeff will be here today."

"Well, it's just your wedding," I taunted. "One out of four is something, I guess. I bet your sister, Patricia, would have been here to support you and me, had she not lived out of state, and had she been able to afford air fare for herself and four kids."

Suddenly the Justice of the Peace interrupted us. "Are we ready to get married?"

"No," I tittered, "but let's start anyway."

"Do you have the rings?" She asked Seth.

"Yeah, I do. We bought matching gold bands," he answered.

"I'll be asking you for them, Seth."

MINUTES LATER. Everyone gathered in a small group forming a circle around the host and hostess. Seth and I stood next to each other with our two witnesses, his younger brother, Frank, and my sister, Holly, on each side of us, and the JP stood in front of us four.

Justice Sombrio followed the marriage ceremony outlined in her little black book, while my fear transformed into a joy while I listened to Seth repeat after the Justice:

"I, Seth Zherneboh, take thee, Jean Wynn, as my wedded wife, to have and to hold from this day forward, for better or for worse, for richer or for poorer, in sickness and in health, to love and to cherish, till death do us part."

The Judge looked at me. "Now, you repeat after me."

And I repeated the same vows Seth had said to me, and when I ended, the judge asked Seth for the rings.

The Justice took the gold bands that Seth and I had picked out together and said to us, "Your rings, by their very shape, are symbols of eternal unity, without beginning or end. They are the emblem of the love that exists between you, and characterize your devotion to one another. Let them always remind you of the commitments you make today." She handed the smaller ring to Seth. "Place this ring on Jean's finger and repeat after me."

And while Seth slipped the ring onto my left hand, he solemnly vowed, "Jean, with this ring, I promise to grow with you, and build our love, to speak openly, and honestly, to listen to you, and to love and cherish you, for all the days ahead; and from this day forward, you shall not walk alone. My heart will be your shelter, and my arms will be your home. With this ring, I thee wed."

I then repeated the same words to Seth while I placed his ring on the fourth finger of his left hand, and again, I committed to love him for the rest of our lives. I looked into the eyes of my husband and felt love for him.

The Justice continued, "I came here to join two willing individuals today in matrimony, and now I leave you as a legally married couple, united to each other *by the binding contract you have just entered*. Your cares, your worries, your pleasures, and your joys, you must share with each other. The best of good fortune to both of you."

"Thank you," we each replied.

She looked at Seth, "You may kiss your bride."

We smiled at each other and kissed, and I heard the family

clap. I pulled my face away from Seth's and acknowledged I was truly thrilled to be married to him while I looked at my four smiling children sitting on the couch next to each other.

The woman announced, "I now present to you, Mr. and Mrs. Zherneboh." The family applauded.

Seth appeared genuinely happy, too; and I figured myself to be the eternal optimist, again, because I felt hopeful about my marriage to Seth that day, and only wanted to believe we would give the best of ourselves to each other and to our children.

I turned my attention to the JP and saw her close her book. She glanced over at me with a smile and then handed me a business card. I read the card and then looked up at her in question.

She whispered, "I'm also a family law attorney, so when you're ready for a divorce, call me."

I chuckled at the woman's offer, but I wondered then, if she saw the judgment that I had buried, not too long ago, in order to take this leap of faith. Did she see Seth as I had? A smooth talker, too self-consumed to care about anyone, not even himself.

I noticed immediately, after the commencement of our marriage ceremony, and after our guests left, that Seth emotionally distanced himself from me before we left for our honeymoon. We barely spoke to each other on the flight from Houston to the tip of the Yucatan; and by the time we sat on the tarmac in Cancun, delayed inside the aircraft for some reason, I felt impatient with his withdrawn and aloof manner. His unwillingness to connect with me angered me, and his way of being with me made me feel as if something was wrong with me. I knew better than to give those negative thoughts of mine any life, but concluded Seth wanted me to believe there was something wrong with me.

Seth sat next to the window, and we both watched the Mexicans take the three-hundred passengers' luggage out of the belly of the jet and load onto wheeled carts while I struggled with my confusion. I decided to rise above my feelings and make conversation with the man who stared out the window. "So my writing professor, Venkatesh, told me about a time when he was a struggling novelist.

He said he had spent ten years writing what he called *a literary work*. He says the average writer spends five years writing their first novel--he spent ten years."

Seth nodded while he continued to watch Mexicans take our luggage off the jet.

"He finally submitted his novel to a publishing company, and to his surprise, he got an advance in the mail. He read the accommodating letter from the publisher and then realized that if he were going to cash the check, he would be giving the publisher rights of ownership to his book. Venkatesh told us that he was not clear when his book would be published, either; so he picked up the phone and called the publisher in New York."

Seth turned his attention to me, and I continued, "He told us, that he did not know, at the time, that to call his agent, at that point in time, was an unreasonable act and a big no no! And, coincidentally, he placed the call just as his publishing agent was standing over his secretary's desk. So, the secretary answers the phone, and Venkatesh asks to speak to her boss, and she hands the man, standing beside her, the phone. His agent is *very important* and has no patience for Venkatesh's personal call. My writing teacher wants to know *when* the publisher will release his book. The irritated agent says they can't make any promises to him *as to when* they will publish his book, but explains to my professor that by him signing the documents and cashing their check, they then have the right to take his book off the market and never publish his story, if they wish! Well, my professor does not like that his book might be bought, just because the publishing company has a similar one coming out in the near future and doesn't want to compete with his book, so Venkatesh begins to argue with the agent demanding to know which way his book will go. The publishing agent is further annoyed and tells my teacher, 'Look, I'll do you a favor. You can keep all rights to your book and the advance, too!' And then he hangs up on the novelist."

"Really? He got to keep the advance, too?"

"Yes, but Venkatesh lost the opportunity to be published; and for years to come, he could not find another publisher interested in buying his book. Meanwhile, he decides he's going to look up his old flame in Connecticut. He has not seen her in a decade, since they broke up, but he admitted to us that he had never gotten over her. He learns she's running an old antique store in New England and goes there to surprise her. He walks into her store and sees her, but she does not see him. She's busy with a customer, and he's hiding behind a tall shelving unit. He sees she is still so beautiful, and then he freezes, rethinks his actions, and considers he's crazy to believe that this fine, successful woman would want anything to do with him, ever again, and then thinks that he should slip out, along with her customer. And, just as he turns to leave her store, she spots him. 'Venkatesh! Is that you?'"

"He feels like a fool and identifies himself as the shy Venkatesh, and they embrace. She is thrilled that he found her, and admits she missed him. She further tells him that she not only runs the antique store, but she's a published novelist, too. He already knew her to be a writer, but neither one of them had any writings published when they were previously together; and now, he says that he feels like an even bigger loser. Silently, he crumbles while she tells him that she makes a lot of money writing romance novels. He feels unworthy of her, because he has spent ten years writing a book that he has never been able to get published, but he tells her how he had *almost* sold his book project."

Seth chuckled, and I continued. "She says, 'I told you not to write that literary garbage!' Then she says, 'You will come stay with me, and not leave my place until you finish writing a book of romance; I'll show you how to write that genre. I'll inspire you!' He can't believe her offer, but, of course, accepts her gracious invitation and quickly moves into her life. They reignite their romance, as well as his creativity. He is completely inspired by her and writes a romance novel in just six short weeks, then sends it off to a publisher, and shortly, thereafter, gets a check for $50,000!"

Seth laughed. "Wow, maybe I should write!"

"Maybe you should?" I nodded. "I want to write."

"Did Venkatesh ever sell his literary work?"

"Yeah, he did, and that's the best part of this story. A publisher bought his literary work, and that book won the *UCLA Book of the Year Award*; and because of him getting that prestigious award, the University of Paris-Sorbonne offered him a teaching position! He taught novel writing; and then, after teaching a number of years in France, Venkatesh came back to the United States to teach at Rice University, where I met him."

"That's an amazing story, Jean."

"His story inspires me. I really enjoy his classes," I said to Seth. "Did you know Rice University ranks on the *Top 25 Best National Universities?*"

"I guess I knew that," he impatiently said as if I were starting to bore him again. "So what? Now that you have attended Rice, you'll write a New York Times Bestseller?"

"I could write a bestseller, if I stay married to you long enough."

"Yeah, and I'm going to be a brain surgeon!"

Seth sounded piqued, and I assumed he was jealous that I had taken *Intro to Novel Writing* in the mornings at such a prestigious university. "While I was taking those classes in June, I realized I love not only writing, but that I love school, too. So now that Doren is a year-and-a-half, and you're still home, all day, I've decided to return to school in the fall. I'm going to enroll into the University of Houston."

"Why don't you take the next level of novel writing with Venkatesh? Didn't you tell me that he offers ten levels of novel writing classes?"

"Yeah, but you know those classes are offered as part of Rice's Continuing Education curriculum. Those writing classes are *not* accredited. I can't get any mileage for my buck. If I am going to spend money to learn how to write, then I want to take accredited courses and work toward my degree, too."

"I don't think you returning to school full time a good idea, Jean."

"And why not?" I asked defensively while already understanding his agenda.

"Because our boys are still very young."

"Well, I guess you'll have to get out of the yard and pull your weight, Seth. Sorry to disappoint you, but one of us has to consider the future of this family."

"Pull my weight! You sleep in every morning while I am up. I feed my sons' breakfast!"

"Well, I guess you'll have to feed them lunch, too, because I won't be home from school by then; I'll be up early and off to a 7:00 a.m. class, and I won't get home until 2:00 or 3:00 p.m. every day."

"I do not want to take care of the kids by myself."

"Then hire a nanny! We can't afford to do what we are doing, Seth! We have three children, and we are not at a place in life where we can retire!"

"I'm in a place that affords me to be home with my children and not have to work."

"Then don't work! But, one day, that $100,000 a year income will stop coming in, and then what? You should be developing a career at your age."

Seth folded his arms across his chest and said under his breath, so as the other passengers would not hear, "You are such a bitch!"

"You're going to call me a bitch now? I'm thinking about the future, you prick. Screw you for *not* considering our future. Why don't you just try being normal, once, in your life, Seth?"

"I am *not* normal!" he emphasized under his breath.

"Well, I *am* normal, and I consider the future. It *does* matter what we do today, and I'm *not going to continue* to put all my effort into decorating our home, while you obsess over our yard, without a plan in place for the future of this family. I told you that I had plans to go to school, before you ever told me that you were going to law school. You dropped out of law school so that you could landscape--not a smart move! I was looking forward to you being a lawyer and making a lot of money for this family *in the future*. So now, I have to take over, because your obsession over landscaping will be the death of us *in the future*."

"I am retired, Jean!"

"No, Seth, you're *not* retired! You're on drugs, if you believe that! You have been hiding out in the yard, for the last twelve months, to avoid your career and your financial responsibility to this family."

"Fuck you, Jean. I've provided you a good income."

"I'm not arguing that fact, Seth. And don't talk to me like that. After three years of insane poverty, I appreciate having money now. Thank you, Seth! Nevertheless, I'm telling you now, that I know, as a fact, your commission check will stop coming in the mail one day, because *Bike World* will put a new CEO in the picture, and that man will bring in his own investment company, and that new CEO will boot you out. I worked for the oil companies for years, Seth; and when management changes hands, so does the company's money. The next person will move the employees' $25 million pension fund into another brokerage house, because when he does, he will then get a big kickback under the table. And then what, Seth? What happens to us when we have made no preparations for the future?"

"We'll be fine," he stubbornly persisted. "*Bike World* took great measure to put my brokerage house into play, and that company will not change anything for years to come. And I have the right to enjoy the fruits of my labor."

"And that might be true, Seth, but as long as we have $8,000 coming in every month, and you're home with the children, I'll be in school earning my bachelor's degree. Like your mother's boyfriend said, 'It's my turn!'"

"Fuck CJ. I want my wife at home helping me with our children!"

"Not going to happen. And screw you, for not supporting me, when I want to go to school. I helped you get into law school. I bought you the LSAT study books, and I was more than willing to handle the kids and home for three years. So, get this about me. It's not my problem that you now feel threatened because I'm in school!"

Our arguing continued for the next two hours while we checked into our beach hotel. I fought him over his contemptuous words; and then, we separated immediately, before we even unpacked. Seth stormed out of our hotel room first; and then, I left and went on a long, lonely walk, along the Mexican Caribbean recognizing my new husband hated being married to me. He had despised me way before we made our relationship legally binding. I summed while I walked down a sandy beach, with tears running down my cheeks, that I must truly be crazy to have believed, for one second, that Seth had ever cared about me.

I now understood Seth had always been with me for the money. He had previously admitted to me one evening, years earlier, when we had parked our mopeds on the beach in Key West, Florida, that he had told Runi that *he had to do what he had to do*. I did not understand, at the time, that Seth was explaining why he was being unfaithful to his lover and taking a long vacation with me, his neighbor. Seth was thirty-two years old when we first met; and at the time, he had to get out of his mother and teenage brother's apartment for his own sanity. He and his mother were fighting, daily, over his constant need to borrow her money because he had no income. When I first entered upon the scene and took notice of Seth, the bank had just repossessed his car; and while looking back at those days, I saw I was the best option for the closet gay, if not the only option.

Initially, Seth believed this married woman would be the next Donna Karan of New York City, or be lucky like Calvin Klein and make a fortune at her first market. I sold my neighbor hard on the concept, because I truly believed I would be the next great designer. He threw the dice and bet on me to be that successful fashion designer in America; and he felt the gamble on my dream worthy enough to invest his time, energy, and the $10,000 settlement check, awarded to him for his bodily injury claim from his car wreck. The fact, that I had a husband, was also irrelevant to Seth. The other man in Springfield, Missouri, understood the demands Seth's mother was making on her firstborn to get a job and to get out of her apartment. Runi was willing to put up with me in this picture, too, if Seth could get ahead financially. Seth gambled on my apparel business taking off and making both of us rich, but he lost the bet at the same time that he learned I was pregnant with his first child. I remember how angry he was at me that day, when we were first released from the Tampa Bay Correctional Facility, the day he realized our dream had gone bust, and that I was pregnant, and that his last $10,000 was gone, and that he did not even own his own vehicle. He felt trapped in a situation he had never wanted—being broke and having a child with a woman that he did not love.

Grim circumstances followed that disastrous week at the Dallas Apparel Market. The convenience store had us falsely arrested while on our sales trip, and the future seemed gloomy. When we returned to Texas, I retained a lawyer to clear our names over the false arrest, to drop the criminal charges, and to sue for one million dollars for malicious and compensatory damages. Our case was strong; and Seth found hope again. Once again, he believed his pregnant girlfriend was a worthy of his time, energy, and money. My neighbor then pledged himself to me in the shower, wanted me to cite wedding vows to him under the running water, and, thereafter, quickly attached his name to my million dollar lawsuit—a legal action which should have involved me and Leonardo, not Seth. My second husband had invested the majority of the money into the apparel business.

My former sales associate and I, while newly showered, quickly retained a Coral Gables lawyer who made promises to deliver to us a million dollar settlement for a false arrest, which ruined our sales season. Seth again placed his bets he would win another lawsuit. He had previously sued an insurance company, though never injured, over a car wreck for bodily injury, and settled out of court for $10,000. Seth had spent that settlement check on us getting to the Dallas Apparel Mart, after Leonardo quit the marriage. His $10,000 vanished weeks before we ever got to the apparel market.

Seth had also received in recent past months, a $7,000 settlement check over a class-action lawsuit concerning his former apartment complex and their landscaping company jeopardizing the residents' health with chlordane. He had spent that settlement check on a car his mother's boyfriend sold him. During our first years together, before we had received the $300,000 settlement check from the Florida fiasco, and while I was pregnant with our first child, Seth struggled as a furniture salesman at JC Penney's for six months. Commission off furniture sales at the mall did not pay him enough to pay the rent, so we had sold off everything in the sewing factory. I liquidated every remnant of my apparel business, then we sold my fine household furnishings, appliances, piano, artwork, and jewels for rent money; and when all my valuables, of any worth, ran out, Seth begged his mother for money.

I knew that no intelligent man, in love with me or not, and who just learned his first child was coming, would leave me when a million dollar lawsuit pended in our favor. How perfect for Seth that a baby would now secure his place in my life—much better than phony marriage vows, in a shower, with a woman who still had a husband in Indiana at the time!

So, Seth stayed with me, three more years while our Florida lawsuit pended; and during the interim, I made the man, in love with another man, financially responsible for two children for the rest of his life. Seth's gamble paid off, over and above the inconvenience of two biological children, a young stepdaughter, and a common law wife, whom he had never loved, when the convenience store settled with us outside of court. We did not receive a million dollars as the legal eagles had promised us, but enough to pay cash for a custom, two-story home, luxurious furnishings, state-of-the-art electronics, the best appliances that money could buy, and two "almost new" cars--a Mustang hot rod, and a Volvo station wagon, with leather seats and a moon roof. The thirty-eight year old Seth had finally won the lottery, after having made such a great sacrifice; but, by the time we had the American dream, he had grown to resent the hell out of me for having made his life too hard for too many years.

I grasped Seth had expected me to rescue him from the start, and *love* had never had anything to do with us. I understood I was *not* the one he truly loved, and that I, on the contrary, was the one who had imprisoned him in a penumbra. Seth was unhappily stuck between two worlds: One world represented all Seth had coveted-- money, luxury, and freedom; and the other world was clearly his careless manifestation, opposing his freedom, and the very thing he had learned to hate as a child--family. Family meant unhappiness to a boy who grew up with acute alcoholism and abuse; and now, Seth had the burden of family with life-long responsibility and liability. The Justice of the Peace had even felt his contempt toward me, which explained why she had given me her business card selling herself as a divorce attorney, shortly after leading us in marriage vows. I, on the other hand, wanted to make my life work.

I wanted to love Seth like a husband. We had had two children together, and Bella, and a beautiful home. I wanted us to be happy, and enjoy the blessing of a comfortable and luxurious lifestyle. I wanted Seth to love me back, but he did not--he was in love with Runi and had no intention of staying married to me.

I strolled along the beach oblivious to everything around me. I was lost in my sad thoughts. I married Seth, a few days earlier, because I wanted us, an intact family forever; and I just wanted to believe Seth loved me, and if not for any reason but one, because his children loved me. Seth and I had everything given to us, for some strange reason, but I knew the contempt he held for me, because I was not Runi, would eventually drive us to the divorce court, and we would lose everything. Someone would lose the children. Someone, if not both of us, would lose the beautiful home. Seth had secured a $100,000 a year income, and the children and I would lose our financial security if he left. And, I knew well, that when we broke up, and headed toward divorce court, that lawyers and judges would enter into this picture, and make rulings that would make all of us angry and sad for a lifetime.

Runi's wife, Joyce, foretold the ending to this fairytale; she had told me that Seth would leave me and take my children, and at that point, he and Runi would come out of the closet. I suppressed my anger, went back to the hotel, and found Seth to continue our honeymoon, and live in my delusion that we might be happy. Seth was right--I was delusional and paranoid.

I went with Seth on a tour bus toward Merida. We went into the jungles of Chichen Itza and walked to the top of the Mayan pyramids. We talked very little to each other. We signed up for snorkeling off Isla de Muyeres; and while we were in the deep blue, Seth swam off into another direction and disappeared. I soon quit snorkeling, when I found myself alone in the ocean, and climbed back into the small, wooden, tour boat that dropped us there. I found myself sitting among seven tourists, and one Mexican tour guide, who had been waiting for Seth and me, and who all were more than ready to go ashore for lunch. The seven, non-English speaking nationals, from around the world, stared at me in question, and soon one attempted to ask me in her broken English where my husband was? I shrugged without an answer while wondering myself how far away could he be in the middle of the ocean. We waited in our rocking, little wooden fishing boat, on the turbulent salt water, under an intense August sun. Our parched skin continued to bake while we peered out looking for Seth, and I felt embarrassed my new husband had no spirit to hang with me on this honeymoon. I quietly wished a Great White would eat him.

After the honeymoon, a short, five-day vacation in Cancun, which included no sex, we went home and relieved Seth's mother from her babysitting job. Ma stayed at our home with our three children and ensured Bella got to school every day.

Business as usual followed. Seth jumped back into his landscaping, and I went back to decorating our home for two more weeks, until I would start the fall semester at the university.

My two boys and I frequently shopped and lunched with my sister and her young son during the weekday while Bella and her daughters were in school. My sister's son was in between my two sons in age, and the cousins liked playing together while their moms visited. Holly and I bargained shopped for home décor and used furniture, and we both liked antiques, too. She lived only ten miles away, and we had grown close, since our youngest children were born, and she no longer worked for the oil companies. We sat at a table in McDonalds and talked while our three little boys bounced around inside an enclosed air mattress.

"Seth gets up, before daylight, every morning, and he goes outside with his cigarettes and coffee and watches the sun rise. Then, he begins working in the yard; and he doesn't come inside the house, unless he has to pee, or I call him to lunch, or dinner. He even put a phone in the garage. He says he does his business out there, but I don't think he does any kind of business."

"Doesn't he have to handle his accounts?"

"Account," I corrected. "He has one account. His company sends him information in the mail, and he stacks the unopened envelopes in the corner in the garage."

"Maybe he corresponds on the computer?" Holly asked.

"We don't have a computer, yet. I recently bought a word processor, but it does not do anything more than allow me to type my novel."

"Oh," she said while looking confused. "What do they pay him a commission check for?"

"He does nothing but collect the check each month out of the mail box. I think he's neglecting his responsibilities. He has a lot of secrets, and doesn't open up with me. But, I watch him make a dozen trips to the nursery, each week, and bring home plants, rocks, fertilizer, stepping-stones, and balustrade. He even ordered a twelve foot Roman column this week."

"Your yard is amazing."

"Yes, it is beautiful, but he's out there every day, until way past dark. He's obsessed with his yard. I think he's doing drugs out there, too. And I'm certain the neighbors suspect we are in the Witness Protection Plan because no one seems to hold a job around here, and we have endless dollars!"

She laughed. "Have you seen him do drugs?"

"He smokes marijuana, drinks alcohol, and chain smokes cigarettes, but his behavior is unpredictable. He quit studying for his classes after the first week of law school, and gouged out these huge holes in his body. I think he's doing crack."

"Why don't you tell him you suspect he does hard drugs?"

"I did."

"And how did he respond?"

"Seth says I'm delusional, paranoid, and that he doesn't do drugs behind my back. He denies any allegations I make, but I know better, because I once found a crack pipe in my van. I suspect he's been doing hard drugs for years. Maybe coke, crack, meth…I don't really know what he does out there in the yard all day."

"That's sad, Jean."

I nodded in agreement. "He won't allow himself to be normal."

"Too bad, he's got a good life," Holly retorted. "I wish Don still worked at home."

"Why, what's up with your husband?"

"I think he's having an affair with a woman at the office."

"Oh no, that's terrible," I said while realizing I had never revealed my concerns to my sister about Seth's promiscuity, or homosexuality. I felt the drug issue was enough to lay on her about my marriage. "Why do you think he's having an affair?"

"He disappears all the time."

"What are you going to do?"

"Nothing, I'm too close to finishing my degree to let his crap distract me."

"That makes sense to me."

"What choices do I have right now?" Holly asked. "I haven't worked in years. I'm in school finishing my political science degree, so I can teach one day, or write for the Houston Chronicle. I dare not upset the apple cart, right now. Sometimes, though, I can't refrain from speaking what I have pieced together; and then, I say something that hits a nerve, and he gets defensive and lies to me; and then, we have these huge fights. We were fighting over her while we were driving to your wedding, Jean."

"In front of the kids?"

She nodded yes in disappointment. "I talked in code. I told him that I wasn't stupid, that I knew he was sneaking around behind my back, and that he would lose everything."

"Then he lost his good sense and let his anger take over, and told me that I like fighting! How else am I suppose to feel about his adultery? Does he expect me to look the other way? He said that he would fight back, meaning that he'll fight me for the kids."

I shook my head and feared the same scenario. "What's her name?"

"Benji."

"Benji? Is she a dog or a stripper?"

"Both. She's beautiful and works in the adjacent cubicle. I met her at their Christmas office party. He was so smitten with her then, and that's all he could talk about last Christmas--Benji and all her troubles. She was going through a divorce, cried on his shoulder, and made him feel needed."

"I remember Don thumping his Bible not too long ago," I said while I considered the man's multiple personalities.

"And before he got on his Jesus crusade," my sister viciously added, "he was a chronic alcoholic for years. Remember?"

I laughed. "I do! And now, he's what? A philanderer?"

"I think he's jealous that I'm finishing my degree and heading up the university newspaper, too. He never did finish his bachelor's degree, and he was only ten hours short of graduating, when he found out I was pregnant. So he quit school and started working for himself, if you remember?"

"Yeah, I do remember. You went to work, and he stayed home with the baby and wrote software programs."

"Yeah, he did that for years, and that's when we were good."

"I also remember that when you came home from work, he went out *without* you."

"He said he needed a break from the baby."

"And he probably did, but I saw your husband in the night clubs every week. Back in those days, I'd walk in with Charley and say hello to him and his good-looking sidekick, Brett; and then, they would quickly leave after wife's sister walked in. I thought you were crazy back then to allow that behavior from him. He should have gone to night school, when you got home from work, instead of going to the bars looking for women with his single friend."

"I agree with you, but Don couldn't drink in school," she slammed.

LATER THAT DAY, I went home with my little boys, and threw my new, purple bedspread, onto the full-size bed, in my upstairs guest room which once served as Seth's study for law school. The new look motivated me to pick up some of the clutter that sat around the room. I began by straightening Seth's desk and sorting through legal pads, papers, binders, and correspondence from South Texas College of Law. My five-year CEO operational schedule, for my next apparel business start-up, hung on the wall; and I decided, right then, to take down the chart. Three children afforded me no time for an undertaking of that magnitude, and had I even attempted to go down that endless career path, I would neglect my children while they grew up. I imagined they would all be in therapy, by the age of twenty, complaining of having everything given to them, except a mother's time and attention.

While I removed the wall-size flow chart, I understood I was saying goodbye to my dream. I carefully folded up the 48" wide strips of white meat wrapping paper, and considered that one day, I would give my heart-felt and well-researched project to Harper or Doren. Perhaps one of my sons would become a fashion designer and pick up where Mom left off with the business.

I noticed more loose papers on top of the nightstand and picked up the mess. I flipped through what appeared to be fit for the trash can and spotted a letter written in Seth's handwriting and addressed to Runi. Seth dated the letter March 7, 1991, two days before I gave birth to our last son. Doren was now sixteen months old. Apparently, Seth had forgotten about mailing the letter he wrote to Runi.

Dear Amigo:

♫♫♫ *Hi; I thought I'd drop by, so nice to see you. It's been too long since I've been holding on. And now, I'm holding on to a prayer; but my prayers never seem to come true; but I'm never letting go, never letting go, never letting go-- it's not that easy.* ♫♫♫

I knew the lyrics to be a Billy Joel tune, and the words relayed Seth's own personal struggle to live with me while his heart belonged to his lover in Springfield, Missouri. I sat down on the bed while coming to terms, again, with my reality of where Seth's heart and head was only two days before I gave him his second son. I continued to read the three-page letter.

One hell of a pristine night here in rocket town! All have retired to slumber, and I'm armed with four torch burners and a song in the heart to fire off a missive to the alter ego... ♫ sittin' on the dock of the porch...♫

Jean and I spent most of the day at the hospital. Jean had to take a drawn out blood test to see if her blood sugar is elevated; i.e., maternal diabetes.

Concern, but no alarm. She is now officially in labor, but obviously not close enough to be admitted. I think she will have the baby tomorrow, so you will hear me phoning before you read this communiqué. And do I have a surprise for you! My God, do you know I love you. Wake up! Now sit down!

I was sad to hear Seth tell Runi how much he loved him, while nowhere did he admit to Runi, that I made him happy, or that he loved me. I read on to understand more.

It's a very peaceful feeling tonight. I remain convinced you and I have a perception of life: of its magnitude, treasures--past and present--and of its vibrancy no other entity in the cosmos can fathom. I accept that now, and no longer frustrate myself trying to attain with others a level anything other than a semblance of that reality--you know my meaning.

I sent off the money to pay in full my debt to good ol' Centroidal Bible College, which will secure the release of my transcript I need for law school. Everything I can do has been done--the Father of Lights will show me the way, now, and hopefully to a $75,000 starting salary with perks out the yahoo. Otherwise, a secure counter position with Git-in-Poke.

Satan was the Angel of Light and Father of Lies. Seth felt *the Father of Lights*, who I knew to be our Heavenly Father, would show him the way. Why did Seth believe that? The Bible college graduate had turned his back on our loving Lord decades ago.

I looked up his reference to *the Father of lights* in the Bible. James 1:12-18 wrote, "Blessed is the man who endures temptation; for when he has been approved, he will receive the crown of life which the Lord has promised to those who love Him. Let no one say when he is tempted, "I am tempted by God"; for God cannot be tempted by evil, nor does He Himself tempt anyone. But each one is tempted when he is drawn away by his own desires and enticed. Then, when desire has conceived, it gives birth to sin; and sin, when it is full-grown, brings forth death...Every good gift and every perfect gift is from above, and comes down from *the Father of lights*...Of His own will He brought us forth by the word of truth, that we might be a kind of first fruits of His creatures."

I moved on, considered the reference to *Git-in-Poke*, and recalled Seth telling me that he had met Runi on the job--they both had worked for the same convenience store called *Git-n-Go*. Seth was married to Deb back in those days, when he first fell in love with Runi. I continued to read his letter:

> *Ah, just took a leak and fired up my next to last lung chaser. As I sit here in the quiet ambiance of no guarantees, I feel I have turned a significant corner in my vitae. A wife and three kids--responsibility breathes hot on my back, but I possess an indefatigable spirit to meet its challenge, that is equally balanced with visions of adventure. Yes, snorkeling in the waters somewhere on the coast off southern Turkey, having just spent several days giving Ephesus an appropriate amount of time on our travel video, contiguous with our week in Greece. You and I take a karmic breather before pressing on to Crete, with expectations of the boat passage to Egypt and a float down the Nile along with the current Pharaoh and his retinue. Then it's on to Petra and...*
>
> *Do you ever have the feeling that this soul journey is really why we were given form on this orb: like it's the meaning of life? Sure you do. Time passes in our lives like the semi-nomadic pastoralists. We pitch our tents and let our desires graze on the nearby plains. If the grass and rain are kind, we linger; a drought and it's time to move on. Many of these moments are enshrined on polished stelae in our minds. Others are recalled only by a pile of stones placed along the way. And still other moments serve as only bridges to connect our travels into one cohesive journey. We have erected many monuments on our journey, my brother, as well as other cornucopic statues. And there are many more to be hewn and set in place, in remembrance of two, homo erecti, who conceived and acted upon the desires of their heart. Salam Aleichem, Seth.*

Seth's letter was full of innuendoes, and overtones, thinly veiling their sexual relationship, and his acquired knowledge gained from earning a Master's Degree in Ancient Near Eastern History--an umbrella term for Assyriology, which is the archaeological, historical, and linguistic study of ancient Mesopotamia (ancient Iraq) and of related cultures that used cuneiform writing. The field covers the Akkadian sister-cultures of Assyria and Babylonia, together with their cultural predecessor, Sumer.

I questioned whether Seth was high that late night when he wrote the letter to Runi while the kids and I slept. This last line of his letter: ...*two, homo erecti, who conceived and acted upon the desires of their heart* told me of their long love affair. According to evolutionists, the *Homo erectus* man debuted 1.5 million years ago, migrated down the Nile, and went into Northern Arabia. *Erectile* meant capable of becoming erect, but what did Seth's word choice *erecti* mean, other than a reference to their sexual connection and orgasms? The Shari 'a, otherwise known as Islamic Law, did not condemn homosexuality, unless displayed in public; and for that reason, I assumed, Seth was a fan of the Middle East.

I did not support the evolution theory either, and put little value on scientific explanations that denoted man to be 1.5 million years old. There was no proof of any species evolving into a more complex species—a horse remained a horse, and a monkey remained a monkey. I considered that even under the most controlled environments, in any lab, and after trillions of dollars had been spent for research, man had yet been able to create a single living cell. I did not believe that a tornado could sweep through a junk yard and by chance, create a 747 jet craft, nor did I believe in The Big Bang Theory. The Bible's timeline indicated that the earth, this earth age anyway, was only 6,000 years old. God created the earth in six days, and on the seventh day, He rested. Perhaps Seth's studies in his Master's program concerning ancient near eastern history had allowed him to conclude there was no God.

Seth and I were not rich back in those days when he wrote that letter, and all he had was me, two kids--one on the way, a law school dream, and a job at Pete's photography studio for gullible wannabes who, on vacant office floors, were more than willing to fuck their way into the spotlight. We had not received our Florida lawsuit settlement when Seth wrote that letter to his boyfriend, and he had not earned a $100,000 a year commission yet. In addition, we were not married back then, either, although he acknowledged me as his wife, to Runi, when revealing in his letter that a wife and three kids was a great responsibility, but added that he possessed an untiring spirit to meet its challenge. I suspected Seth *did not* possess the character of a loving and responsible husband and father, but was experiencing euphoria due to a crack pipe when we wrote the love letter. Sixteen months later, his challenge to find peace with *what is* should have gotten easier, due to our good fortune, but I saw no evidence of any change of heart in my husband. I prayed Seth would be content *with the rain and the grass* and not get lost on the Nile River in the debauched Roman Empire; but yet, he had continued to instill no sense of security with me; and I had no choice, but to go against his wishes, and enroll into the university. After all, Seth admitted to Runi in his letter, there were no guarantees. I had built my dream on sand, because I remained ignorant to God's Word. I had mated with a man who considered himself a god, and who held himself accountable to no higher being, or standard of morality, other than his own inventions.

LATER THAT SUMMER MONTH. I pulled into my driveway and spotted an unfamiliar, newer model car parked in my driveway. I grabbed my brown paper bags of groceries and entered through the glass kitchen door. I heard Seth and another male talk and laugh while I sat my food down on top the island, and before quietly stepping into the threshold of the den to view our guest. A blonde, with a conservative haircut, and wearing an expensive business suit, in silver and black tones, stood with his back to me in front of my husband. The track lighting on the ceiling, which spotlighted Seth's antiquities displayed in the built-in shelving unit, also shone on the stranger who appeared taller and broader in contrast to Seth; and although Seth saw me looking on, he kept on talking to our guest, as if my presence made no difference. "This piece dates back to the Neolithic Age," he explained to the stranger while he held out a small clay bowl for the man's examination. I watched our guest take the antiquity from Seth and turn it over in his hands for inspection while Seth continued to talk. "Only *Homo sapiens* existed by then, and they were an agrarian culture, and probably ate their cereal out of that bowl."

"Fascinating," our guest said, just before turning his attention to me. He smiled at me and then asked his host while locking eyes with me, "How old is this artifact?"

"Thirty-three," I softly replied with a smile and answered his question while Seth remained oblivious to our interaction. "The Neolithic Settlement existed sometime between 7000-5000 before the Christian Era. I found the bowl in a settlement called ˈAin Ghazal in Jordon, North-Eastern Jordon, on the outsides of Amman. I was doing a dig while working on my master's degree at Southwest Missouri State University."

"He's impressive, right?" I interjected with a smile while continuing to lock eyes with what appeared to be a very proud, blue-eyed, and handsome German.

"Very impressive," the stranger said to me.

I stepped down into the sunken room and headed toward him with an extended hand, while the stranger gave Seth his clay bowl and then reached out to shake my hand.

Seth smiled at me and proceeded to make introductions. "Baby, I want to introduce you to one of my oldest friends, and my former college roommate, George Harmsworth. George and I go all the way back to Centroidal Bible College days."

I shook George's hand, "What a pleasure, sir. I'm the better half, Jean."

George chuckled. "Obviously."

"George is one of the inner-circle," Seth added with a smile.

"You don't fit the mold," I slammed back while certain George did not understand my meaning. "Where are you from, George?"

"East Windsor, Connecticut," he answered. "Just outside Hartford."

"You've come a long way to see us. I wasn't expecting any company this evening."

He chuckled. "Well, actually, I had to make a sales call on a client in San Antonio, and just got a wild hair, after my last meeting, to drive to Houston and see this old man. I called Seth while I was in

San Antonio, couldn't believe I found him, and he told me where he was living, and that he was married, and well, I guess my curiosity got the best of me, and, here I am." He laughed.

I didn't recall Seth as ever having mentioned this friend. "I'm glad you're here, George. I just went to the grocery store, and I'm about to fix dinner. I would like very much if you would join us."

"No, please, don't cook. Let's relax over dinner and drinks," he suggested with a smile. "And dinner will be on the company tab anyway," he chuckled.

"Well, by all means, George," Seth interrupted, "Let's eat out on the company tab!"

"Okay," I nodded with a smile. "Let me put my groceries away, and feed my kids, before we grownups go out."

"I'll be glad to pay the babysitter," George offered.

"No, that's alright. My daughter, Bella, will watch her brothers. She's nine going on sixteen."

"Oh, okay," he said as if surprised I would leave them with a nine year old. "Seth took me upstairs to meet your children," he admitted to me. "He's pretty proud of them."

"Yeah, Daddy is proud; one of his few accomplishments in life," I sarcastically spouted while feeling since their birth, Daddy had taken no further interest in his wife, or kids. We were Seth's property he had accumulated over time.

"She doesn't like to brag about me," Seth interrupted. "George, have you ever read *The Prophet* by Kahlil Gibran?" Seth pulled a book out of a collection of books off the shelf above his antiquities.

George shook his head, "I know of the book, but haven't read it. I'm aware *The Prophet* was extremely popular in the 1960's counterculture."

"Rightly so;" Seth spouted, "this is a book everyone should have in their library, if they don't already." Seth flipped through the pages. "I first read *The Prophet* in my college days. I've given a few copies away since then, too--that's how much I think of it!"

"Gibran was a Middle Eastern poet, right?" George asked.

"A poet?!!! Gibran is the third, most-widely read poet. He's in the same club with Shakespeare and Lao-Tzu. He was born in Lebanon and immigrated with his family to the United States, settled in Boston. *The Prophet* is a collection of philosophical essays. His most notable line of poetry is my favorite line: '*Half of what I say is meaningless, but I say it so that the other half may reach you.*'" Seth laughed and then handed *The Prophet* to George. "Read it, my friend--my gift to you."

"Thank you," George replied while he flipped through the book.

"May I see that book for a moment?" I asked George.

He handed me the gift, and I began to flip through the pages of prose. I had read the book on the toilet, and recalled a particular passage I thought Seth should hear again. I opened to the poem called *On Children* and read aloud:

"*Your children are not your children.*
They are the sons and daughters of Life's longing for itself.
They come through you, but not from you,
And though they're with you, yet they belong not to you...."

Seth interrupted me while I began the next stanza, "Hear the wisdom. Gibran's words are imbued with equally powerful simplicity!"

"So are the words in the New Testament," George added, while I concluded to not finish reading the poem, but, instead, flipped to the front of the book to silently read about the author before the book was out of my hands forever.

"'He is able who thinks he is able.' Buddha." Seth laughed.

George continued, "Perhaps we do not know the God of the Bible, our Father, and Creator to whom we owe life itself? The Bible is our means of such acquaintance; and through the Bible, every man is free to form his own friendship with the Divine."

I was not paying attention to their banter while I read the introduction of *The Prophet*, and to my glee, found something very interesting to share with my husband. "Did you know, Seth, your favorite poet, and I, are born on the same day?"

Seth shook his head in disbelief and took the book from me while George asked me, "When is your birthday?"

"January 6," I answered. "That day is celebrated as The Epiphany, or known as Three King's Day in Western Christian tradition. Epiphany is the climax of the Christmas Season, and we count the Twelve Days of Christmas from the evening of December 25th until the morning of January 6, which is the Twelfth Day. The evening of January 5th is really the Twelfth Night according to old tradition, when the custom of counting days begins at sundown. In some cultures, like in New Orleans, a King's Cake is baked as part of the festivities of Epiphany, and the cake is part of the observance of Mardi Gras in the French Catholic culture, too."

George smiled, "You are informed!"

"Well, yeah, my birthday matters."

"I guess the *whole world* celebrates your birth, too."

"Too?" I asked George.

"I'm a New Year's Eve baby," he grinned and waited for my reaction.

"Oh, I get it! The whole nation celebrates your birthday!"

"Yeah," he smiled.

"You and I are pretty special people."

"Yeah we are!" George admitted.

We both looked at Seth, who strangely stood there quietly listening to us.

I continued, "Seth's a Capricorn, too--that makes him special by default."

George chuckled, and Seth quipped, "Yeah, I'm special, too." He mocked. "I rode the short bus home every day after school."

Our guest laughed again, and I continued, "We have three strong-willed Caps in the same room!"

"I don't do astrology," George retorted.

"I do," I challenged. "Where the stars, and moon, and sun are aligned, when you are born, is important to understand because it's like walking out onto stage when it's your cue--everything is in place. And, I think before we came here, before we were conceived of, we first agreed to come here, too, and suffer what we suffer."

"Who did we have an agreement with?" George asked.

"We have an agreement with God to come here and play out our lives with the people we know here. I think we come here to get complete about what we *did not get complete with* in a previous life."

"Interesting," George said while pondering my words.

I continued, "We chose to live the life that we are living."

George laughed. "I don't know about that!"

"I do," I said. *"The hairs of your head are all numbered."*

"Matthew 10:30," George confirmed and then added, "And in Jeremiah 1:5: *'Before I formed thee in thy belly I knew thee; and before thou came forth out of the womb, I sanctified thee; and I ordained thee a prophet unto the nations.'"*

"Okay," I nodded while not aware of the last line he cited from the Bible. "If you say so, George. I was raised a Catholic! Didn't study Scripture, until it was too late."

"It's never too late," George solemnly replied.

"Sometimes it is too late," I refuted while I considered what I could not undo. "We three Caps have a deep understanding of basic human nature. Capricorns are intuitive, and we have a strong focus on goals."

I looked at Seth and reconsidered my words. "Well, *most* Caps have a strong focus on goals," I corrected while I considered the drugs that I suspected my husband did on a daily basis, for the last decade, had kept Seth committed to nothing, other than to his addiction, and to his own selfish needs.

George added, "I will admit Capricorns are goal-oriented. I certainly am."

"And sometimes a little suspicious by nature," Seth told George, and then glanced at me, as if to insinuate I was a suspicious and paranoid person.

My anger flashed when I computed Seth's insinuation and gave him a look of disgust. "I am not suspicious, or paranoid, Seth!" I turned my attention back to George, "Capricorns tend to have a slightly dominating nature and tend to ruffle feathers. Is this true of you, too?"

George chuckled. "I try not to be dominating, but sometimes

my lack of diplomacy has been known to rile members on the Board of Ed. I get very irate with their policies sometimes. For instance, the money we spend to accommodate just one handicap child is ridiculous! And I tell the Board so, too."

"You might feel differently, if your child was handicapped, George," I provoked.

"I might," he admitted. "But we've been known to spend $50,000 at one elementary school for wheel chair ramps needed for only one or two children! We just need to consolidate this population of children, who have a diversity of learning dysfunctions. I know of a situation, which employs one full-time teacher, and one teacher aid, for four children, who have emotional disorders due to parental divorce. That type of classroom situation is in every school in our district. Why not consolidate the population and bus these children of divorce into one school?"

Seth piped in, "I'm a tax payer, and I want my kids given the best opportunity when the day comes they attend school."

"You and all parents," George groaned. "When is your birthday, Seth?"

"December 26."

George laughed, "You're five days older than me! I was right to call you the old man."

Seth laughed, and George looked around our beautiful home. "I'd have to say, old man, you are doing alright for yourself."

"Thanks," Seth replied. "I'm a lucky man--"

George interrupted and said in all seriousness, "But what I don't understand is how you managed to land her?"

Seth smiled. "You and I were roommates, George. You have known me a long time! You understand more than you'll admit!"

George laughed.

I inserted, "Seth moves fast."

Seth snickered, "I'd say it was the other way around--she knocked me off my feet! I met this beautiful woman, and had her physical beauty *not been enough* to capture my heart, she then tells me she's a clothing designer! And that was the end of my life as I knew it!"

I nodded to George in agreement while I considered how I had facilitated Seth's move out of his mom's apartment, and supplied him with a new red van to boot. "That was the end of his life, as he knew it," I confirmed. "It really was the end of my life, as I had known life to be, too."

George laughed at us while I considered Seth's words. My physical beauty *had not been enough* to capture Seth's heart; but more accurately, my earning potential had been the very reason for why Seth had ever pretended he cared about me.

George assumed we were kidding and added for my information, "Seth always moved fast."

"You snooze you lose!" Seth declared to our guest.

I asked Seth's friend, "So how does your family tree look these days?"

"I have two daughters," George answered. "Esther is five, and Ruth is seven."

"They were named after women in the Bible," I affirmed.

"They certainly are!" He proudly answered.

"George, you haven't changed at all! You're still the ol' preacher man I knew you to be in college."

George forced a smile toward Seth that looked uncomfortable.

"I like old fashion names," I eased in. "I bet Esther and Ruth are adorable."

"They're great!" George looked sad for a moment. "I guess you guys should know that I'm going through a divorce."

"I'm sorry," I said while I saw Bella coming downstairs with Doren on her hip.

Seth interrupted, "Hey," he shrugged, "when one window closes, another opens. So, who walked away?"

I shuddered at Seth's invasive impropriety and diverted the conversation. "Here come my babies!"

"I'm not a baby!" My daughter said as she walked up carrying my youngest child, who was now one-and-a-half years old.

George said to Bella, "You'll always be your mama's baby."

Bella smiled at George and then said to me, "Doren wants to

see Mama."

I grabbed Doren as he lunged for me and then placed him on my hip. "What's up, pumpkin?" I asked my youngest.

Doren smiled back and rested his head on my chest.

George stroked my son's blonde hair and said, "He looks like you, Jean."

"I don't think so," I said. "He looks like his father's side. Seth's mother is blonde, but she has blue eyes. Seth has green eyes, which are really a form of brown eyes, and I have brown eyes, too. Three of my children have brown eyes; my oldest has blue."

Bella interrupted, "Mama, may I have an apple?"

"You may," I answered.

Bella zipped off to the kitchen.

George stepped back into our adult conversation and whispered, "I never expected everything to be as hard as this divorce has been for all of us." George turned to Seth, "Liz is so angry at me, and the kids are suffering, too. She's filling their heads with negative stuff about me, telling them I was unfaithful. I hate the whole thing, but I couldn't breathe anymore. I had to get out of there."

"You have to do what you have to do," Seth retorted. "I remember Liz. She was pretty straight laced, a *good Christian* woman, George."

The estranged husband rolled his eyes. "The woman is rigid. She works day and night—she's a workaholic."

I realized then that George was the cause for his marriage to break up.

"You and Liz were together a long time," Seth added.

Suddenly we heard a thumping sound in the stairwell, and everyone turned to see Harper happily bouncing down the stairs on his behind. When he got to the bottom stair, he trotted over and grabbed my leg.

"Did you get lonely up there, Harper?" I asked my third child.

Bigger brother reached up and begged me to pick him up, too. I did; and then, while holding both my sons, I walked across the room, sat down in a chair, and placed both boys on my lap.

George continued to talk. "We were married fifteen years when I walked away." He pulled out his wallet from inside his suit jacket and took out a photo. "I do not regret leaving her!" He handed the photo to Seth. "This is who has changed my whole life."

Seth studied the picture. "What's her name?"

"Gail. She works in my office. I hate to be a cliché, but she's my secretary." He chuckled.

"Romance in the office can spice up a work day," Seth wisecracked.

George snickered while I recalled the elevator ride when Harper and I stopped on an isolated floor of Seth's office building and surprised Daddy and a beautiful young model.

"Nice rack!" Seth added while still staring at the picture.

"I have to agree with you there--Gail's got a body."

"She's hot, buddy."

"Thank you," George proudly beamed.

"I could take her away from you," Seth nonchalantly informed.

"Pardon me?" George angrily baited while I felt insulted, too.

"I could take her away from you," Seth repeated in the same nonchalant manner as if challenging his old college roommate. He smiled.

George did not answer and appeared disturbed.

"Now, come on, ol' George! You know I could steal her away."

"Not you," he huffed. "Not in your wildest dreams, Seth!"

Seth laughed him off, "Would you like to test those waters?"

George angrily asserted. "You know, you haven't changed at all, you bastard!"

"Why mess with perfection?" Seth shrugged in question and then laughed.

I felt George's indignation caused by the antagonist; and yet, both of them repulsed me while I sat there with two babies in my lap. I wondered how I would feel--*not if, but when*--Seth left us for greener pastures, like George had done to his wife and two kids?

"You're still a competitive asshole!" George declared to his old college roommate.

"I agree!" I added for George's benefit. I wasn't sure if our guest was about to wallop Seth in the face, or not.

George turned to me clearly upset with Seth's audacity. "You know, Jean, when I was in school with this guy, I would beat him on the basketball court, on the tennis court, at any sport we ever played. And he'd always be amazed that he lost to me, and he would throw a temper tantrum every time he lost. He was 130 pounds with his clothes on, and I was 175 pounds of solid muscles back in those days." George shook his head, snickered, and then turned to his college buddy, "I could never understand why you *ever* thought you could beat me?"

I laughed along with Seth, but obviously for different reasons. I, too, wondered why the short beanpole thought he was ever competition for this stocky German.

George turned his attention back to me. "One afternoon, Seth lost a tennis match to me, and got so angry on the court that he slammed the tennis racket so hard into the pavement that the wood frame splintered. And we fought all the way back to our dorm room over him cracking *my* racket; and when we got inside our room, I had this prized onion sitting on my desk and--"

Seth cracked up and hollered, "Your onion! I forgot about that day!" My husband took control of the conversation and spoke to me. "George had this enormous onion; and I wanted to yank his chain, so I took a big bite out of his prized vegetable!"

"That was the last straw!" George admitted to me.

Seth laughed, "Oh right. You went psychotic on me when I bit your onion. You should have seen your face, when I took a big bite out of that damn onion!" Seth laughed.

"You should have seen *your face* after I punched you!" George laughed at Seth and turned to me, "I was pretty pissed off that afternoon. Is he still a poor loser?"

"I suspect Seth hasn't changed that much since the seventies; after all, he just admitted he had no reason to mess with perfection, remember?"

George snickered along with me.

"And for the record, George," Seth defended, "you did not beat me at *every* game. I ran circles around you when it came to the women at CBC."

George turned his attention back to me. "He *thinks* he did! Every Friday night, I'd watch Seth call a slew of coeds, from our dorm room. He called his technique *a self-indulgent sport*, and most of the girls would hang up on him as soon as they recognized his voice."

"He paints a non-truth!" Seth defended.

George laughed. "Okay, I will admit that if they politely refused his offer, then Seth would have the audacity to ask them if he could speak to their roommate."

I laughed.

"I was a working on my game, George."

George turned to me. "He would beg, and he played underhanded, too. I dated one girl the whole time I attended CBC."

"--Deb," Seth injected while he rolled his eyes and sounded as if the subject matter was irrelevant.

"Yes, Deb!" George firmly repeated, as if the subject still mattered. George turned to me, "And this dog stole her from me in our senior year and married her."

Seth laughed, "Oh man, haven't you heard, all is fair in love and war? You aren't still hanging on to that war injury, are you, buddy?"

George was not laughing or smiling. "You did me a favor, *buddy.*"

"That's right! You left after graduation, went back to your hometown in Connecticut, and married the girl of your dreams with the same last name!"

"Was that Liz, your current wife?" I asked while now aware Seth had a history of stealing other men's women.

"Yes, I had known Liz my entire life. Liz and I went to the same elementary school there in East Windsor, Connecticut. We had the same last name, but we weren't related."

"Are you sure?" Seth teased. "Are your children intelligent?"

"Very!" George snapped and appeared chafed when he

hurled back at me, "Deb, Seth's first wife, had a wart on the end of her nose!"

I turned to my husband, "You never told me your first wife was a Wart Hog, Seth?"

George and I chuckled while we watched Seth grow uncomfortable.

"Yeah, I heard her squeal a few times," Seth nonchalantly quipped.

"I did, too!" George sternly refuted and then glared at Seth.

There was a lull in the room. George appeared upset by Seth's last statement; and the two men locked eyes, both obviously angry about something.

Seth returned to his cocky stance. "George, I think you're still sore over your girl dumping you for me?"

"I had to let you win at something, old man!" George turned to me again, "Your husband had a bad boy reputation fifteen years ago."

"He still does," I admitted.

Seth interrupted, "George, you've made strides. I'll give you credit. You've done alright for yourself."

"Thank you, Seth." George admitted to me, "I was a geeky, Bible thumper, with bad hair, back in those college days--a late bloomer."

I laughed at his honesty. "Well, you're very handsome now, George! You ought to be a model!"

George blushed and appeared uncomfortable with the complement from me, the married woman. "Thank you, Jean. I never considered myself a model."

"Are you kidding?" I asked. "You're like the All-American blue-eyed blonde with a great physique!"

George nervously laughed. "Oh, well, thank you!"

"Now, come on, both of you," Seth interrupted. "Take a look at these chiseled features of mine. Don't you think I could be a GQ cover model? Isn't this GQ look what you like, Jean?"

I clearly heard Seth reference our mutual fantasy boy whom we both kissed, the Clearwater, Florida bartender, who had actually been on the cover of GQ. "Seth, you have the cleft chin, and the sloping overhang, but you're *too small* to be anybody's cover." I was referring to him using me as his cover for his secret life.

George laughed. "What are you weighing these days, Seth?"

"150, 155 pounds," Seth answered. "I'm bench pressing three hundred pounds now."

"So you figure you could fight in the Super Welterweight Division now?" George challenged and then laughed him off.

Seth laughed, "Now, George, you know I'm not a fighter, I'm a lover. I use my head, not my brawn."

George turned to me, "That's news to me."

"Me, too," I confessed to George.

Seth laughed at our willingness to gang up against him. "So I see how this is going. You two are going to keep me out of the admiration club, huh?" Seth chuckled.

George and I laughed.

"Well, how about some one-on-one, George; and we'll see who *the man* is here? Up for a game of hoop?"

"You never know when to quit, do you, Seth?" George laughed.

"He never plays any one-on-one on the basketball court!" I revealed to George. "You better take a patch kit--Seth might *bite the ball* when you whoop his ass."

George laughed.

"I'm out there all day in the yard, George, with a shovel, not fingering a keyboard for a living like you do every day! I think you underestimate my natural born talent!"

"I doubt it, Seth!" George slammed. "Where can I change into some court clothes?"

LATER THAT EVENING, Seth and I directed George to the nearby Woodlands Country Club for dinner. Since Seth still demonstrated a need to compete with George, fifteen years after college, it went without say that George and I would continue to gang up against the arrogant roommate, who bragged earlier that evening, in our living room, that he could take George's new love from him after gazing at her picture.

George and I sat together all night looking into each other's eyes, and for the most part, ignoring Seth while we unearthed our lives and personalities for the other. I respected George simply for the fact that he was the first man I met who did not revere my husband, but, instead, viewed Seth as I did--a self-indulgent game player. This handsome stranger and I were teaching Seth a lesson, without any kind of overt agreement; and although Seth attempted to dominate the conversation, as he always did when I was present, on this particular night, George would have nothing to do with Seth being rude to me; and I appreciated George's loyalty to me.

"What do you do for your company, George?" I asked.

"I'm vice president of sales and marketing. We sell jet engine parts."

"Impressive!" I said while I casually looked over at Seth and watched him cut into his steak, without any show of reaction. "Your friend here is a high roller, Seth."

Seth looked up from his food, "He certainly is, Jean! He was telling me about his job, before you got home today."

"Oh, I hope I'm not boring you, George, by asking redundant questions?"

Seth snickered, "George loves to talk about his success! No offense taken, I do, too! When you got it, you got it!"

"I don't mind letting anyone know who I am," George said while remaining cool.

"You have good cause to be proud of your life, George," I defended while I suspected my husband, with all his bravado, was jealous of his former college roommate. "Have you been with your company long?"

"Actually, ten years. I started in a very humble way. I was driving a truck for the company with my college degree; and after a year, the owner took me aside, and told me he would mentor me. I'm grateful for the opportunity he gave me. I was a youth pastor for a church, before I grabbed that truck-driving job. My wife insisted I could no longer afford to stay in the ministry. She wanted to stop working and have children, and I wasn't making enough money as a youth pastor."

"You are so multi-dimensional," I added. "A youth pastor, too? You must be a good man."

"George has always been a righteous man," Seth inputted.

"Not always, but I try, Seth." He turned his attention back to me. "After I graduated from Centroidal Bible College, I took a job as a youth pastor at a church in Massachusetts. I held that position for five years, but my wife wanted to move back to our hometown in Connecticut, and be closer to her parents, so we did! And that's how I got into the aerospace industry."

"You're very successful," I said while hoping my under-employed, drug-using husband would pay attention to what was possible in life, with a little effort on his part.

Seth sat on the other side of George and interrupted with a chuckle. "Do you remember those good ol' days back at CBC, George? You would stand behind the pulpit, on Sunday morning, and preach the gospel, and I was the singing evangelist, who played guitar in the same church service."

George laughed. "Those were fun days."

"What a funny vision of you two!" I looked at Seth, "I can't imagine you leading up a church service!"

"Of course you can! George and I go way back, Jean!" Seth reminded, and then turned to his old friend. "Why do you think we ever got along?"

George snickered, "I didn't think we did."

I chuckled. "Did you two share a dorm room all four years?"

"No," George admitted. "One year of Seth was enough for me."

Seth laughed. "Brother, you and I had a lot in common. Both of us came from dysfunctional homes. My old man was an abusive, chronic alcoholic, a blue-collar iron worker, who couldn't hold a steady job, and your old man ran away and never looked back."

"Yeah, I had some challenges growing up." George somberly admitted and turned his attention to me again. "I had a mother who was incapable of working, and had an IQ of a moron. I answered the front door a few nights, after midnight, and found some creep wanting to come in and see her," he sternly recalled. "I threw a few of her *boyfriends* off the front porch. We lived on welfare. My father finally left for good, when I was eight years old; and, for a year, after he left, I'd peer out the front window, every Friday night, waiting for him to walk up and take me for the weekend, before I didn't wait anymore. He did show up once, or twice, before he soon had more important things to do with his weekends. I was his only child, but I was the oldest of my mother's six kids. My grandparents were my saving grace, especially my grandmother."

"Your mother's parents?" I asked.

"Yes. Grandma took me to church every Sunday, and the minister of that church led me to Christ."

"What church?"

"The Church of God; and then, I went to Centroidal Bible College to be a minister because of that pastor's influence. He called me his son. He had two daughters, but no biological son, and I felt he truly thought of me as his son. And I wanted to be the pillar of the community, like him, after enduring the pain of living in *the poor house of crazies* my entire childhood. I really wanted to be respected."

"Wow, George, you're a man of great strength," Seth sarcastically retorted.

"Yes, I am!" George reaffirmed and then chuckled, "After I separated from my wife, I moved into that same house I grew up in! My grandfather had bought the house for his daughter and grandkids after my father left, and my grandfather had always kept the homestead in the family. My grandfather made me the executor of his estate, with orders from the grave to never sell the property. I bought the old homestead, and then rented the property to my crazy siblings. My siblings were living in the property all these years while I was married, but, after I left Elizabeth, I threw them out. They didn't pay rent, they don't work, and they had torn up the place. I've spent months cleaning up, after their destruction."

"Where did they move to?" I asked.

"Who cares," George said. "I've had the buzz saws going for months. I re-built the back porch and steps, and the front porch, too. The house is shaping up nicely. Nice location, too, sits on a hill looking down at a pond in the back yard."

"Sounds like a great place to live!"

"It really is. The house has a lot of charm, was built in 1885."

"I once owned an antebellum in Evansville, Indiana, built post-Civil War," I added. "Great house, but I do understand the amount of updating that is required of these hundred-plus year old houses!"

"It's endless!" George nodded.

"Do you miss the ministry?" I asked.

"Sometimes I really do," he said to me. "Business is so cut throat. I would like to start going to church again. I stopped attending Sunday services, when I left my wife," he ended with regret. "I think my wife and I became too much of this world. The company promoted me, often, and gave me frequent pay increases; and then I set Elizabeth up in her own business, and that was the beginning of the end of our marriage. I built her an 8,000 square foot aluminum two-story building. She and her best friend work the business together--they're partners. Those two women ship out all the parts I sell to the aerospace industry. Her business caters to all the aerospace companies; she doesn't need me anymore. She's got business coming in from everywhere now."

"You were a very supportive husband, George. I admire that about you." I looked to Seth for his reaction, but noted no internalization of my words while he looked down at his plate to cut more off his steak.

"The business I built for her allowed her to work *and* be with our children, too. She would take our children to work with her, and that aspect of her business was good; but we grew more and more unhappy, the wealthier we became over the years. I spent years coming home from work and building our dream home, hammering and sawing until late at night. My wife's parents gave us a parcel of their land, after I quit the ministry." George turned to Seth. "I built a two-story, Connecticut Dutch Colonial, with a three-car garage. I dug the earth out to build the garage. Whew, that was a challenge!"

"Sounds magnificent, George," Seth offered.

"I put my sweat and tears into that project for over a year.

The gambrel roof was a challenge, too, with its flaring eaves." George took a whimsical breath, "And after eight years of marriage and fertility clinics, we finally had our two daughters, too. We appeared to have it all."

"Sounds like you did have it all, George," Seth added.

"I wasn't happy."

"Are you going to sell the house now?" Seth asked.

"Na, I'm walking away from everything. Liz and the girls can keep the house and have it all."

"You *do* feel guilty, bro!" Seth shot back. "Jean says guilt sucks."

I felt embarrassed by those long-ago spoken words. "I use to believe that way, George, but no more." I quietly considered why I had once been so callous. I summed that the guilt I had suffered, from making the grave mistake of being an unfaithful wife, and getting pregnant out of wedlock, was reason for why I gave my alcoholic husband custody of my firstborn child. The decision to give up custody of my son, over guilt, had led me to become bitter and callous. I had felt for years that guilt sucked, following that decision to split up my children; and because of the pain that I felt, I paid no heed to guilt thereafter, and aborted my unborn child. I was unconscious. I had somehow managed to not feel accountable all those years, after losing custody of my firstborn. I was angry, and I grew more offended, and bitter, with myself, until I finally created a relationship with God, out of my desperation for peace and forgiveness. I would reserve that disclosure for the day George and I talked intimately, if ever.

George picked up on my uneasiness and broke through the silence. "Guilt is one of Satan's biggest weapons against us. Guilt tears us down; it makes us feel dirty, unworthy, robs of us of our faith and confidence in Christ Jesus."

I wondered if George suffered from guilt, after he had an affair with his secretary. Did he leave his wife and children over his guilt, after having sex with his secretary?

George continued, "Jesus not only came to cleanse us from our sins, but also to set us free from the guilt of our sins. If you want to live a life of spiritual victory, you need to have a conscience freed from the guilt of your past."

"I know, all too well, how guilt can lead us to do things we might not do otherwise," I admitted to George. "I gave custody of my firstborn to my alcoholic husband out of guilt."

"I'm sorry," he replied. "There are two kinds of guilt in the Bible. Sorrow leads a person to repent and become convicted, and conviction comes with knowing God's Word. Once a person repents, the guilt lifts, and they feel relieved and joyful while knowing Jesus Christ has forgiven their sins. Then there's another kind of guilt, and that's condemnation, when you condemn yourself, or others condemn you—Satan's tool. Satan loves to torment God's people by reminding them of their pasts, and continually holding their sins before them, sometimes even after they have asked for God's forgiveness and God has forgiven the sinner. This guilt is condemnation, and there is no good that comes out of it, whatsoever."

I found George's words comforting, because I had been struggling with accepting the fact, that God had already forgiven me for my horrid acts.

George continued, "When God's only son, Jesus Christ died on the cross, the blood of the cross washed us of our sins."

"Amen, brother," Seth mocked.

I ignored Seth, as did George. "I asked God to forgive me," I said to George, "…but then, I had trouble believing I was worthy of being forgiven."

George folded his arms across his chest and rested them on the dinner table. "I will admit I'm feeling guilty, these days, over my actions. I suspect that me leaving my wife and the kids the house, and everything else, compensates for my guilt. It's the right thing to do. My girls will have a nice home to grow up in, and they will be growing up next door to their grandparents, too."

I noted a sad looking man and wondered why he would make himself sad by leaving his wife, children, and the beautiful home he had built from the ground up. Had he walked away because he felt too guilty to stay?

Seth piped in, "Look at the bright side, George. You still

have your job and the big bucks."

George turned from me to Seth, "I know. I am grateful I have a good job. My boss gave me a $45,000 car allowance last year, and told me to go pick out a car. A bonus for the hard work I do."

"Wow, you're the man!" Seth acknowledged. "You're flying over there!"

"I have to admit, it was fun car shopping. After looking at Mercedes and BMWs, I bought a Lexus LS400, out for its second year in '91. The LS400 competes with the BMW 7-Series and the Mercedes S500-Class. The Lexus has a 4.0-liter V8 engine with 250 horsepower and torque out the wazoo!"

"What do you get miles per gallon?" Seth asked.

"I get eighteen miles per gallon in the city, and twenty-three miles per gallon on the highway. And the 0 to 60 miles per hour is at 7.9 seconds."

"That's fast, brother! I bet my Mustang could get there faster."

"Oh, no way!" George shot back.

Seth laughed, "Put your money where your mouth is."

"Forget it, Seth. Your old Mustang is not luxury class, and it is not going to outperform my Lexus. You are so arrogant!" George turned to me, "Does he compete with everybody?"

"Just you and me," I answered.

"George, are you threatened?" Seth asked.

George rolled his eyes as if the question was ridiculous. "By your car?"

"No, by me," Seth straightened.

"Seth, I can beat you at anything. Name your game. What is it?"

Seth laughed, and I could clearly see George was annoyed.

George turned to me, and then momentarily back to his antagonist, "I should be able to get 380,000 miles on my Lexus, and your car, Seth, will die at 150,000 miles, and your trade-in value will be zilch. Of course, I won't keep my car that long—I'll sell my car in 4 years and still get $10,000 if I'm desperate enough!"

"Slam dunk!" I spouted. George smiled back at me while

Seth ignored me.

"So brother, how much are you making over there at that company as vice president of sales and marketing?" Seth unabashedly asked.

"I'm making $150,000 a year," George answered without flinching.

"Okay!" Seth cheered. "Maybe you should re-think your exit strategy from your marriage?"

I knew Seth was implying that George should not be so generous and leave his wife with the kids, and the big house, in the divorce, but that he should take his big salary and fight for custody of his kids and possession of the home.

"It's too late—she's too angry. Liz won't forgive me for sleeping with Gale."

I was aware that George did not understand what Seth was implying, that Seth was always looking for an angle to take more for himself. I shook my head in disgust and peered at George. I saw a sad man, who I assumed regretted having left his wife, but had done so over his guilt, after having an affair with his secretary, a woman I now doubted he loved enough to marry. Or perhaps he was too guilt-ridden to marry the other woman?

"Well, George, ol' man," Seth continued, "I guess you're going to have to take that beauty queen *you have in your wallet* for a drive in your $45,000 Lexus and find reason to smile."

"Gale wants to get married, as soon as I get a divorce, but I'm not sure I'm ready for that kind of commitment, again."

I heard him confirm what I suspected—that he was too guilt-ridden to marry the other woman. And, he just confirmed, to me, that he did not leave his wife and kids for the other woman, but, instead, he had left them, and the beautiful home he built, over his guilt. I considered a *committed* relationship was without end, and what George and Seth had created, with their wives, was temporary and conditional. Had George not been feeling guilty over his unfaithfulness to his wife, he might have been able to save his marriage at one point, after his affair. Had his wife been able to forgive him for the affair, then she might still be married to him today. Neither George, nor his wife, really possessed what it took to be in a committed relationship. The Holy Spirit led neither. Was not love forgiveness? I then advised, "I think you should cool your jets with her, George."

"You might be right. My best friend says Gail is a rebound, and that she is only after my money."

"Aren't all women?" Seth asked George.

"No," I angrily defended, and then said to George, "Some women want strength of character in their man."

Seth scowled at me, and I continued to set the record straight for George. "When Seth moved into my life, he admitted to me that he had never spent forty dollars on a dinner in a restaurant! He was thirty-two years old. And he moved into my apartment with one box of belongings. I really thought he had just been released from prison to be as old as he was and to have nothing! He was moving out of his mother's apartment."

George laughed. "Seth, I didn't realize you were so far down."

Seth appeared as if not at all bothered by what I had revealed about him and defended, "I had been living with my mother and brother when I met Jean. I had been on hiatus for a year. I was floating in the abyss, but the year before I quit working, I had won the salesman of the year award."

I interjected, "So I met him while he was unemployed and sharing a bed with his pimple-faced, sixteen year old brother. Seth was smoking dope on his mother's front porch, when the bank repossessed his *one-year-old* Nissan sports coupe. I happened to be walking up to their apartment, that day, and saw the whole thing," I added for George's knowledge. I saw Seth was uncomfortable with my disclosure. I knew my husband did not appreciate me sharing that type of honesty, revealing the longevity of his *stick-to-it-ness*, but I really did not care. Seth was trying to convince George that I was a gold digger, when he asked his former college roommate to consider that all women were after a man's money.

George looked at Seth with sympathetic eyes, "Well, it appears you're back up now. I don't do drugs myself."

"Recreation is all it is, George. I'm living everyman's dream."

Seth reminded.

George turned his attention back to me and smiled, as if he agreed I was every man's dream. "Seth is lucky to have you."

"Yes," I nodded.

"Seth told me that you are going back to school?"

"I intend to start the university this fall. I have a handful of college credits. I have a ways to go before I get the bachelor's degree."

"Good for you! What do you intend to study?"

"Business," I answered while I wondered if Seth had expressed to the college graduate that he did not agree with my return to school. I doubted Seth would disclose to his friend that he was an insecure control freak. "I'm thinking I might go all the way and get the MBA, and then create an apparel business again, but on a bigger scale."

"Seth was bragging to me about your business acumen. You designed clothes?"

"I did. I designed, manufactured, and sold them wholesale."

"He said you sold them at the apparel markets and along the coast?"

"All over," I said while not wanting to talk about the past anymore.

"Impressive." George nodded. "And you have four children, too."

I nodded with a smile.

"And from what I saw this afternoon, you are quite the decorator, too. There's nothing you can't do, is there, Jean?"

I chuckled and said, "Oh yeah, there are a few things I find challenging, and have not mastered, like simple math. I keep thinking that the root of 25 is 5."

"It is," George confirmed as if not understanding me.

"I know," I nodded. "I was referring to my family—we number five—Seth, me, and the three kids, and we're supposed to be the childhood root of happiness, right?"

George shot me a look as if he understood. I did not want this man to influence my husband to leave me. I switched gears. "I was thinking about calling my interior decorating business 'Decorator Extra.'"

Seth intercepted the game ball and took the lead on flattery, as if trying to convince his former college roommate that he was in love with me. "Jean is an amazing wife, mother, decorator, cook, business woman."

I looked at my husband and questioned his sincerity.

"Apparently," George agreed. "Are you in the business of interior decorating?"

"Not professionally, not yet anyway," I replied. "But, I have to admit, that without an artistic outlet, I would die. Our house was a white canvas when I began splashing color everywhere. I am creative, and I believe my creative inspiration is a gift from God."

"God gives everyone special gifts," George informed.

"Jean has done an amazing job on our home—she has created a resort in paradise," Seth bragged, "while I have turned our yard into an actual paradise! What do you think about my creative genius, ol' chap? I consider landscaping my vocation, my calling. You haven't said much about what I've done with the place?"

"I certainly did, Seth! When we walked around the grounds, this afternoon, I said then that you demonstrated excellent workmanship."

"Thank you, George," Seth said while lifting up his wine glass—"To friendship."

George and I followed the gesture and repeated, "To friendship" while we clanked in cheer. I glanced at George and saw him smile at my husband, and then he locked eyes with me and said, "You've got it all, Seth."

"I do, don't I?" He shouted, as if suddenly struck with his good fortune. "I'm a lucky man. I have the American dream. God is good! And I'm sitting here tonight, with one of my oldest and most faithful friends; how sweet life is!"

George reserved matching Seth's level of enthusiasm, while I remained aware our handsome visitor drew me to him. I considered I could not make Seth love me, no matter how much he gloated about me, or about the life God had given him. I was a possession of Seth's, an element to ritually toast, but while I understood Seth did not necessitate God as part of his life, neither was I a necessary part of Seth's detached nature, either. My sad thought made me aware, again, that I built my castle on sand. I shifted from thoughts of my ill-fated choice, and focused on the more positive aspects of my life. "I like being home with my kids, too," I said to George, "...and me going to school full-time, right now, while they are young is good because I get home in the early afternoon, and Seth is home all day."

"If you had a teaching degree, then you'd be home every day when your kids got home from school."

"Teachers don't make very much money," I said while not interested in any teaching profession.

"They do in Connecticut!" George bragged. "I'm the Vice Chairman of the Board of Education. I know about teachers' salaries. Teachers are earning on average $50,000 a year where I live."

"Wow, that's good money," I admitted while considering a life in Connecticut with George—me working as a teacher, and George, the vice-president of an aerospace company. I liked the picture, but my thoughts were premature, and I was acting like an immature schoolgirl. I snapped out of my fantasy.

Seth lit up. "Congratulations, George, on your Vice Chairman position! That's impressive, too!"

"Thank you, Seth." He turned his attention back to me. "We Board members meet every month and spend the tax payers' annual $10 million on school projects. A nine-member Board of Education governs the school system in East Windsor, each of us serving a four-year term. We appoint the superintendent of the schools, too."

"Are you elected or appointed to your position?" Seth asked.

"Elected," George answered. "I'm serving my third term."

"Sounds like you're a natural born politician!" Seth admitted.

"I like politics. I especially like planning and development. I'm also a member on the East Windsor Economic Development Commission."

"You're an over-achiever, George," I summed.

George chuckled.

"What do you do for the Commission?" He intrigued me.

"I work with town officials marketing the town to attract new business."

"You're a popular man, George," Seth mocked.

"I'd say you're to be admired, George!" I defended. "You are Vice President of Sales and Marketing for your company, Vice Chairman of the Board of Ed, and a member of the Economic Development Commission, too! You're amazing. Gail is lucky to have you."

George remained humble. "I like to be involved and active in my community."

Seth was quick to interrupt, "I'll be happy to invest the *pillar of the community's* school district employees' pension fund."

"Oh, I don't know--" George weighed and then recoiled.

"You must have some of that money lying dormant in some old account?" Seth persisted. "I'll make the opportunity worth your effort. I am a registered licensee with the NASD in California, Texas, Ohio, and Wisconsin. Do you remember Brian Flannigan from CBC?"

"Yeah, how is he doing?"

"Brian's CFO now for a Fortune 500 company, and I'm the Managing Broker over his company's $25 million employee pension fund."

"You don't say."

"Yeah, that was a sweet deal. I earned $100,000 a year in commissions on just that one deal."

"Not bad."

I quietly sat there and listened to how Seth led George to believe he had other accounts, and saw Seth clearly competing with the $150,000 a year aerospace sales pro.

"I deal with commodity futures," Seth continued while he leaned back in his chair. "As I told you earlier this afternoon, I'm a registered options principle with my company--*Inroad Investments and Securities*. I'm a financial and operations principal, and General Securities principal. I have a Series 6, 63, and 7."

I knew, as fact, that Seth did not have a Series 7, which would allow him to make stock trades because he had not taken the stockbroker exam; and again, his ease to tell lies in order to build himself up bothered me.

"I commend you, Seth." George granted him. "Sounds to me, you are positioned to be a huge success."

"*Positioned* is a good word," I mumbled for George's hearing.

George looked over at me in question, and I diverted the conversation. "I have a problem with kids in school today--" I began when Seth interrupted me and took back control of the conversation.

"--I'd appreciate an opportunity to come into your aerospace company, George, and look at your employees' pension plan," he emphasized. "Or let's see how I can invest the school district's pension fund and make it work for all of us. That fund must be huge, too."

"Oh, Seth, both the aerospace company, and the school district, have all their accounts wrapped up. Thanks for the offer though. I'll keep you in mind should something come up." George turned to me, "I'm sorry; we interrupted you, Jean. Please, continue, you were saying you have a problem with kids today?

I detected George wanted to keep his distance with Seth, and not mix his pleasure with business. I guessed George probably had not trusted Seth since their college days, when Seth had stolen his one and only girl, Deb. I continued, "As the Vice Chairman of the Board of Ed, what do you feel is going on with students today?"

"Good question, Jean. I have noticed a consistent pattern. Too many students don't know how to show respect to others. These kids don't know how to behave on the playground, or in the lunchroom, nor do they know how to pass in the hallways. They don't complete their homework. They lack drive and desire, and they have no goals. They don't use their brain to think critically. If they do their work, at all, then they do it with minimal effort; and as a result, they fall behind grade level. And when teachers bring up these problems to the parents, the parents say they will ensure their child improves, but nothing ever happens. My question is why are parents not teaching their children the value of having an education, or how to be respectful? Are the children a reflection of their parents, who were also raised this way?"

I shrugged without an answer.

George turned to my husband. "What do you think, Seth? Are you going to raise your children the way you were raised?" He politely smiled at Seth.

I chuckled while realizing George understood Seth did not respect others.

"No, I'm not!" Seth retorted. "I want the best for my boys; they're my world—I was raised by ignorance. My blue-collar father was an ironworker and a mean drunk, and my mother fought with him for eighteen years over his drinking and unemployment. She was at fault, too. Are you kidding? My kids will not experience anything similar to what I experienced while growing up. I have the education, and I've earned the right to stay home with my boys and be a better role model."

I found Seth's response carefully structured. Perhaps he felt unworthy to be a good father, and though he knew he had "earned the right" to be a better role model than his own parents, he also remained aware he did not possess the tools to instruct his kids properly, any more than his own parents had possessed the right tools. Maybe the underlying reason he ignored the kids and me, and hid out in the yard 24/7 and did drugs, was he felt unworthy to be a good father.

"You're a lucky man to have the opportunity to work out of your home, and be home with your kids every day, Seth." George reminded us.

I knew George did not understand the entire picture. I wondered if Seth felt guilty about something that made him feel unworthy to be a husband and father. Was that something his sexual relationship with Runi? Or did Seth's dysfunction stem out of the anger he had held on to for a life time—an anger that stemmed from a childhood of abuse and alcoholism. Seth did not understand either, how his decades of drug addiction, and a lifestyle covered with lies, would impact his kids' wellbeing in the long-term. Ironically, he had no regard for his deceased father; and yet, he was no different from the old man, who had fallen off a fishing boat and drowned when Seth was eighteen. Seth was selfish like the old man he admonished.

7
ULTIMATUM

A WEEK LATER. Saturday night's enthusiasm waned under the full moon. I felt bored most of the evening while out sucking down alcohol with Seth and our best friends, Pete, Karen, Chad, and Jenn. I also felt forced to listen to conversations dominated by Seth that did not include my input. We exited off the floating nightclub on Clear Lake and headed toward Pete's white convertible Mustang parked on shore in the adjacent parking lot. While we walked across the pavement, I listened to my husband talk to the boys, as if he was a high-powered businessman, instead of the bum I considered him to be. I had grown especially tired of his braggadocios demeanor.

"So Seth," Pete asked, "Is the stock market about to take a tumble?"

"You'd be silly not to be buying stocks," my husband answered. "Corporate profits are swelling, and the economy is starting to boogie."

Pete turned to me, "What is he, the Einstein of the market?"

I tittered and reserved any comment.

Seth continued, "I consider myself more like Pied Piper. I sell the dream and ignite a bull run!"

Pete laughed.

"Oh brother!" I groaned while I considered we had not saved a dime since having received the sum of $300,000 from the lawsuit settlement over the false arrest in Florida; and since Seth began receiving his $100,000 a year annual commission on a quarterly basis.

"I've been thinking about building up a speculative portfolio," Seth said to Pete.

I wondered with what money my husband would use to invest? The next quarterly commission check?

Pete asked, "What if you experience a sudden collapse in prices and your bubble burst?"

"The way I see it, Pete, there's no return on bank CD's offering 3.5%. And just over the last six months, the market has returned 12.5%."

"I've read that analysts project a possible fall, Seth. Maybe it is time to move more cautiously."

Seth snickered as if Pete talked foolishly. "No cause to dump your shares and run, friend. Just maybe good reason to stash new money elsewhere and prune the most over-valued shares from your portfolio."

I snickered and interrupted, "Do we have a portfolio I don't know about, Seth?"

"Not yet, but I've been studying up on the market; you know I read the Bible--*The Wall Street Journal*. I'm doing my homework before I dive in." He turned his attention back to Pete, "I'm looking at a hedge fund because the market tends to look ahead six months, and it anticipates profits and prices stocks accordingly."

"But, the other sticky problem for stocks," Pete challenged, "in an economic recovery, is rising interest rates, which will cause problems for industrial production increase."

"Yes," Seth agreed, "but that blip usually lasts only until companies have brought their inventories in line with sales--a process that takes three to six months."

"Three to six months can cause a bear hug!" Pete said. "I'd say there's a great risk of losing your ass over six months."

The two men continued to impress each other with their market knowledge while I turned my attention to the rest of the gang. Karen hung onto Pete's arm for balance and was quiet. Pete seemed content these days with his newfound love who was all of twenty-one years old. Chad and Jenn hung onto each other all night and appeared intimate. My husband no longer worked at Pete' *Talent House*, but nevertheless, the three men who had run the business--Seth, Pete, and Chad—had remained close friends who constantly talked money and new ways to make a buck.

Just after Seth and I bought a home in The Woodlands, Texas, Pete then followed in suit, and bought a smaller, single-story, within a mile from us. The six of us gathered every weekend, that first year, at either our house, or at Pete's, with only one agenda: to eat, drink, talk business, play techno music, and, if at Pete's house, bet on pool games. Seth and I did not have a pool table, and I did not want one. I was pretty sure had Pete not owned the talent agency, and had not just bought a beautiful home in The Woodlands, Texas, the gold-digger on his arm would have gone off to greener pastures. I did not care for Pete's young girlfriend, Karen. She consistently came to my home every week, though she snubbed me. She would not make conversation with me. I have never understood that attitude, but held little regard for anyone who felt I intimidated them. I did what to you? I caught her rolling her eyes at Pete over something I said one night, and I judged her two-faced. Pete was my friend, and Karen was not comfortable with that fact, and, as a result, she treated me as if I was not good enough to belong to the group that had originated before her conception. I further faulted her for being ignorant because she was impressed with Seth and paid homage to him. Karen was Pete's latest in a long string of gorgeous women, and Pete seemed to be smitten over the twenty-one year old. I feared the thirty-year old, never-married, gracious bachelor, who had let the naïve youngster move into his Woodlands home, would find himself making another child support payment in the near future, if he leaped too fast.

The three guys stood beside Pete's car and lit up a joint. I stood looking on, along with Karen, and the sweet, but crocked, Jenn. Pete and Seth both had the same muscle car, and they liked to compete with each other on the streets. Pete had a 1990 white convertible Mustang that we rode in that night, and Seth drove a 1989 black 5-speed Mustang with hardtop that he had left in our driveway that night.

"I have something to show you, Seth," Pete said just before he got into his sports car and turned the ignition key. The music blasted from the radio. He popped open the trunk of his car and *Boyz II Men* blasted from the trunk speakers. Everyone gathered behind the car to look at his new acquisition. "Those are Polydax 15" woofers. I've got two 4-ohm woofers wired up to form an 8-ohm system. Twice as much current will flow through a 4 ohm speaker, as compared to an 8 ohm speaker. And all to accommodate my Yamaha stereo--the best money can buy!" He bragged to Seth and Chad.

"Nice sound, dude," Chad acknowledged.

Seth balked, "Speakers are in general notoriously inefficient."

"Eh, you're jealous, Seth!" Pete retorted as he slammed close the trunk and walked away and toward the front of the car. Seth, Chad, and Jenn remained standing behind the trunk and shared a joint. "What do you have in that Mustang of yours, Seth? An AM radio?" Pete shot back over the loud music as he opened up his driver's door and sat down.

I laughed along with Jenn and Chad while I walked up to the the front of the car expecting to leave. Pete popped out the cassette and threw in a different sound.

"I've got decent equipment, hombre," Seth spouted while choking on marijuana.

"Come on, guys," I groaned. "I'm tired, and I want to go home." I stood by the passenger door and waited for Pete to unlock the door.

Pete got back out of his white Mustang convertible, without unlocking the door, walked around the front and over to me. He handed me a joint. "Take a hit, Jean."

I took the reefer from Pete and held it at my side—I didn't want it. "I'm already high as a kite," I said to my friend while I stared up at the clear night sky. "Look at the full moon, Pete. We're so miniscule in the bigger picture. Frivolity is a waste of time, and time is short."

Pete nodded in agreement. "Are you going somewhere soon?"

"Are you kidding? Where would I go?"

"I don't know," he answered while flashing his trademark smile.

"I don't care to spend my time getting stoned or drunk. There's more to life. There must be."

"You don't like to party anymore?"

I nodded no, and then looked at Chad and Jenn who remained behind the car. They held each other up in their drunken stupor while Seth stood near them and held court. Seth talked over their dizzy heads. I got, in that moment, that one reason I was bored in my unhappy marriage was because my husband never stopped to hear what I had to contribute to any conversation. When I began to talk to a friend while in Seth's company, or if I captured the interest of a group of listeners that included Seth's company, then Seth would shift the attention back to him, or lead my listeners away by asking them to join him outside. If he stayed in my company, then usually, he would begin talking over me, until he pushed me completely out of the conversation. If I would not relent, then he would create a separate conversation with a member, or members of the group that might be trying to talk to me. He left me with the feeling he did not value my thoughts. He acted as if what I had to say was irrelevant, when he did not listen. I had never known Seth to focus on my dialogue with anyone, or to add to my dialogue. He constantly competed with me, and Pete's rude girlfriend had taken her cues from my husband, and treated me the exact same way.

Pete and I tuned in to hear Seth impress Chad and Jenn with his knowledge about car speakers. "...There are two major ways you can blow a speaker. One way is mostly limited to woofers caused by too much cone excursion, and the other way to blow a speaker is thermal failure--the voice coil overheats and melts. Drive a speaker with too much electrical power, which this cat over here will do before we get home;" Seth pointed back over to Pete, "...and, he'll be off to the audio store again."

"It's just money!" Pete snapped back in his defense.

I turned my attention back to Pete, who rolled his eyes at Seth for my benefit. I continued, "I'm waking up, more every day, Pete. There is not a better place to go than to the land of the conscious." I took a drag and handed the reefer back to Pete. I felt like I was double-minded when I submitted to the drug. I had no integrity...or was it conviction? Maybe my commitment was missing.

Pete inhaled the reefer while I continued talking under my breath to avoid the other parties hearing me. "It's no good anymore," I said and then nodded over to Seth. "Drugs and alcohol have been the demise of us, and nobody's home anymore." I considered my words had no impact on my friend because I got high, too. "Seth doesn't have any sense of urgency to grow his business network. He's abusive—has been for a long while. He's not in love with me, never has been—and now, well...I'm--"

I hesitated to tell Seth's best friend that I was not in love with my husband, either. I had never felt more alone, or unfulfilled, than I had with Seth. "I'll just stop there."

Pete choked out the smoke from his lungs and then grabbed hold of his composure. "Just watch your back, Jean," he warned and then walked around the hood of his car and over to the driver's door. I stood still and repeated his words in my head while I watched him open his door. He stared at me while I digested his warning. He then sat down behind the steering wheel. I knew he had more to say to me, but that tonight was not the night--too many ears. He hit the electronic lever and unlocked the passenger door.

I got into the backseat of Pete's car and watched Pete sort through a selection of cassettes in his glove box while I considered his warning again. I felt I had reason to worry. Pete slid a carefully chosen cassette into the tape player in the dash before starting his powerful engine. "Get in everybody and get ready for the ride from hell!" He jokingly said to his five passengers while we squeezed into his small sports car. Jen sat on Chad's lap, in the back seat, and I sat on the hump, in the middle of the back seat, with a view between the front bucket seats. My husband sat on the other side of me. Karen sat up front in the passenger seat next to Pete and held his hand. We crawled from the lake to the freeway at 30 MPH to avoid any DUI, but once Pete drove onto the on-ramp of I-45 and headed north for The Woodlands, Texas, he floored the accelerator and quickly reached 100 MPH.

"Yahoo! My hair is on fire!" Seth squealed while I anxiously watched the needle on the speedometer creep up to 120 MPH. ZZ Top lyrics to *I Wanna Drive You Home* blasted for the fifty-mile drive home—

♪ *She is an American car,*
She isn't legal so she can't go far.
She got her mind stuck up in second gear,

Where she going ain't exactly clear,
Baby please, baby please, I wanna drive you home... ♪

I sat on the edge of my seat without a seatbelt available for me. "Whoa!" I yelled as Pete quickly approached a rear bumper.

Our driver did not respond to my plea to slow down, but, instead, appeared in a trance behind the steering wheel. Whether Pete was focused, skilled, drunk, stoned, or whatever state of mind he currently held, I was un-nerved by his insane driving. "Slow down!" I yelled again while in fear. I heard Karen and Seth laugh at Pete's daredevil antics.

"Who is the man now?" Pete yelled while he continued to ignore my pleas.

"Oh you definitely have balls, dude!" Chad confirmed.

I glanced at Chad on my left in disgust; and then turned my attention back to the road to see us barely miss the back-end of an approaching car, just before Pete swerved onto the shoulder and continued to drive 120 MPH. He drove on the shoulder for about a mile before he got back onto the freeway and then zigzagged through five lanes of traffic. My heart missed a beat. "You're going to get a ticket, Pete!" I screamed over the music.

"He has a radar detector, Jean," Chad comforted.

"Oh, that will save my life!" I sarcastically spewed.

"120 MPH, Seth. That makes record." Pete yelled to the back.

"Any Sunday, hombre!" Seth hollered over the wind and music.

"Put your money where your mouth is," Pete answered as he continued to race down the freeway at illegal speeds.

"I will," Seth answered. "I'll show you performance, if you want performance!"

I gave Seth an angry look and then turned toward Chad and Jenn. I could see by their stoned looks that they were too high to be scared for their lives while I recalled I once considered myself immortal, too. I looked at Seth again, and he acted oblivious to my fear of dying that night. "Seth, tell your friend to slow down!" I angrily demanded.

My husband looked at me and laughed while Pete raced down the freeway like a fool. "Where's your sense of adventure, Jean?"

I was furious and yelled, "Slow down, Pete!" I saw my life ending that night in a deadly car crash while I sat there feeling powerless in the backseat, without even a seatbelt, and considering what would happen to my children if we died that night? No one in the car seemed to care I was frightened for my life, or that there were three children asleep at home who assumed their parents would be there in the morning when they woke. Pete did not consider his little girl's happiness, either, while he drove like a suicidal maniac. After too much NASCAR tension, Pete finally took the exit off I-45 for our hometown, The Woodlands, Texas, and crept along the sleepy streets until finally pulling up into our driveway inside a cul-de-sac. I had not said another word to any of them since my last plea on the freeway. I glanced at the clock on the dash and read 1:00 a.m. Sunday morning.

"I think you made that drive in record time, Pete!" Seth boasted as he hopped out of the backseat.

"I'd say thirty minutes is a record!" Pete informed.

I was furious while I scrambled behind Seth to get out of Pete's suicide machine. I considered not saying another word and just walking into my house while I angrily jumped out, but I had had enough of their disrespect.

Jenn and Chad politely bid their adieus to us while they remained fixed in the back seat; and Karen, with her phony smile, forced a goodbye on me.

"Goodbye Seth, Jean," Pete said to us while he sat in the idling car looking cocky.

"I have something to say to all of you," I firmly announced while noting I had everyone's attention in the car. "I don't want to be around you guys anymore--not really, but I realize I don't have any backup support here." I glanced at Seth and then continued, "So if you're going to come around, and visit with this asshole, who does not respect anything I say, from now on, things are going to be different around here. You will obey my rules when you come over."

Karen interrupted, "I guess if you don't like us, we won't be coming over."

Pete stopped her by gently touching her forearm. "Wait, before this gets out of hand. I'm sorry, Jean, if I scared you with my driving."

"Apology not accepted!" I firmly replied. "Karen, you can come over with Pete, or not--I don't really care, but leave your drugs at home. I don't want any of you smoking pot in my house, or outside my house. I have young impressionable children. I've asked this of you all before, but obviously, I haven't made a tough stand. If you come around here with drugs, I'll call the cops. Moreover, Pete, piss off! I thought we were friends?"

"We are, Jean!"

"You disrespected me when you pretended to not hear my wishes that you slow down! And let me wise you up; trying to keep up with Seth, and compete with him, makes you stupid!"

"Oh, she just insulted you!" My husband heckled as he usually did when I stole the spotlight.

"Your turn is next, Seth!" I snapped.

"She might be right about you!" Pete said to Seth, in my defense.

I turned and walked into the house through the front door. I heard Pete's music from inside as he backed out of our driveway; and then, I heard him screech away. Seconds later, Seth entered through the front door.

"These people we hang with are a bunch of losers!" I angrily blasted as he walked through the room toward the kitchen.

"Did you take your medication, Jean?" Seth slurred.

"Screw you! You are the one who takes the drugs! And you don't stand up for me. Did you want to orphan your kids tonight?"

"Oh shit, you're paranoid. We got home safely!"

"Safely?! And you call me paranoid? Again! I'm clear you are deliberately building a case against me—a case called Jean is paranoid and delusional! You're an idiot to believe, for one second, that anyone is going to buy that bullshit you spread about me, especially me. In addition, for good reason God instilled in me the fear I felt tonight in that car—that fear was necessary for the preservation of my life, and for my children's well-being, too! You are so irresponsible on so many levels, Seth."

"You're just fucking crazy, Jean. You just can't be cool, can you?"

"There you go again, building your case. I'm *not* fucking crazy. You, on the other hand, are a strung-out drug addict *and* crazy. You don't know if you're coming or going, Seth! And, you might be right--I'm living with a pathological liar and chronic drug user. I might be crazy, if I continue to stay in this shit relationship."

"You've never seen me do anything, but smoke weed; and you're smoking right along with me, baby!"

"If you're not a drug addict, then why are you paralyzed and hiding out in the yard? Are you too lazy? All you do is landscape. You act as if you're retired. We have young children who need college funds, and we need a retirement fund. And you're acting as if the money you have coming in will always be there. You have one account, and what happens when that account is closed? The money will stop one day."

"I'm a piece of shit to be with you!" He screamed and then picked up a heavy wood coffee table in the center of the room and slammed it to the floor. "I am retired! Leave me alone!"

I watched the table legs at one end snap completely off, and I yelled, "You broke my coffee table! You asshole! I looked for that table for weeks! I'm sick of your barrage of insults and abuse. Your crap never ends. You constantly destroy something of mine every time you get angry!"

I walked over to his rock shelf and picked up his prize possession--a small 5,000-year-old clay bowl that he excavated from the earth while doing an archeological dig in the Middle East, as part of his master's program curriculum.

His eyes popped when he realized what I was about to do with his antiquity he snuck out of the Middle East. He screamed, "Don't do it, bitch!"

"You called me a bitch? Again? That is not respectful! I've had enough of your name calling, too!" I threw his ancient artifact, with all my might, into the brick wall, on the front of the fireplace, and watched the bowl explode into granules.

He screamed at the top of his lungs, "You fucking bitch!" He then picked up the nearby Chinese, tri-fold, privacy screen, in the front window, and slammed the wood and rice paper against the floor, turning my décor into rubbish.

"I'm putting an end to your destruction; I'm calling the police," I cried while I dashed for the phone in the kitchen. I dialed 911 and heard, "What is your emergency?"

"My husband is tearing up my house, please hurry. He's high as a kite, and I fear he will hurt me next!"

The police showed up minutes later in a pair of blue uniforms. They separated us. One office took Seth outside to lie, and the other took me into the kitchen. In the end, the police forced Seth to leave the house that night, and told him to not return until the sun came up. He did not go to jail.

ONE DAY LATER, I walked into the kitchen and found a bouquet of spring flowers with one hundred dollars cash and a card from Seth. I put the money into my jeans pocket and read his words:

Jean, I am so sorry I broke your coffee table. I know you spent time and effort to find it. Although, it was unintentional, I broke it out of anger and selfishness. Please forgive me, and I hope this will be enough to replace it. Also please, always know, I love you, Jean! Seth.

I peered out the wall of windows in the kitchen and saw Seth working in the back yard. Seth's written words were insincere. When he picked up my coffee table and slammed it into the floor, he *intentionally* did so to break the object, and his anger *justified* his action. He had been breaking my possessions since the beginning of the relationship starting with my $600 white neon and black Plexiglas sign, the *Jean Wynn, An American Designer* logo sign I had once hung at the Dallas Apparel Mart.

I harbored a lot of anger and resentment toward Seth for many reasons. I felt he had stolen my dreams, first the apparel business, and now, my opportunity to have a loving relationship with a man whom I had given two children. He had stolen his children's opportunity to grow up with two parents who loved each other. I looked at the flowers on the kitchen island and felt contempt toward him. I wanted more than flowers--I wanted his respect. Maybe I needed to respect myself first, and leave the abusive man? I recalled having read recently that abusive men often like to reel their victim back into their good graces, only for him then to repeat the cycle of abuse. I wondered how many days or weeks of peace we might endure before he went crazy on me again.

SEPTEMBER 1992. I started classes at the University of Houston that fall of 1992, a few weeks after my passionless honeymoon. I enrolled into fifteen hours of freshman/sophomore classes that supported me getting a business degree: accounting, microeconomics, old world literature, government, and sociology. I still considered the idea that one day, I would eventually enroll into a MBA program; and as part of my thesis, I would recruit heads for the different divisions of my apparel business from my business classes; and together, we would build a company from the ground up. I figured by then, my three children would be more self-sufficient.

I loved the buzz of the campus while I walked toward the Student Center in the heart of the university and struggled with the weight of a book bag I carried off my shoulder. I was meeting a new friend, Adriana, whom I had met in my sociology class earlier that morning. I swung open the door to the big, noisy break room and spotted my classmate sitting alone at a table in the midst of a large crowd. I walked up to her and shouted, "Hey, girlfriend!"

The middle-age student looked up and smiled as if thrilled to have company. "Hey, Jean, have a seat!" She pulled out a chair from the table.

"So how did your first day of school go?" I asked while I threw my back breaker on top of the table and sat down in a chrome and plastic chair.

"Great! I'm hyped up for this semester," the thirty-something year old, petite blonde replied. "I am thrilled to be in college!"

"Have you attended college before?" I asked the woman with a short do.

"Nope, I've been working in the insurance business for thirteen years."

"What about you? Have you been in school?"

I snickered and rolled my eyes at my past pursuits. "Yeah, I'm on the twenty-year plan."

Adriana laughed, and I continued, "I enrolled into community college while I was married to my first husband, and then did a semester at this university while I was with my second husband; and now I'm on husband number three, and here I am again, still a freshman!"

"Life is distracting sometimes, huh?"

"A bit," I giggled. "Three husbands and four kids is a big distraction. I blamed them for my lack of success while, in fact, I had no sense of commitment each time I quit school or a husband."

"Do you have a sense of commitment this semester?"

"I have a great sense of urgency to finish a degree, as if there may not be another window of opportunity."

"It's all about attitude," she added.

"Thirteen years, at an insurance office, is a long run," I affirmed while wanting to avoid talking about those particular *distractions*.

"Too long," Adriana added. "I'm done with the business world. I want to teach school now."

"Really?" I was intrigued with her choice to work for peanuts, and then thought about the sexy George from Connecticut, who was the Vice Chairman of the Board of Education. "A friend of mine says school teachers average $50,000 a year in New England."

She nodded, "Maybe I'll move there. I want to be home when my daughter gets home from school. She's eleven years old and my only child. I'm divorced."

I nodded while digesting her situation. "I would think a business degree, at this point, in your career, would allow you to get the promotion, and larger salary, if you stayed in the insurance world. You've got a lot of good experience."

"You're probably right," Adriana nodded, "but I'm burned out with the business world."

"I understand," I said while appreciating her position to throw the dice and venture into a brand new direction. "I'm going for my business degree. Money is the bottom line with me. I have at least three years, to do here, before I get the bachelor's degree, and salary potential is my motivation for the direction I eventually take with my career. I figured work is work, so if I'm going to work every day, I best be paid a lot of money. I find no fulfillment in any job when I can't pay my bills."

Adriana chuckled, "You've got a good point there, but I just don't have a heart for numbers and the bottom line anymore. I did bookkeeping for years," she groaned.

I figured Adriana had never experienced poverty, and the value she placed on money was not at the level I now placed on money. I had recently lived in poverty for the first time in my life, and did so for three years with children to care for, too; and those impoverished years were hell on earth with Seth. And since our boat had come in, and my $300,000 apparel business lawsuit settlement was, for the most part, spent on the desires of the heart, I came to appreciate having money. Seth and I had the American dream. We owned our custom, two-story home, along with beautiful furnishings, state-of-the-art electronics, the best appliances money could buy, art, landscaping, and new cars; and best of all, all our possessions were paid for in full with cash. Now, I wanted personal security, which included a degree, job opportunity, and a good income for me, in the future, when Seth would finally leave me.

"With money comes freedom," I continued while I considered how nice our indulgent lifestyle supported by Seth's $100,000 a year income had been for us, too. "With money, I can sleep at night!"

"Money does indeed make life easier," Adriana nodded. "I have a 401k, and some in savings--not a lot of money, but if need be, I can pay my rent and utilities for a year."

"Good for you!" I declared. "We don't have any investments, nor do we have savings of any kind, either. We've got some catching up to do in that department." Seth and I had spent our money as fast as we could pull the checks out of the mailbox over the last nine months.

Adriana continued, "I lost a majority of my investments in the stock market in '87 on Black Monday; and then, the savings and loans industry began to collapse, which sent me and the rest of America into a crisis, and I pulled what money I had out of the stock market."

"Well, teachers have good benefits. You can start again. What does a first year teacher earn now in Texas?"

"About $28,000 a year."

"After taxes, that leaves you with two grand a month!" I affirmed. "That's not enough money for our spending habits; much less, would we have any extra for any investment portfolio we need to build."

"I will live simple. I think our economy is finally pulling out of the recession," Adriana added.

"Hopefully, by the time I get my degree, America will have a strong economy again. My husband thinks the stock market is a good place to make money right now."

"I think so, too;" Adriana submitted, "but I don't have any money to invest. My father is paying my bills while I'm in college."

"He's very generous," I acknowledged.

"He's kind and generous. My daughter and I can manage on a teacher's salary. I also get $500 a month child support from my ex."

"You can't depend on him though. He might lose his job or just stop paying," I challenged.

"He might. The government raised a first-year teacher's pay up to $28,000 a year, because of Ross Perot's efforts in 1984, under Governor Mark White. Perot's own money paid for one of the biggest lobbying efforts Texas has ever witnessed."

"I liked the billionaire," I said. "The problem with that kind of small start salary is that teachers' salaries increase at a very slow rate over the decades. And teachers now have to pass a competency test to keep their jobs, too." I said. "At least you'll be fresh out of school when you have to take that test."

"I know--good thing for me. And high-school students have to now pass a proficiency test to graduate," she contributed.

"And if they don't pass, then what?" I asked.

"They don't get a diploma. They get a certificate of completion."

"I see. So with a certificate of completion, a kid will now have to take more pre-requisites and spend more money on college?"

"Probably," she laughed. "And the no-pass, no-play rule forbid Texas students to play sports if they fail a course. I agree with that new policy."

"Me, too. No more passing kids through the system who can't read," I supported.

"I would have liked to have seen Perot win the presidency," Adriana said. "He's proved that business methods and plain speaking is what it takes to forge policies."

"He's a successful businessman, but he might not have succeeded with education reform had he *actually been in* government. He did not have to worry about making anybody angry when he lobbied for all those reforms, but no matter how much we all liked him, no independent ever wins," I said. "When Perot dropped out of the race this summer, he had 39% of the vote. That move really angered his supporters, but rumor has it the Bush campaign would have released digitally altered photos and sabotaged his daughter's wedding if he continued to run for the presidency."

"There's rumor he might re-enter the race again. He's on all fifty state ballots now."

"He should re-enter; he's got a good chance," I said.

"But the problem is Perot won't get any Electoral College votes."

"Too bad," I added. "George Herbert Walker Bush has alienated much of his conservative base because he broke his 1988 campaign pledge against raising taxes, when he did raise taxes while we were in a recession."

Adriana mocked Bush, "Read my lips: no new taxes."

"He lied, and there has been an economic malaise since the beginning of the Gulf War in 1990, too."

"The spike in the price of oil increased inflation, too," Adriana added.

I nodded in agreement. "Americans don't like George Bush anymore. I don't think he'll win a second term."

"So you will vote for the Arkansas Democrat?"

"There's no other choice, is there?" I answered. "Perot dropped out of the race in July."

"Clinton plays a mean saxophone. Did you see Clinton on the Arsenio Hall Show?"

"Who hasn't?" I asked.

"Impressive horn player, right?" Adriana questioned.

"Yeah, The Blues *Other* Brother probably will win the presidency due to that one, single TV appearance."

"Probably" she giggled. "This campus is pro-Clinton. Students have tables set up, outside today, and their goal is to get all of us to vote Democrat. I registered."

"I always vote," I added, "but not always for the same party. I will vote for Clinton."

"Me, too," Adriana admitted. "Were you working before you started school?"

"No, I've been a stay-at-home mom for years. I have three children at home--two boys and a daughter. I have another son, too, who lives with his father."

"How old are your children, Jean?"

"My baby boy is one-and-a-half years old; then, I have a three-year old son, and a nine-year old daughter. My oldest is twelve-years old and he lives with his father in Clear Lake City."

"Wow, that's a large family."

"Yep," I nodded, "My greatest accomplishment yet! How long have you been divorced?"

"About five years," Adriana replied. "It's hard being a single parent. I'm fortunate to have my father."

"You are! My father and I are not close, and he's very tight with his money. I'd be afraid to ask him for any money."

"But you have a husband who affords you to go to school?"

"Yes," I grimly replied while I considered the fragility of my relationship with Seth. "For the time being, I have a husband," I confessed. "I don't have a choice, but to get this degree. I fear one day, I will wake up, and not have an income of any sort."

"Why is that?"

I hesitated to burden my new friend with the entire truth. "My husband, Seth, is obsessed with our yard, and I suspect he's got a drug addiction problem, too."

"He doesn't work?"

"Only in the yard. He collects a commission check each month, which affords us a very nice lifestyle, but there are no guarantees how long his commission check will keep coming, either. He's a licensed investment advisor, but he has closed one single deal in all our years together; and if this deal goes south, then we are in big trouble because he has not generated any further business, nor is he trying to build up any kind of network for future business. I'm hoping I can get my degree before his commission is axed, and we're dealing with poverty." I stopped short of saying *again*.

"I would think being married to a drug addict is reason to leave him, Jean?"

"It is, but not now," I said. "First things first; I've got to be able to support myself, and the thought of leaving Seth and tearing apart my children's hearts does not settle well with me, either. My little boys love their daddy despite what I think about him. I worry about the frequent shouting matches they witness and wonder how we are scarring our children in the long term."

"For the sake of your children, don't let that fighting go on too long."

I drove thirty miles home from the University of Houston and pulled into my driveway with excitement bursting forth, eager to share my first day of school with Seth and my kids. I turned off the ignition, grabbed a stack of new books, and hurried through the kitchen door. I saw my third child playing with a car on the floor and my husband loading the dishwasher. "Hi everybody!"

My three-year old son ran up to me happy to see me and showed me his Hot Wheel racecar. I set my books down on the countertop and picked up Harper. "Wow, you have a new car! Does your car go fast?"

He nodded and then made motor sounds while he raced the car through the air.

I giggled, "You're ready to drive in the Daytona 500!" Daddy did not acknowledge me. "How are you, Seth?" I asked the man who obviously was cleaning up after a breakfast and lunch he had prepared for himself and his sons.

He did not answer so I took the bait, "What's the matter?"

"Plenty," he angrily snapped back.

I felt I was walking into a trap. I looked at Harper and asked him, "Where's your younger brother?"

Harper pointed to the adjacent den, and I spotted Doren playing with his car and miniature garage on top of the hearth.

"Can you say, 'Doren is over there?'?" I asked my three-year old son who was reticent to talk.

"Ober 'der," Harper repeated.

"I see Doren *over there*. Let's go say hi to Doren." I then walked into the den carrying my third child, sat Harper down next to his younger brother, and squatted down to hug and kiss my baby, who leaned on the hearth while busy with his toys. "Hi Doren!"

My year-and-a-half old son excitedly jumped up to show me his car.

I examined the toy he gave me. "You have a new car, too, and it's red! Can you say *red?*"

My youngest uttered, "Red."

"That is correct! Your car *is* red!"

Harper held his car up for my view and said, "Blue."

"You're right, Harper. Say, *I have a blue car!*"

Harper refused to respond and continued to roll his car on the hearth while making motor sounds.

I felt my three-year old son's verbal expression was too limited for his age, and speculated that the frequent verbal wars around the house between his parents had somehow traumatized him. I intended to have a specialist look at Harper in the near future, if he did not start making sentences. I rolled Doren's car down the garage ramp, and he grabbed his car from me.

"We need to talk, Jean," Seth said from the threshold of the den and kitchen.

I turned my attention toward my husband and saw him walk back into the kitchen as if he expected me to come in there. "Do you want this car?" I asked Harper while I held up a purple speed mobile I picked up off the floor.

Harper nodded yes.

"Say, *I want the car, please.*"

"Car!" the three-year old replied.

I handed my son the *Hot Wheel* and replied, "Okay, you can have the car." He took the purple racecar, and I got up. "I'll be right back, boys."

I walked into the kitchen and stared at the man in jeans and T-shirt, who continued to fill the dishwasher with dishes from the sink and countertops. Seth looked up at me with disdain and growled, "I resent you going to school."

"Get over it!" I fired back.

"I don't want to be home with these kids all day."

"No one is making you stay home with the kids. Go get a job."

"I don't want my children in daycare."

"Me, either. We'll get a nanny to come here if you *have somewhere to go* one day. A nanny will be a better deal than the cost of daycare for two babies every week. She can load the dishwasher, too!"

"I want you to quit school."

"I'm not quitting. I just started."

Seth slammed the dishwasher closed. "You, being gone, is not going to work for me!"

"I'm gone early in the morning and home by 1:00 p.m. every day. You've been obsessing over the yard, landscaping from morning until midnight, and ignoring all of us for over a year. It's *your turn* to cook and change diapers. I was there for you when you went to law school *all three weeks*. I didn't tell you to quit and stay home, that choice you made. And for your information, I was really looking forward to being married to a successful International Lawyer, but since you have chosen *a different route to success*, I'm going to finish this semester; and then, do another one, and then another one, and then another one, until I earn a bachelor's degree! Therefore, *I don't care* if you resent me going to school or not! I'm going to have to get a good paying job one day when we go broke, and I'll need a college degree to do that!" I walked out of the kitchen trying to not let his tantrum get the best of me while I headed back into the den to spend time with my sons. "Where's Bella?" I asked Harper.

"Upstairs."

Seth blasted from the kitchen, "We'll see who takes care of the future!"

I did not know what he meant by his threat. I peered into the kitchen and watched him walk outside through the glass kitchen door. He stood just on the other side of the door and lit up a cigarette while appearing disturbed.

The second day of classes at the university was smoother than the first, and I grew more and more excited about my new academic journey and all the possibilities I was creating for my life. I fantasized about graduation day, and then about interviewing for a high paying job after I earned my degree, but told myself, "One day at a time, Jean; one day at a time." The goal of attaining a bachelor's degree seemed too far off into the future when I considered three-plus years, but my immediate goal felt feasible. I would ace every class this semester.

I drove home that early afternoon and talked to myself. "All good things come to those who have patience and persevere," I reminded myself while I considered how I would react to Seth if he continued to not support my academic endeavor that evening. I would not accept anything from him but his support. I shifted to thoughts that were more productive and recalled that morning's lecturers, and then reminded myself of the reading homework I had to do that night. I began composing in my head the composition I needed to write for literature class; and before I realized, I was already thirty miles down the freeway and pulling into my driveway.

I saw Chad's car in the driveway and figured he was keeping

lonely boy company that day. I walked through the kitchen door and found Chad sitting at the dining table reading a book to Harper who sat on his lap. Doren was on the floor nearby building with toddler tinker toys.

"Hey Jean," he smiled.

"Hey, Chad. Hi, Harper! Hi, Doren!"

"Hi, Mommy!" Harper yelled from Chad's lap. "Chad is reading *The Stinky Cheese Man!*"

"Hi, Doren!" My baby ran up to me, and I squatted to kiss and hug him.

Chad continued, "I've started something here. I've read this book twice to Harper, and he wants me to read it one more time."

I laughed. "He loves that book. I then said to my third child, "Harper, Chad might want to take a break."

Harper jumped off Chad's lap, "I get a nuder book," he said before leaving the room to run upstairs.

"Where's Seth?" I asked while I stood up with my baby boy on my hip.

"He's running an errand."

"What kind of errand?"

Chad shrugged, "He didn't say."

"I would like to ask you a favor?"

"Certainly."

"I have a paper due tomorrow, and I need to write for a few hours. Will you stay until Seth gets back, unless you're busy? If you are, I understand."

"I would be happy to stay."

"Thank you. I'll be back in my bedroom working if you need anything; knock on the door." I sat Doren back down on the floor. "Mommy has to go do her homework."

"Go do what you have to do," Chad kindly offered. "We boys are tight."

"Thank you so much," I said to the supportive man as I walked out the room.

Hours later, I found myself proofing a seven-page literature paper due the next day in class. Writing came natural to me; and in the right space, I could hammer out the perfect words. When I had peace, my creativity flowed. I heard the bedroom door open and saw my husband walk into our room. I glanced at the clock and realized I had been behind closed doors for three hours. "Where have you been?" I asked.

"We have to talk," he seriously replied.

Harper and Doren followed Daddy into the room. Seth turned to them, "Harper, go with your brother, Doren, into the other room and let Mommy and Daddy talk in private. I'll be out in a few minutes," Seth kindly requested while he held the door open for their exit.

"Go, Doren!" Harper bossily said to his little brother.

My sons walked out together, and Seth gently closed the door. He walked up to my desk, "I went to see a lawyer today, and I withdrew all the money from our bank account. I'm done; good luck getting to school now without gas money."

"You did what?" His words were shocking.

"I'm sick of your shit, Jean."

"You're done? You're done with what?"

"You! You have one choice. Either you quit school, or I'm leaving you."

"I'm not quitting, Seth. You dropped out of law school--that was your choice. I'm entitled to get my first degree; you already have two degrees! And I didn't stop you from getting your third degree--you stopped yourself. Now, I expect you to support me."

"I'm giving you an ultimatum, Jean," he said while he walked toward the closed door. "I'll go pay the lawyer tomorrow and serve you a divorce petition, if you continue going to school."

Tears began rolling down my cheeks, and I mumbled, "I hate you, you deceiving son-ov'a-bitch!"

"Oh well," he smirked and then walked out of the room.

I had no gas money to drive the 70-mile roundtrip to school and back every day. "I can't believe this," I mumbled to myself while I sat there, alone, in tears, and staring at the words that I wrote on my computer screen. I began to uncontrollably weep when I realized a control freak that cared about no one, not even about himself, had just shot down my dream, again. First, my apparel business dream, and now my dream to get a college degree. I got up from behind my desk, threw myself across our king-size bed, broken hearted, and cried out to the heavens, "God, help me; I hate him."

 The following morning I woke up and stared at the clock. 7 a.m., and Seth's side of the bed remained unmade. I figured he slept in the guest room upstairs. Classes started in five minutes, and I felt despair while I knew I had no choice, but to withdraw. I had written a $1,200 check for that semester, and if I dropped now, on the third day, I would get a full refund. I crawled out of bed feeling depressed while I freshened up in the bathroom, and then threw on jeans and a T-shirt and headed out of the house.

 Seth was sitting on the slider swing outside the glass kitchen door, between the house and the garage, smoking a cigarette and drinking a cup of coffee. "Are you going to withdraw?"

 "Fuck you!" I angrily muttered as I passed under the catwalk and entered into the garage where I parked my green Volvo next to his black Mustang.

 I started up my station wagon and slowly backed out of the garage. I peered at Seth, who smugly sat in his slider swing without a care in the world; and I became aware, in that moment, that I despised him. I had bought the house, the beautiful furnishings, the best appliances money could buy, state-of-the-art electronics, my Volvo, and his Mustang, and all with cash from the apparel business settlement. I had spent every dime I had won in that lawsuit against the convenience store. In addition, I had given Seth two perfectly healthy sons, and had supported him one hundred percent when he wanted to go to law school; and now, he gave me an ultimatum while he did drugs, landscaped, and collected $8,000 a month out of the mailbox. I hated him.

 I drove from The Woodlands to the University of Houston and stood in line at the registrar's office to formally withdraw from school. I no longer felt part of the academic scene buzzing around me. My hope was gone, and I felt anger because I had no control over my life. I felt trapped in Satan's den. My potential threatened the man with no faith in anyone or anything. I abhorred the word *potential*, but more accurately, Seth's mindset was depleting. I had once felt that I had the potential to be a great clothing designer and manufacturer, but as the years with Seth passed, I saw nothing amazing materialize in either of our lives—except all the destruction, due to his mental illness. In that moment, I admonished myself for being stupid enough to have ever given him the time of day. Why had I ended up having children with this horrid creature who created only chaos in our family? I used no discernment when I chose Seth to be part of my life.

I stepped up to the clerk's window and could barely utter the first two words before I broke out into tears. "I need to withdraw," I said and then clutched my face and wailed, "My husband won't let me do this!"

The black middle-aged woman's face appeared compassionate. "Oh, sweetheart, I'm sorry."

"If I don't quit, he'll divorce me, and leave me and the kids penniless."

The woman shook her head in disapproval, reached across the counter, and touched my arm. "Pray," she said. "Pray for peace. I'll pray for you, too. Pray and God will answer your prayers. God loves you."

"I will pray," I sobbed while I feared that if I prayed for peace, then God would answer, and I would find myself with no income, and three children to raise by myself. "Thank you for your kind words," I said to the angel who rendered me hope and a moment of peace with her words. The woman filled out my withdrawal form, and I walked away reminded that God was ultimately in charge, not Seth. What God could do for me, I could not fathom. Anything was possible.

I walked across the sprawling campus, like a mad woman, and could barely manage my composure. A no-win situation dictated my feelings. The Lord reminded me that vengeance was his, but I wanted to assist him. I wanted to kill my husband. Seth had forced me into submission out of his need to control me, out of his insecurity that he had given me enough reason over the past four years to walk away. He had constantly ripped at the core of my life's designs, and my frustration shackled my spirit to no longer act tolerantly. I would contend with his demonic spirit on his level!

I understood I did not know how to love when I was married to Leonardo. I took Leonardo, my generous, loving husband for granted, when I did not have faith in the Lord to work out that which I could not understand. I did understand what Cliff had brought to the table that summer, in Florida, either, when he wanted Bella and me to go to Switzerland and be with him—another opportunity to exercise faith. Now, I was learning what love was *not!* And here again, I had another opportunity to exercise faith in the Lord.

Seth's ego was at the root of his diabolism; and for the first time in my life, I began to understand the personalities of darkness. Satan had tricked me from the beginning. Seth was like Mephistopheles, a devil in disguise wearing the form of a gray friar. I had learned the day before in literature class the Greek translation for *Mephist* meant "liar" and *tophel* meant "destroyer." The diverting fiendish spirit in my home was swaying my feelings to match his methods, and I felt as if Termagant had taken residence inside my soul. There was no more compromise, nor pleading, on my part, for Seth to understand a greater way of being. My husband was forcing me into war, and though being loving was my nature now, I had no choice, but to take on the enemy. I would lose evil's domination over my life; and for my children, I would be a woman of strength who did not live in fear. They would eventually know peace, but only if I first went to war with the devil that lived in our home.

I was so furious when I got into my green station wagon that I could barely sit behind the steering wheel while I drove home. I turned on talk radio in hopes my anger would diminish if I shifted my focus. I heard a male personality argue with another male: "Bill Clinton is a natural-born politician. It's no wonder the Democratic Party has made him their candidate that stands for them this November! He is a master of substance, a policy wonk, who does talk about the minutiae of government for hours on end. I've never seen anything like it," he marveled.

Another man jumped into the conversation, "Clinton seems to be up on every social program in America. And he makes promises of a massive reinvestment program. Clinton is intellectual, canny, and particularly clever about people and how to manipulate them."

A third male added his two cents. "Let's keep in mind that since 1982, ten years ago, when Clinton was re-elected as Governor of Arkansas, he has been permanently campaigning. Clinton keeps a close eye on the public opinion polls and steers clear of politically risky public stands. He has shrewdly positioned himself as a *New Democrat* out to reinvigorate liberalism by stressing opportunity and responsibility, and he skillfully paints the Republicans as both heartless and inept. But Clinton has no experience in foreign policy, and at best, will be a nimble peacemaker. He will be standing for the party of moral relativism, of toleration and hesitation, in the face of worldwide terrorism. Bush is tough on totalitarianism, and the voice of appeasement of today's liberals back Clinton! Liberals now refuse to acknowledge that our designated Operation Desert Storm was a beneficial thing, or that we had any solid reason to be in Kuwait helping them stop Iraqi forces, other than we did so for our own personal agenda to maintain control of the oil market. These anti-Bush people say the Gulf War was unnecessary. But, I say, it *was* necessary; and if we are to condemn the effort of our government, it should be because we stopped short, and that the war should have lasted until we killed Saddam Hussein. The Gulf War was an incomplete triumph, *not* a blunder on America's part. We left Saddam Hussein alive, and we allowed for dangerous possibilities to occur. Bush stopped the fight because we might have split our alliance, especially with the skittishness of the Soviet Union. Moscow was reaching out to Baghdad, and we could not afford to *not have* an alliance with the Soviet, both for Arab cooperation, and for the winding down of the Cold War. We stopped short, okay, but these liberals are more tolerant of Saddam Hussein than they are of George Bush! They don't see that Iraq is a breeding ground for evil, nor do these liberals consider that Saddam Hussein has terrorized and plundered his own people. And unless we, the people, acknowledge a moral code of good and evil, and stop with the nonsense of tolerating what is downright evil, then we have a good chance to end up like Nazi Germany, paying homage to a charter that says God is dead and establishes the state as god. And, when government considers itself God, and surrenders a moral code of good and evil, in lieu of toleration, we risk evil controlling us. We've got to evaluate the behavior code of these vicious mass murderers like Adolf Hitler and Sadam Hussein in moral terms, and fight evil's domination over good, and this country needs to re-elect George Bush for a second term."

I turned off the radio. The debate over Clinton versus George Herbert Walker Bush hit too close to home. My hands shook over the state of affairs in my world. Seth forced me into a risky situation against my will. I had never wanted to have two more children, only then to find myself a single mother without a sufficient income. The thought of having no degree, and no ability to make enough money to support three children and myself frightened me. Daycare alone would eat my lunch each pay period. I believed that if Seth pressed for a divorce, and he forced me into a courtroom, to fight for custody of our two children, I would get a fair shake, especially after I told the judge that my husband was an over-educated, abusive, drug addict with a boyfriend! I believed, without a doubt, the court would give me permanent custody of my two youngest children in the divorce, if I told the judge that the father had refused to work during the marriage. I truly believed a court would force the bum to get a job and pay me child support. If he wanted to seek a divorce, then he deserved what he got!

The long drive back to my country club neighborhood in north Houston concluded with me resenting the hell out of Seth for depriving our children and me of a happy home life. I threw my car into park in my driveway, left my now useless textbooks in the front seat, and raced into the house looking for my target. I flung the front door open and heard the door crash into the wall while I scanned the front areas for Seth. I was on a mission to kill. I heard the commode in the master bedroom flush. I flew through the living room and master bedroom on adrenalin, and then into the large vanity area of the master bath. I saw light filter out from underneath the door of the water closet and did not hesitate to corner my prey. I flung the door open, surprised the jerk who sat on the commode wiping his ass, and grabbed Seth by the dark, thinning hair on the very top of his head, and with the strength of a sumo wrestler, I threw the 150-pound lightweight, face down, on the floor. "Fuck you!" I yelled while I physically held him, face down, on the floor, by the hair, and pressed my foot into the back of his neck while I continued to read him the Right Act. "All laws that restrict me as a woman, and as your wife, are null and void! I have the same rights as you, asshole! I have a right to life, liberty, property, security, and the pursuit of happiness! You are violating my rights, and that violation is a crime of honor! I have the right to be free from all forms of domestic violence; do you understand my rules? I have the right to attend college and learn, too! I'm giving you an ultimatum now, you son-ov'a-bitch--"

Seth dug his feet into the floor and tried to jump up while I continued to hold tight to his Mohawk and vent; and out of his rage, over me taking him down, the red-faced man sprung up from the floor, grabbed me by the hair, and plowed his fist into my nose with all his might.

I let out a bloody scream while pain surged through my face, and immediately let go of his hair and reached for my nose. Blood dripped down my fingers.

"Fuck you, bitch!" He yelled.

"How do you like being assaulted, asshole?" I wailed. "I've had enough of *your* shit, too. I want you to leave! Get the fuck out of here!" Tears streamed down my face.

"I'm not leaving, bitch; but you will, though! And, if you think you're going to take my kids away, boot me out of my house, and tell some judge that I'm the abuser, you've got something to learn. Whatever you accuse me of, Jean, I will accuse you of the same."

"I am *not* like you, not even close!" I answered.

"I will reiterate, Jean. Whatever you accuse me of, I will accuse you of the same. If we go to court, I will win custody of our children because you're a paranoid and delusional nutcase!" He hammered the bi-fold doors with his fist as he walked out of the vanity area.

"You will never get custody of my children, you creep from hell!" I shouted just before hearing the front door slam shut. I figured he would head to his lawyer's office and begin a divorce action. I feared losing my children to the snake.

My face throbbed while I examined my bloody nose in the mirror. I looked hard at my worn and haggard reflection. I hated who I had become since 1988--a weak woman, who was allowing a mentally sick reprobate to cripple her. My nose was swollen and obviously broken.

I dialed our family doctor within minutes after Seth left the premise. The receptionist answered, "Dr. Hawkes' office."

"This is Jean Zherneboh. My husband broke my nose, and I need an appointment today." I intended to document my husband's abuse for the eventual divorce hearing that he most likely would begin setting up that day at his lawyer's office.

8
BREAKING THE CAMEL'S BACK

MONTHS LATER, NOVEMBER 1992. I heard the male voice on the other side of the phone say, "I just had to laugh when Seth called me and offered to invest *my money* in the stock market. What is your husband thinking, Jean Ellen? Is he taking drugs?"

"Maybe. I had no clue, Dad, that Seth called you; he didn't say anything to me. I didn't know he wanted to invest your money; he doesn't share his ideas with me."

"Well, he's ridiculous if he thinks I'm going to give him my hard earned money. I told Seth that I had no idea he was an expert in the stock market."

"He isn't an expert, Dad. He's never invested a penny, a day in his life, into any fund anywhere."

My father chuckled, "Well, I knew that to be the case with yall, though he sounds informed about the market."

"He's been studying the stock market trends."

"I asked your husband if he thought I was stupid enough to give him my life savings. He just laughed. I told him that I had been investing in the stock market for decades, that I had earned some hefty returns, and that I did not need help from a neophyte. He's got a lot of gall, to want to risk my money," my father chastised. "Seth has always chosen the easy road. That man needs to get a job."

"I'm sorry, Dad."

"Only thing to be sorry about, Jean Ellen, is that your husband is not a responsible man. I was telling my friend, Harold, over at the Men's Club, at the church, about my son-in-law a couple of nights ago, and he says Seth's got chutzpah."

"What's that mean?"

"He's got supreme self-confidence, too much nerve. Your mother couldn't believe Seth would even ask me such a thing. Something is wrong with that man; he's not thinking straight. And, I don't think *now* is the time, for a novice like Seth, to be investing his money, or anybody else's money, in the stock market, either. I don't trust the stock market anymore. I pulled all my money out recently and sunk my retirement into T-bills."

"Why?"

"There's going to be another stock market crash like the crash in 1929 that launched The Great Depression. There's too much corruption in the government, these days--that was the case back then, too. All these oil companies are contributing to political campaigns. Exxon and Mobile Oil merged here lately. Too many big oil companies are merging and creating a monopoly power. There are anti-trust laws in place which prevent mergers of huge companies, like these oil companies that each earn $10 billion dollars a year; but because these big oil companies contribute millions to the political campaigns, anti-trust laws are not being enforced. You'll see, Jean Ellen, the price of oil will rise over the next decade, and not because there is a shortage of oil, or because production costs are rising, or because of the unrest in the Middle East. There's always been unrest over there. And the U.S. has plenty of oil reserves, and so does Canada, Russia, Saudi Arabia, and most of the Middle East. There is no shortage of supply. Oil will rise because there is a monopoly of power."

"There was a shortage of oil in the 70's. I remember people waiting in line at the gas pumps for hours to get gas, Dad."

"Back in 1973, when the members of the Organization of Arab Petroleum Exporting Countries proclaimed an oil embargo, in response to the U.S. decision to re-supply the Israeli military during the Yom Kippur War, OAPEC declared it would limit, or stop shipments in the US, and other countries, if they supported Israel in the conflict. Arab oil producers lifted the embargo in 1974 when Israel agreed to withdraw from the Golan Heights. In addition, independently, the Oil Producing Exporting Countries, the OPEC members, agreed to raise world oil prices in the 70's, too. Now, as it stands, big business has bought out governments around the world through campaign contributions, and that's official corruption. And if you compound the political corruption with the wage gap; then, we've got the beginning of the end of capitalism."

"That sounds a bit farfetched, Dad."

"When there is official corruption, then the house of cards fall. Worker productivity is going up, but the real wage is not rising, and that wage gap causes a decline in demand. Capitalism only works when productivity and wages rise together. Over-production means layoffs. The government is not, and will not, increase wages because increased wages means loss of business profits. Big businesses own the government. The government is creating debt by creating credit. The government is creating debt, instead of raising the minimum wage. Government lowers interest rates, and people borrow money and get in debt. New debt raises demand. And that surge of new money injected into the economy creates stock market bubbles, but bubbles pop."

"Why do bubbles pop?"

"Simple, debt cannot keep rising! Supply will eventually become greater than demand, and the bubble pops. People eventually max out their credit line and can't borrow any more money and spending stops. We'll have a few stock market bubbles over this decade; and then, people will stop investing. The country will eventually have too much debt, and there will be no more spending; and when that happens, we'll have another Great Depression. No system can live on new debt creation forever. Political corruption will be the downfall of the entire world market, and I predict that situation will happen in my life time."

"Seth has been telling our friends that now is the right time to invest in the stock market."

"The stock market is a risk, always has been, but will be especially volatile this year and next year. You tell Seth to use caution. The bubble might burst soon. Alan Greenspan lowered the Fed rate from about 10% to almost 3% in the last two years, in an effort to stimulate the economy and keep George Bush in for a second term, and Greenspan has channeled $700 billion into the economy through our banking system. After our government lowers the interest rate, the normal lag time is usually six to twelve months before we see the stock market rise; and we're seeing the economy take off now, just as Clinton takes office. Bush's manipulation of the economy came a day too late. So, tell your husband to take great caution because that bubble will burst."

"I will, Dad. I don't think Seth has much money of his own to gamble anyway."

"You and Seth are not living right, if you don't have money put away each month. There's something wrong with that picture, if he's bringing in $8,000 a month and you're not saving any money. You have a paid for home! What are you and Seth doing with all your money, Jean Ellen?"

"I'm not sure. Seth is always buying something for the yard, and I've been buying paint, wall paper, and décor for a year."

"That doesn't sound right to me," he grumbled. "You and Seth need to slow down your spending, and remember to keep God first in your life. God requires all who love Him to keep his commandments; and if you and Seth pattern your behavior after your Lord, then your lives will be most valuable."

"I know that, Dad."

"Jesus said in John 15:10, 'If you obey my commandments, you will remain in my love, just as I have obeyed my Father's commands and remain in His love.' You and Seth need to live right, and go to church and tithe. If you think Seth's on drugs, then that might explain where your money is going each month."

"I haven't actually *seen* Seth do hard drugs, Dad," I said in order to retract my suspicions about Seth's addiction so I could put my father's mind at ease. I didn't consider the marijuana a drug worthy of mention, nor did I believe the pot would make Seth crazy, but perhaps I was wrong. Marijuana was different than in bygone days—stronger and more potent.

"Well, that's good. Put your savings into a three-month treasury bill; that's a safe bet for right now. As of this November, T-bills have a 3.13 value right now. You and Seth need to save for a rainy day because that commission check he gets every month will stop one day."

"I know! I tell him that all the time."

"You kids need to prepare for the future," the elderly man warned. "Well, Jean Ellen, I've got a Men's Club meeting over at the church here in a little bit, so I better get off this phone now and get ready."

"What do you men discuss at your meeting?"

"We play poker and drink beer," he chuckled.

I laughed, too. "Well, that sounds like a bunch of Catholics having fun. You better hurry up and get there; that is an important meeting."

He chuckled. "Come see your mother soon."

"I will, Dad. I'll see you soon, too."

"Bye daughter."

"Bye Dad." I set the phone down in the cradle on the counter next to the glass kitchen door and thought about the man who became wiser as I got older. I appreciated my father more than ever these days. He had always been a responsible husband and father, who consistently held tight to a code of morality that he claimed would allow him to hold his head up high on Judgment Day. I had been conflicted about Judgment Day, most of my life, fearing a court hearing after this life was done here on earth, but today I have re-evaluated my teachings. I believe that Jesus died on the cross, and rose from the dead, so that I may have life—now and for eternity; and when I chose to become a believer and walk in faith, my heavenly father forgave me of all my sins and gave me a clean slate. I do not agree that I will stand before God on Judgment Day and that my sins would be re-addressed.

I had heard Seth talk with Pete about investment strategies over the last year, but I had no idea Seth would even consider, for a second, learning how to play the stock market with anyone else's money, much less ask my stoic father for a dime! Seth's temerity was embarrassing.

My husband walked in through the glass kitchen door from outside.

"You're covered in dirt, Seth. Don't come in here!"

"I'm dying from thirst," he retorted while he headed to the kitchen sink leaving a trail of dirt on the floor. He grabbed a glass out of the cabinet and turned on the kitchen faucet. "I just dug up most of the grass beside the driveway. I bought some timber, and I'm going to build three garden boxes along the driveway." He took a swig of water and set his glass down.

"My father told me that you requested of him to let you invest his money in the stock market."

Seth snickered. "I did, but your old man told me he took care of his own affairs."

"Are you crazy?" I asked. "You're making me look like a fool. I told my father that I had nothing to do with you calling him."

"I'm sure you did, Jean," he sarcastically retorted. "You told me that your father had a half million dollars."

"So what if he does? He's not stupid. Dad told me to tell you to get a job."

"I've got a job, Jean!" He defended. "I'm investing Ma's money."

"Your mother is letting you invest her money?"

"Yeah," he smiled.

"She's not too bright. How much money did she give you to

invest?"

"All of her money. Well, not all of it, yet; first, Ma has to pay some penalties for making early withdrawals. I expect to get the majority of her money sometime this coming week; and then, I'll make my first trade."

"She's doing what?" The unfolding of events blew me away. I knew the woman had always felt guilty about raising her four children under the same roof with their abusive and chronic alcoholic father, but this insane act took the cake for the enabler.

"Ma's pulling her money out of her investment portfolio. I can do better for her; I told her so."

"And she believes you?" I shook my head in disbelief. "How much money is she giving you to invest in the stock market?"

"$85,000."

"$85,000! What if you lose all her money?"

"I'm not going to lose all her money!" He growled.

"What if you lose just $20,000? Won't you feel guilty, Seth?"

"Leave me alone, Jean! This transaction is between me and Ma."

"No, you gambling your mother's money, in the stock market, involves me, too."

"No, my business with Ma does *not* involve you, Jean!" Seth retorted.

"If you lose your mother's money, we're not paying her back."

Seth stepped up to me and screamed, "If I lose Ma's money, I *will* pay Ma back if *I choose* to pay her back. I'm earning the money around here, not you!"

"You get more stupid every day, Seth. Why would you put us in a position like that?" I saw Harper peaking around the corner of the kitchen door, but continued my argument. "You are willing to risk losing your mother's entire life savings because you're too damn lazy to get a job. Or is the problem your drug addiction? Are you insane enough to gamble your mother's life savings because the drugs have fried your brain?"

"Fuck you, Jean," He yelled before kicking me hard in the

shin.

Pain streaked up my leg. I hollered "Ouch!" and then angrily reacted and pushed Seth, with both hands, away from me and into the counter. He regained his balance and then kicked me hard into the other shin.

"Ouch!" I cried out while grabbing my lower leg.

My three-year old son ran from around the corner and into the kitchen. He pushed at his father's knees and yelled, "Stop, Daddy. Don't hurt my mommy!"

Tears rolled down my eyes at the sight of my upset child. I squatted down and hugged my three-year old son to comfort him. "I'm okay, Harper," I said while I stood up with him in my arms. He *could* talk if forced to talk!

"Put him down, Jean!" Seth angrily ordered. "Harper, this is between Mommy and Daddy."

I grumbled, "You get out of here, Seth."

"Go 'way, Daddy!" Harper sternly ordered from my arms.

Seth kissed Harper and murmured, "It's okay, son."

"No, your behavior is *not* okay, Seth!"

"You are not right with him," Seth growled.

"You're not right with *me*, Seth!" I refuted.

"I love you, Harper," Seth said before walking back outside.

I questioned how a man could love his child and hurt the child's mother? Seth had been assaulting me since the beginning of our relationship when I was pregnant with this child—he pushed me into the back of the closet in our first apartment; and now, he wanted to send this same child mixed messages about love. "I'm sorry, baby," I whispered to Harper while I wiped the tears off my cheeks. "It's not okay for Daddy to hit Mommy."

FOUR MONTHS LATER. MARCH 1993. I walked down the street to the mailboxes and found an envelope from Texas Commerce Bank in our box. A monthly statement and returned checks, written on our joint banking account, rendered to me an answer. I curiously studied each check to see what Seth was spending money on, and to see whether he had secretly retained his lawyer yet; and I discovered my husband had written his mother and his baby brother checks in the amounts of $330, $500, and another $500, totaling $1,330. On all three checks, the memo line was blank, and I suspected Seth was sliding money out of our account for a future, which did not include me. I would keep my discovery to myself and not let on to Seth that I knew he was secretly moving money out of our account. I then went back home, called our bank, and asked them to not send our checks directly to our house anymore, that I would personally pick up our returned checks from the bank each month. The bank agreed to my request.

The following months of April, May, and June, I discovered Seth had written his mother and brother more checks and bigger checks that totaled $5,000. I knew if I asked Seth about these banking transactions with his mother and baby brother, that he would lie and tell me the money he paid his family had to do with his mother's stock investments. I also considered Seth might be investing our money in the stock market just for his own gain while excluding my welfare.

I felt disturbed about Seth's secret life that continuously unfolded for my understanding each month. One day in the month of June, of 1993, I walked through the house and looked out the wall of windows in the kitchen. My husband was erecting a twelve-foot Roman column on a cement slab outside; and I instantly recalled the letter Seth wrote to Runi before Doren's birth, in which Seth described a dream trip he wanted to take down the Nile with his boyfriend. I figured Seth spent $1,000 to erect the phallic symbol of his love for the man in Springfield, Missouri.

I suddenly had a great idea to appease my angst that my needs did not matter to my partner! I would spend some of our money, too! I jumped into the shower and then dressed for the gym. I would go to the bank and withdraw enough cash to get myself a lifetime membership at *Bally's Total Fitness*, and I would not tell Seth about how I treated myself to luxury and self-indulgence until I got back home! I would get into the best shape of my life. I believed spending $1,200 to lift weights, and to do aerobics, at the nearby gym, in The Woodlands,

Texas, was a start. In addition, the expenditure would suffice, in lieu of a $1,200 semester at the University of Houston.

The following day, I was on the phone in the kitchen talking business when Seth walked in through the glass kitchen door and asked me who was on the phone.

"A contractor," I happily replied. "I want to update our stairwell, Seth." I turned my attention back to the man on the phone. "Okay, sir, I'll see you here tomorrow at noon." I set the phone down in the cradle and smiled at Seth. "What do you think? Are you up for some remodeling around here?"

"What is it you want to do again, Jean?"

"I want a bid, from a contractor, to replace that 1970's stair railing, and I want a glass block wall installed in its place that goes all the way up to the ceiling, and I want lights to shine through the glass."

"Cool," Seth responded while he looked into the den and envisioned my idea.

"I think our house needs some updating. I also want this island here in the kitchen removed and a bigger one built in its place. And I want a new stovetop, too. I want to be able to sit eight people around the island, so we need an overhang for laps. And we'll have to move this over-sized refrigerator back into the wall to create more space between its doors and the new island. A hole can be cut into the wall behind the refrigerator, and the refrigerator can be partially moved back into the utility room."

"That's a great idea," Seth added as he walked from the kitchen and into the utility room to study the adjoining wall.

"Yes, it is. The contractor will have to move the plumbing in the wall for the ice maker."

Seth nodded, "That will be costly."

"I want the Saltillo tile in the kitchen, too. We have Saltillo in the foyer and front sitting area, and I want the Saltillo installed in the kitchen and in the den, too. I want to get rid of the dyed carpet in the den. And when the contractor rebuilds the base of this island, we will have to replace this old linoleum anyway."

"That's true," Seth said while he stepped into the threshold of the kitchen and den and tried on my flooring idea. "Saltillo will be beautiful throughout the living areas."

"I think so. These renovations will increase the value of our home, too." I knew Seth was all about increasing the value of our real estate so that when a court ordered us to sell the marital property in the future, his share of the equity would be bigger. I also knew I could tie up our monthly income for months with a contractor steadily working on the house; and the costly renovations would not allow Seth to slide any more *free* money into his mother and baby brother's bank accounts because there would be no more free money. "So you agree we should make all these renovations?"

"Yeah, let's do it," he answered while not yet aware of how I would block him from saving for the day when he left me high and dry.

"Great! The construction mess will be worth every penny." I smiled while believing I would beat him at his own game. "I also have another plan, Seth."

"What's that?"

"I'm going back to school in a few weeks."

His expression instantly became soured, and his body language defensive, while I watched him fold his arms across his chest. "You just insist I have to watch these kids all day long, don't you?"

"Hold on, Seth. Don't get your panties in a bunch," I sarcastically whipped. "I'm going to take another creative writing class at Rice University."

His face instantly relaxed while I was aware these non-accredited classes did not threaten him in the least.

"I need a creative outlet. I've done all the wallpapering and painting around here that I'm going to do; the contractor can do the rest. I can't go shopping and do lunch another day with my boring sister--she's depressing me. All Holly talks about these days is her husband's affair."

Seth did not react to the sad information I leaked about his cheating brother-in-law, and I suspected Seth's lack of commentary on the subject meant he and Don were probably plotting their divorces together. I did not push for commentary from Seth and understood, more every day, the value of holding my cards close to my chest.

"So I have already enrolled into another writing class at Rice University. The next level is Novel Writing Level Two and the class is only three weeks long. I took Novel Writing Level One already over a year ago. Time flies when I'm having fun."

"A year already? Wow."

"I'll be gone Monday through Friday, every night from 6:30 p.m. to 9:00 p.m., but only for three weeks."

"Your previous writing class was in the mornings."

"Yep."

"Doesn't Rice offer a writing class in the mornings?"

"Nope, not this time. This is how we'll do our schedules. I'll watch the kids during the day while you landscape; and then, you watch them at night while I'm at school."

"I guess so," he grumbled while he acquiesced to another expense strictly about my desire.

"I'm going to write a book one day," I reminded him. I knew Seth would cause no fight, over me taking another non-accredited class that would not apply toward any bachelor's degree; and in addition, I knew Seth liked me gone in the evenings, so he could talk to his long-distance boyfriend in private.

"I wish you the best of success with that book, Jean."

"If we stay together, I may never write the book, Seth; but if you leave me, I will write a best seller."

Seth laughed. "Why would you not write a book if we are together?"

"Because," I answered, "the story I would write would be about us, and you would try to stop me."

"Why would I stop you?"

I snickered at his pretense. "Truth is hard to hear when you're wrong." He had blocked my success with the apparel business, with me getting a college degree, and he would block me in my next pursuit that threatened him.

The following month, after my three-week writing class ended, I enrolled my daughter into another summer camp at the exclusive Theatre Under the Stars' Humphrey School of Musical Theatre. I walked out of our home one early morning with my daughter, Bella, and her two brothers, Harper and Doren, at my side. Seth sat on the slider swing performing his early morning ritual of drinking fresh brewed coffee and smoking cigarettes when we exited the glass kitchen door.

"Where are you all going so early in the morning?" He cheerfully asked.

"We're going to Bella's song and dance class," I answered.

"Oh, I'm sorry, Seth; did you forget that I enrolled Bella into another song and dance camp at TUTS?"

"You never said a word," he quipped between drags.

"Oh, I thought I had. Well, I did; we did, enroll her, one more time," I nonchalantly explained while well aware that I had never intended to ask Seth if I could spend $355 for Bella's month-long camp. "Bella's going to be a star one day, and I want her to have the best training." I looked at my grinning daughter, "You deserve the best! Right, Bella?"

She nodded in agreement and flashed her crooked smile at us. Bella and I had shared a secret, since enrollment, that we would not tell Seth anything about her song and dance camp, until the morning of her first class, which would be way after the check cleared.

"Right, Mom!"

I turned to Seth. "We're going to have to take Bella to see an orthodontist soon, too. I watched Seth nod, as if contemplating the expenditure. "When we get home, I want you to show *our* daughter how to sing with her sheet music. Will you do that for us? Please?"

"I'd take delight in mentoring you in song, Bella. Do you know I once was a lead singer in a road band?"

"He was?" Bella looked to me to confirm his statement.

"Yep, a long time ago, when I first met him. I helped Seth pay for the ad, so that he could form a band." I looked at Seth, "That was the very first day that I met you. Interesting. I always encouraged your success, didn't I? I've been there for you."

"You were quite incredible back in those days."

"I still am incredible," I affirmed for my children's

understanding.

"Why did you quit being in a band, Seth?" Bella asked her stepfather.

I snickered while recalling Seth telling me the band fell apart over drugs, and over their lead singer not knowing his lyrics. "He'll tell you later, Bella; we've got to get, or we'll be late for your first class." I turned my attention back to Seth, "The boys and I will drop Bella off at school, and then we're going shopping. We will not be back until mid-afternoon. We're going to hang out in the city today."

"Have fun," he offered while we walked under the catwalk toward the garage. "We're trying. Oh, by the way, Seth, the contractor will be back over this morning to install the island's new counter top and stovetop. He's expecting you to write him a check today."

"Okay," Seth calmly responded.

Seth never questioned the money I spent, nor did he ever reconcile his checkbook to know how fast I could spend his money. The fact that I was picking up the returned checks each month from the bank had gone unnoticed by the irresponsible husband. I knew Seth not to care if he filed a tax return on time or not, and to throw his unopened mail from his employer into the corner of our garage. Seth kept an old chest-of-drawers, once used by our infant boys, in the corner of the garage; and there, on top, lay his unopened business correspondence, which had been mounting up since spring of 1992, over a year. The mail was now a two-foot high pile of letters, reports, and envelopes. Seth had installed a phone line in our garage, too; and this space was his office, where he supposedly managed his one and only account, the $25 million dollar employee pension fund for *Bike World*. This corner in the garage was also, where he managed his weekly stock market transactions that he made with his mother's $85,000. I was never privy to any telephone calls he made in the garage.

Seth bragged to all, that he was an important financial and operations principal, and General Securities principal, with Series 6, 63, and 7 licenses for *Inroad Investments and Securities* who paid him $100,000 a year. He threw in the fictitious Series 7 stockbroker's license for added impact. His company advised him that he could only sell investment company products until he took the broker's exam, but after having stopped all work efforts, after closing one deal, and "retiring," Seth saw no point in getting a Series 7 license. Any individual seeking to become a stockbroker must take the General Securities Representative Exam, commonly known as the Series 7 or Stockbroker Exam. The exam is a six-hour, 260 question exam, which covers a broad range of investments including stocks, bonds, options, limited partnerships, and investment company products such as open- and closed-end funds.

As the months passed, and he played the stock market with his mother's life savings, he then bragged about the hefty gains he made in the market, too. Seth found pride in titles like law school student, and investment broker; though, I prayed the *investment broker* title would last for a longer period than the three weeks Seth wore the title of law school student.

AUGUST 1993. My oldest and dearest friend whom I had known since the fifth grade was on the other side of the phone sharing with me her enthusiasm and glee over our recent reunion. I had not seen Sabrina in years and suddenly she popped into my life with a small child.

"Jacqueline is two now," she answered from somewhere unknown to me.

"Wow," I exclaimed. "I'm so glad you finally called me. I tried to call you years ago, but you had a disconnected number. I didn't know where you went. Now, suddenly, you're back in my life, and telling me that you have a two-year old! What a great day!"

"I'm sorry I disappeared. We have a lot of catching up to do."

"It's alright. My youngest is two years old, and Harper is four now. Harper was still in diapers when I had my last child. I had two babies at the same time--what a hand full!"

"The last time I saw you, you were pregnant with Harper."

"That's right, Brini," I confirmed. "It's been five years?"

"Too long. I'm thrilled I can now join your mommy club,

Jean Ellen. I want to meet your children."

"And I want to meet your daughter, Jacqueline. Our children are close in age; they'll have fun playing together. I'm delighted you finally had a child, Sabrina."

"Me, too! Jacqueline is the best thing that ever happened to me. She is a miracle child, too."

"How's that?"

"Well, you know, I had to have one of my fallopian tubes removed back in my early twenties before I married, and the doctor said then, that the chances of me getting pregnant had been cut in half."

I suspected Brini's emergency surgery stemmed from complications from one too many abortions. "You beat the odds, Brini! How does your old man feel about having another child?"

"Are you kidding? She's daddy's little girl. Goose didn't care if I got pregnant on our honeymoon or not, and neither did I; but, after eight years of marriage, I began to wonder if I could get pregnant at all. I desperately wanted a child around our fifth year of marriage, but no matter how hard we tried, I never got pregnant. I became depressed and very disillusioned over the thought of never having a child of my own."

"How long have you been married now?"

"Ten years."

"Whoa! It feels like yesterday when I stood up for you in your wedding. We were so young. I came to your wedding with Leonardo."

"I remember."

"Bella was three months old; she's ten years old now."

"Wow, ten years already."

"She's brunette with big brown eyes, very pretty. I have her in song and dance classes over there off Post Oak Boulevard. She's taking classes at Theatre Under the Stars' Humphrey School of Musical Theatre, or commonly known as TUTS. I'm grooming her to be a performer."

Sabrina laughed. "I remember when your mother took us when we were kids to see those Broadway musicals produced by

TUTS."

"I forgot you went with us, Brini."

"Yes, I did! How are Joseph and his father?"

"My son is enrolled into year-round baseball--that's how Todd keeps me from spending the summer months with him."

"That's not right."

"No, it's not, but Joseph seems to be very interested in baseball; and Todd and I would like to see him go all the way to the top. Therefore, I'm sacrificing my summer visitation. Maybe Joseph will get a baseball scholarship, play in college, and then play in the big leagues one day. I hope so."

"Did Todd ever remarry?"

"No, he's been dragging along this Italian girl for years. She is being a fool for the drunk. I've run into Todd in the past years, while out late at night at the bars on the lake, and I'll ask him who is staying with Joseph while he's out carousing, and he tells me his girlfriend is there at his apartment babysitting."

"So he's still got a drinking problem?"

"Every time I see him at the ball field, he's got a drink in his hand."

"My father was an alcoholic," Brini reminded. "Why don't you go back to court and get custody of Joseph?"

I hesitated to tell my old friend that my marriage was on the rocks. "I've thought about taking Todd back to court often, but Joseph seems happy. I don't want to upset that apple cart after ten years."

"And Bella? Tell me about her."

"She's a wonderful child. I enrolled her into a seminar called the *Landmark Forum for Young People*. After three days in the seminar, she turned her entire act around. It was just like flipping on a light switch. Her transformation amazed me. Before the seminar, Bella didn't care about her grades, or whether her room was neat, or about her appearance. I got weekly calls from her teachers. One teacher told me that she moved Bella into the hallway, and that my daughter didn't care that she was sitting out there by herself. The teacher did not know what to do with my obstinate child."

"Wow; what was going on at home?"

"Our home life has been hard on her, and until recently, we had grave money issues. Bella did this expensive three-day seminar in the fourth grade, a year ago, after we finally came into some money. She is now a neat freak and makes straight A's. She folds her socks and places them neatly in her drawer. She is recording herself on a tape recorder these days, singing Madonna tunes, and wants to be a professional singer."

"Is she talented?"

"It doesn't matter if she is talented or not at this age. I'm giving her an opportunity to get over her shyness, and to choose to take advantage of the opportunity to learn how to sing and dance. She has no choice in the matter over whether she stays in these classes or quits. I was shy as a child, and my parents pandered to my fear-based personality. Mom enrolled me into dance, and I moaned every time I went to class until she finally let me quit. I expect more from my children."

"You're a great mom, Jean; I've some learning to do from you. I was twenty-four when I married, and Goose was forty-one years old. I figured when I couldn't get pregnant after trying for eight years, if it wasn't me, then maybe Goose had slow swimming sperm."

"Well, obviously nothing was wrong with either one of you," I celebrated.

"I took an art class," she continued. "I got involved with Jack."

"Uh huh," I replied while stunned by her revelation. "So is Jacqueline named after Jack?"

"I didn't care how I got pregnant after trying for nearly eight years."

"Wow," I muttered. "Does Goose know?"

"He has no idea," my friend answered. "He's thrilled with his daughter, and relieved, too, that I finally had the child I desperately wanted for so many years."

"So now you have a love child, too," I said while referring to mine.

Sabrina snickered. "Jack was this tall, thin, blonde, sexy

artist."

"Is it over?" I asked.

"Way over; I ended the relationship when I told him I was pregnant. He disappeared; I think he moved to another country—or went to prison."

"Good riddance," I spouted while having no respect for any man who ran from his responsibility. "Usually girls look like their fathers," I added. "Bella looks like Mario. Does Jacqueline look like Jack?"

"Fortunately not, and I was a blonde tot. I have a picture of me at the age of two with long blonde hair. Jacqueline and I look a lot alike."

"I would love to meet your daughter, Sabrina. Too many years have passed. Why did we let that happen?"

"I don't know," she sadly answered.

I considered the reasons Sabrina may have moved away without letting me know. "The last time I saw you, Leonardo and I had just split up, and I introduced you to Seth. That was nearly five years ago."

"I remember," she said as if horrified. "You introduced me to your good looking neighbor; and then, I learn you've dumped your successful chemical engineering husband with a Ph.D. for a guy who doesn't have a job or car. And then you tell me that you're pregnant. I thought you had lost your mind, Jean."

"I never found my mind until recently, but hindsight is 20/20. I actually believed, at the time when I hooked up with Seth, that my apparel business would take off and make a lot of money. Seth was going to work with me in the apparel business, and it did not matter to me, that he did not have a job or car--we were on our way to success, or so I thought. Moreover, I couldn't move away from my son, either. Joseph was only six years old, and he lived next door to me at the apartment complex. I was already pregnant with Harper when I got the harsh reality of my life—that I was not going to make any money with my apparel business. I regret I hurt Leonardo, though, but I got what I deserved--Seth."

"I'm sorry to hear that you are not happy with Seth.

Leonardo should have never forced you to choose between him and Indiana, and your first-born child who lived next door to you."

"You're right, that was too tough of a decision for me to make, but nevertheless, I lied to Leonardo for too long, while in that two-year computer relationship. And in hindsight, I see differently, now that I've gotten to feel what it's like to be the receiver of great deception. I didn't love myself; much less could I truly love Leonardo back in those days. I still believe that Seth and I can get over whatever this is, that we're struggling with," I added while sure I was wrong.

"I remember him being intelligent," Sabrina prompted.

"I don't know anymore. When you came to my apartment that evening, Brini, nearly five years ago, little did I know then, just how hard my life would be for years to come? It's a long story."

"Are you okay?"

"Well," I hesitated. "I don't know."

"You don't know?"

"I'm okay," I spouted for the sake of simplicity. "Seth and I have a nice place here in The Woodlands. We bought a beautiful, two-story home in '91, paid cash; and I've had a contractor in here, for the last two months, costing us a lot of money." I wanted to take the emphasis off my failing marriage and not burden Sabrina with all my troubles—not yet anyway.

"I would love to come see you and Seth, and your children, and your new home. The Woodlands is very nice—I'm happy you have a nice home for yourself and the kids."

"Bring Jacqueline and come see us. Are you still living over there off Westheimer in Houston?"

"Oh, no, I wish. Goose moved his law practice to the Golden Triangle. He decided he would rather be a big fish in a small pond, than a small fish in a big pond. We're living in Port Neches."

"Where?"

"Outside Beaumont, Texas. It's home to Bubba and the pickup truck."

I chuckled. "Did you forget that I once worked in the refineries for years? I met Leonardo at the Shell refinery in Deer Park, Texas-yahoos everywhere. Todd worked at the same refinery."

"I remember, Jean. The cities of Port Neches and Groves merge, and these blue-collar towns are located in an area called the *Texas Coastal Prairie*. Port Neches is on the Neches River, and the city's biggest employers are refineries. I thought when I married the lawyer that I was going to be living in Houston for the rest of my life, adjacent to the fabulous River Oaks, shopping at the same boutiques, and living among Houston's crème de la crème; and then, five years into the marriage, and he moves me away from everything civilized."

"Culture shock, huh?"

"You and I grew up in southeast Houston, Jean. I didn't want more of the same, and that's what Port Neches feels like to me to this day. I became depressed after we relocated to Port Neches. I put on a huge amount of weight, and since the baby, I haven't shed a single pound, partly the reason for why I've been hiding."

"When I saw you, five years ago, Brini, you did not mention moving anywhere; and you were trim and gorgeous."

"No, I didn't say a word to you. I was really hoping that if I didn't speak Goose's plan aloud, that I would wake up from the nightmare and find myself still living in our beautiful Houston home, but we moved to Port Neches shortly after you and Seth got together; and I ate, and ate, and ate to repress my ill feelings about my new life. I didn't know anyone in Port Neches for years; nor did I want to. I was really angry about the move."

"When you came over to my apartment that night, Sabrina, and met Seth, you brought with you that guy from our old neighborhood. What were *you* doing with him?"

"Carl," Sabrina snickered.

"Yeah, Carl--Eddie's brother. And you told me that evening, that you were sleeping with Carl. I was worried about you. I remember you and I talked in private that evening in my bedroom. You were high as a kite and admitted to doing a lot of drugs, too. You seemed very unhappy."

"I did?"

"Yes."

"I grew up with those boys--Carl and Eddie are from the same side of the tracks. I was dealing with that upcoming move to

Port Neches, and not very well."

"How is Eddie these days?" I asked while recalling Sabrina had always been in love with Carl's brother, but had married the lawyer instead of the boy from our hood.

"Still acting like a loser. He never got his act together!" She spouted.

"The last time I saw Eddie was at your pool party at Goose's house, just before you got married ten years ago. Eddie was really hurt that night because you were marrying Goose."

Sabrina shrugged off the consideration. "Eh, well, Goose is a great guy. I told Eddie, 'You snooze, you lose.'"

I recalled my own connection to Sabrina's former live-in, Eddie. The tall and lanky free spirit from southeast Houston came over to my Shore Acres, Texas home, shortly after I split with my first husband, Todd. Eddie kept me company one night, just before we all showed up at Sabrina's fiancé's home for what Sabrina called her final bang before she walked the plank. Goose was away that weekend on his Catamaran, and Sabrina had invited every single male she knew in Houston over for a pool party--the same weekend I introduced Mario to his three-month-old little girl.

Eddie's need to get revenge was satisfied with my help. He had agreed to change a lock on my garage door, so I could keep Todd away from my new wardrobe, after having replaced the one he previously shredded; and in lieu of Eddie's good deed, I offered to cook Sabrina's ex-beaux dinner. Eddie installed a deadbolt; and we shared a meal, followed by alcoholic libations, and dancing to sultry music. We seduced each other that night and violated the principle of respect. I knew when Eddie came over that night, that he was out to hurt Sabrina, but the spirits moved me to a place of unconsciousness. I had crossed the line with my girlfriend; and no matter what my excuse, I did not want Sabrina to hear about my interlude with her ex-boyfriend, even if she was marrying Goose within the month.

After I sobered up the following morning, Eddie swore to me that he would keep our one-night fling a secret and not tell our mutual friend, but he broke his promise as I suspected he would when I sobered up. Weeks later, Sabrina called me and angrily spewed that I broke a taboo, that Eddie was sacred and forbidden fruit. I agreed. I told her that I was wrong to sleep with the man she loved, even if she was marrying another, and I told her that, in just those words. I believed Brini had finally forgiven me for sleeping with Eddie by calling me today.

I got off the phone that day with Sabrina and was thrilled my best friend and I had reconnected. My sons sat at a small table in the heart of the family room. Harper cut with his small scissors pictures of cars out of a hot rod magazine, and Doren scribbled in his coloring book. Bella was at her elementary school, and Seth had ventured off, on foot, down the bike trail behind our home, an hour earlier to collect moss.

A paved bike trail ran behind our lot, a pie-shaped wedge situated on a cul-de-sac and densely wooded with East Texas Piney Red Woods. The trail ran behind our property and continued for sixty-plus miles throughout The Woodlands; and frequently, Seth, and I, and our children, rolled the bicycles out of our detached garage and hit this trail for a few hours of fun and exercise. Doren and Seth each sat behind a parent in a child's bike seat, and Bella and Joseph rode hard their own bikes behind us. I looked out the wall of windows in the kitchen and appreciated my view of the piney forest. I had no grass or fence, and the natural setting was what made The Woodlands an exclusive community and a place I loved to call home.

I stepped into the family room and said, "Boys, I have to take you both to the doctor today for a checkup."

Seth walked in through the glass kitchen door, and I said to him, "I have doctor appointments for both the boys today. I'm concerned about Doren's chronic earaches, and Harper's language development seems stalled. Do you want to go with us?"

"No. I just picked up a barrel of moss, I want to plant it, and I'm expecting a call from my stockbroker this morning."

I shrugged off my ill feelings about his daily obsessions. "That's fine," I said while feeling irritated by what he chose to do with his life every day—collect moss and gamble his mother's life savings. "I'm going to my parents' house after the doctor appointments. We'll be home later this evening. Bella will be home at 3:20 this afternoon. Get her something to eat, please."

"Will do. Tell your father that I've turned Ma's $85,000 into an amount over a million dollars of gross proceeds."

"Is that really true, Seth?"

He grinned, "I'm buying on the margin. Hold on; I'll prove it to you!" He stepped out the glass kitchen door, and I watched him walk into the detached garage. Seconds later, he came back out of the garage and stepped back into the kitchen with a piece of paper in his hand. He obviously retrieved the document from his rat nest he kept in the corner of the garage.

"Why don't you just use the upstairs bedroom as your office again?" I asked.

He ignored my question and handed me the paper. "Here, see for yourself what your man can do!" He proudly instructed.

I took the document and read the letterhead. PaineWebber, Inc. in New York reported gross proceeds less commissions to be $1,084,574.69. Beneath this total amount was a breakdown of what stocks Seth had bought and sold over the last ten months and their net proceeds. "This seems like a lot of money you've made for your mother, but I don't understand what you mean when you say *you buy on the margin?*"

"I'm allowed to buy stocks by borrowing money from a broker. The margin is the gap between the market value of a security and the loan a broker makes."

"Margin sounds risky, Seth. Why don't you pull your mother's money out of the stock market today before you lose a dime? She's good where she's at, isn't she? Why take any more risks with her life savings. You've made her some money; get out while you're ahead."

He snickered and then, very dramatically, took on a thespian sound and posture. "The point is, dear lady, that greed, for a lack of a better word, is good." Seth stopped talking. "Perhaps you remember Gordon Gekko's words from the movie *Wall Street?*"

"I remember the movie."

"Gekko said, *'Greed is right, greed works. Greed clarifies, cuts through, and captures the essence of the evolutionary spirit. Greed, in all of its forms--greed for life, for money, for love, for knowledge, has marked the upward surge of mankind.'* And greed, you mark my words...will save my ass!" Seth tittered and then continued on a more serious note, "Leave me alone, Jean. You don't understand what I'm doing."

"I understand more than you think," I retorted while I watched him walk over to our cappuccino machine.

Seth continued to talk to me while he poured himself a cup of coffee, "Bud Fox says, *'Life all comes down to a few moments; this is one of them.'"*

"Why are you expounding on the philosophy of the movie's Wall Street traders? Your arrogance irritates me. This is not Hollywood, Seth! You're not a billionaire or millionaire. You will hit the bottom hard, if you continue to play this game; and when you do, you're going to take us all down with you!"

I watched him pour liquor from a bottle of Bailey's Irish Cream into his cup of coffee and then take a sip as if my words made no difference. He walked over to the glass kitchen door and said to me just before he exited, "You'll have reason to love me one day."

He walked out while his words reverberated in my head. He assumed I did not love him.

LATER THAT EVENING, I sat in my parents' small living room, in the same house we moved into when I was in the first grade. My father sat in his usual corner of the same thin-cushioned, and worn-out, streamlined couch that had been reupholstered a couple of times over the last thirty years. His oversized and dirty wooden ashtray, and pipe tobacco, sat on a 1970's modern-style end table; and a 1950's beige, ceramic fruit lamp, that my mother had inherited thirteen years earlier, when my maternal grandmother passed away, sat on top that table, too. I watched Dad strike a match and put the fire to his tobacco in the bowl. My mother described his pipe smoking as a filthy, lifetime habit. Once the sixty-year old, silver-haired man ignited the tobacco, he continued educating me about the stock market.

"His broker could make a margin call. And, if that happens,

Seth will have to deposit enough money into his margin account to bring it back to the margin limit, or to the minimum maintenance requirements. This usually happens after the value of the securities in the account falls below the limit."

"Seth told me that he's *buying on margin*. What does that mean?"

"A margin is the amount of collateral above 100% that a buyer deposits with a broker when borrowing money to buy securities. He could get notice from his broker to pay up, if he's purchased stock on margin, when his account balance drops below the minimum margin requirements due to falling stock prices."

"So let me sum up what you've said so far. In order for Seth to create a margin account, he had to deposit a minimum between $2,000 and $5,000?"

"Yeah, and that deposit is used as collateral against his trading activities," my father continued.

"That might explain why Seth was writing checks out of our account. I discovered he wrote checks to his mother and brother amounting to about six thousand dollars over the last several months. He did that behind my back."

"I don't know, Jean Ellen, what he's doing. It's hard to say with Seth. I have used margin debt to leverage my returns several times over the years, with successful results. He should have written checks to his broker, not to his mother and brother."

I nodded while still confused as to why Seth was secretively sliding our money over to his mother and teenage brother.

My father continued, "At no time did my margin debt exceed 25% of my net account equity. This is my personal comfort level, but that 25% also depends on my risk tolerance--my portfolio return versus the interest on my debt; and, as well, on my degree of bullishness about my investments, and on the general market conditions. If I am using margin, I have tighter stop-loss limits. I recommend Seth not use margin, unless he follows the market and his investments on a daily basis, and if he's well informed about the factors that could influence his asset value. And your husband should *never* use margin debt as a long-term investment strategy. Did he ever purchase a computer for his office?"

"No," I shook my head while considering the rat nest he called his office in the garage.

"I'm not so sure Seth is well-informed about the factors that could influence his asset value."

"I don't know how he's following the market, Dad, but he's got a broker in New York that he talks to every morning. Seth thinks he's Gordon Gekko."

"Who?"

"Gekko was a billionaire trader in the movie, *Wall Street*. Michael Douglas played Gordon Gekko."

My stoic father puffed on his pipe and looked at me as if I was crazy. "Seth should have a cash reserve outside of his brokerage account that exceeds his margin debt, so he can pay off the debt at any time, if necessary."

"Oh my God," I groaned. "He has no cash reserve. We live from pay period to pay period."

"You've told me that, Jean Ellen, but if Seth maintains the margin debt for more than a few weeks, he needs to contribute cash to his account on a monthly basis, so that he is paying off the debt the same way he would pay off a credit card."

I feared the worse and felt frustration. "I don't know what he's doing, Dad."

"I think your husband is taking too big of a risk with his mother's money."

"I agree," I said while feeling frustrated with the money game my husband played with his mother's life savings. "I'm going to find Mom and talk to her for a while. My hands are tied, Dad; Seth has the sense of a Billy Goat."

"She's back there watching her soap; she's not feeling well these days. I'm going to take myself outside and see what my grandkids are doing back there."

"They were enjoying that tire swing last time I took a look out the kitchen window, Dad. Uncle Henry was pushing them."

I walked down the hallway and toward my mother's bedroom. She was sitting up on her bed reading a book and watching her TV. "Hi, Mom."

"Well, Jean Ellen, I heard you up there talking to your father," she beamed.

"What are you doing?" I asked.

"Oh, I'm watching my old soap, *Guiding Light.*"

"I don't mean to disturb you; I'll sit quietly."

"Jump up here," she patted the bed. "The storyline isn't really holding my attention these days. Do you know I've been watching this soap since you kids were born? *Guiding Light* is the longest running soap; first broadcasted in 1937."

"I watched *All My Children* for a year after Joseph was born before I went back to work; now, my life is the soap."

My mother chuckled.

"Dad says you're not feeling well."

"I'm not doing well, Jean Ellen. I have another doctor's appointment later this week. I have Hepatitis C."

"What's that?"

"A liver disease."

"Oh no! How did you contract that disease?"

"Well, the best I can sum is when I had a blood transfusion after giving birth to your brother, Henry, I got some bad blood. That was thirty years ago."

"Have you had symptoms for thirty years?"

"No; I did not have any symptoms until recently. Only when my Hepatitis became acute, did I start feeling tired and having aching muscles and joints. Lately, I've had a poor appetite, nausea, and a low-grade fever, which is why I finally made a doctor's appointment."

"So what does this mean now?"

"The doctor said patients remain asymptomatic until decompensation occurs."

"I don't understand *decompensation*, Mom."

"My liver is not functioning normally anymore. I have toxins in my blood stream."

The impact of her words startled me, and I just stared at my dear mother speechless.

"Your father and I went to see a liver specialist last week, and the doctor ran tests. I have an abnormal protein count and an accumulation of bilirubin in my blood which is making me jaundice."

"Why?"

"I have Cirrhosis of the liver, and the cirrhosis is a late stage of Hepatitis C. The disease has been scarring my liver for thirty years. And as a result of this disease, fluid is collecting in my abdomen which is why I've suffered with this painful bloating for so long, and why my clothes don't fit anymore."

I shook my head in disbelief while I summed the worse for my mother. I continued to pry in hopes she would tell me something that would make me believe she was not terminal. "What can they do for you, Mom?"

"Nothing. There is no cure for this Hep-C. If a person drinks too much alcohol and develops cirrhosis of the liver, that person can stop the cirrhosis from getting worse by stopping the drinking, but this kind of cirrhosis is progressive."

"So you're telling me that you can't stop the disease?"

My mother nodded no. "The doctor says I have about five years of life left. All my organs are eventually going to shut down."

"Oh my God," I sputtered while my eyes welled up at her news. "Can't you get a liver transplant?"

"A new liver costs so much money," she sadly replied.

"So what! Dad has enough money to buy you two new livers."

"Maybe not," she said. "The cost of a liver transplant is between $100,000 and $400,000, depending on how long you spend in intensive care and what complications occur during surgery. I would be in and out of the hospital several times, as my body becomes accustomed to the new organ, and I would have to take medication to prevent my body from rejecting the new liver. Maintaining my new liver and health can also cost me tens or even hundreds of thousands of dollars over the decades."

"But if the liver transplant is successful, the new liver will begin filtering the toxins out of your bloodstream again, and you will be healthy. And not getting a transplant will also incur you major medical costs over the next five years!"

"I don't want to wipe out your father's hard-earned retirement. I could get a new liver, but my blood is still infected with Hep-C."

"Well, it took you thirty years for your liver to get into this non-functioning condition; another thirty years with a new liver is a lifetime."

My mother leaned over to hug me. "This is all brand new to me, Jean Ellen. Let's just see what I learn from this next doctor visit."

I wiped the tears off my face. "I love you. I don't want you to suffer."

"Me, either! The worse part about this situation with my health is the thought of leaving my children and grandchildren."

I related to her consideration, and the thought of leaving my four children behind, and not being around to watch them grow up, get married, and have their own children was distressing for me, too.

"Your sister calls your father every day crying on the phone. I don't understand how a man can create two children with his wife and then walk away from his responsibilities. Is there something more important than family? Holly is devastated by Don's infidelity, and that nasty man served her divorce papers on the same day she was to walk in cap and gown for her college graduation."

My anger spewed, "Don doesn't care about anybody, not even himself. I suspect he is jealous his wife went back to school and finished her degree; he was short a few credit hours when they got married because she was pregnant."

"That man ruined Holly's graduation day, and tore his family apart. He is a disgrace."

"She told me about being served divorce papers that morning of her graduation; I couldn't believe what I was hearing. I went to her graduation ceremony at the University of Houston and watched her walk. Graduation is a rite of passage, which marks the end of one stage of a person's life and the beginning of another--for most people it's not symbolic of a marriage ending. I never trusted Don. One day he's an alcoholic, out late at night, every week at the bars without her; the next stage, he dries up and is a Bible thumper; and now, he's leaving his family and marrying somebody else. He's a fake. I'm proud of Holly's accomplishment to get her bachelor's degree--he fought her all the way. At least now, she can take her political science degree and teach."

"Your father is so worried about Holly and his grandkids. Don is fighting her for custody of their two kids, too, and Holly is so upset. And now, your father is supporting her and her three children because Don has taken off and cut her off financially. Holly can't make the house payments anymore. Your father might have to buy her house off the auction block in the near future; and he's already paying for her new lawyer, and for an investigator that Holly says she needs. Your father doesn't want that bastard to take her kids away from her. He's really stressed over Holly's divorce and my illness; all of this stuff hit him at the same time."

I shook my head in disappointment while making note to self to not add any further stress to my mother or father's already over-burdened life. Doctors, a lawyer, and an investigator now forced a man, who held too tightly to his money all his life, to now pay out tens of thousands of dollars, if he wanted to keep his wife and grandchildren in the family. "It's not supposed to be like this," I sadly summed. "America morally declined when the U.S. Supreme Court removed prayer from our nation's schools, and the family structure was hit the hardest."

"I believe that is the truth, too, Jean Ellen. America's family, youth, education system, and national life all declined since 1962. The removal of prayer from our schools was a violation of the Third Commandment which commands us not to take the name of the Lord in vain."

"I don't understand, Mom; there is no mention of God's name whatsoever in the public schools."

"Worse than taking the Lord's sacred name in vain is treating the Lord's name with contempt, denying it rightful place, and stripping it from public use and even from the lips of children! And this nation is so glib, in the way everyone makes promises to each other when they marry, and then they don't perform, and these same people never realize their lack of integrity is sapping their moral energy. And, we're a nation rife with broken marriage covenants, but moral law never alters."

I nodded in agreement. "I can see now, while looking back, that I was glib about not honoring my marriage vows to Todd, even if he was, and still is, an alcoholic; and ever since I divorced him, my life has been a struggle. I still don't have it right."

"I know you don't, Jean Ellen. I wish you would get your degree, like your sister, so you can get a good paying job."

"I'm going back to school in September. I haven't told Seth yet, but I'm enrolling into the University of Houston again. If my sister can finish her degree, while married to a man like Don, then I can finish mine, too. I'm not going to let anybody, or anything, ever stop me again."

"Wonderful! You stand strong. I want to know my daughter and grandkids are okay when I leave this planet."

"We're going to be just fine," I assured the meek woman. I was not so sure how Seth would react when I enrolled into another semester at the University of Houston and promised to cut off his balls if he tried to sabotage my effort, but regardless of any contest, I would not give my precious mother any more reason to worry about me.

Bella and I walked out of her song and dance class, and down the hallway to exit the building. Her class recital was quickly approaching, and I seriously considered the next direction to take my little star. Maybe I would give her private vocal lessons after school.

As the two of us headed out of the building for the parking lot, I spotted, in big, bold, black letters, the word AUDITION on a poster in the hallway and halted. "Look Bella!" I pointed as I walked up closer to read, "Theatre Under the Stars is casting for the pre-Broadway World Premiere production of *Beauty and the Beast* to be performed at the Music Hall December 1993. Auditions July 24-25th at 6:00 p.m." I turned to Bella, "Wow! That would be fun to do. What do you think? Want to try out for a part in the play?"

She shrugged and showed no enthusiasm for the opportunity.

"An audition would be a stretch for you," I encouraged.

"I don't want to do any audition, Mom," she argued.

"Oh, Bella," I groaned in my disappointment at her quick response to say no. "I want you to audition. We'll pick out a song together for you to sing. We'll get the sheet music, and I'll call your music teacher at your elementary school, and see if she'll work with you after school. She can play the piano and accommodate you while you sing."

"I don't want to audition, Mom," she insisted.

"I want you to try, Bella. Your shyness is a choice, not a genetic dysfunction. I want you to go beyond the limits you have set for your life."

"I haven't set any limits!" The ten-year old retorted.

"Okay, then set some! Be extraordinary and be okay being in an uncomfortable place in life."

"I don't want to be uncomfortable," she argued.

"And for that reason is why you *will* do this audition. Do you know why you don't want to?"

"I just don't want to," she stubbornly answered and folded her arms across her chest.

"I know why you don't want to do this audition, Bella."

"Why?"

"Because you fear looking bad."

Bella considered my words without reply and rolled her eyes at me.

I continued, "You, trying something new, is you being fearless. And it is okay to fail, if you do fail, but you might not."

"I don't want to try!"

"You've been singing with your class, Bella. You're putting on another song and dance performance with them this weekend for a room full of parents. You don't have a problem with that?"

"So!"

"Well, singing as a soloist is uncomfortable for you because it's something you've never done before. You're in unfamiliar territory, but, sooner or later, you will have to sing as a soloist, if you want to be a singer when you grow up."

"I don't want to sing as a soloist!"

"Not acceptable, Bella! You told me that you wanted to be like Madonna."

"Maybe I don't, now." She grinned while aware of her personal conflict.

"I want you to audition just because you can. I want you to create a new way of being; I want you to be courageous. Can you choose to be courageous instead of shy?"

She grinned in spite of herself. "Okay!" She acquiesced.

"Great!" I smiled. "When you are brave enough to step out of your comfort zone, Bella, and try something new, then endless opportunities suddenly appear. You'll find the breath of life in a journey of faith. I was shy as a kid, and I let so many opportunities pass me by. I want more from you, Bella, than you hiding in the shadows as I did. Fear stems out of not having faith in God."

WEEKS LATER, I ran on the treadmill for one solid hour as I had been doing at Bally's Total Fitness gym for five days a week, and now for six straight weeks. I liked the woman I saw in the mirror at the gym, these days--no sign of ever having four children, or a weak mind. I toned my body, and I was in the best shape of my life, at thirty-four years old. What I discovered about myself, over the last six weeks, was that I had endless excuses for why I should not go to the gym, and with each reason that I substantiated good enough to blow off my commitment that day, I found strength in being my word, and went to the gym anyway. I did not take no for an answer. My commitment to be my word empowered me, and was a conscious and daily practice for a new way of being. I was being authentic and not a liar. I was learning I could trust me, inside of the struggle to consistently be my word, and I trusted me because I knew God loved me. I stopped losing sleep over what I had done in the past, and accepted the fact that God forgave me through the blood of Jesus Christ on that cross. More specifically, God forgave me the day I chose to walk in faith, renew my mind in the Word, and trust God had my back. I could walk with my head held high. I also stopped losing sleep over who Seth was for me and his children. I didn't have to trust Seth; I could trust God.

I reviewed the calorie counter on the treadmill dash and saw that I burned 650 calories in an hour. My lunch no longer mattered. I wiped the sweat off my brow and headed toward the locker room for a steam and shower. An hour later, I drove home feeling de-stressed and hoped to hear good news from a discouraged contractor that I had left hours earlier.

I pulled into my driveway, got out my car with my duffle bag; and as I entered through the glass kitchen door, I heard the phone, next to the door, ring. I picked up the receiver as I stepped inside. "Hello," I answered.

"Hello. This is Mrs. Sobieski, Bella's music teacher. I got your note, Ms. Zherneboh; and today after school, I gave your daughter a top hat and cane. I played her sheet music on the piano in my classroom, but she refused to dance or sing to '*Something There.*'"

"Oh, I'm disappointed to hear that, Mrs. Sobieski."

"She's really shy," the teacher continued. "I think she was about ready to cry. I didn't want to push her to tears."

"Oh boo hoo! My daughter won't fall apart if somebody pushes her to get out of her comfort zone. She chooses to be shy; and of all the choices she could make, this one is not acceptable."

"I didn't want to make the experience an unhappy one for your daughter."

"I appreciate your effort, Mrs. Sobieski. I'll talk to Bella tonight. Maybe she will cooperate for you tomorrow."

"I'll be happy to try again, if she's ready."

"I appreciate you calling, and I'll let you know if Bella is willing to try again."

"Thank you, Ms. Zherneboh, and good luck with your daughter."

"Thank you," I said while I hung up the phone and saw the contractor packing up the last of his tools in the kitchen.

"I'm done here for now," the tall and lean man in his early forties said to me. "I spent too many hours trying to weld that damn pipe in the slab," he said with great frustration. "I had to cut the water pipe to your ice maker down so I could slide the refrigerator over that pipe, and I couldn't stop the leak. I'm going to have to charge more for that job. I had to weld and re-weld for about four hours today. I finally managed to get a good weld on that pipe, but it took me all damn day." He grumbled.

"No problem," I answered. "I feel your pain."

"Your water dispenser should be working fine now," he answered. "I'll see you tomorrow morning. You can pay me the balance of $2,500 tomorrow."

"I'll give you the cash tomorrow. Thank you for all your hard work; see you in the morning." I said to the carpenter who walked out the glass kitchen door.

I watched Seth, through the glass kitchen door, walk up to our contractor, greet him and speak, and then enter the kitchen.

"Well, well, well, it looks like we're getting close to completion," the man covered in dirt said to me, while he took a cup out of the cabinet and filled it up from the water dispenser on the front of the refrigerator door.

"I have to order the Saltillo tile this week."

"I've ordered a truck load of pebble from The Rock Store. They'll be dumping a ton of the stuff in the driveway tomorrow."

"Okay. What are you doing with those pebbles?"

"I'm laying pebble down between the pebble stepping stones."

"Oh, that will be pretty, but I thought you planted moss around the stepping stones?"

"I did on the backside of the house, but on the side over here by the kitchen door, I'm spreading out pebbles where all that dirty bark lies."

I nodded while I looked out the glass kitchen door and pictured what he schemed. "I need your help, Seth. You're the professional singer. I want you to help me get Bella past her shyness."

"Lead by example, huh?"

"Exactly! Bella's dealing with being shy; and all of life is going to pass her by, if she stays on this boring track. I gave her sheet music to a song I want her to do for the audition; so please sing with her *that* song."

"I'd be happy to. Where is she?"

"I don't know; I'll find her," I said just as Bella descended the stairs.

"Bella, bring Seth and me your sheet music; we're going to coach you, and bring your top hat and cane, too."

"Oh, Mom," she groaned before going back upstairs to retrieve what I requested.

I looked at Seth, "Her piano teacher tried to work with her today after school, but she refused to participate."

Seth and I stepped into the front living area where I had hung wallpaper of a print called Giverny Gardens by the Impressionist Claude Monet. The print was in hues of gold, pinks, greens, blues, and turquoise and hung on two of the three walls. I painted the other wall gold to match the gold in the Saltillo tile. Two gold tufted velveteen swivel chairs with skirts sat on the wall that separated this front room from the kitchen; and an over-stuffed sofa in a tan and floral island print sat in front of four, narrow, floor-to-ceiling windows that looked out to the front yard gardens. A large upright piano I had painted glossy white sat on the third wall that separated this room from our large family room, and Seth's acoustic guitar stood on the floor in a guitar stand next to the piano. I called this room our music room--a place where I would play my own piano compositions for hours. I never learned to read sheet music fast.

Bella descended the stairs with her papers and accessories and joined us. "I don't know if I want to be a singer anymore, Mom," she huffed.

"Put it to rest, Bella!" I refuted, "Until you know for sure what you want to do with your life, you are going to conquer your fears about singing to other people and sing! Are you going to throw away this opportunity to be a singer and have fun?"

Bella shrugged while unwilling to commit.

"If you throw away years of song and dance classes, then what will you do? Do you want to work for McDonalds for the rest of your life?"

Bella considered her options. "No, I don't," the ten-year old whined.

"Okay, then please give Seth and me a copy of your sheet

music so you won't have to flip burgers for minimum wage."

Bella did as I instructed and handed her parents each a copy of her sheet music.

"Just be brave, Bella," I coached as I reviewed the words on the paper. "You know this song, *Something There*; you've watched Disney's *Beauty and the Beast* for years."

"I'll be the beast," Seth proudly informed us.

"How appropriate!" I retorted just as Bella bravely belted out the first stanza as if she were jumping into a deep pool while knowing she could not swim.

Bella sang Belle's part to me: "♫*There's something sweet and almost kind, but he was mean,*" Bella looked directly at Seth and then continued to sing to me: "*And he was course, and unrefined, and now he's dear, and so I'm sure, I wonder why I didn't see it there before.*♫"

Then Seth sang the Beast's words to me: "♫*She glanced this way, I thought I saw. And when we touched, she didn't shudder at my paw. No it can't be, I'll just ignore, but then, she's never looked at me that way before.*♫"

Seth picked up the guitar and began strumming while Bella and I then sang together: ♫*New and a bit alarming, who'd have ever thought that this could be true, that he's no prince charming, but there's something in him that I simply didn't see.*♫"

Then I sang the part of Lumiere to my daughter: "♫*Well who'd have thought.*♫"

Bella continued with her part: "♫*Well bless my soul.*♫"

And I picked up: "♫*Well who'd have known.*♫"

Bella continued: "♫*Well who indeed.*♫"

Then I sang to Seth: "♫*And who'd have guessed they'd come together on their own.*♫"

And then Bella sang to Seth: "♫*It's so peculiar.*♫"

Bella and I sang to each other: "♫*We'll wait and see a few days more. There may be something there that wasn't there before.*♫"

I sang to Seth: "♫*Well perhaps there's something there that wasn't there before.*♫"

Bella sang to her step-dad: "♫*There may be something there that wasn't there before.*♫"

We laughed at the end of our Broadway number. Bella grinned while seemingly proud of her accomplishment to sing before us, and I smiled, and along with Seth, we applauded her efforts. "See, you have it in you!" I confirmed for my daughter while I considered the words of that particular song. Perhaps there was more to Seth than we could see? Perhaps he really felt like an undeserving beast in our eyes?

"I still don't like to sing for strangers!" My daughter insisted.

"Bella," Seth added. "You have a beautiful voice, believe in yourself."

I looked at Seth and nodded in approval. "I agree, too. I believe everyone in the world would like to hear you sing, Bella!"

I turned toward Seth, "Perhaps you can do the audition with her?"

"I would love to!" Seth quickly agreed. "What do you think, Bella?"

"Not with you! I'm not doing the audition with him, Mama!" She declared, and then took her hat and cane and ran upstairs.

Seth looked at me in confusion.

I shrugged with no further answer. "I can lead a horse to water, but I can't make the horse drink."

"You're a good mother, Jean."

"I keep hearing that. Sabrina told me that recently, too, but I feel the job I do is not good enough." I knew the constant fighting between Seth and me was tearing at my children's well-being.

JULY 1993. Sabrina and I sat in folding chairs in the front row of a Houston hotel ballroom and listened to the seminar leader along with one hundred other attendees. "I want to welcome all of you to the Landmark Education Self-Expression and Leadership Seminar," the thirtyish male in crisp office attire said to the room of one hundred. "This seminar will take place once a week over the next three-months and will provide you, the participants, with the tools to create an environment outside the personal and conceptual, in which you expand your natural capacity for leadership, and communicate in a way that elicits the alignment, cooperation, and partnership of others."

Sabrina whispered, "This stuff is right up my alley. I have a degree in communications."

"You have a BS in BS," I whispered while referring to her Bachelor of Science in Communications.

"Genius is the ability to produce fantastic amounts of equally fantastic bullshit that all makes perfect sense."

I giggled, "You must have learned that BS from your lawyer husband."

"No!" She defended while I knew well that my dearest friend, since the fifth grade, had the art of bullshit down way before she finished her degree while married to Goose.

The seminar leader continued, "Informative, or additive learning, increases *what people know*, adds to their skills, and extends *already established capabilities* by bringing new knowledge to an existing worldview. By comparison, transformative learning gives people a basic structure in which people know, think, and act in the world. Participants find themselves *able to think and act beyond existing views and limits* in their personal and professional lives, and their wider communities. This shift of awareness is the most powerful attribute of our technology. Now that all of you have completed the Landmark Forum, we continue our inquiry about what is possible. Many people have methods for producing outstanding results; and at the same time, people recognize that there are certain realistic limits to what seems possible. We have an opportunity to go beyond those limits, and to have breakthroughs, and achievements, that are extraordinary and outside the limits of what is already predictable, attainable, or known."

Sabrina and I sat in those folding chairs for three hours, that night, with a short break; and at no time during that evenings' discussion, were we anything, but glued to our chairs in complete fascination.

We left the seminar about 10:00 p.m. and headed toward a nearby watering hole in the city. Sabrina had driven over from Port Neches, Texas, earlier that day, a two-hour and ten-minute drive from her house to mine. Seth had agreed to watch Sabrina's two-year old daughter, Jacqueline, along with our two sons, Harper and Doren, on this Monday night, and every Monday night for the next three months.

I confided in Bella that I worried Seth would get too involved in his yard and forget about the three toddlers, and my daughter assured me that she would watch the three youngsters closely while Sabrina and I were gone for the evening. I agreed to give her payment for services rendered. I still suspected Seth used hard drugs, but other than him being an insecure person demonstrating a contradictory personality with a need to control my life, I had no current hard evidence to prove my suspicions that he was in the yard 24/7 landscaping *and tripping.* Not since I had found the crack pipe in my van after Seth had picked up Runi from the airport three years earlier, had Seth been careless. I knew Seth to pour liquor into his morning coffee cup and to smoke weed every chance he had with his current friends, but I could not prove what substance made him fear getting out of the yard for the past two years. Maybe it was the marijuana.

We girls pulled into the front of Jimmie's Ice House in The Heights, located in northwest central Houston. I threw my green Volvo station wagon into park, and Sabrina and I both pulled down the visor mirrors and freshened up our lipstick before meeting our new friends.

"This is a gem of a dive bar," Sabrina informed me in her thick, east Texas, southern drawl, while she looked out at a dimly lit parking lot covered in oyster shells and at a gray shack in the rear. "I bet the beer is cheap."

I took in her perspective. "Let's be honest, this place is kind of a dump, but in an awesome way."

"I bet the bathroom is a bit scary," Sabrina rattled.

"Let's go get us a couple of Coronas; and then, we'll find out," I snapped as I threw my lipstick back into my purse.

"I hear ya, sista!" She smiled while flipping up the visor. "It's great to be back in Houston and be hanging with you again."

"It's great to have you back in my life! Let's go celebrate," I said while we simultaneously jumped out of my car.

We walked across the oyster shells and spotted a pack of familiar faces both sitting and standing around an old picnic table on the patio beside the gray shack.

"Hey Brini, Jean," Cullen called from across the way.

"Hey, Cullen!" We both yelled while we waved back and ventured over in their direction.

Brini greeted the smiling redheaded Cullen with a hug.

I was more conservative than Brini with men I barely knew and walked up to a very tall and lanky blonde male standing beside Cullen. I politely greeted the familiar face while Brini hugged the red head. "How's the beer, Fred?" I asked our fellow seminar student.

"Cold," the smiling blonde answered.

Brini interrupted us, "I'm going up to the bar and getting us a couple of cold ones. Would you like another one, Fred?" She asked the tall blonde.

"I just got one, Sabrina. Thank you anyway," he answered.

"Alright then," Brini said before walking away.

"Thanks, Brini," I yelled as she walked away. I sat down on top of the picnic table, placed my feet on the bench, and faced Fred who stood next to me.

Brini turned and winked at me as she made her way to the bar.

I wore long shorts and pulled them down toward my knees for modesty sake after sitting down. The evidence of abuse startled me; until just then, the battle scares remained obscure to me. I glanced at the three people who sat around the table to see if they were looking at the bruises on my shins. No one seemed to pay attention to my legs, which were within their sphere of notice. I diverted my concern while thankful it was dark outside.

I looked back up at the tall, thin male whom I had initially spoken to that evening in the lobby of the building where our weekly seminar occurred. Fred appeared intelligent, looked like a writer or software engineer in his forties, and he wore no marriage band.

"So where are your children tonight?" Fred asked me.

"My husband is at home with them. He's got Sabrina's child, too."

"Oh, you're married; I didn't see a ring."

"Yeah, I am. I lost my ring," I lied while remembering I threw my gold band into the woods behind our Woodland's home after our miserable honeymoon in Mexico.

"Are you a new Landmarkian?"

I snickered at the title he gave us alleged cult worshippers. "No, I did this work in the 80's. Fortunately for me, Brini sucked me back into the seminars."

"I did the Forum in the 80's, too," he nodded with a smile.

"Have you been actively involved in these seminars ever since?" I asked while noticing a twenty-something year old blonde female sitting nearby my feet and looking up at Fred and me. The pretty woman had a kind face with white straight teeth and soft twinkling blue eyes.

"No, I just got involved again this year," Fred answered.

"I see," I said to the 6'5" man with thinning wispy blonde hair. I turned to the smiling face looking up at me and who sat at my feet and waited for an introduction. "Hi, I'm Jean Wynn."

"Hi!" She beamed. The young woman had twinkling blue-eyes and a short blonde bob, and appeared to be slightly larger than average build. "I'm Linda Sherrill. Do you know, Theo?" She asked me while pointing to the woman sitting beside her.

"No, I don't, but I saw you both at the seminar tonight," I said while I extended my hand to the other woman with long red hair. "Hi, Theo; I'm Jean. I enjoyed listening to you tonight talk to our seminar leader about your relationship with your father. I could relate. I think all my relationship issues stemmed out of my dysfunctional relationship with my father, too."

Theo nodded with a smile, "Thank you. And speaking of dysfunctional, this dork here is my boyfriend."

"Hey!" the man objected to his girlfriend's remark with a grin while he extended his hand to me. "I'm Dysfunctional Dan."

"I'm kidding, baby," the red head said to her boyfriend.

I chuckled and said hello to Dan who wore a full black beard and looked like a young scientist or professor. "I'm Jean."

Sabrina came up and handed me a cold beer.

"Thank you," I said to my sidekick.

"You're welcome!"

"Nice to make your acquaintance, Jean," Dan replied just as I was about to take a swig.

"Yours, too. This is my oldest friend, Sabrina," I said to Linda, Theo, and Dan. "Sabrina and I go way back to the fifth grade." The same group found our longevity amazing and introduced themselves to Sabrina.

Cullen stood next to Fred; and they bantered with a third entry, a very sexy, middle-age male from the seminar group, whom I wanted to talk with some more. I got off the table, walked over to him, and got the intriguing man's attention with a smile.

"Hi, Jean." He returned the smile.

"Hi, Chris."

"I see you two already know each other," Cullen said to the two of us, who stood on both sides of him and grinned at each other.

I turned my attention to Cullen and Fred and filled in the missing pieces. "By the luck of the draw, I was sitting beside Chris tonight; and as a result, we are now phone partners for the next twelve weeks." I was drawn to the well-built man with a defined chest and muscular arms, soft blue eyes, and lots of curly, sandy brown hair; and as for me having sat beside Chris that night, in the seminar, that move had been intentional on my part when I selected my seat.

"Lucky you," Cullen teased Chris.

"Yeah, lucky me," he murmured while he grinned at me.

I thought the same of the man with the bronzed and rugged face. "I guess we're going to get to know each other pretty well by the time this seminar is over," I said to my phone partner.

"No doubt," Chris nodded.

The seminar leader assigned everyone, in the one-hundred-plus member group, a phone buddy, that first night of the ten weeks of sessions. We were to confide in our partner, and to open up with the stranger, once a week on the phone, until the end of the seminar. I was to share with my phone buddy, and tell him how the seminar was going for me, and how the seminar was affecting my life; and he was to do the same with me.

"Isn't your phone buddy, Sabrina?" Chris asked the chubby red head.

I looked over at Sabrina, but she was enthralled in a conversation with Theo and Dan.

"Yeah," Cullen answered while beaming like a schoolboy with a crush.

Chris chuckled, "Down boy, she's married."

"I know that!" The Irish man cried as if upset by that fact.

Chris, Cullen, and I laughed while we watched Sabrina interact with other fellow seminarians.

I concluded, that although Brini had piled on one-hundred-plus extra pounds, since her lawyer husband had moved her to a poor, blue-collar, refinery town, ten years earlier, and since she had given birth to her first and only child, two years earlier, she still had that Queen Bee attitude, believing she reigned over all females in any social setting. I liked her confidence she projected in spite of her obesity. I personally always withdrew from social settings, when I gained ten pounds past my ideal weight, because I felt unattractive; and periodically, over the decades, I did stop socializing, until I lost the extra pounds that made me feel less than perfect. Sometimes, I went into hibernation, for a month, or two, and would not come out of hiding until I had run off the ugly. My self-image revolved around me maintaining a svelte figure.

A few beers and an hour later, Brini and I found ourselves drowning in seminar lingo with the group of eight. "I find it very freeing," I said, "to understand there is a big difference between what actually happened in a person's life, and the meaning or the interpretation they made up about what happened."

"It works for me," Sabrina added. "I've realized how much drama I've kept attached to my childhood experiences. Our leader concluded the very first seminar with the fact that life is empty and meaningless, and it's empty and meaningless that it's empty and meaningless. That statement upset me for about five minutes, until I realized that the meaning I had attached to my earlier experiences really sucked. I find it liberating to realize I created the meaning I attached to those early-on experiences; and I can toss that crap out the window now, re-create my life, and attach an interpretation to my current life experience that empowers me. I made up this whole story that supported me being a fat girl," Sabrina admitted to the table of listeners. "I'm committed to being thin from now on." She held up her beer, "Here's to being a thin and beautiful woman!"

The crowd raised their beer bottles up in the air and cheered on Sabrina's commitment to lose one hundred pounds.

I chuckled. "Here's to being free from being a meaning-making machine."

The crowd cheered, and Linda added, "Here's to being free to be!"

Fred chuckled. "I had to laugh when the seminar leader said that the only difference between us, and the nutcase who walks on the streets downtown talking to himself, is that the nutcase just says out loud what he's thinking."

"The nutcase is not worried about how he looks!" Theo reminded us.

"He's free to be and we *normal* people call him crazy," Dan added for our consideration.

Linda jumped into the conversation. "I have for too long pursued a *someday* satisfaction, but I'm committed to having a breakthrough in my love life *now!*"

"Who are you involved with?" Theo asked Linda.

"No one yet," Linda giggled.

Cullen teased, "I'll volunteer to help you with that breakthrough, Linda!"

Linda chuckled and looked at Sabrina and me for an answer.

"Why not?" Sabrina replied. "You're young, free, and single. He's cute."

"And everyone needs a coach to do anything better," I added.

"I set myself up for that one!" Linda retorted and then turned to Cullen, "Okay, I surrender to the possibility."

We chuckled.

Chris nudged the redheaded Irish Man, "Wow, that's more than you had two minutes ago."

"I'm in!" Cullen teased and appeared delighted with the opportunity.

The crowd chuckled again.

"You two girls are lucky you're both married!" Linda quipped.

I looked at Sabrina, and she smiled back at me while I noted how quick perfect strangers were to judge.

The banter and the night wore thin, and the crowd dissipated around midnight.

I had been perched up on top of that picnic table the entire night for the most part; and now, I was talking to Sabrina alone who sat on the bench at my feet. I noticed my oldest friend staring at my legs and looked down to see what she saw. She was looking at the blue and green bruises on my shins before her eyes met mine in question.

"I've wanted to ask you all night, is that Seth's doing?"

"No, no," I thwarted, "these bruises are from all the house construction. I've been down on my knees." *In prayer* was the complete truth.

"Looks like to me you've been *hammered* alright," she angrily shot back and gave me another opportunity to be truthful.

I knew Sabrina's looks, and she knew better. I flatly refused to talk and changed the subject. "There is the contention that Landmark is a cult. Did you see when *60 Minutes* featured Landmark as a cult?"

"No!" Sabrina angrily snapped while now bothered by me lying about my war injuries.

"Yeah, two years ago, in '91, I saw the show on TV. My brother Henry couldn't call me fast enough that night to tell me that *60 Minutes* was alleging Landmark to be a cult."

"That's total insanity; no such thing!"

"I know; it's crazy—but he does not approve of anything, but the teachings of the Catholic church. It's always been my pet peeve when people, who haven't read the book or done the seminar, make a judgment about it. For instance, I read the controversial L. Ron Hubbard's *Dianetics*, too; and since, I've run into more people who condemn *that* book, and when I ask them if they've read the book, they *always* say no! I have!"

"The world is full of people who judge what they do not know the first thing about," Sabrina huffed.

"I told my brother that the seminars I attended were just

simple, common sense courses delivered in an environment of startling integrity. Where do you find that sort of thing in today's world?" I asked Sabrina.

"Nowhere!" Sabrina adamantly defended. "Tell your brother that this technology is simply good techniques of self-evaluation with an emphasis on action and on being a cause in the matter!"

"I've never heard anyone in the program mention God," I continued, "or call the Landmark Education Corporation a church or a religion; but yet, this program drew me closer to understanding more clearly what I read in the Bible over the years about the carnal man. I've never had any priest or minister cut through the crap like this group did for me regarding understanding our ways before we are born again in the spirit of Jesus Christ. I don't know why people call Landmark a cult, but I know there are people in the world who tell lies for all kinds of reasons, and maybe these liars just can't accept that life can be free of burden? Maybe they've never read the Bible, either?"

"Egos resist change." Sabrina supplied.

"We've learned how not to live in the ego through these seminars, but we're not the majority."

"Exactly!" Sabrina agreed. "I guess if this expectation doesn't work for someone who's done these seminars, then it's possible that person might have a need to condemn the course. My Christianity was not any less diminished when I was empowered in a three-day seminar to be anything I want to be!"

"I believe it's possible that some of these attendees have defamed this group because they cannot handle making commitments and keeping them. They do not recognize that integrity is the pathway to trust. But, for whatever reason, these people might have for not wanting to experience a transformation, they refuse to collapse their old worldview and stubbornly hang on to their miserable lives because they love to wallow in their crap, thus the reason they condemn that which makes them uncomfortable."

Brainwashing is a scary process," Sabrina sarcastically quipped.

I knew Sabrina to have a problem with obeying God's Ten Commandments; we were both sinners. She was unfaithful to her husband for starters. "We all have racquets;" I continued, "and some don't want to give up their act for solid reason! But we all need to be scrubbed and re-programmed."

"I agree," my friend said. "These seminars are about love--loving ourselves and one another."

"But" I added, "We can't love others when we're emotionally dysfunctional, and anyone operating out of ego is emotionally dysfunctional. We have to change our thinking if we want to change our lives. I have hope in something greater than me and my ego."

"Oh pooh!" Sabrina extorted. "Getting caught up in *hope* is contradictory to having personal power!"

"How much personal power do I really have without God or without His Word?"

"How great is your belief in self?" Sabrina questioned.

"Not very," I sadly admitted. "I've made a life of bad choices because I did not adhere to God's rule book, and I did not adhere to God's Word because I had no reverence for a greater authority over my life. I have bruises on my legs now because I did not have God's blessings in my life when I found Seth. I was not living the plan God had in store for my life."

"Oh pooh, again! You have bruises on your legs because your husband is a creep!" She angrily corrected.

"Exactly, and Seth was *my* choice, not God's choice for my life! Had I lived a life according to God's Word, I would have never married Seth and bred with a monster."

Sabrina's anger surfaced over my admission. "You're in a bad place, Jean Ellen."

"On the surface it may look like that to you, but I have *hope*."

Sabrina rolled her eyes at my use of the word *hope* again.

"Okay, let me replace the word *hope* with faith. I have faith in a supreme being—I have faith in God the Father and in his Son, Jesus Christ. I don't *hope* God answers prayers; I *know* God answers my prayers. I have a supernatural power on my side that goes beyond the limits of my human thinking or ability, and prayer is my first choice to do the will of God. I don't *hope* there will be a better tomorrow; I *know* there will be a better tomorrow. I don't *hope* God delivers me from impossible situations; I *know* he will deliver me from impossible situations. Jesus told us to have courage, and to be strong, for our Father is with us. Nothing is impossible for those who believe in Jesus Christ and our heavenly Father. Jesus said, 'I am the way and the truth.'" I took a breath and wondered if my preaching turned off Sabrina. "God's Word gives me hope, no matter the circumstances. And my happiness is not contingent upon the circumstances in my life. There lies the difference between me knowing God, and me considering myself a god who creates my own life. I don't agree life is meaningless and empty. I believe God put the meaning and the purpose in our life, when he sent his son, Jesus, to this world. I personally connect to Jesus. Jesus said, 'I am the joy, a joy the world didn't give, and a joy the world cannot take away.'"

"Thank you for those words," she kindly replied. "I've drifted away from my childhood teachings, Jean Ellen."

"I did, too, and that's a good thing. I'm going back home, but to my heavenly father's home." I smiled.

"Amen."

"And speaking of going home, let's go, Sabrina," I said as I got up from the picnic table. "You're welcome to stay at my house as long as you want. Stay all week."

"Thank you. I have to leave in the morning. Goose has a dinner tomorrow night, and he wants me to go with him, but I'll be back in a week for the next seminar. I'll stay overnight with yall, every night we do this seminar."

"I'm really going to enjoy you coming over here every week for the next ten weeks, Brini."

"Me, too."

LATE AUGUST 1993. "We'll be two houses down, if there is any emergency, come knock on the door, Bella," I said as we stepped outside into the dark and onto our front porch.

Seth and I walked toward the corner house of our cul-de-sac with expectations to have dinner with a neighbor we barely knew and her guests. My husband wore crisp tan slacks and a short-sleeve dark dress shirt along with brown leather loafers and belt. He had his stylish and well-manicured five o'clock shadow going which accentuated his dark, good looks and green eyes. I wore a fuchsia, orange, red, turquoise blue, and yellow floral knee-length sundress cinched in by a black leather belt with a rainbow-colored rhinestone peace sign buckle--my favorite outfit. My long chestnut brown hair flowed past my shoulders and I stood 5'9" in summer black flats. We knocked on the front door, and our hostess greeted us with a smile.

"Hey Jillian, we journeyed far;" Seth dramatized, "do you think we could partake of some wine and bread?"

We chuckled, and our hostess replied, "It would be my pleasure! Come in Seth, Jean."

"How are you, Jillian?" I asked the neighbor I barely knew as I stepped inside the threshold.

"Wonderful! I want you both to meet someone." She walked across the room and brought over to us a stocky man with silver hair. "This is my father, Bill Sherrill, who has just moved here from Washington D.C. He came back home."

I warmly smiled at a 5'7" distinguished and friendly gentleman in his sixties.

"Mr. Sherrill," Seth repeated with a nod.

"Nice to make your acquaintance; you may call me Bill," he said to us while he shook Seth's hand first.

"It's a pleasure to meet you, sir. I'm Seth Zherneboh, and this is my wife, Jean."

I shook the hand of Jillian's father. "It's nice to meet you, too, Bill."

"May I say you're a very beautiful woman, Jean?"

I smiled, "Thank you."

"Excuse me, but I have to check on something in the oven," his daughter advised and then scampered off.

"May I get you two a drink?" he asked while leading us to the bar.

"Of course," Seth confirmed.

"Red is good for me," I said while I looked at an assortment of wine bottles on top of the bar.

"I'll have the same," Seth confirmed.

"Is pinot noir good for you?"

Seth and I both agreed, and the man poured our drinks into stems while I scanned the room. I recognized everyone--they all lived in the cul-de-sac, and we all knew each other.

"So Bill, are you retired?" Seth asked.

"For now!" he boasted. "I was the Governor of the U.S. Federal Reserve Board when I retired."

"Impressive," Seth added while I agreed.

"I imagine you have some stories?" I prompted.

He chuckled, "A lifetime of stories. I also served in the US Marine Corp in World War II."

"Wow," Seth said while not taking over the conversation.

"I'm doing lectures now that I'm officially retired, conducting seminars to educate those interested in the workings of the FDIC."

"What do you lecture about?" Seth asked.

"I update anyone interested on organizational changes and teach negotiation and critical thinking strategies related to the Federal Deposit Insurance Corporation's mission. I assist with planning and development and implementation of outreach activities," he said while he handed a glass of wine to me.

"Thank you," I murmured.

"Sounds like law school," Seth replied while taking his glass from the host's father. I said thank you as I reached for my drink.

"You're both welcome," Bill said. "And yes, Seth, it does sound like law school. All of what I was once involved with was very legalistic."

"I attended South Texas College of Law," Seth pointed out. "And you sound like a professor of jurisprudence."

Bill chuckled, "I didn't go to law school. I got an MBA from Harvard."

"Very impressive," Seth nodded in approval. And where did you get your undergrad?"

"University of Houston. Houston is my hometown."

"What kind of law do you practice?" Bill asked Seth.

"Oh, well, I'm dealing with securities now. I did a year of law school and figured out I could make just as much money in the financial industry."

Bill nodded while I felt repulsed by my husband's lie. Three weeks was hardly a year in law school. I casually walked away not wanting to listen to anymore of Seth's created illusion. I walked over to the cul-de-sac psychiatrist, John, and his wife, Pam. I had gone jogging with the full-time homemaker once in the two years that we lived in the same cul-de-sac and could not keep up with her pace that day. I never went jogging with her again. I had run for years, but not at the pace she kept, and trying to stay up with her was too hard—I did not like to compete with anyone except myself. I preferred to run alone and get lost in my own thoughts.

"How are your daughter's ballet classes going?" I asked my neighbor.

"Oh wonderful," Pam said in delight. "She's auditioning this week for the Royal Academy of Dance, an old school in France founded by Louie XIV. If she gets the audition, then she will tour with this dance company after high school."

"Wow. I wish her the best. I love to watch the ballet. The dancers make their movements appear effortless. How do they stand on their toes and appear so graceful? I try to balance on one leg, and I'm wobbling all over the place."

"Me, too. It's all about dancing en pointe. The 20th century Russian ballerina, Anna Pavlova, actually made the modern pointe shoe what it is today. She had slender tapered feet, which resulted in excessive pressure applied to her big toes when she danced, and to compensate for this problem, she inserted toughened leather soles into her shoes for extra support and would flatten and harden the toe area to form a box. Her peers told her that she was cheating."

I mulled over her words. "I took ballet when I was a kid, but my pink slippers did not have the box toes. I was too shy to perform and quit before I graduated to box toes."

Pam smiled, "How is Bella doing with her dance lessons?"

"She just finished another summer camp ending with a school performance. The choreography for their song and dance number was amazing--I was impressed."

"Great. Sammy learned how to play golf this summer," Pam

offered.

"Sam told me about his golfing lessons when he was over playing with Bella. He's heading into the direction of a pro according to his enthusiasm." I peered over at Pam's husband who stood beside us quietly listening. I did not trust John because he talked to Seth for hours every week in the driveway; and once, or twice, out of curiosity, I would wander up to the two men and listen to their conversation. On more than one occasion, I had heard Seth telling whopper lies to the unsuspecting neighbor, tall fish tales about his job responsibilities and finances, while I remained amazed that my husband unabashedly did so in front of me. I told Seth later, when we were alone, that one day I would show him up to be a liar; and he laughed off my threat. I questioned if lying had become a norm and I was out of step? No matter, I knew I would not cause this family further humiliation. I wasn't sure if the psychiatrist was psychoanalyzing Seth, or whether the doctor was a closet gay, too, but I greatly suspected his aloofness with me was due to a lie Seth created about me. I felt uncomfortable in John's presence and needed to leave. "I have to find the ladies' room," I told the couple. Pam pointed me into the direction of the hallway.

I came out of the bathroom and walked back into the living area and over to the Continental pilot and his wife, Linda, who were standing in a small group.

Bard was telling a joke when I walked up: "The plane's cabin was being served by an obviously gay flight attendant, who was obviously enjoying himself. He came swishing down the aisle and said to the man and the woman seated beside him, 'Captain Marvey has asked me to announce that he'll be landing the big scary plane shortly, lovely people, so if you could just put up your trays that would be super.' On his trip back up the aisle, the flight attendant noticed that a woman hadn't moved a muscle. 'Perhaps you didn't hear me over those big brute engines. I asked you to raise your trazy-poo so that the main man can pitty-pat us on the ground.' She calmly turned her head and said, 'In my country, I am called a Princess. I take orders from no one!' He returned, 'Well, sweet cheeks, in my country, I'm called a Queen, so I outrank you. Put up the tray, bitch!'"

I chuckled along with the group and turned to Linda, who stood beside me and smiled back. "How's the construction going?" She asked me.

"It's nearing completion. You should come over and see what we've done to our place."

"I would love to," she answered. "I'll have to come over soon. We're moving away."

I shuddered to think my next-door neighbors were moving away due to their neighbors' dysfunction. "Where are you moving to?"

"To Atlanta, Georgia. Bard is being transferred to the Atlanta airport."

"How do you feel about moving away?"

"Bard and I are delighted. We have family there, but our daughters are upset. They don't want to move away from their friends. We have a senior in high school and one in college. Our seventeen year old might go live with her big sister and finish out her senior year here."

"What do you think about that?"

She exhaled, "I don't know. I'm torn. I told my employer that I'm leaving, but I have mixed emotions about giving up my job."

"You've been managing that retirement home a long time, right?"

"Nearly fifteen years," she answered.

Marilyn moseyed over to Linda and me. Marilyn was my favorite neighbor who lived next door, on the other side of me, in a two-story house painted dark green with a white picket fence. Marilyn grew edible herbs and flowers in her front yard and loved my baby boys. The woman had three grown sons and no daughter, nor grandchildren. Her husband, Jim, the prominent house builder, was not present, as usual. I gave the tall, lanky snob the award for the most unfriendly neighbor in the cul-de-sac. I had never seen the pores on his face. Marilyn, on the other hand, had invited herself over for coffee and chitchat when she saw Seth pull out of the driveway in his car and drive away. She educated me about holistic health, spiritual matters, and about her church of no denomination.

"How's the fund raiser coming along?" Linda asked Marilyn.

I looked on with great interest, as I had no clue what fundraiser Linda was asking about.

Marilyn nodded in approval, "It went better than we expected. We sold all our tickets to the December banquet."

"Bard and I just could not make plans that far into the future; otherwise, we would have loved to attend your charity event," she confessed.

"Oh, I completely understand."

"We're going to list our house this week," Linda admitted. "Hopefully, we won't be stuck with a house we can't sell."

I interrupted and asked Marilyn, "What are you raising money for?"

"Our foundation is for abused women. I sit on the board of The Women's Center," Marilyn said without any show of emotion.

I cringed at her admission and felt embarrassed because I was certain she had heard one too many brawls through our thin walls while she tended to her herb garden, and I was certain, too, that she had seen the cop cars in the driveway. I was sure she smelled the marijuana floating over to her yard when our friends came over. She knew there was trouble on the home front, even if I did not want to discuss my personal problems with her over coffee, or with anyone for that matter. Now I understood that she had been attempting to establish trust with me so she could counsel me to leave my abuser without me taking offense to her intrusion. I suspected everyone on the block had heard about us, and I was embarrassed that my neighbors saw me in this horrid light.

And, when I thought I could not bear any more anguish that night, the person I feared the most walked up to join me, Marilyn and Linda. We all greeted our cul-de-sac neighbor with warm hellos. Susan was my relative by marriage, although now a widow. Her husband had died several years ago and left her a life insurance policy to buy the house on the other side of Marilyn's house. Seth and I looked at her Spanish-style home before we decided on the contemporary home we currently remodeled. Recently, my relative-by-marriage admitted to me, she had run out of her inheritance and had to get a paying job. She went to paralegal school for six months after moving into the cul-de-sac and had inspired me to consider the same career--$50,000 a year was a decent income for a short education.

I often saw Susan talking to Marilyn in their front yards, and I now I assumed Susan had the scoop on my awful situation, too. Susan had been married to the brother of my aunt, and my aunt was married to my mother's brother, the ophthalmologist. I had never seen the gossiper around my mother's family at any time in previous years, but Susan told me plenty of unflattering stories about the eye surgeon uncle and his cute wife. I knew the pipeline flowed both ways. I stood there and concluded my suspicions accurate that my neighbor shed less-than-desirable light on me and the disaster I called my husband, when I recalled a family reunion that same summer of '93.

My uncle the eye surgeon had walked over to my house from Susan's and had invited me to the family's annual horseshoe party on the river in Wimberley, Texas held every July 4th, but my first ever invite. He had never exchanged more than five words with me until this day when he stood in my kitchen and invited me and my husband and our children to a family reunion on my mother's side of the extended family. I was somewhat *honored* he considered my little family. Uncle Chris was my mom's youngest brother, the youngest of eight siblings; and he reminded me that day, in my kitchen, that I had missed the funeral of my first cousin's sixteen-year old son. I told Uncle Chris that I did not like funerals, and he gently lectured that family needed to be there for each other in those sad times. I wholeheartedly agreed with him, but I had too much pride to explain to the millionaire that I had an eviction notice on my door every month during those years, and that the bank had repossessed our only vehicle, and that we walked everywhere, and that we had no phone, and that we ate donations from a food pantry. The doctor stood in my beautiful two-story home and had no clue where I had come from while he admonished me for my callousness toward my cousin's loss. Therefore, to make up for appearing insensitive, Seth, I, and our three children drove to the annual horseshoe party on the river.

IN HELL WITH EYES WIDE OPEN

My mother was too sick to attend her own family's party that July 4th in Wimberley, Texas, and my father stayed home with her; and out of us four siblings, I was the only one willing to drive three-and-a-half hours and go around this well-known group of snobs. I brought my pregnant cousin, who had lost her sixteen year old son in a car wreck, three years earlier, a small ceramic angel, as my way of saying to her, 'I'm sorry I did not send you a sympathy card.'

Her drunken husband, who stood next to his pregnant wife, seemingly came on to me in front of her, while giving me the blow-by-blow details of how his vasectomy reversal improved his sexual performance. His inappropriate conversation, directed at me in front of his forty-something year old, pregnant wife, pissed me off. While he wanted me to hear about his past erectile dysfunction being an ongoing problem due to a previous vasectomy, I grew uncomfortable. He alleged that until he had a vasectomy reversal, he also had a weak urine stream. I anxiously stood there and related to the insecurity I felt while pregnant with Seth's first child. I knew that his wife who was nine months pregnant was insulted. She already had little respect for me when I had not shown up for her son's funeral. Her husband's conversation greatly disturbed me, too, and later that day, when his pregnant wife, and her two sisters, and three younger brothers, treated me as if I had a contagious disease, I understood that they would continue to snub me, probably for the rest of my life.

The morning wore on too long for me, and I could not fit in with my peers no matter how I designed the conversation—nothing had changed between them and me since childhood. These same cousins, and their entourage, clearly treated Seth and me, and our children, as uninvited guests that day; but I found acceptance from my aged aunts and uncles, who were kind to my family and me because they loved my mother. Late into the morning, and far into feeling rejected, one of the first cousins, who had been ostracizing me, asked me if I wanted to participate in the horseshoe event. The unexpected gesture spoke kindly to my heart. I enthusiastically agreed to play in their tournament, and I was happy with the invitation until I found myself partnered with a cousin's guest, a flaming, pot-bellied male, with red hair, who deemed me unworthy of recognition and treated me as if I were invisible. Obviously, the unloving family members thought, that out of fifty relatives there that day, paring me up with an arrogant and gay stranger to play horseshoes with, funny. I, on the other hand, felt insulted that they prevented me from creating any bond with any of my bloodline that day.

Uncle Chris told me to bring food to the potluck, the day he unexpectedly showed up in my Woodland's home. Wimberley was in the Texas Hill Country, the home of Germans and good beer, and because I was emphasizing our culture, I brought sauerkraut and sausage to the July 4th family reunion that feature a horseshoe tournament. At noon, Seth, my children, and I joined family members and sat down at a long table in my Aunt Jean's backyard, overlooking the Blanco River from high above. There was sauerkraut and sausage, and more sauerkraut and sausage, on the table, and I wondered how it was possible a family this large in number would have such a limited menu. We had all waited, very late into the hot afternoon, for those, organizing the party, to bring out the food, which had been a challenge for me who had two, very young, hungry, and tired children. While I finally sat down at the table of kraut, sausage, and beans, and scanned the sunburned and sweaty hungry bodies, I noticed my pregnant cousin, her younger two sisters, their three younger brothers, my Uncle Chris, and his cute wife, were all missing, among a few others I shall not name. When dinner was over, the missing members of my family showed up freshly showered in elegant clothing with their fine foods and offered us none of their private selections, or a seat at their banquet table. I walked up to their feast and peered at salads and relishes, casseroles, vegetables, breads, trays of beef, chicken, ham, and cheeses, and desserts. My pallet salivated, and the child I held reached toward their food. I pulled my four-year old Harper back from the table. No one at the table acknowledged that I stood near with my son, while they carried on conversations with one another, at the very table that we had been sitting at an hour earlier. I questioned why I had come to their party after a lifetime of them snubbing me? I leaned over their private table, grabbed my Tupperware tub with leftover sauerkraut, and walked away from their pretense.

I walked over to a kinder face, who had already eaten, at the table of meager, and told the elderly aunt, whom I had adored since childhood, that my children and I were tired, that we were leaving to find a nearby motel, and that we would return the following day for the horseshoe playoffs. Aunt Millie had witnessed the game called *we're important and you're not* and knew I would not be back in the morning. She acknowledged me for being brave and thanked me for coming. I kissed her and sweet Uncle Frank goodbye.

I walked to my car and angrily spewed under my breath to my husband that we were driving back home. I reserved my harsh words until we drove off their property, and then summed for my confused husband that this family had never been anything but a bunch of arrogant and unfriendly snobs to me since I was a young child, and that they could kiss my ass!

My sister, Holly, said to me on the phone after I returned home and told her about our horrible family, "Why do you think we didn't go, Jean? We knew they would treat us badly."

I snapped out of that awful memory of July 4th and looked at the three neighbor ladies--Susan, Linda, and Marilyn--who stood beside me with cocktails in their hands. I was in a bad place with myself. Everything had mounted up to my humiliation. The neighbors had not missed a beat. They knew Seth obsessed over his yard, and that he did not hold a job like the other men with wives and children. They knew Seth was not concerned for his family's financial future, and that the marijuana smoke that drifted into the neighbors' yards, when our friends were over, rendered explanation for why Seth did not want to work for his sons' college education, or for our retirement. I had called cops to our house after I finally had enough of Seth's destruction and assaults on my body. The neighbors in the cul-de-sac saw the police cars in the driveway more than once. My perception of how the neighbors and family judged us mortified me. I was certain that they stigmatized us as *the dysfunctional white trash* on the block. And these friends and relatives had only the tip of the iceberg-- our problems went far deeper.

My mama raised me to hold my head up high and walk proud, but I no longer felt I had anything to be proud of. "Excuse me, ladies," I humbly said as I walked away and over to Jillian's father who stood alone in the room. I hoped he would welcome my company while I walked up to him. I asked him if he was enjoying Houston.

"I am, I love Houston," he happily answered while I spotted my nemesis on the other side of the room talking to the psychiatrist, John. I wondered what lies Seth filled John's head with on this night.

Our hostess, Jillian, Bill's daughter, asked all of us to please join her in the dining room just as I was settling into a conversation with our honorary guest.

Bill and I led the group of eight to a long, wooden, dining table, with big cushioned chairs; and while I considered the safest place to position myself, Bill asked me to sit beside him. I was relieved by his friendly invitation and sat next to the stranger in hopes I could escape the ill feelings that manifested in the pit of my stomach like a rock, over how the neighbors and my family perceived me. I wanted to tell all of them that if I could figure out how, I'd leave the bastard that didn't care how far down he took his children and me.

Jillian sat at one end of the table, and her father, Bill, at the other. I sat next to her father, and on the other side of me sat Marilyn. I was in favored company. I looked down at the table setting and counted the forks, from left to right. I had a small appetizer fork, a fish fork, and a meat fork. My napkin sat in the center of my plate, and to the right was a meat knife, a fish knife, and a soup spoon. A water stem sat above the knife, along with a wine glass. The hostess covered the table in gold linen cloth. A servant served the first course, the appetizer, then served the stuffed olive canapés, and thereafter, served the main course, scallops in wine sauce. I found Jillian's father warm, complementary, and his conversation stimulating throughout the elegant five-course dinner.

Bill held my undivided attention while I listened to him educate me about the financial market. "1988 marked a turning point for the FDIC. For the first time since the agency's creation, the FDIC suffered an operating loss to the tune of $4.2 billion. That loss was due primarily to the $7.3 billion cost associated with bank failures and assistant transactions."

"How many bank failures were there?" I asked him.

"Two hundred S&Ls failed in 1988. A new record was established for the highest number of banks to fail in one day, when forty bank subsidiaries of First Republic Bank Corporation were closed and sold to NCNB Corporation."

"I recently read that the U.S. banking industry had its best performance since 1988, just this year."

"The FDIC Chairman, and Andrew Hove, recently stated that the Bank Insurance Fund has a balance of $13 billion this year. That is a significant improvement over the negative balance of $101 million at the close of 1992, and the $7 billion deficit at the end of 1991--the only years since the FDIC began operations in 1934 that the insurance fund had a negative balance."

"And where do you see our country's financial future going?"

He chuckled, "I believe without a doubt we're heading toward a world-wide financial collapse."

"Really?"

"Yes, I do. And I believe one day the slate will be wiped clean, and all debt will be forgiven."

"Why?"

"Because our government is not regulating the bank system, and we're a debt ridden society, which cannot keep going in the same direction we're heading without a big crash. In 1990, when S&Ls were failing at the highest rate since the Great Depression, the FDIC, which at the time had $13 billion, predicted it would run out of money. Three hundred fifty-four banks reported annual losses every consecutive year since 1986. The industry had one foot on a banana peel and the other in the grave."

"I thought when banks were making more loans than the previous year, as is the case now, then that was a sure sign of recovery?"

"Making loans is a temporary fix to stimulate an economy if the wages are not increasing. And here's another problem: Since the 1980's, securitization--the packaging and sale of loans by investment banks--have exploded. What was once the exclusive preserve of banks--mortgages, car loans, and credit card receivables--are now packaged and sold off. While banks still originate these types of loans, securitization eliminates profits gained from holding them, from earning interest over many years. Therefore, with their earnings declining, banks have responded, much like the S&Ls did in the recent past; and now, banks make riskier loans for which they can collect higher fees and interest. In particular, they have poured money into commercial real estate and highly leveraged companies. In 1989, for the first time ever in the U.S., real estate loans alone exceeded the banks' commercial and industrial lending. Unfortunately, what bankers are also discovering, just as they did in the early 1980's, after their disastrous lending spree in the Third World, is that in an economic downturn, such risky loans go bad far more quickly, and in far greater numbers, than the more conventional variety. So far, banking woes have not directly cost U.S. tax payers money, but mark my word, one day the tax payers will get hit hard."

I nodded, "And then what?"

"We taxpayers will have to bail out the banks like we did the S&Ls. The banking industry does not see future failures sufficient to imperil their fund, but that depends on the economic environment, doesn't it?"

I nodded while completely fascinated with my education.

"We're assuming that the economy will remain what it is now," he said.

"Certainly the banks use some kind of formula to predict expected losses?"

"They do. In the slowdown scenario, it's assumed 30% of loans already on banks' books, as *nonperforming loans*, will go uncollected, whereas in the recession case, it is assumed 50% of these same *non-performing loans* will be written off. In the less dire scenario, the average bank earns a return equal to .75% of its assets; but while in a severe scenario, the average bank earns a return equal to .50% of its assets. Under the slowdown scenario, the entire U.S. banking system suffers a net loss of some $19.5 billion in equity capital, and that translates into a $5 billion hit to the FDIC insurance fund. And once the FDIC fund slips below $10 billion, then the banks risk becoming effectively insolvent because, as the fund dwindles, big uninsured depositors, with more than $100,000 in a bank account, will become alarmed and move their money from weaker banks into either strong banks, or T-bills."

"My father told me that he put his retirement into T-bills," I offered. "He's not playing the stock market anymore."

"He's a wise man," Bill confirmed. "Tax payers will eventually have to shell out at least $40 billion dollars in the future for bank failures, which is $100 billion less than the S&L debacle."

"Why does Washington allow banks to put us taxpayers at risk like this?"

"Banking regulators lack the kind of clearly defined, early warning policy that the SEC uses to police Wall Street; and by the time the White House, and Congress, will finally step in, the banks will have gone too far."

"Are we truly coming out of a recession?" I asked the banking expert.

"We're having a moderate economic recovery, Jean. The economy was slow all year, until recently. The housing industry picked up recently reflecting the drop in interest rates. The decline in interest rates helped put more disposable income into consumers' pockets. When the government lowers the interest rate, as they did earlier this year, then consumers spend more, businesses spend more on capital equipment, and manufacturing productivity increases."

"My husband has made a bunch of money in the stock market recently," I said.

"Seth was telling me about his gains; and I warned him to be careful for the very reasons I already gave you, Jean. Seth needs to understand the credit cycle and know when to pull out."

"That's what my father said, too. I don't know if Seth really understands the market."

"No one really understands the stock market, Jean! It's a guessing game sometimes."

I sensed doom looming.

THE FOLLOWING MORNING, I sat at my kitchen table reading the Houston Chronicle. I flipped through the Travel Section and noticed a picture of a skier spraying snow down a steep mountain.

I read the ad and considered how I had not been skiing in a few years since Seth and I had made a trip to Aspen. Seth walked in through the kitchen door, in dirty jeans, and looked exhausted from whatever work he was involved with outside.

"Let's book a ski trip, Seth, while the prices are cheap."

"In August?"

"I'm looking at an ad for lodging in Steamboat, Colorado. We can rent a ski-in/ski-out lodge with three bedrooms and three bathrooms and split the cost with whoever wants to go with us."

"Who did you have in mind?"

George snapped to the forefront of my mind. "Let's ask your old college roommate, and dear friend, George; and I'll ask my best friend, Charley, and maybe even some of the people I've met recently at Landmark. Someone will want go with us!" I was even considering asking my sexy, phone buddy, but, maybe not. George was more than enough to fill my need for quality male company."

"Are you trying to hook up Charley and George?"

Seth's question surprised me, as I had never conceived of sharing George with another female. "Hey, that might be a great idea!" I snickered while I considered Charley my decoy. "Is George still dating the cliché, what's her name?" I asked while wondering if Seth would remember the name *Gail*.

"I don't remember her name, and I haven't talked to George since his visit here."

"Well, call George up! Why don't you ask George if he and his girlfriend would like to join us?" I asked while knowing Seth would take the bait. I knew George would never give Seth the satisfaction of meeting his centerfold, but rather, George might like to spend time with Seth's centerfold—me, and prove to Seth who could take whose girl.

"George might go for a group ski trip."

"Of course he will, Seth!"

"And if he's not dating his secretary anymore, then he might find Charley interesting," Seth considered.

"No doubt! Call George right away and ask him if he wants to go to Steamboat with us. If so, I'll book the lodge, and he can reimburse us. Airfare to Colorado should be very cheap if we buy in the summer."

The phone on the buffet next to the glass kitchen door rang. I picked up and answered and heard a breathy male voice with a smile, "Hello, Jean. This is your fellow Landmarkian, Fred. How are you?"

"Fred!" I gleefully responded. "What are you doing?"

"I'm inviting you to my backyard barbeque this coming weekend. The gang is getting together at my place on the water."

"I'll be there. Where do you live?"

"On Galveston Bay in a town called Shore Acres."

"I know exactly where that is! I had a home there once many moons ago."

"Where are you at?" Fred asked.

"In a good place," I teased.

He laughed. "How many miles is that from me?"

"Not many," I quipped. "Aren't you in the same place?"

"I am."

"You are about one hour away, if I don't use my interstellar ship to get there."

He laughed. "And your expected arrival time, if you come in your space ship?"

"I travel at the speed of light, whatever that may be."

"186,000 miles per second," Fred answered.

"That's fast, isn't it?" I giggled.

"Yep, and you can't go any faster."

"No?"

"No. It's not possible to travel faster than the speed of light, so the laws of physics tell us. But don't tell the writers of Star Trek that fact," he chuckled.

"I won't tell anybody that warping space is not possible! It is fun to think about though, and speaking of travel and fun, would you like to go on a ski trip with a group of us?"

"I love to ski. Who's going?"

"Me. Well, Seth and me. I'm not sure yet, but I'll make sure there are some single people going, too."

"Sounds like fun, when?"

"I was thinking the first week in December."

"Yeah, sounds like a lot of fun, count me in."

"Great! I'll book the lodge, and you can reimburse me," I said to Fred. "I was thinking we would rent a three-bedroom, three-bath ski-in/ski-out condo. Would you be willing to share a bedroom?"

He laughed, "With you? Yeah!"

I chuckled and reserved comment because Seth was standing nearby listening to our conversation.

"I'm teasing you, Jean. I don't mind sharing a bedroom, as long as I don't have to share a bed with another male."

I laughed. "Twin beds are more of what I had in mind for the single people."

THE FOLLOWING WEEKEND, I found myself sitting on a grassy green lawn that rolled down to the water's edge. We all sat looking out onto Galveston Bay under a clear blue sky. I wore the same attire as the other women who sat with me: shorts over suits, a sun visor, sunglasses, and lotion. Sabrina, Charley, and my newest Landmarkian friend, Linda, and I, each held a paper plate in our lap while we talked about the various men who stood in groups around the yard, and about our love lives--or lack of, and our children--or lack of.

Upon my invitation, Charley jumped on the opportunity to go on a ski trip with George, Fred, Seth, and me in December. Before all of us stayed together in a condo, in Steamboat, for four days, in December, Fred and I felt inviting my best friend to meet him at his backyard barbeque a good icebreaker. Most of the guests were attendees from the Landmark seminars, and Charley knew no one but Seth and me. She arrived with the boyfriend du jour and easily blended with the partygoers, and told me, on the sly, that Fred was not her cup of tea. Fred rented the bungalow on the back of the oceanfront property, and I knew Charley wanted a great deal more in life than Fred could offer her.

I was thrilled Charley was back in my life again, and I would spend even more time with her during the holidays. I had not seen much of Charley since I had my last two children and had moved way north of Houston to The Woodlands. She knew Seth from the apartment complex, where we all lived in the late 1980's, and had no regard for the man, after hearing what a poor provider he had been for the kids and me, the first three years of our relationship. She was going on the ski trip strictly for me, and we schemed to ditch my husband, while in Steamboat, and find our own fun in the hot tubs and at the bars.

Sabrina and I looked across the yard and saw Seth talking to Dan, the young scientist from our group, Theo's boyfriend. Seth did not know these people from Landmark, either, before today; and I figured he was filling their heads with tales of his greatest accomplishments. Sabrina turned to me, "I can't believe you brought him!"

I found her statement off the wall. "Why not?"

She rolled her eyes at my absurd pretense. "You know why not!"

Linda chuckled. "I'm curious," she said to Sabrina, "Why can't you believe Jean brought her husband?"

"Where do you think she gets those bruises on her legs?" Sabrina asked Linda.

"Sabrina!" I objected. I did not like the corner she painted me in. "Okay, we have arguments, and he kicks me," I explained to Linda and Charley.

"I'd kick him right out," Sabrina huffed while I watched the girls lean over and examine my injured legs.

"I've never liked him," Charley confided to Sabrina.

"So you know Seth, too?" Sabrina asked Charley.

"Jean and I once called Seth the apartment gigolo. He broke up her marriage to Leonardo because he wanted to be part of her apparel business, but he's never been in love with her. Seth just loves Seth, and I told Jean he would leave when the money ran out."

"He might or might not," I murmured. "But because I don't believe anything he says anymore, and he gives me no sense of security, *I am* going back to school this fall. I'm going to finish my degree so that I can provide for my children when the day comes and he does leave."

"So what makes you think he will let you finish *this* time?" Sabrina asked.

"Nothing, but I've changed. I swear I'll kill him." I had changed, too; I had changed for the worse. I knew Seth could make me crazy like the time, a year earlier, when he forced me out of school, and I pulled him off the toilet by the hair on the top of his head and slammed him face down on the floor.

"I know a good divorce attorney," Sabrina quipped.

"I'll keep your husband in mind," I replied.

Linda laughed, "She's going to need a criminal lawyer!"

We giggled.

Charley asked Sabrina, "What's Jean going to do with two babies if she goes to work. She wouldn't make any money by the time she paid daycare every week." Charley turned to me, "You need to start hiding some of that money Seth brings in every month."

"That's right!" Linda piped in, "Get a divorce, too, Jean, and have the judge make orders that the asshole pays you enough child support to pay for the daycare. What's the problem here?"

"I could do that, but I don't want to hurt my children. One day their father is there, and the next he's not--they love him."

Sabrina huffed, "He shouldn't be anywhere near you and your children if he's kicking you!"

"You're absolutely right, Brini," I sadly said while recalling how upset Harper was to witness his father kicking me in the shins.

Linda reminded, "Like they say in the seminar, Jean, you've got to make a stand for who you are. Are you a woman who will allow a man to hit her?"

"No, I'm not! I won't put up with his abuse anymore."

"What are you going to do if he hits you again?" Sabrina asked.

"I won't put up with it!" I adamantly repeated.

"He'll hit you again, Jean," Charley fueled.

"I know, and he's going to be very sorry when he does."

"You might as well get rid of him now," Charley continued. "Take him to court and get child support; the judge will give you the house, too."

I did not want to deal with that situation and stared off at my husband. The rest of the women turned their attention to Seth, too, who stood on the other side of the yard talking to sexy Chris, my phone buddy.

"I wonder," I said to the girls, "if Seth realizes that the hunk he is talking to is a man I have daytime and night time fantasies about."

"Seth probably has fantasies about Chris, too," Charley snickered, and then rolled her eyes and shook her head in disappointment at my situation. Everyone else chuckled.

SEPTEMBER 1993. I enrolled into the fall semester at the University of Houston full-time, and then told Seth, after the fact, that I would attend classes Monday through Friday each week from 7:00 a.m. until 3:00 p.m. Seth assured me that Bella would get on the school bus each morning after I left, and that he would feed, change, and look after his sons while I was away. His calm reaction caught me off guard, but, obviously, Seth was too preoccupied with moving his mother's money from stock to stock on a daily basis to concentrate on a war. I suspected he was worried his New York stockbroker would make a margin call, and if that happened, Seth would then have to deposit enough money in his margin account to bring the account back to the margin limit, or to the minimum maintenance requirement.

Seth's other brokerage, *Inroad Investment and Securities*, paid him an annual $100,000 commission in monthly checks, which we received in the mail, and was making demands on Seth at the same time I started the fall semester. *Inroad Investments* demanded he pay all his brokerage fees upfront for the upcoming year in 1994. A measly amount of $725 was due from Seth, which startled him and created cause for concern. Twelve months of fees paid in advance allowed Seth to legally conduct business with *Bike World* in Texas, Ohio, California, and Wisconsin with his NASD registered Series 6 and 63 licenses. Supposedly, while I was at school one morning, Seth called *Inroad Investments* seeking explanation for why he received a bill for only a portion of the 1994 fees. He explained to me later his company simply erred and billed him by mistake for seven months instead of twelve months. I challenged Seth with the consideration that perhaps *Inroad Investment* was pulling a quick one, and getting rid of him in the near future. Seth reassured me that his college buddy, the CFO of *Bike World*, Brian Flannigan, had his back, and would give him a head's up, if the relationship between Seth's brokerage and *Bike World* was to be severed at any point. I wondered if Seth's employer was looking to get rid of their non-performing and over-paid account manager who managed nothing. Perhaps *Inroad Investment* was keeping *Bike World* employees' $25 million pension fund, but cutting out the middleman? Maybe Seth was just the last to know about his company's intention to ax him; or maybe I was the last to know? The possibility we could find ourselves with no income in less than a year frightened me.

  I had promised Seth that if he took an issue with me going to school and sabotaged my effort in any way, at any time, that the result would be his loss. Seth took my threat, without any show of upset; and although he was not admitting to me, as having any financial problems, I strongly suspected he had painted himself into a corner with the New York stockbroker and his mother's life savings. My being in school was the least of his concerns. I had learned enough from my father about the hazards of playing on the margin, to know, that *when*, not *if*, the New York broker made a margin call, Seth would need a huge amount of quick cash; and we had no credit, or cash saved anywhere to facilitate a last minute demand. He had grown his mother's $85,000 investment into an amount well over one million dollars, and I suspected her money was now at risk. How great the risk, I had no clue, but for mama's firstborn to lose any portion of her meager $85,000 she called her life savings was unsatisfactory.

  Seth, more than once, had told me to back off, that his business with his mother's money did not include me. For the sake of keeping the peace, and turning my attention to my studies, without any additional stress over a matter I had no control over, I discontinued all argument with my husband about what I considered a looming disaster. I no longer expressed my fears or anger to Seth about him putting us in a no-win position, if he lost even a fraction of what he gambled of the old lady's life savings. He most likely would get notice, from his broker, to pay up when his account balance dropped below the minimum margin requirement, due to eventual falling stock prices. And then what? Were we expected to financially support an elderly woman who did not like me?

I had enrolled into another fall semester, the second one I would attempt in two years; and I dared Seth to stop me, a second time, from completing this semester. I watched my husband like a hawk because I did not trust him. My patience had grown thin with his determination to keep me down, and the very sight of him enraged me, which I managed to suppress unless he talked to me. I had enrolled into another fifteen hours and felt completing these classes with top grades no problem. I was determined to be independent and a self-sufficient woman who could take care of her children without a man in the future. I knew Seth's modus operandi was to take me to court one day and tell the judge that I had no earning potential, and that he should have the kids and the house, and that I should *pay him* child support.

My most challenging subject matter this semester, other than my husband, was my microeconomic principles class; and though I had found the topic enthralling, when talking to Bill, our neighbor's father, I had no understanding, until the last few weeks, of how the economy was truly regulated. My dinner party discussion with the hostess's father encouraged me to take this difficult class, along with more accounting principles, psychology, history, and government.

The professor of economics at the university summed up the two-hour lecture. "Some have suggested that a lower rate of home ownership would be deleterious to our common weal. However, if we are to increase homeownership in the future, I feel there will NOT be a market failure, but, instead, a government failure. If the Federal Reserve drives down the cost of borrowing money to unprecedented lows, and if banks make loans available to those, who under prevailing conditions, cannot afford their mortgages, and if private agencies, charged with determining the risk and value of securities, are exceptionally generous in their assessment of the financial products, known as *derivatives,* whose collateral resides in the value of thousands of mortgages bundled together, then, yes--there will be a government failure. When these lending institutions offer financial products, with the assumption that housing prices will keep rising, this country is heading for a crash."

I raised my hand.

"Do you have a question?" The professor asked.

"Do you think that scenario could happen?"

"Absolutely," the bearded thirty-something year old answered. "Our government could cause failure to our financial system, and push the global economy into the worst contraction since the Great Depression. The government will tell us that this contraction is *a market failure* because the promise of capitalism has always been that the self-correcting mechanisms, built into the system, would preclude the possibility of a systemic market failure. If government subsidies push house prices up so fast, that marginal buyers can no longer afford to chase prices even higher, then this is a result of bad public policy, and *not* a market failure." The professor peeked at his watch and then informed, "That's it for today; I will see you guys the day after tomorrow." He said as he closed his notebook and walked away from the podium.

I shut my book, too, and made plans to study that night when I got home while aware I had the first exam of the semester coming up soon. I quickly packed up my belongings and followed the crowd out the classroom, and had barely stepped into the hallway when I spotted Bill, Jillian's father. I was as surprised to see the distinguished man, as he was to see me. We greeted each other with a hug as if old friends.

"That's right," he acknowledged. "You told me you were taking classes here."

"I am! What are you doing here?" I asked my neighbor's father.

"I was offered at the last minute a position to head up an entrepreneurial club here. My alma mater learned I had an MBA from Harvard, and that I was the former Governor for the Federal Reserve Board, and they came begging me to work for them."

I chuckled.

"Okay," he humbly bowed his head, "I needed to do

something with my life, so I applied for the position, did a lot of begging, and they took pity on me."

"Congratulations, Bill!"

"Thank you, Jean. I would love you to come to our meeting tonight. Maybe you would like to join our club? Our members are seniors graduating from this business school. You're walking the halls! What about it?"

"Oh, I'm not a senior," I confessed to Bill. "I'm just a freshman."

"That's all right. You have so much to bring to the table, Jean. When you told me about your apparel business that night over dinner, I was fascinated! You've done more than any of these seniors have accomplished. Please, come! Teach us! I make exception for you."

"Oh," I giggled. "I'm flattered, Bill. I would love to come to your meeting."

"Great! We're holding a meeting tonight in room #1 in this building at 5:00 p.m."

"What does your club do?"

"We put ideas into action."

"I like that!" I nodded.

"I know you do! Our club invites speakers and lecturers to talk to us about entrepreneurship; for example, we'll tour office space in a commercial building and negotiate with the owner over rent, over the price per square foot we're willing to pay, and when we're done negotiating, then the owner will tell us how low he was willing to go."

"That sounds like fun!"

"We have a lot of fun! Everyone in the club is either working on a business degree, or on a MBA."

"Wow," I said while considering how often I had dreamed of being in a class of business-minded students who would be willing to collaborate with me and help me kick off another apparel business. "I'll be there at 5:00. Thanks for inviting me."

"You're most welcome, Jean."

"I have to race off to another class," I informed the man with silver hair. "I'll see you later, Bill."

"I look forward to it, Jean!" he said as I disappeared through the crowded and noisy hallway.

At 5:00 p.m. that evening, I sat in classroom #1 inside the university's business school with forty other students and Bill heading up the meeting. "I would like to introduce Jean Wynn to everybody," Bill kindly said to his audience while he pointed into my direction.

"Hello," I shyly nodded at my intrigued classmates.

"Jean is an amazing woman," Bill continued. "I had the honor of sitting beside her recently at a dinner party and hearing about her apparel business startup." Bill chuckled, "I'll advise all of you to get to know her; she can teach us a few things."

I snickered and thought of myself as the author of failure regarding business and personal relationships while the seniors turned and smiled at me. I knew they held me in high esteem because Bill respected me. The moment reminded me of my failing relationship with my husband, who did not make me feel appreciated. I refused to take Seth's lack of support personal because Seth did not love Seth, much less could he love anyone else. Seth did not care about his own success; much less did he care about mine.

Bill continued, "Let's begin our meeting now. Firstly, we define our mission and vision to become a true entrepreneurial organization. The Events and Dinners with Business Gurus Program is the first week of every month; and the Action MBA Event and Young Entrepreneurs Dinner is the third week in every month. These meetings are where we strengthen our ties with outside organizations; and we understand, that without their generosity, many of our accomplishments would not be possible. We believe the world of tomorrow belongs to those with the vision and passion of today."

I sat quietly and listened to engaging dialogue between the seniors and Captain Bill. The business-minded students directed many questions at our revered leader over the next two hours. I was thrilled to be in their company and inspired to start another apparel business. I could hardly wait to run home and tell Seth whom I had met that day at school, but while excited about sharing my news with my husband, I understood that my so-called *partner* would be jealous and threatened by my opportunity at the university. I reconsidered hiding the turn of events from my husband, and instead, decided to rub salt into his insecure wound and watch him squirm.

A MONTH LATER and another Monday night forum, Sabrina drove back over to my house from Port Neches, Texas. Our group meeting began in an hour, and she showed up minutes before we had to get into the car and drive across the city to be at our meeting on time. Integrity was the emphasis in our group meetings; and being on time, for each meeting, held every Monday night, for the past month, was exemplary behavior and mandatory. She barged through my front door in all her fashionable splendor, dropped her undisciplined two-year old child, Jacqueline, off with Seth and my three children, and left with me in my green Volvo station wagon. We drove against the 5:00 o'clock traffic and into Houston via I-45 South. We had plenty of time to get to our meeting by 7:00 p.m. We participated in a three-hour discussion which centered on the integrity of one's word; and after the engaging seminar, we both agreed to skip beer at the ice house with our new friends, in lieu of needing sleep. Sabrina and I arrived back at my place at 11:00 p.m.; and as was her weekly ritual for the past month, she would spend the night in my upstairs guest room and make the two-and-a-half hour drive back home the following day.

  We entered through the front door and were surprised to hear music blasting from Seth's prized speakers that sat on the floor at the base of my newly constructed glass block staircase. We strolled through the large living area, with partial tile laid down over concrete, and toward the kitchen, with the same unfinished concrete flooring, and spotted a small, late-night party going on just outside the glass kitchen door. Seth, Pete, and Chad were sitting on the pebble patio under the catwalk between the house and the garage. My husband saw Sabrina and me through the glass kitchen door and jumped up to greet us. Pete and Chad followed Seth into the house.

  "Where are the children?" I asked Seth who stepped inside with a drink in his hand.

  "Bella put them in bed upstairs hours ago."

"And they can sleep with this music blasting?" I challenged as I stepped back into the living room to turn down the music.

"Doesn't seem to be a problem," Seth confirmed.

"I wish I could sleep that sound," Sabrina chuckled.

"Care for a drink, sweetheart?" My husband asked Sabrina.

"Thank you, I would love a drink." She smiled at Seth while I watched her go into a familiar posturing she did for all men.

"Jean?" Seth asked.

I nodded yes to his offer to make me a drink.

Pete, the debonair man with dimples and a groomed five o'clock shadow stepped up to Sabrina. "Let me make some introductions here," Seth's former boss offered while he took the stranger's hand. "I'm Pete."

"Pleased to meet you, Pete. I'm Sabrina, Jean's oldest friend." She said while shaking his hand.

"And this gentleman here," Pete pointed to the twenty-two year old with a sloping brow and curly blonde hair, "...is Chad."

"Pleased to make your acquaintance," Chad said while he stepped up and extended his hand to the thirty-four year old woman.

Sabrina returned the charm in her usual southern belle manner and shook Chad's hand, too. "The pleasure is mine."

Seth interrupted, "Brini, would you like a beer or something harder?"

"What do you have that is *harder*?" She coyly asked Seth.

My radar flashed when I picked up on the flirtatious interplay between my husband and the queen bee. Sabrina's change of attitude toward my abusive husband surprised me, and I interrupted them, "I would like a beer instead of a mixed drink, Seth."

"Why certainly, Jean." He answered before he opened the refrigerator door and handed me a Coors.

"Thank you." I took the beer and popped the tab.

Sabrina piped in, "I'll have whatever you're drinking, Seth."

"Good choice!" Seth then grabbed Sabrina a glass from the cabinet, filled it with ice from the refrigerator door, and poured Jack Daniels from a lead crystal decanter. "Do you like it stiff?" He asked her while he cocked his eyebrows.

"Of course!" She snickered and shot Seth a come-hither look.

I turned to Pete while feeling annoyed by their flirting. "I smell reefer."

Pete asked, "Would you like a hit?"

"Did you guys smoke around the kids?" I asked while already knowing the answer.

"No, we didn't!" Seth intercepted.

I looked at Seth who remained straight-faced and then at Pete's dimples and glazed over eyes.

Pete happily asked Chad, "Where's that joint, dude?"

"Smoked up!" Chad pulled a new joint from his shirt pocket. "But fear not, the supply is endless."

Sabrina smiled. "You guys know how to have a good time! Light that sucker up!"

"Not in the house!" I sternly ordered while remembering how I had, in the past, threatened to call the police on them if they smoked weed on my property ever again. I did not want to start a fight that night.

"Of course not in the house, Jean," Pete kindly replied.

Sabrina seemed to love the attention of the male company while I wrangled with the idea of not protesting over them, once again, violating my no drug policy.

My friend with the mole above her lip and long dark tresses sassed, "Well, we just spent three hours looking at our *lack of* integrity tonight."

"That's not what I looked at tonight in the seminar, Sabrina! I looked at my integrity, and I saw how my life *was working* these days because *I am my word*." I felt like a hypocrite now. I had no integrity because I was allowing our friends to smoke weed on my property.

Sabrina shot me a look, as if confused, and then quipped, "Okay, you looked at your integrity. I looked at my lack of integrity--same thing!"

"No, it's not!" I argued with the obese woman.

Seth handed Sabrina her drink and interrupted our debate. "We boys discussed the usual--stock options, money, and opportunity.

Interested in any of that stuff?"

"Oh baby," Sabrina seductively moaned, "now you're talking my game." She took a sip and peered over her glass at Seth.

"I heard you were a smart woman, Brini," Seth commended.

I wondered where my husband was going with his flattery that night. Seth had known, since 1988, our first year together as a couple, and the same year he first met the married Sabrina, who came to my apartment with a strange male, her ex-lover's brother, that Sabrina was an unfaithful married woman.

"What do you do, Sabrina?" Pete asked.

"Whatever I want to do!" She bragged and smiled. "I've been married for eleven years to Goose, who is an attorney in Port Neches. We have a two-year old daughter now, and I'm proud to admit that I'm a wife and stay-at-home mother."

"I met your daughter, Jacqueline," the handsome Pete revealed. "She's beautiful like her mother."

"Thank you, darling. She's smart, too. I married into a Texas A&M family, and she's got exceptional genes."

I stared at Brini and questioned why she was talking about Jacqueline's genetics being connected to her husband, when, in fact, she had confided in me that the sperm donor was a fellow art student named Jack.

"Go Aggies!" Chad cheered and disrupted my consideration that Sabrina was perhaps a compulsive liar like my husband.

"Did you graduate from A&M, too?" Sabrina asked the twenty-two year old, tall blonde with blue eyes.

"No," Chad answered. "My father graduated from Texas A&M."

I waited to hear whether, or not, the son of a millionaire would admit that college was not in his life's plan, but that, instead, he was majoring in being a drunk and pothead.

"I didn't go to college," Chad admitted to my surprise.

"Well, there's always tomorrow!" Sabrina shot back. "I went back and finished my bachelor's degree in communications just after I married Goose."

"Did you go to A&M, too?" Chad asked Sabrina.

"No, I graduated from Lamar University, but I married into this big A&M family, and I proudly stand behind the maroon and white with my husband and his family. They generously donated to A&M over the decades; and due to our standing and alumni affiliation, an A&M University extension program called the Texas Master Gardener Specialist Program recently accepted my application for membership. I've become very interested in horticulture, gardening, and small-scale food production."

Seth blurted, "That's my girl! I'll have to show you the most recent additions to my gardens and get your expert opinion."

"I would love to see your latest creations," Sabrina winked at Seth and continued talking to him, "The Master Gardener Specialist is an intensive training program. I'm learning so much about gardening. This month we're studying basic ornamental horticulture."

"You could teach me a few things, Brini," Seth seductively interrupted.

"I can teach you a lot! My mentor is a certified Master Gardener, and I'm learning how to grow all kinds of vegetables, and I'm learning about entomology--"

"What's entomology?" Chad asked.

"A branch of zoology concerning insects."

"Oh," he responded.

"And I'm learning about plant propagation, Earth-kind landscaping, greenhouse management, irrigation efficiency, and harvesting. Once I get my Master Gardener's certification, then I have to do fifty hours of volunteer work in the community, on city landscapes, and whatever."

"I'm impressed, Sabrina," Seth acknowledged.

She smiled at him and retorted, "Well, you know, it's all about the education."

Her alignment, with the man bent on keeping me from getting my degree, flabbergasted me. I knew Sabrina well enough to know she was on automatic pilot and was naively playing up to my manipulative husband's overtures. Her sudden interest in gardening and touting her higher education to Seth felt like betrayal to me. She was throwing her Bachelor's degree in the face of a man who felt superior to me because I had no college degree. I had given her the details about that subject matter. Had she changed her feelings about the cad because she knew his investments were up to a million dollars?

I looked at Pete and our eyes met. He knew my husband and oldest friend's interaction bothered me.

Pete turned to Sabrina and interrupted, "Well, well, well, what do we have here, two horticulturalists in one room? You two can talk landscaping all night long, I'm sure."

Chad interrupted and threw at Sabrina, "I tell Seth that he should get his gardens featured in *Southern Living*. Don't you agree?"

Sabrina nodded, "I've seen his talent, and I have to agree with you, Chad."

Seth gloated, "I am a Renaissance man. What do I *not* do?" He asked the woman married to the lawyer. "I dropped out of law school!" He chuckled. "I didn't need it! I'm the managing broker over Bike World's $25 million dollar employees' pension fund. I'm collecting an annual $100,000 in commissions, and, in addition to that income, the value of my investments in the stock market is climbing every day! I'm living the American dream. I have a beautiful home completely paid for in full, three beautiful kids--a beautiful wife. I'm a lucky man."

Pete chuckled. "I have to admit, Seth, you are one smart son-ov'a-bitch."

I did not agree with the homage the room was paying Seth, and wondered why they all blew their trumpets in my husband's honor?

Sabrina looked around the kitchen while I knew she was internalizing my husband's pretensions. "You got it all, Seth."

She looked back at me. "Your kitchen should be featured in *Southern Living*, too."

"Thank you, Brini. I brought the outdoors in." I was referring to the floral prints found in the wallpaper and matching custom swags, I had ordered for the kitchen's wall of windows that looked out onto a twelve-foot Roman column made of cement. The white background of the paper accentuated the dark teal colored cabinets.

"Do you like smart?" Seth asked Sabrina while walking up closer to her and then lowering his voice as if only talking to her.

I could hear what Seth said to Brini: "I have some *insider* information; and due to my privileged relationships in New York, I now have my initial investment up, over one million dollars."

"Really" she considered his words and then turned to me, "You didn't tell me, Jean."

"Of course I did! You forget?" I became aware of her pretense. I had confided in Sabrina over how my husband risked his mother's fortune. "I'm certain Seth will refresh your memory."

Sabrina flipped her attention back to Seth. "Tell me more, darling. My husband would be interested in *insider* information. Anytime Goose makes money, I'm thrilled. We will all gain."

I had relayed to Sabrina that the money Seth played with was not his; and I expressed my fears to her that my husband's New York stockbroker could make a margin call any day, and that he would most likely loose every dime of his ma's life savings. I also was aware Sabrina had no understanding of finances or investments—Goose had purposely kept her in the dark about the money he earned. She did not even pay the household bills; therefore, I figured she did not understand the risk at hand when I told her that Seth played on the margin.

"Come on outside, Sabrina," Seth instructed as he walked back out the glass kitchen door. "I need a fag. Anyone care to join me for a smoke?"

"I'm right behind you," my girlfriend answered while Pete, Chad, and I followed them outside. We stood just beyond the glass kitchen door, under a catwalk, with a slider swing sitting on a wide pebble walk. Sabrina held out her wrist for Seth's view as they stepped into the late night air. "Have I shown you the bauble that Goose gave me for our eleventh year anniversary?"

I watched Seth light up a cigarette, then take her wrist, and examine her jewelry while I considered my husband and oldest friend had much in common--both were braggadocios and often twisted the truth. I wondered if Sabrina's husband truly gave her the pearl bracelet she held out for Seth's view, or whether she bought the piece herself. Since she had born a child out of wedlock, I often questioned if her marriage was truly as solid as she had painted her relationship to be with Goose. Was the good-looking attorney really happily married to his unfaithful and fat wife?

"That's some diamond," Chad said to Sabrina while looking at her ring finger. Chad continued, "My father gave my mother a four carat diamond for their twentieth anniversary."

"Your father knows how to do it right," Sabrina quipped.

"What's that stone worth, a month's wage?" Seth asked Sabrina.

"Twenty-four months if you make $7 per hour," Sabrina snapped. "Goose is a *very generous* man. My husband gave me this diamond for our engagement; and I knew then, exactly what I was marrying. My mother didn't raise a fool."

Pete retorted, "A fool despises good counsel, but a wise man takes it to heart--Confucius."

"We love wisdom," Brini quipped and then said to Pete, "I watched my mama struggle while she raised three kids by herself on a private school teacher's salary."

I whined to Seth, "Why don't you buy me something *nice* like that for our anniversary? Do you even know when our anniversary is, Seth?"

He laughed while I knew Seth recalled that day, after we got back home from our honeymoon, when he stood in this very spot under this catwalk and watched me throw my gold band into a clump of trees in our backyard. He had verbally degraded me for the last time. I had had enough of his abuse and reneged on my marriage vows when I threw away the gold band. I needed no court to tell me that I was free to not play the role of wife!

"It's in the summer, sometime," Seth tried to recall. "I remember, we went to Cancun and went snorkeling."

I snickered. "That's all right; I don't want to remember when we got married, either."

"You don't know when your anniversary is?" Sabrina huffed as if surprised.

"No!" I reiterated while wondering what happened to the

woman who lectured me at Fred's place on the oceanfront about leaving the man who kicked me in the shins.

"Hey, Seth, why don't you buy your wife a big diamond, too?" Chad suggested.

Sabrina prevented Seth from having to respond to the consideration when she shot back with a question. "Seth, you're doing okay for yourself, right?"

"Of course I am, Sabrina. Look around! What do you think?" He hissed as if she was ridiculous to ask such a question.

"I see a man who is doing *quite well* for himself," she confirmed and then looked over at me. "This is your wife, who gave you two sons. My god, buy her something special!"

"Hey," I corrected, "I gave him a house, too! That's irrelevant, though."

"Like I said, Sabrina, you're a smart woman," Seth quickly stirred and skimmed over my last statement.

"I'm going to have my husband call you, Seth."

"Better than that, Sabrina," I interrupted them. "I'm having the group over here for a barbeque in a couple of weeks. Invite Goose over, and he and Seth can talk stock options all afternoon."

"Great idea, Jean," Seth added and then looked over at Sabrina, "I look forward to meeting your husband. Maybe he and I can do some business together."

"When you help Goose make money, you help me," she reminded Seth.

"I'm all about helping you, Sabrina." Seth illuminated for her understanding.

"I'll love you forever, darling," Sabrina sparked.

Their overt flirtation in front of me threw me into a tailspin, and I was feeling played for an idiot.

Seth smiled at Sabrina. "Let me take you on a tour of my gardens," he offered while he stood on the edge of darkness with his smoking cigarette.

"I'd be delighted," she said as she walked up to him.

I watched my oldest friend and husband disappear around the dimly lit house while I remained in the spotlight with Pete and Chad.

I could not hear my husband and best friend's chatter over the music that flowed through the glass kitchen door from the living room.

"How's school going, Jean?" Pete asked.

I felt disturbed by all of them and spouted. "On the upside, the professors stimulate me with their lectures, and on the downside, the university feels too big. I have to bring my driver's license with me in order to take a test. Some of my classes are in a huge auditorium and feel so impersonal. Those professors don't even know my face after a month, and I have not made a single friend, either."

"Wow, I'm surprised to hear that, Jean. You? No friends?"

"None!" I impatiently answered Pete while I grew suspicious of my husband and best friend's current act. I knew I kept my distance with people these days because I did not trust my situation. The year before, I had made a friend, on my first day of school, and two days later, I had found myself withdrawn from my classes and with a broken nose. I prayed I would not run into Adriana this year. I felt humiliated by my life and did not want to explain to her how Seth forced me to quit school. I feared every day I would come home from school and discover Seth had pulled the plug on my life again.

I felt disturbed by my husband's walk in the dark park behind the house with my oldest friend. "Excuse me;" I said to Pete and Chad, "but I need to go check on my kids."

I walked inside my house, turned off, again, the loud music that blasted from an expensive stereo in the living room, and glanced at the clock hanging on the wall inside the walk-in bar to see midnight. I had smoked dope with all of them, against my convictions that night; and after all I had said to Chad and Pete, about them not bringing their drugs to my home, I now appeared to be a hypocrite. My word was crap, and though I was stoned from the weed and beer, I felt something brewing between my husband and Sabrina--they were just too friendly. Maybe I was just paranoid from the drugs? I reasoned that my bi-sexual husband, who seldom desired to have sex with me, *would not be* attracted to a woman twice my size? And that surely Seth would not sleep with my oldest friend, nor would she sleep with my husband. I went upstairs to peek on the children and then headed back down and went to bed without saying goodnight. I figured everyone would continue to party for several more hours.

NOVEMBER 1993. Two weeks later, on a Sunday afternoon, I threw a backyard party for the group, those loyalists that enjoyed beer with Sabrina and I at Jimmie's Ice House after the Monday night Landmark Education seminars. Unfortunately, my group leader and weekly phone buddy, the sexy and tall, blonde and blue-eyed, and well-built Chris did not make the invite. I suspected he felt our chemistry was transparent and that his absence would prevent any riff with my husband.

My new seminar friends, Fred of Scandinavian descent, and with high cheekbones and milky white skin, showed up for my barbeque, along with the blonde and blue-eyed easy-going Linda, and the redheaded flower child, Theo, and her boyfriend, Dan, the bearded scientist.

Linda was pretty, currently single and never married, and living nearby The Woodlands in the rural town of Tomball on her parents' land in a newer double-wide her deceased grandmother once occupied. We had been talking since Fred's oceanfront gathering, and she had revealed to me her growing dissatisfaction over her current life. She had lost her best girlfriend only weeks earlier, and had expressed to me her loneliness and her need to find companionship. I liked Linda because she was smart, fluent, and straight up with me; and quickly into our relationship, I began to open up with her regarding my marriage.

Sabrina and her husband, Goose, drove two-and-a-half hours with their daughter, Jacqueline, from Port Neches that day for my gathering. And, of course, the boys from *The Talent House*--the young Chad, and his high school sweetheart, twenty-year old Jenn, who still lived at home with her parents, and the thirty-two year old Pete and his new live-in, Karen, the beautiful twenty-one year old who greatly disapproved of me, all showed up for the mixer.

My husband sat on the back patio next to the grill ensuring the cooking meat did not burn while he chatted with Sabrina's husband, Goose, who picked his brain for stock market tips. I flittered all over the place watching three young children, preparing side dishes in the kitchen, and serving cold beers to the guests who gathered in a large circle on the backyard patio.

Fred found me in my lonely kitchen chopping vegetables for a salad. "Care for some company?" He asked.

"Yeah, have a seat!" I said as I pointed to a bar stool at the island. "Let's have a cold one."

"Love one," he replied as I headed toward the refrigerator.

The first time I really made a connection with the man was in our first seminar together, when he stood up in front of his chair in a sea of a hundred sitting participants and announced to all of us over a microphone that he was committed to writing and finishing a screenplay within a year. He informed us that he was an active screenwriter, and that he would sell his current script to Hollywood; and I was immediately intrigued with his lofty ambition. I quickly learned thereafter, over beer and conversation at Jimmie's Ice House, after our weekly meeting, that Fred was a carefree spirit who graduated from college and then drove an eighteen-wheeler after he got his degree. Now, somewhere in his mid-forties, he earned a living making videos with computerized graphics for a gas company. I instantly clicked with him that evening in our first seminar when he verbalized his commitment and made himself accountable to the entire group to be who he said he was--a screenwriter who would sell a script in a year. When Fred announced to all of us seminar participants that he was writing a script, I knew I had found my support system as a writer. I, too, desired to be a great writer one day; and without hesitation, I sprung to my feet and yelled across the room of applauding attendees, "Fred, I want to talk to you about your writing project after the seminar! I'm a writer, too."

He flashed a big smile at me that night and agreed to my request with a nod as he sat back down. We formally introduced ourselves to each other in the lobby after our three-hour seminar ended at 10:00 p.m.

I informed Fred later that evening that I had three young children at home, and that I suspected my husband would leave me in the near future, and when he did, I would have to support three kids and myself. I further informed my new writer friend that my solution to my dilemma over not having worked outside the home for anyone since 1987 was to write a best seller and make some major money. We exchanged phone numbers and continued talking on the phone and at Jimmie's Ice House after our weekly seminar meetings.

I revealed to Fred that I had taken short, three-week long, non-accredited writing courses at Rice University, and that I did not have a college degree. I told my seminar friend that I had been writing a love story on my word processor, which involved a man in Switzerland, named Cliff, who inspired a woman to dream. I called my novel, *Yellow Bird*, named after a poolside drink my lover and I had shared together over the weeks we had spent together in Florida.

Now, a month after our initial meeting, Fred sat on a barstool at the island in my kitchen, while I stood on the other side of the island and prepared a large garden salad. He took a swig of beer and I continued, "I want to sell my story to Hollywood one day, too, but for no less than three million dollars, or I'll produce the adaptation of my novel and be the creative director on the movie project. My story will be movie of the year." I looked up in all seriousness. "I realize I have a lot of work to do before I accept my Oscar; like, for starters, I must learn how to write!"

Fred chuckled, "Subscribe to *Writer's Digest*, the magazine offers good pointers. I'll be happy to critique your writing."

"Oh, you're wonderful!" I said in pretense while feeling that if he were to truly read my writing, he would conclude me to be a neophyte with no writing ability, or worse, he would see the real me through my words. "I've finished a couple of chapters."

"Bring them on!"

I shuddered at the thought of anyone reading about me. "I have to admit something to you, Fred. I've been struggling with something. I'm not able to open up about me. Tess is the main character in my novel, and she is me," I revealed. "All my characters are people I actually know; and I expose all their flaws without any hesitation, but when it comes to me exposing me, I have a very difficult time being that honest."

"Don't try to stay in your reader's favor, it's okay if they judge Tess to be something less than perfect. They will relate to her flaws."

"Good point. I had a breakthrough recently. I get I have to write without judgment. I'm hard on myself. I deal with my ego—I feel embarrassed, stupid, and wrong when I try to write about my past."

"Let the reader make up their own mind about your characters—be unabashed. Remember, it's our human nature to need to look good for others, and not appear like the failures we are at times; but, we limit our possibilities when we play the looking good game, and you'll limit your self-expression as a writer."

"I feel like a fraud. I'm the most screwed up person I know."

"Everyone falls apart sooner or later. Be unabashed and people will respect your courage to be honest."

"I think that for me to be authentic, feels like a big risk," I affirmed. "The next time I sit down to write, I will work on my courage to show myself up to be less than God-like."

Fred chuckled. "There you go!"

"So how's your writing coming along?"

"I submitted my script in a contest, the one about the Bolivian drug cartel and the American female tourist; and I came in second place, out of hundreds of submissions."

"Wow, congratulations!"

"Yeah, thanks," he beamed. "So now there's this director downtown who wants to do a reading of my script, live, on stage with actors."

"That's cool."

"And then depending on how the reading goes, he might produce my play."

"Wow! That's awesome, too!"

"Yeah, it is," he snickered.

"Hey, I'll race you to the top of the marquee!"

He chuckled. "Okay, you're on!"

I leaned over the island and shook the blue-eyed man's hand, while I understood we were making a pact with each other to be there always for each other as writers.

Sabrina entered into the kitchen with a couple of empty beer cans in her hand and caught us sealing the deal. "Okay, what are you two cooking up?"

"Baked potatoes, brown beans, salad," I answered.

"Ha, Ha," she retorted. "Where's the garbage can?"

I pointed her into the adjacent utility room and watched her drop the recyclables. She continued, "I've had all I can bear out there. Seth has been telling me and my husband about his investments—Goose is picking his brain and taking notes."

"I don't even know what stocks Seth has sunk his money into anymore," I admitted to Sabrina. "I once read what stocks he bought when he showed me as proof that he was not lying, and that his investment had indeed soared to over one million dollars."

"Seth mentioned having purchased shares in a communications company, in a gaming company, in an airline, and in pharmaceuticals, just to name a few," Sabrina relayed with rolling eyes. "Goose is paying attention, and that's all that matters."

Fred jumped in, "The market is tumultuous right now. Stocks plunged last month in Tokyo, and their brokers attributed the fall to the political turmoil in Russia. In addition, earlier this month, European stock markets plummeted after a yearlong climb that had taken many exchanges to record levels. London, Paris, Frankfurt, all those exchanges are down now."

Sabrina inserted, "Goose says that here in the United Sates the Dow Jones has been confusing this week, too. Supposedly there was two days of sharp declines that followed two days of record closes."

"The global economies are all connected," Fred added. "Some analysts say that a correction in the European markets was overdue, but overall, the London, Italian, French, and German exchanges have all been rising and strong, despite a severe European recession. The rises occur mainly because of falling interest rates over there, and expectation of further interest rate cuts have prompted investors to bet on an European economic recovery next year, sometime in '94. They're hoping to earn higher returns through the stock market."

"I don't keep up with overseas economies," I said. "But here in America, there are signs a recovery is picking up steam, which has caused concern that inflation may rise in the United States."

Sabrina added, "Great, my house will go up in value!"

"Do you want to sell?" I asked.

"I wish;" she grumbled, "but my husband won't leave Port Neches."

"Most likely your house will go up in value," Fred confirmed. "Low interest rates in America have fed the stock rally frenzy this year on Wall Street, and our economy has a direct impact on Europe, too."

"I find it all complicated;" I groaned, "and I took a class at the community college specifically called *Understanding the Stock Market*. It's all just a calculated gamble."

Fred began singing Kenny Rogers' The Gambler: "♪You got to know when to hold 'em...♪"

Sabrina and I jumped in and finished the catch-phrase lyric. "♪...And know when to fold 'em. ♪"

Fred chuckled, "The continuing recession around the world has kept pressure on various central banks to lower interest rates, and that in turn helps stock markets. Supposedly the recession in France and Germany has hit bottom, and that could have a positive effect on global markets, too."

"I hope you're right, Fred;" I said, "and I hope you don't mind if I change the subject." I then looked at Sabrina, "After you showed my husband your pearl bracelet that Goose bought you for your eleventh wedding anniversary, Seth has since gone out and bought me some very expensive Tiffany lamps."

"I saw those beautiful lamps when I came through the front door today," she expounded. "Seth proudly showed us his gifts."

"He bought the lamps because he liked them, or the sales agent."

Sabrina hissed, "Listen to you. He's stepping up to the plate, isn't he?"

I shrugged while not believing he cared about me enough to do anything selfless. "I was surprised to see him drag those lamps into our home. Come see, Fred."

Sabrina and Fred followed me as I led them into the front room just off the kitchen. "He's definitely got good taste," I admitted while pointing to the ornate floor lamp with a thick milk glass shade colored with muted shades of pink and white striations, and then to a matching smaller lamp that sat on top of my white piano. Rose-colored and black glass beads dangled from both pink shades. "I don't know whatever possessed him?" I quipped.

"Oh stop!" Sabrina spouted. "Seth gets that he's taken you for granted for too long."

"Oh, I don't know about that, Sabrina," I groaned. "I think he bought those lamps because he liked the lamps himself."

"Would you give the guy a break?" Sabrina pleaded and then looked at Fred. "And she wonders why they don't get along!"

"I don't wonder! I know exactly why we don't get along," I defended while looking at Fred.

Fred laughed and looked at Sabrina. "They're married! They're not supposed to like each other."

Sabrina and I chuckled; and I quipped, "That sounds like something a confirmed bachelor would say."

Sabrina looked at Fred, "How is it that you have remained unmarried your entire forty-something years?"

"He's smart," I answered for Fred.

"I'd have to agree with Jean," he laughed.

WEEKS LATER, NOVEMBER 1993. I woke up and saw Seth was not on his side of our unmade bed. I peered at the clock on the nightstand and noted 7:00 a.m. on this Friday morning. I needed to wake Bella up and get her on the school bus. My daughter was finally making good grades in school now that she was in the fourth grade, and I attributed her progress, and change of attitude toward her entire life, to me having enrolled her into a $450 three-day seminar for young people between the ages of 8-12 at Landmark Education Corporation's Houston site. Bella attended her first seminar over a long, three-day weekend, beginning on a Friday. She had learned the same carnal technology that I had been given in my three-day seminar for adults; and now, mother and daughter shared the same understanding in a conversation called the power of one's word and how the stories we tell ourselves limit our lives. Bella, having learned about her biological father, Mario, from me, at the age of eleven, had experienced a transformation from being a foregone conclusion over the three-day seminar. For the first time in her life, Bella became conscious of her choices, and now chose to be a victor with a winner's attitude after three intensive days of thought-provoking considerations presented to her by their seminar leader. The eleven-year old now cared about taking a shower, about washing her hair frequently, about keeping her room immaculate, and about being exceptional, instead of average. My daughter had examined her life in a way that left her empowered to be responsible for her life, and had discovered a new appreciation and respect for herself and for others. Bella gained clarity in what it took to communicate and effectively relate to others, and she had found a new freedom in life. A light had flipped on during the seminar for the young girl who once acted as if nothing about her life mattered. She now paired her socks neatly in her top drawer, and did all her homework every evening without me having to nag. Since her recent brainwashing, she suddenly made straight A's in school, and began drawing charcoal portraits of the country singer Garth Brooks, and of the Hollywood movie star, Antonio Banderas; and she began singing Madonna songs every night behind her closed bedroom door. God had finally answered my prayer. I hoped that she drew her strength from God.

 I lay there in bed that early morning and noted that the red light on the phone that sat on the nightstand was illuminated which indicated that someone was using another extension in the house or garage. I figured Seth was outside, in the garage, smoking a cigarette and drinking coffee while talking to his New York stockbroker just as the sun came up in Texas; the east coast was an hour ahead of us.

 I salivated for a cup of hot coffee sweetened with vanilla flavored creamer and pulled myself out of bed. I threw on my robe, slid into my house slippers, and headed upstairs to wake my daughter. Bella was up and dressed, and ready for school, and reading a book on her bed about the music industry. I said good morning to her, and then peeked into my sons' bedroom and saw them sawing wood. I climbed back downstairs, traipsed across the living area, and entered into the kitchen from the den through the frosted bi-fold doors. I walked over to the stainless steel sink to run hot water for the coffee pot and peered out the window in front of me. I spotted Seth pacing in and out of our two-car garage while on the phone. I heard the coffeemaker rumble and noticed that Seth had already brewed a pot of coffee. I turned off the faucet and reached into the cabinet for a cup when Seth suddenly barged through the kitchen door. He held his empty coffee cup at his side and looked as if death had called him by name.

"What's the matter?" I asked with great concern and walked toward him.

"I lost all Ma's money," he said as if in shock.

"Oh, my God!" I exclaimed.

"I can't believe that imbecilic woman!" He bellowed and walked past me.

"Why? What happened?" I turned and watched him pour coffee into his cup.

He just continued to shake his head in disbelief and then angrily cried, "My broker screwed me!"

"And how did she do that?"

"I put all my eggs into one basket," he explained.

"And...?" I prodded while hearing him blame his stockbroker for a poor investment that was ultimately his decision.

"And...I lost every damn cent!" He snapped.

"Wow," I sighed while feeling disappointed in Seth and sorry for his mother. I considered asking my husband if his broker made a margin call, and if he lost his mother's investment because he could not meet his broker's cash demand, but I stopped short. I knew which way was up; I knew the answer. Many experts had forewarned him, and I instantly became angry with Seth *and* his mother. The aged, but not-yet-retired, and poorly paid secretary had the sense of a nincompoop due to a lifetime habit of enabling her oldest son, and not having learned how to say no to him. I suspected all along that my husband would lose his ass, but I didn't want to have a discussion that morning called *you arrogant buffoon!*

Seth ripped through the swinging saloon doors of the walk-in bar adjacent to the kitchen and came back out with a bottle of Bailey's.

He poured the liquor into his coffee and then headed back out the glass kitchen door without saying another word to me.

I figured he was ready to cry, or get drunk, while certain that I would not have wanted to make that next phone call. How would he tell his mother that he lost her life savings? Would he pick up the phone, or drive to her apartment, and then say what? Would he say, "Hey, Ma, sorry, but you no longer have a dime to your name." Then what was to unfold after his grim disclosure? Would she expect him to take care of her? Would we be saddled with an old woman in the future when she no longer could work?

I grabbed a mug out of the cabinet and was considering adding Bailey's to my coffee, too, when Seth suddenly barged back through the glass kitchen door and said, "I'm going to sue my broker for losing my money in the stock market."

"You can do that?"

He shook head, "Yeah, I heard about a case in law school. My broker gave me insider information. I was told by her that I could not lose."

9
THE BETRAYAL

A WEEK LATER. Seth seldom seduced me, and I rarely felt amorous even with Seth around 24/7; but, on this particular day, while shopping at the mall, I popped into *Victoria's Secret* to check out sexy lingerie. I had been working out five days a week at the club, and I sculpted my body to be hard and in perfect shape. I felt lonely and empty. There wasn't an ounce of fat anywhere on my sinewy form. My long slender legs were tan and my thin waistline was that of a woman who had never bore a single child. I fantasized that Seth tore off the sexy garment that I chose to wear that night, while I sorted through the racks of silky nightwear, bras, and panties. No matter what I donned, most likely, the garment would be on the floor within minutes. I stopped and considered a beautiful, black teddy and wondered if Seth would find me attractive if I kindled his fires with a garter belt and stilettos, too. Our sex life had always been on the back burner, for one reason or another, and had felt conditional for years; either Seth was disinterested, or I was too angry, too exhausted, or too busy. I spent one hundred and twenty-five dollars that morning on an ensemble that I hoped would turn on my husband. I figured we might grow closer together if we spent more time in each other's arms. I plotted to seduce him that afternoon. I would wait for Bella to come home from school, and then ask her to watch her younger brothers while I got Seth out of the yard and we "took a nap."

I went home, and as planned, I showered, shaved my legs, washed and dried my hair, and sweetened my body with oils and perfumes. I then dressed in a black teddy, silk stockings, and sexy black stilettos. I pulled a robe over my scantily clad body and then stepped into the living room where I knew Bella sat and watched TV. I asked her to go outside and find Seth, and to tell him to come in and talk to me. "Tell him it's very important," I added while she walked out of the house.

I waited in the bedroom, and within minutes, Seth entered through the closed bedroom door and found me lying in the center of the bed on my side in my black seduction costume. I smiled. "I think you should take a break from that yard, baby, and spend some time with me," I enticed with a breathy voice.

Seth looked at me as if I was crazy and jeered, "You're the last thing I want right now, *baby!*" He then walked out of the bedroom.

My anger flashed as he slammed the door behind himself. I sat up, felt humiliated, and rejected, while understanding that I had just given Seth another opportunity to tell me that he was not attracted to me. Nothing was new about his disinterest in me. Seth had never craved me on a sexual or intellectual level, and, in fact, he degraded my intelligence and took enjoyment in telling me that if he were to have met me at a bar, and bought me a drink, our conversation would have run the length of one alcoholic beverage before he would be bored. There were too many reasons for why I no longer wore a gold band.

The irony of his berating words was that I had grown completely bored with him.

I had discovered over the years, during our sexual encounters, that if Seth knew I had an orgasm, then he would distance from me by not having sex with me for another month, or longer, ending any intimacy we may have created in the moment of passion. Recently, the Houston Chronicle ran a series of articles about controlling behavior in a battering personality. Seth liked to leave bruises on my legs, therefore he fell into this category; and I read the column with great interest. A psychiatrist wrote that when a batterer's behavior gets worse, he might not let the woman make personal decisions. Obviously, I was not going to call the shots when we had sex either.

I slid down to the edge of the bed when the phone rang and distracted me from my depressing thoughts. I grabbed the receiver and sadly answered, "Hello."

"How are you, Jean?"

"Chris! Good timing," I answered while thrilled my sexy seminar phone buddy was on the other end.

"Why is that?"

His voice was sultry and caring. "I was just sitting here on the edge of my bed feeling very lonely."

"Where's your husband?"

"He's here; he never goes anywhere," I bemoaned. "Seth is preoccupied with anything but me."

"And what are *you* preoccupied with, Jean?"

"My unhappiness these days," I disclosed while hoping he had a quick fix.

"Do you want to talk about your unhappiness?"

"Not really, I don't know what to say, other than I don't know which way is up these days. I don't know what to do with my husband? Seth gives me mixed messages. Maybe you can help me? You're a man."

"I've never been married, nor do I have children. I don't know what that situation is like."

"But you talked to Seth when we were at Fred's house?"

"Seth didn't talk about his relationship with you; he just talked about himself."

"His favorite subject," I cracked. "I refuse to divorce him, but staying with him is such an empty feeling."

"All I can offer you, Jean, is some advice."

Chris was staying at arm's length with me, but getting more from him than advice was a nice fantasy.

"Find happiness within your own self," he continued, "and be aware that nothing stays the same."

"I appreciate your advice," I said while disappointed with his strength of character. "I find it difficult to be happy with a mean and cold partner. You can understand my need to have a warm loving spirit who loves me, right?"

"I understand perfectly well."

"And I *can* imagine having a different partner, and I *can* get lost in that fantasy. I like the idea of being with someone who desires me, who doesn't want to live without me."

"And why do you call that possibility a fantasy?" He asked.

"Because I can't move from this place I've created. I truly believe Seth and I need each other for our spiritual well-being, and our children need us to need each other, too. I don't want to split up my family! I don't want to cause anyone emotional suffering--not my kids, not Seth, not myself. I don't want to wake up and wonder what my youngest children are eating for breakfast. I've experienced that pain with my firstborn. I'm certain Seth would not want to cry, either. Divorce is too painful, and anything that is *that* painful has to be wrong."

"You may be doing your children a disservice if their parents are fighting."

"You're right! We just have to stop fighting. My children want both their parents under their roof, and they want happy parents, too. I need Seth, too. I need his emotional support and his financial help. I don't hold down a paying job; I haven't worked in years. I need him to help me raise these children, but Seth acts like he doesn't need me."

"Maybe he doesn't need you, Jean."

"I don't think he loves me," I sadly admitted.

"Maybe he doesn't love you," Chris offered.

"If so, then why do I feel I need him?"

"Do you expect Seth to love you back?"

"Yes!"

"Does he love you?"

"I don't know," I said while considering the Tiffany lamps Seth recently gave me.

"I grew up in a Christian home with parents who loved each other, Jean."

"I did, too," I said while doubting my parents truly loved each other. I questioned if because *I thought* I did not have parents who loved each other, therefore, did *I believe* I did not deserve to have love as a married woman?

Chris continued, "And I suppose when we grow up with two parents who love each other and need each other, then we expect to have the same when we marry and have kids."

"I do expect Seth to love me," I said.

"But maybe Seth doesn't expect you to love him," Chris challenged

"Why wouldn't he?"

"Maybe he concluded when he was a kid, due to his parents' awful behavior, that they didn't love him. We've often heard others admit, in our weekly seminars, that they believed their parents didn't love them. We've learned that if a person feels unlovable as a child, then that person expects no one else will love him either, that is, if his *own* parents didn't love him."

I added, "Worse than believing your parents don't love you, is to believe God doesn't love you, either. I don't really think my parents loved each other, Chris. I witnessed a lot of unhappiness growing up. My parents did not appear happy in love to me; on the contrary, my mother consistently expressed her unhappiness with her marriage over the years to me and to her women friends. I think when I was a kid that I concluded God did not love me because had God loved me, he would have placed me with happy parents. I had no use for God; and as a result, I easily fell to temptation and lost opportunity to have love--I ended up with Seth. My feelings and emotions have ruled over my life."

"Maybe you and Seth are more alike than you understand?"

"Maybe we were the same *at the beginning*, but I've woken up and matured. I'm in hell with my eyes wide open. Seth grew up in a sick environment, with very dysfunctional parents. His father was a mean, abusive alcoholic, and his mother was always angry and warring with his daddy. I've heard Seth refer to his mother as a rage-aholic. Seth can't believe I could ever love him, and that's why he thinks that if I get my college degree, I will leave him. I believe Seth went to Bible College hoping that he would find a family there, and be in a place where he was truly loved and respected."

"Or he hoped that a church congregation might one day love him. And it's possible, too," Chris added, "that Seth told himself when he was a kid that he would never get married because a spouse would never make him happy. You're the spouse, Jean--you don't represent happiness to that little boy that still controls Seth's life."

"Wow, I'm his second spouse, too. I'm not off the mark when I claim not to know what to do with Seth. What can I do?"

"You might not ever be enough for the little boy, Jean. Seth is still angry, and deep down still feels unlovable, and marriage was and probably is the last thing he wants in his life."

Seth's last words to me, in the bedroom, only a few minutes earlier, echoed in my head: *You're the last thing I want right now.* Chris was right--Seth was still that little boy who had sworn off marriage. Seth's father had died in a drunken boat accident when Seth was a senior in high school, and I suspected he had forgiven the dead, but obviously, was still angry with his mother for not loving her son enough to leave his drunken father and take them out of that miserable situation, early on. Perhaps Seth's act of losing his mother's life savings in the stock market was his passive-aggressive retribution for the eighteen years of hell she had brought into her firstborn's life?

THE END OF NOVEMBER 1993. Sabrina and her two-year old, Jacqueline, arrived from Porte Neches early that Monday morning to spend some time with me and my family before she and I headed out to our Monday night seminar at 7:00 p.m. Jacqueline was in between Doren and Harper in age, and I took delight in watching them play together that morning while knowing that the loyalty between these three children would continue into their adult lives because their mothers had been the best of friends for a lifetime.

Sabrina insisted on cooking lunch for us three adults that day. I sat on the barstool at the island while sipping tea and watched her add lemon to mashed avocado while Seth remained outside most of the morning gathering moss for his green carpet.

"The avocado is seasoned with pepper and only a bit of salt; there will be enough salt in the lox." She took the split bagels, spread each half with the green mixture, and topped with the fish. "The onion, tomatoes, and capers are the key combination of good taste," she announced as she finished topping off a platter full of bagel halves.

Seth walked through the glass kitchen door and Sabrina lit up. "Oh darling, just in time," she gleefully announced. "I've made you something very special--a BLA."

"You mean a BLT?" Seth corrected.

She rolled her eyes, "No, I don't mean a BLT. It's a bagel with lox and avocado, silly. It's a traditional Jewish recipe handed down my family." Sabrina sat a decorated toasted bagel half on a small plate and served my husband first, while again, I remained intrigued with their friendliness.

"Yum," he said. "Thank you, sweetheart."

She beamed, "You're so welcome, darling."

Seth sat down at the nearby kitchen table with his plate. "Where are the kids?" He asked us.

"Upstairs," I answered while I remained perched on my barstool at the island. "They're so cute together."

Sabrina jumped in, "The kids already ate, and they're happy and content. Jean cooked spaghetti for the kids. If you'd like some of that, too, we've plenty left over."

"Maybe later," Seth replied. "What I'd like is another one of your scrumptious culinary delights."

Sabrina jumped at Seth's request and walked over to where he sat with a platter of bagels. "Here you go, darling. Mama loves to see somebody enjoy her creations."

"I'm enjoying," Seth answered with a mouth full of food and then swallowed. "I would guess that you are an amazing cook."

"Of course I am!" Sabrina boasted while she stood at the bar across from me. She bit into her delicacy, which inspired me to take the first bite of lox, avocado, tomato, and capers on bagel.

"I love the burst of flavors," I said. "This is very good."

"Thank you, darling." Sabrina turned her attention back to Seth. "I've had the life of privilege. I stay home, and I take care of my husband who takes *very good care* of me; and, as they say, the way to a man's heart is through his stomach. I love to serve. I think of myself as a Jewish mother."

"Are you Jewish?" Seth asked.

"No, I'm Christian. Goose and I got married in the Methodist Church."

"You and Jean went to the same Catholic school while growing up, right?"

"Yes, we did. My mother taught at that Catholic school that Jean and I attended. We went to mass together, every Sunday, or at least, we popped our heads into the front doors of the church to see which priest was conducting mass, so that when her father asked us who said mass, after we came back from the beach later that evening, we would be right, and keep the peace." She laughed. "Hank did not allow us to go to Galveston Beach on Sundays without us first going to church."

I giggled along with Sabrina.

"Ol' Hank is a good man," Seth patronized.

Seth knew my father had his number when my father brought my arrogant husband down a peg or two for having the audacity to ask if he could gamble his life savings in the stock market.

"So why did you get married in the Methodist Church?" Seth asked Sabrina.

"A compromise," she said flippantly. "Goose attended First Methodist on the edge of River Oaks, which was only a few blocks from his palatial home, which was where we first lived together."

I had always known that Sabrina would never hold any marriage ceremony in the beautiful Catholic church in our crumbling and decaying neighborhood of southeast Houston simply because she did not want Goose to clearly understand how disadvantaged she had been as a child with no responsible father in the picture.

I inserted, "I think I'd like to call myself a Jewish mama, too. I like what the stereotype represents."

"What's that?" Seth asked me, "--a controlling woman who smothers her children?"

I shook my head in disapproval at his incivility while Sabrina came to my defense. "That *is not* what a Jewish mother is!"

"Well, yes it is, to a degree," I added for Sabrina's consideration. "She engenders enormous guilt in her children via the endless suffering she professes to have experienced on their behalf! That could be me!"

Sabrina argued, "No, that *is not* what the Jewish mother does, Jean. The role of the mother within the family is associated with virtue. Immigrant parents, mothers especially, sacrificed for their children. Jewish parents pushed their children to succeed, resulting in a push for perfection, and a continual dissatisfaction for anything less. For instance, Mona Lisa had a Jewish mama, and the woman said to her daughter over her portrait, 'This, you call a smile, after all the money your father and I spent on braces?'"

Seth and I laughed.

"That's a Jewish mama!" Sabrina stressed.

"I do that, Sabrina!" I affirmed. "I'm a woman who tries to control my life and the events around me;" I looked at Seth, "and sometimes that is too hard for even the brightest."

Sabrina looked at Seth, "It's important that the woman has her husband's support. "*Oy vey!*" She said in a Yiddish tone of voice, "I've watched my mother suffer while trying to raise three children on a private school teacher's salary! I love my father, but I do not respect him for jumping ship and abandoning his responsibility."

I understood, if Seth did not understand, that my friend was referring to Seth not having had my support, when he chose to risk his mother's life savings and then lost all of it.

"And by the way, Seth," Sabrina continued, "I'm still feeling the aftershocks at home. You gave Goose a bum's steer with those stock tips. I sold my friend in The Woodlands as reputable, and my husband lost quite a bit of money due to trusting me. I'm having a hard time living it down."

Seth growled, "My stockbroker gave me a bum steer!"

Sabrina rolled her eyes.

"I'm suing my broker in New Yorker," Seth added.

"I heard that from Jean; and I told Goose that you were suing your stockbroker, and he said you have no case."

"Not what my lawyer told me," Seth quipped.

Sabrina rolled her eyes again in disapproval.

I was compelled to make Seth's hard, life lesson bigger, and jumped into the middle of their exchange. "I consider myself intelligent, articulate and aggressive;" I said to Sabrina, "and I'm not going to passively accept life. I try to shape my family, my friends, and the events in my life to match *my vision* of an ideal world, and when they don't listen to me, then--"

Seth interrupted, "*Your vision* of ideal is not necessarily everyone else's vision!"

"Well," I shrugged, "after all is said and done, who was right? I was!" I slammed back at Seth and then angrily emphasized what I considered the obvious to Sabrina. "I have a vision of what greatness is, and anything less is, well, just that, less than exceptional."

Sabrina nodded in agreement with me and said to Seth, "Jean and I are on the same page; you've got to respect her. I've watched Jean mother her first two children for years, before I ever had my first child, and I learned a lot from watching her."

"Oh, you must have learned what *not* to do?" I chuckled. "My first two were my practice children."

"You're a good mother," Sabrina confirmed.

"Thank you, Brini."

"You go forward with gusto, Jean. I was impressed with your apparel business, too. I'm impressed with your home; it's beautifully decorated."

"Thank you; I appreciate your acknowledgments, Brini. I pride myself on being a caring mother these days, and I'm a good student, too. I'm making straight A's this semester. I push my daughter to be more, as I do myself; and I'll push my sons into activities when they get a bit older, too. I don't ask Bella if she wants to be in song and dance, I tell her that she will go. End of story. She's too young to know what she wants. I put my fourth grader into the same three-day seminar that I did as an adult; she sat there all day with her peers and learned the technology she has since used to turn her life around. I think that my daughter being a straight A student now is a miracle. I wish someone had given me that seminar at age ten. But, I ask, do you think she wanted to sit in a seminar all day for three days at ten years old?"

"Oh, heavens no!" Sabrina answered.

"Of course not! I am a Jewish mama who wants more for her children than what I have had in my life because I was less privileged, and unable to take full advantage of the American education system myself! I wasn't encouraged to go to college by my father; on the contrary, he told me that I was not college material!" I earnestly looked at Seth and continued, "Perhaps the consequence of what I've had to deal with over my years is the transference of my aspirations onto my children!" I looked at Sabrina, "As you know, I go to school every morning of the week. Do you know what I'm sacrificing for my family?"

I waited for her to jump on board. I hoped she would poignantly let my husband know that she had had the privilege to stay home with, or without a child, in her eleven-year marriage, without a single worry that her lawyer husband might walk out the door at any given moment. I hoped Sabrina would spew some of those harsh words she spoke to me about what she thought about my abusive husband onto him.

Seth cut into my assault. "Oh listen to Mama Rachel tell us that she tossed aside her hopes and dreams one more time."

"Shut up, Seth!" I angrily blurted while still reeling from my reality.

Sabrina cushioned the moment with soft words. "Of course, I know what you are sacrificing, Jean! You are going to school full time, and that feat is amazing in itself, considering you have three young children at home."

Sabrina walked over to the kitchen table where Seth and her purse sat. "I want you to see something, Seth," Sabrina said while she reached into her purse and pulled out her wallet. She handed Seth a photograph and then stepped back and waited for his reaction.

"Wow!" He exclaimed. "That's some sexy mama. You're incredible!"

"That picture was taken the first year I was married."

"So that's what you looked like ten years ago, huh?" Seth asked. "I would have snatched you up, too!"

"I want to see it," I exclaimed while walking over to where my husband sat and peering over his shoulder. I was surprised to see a frontal nude of a twenty-three year old Sabrina in a swimming pool baring her very large and perfectly formed breasts and shaved twat. I looked up at my friend and reconsidered who she really was for me?

She caught my disapproving look and meekly defended, "I just wanted Seth to see that I haven't always been a fat girl."

"Sabrina!" I begrudging espoused. "You're *not* a fat girl. You're a beautiful, mature woman."

"Well, look at you after four children! I hardly compare. Do you remember, though, back in the day, when we went uptown to that Houston bar?"

"Yeah," I answered. "That was great fun."

Sabrina turned to Seth and continued, "Jean and I were the two most beautiful women in the place. We had every man's attention."

"You were very beautiful, Brini," I confirmed while realizing she missed those days of her reigning glory.

I confirmed to Seth, "She absolutely had every man's desires that night."

I turned back to Sabrina, "I remember borrowing a dress of yours before we went out that night, a size four. I wore that dress to work the next day--my lucky dress. I got Leonardo's attention that day at work." I glanced at Seth for his reaction, but he held a poker face.

"That's right!" Sabrina affirmed while I also recalled having run into my high school crush in that same uptown bar on that very night. I had gone back to Mario's apartment that night while wearing that *lucky* dress and conceived my daughter. "We were all *small* eleven years ago," I consoled while wondering whatever possessed me back in those days to have sex with someone I just met, even if he and I grew up in the same neighborhood and went to the same Catholic school and church for twelve years.

"What do you mean, *you were?* You're practically anorexic now!"

"I'm not anorexic--I eat all the time." I hoped that my ability to stay in perfect shape after four children did not make the queen bee feel inferior.

Seth intervened, "You're still beautiful, Sabrina; I wouldn't push you out of my bed."

Sabrina took delight in my husband's words. "Thank you, darling," she said while I felt threatened again by my husband and best friend's amorous advances. I wasn't sure who was seducing whom, but I knew what provocative displays of sexual overtures were when I saw them!

I watched Sabrina take her nude photograph from Seth and put it back into her wallet; and while I questioned whether I was being paranoid, or not, I saw them give each other a come-hither look.

I wanted to shift the direction because I was feeling stupid. "You talk about the Jews in your family," I asked Sabrina, "Is Goose's family Jewish?"

"No, he's a practicing Christian; in fact, Goose holds Bible studies in our home every month. Sometimes I stay and study with the group, other times I take off for the evening."

Seth asked, "Who is Jewish then?"

"My brother married a Jewish princess," she answered.

"Did your brother convert from Catholicism to Judaism?" He inquired.

"Of course," she answered. "He studies the Torah and has learned Hebrew, too. Jews maintain a belief that Hebrew was God's language. They are raising their children in the Jewish faith. The religion of the child goes by the mother, while the tribal affiliation goes by the father."

"What tribal affiliation does your brother affiliate with?" I asked.

"None, silly" she answered, "We're Catholic!" "But for the most part, tribal identities have been lost through the generations anyway, and the majority of Jews do not know which tribe they are from. The Jews believe that when the Messiah comes, we will all find out which tribes we are from. The main emphasis is that both the father and mother must take active roles with the child. The mother is entrusted with the awesome duty of instilling in the child, faith in God, observance of mitzvoth, and Jewish pride."

"You're pretty astute in your understanding of Judaism," Seth noted.

"I guess I've become a Jewish mama, too," she said with self-importance.

Later that evening, I found myself behind my steering wheel, driving to our 7:00 p.m. seminar, and rattled by the thirty-four year old woman who sat beside me in my green Volvo station wagon. *I had not been living in fool's paradise*; and I felt Sabrina, and my husband, were so arrogant, that they believed I would not decipher between their acts of honor, and their acts of disrespect. Long ago, the dark side seduced me, and though I had come over to the other side since, any delusion on my husband and best friend's part that I believed what they *had preferred* I believe about them, clearly evidenced that they had no personal relationship with our Lord. Had they ever known the Light of our Heavenly Father, then they would have known that I had the gift of discernment. Her lecherous and lewd addiction was apparent. I had seen these mechanical movements for a lifetime. Now, she canonized me as a saint, after a lifetime of friendship--a deceptive ploy on her part to distract me from the obvious. My husband's abomination toward God and his monster's need to mock our martial union with his fleshy and libidinous vulgarities toward another, dared me to counteract their wantonness with charges of wrongfulness using barefaced honesty.

They had no consanguinity with me, and my world suddenly felt fragmented and splintered by their adulterations. The annihilation caused by their *coup de grace* bulldozed down my wall of security and left me feeling exposed. The great loving spirit came to my aid and whispered into my ear that theirs was double-talk, and via hocus-pocus. Their intent was that one-day I would feel loved and the next day broken-hearted, but, out of their contemplative contempt for my strength, I could and would return to the battlefield and mobilize against them.

I was in no coma; I was reassured that I saw it right, yet no definite indictment could I render over these rumblings. Perhaps I could still believe that my world would not shake, nor would the mountain erupt, and that the playboy and playgirl's conceits of power and puffery would dissipate like a billowy cloud. I silently prayed while I drove my car down the Houston freeway: *Please, loving father, be with me while I feel betrayed.*

I would remain cool. "Sabrina," I scrambled for the right words. "I just want you to understand something. I'm happy where I'm at, and with what I'm doing with my life. I realize I've shed some bad light on my husband in the past, but I'm in a good place right now with him and my kids. I'm in school making the grade with the goal in mind. I have a promising future, and I need to stay on this fast track and get my degree. I'm feeling more confident these days as this semester comes to an end."

"I wish I had some of what you have, Jean," Sabrina quipped. "I'm depressed; and I'm eating all the time, trying to find comfort in food."

"What's really bothering you?" I asked while wondering if she wrangled with her conscience after having had a child with a man named Jack from art class, or was her depression stemming from her long ago abortions. I had never asked Sabrina how she coped with her abortions, but I felt certain that she struggled with the same emotional issues that I had once suffered—guilt and unworthiness.

"This weight is my biggest problem! I don't feel attractive anymore. Goose is gone every weekend out on the catamaran. We don't spend time together anymore."

"Why don't you go on the boat with him?"

"I just don't want to spend every weekend out on the water."

I questioned if Sabrina was too embarrassed to wear a swimsuit and therefore stayed off the water. "Why are you holding on to that weight? Your daughter is nearly two."

"That's what I've been asking myself, too, Jean. I find being married to Goose after eleven years not very fulfilling anymore. And I've packed on over a hundred pounds since we got married, and it's like I, I," she hesitated. "I've never told you this before, but when I was still living in my mother's house, my oldest brother, Dalton, molested me."

"Wow," I said. "I had no idea you were dealing with issues of that magnitude while we were growing up. I'm so sorry, Sabrina."

"My mother caught my brother with his pants down, with an erection one night, with me in bed with him, and my pajamas unbuttoned. I was eleven, and he was sixteen. All he would say to her was that I was trying to tell him something and nothing happened. I told my mother that he made me touch him, and in turn, he touched me back. I told my mother that I told Dalton no and that I tried to get away from him, but he would grab me and hold me down. She asked why I didn't scream or come to her, and I told her that I was scared and felt I would be in trouble if I told the truth."

"Sabrina, you were too young to understand that your brother, an older and more powerful sibling, was being sexually abusive."

"Yeah, of course, I was. At first, Dalton had my trust just by being my big brother. I looked up to him, and I wanted his attention. My mother had given him a lot of responsibility and power because he was the firstborn, but Dalton abused that trust. Moreover, Mom was not paying attention for years, and I felt pressured and trapped by my big brother who babysat me. He made me have sexual intercourse with him, and I began to feel betrayed, and powerless, and ashamed."

"Did he commit sexual abuse for a long time?"

"Yes."

"But your mother had caught him in the act when you were eleven, right?"

"Yeah, but by then, too many years had passed. My mother was so ashamed when she caught Dalton, and she ordered us to protect the family secret. My brother did not get help, and I suspect he's doing the same thing to his own child now."

"That's horrible! Does the child's mother know about her husband?"

"I've tried to explain to her, but my brother tells his wife I'm crazy, and she wants to believe her husband. He continued sexually abusing me after Mom caught him, and threatened to hurt me if I talked again. He caused me further emotional abuse. He would tell me that no one loved me and that terrible things were going to happen to me if I said anything more. I started lying."

"Why do you think your brother became a sibling abuser?"

"There are a number of factors. My father abused my mother physically, emotionally, and sexually, until he finally ran off to Las Vegas. I was young when my father left; I understood very little."

"Maybe your brother was sexually molested by your father?"

"I don't know."

I felt Sabrina blamed herself for what happened, and maybe she felt guilty because she had experienced pleasure while being sexually abused by her older sibling. "What your brother did to you was not your fault. He took advantage of his size, power, and authority, and your mother wasn't paying attention, or didn't want to know. You can't beat yourself up for his behavior."

"I know all this on the surface. I don't get along with Dalton today, and he knows why I feel the way I do about him," she spewed.

"I can certainly understand why you wouldn't have a kind word for him," I answered.

"My brother is five years older than me. He didn't want me around when we were kids, but I adored him and wanted his attention! When I was three, or four, my brother tried several times to have sex with me, but I can't remember if there was any penetration. When I was eleven, my brother asked to see me naked several times and touched me. He asked me to touch him, too, but I would say no until I finally gave in. My brother told my mother that I was crazy back in those days when he was molesting me, just as he tells his wife now. He tells his wife that I'm *a crazy whore*. Oh, and get this! Dalton is now a marriage counselor!"

Her story troubled me. "Let your brother go, Sabrina, and let go of the story you carry about him and about that time in your life. You were just a young girl."

"My brother's young son, who is only twelve, tried to commit suicide recently."

"Oh my," I responded. "You have to say something to the child's mother."

"I can't," she said. "Dalton will hurt my relationship with Goose."

"You can't still fear him, Sabrina!"

"I do!" She exclaimed. "My relationship with my husband is strained right now. He's angry that I brought him over to your house and introduced him to Seth, who sold him a bill of goods. Goose invested a lot of money into Seth's stock recommendations, believing your husband had some kind of insider information. Goose is distancing from me even more now; I feel it."

"I'm sorry that your husband got caught up in Seth's web, but I don't think my husband intentionally lied to him, or wanted to mislead Goose. Seth lost his mother's entire life savings. He did not believe for a second that his investments were a bad risk."

"I understand," Sabrina replied.

"Seth has a pending arbitration sometime in the future. I don't know when the arbitration will happen, but his law firm believes his New York brokerage will compensate Seth for his investment losses in the stock market. Seth's lawyer is suing for no less than $500,000, and Seth says he's confident he will get this kind of settlement in the upcoming arbitration."

"Half a million dollars is a lot of money, Jean!" Sabrina smirked and nodded in approval as if impressed.

Since we were teenagers, Sabrina had always been about the money when it came to men. "He had his investments way up, over one million dollars, Brini. His lawyer might get more than $500,000, but $500,000 is the minimum his lawyer is asking for in the arbitration, and I hope Seth wins a lot of money in his arbitration, so that he can give his mother's life savings back to her."

"How much of her money did he lose?"

"Everything the woman had in the whole world. $85,000!" Brini perked up when she got the bottom line, "So Seth will walk away with $400,000 in his pocket?"

"I don't know what he feels he owes his mother over and above her initial investment. We don't talk. He's too angry."

Sabrina quipped, "He probably doesn't feel he owes his mother a penny more."

I shrugged not knowing what my husband was thinking while I considered that Seth only thought about himself. "He will probably keep $400,000 for himself; and if his lawyer wins more in arbitration, then Seth will probably keep more."

"He'll have to pay his lawyer a portion, too," Sabrina advised. "Probably one-third."

"Yep, and that's probably why he wants to sue for a million."

After our seminar, I did not want to race home in case Seth was entertaining Pete and Chad again on this late Monday night; instead, I was hoping with a delayed arrival, that Sabrina and I would find my husband and the kids sound asleep. I did have classes in the morning, but I would sacrifice my sleep for my agenda.

I pulled off the freeway, a short distance from The Woodlands, and headed down FM 1960 toward a neighborhood watering hole that I had stumbled upon, in the past, when I chose to walk out on a fight with my fear-based, malcontent husband, instead of allowing Seth to catch me up in a non-ending anger dance. Seth lacked compassion and empathy for me, and had proved only able to express one emotion--anger. His common approach with me was defensive, and in the form of disrespectful words and occasional physical assaults; and, in turn, I grew angrier every year that we remained together. I felt suppressed by him, and heard myself screaming too often, while he talked over me, and refused to listen to what I had to say. His was but a game he used to avoid intimacy and commitment; we could not even agree to disagree. I often watched him purposely dance around my effort to have a two-way communication about something I felt important. His verbal tactics prevented me from resolving any of my issues with him, which I considered *our* issues. Seth did not give me respect, or the floor, when I spoke; instead, he cut me off in mid-sentence. He was unwilling to align with me and care about what was bothering me, and, instead, berated my character, and told me what *I was not* for him and the children. He grated at my psychic so that I would feel inadequate, or like a loser. The drug addict, who never left the yard, was apparently a bully, and his meanness shone bright. In these times of loveless exchanges, he would smile while he insulted me and asked me in a demonic voice, "Have you driven a Ford today?" His inappropriate laughter, during our arguments, gave me insight to his mindset. I was certain that my husband's secret drug addiction caused his insanity. Certainly, his love for Runi was the real issue for Seth's unwillingness to be there for me on any constructive level.

"I'm taking you to an upscale neighborhood bar called Chase's," I announced to Sabrina. "I've dropped in here a dozen times over the past year, and we might run into some familiar faces in here tonight--you'll like it. I have friends here."

"All right! Sounds like fun."

I pulled into the suburban nightclub's parking lot and parked. "And I need to talk to you, Sabrina, without Seth around. Let's sit at the bar and have a drink. I'm feeling very sad these days about my mother."

"What's the latest update?" She asked as we got out of the green Volvo station wagon and walked into the dark club.

"I'll tell you after we sit down and get our drinks ordered."

We parked ourselves at the bar in the center of the nightclub. The dance music played to about thirty people who filled the lonely room on this late weekday night.

"What are we going to have?" I asked my friend when the

bartender walked over.

"Bring us a couple of Yellow Birds," Sabrina ordered.

"Two Yellow Birds," the bartender acknowledged and then walked away.

"Ever since you introduced me to that yummy concoction, I've been ordering Yellow Birds," Sabrina informed me.

Her confession made me remember those summer days in Clearwater, Florida, and the handsome Swiss man, Cliff. I wished I had made a life with him in Zurich, Switzerland. He was just a sweet memory now. I tore myself out of my favorite memory and began telling Sabrina about a woman she called Mom, too. "My mother is doing poorly; she's terminal. And there's not a cure for Hepatitis-C, and everything they do for her is just to make her life more comfortable."

"I'm so sorry, Jean. You know I love her."

"I know. Mom always loved you, Sabrina."

Sabrina wiped a tear off her cheek. "Is she on a donor list for a new liver yet?"

"No."

"Why not?"

"She and my father can't afford a liver transplant. Mom says that type of operation will wipe out their savings."

"So what! That's not the priority here; she is!"

"She believes my father should not lose his retirement taking care of her," I angrily shot back. "The cost of a liver transplant is between $100,000 and $400,000, depending on how long she would spend in intensive care and what complications occur during surgery. She would be in and out of the hospital several times, as her body becomes accustomed to the new organ, and she would have to take medication to prevent her body from rejecting the new liver. Maintaining her new liver and health could also cost tens or even hundreds of thousands of dollars over the decades."

"Doesn't your father have health insurance?"

"Yes, but I don't know what his private insurance plan provides. I don't know how much his carrier would cover if she went the transplant route, or even if his carrier will continue to insure her now that they know she is terminal. And he has a few years before he retires, so he's not eligible for Medicaid yet, and she's younger than he is. He talks about taking an early retirement, and then he'll have his pension."

"How old is your father?"

"Sixty," I answered. "…and my mother is fifty-eight years old—she's never worked other than a couple of seasonal part-time jobs here and there."

"She's young!"

"I think so, too. Dad has savings, but not that much. I mean, I understand what Mom's saying. A disease like Hep-C can wipe out everything my father saved for their retirement years, and then what will they do for money? She gets a new liver, and they don't have grocery money when they are in their seventies?"

Sabrina angrily retorted, "This is not right!"

"No, it's not right. Our government needs to offer all of its citizens, especially the middle class, a healthcare plan that insures them for whatever reason! What my father pays already, toward this disease stretches my logic, and his dollars. While his wife is dying, he also bails out my sister and her three kids these days, and has been doing so since Holly's husband walked out the door. Holly is a basket case these days, according to Mom. My sister is on the phone with Dad, every day, crying the blues over her situation. Mom can't handle her drama."

"He sure doesn't need her drama right now, either!" Sabrina slammed.

"I know, I know!" I sighed. "My father is paying Holly's bills, too; and I hear she is about to lose her house over there in Champion Forest. Dad plans to buy it off the auction block."

"That's at least $150,000!" Sabrina protested. "Why doesn't your father spend that money on Mom?"

"That's what I thought, too. I hear he's worried about Holly's three kids. She could move into something more affordable. She doesn't need a five-bedroom home in one of Houston's most expensive neighborhoods, but Dad has always come to her rescue. The first time he bailed Holly out, she was seventeen and pregnant.

He bought her that small house over there by Almeda Mall."

"I remember," Sabrina nodded. "I was going off to college, and Holly was already married with a newborn."

"Yeah, Holly had sex and was pregnant before I ever saw a naked man. She had a shotgun marriage when she was seven months pregnant, too. And my father always takes care of his baby girl. Now, he's going to buy her a second house."

Sabrina rolled her eyes, "And your sister has always treated me as if I was some immoral whore."

"She's bitter over the fact that her first husband went out the front door to get the paper and never back home, and now her second husband has left her, too—for another woman."

"She's a hypocrite," Sabrina said. "She's working your father, too, these days."

A cowboy walked up and interrupted our conversation. "Excuse me, ma'am," he said to me with a big smile, "Would you care to dance?"

I looked up at Sabrina to hear her instruct, "Go dance!"

I looked back at the cowboy, "Let's go!" I grabbed the man's hand, walked toward the dance floor, and looked over my shoulder at my fat friend who sat alone at the bar. I hoped someone would ask her to dance.

After the song was over, I found Sabrina where I left her and sipping on a near-empty Yellow Bird. I sat back down beside her without the cowboy. "I know that guy I danced with," I admitted. "His name is Lance. He drives a classic, red, and white Corvette, that same car Cocoa-Cola used in its advertisements featuring Santa."

"Yeah, I remember those ads. How well do you know the cowboy with the Vette?"

I giggled. "Okay, I'll confess. One night, I left with him in his car from here and ended up at his house. I didn't know I'd end up at his house when he asked me if I wanted to ride in his car. He has a nice house, too. He gave me the tour, but we didn't fall into bed or anything like that." I concluded while wondering if she would believe me.

"Uh huh," she answered as if not believing we did not have

sex.

"Really! He's quite the gentleman. He knows I'm married, too; so we're just friends."

"Kissing friends?"

"I won't deny he hasn't kissed me."

Sabrina arched her eyebrows in approval.

"I remember that he's a boot fanatic. He must have at least thirty pairs of boots in his bedroom closet."

"So you have been in his bedroom! I knew you were lying to me!"

"I did take a tour of his house, but I didn't screw him! I swear to you, Sabrina."

"Why not?" She asked. "He's cute, sexy; he likes you."

"Because, I'm married!" I defended. "He's got a very successful landscaping business, too. He's a gentleman, and we're just friends."

Another man interrupted our conversation by tapping me on the shoulder. I turned and instantly recognized his face. "Hey, Jay Stephens!" I squealed at the sight of the heavy-set man nearing forty with thick blonde hair and green eyes with shaggy eyebrows.

"How are you, Jean? I haven't seen you in here in a month of Sundays."

"I've been attending classes at the university, and that's keeping me out of trouble," I laughed.

"Are you divorced yet?"

"Hopefully not heading there anytime soon," I answered and then looked at Sabrina for her reaction. "Jay, I want you to meet Sabrina, my best friend whom I've known since grade school."

Jay smiled, "A pleasure to meet you, Sabrina," he said while he shook her hand.

"The pleasure is mine, Jay Stephens," Sabrina said with great charm. "And what do you do for a living, Jay?"

I have a TV show called "Weekday Magazine." He looked at me, "I want you to work for me."

I chuckled, "I don't want to work right now, Jay. I'm in school full-time. When I get my degree; I'll come and talk to you."

"I'm going to hold you to it," he firmly stated and then turned his attention to Sabrina. "She always tells me no. I have a talk show on the radio, too, and I've asked Jean to be my guest--she refused. Her story about her apparel business start-up is great fun. Have you heard her story about her first runway show on a 747 stalled on a tarmac at the Houston airport, and the master of ceremony was the Harlem Globetrotter? They were flying to New York City!"

Sabrina smiled and nodded, "I have."

"And the story about how she was falsely arrested while doing her sales calls? What a hoot!"

"Yes, I've heard all her stories," Sabrina admitted. "Jean is brilliant."

"She's hilarious, too! She's had me in stitches for hours upon hours," Jay added for Sabrina's knowledge, and then turned to me, "Please, come dance with me, beautiful."

I looked at Sabrina wondering at this point how well she was dealing with my fan club. Until that night, this side of my life had remained my secret.

I looked at Jay, "You should dance with my friend!"

He turned to my girlfriend, "Nothing personal, Sabrina, but I don't want to dance with you," he retorted. "It's Jean that has stolen my heart!"

I looked at Sabrina and softened his blow, "I was hoping you'd save me!"

Sabrina saved face and happily ordered, "Go dance with him!"

"Okay," I said begrudgingly as if dancing with the handsome radio and TV talent a painstaking ordeal.

Jay pulled me to the floor and grabbed me around the waistline for the slow dance. "Don't put me in that spot ever again," he whispered, "to have to choose between you or your fat friend. I don't dance with fat women!"

"Oh, aren't you the snob!" I tossed back while judging him less than nice.

"I guess I sound that way, but I just know what I like, Jean. And it's you that I want tonight."

"I promise you, Jay, the minute my husband walks away from our marriage, you'll be the first to know."

"I don't think any man in his right mind would walk away from you, Jean."

"Believe me, Jay, when I say my husband is not in his right mind."

He chuckled.

The night wore on; and I continued to dance with an assortment of faces, some familiar, and some not. No one danced with my oldest friend, and she appeared not bothered by the fact that she was no longer queen bee. We walked out at closing toward my car and ran into a group of drunken males who stood in the parking lot in our path, and who were at least ten years younger than we were. A skinny blonde and blue-eyed male, no taller than me, brazenly walked up to us while three other college-age boys followed him. "Hey pretty thing," the drunk said to me. "How about joining us for breakfast over at Denney's?"

"I can't," I answered. "I need to go home and get some sleep. Thank you anyway."

"Oh, you, come on, come with us," he drunkenly begged, and then turned his flirtations over to Sabrina. "You sure are a pretty woman," he said to her. "How about it, beautiful? Wanna go to breakfast with me and my boys?"

Sabrina grinned and looked at me, "Why not, Jean?"

"I don't want to," I adamantly replied. "I have classes tomorrow."

"I think you're being a party pooper, Jean," she said to me while the drunk looked her up and down as if she was a piece of rib eye steak.

"I can't, Sabrina! It is already two o'clock in the morning; and if we go to breakfast with them, I won't get to bed until 4:00 a.m."

Sabrina motioned me to the side and drunkenly whispered, "Come on, Jean. We're going to have fun; let's stay out all night."

"No, we're not going to have any more fun, Sabrina. And they're babies for starters," I argued while I walked toward my car completely disinterested in spending another moment discussing the issue. I unlocked my car and started up the engine.

Sabrina opened the passenger side door and angrily spewed while she sat down and strapped on her seatbelt. "It's always just about you!"

"Okay, whatever; you're drunk. I have to go home, Sabrina. You can stay and take a taxi back to my place, or one of them can drive you back over to my house."

"No, thank you," she answered. "Let's go!"

"I have kids and classes in the morning," I said while I backed out and drove out of the parking lot. "I don't have the luxury of not working and not worrying about my future, like you do."

"Well, all night long, I sat by myself and watched you dance. If you noticed, no one wanted to dance with the fat girl! And then, when it's my turn to have some fun, you want nothing to do with it!"

"How could we possibly have a good time with a bunch of boys who probably still live at home while they take their freshman basics at the community college? What would I possibly have to say to any of them?"

"That's not the point?"

"No, that's not the point, Sabrina? You're angry with me for other reasons. I'm not your problem, Sabrina. You are angry at me because a few guys danced with me and not with you, and that is total crap on your part!"

"A few guys!" She huffed. "You have had this secret life going on with every man in Houston; and tonight, I just caught on."

"Every man in Houston? What's your game these days, girlfriend?"

"I caught on tonight, Jean!"

"What did you catch on to, Sabrina?" I fumed while I watched her intentionally take us down a bad road. "Did you catch on that my husband is an asshole? I don't think you did!"

"I don't want to talk to you anymore, Jean."

"That's interesting, Sabrina. I take the conversation back to my husband, and you don't want to talk about him. That's a first— you don't have anything bad to say about him anymore. Why not?"

"I just want to go to bed, Jean. I've had a lot to drink."

"Obviously, you have had too much to drink because you're acting stupid, and I'm not going to act stupid with you." I said as I got back on the freeway and headed home. I flipped on the radio to avoid any further argument, which I was certain, stemmed out of Sabrina's insecurities and jealousies.

We drove toward my house without saying another word to each other for twenty minutes; and when I got home, I had barely pulled into the driveway, when Sabrina jumped out of the car in a dramatic huff, slammed the car door, and stormed ahead of me through the unlocked front door. I gladly kept my distance.

I stepped into the house and spotted Seth standing in the center of the living room listening to soft music with a drink in his hand. "Why are you still up?" I growled as I stepped down into the sunken den.

"Oh listen to her majesty; she's so nasty," Sabrina quipped while I watched her throw her purse on the couch and walk up to my husband.

"Well, I was enjoying some quiet time in my beautiful home," he kindly replied while looking a bit confused.

"Well, enjoy your quiet time; I'm going to bed. Sabrina wants to have some fun!" I angrily slammed back. I peered at the clock on the wall in the walk-in bar and saw the hour was already 2:30 a.m. and continued to explain my soon departure. "I have classes at 9:00 a.m. in the morning, and I'm going to be there no matter how tired I feel in the morning. I'm sure Sabrina will be more than happy to catch you up with how our wonderful night went!"

I then walked away from them, headed toward the master bedroom at the bottom of the stairs, and fell into our king-size bed without much ado. I was angry about having been castigated by Sabrina; and I was angry about having no sense of security with either my husband, or with my so-called *best friend,* while I went to bed and left the two lovebirds alone, to do whatever. Both of them disrespected me and were liars, and they were going to do what they wanted to do behind my back anyway. I wasn't going to lose sleep over two people I could not trust, and mess up what mattered--the end of what would be the first semester I had ever completed at the university.

THE FOLLOWING MORNING, the sun filtered through the closed drapes on the wall of windows and sliding glass doors. A nagging alarm clock cut short my sleep. I peered at the clock and saw 6:30 a.m. I needed coffee before dressing and heading out the door for a thirty-mile drive to the university. I sat up and noticed that Seth had not turned down his side of the bed. I jumped to one conclusion; he had spent the night in the guest bedroom with our guest.

I quietly walked out of our master bedroom and stood in the center of our large den looking up at the staircase and considering going upstairs just when Seth came quietly tiptoeing down. I already knew what was up with him and my so-called best friend, and I felt hurt and angry. The guest bedroom was at the top of the stairs landing, and he was leaving Sabrina's bed. He had on the clothes that he had worn the night before; shorts and a tank and was barefoot. He was startled when he realized I stood their witnessing his dissension, but played it off with a friendly hello, loud enough to warn Sabrina that I had caught him sneaking down the stairs.

"Well, top of the morning, Jean!" He calmly said as if nothing was unusual about him not having come to bed last night, and me catching him coming downstairs.

I had nothing to say to my unfaithful husband while Sabrina was still in our home, and I simply shot him a go-to-hell look as I turned away and walked into my newly remodeled kitchen to make coffee.

Seth followed me into the kitchen. "Our boys are sleeping soundly," he said while attempting to make polite conversation while I filled the coffeemaker up with water and coffee grinds. "I went up there to look at my boys, and I just stared at them…for a long time. They have the sweetest faces when they are sleeping; they're so innocent looking."

"And you're not!" I angrily snapped. "So stop it!" I grumbled under my breath while I heard Sabrina come down the stairs. Obviously, their plot to get out of bed early enough and not be caught by me backfired on them.

"Stop what?" Seth asked as if confused.

Sabrina arrogantly walked into my kitchen, snubbing me with her chin up in the air as if still upset about last night's fight, but I knew that she could not look me in the eyes. She rendered an adoring face to my husband with her classical smirk, and sweetly greeted him, "Good morning, darling."

"Top of the morning to you," Seth kindly replied.

I seethed over their repugnant pretense. "I thought you two had already given each other a proper good morning!" I looked at the two of them for their reaction. I busted them, and they both knew it.

Sabrina suspected I was onto their game and shot back, "Don't give me that self-righteous attitude while you pretend to be so virtuous, Jean!"

"You've got to be kidding me!" I snipped. "I'm not pretending anything. I'm genuinely upset with both of you, and rightly so! I find you both repulsive and sleazy."

"No, I'm not kidding, Jean!" She replied out of sync while skipping over my reality.

Sabrina would never address the fact that she had slept with my husband. She had told me when her brother molested her that she had learned to lie at an early age.

She turned to Seth, "Seems your wife has lots of boyfriends over there at Chase's night club."

"Oh, you didn't just say that to him," I shook my head at her audacity and sarcastically spurned, "The woman uses a diversion tactic, interesting."

"And watch out for the *Cocoa-Cola* cowboy," Sabrina warned Seth. "He drives a red and white Corvette."

Seth smiled and then said, "Oh, yeah?" while looking to me to fill in the gap.

I added for my husband's data bank, "And the cowboy's got thirty pairs of boots in his bedroom closet, too! You are both unbelievable!"

"No, Jean," Sabrina repudiated, "You're the one who is *unbelievable!* Last night, you had every man's attention, and that wasn't enough, was it?"

"I'm sure that because men asked me to dance, and not you, Sabrina, that reality was more than your psychotic self could handle, wasn't it?"

"You are so selfish," she alleged. "You couldn't take me to breakfast after I sat there for hours, alone on my barstool all night long sucking down Yellow Birds while I waited for you to get off the dance floor."

"Eck! You got some audacity, Sabrina." I said while I stood there and watched the woman turn the tables on me. I had caught my best friend sleeping with my husband, and now she was running scared because she had an unsuspecting lawyer husband in Port Neches whom she feared I would call.

"Let's just get to the bottom line, Jean. You are a huge liar!"

"I am?" I snickered. "That's hysterical coming from you, a psychopathic personality!"

Sabrina turned to Seth, "She's going to leave you as soon as she gets her degree."

I had told Sabrina that I felt Seth feared I would leave him when I got a degree. "Oh, you bitch! I've heard enough! Your brother is right, Brini; you are a crazy whore! Get out of my house!"

"I can't get out of here soon enough," she said to Seth as she turned to leave the kitchen.

"Run home, Sabrina, and try to save your marriage," I threatened as she traipsed across the living area.

She stopped in mid-tracks and turned back to my husband. "I feel for you, Seth. If you need me in the future, call me. I'll be happy to help you anyway I can."

Now I heard Sabrina's threat, and how perfect for Seth!

Wisely, Seth had nothing to say to Sabrina as she walked out of the kitchen, and I had to admit that this was yet her best performance I had ever seen in the twenty-three years that I had known her. I was certain, too, that Seth had everything to do with the play, and Sabrina had fallen victim to my unscrupulous husband. "And while you're up there, don't steal anything more than you already have!" I yelled while I watched her angrily run upstairs for her belongings and sleeping child.

I turned and looked at my smug husband who quietly remained in the kitchen, "You think you're so smart, huh?"

"What are you talking about, Jean?"

"Oh right! Pretend you don't know what you've done. You won't screw your wife when she throws herself in front of you in a black teddy, but you like that fat, lying bitch, huh? You calculating bastard!"

"I didn't touch her!" He defended while he poured a cup of coffee and then headed out the glass kitchen door for his morning cigarette.

"Yeah right," I mumbled to myself after he left the room. "Then what is she running from, if not from guilt?"

DECEMBER 1993. I woke up in the back of my station wagon. I had been attending classes since early morning; and after the last lecture, that mid-afternoon, I had gone out to the parking lot and crawled into the back of my car to sleep. When I left my Woodlands' home at 7:00 a.m. that morning, I grabbed a blue throw pillow off the sofa with plans to take a power nap after my last class, and then study at the university until late. I could not risk going home and having Seth pick a fight with me.

I crawled back out of my station wagon, yawned, and moseyed over to the library to study for a test I had the next day while I wrangled with my business ideas. Since inducted into the seniors' entrepreneurial *think tank* by my neighbor's father, I faithfully attended weekly meetings led by the Harvard graduate and former head of the FDIC. I constantly considered business strategies. The entrepreneurial club activities centered on networking to build business relationships. I needed to meet a business professional who could provide me a centrally located space to lease and to use as a hub where I would receive and document my overseas clothing shipments before distributing my clothing orders to stores across America. I had to figure out the timeline to coordinate my overseas clothing manufacturer with the overseas shipping company, and the time required to ship my orders from point A to point B, and the time I needed to get my clothing line to stores in America. The overseas clothing manufacturer needed time to sew up my orders resulting from the efforts of fifty sales reps across the USA. There was a small island off the coast of India call Sri Lanka, in the Bay of Bengal, which cheaply manufactured clothes for Liz Claiborne and other big designers, and after doing research, I guesstimated I needed to allow the overseas manufacturer three months to sew, and another three months for the boat to cross the seas. Once my clothing order arrived to America from India, I then had to distribute my orders to the retail stores in a timely manner to meet buyers' expectations of promised delivery dates. I needed financial backing, too; I considered as I stepped into the library just as the sun was sinking. I had no more time that evening to think about my future apparel business; I had an economics final in the morning.

 I found a quiet study cubicle in the corner of the basement of the university library and entered with a wonderful thought that I had only a few more days of exams before I would conclude this semester. I sat my books down on top the desktop and closed the door for what I estimated would be three to four hours of study time without interruption. I had made straight A's on all my previous tests and term papers, and because I had stayed on top of all my studies, I knew that with no stress and a little bit of studying, I would ace the finals, too.

 My mid-range plan was to get the bachelor's degree, and then the MBA, and then start up the apparel business again; but this time, I would enroll team members from my master's program. I considered how relieved I felt, and, too, how proud I felt, for having completed the semester. The Christmas holidays were upon me, and not having to study or do homework would be a nice reprieve while I looked forward to relaxing with my family, cooking, shopping, and working on my ongoing writing project, my novel. *Yellow Bird* was a reality that would financially benefit me in the long-term. While I attempted to learn how to write, and struggled with grammar and sentence structure, and with how to tell the greatest love story ever told, about a Texas southern belle and a beautiful man from Switzerland, I found joy in getting lost in their perfect world and escaped my sad reality at home.

After a long evening of sitting in the lonely library, I quit studying and trusted that I had enough information. Since my last class that afternoon, I reviewed my entire microeconomics textbook, three months of class notes, predicted the rise and fall of interest rates, plotted graphs, memorized how to plot the saturation point of market infusion, re-learned when the best time markets should utilize research and development investment dollars, and how R&D jumpstarts a sluggish economy. I threw my books into my black, leather bag and called it a night. I would drive home, get a good night's sleep, get up early, review my notes again, and then drive to school and take the mid-morning semester final.

I pulled my Volvo station wagon into my detached two-car garage, grabbed my books, and entered into my home through the glass kitchen door. Seth was still up at 11:00 p.m. and standing in the kitchen pouring himself a cup of coffee when I walked into the house.

I smiled, "Hello, Seth."

"Hello, Jean." He replied before entering into the walk-in bar and coming back out with a bottle of Bailey's for his coffee."

"Don't you think the coffee will keep you up all night?"

"I don't care," he angrily snapped. "Where have you been all night?"

"I was at the library studying until they kicked me out. I have an economics final tomorrow."

"Sure you were!"

"Don't start with me, Seth!" I warned. "I'm tired and I'm going to bed. I don't want to fight with you. I have to get up early and study some more for my exam and be at school by 10:00 a.m."

"Your kids are in bed and doing fine," he announced as if he was letting me know I paid no attention to them.

"Good! I'm happy that you're holding down the fort for me this week while I focus on studying and taking finals. Thank you!" I felt his resentment that I had a life outside the home. "I'll be done with this semester by the end of the week." I then walked out of the room, went to bed, and left him with his spiked coffee to sing the blues alone.

The following morning, I leaped out of bed with the alarm clock and headed straight for the kitchen with my book bag. The sun was rising and I saw Seth through the glass kitchen door smoking a cigarette and drinking coffee in the slider swing under the catwalk. He saw me flip on the kitchen light.

He had brewed coffee, and I poured myself a hot cup and sat down at the kitchen table. I was opening my book and notebooks when he entered into the kitchen from outside with a blue sofa pillow in his hand. "What's this?" He asked me.

"A blue sofa pillow?" I answered. "Did you go to sleep last night?"

"No, I didn't sleep last night. I found this pillow in the back of your car."

"So what?" I said with great irritation while understanding he was picking a fight.

"There is a cum stain on it."

"You're crazy. Maybe a drool stain from me napping on the thing yesterday."

"Yeah, you were at the library last night," he angrily huffed in disbelief.

"I was at the library!" I defended while I sorted through semester notes.

He flung the pillow at me, and my anger surfaced. "Get out of my face, Seth."

"If you think I'm going to pay for your education and babysit while you're out whoring around, then you're crazier than I thought."

I took a deep breath while I realized he was setting me up to fail my exam. I sat there calmly and began flipping through my textbook pretending he was not in the room. I glanced up and saw him pouring himself another cup of coffee. "I'm faithful to you, Seth," I calmly informed him while I kept my eyes in my textbook.

"I don't believe you were studying at 10:00 p.m. last night. Where were you really?"

I seethed. The man who had slept with my best friend had

the audacity to question me! I bit my lip, ignored him, and pretended to be reading while I hid my anger over his game to defeat me; and while I re-read the same sentence three times, suddenly, I felt hot coffee splash on me, and saw that the brown liquid land on my notes and books. I took a deep breath while wanting to yell and scream, but remained calm. I stood up with coffee dripping down my chest, and shot him a go-to-hell look, walked over to the island, grabbed a towel, and began wiping myself off, when he suddenly rushed me and pinned me against the wall, with two hands around my neck. I tried to push him off, but he held me tight. His eyes were wild and I screamed, "Let go of me, you bastard!"

He tried to cup his hand over my mouth but I bit him. He did not let go until I spit in his face. I ran for the telephone sitting on the buffet at the other end of the kitchen table and dialed 911.

"911 What's your emergency?" A female dispatch asked.

"I'm being assaulted by my husband." I kicked at Seth while he tried to hang up the phone.

"Are you still on East Timberwagon Circle?"

"Yes, hurry!" I ordered while blocking my husband's attempts to pull the cord out of the wall.

"We have a sheriff on the way, ma'am."

"Please, hurry!" I begged while I watched the crazed man pace in and out of the kitchen and den and shake his head in disbelief that I would call the cops.

He grumbled under his breath, "You bitch!" Then he darted out of the kitchen, ran across the den, and then fled out the back door. I hung on the phone, and watched him through the wall of windows head into the woods and disappear down the wooded bike trail. "He left the house," I informed dispatch. "I'm going to hang up now."

"The sheriff should be there any minute now, ma'am. I would like you to stay on the phone."

"I don't want to," I said while I hung up seething from Seth's attempt to hurt me. I sat back down at my study area, dabbed coffee off my notebook and notes, and considered who could watch my two baby boys while I took my test when Seth suddenly barged back into the house through the back door.

He appeared determined. "It's your word against mine, bitch," he smugly challenged.

I saw that his blue T-shirt was now torn, and he had put bloody claw marks on his own neck and chest. "You're a sociopathic personality! That's not going to fly!"

"We'll see," he growled just as we heard the police knock on the front door.

"Montgomery County Sheriff, please open the door," a male voice bellowed.

Seth ran for the front door to be the first to explain what happened while I calmly followed him.

He swung the door open. "Good morning, officers."

"What's the problem here?" the officer asked while looking at me and sizing up the situation.

"Officer, sir, my wife attacked me," Seth answered.

"He's a liar!" I calmly refuted while standing at the kitchen threshold. "I'll give you the truth, officers."

"Not yet," the lead officer sternly replied.

A second officer in a blue uniform walked in behind the sergeant. "Sir, please step outside with me."

"Yes, sir," Seth politely said as he led the officer out the front door.

"Talk to me in the kitchen," the lead officer instructed.

I led the massive form in a crisp brown uniform and black leather-riding boots into my kitchen. "I swear I'll tell you the truth, officer," I calmly began. "I got up with an alarm clock, poured me a cup of coffee, and began to study for a final I have today at the University of Houston and my husband went crazy. As you can see for yourself, I was sitting down over there at the end of the kitchen table where my textbook and notes are laying, when Seth first threw hot coffee on me."

I watched the officer examine the coffee spills on my papers and books while I continued to explain, "I stayed calm because I knew his game was to upset me so that I would fail my test. I got up, got a towel, and began to wipe the coffee off my books, and me, while I saw that my husband got angrier because he couldn't get a reaction out of me. So, while I was standing up and wiping the coffee off the table, he charged me, pinned me up against the wall, and strangulated me. I screamed, but he cupped my mouth; and then, I bit his hand and spit in his face. He then let go of me and I ran to the phone. He's crazy this morning. He told me that he didn't go to bed last night, and he's acting like he's high as a kite, too."

"Does your husband take drugs?"

"Not that I can prove," I answered. "He started fighting with me the minute I got up, alleging I was having sex last night, instead of being at the library studying for this morning's final. He pulled a pillow out of my car and told me that the drool stain on the pillow, I use for my afternoon naps in the back of my station wagon, was cum, and proof that I was having sex in my car. He doesn't work, doesn't have a career, and he hates the idea that I might have a career one day because he fears I will then divorce him. And I will!" I fumed. "I have an exam at 10:00 a.m. this morning, and I just wanted to study. He threw his coffee on me and pinned me up against the wall and tried to strangulate me, officer." I repeated while my tears welled up as my realty hit harder. I stood strong, regained my composure, and wiped a single tear off my cheek.

"I see that your lip is busted, is that from his assault?"

"I guess so, when he cupped my mouth. He ran out the back door when I called you guys, and then came back in with scratches on his neck and chest, and a ripped shirt. He told me that he would say I scratched him, but I didn't. I didn't rip his shirt, either." I then demonstrated for the officer how Seth had put those marks on his neck. I put my right hand up to the left side of my neck and lightly dragged my nails down my neck and chest. "That's how he made his scratches! Go see for yourself that his bloody marks run in the same direction as his hand."

"All right ma'am, stay in here. I've heard enough."

I sat back down at the kitchen table while I watched the police officer walk out of the kitchen. I heard the front door open and close. I sat in total dismay that I could not get up and study for a final without Seth's insanity stopping me and my tears welled up again.

The police officer came back into the kitchen minutes later and said, "Ma'am, we're placing your husband under arrest, and we're taking him to jail."

"Good," I quipped while feeling my troubles were just beginning.

"He'll be locked up at least twenty-four hours before he can bail out, and I advise you to get a restraining order and serve him behind bars. I also suggest that if you do not serve him with divorce papers, at the same time you serve him a restraining order, that you then call this shelter for women and children and go somewhere safe. I'll leave the card right here on your counter," he said.

"I'm *not* leaving my home!" I impatiently spouted.

"Then I suggest you get the restraining order immediately," he said while taking out another business card from his shirt pocket. "I'm going to leave now, but please call me if you have any problems-- here's my card," the officer said while he sat his business card down next to the business card he left me for the women's safe shelter.

"I will," I replied with a nod while I got up to follow the police officer to the door. I walked through the brightly lit room off the foyer and looked out the floor-to-ceiling windows and saw Seth handcuffed and being put into the back of a cop car by the other officer.

The officer turned to me before he walked out the door and said, "We're charging your husband with a Class-A Assault. A detective will be in contact with you. I will forward this case to the Montgomery County Attorney's Office for review, and they will decide what to do after they investigate. You have no say in the matter. Most likely the county attorney will prosecute because we've been out here before."

"I hope so," I calmly said while still in shock over Seth's play to ruin me.

"Take care," he said as he pulled the door closed behind himself.

"Thank you, officer," I mumbled while considering my options that morning. I walked into the kitchen and examined the business card for the women's shelter that the officer had left for me.

No way would I move my kids and me out of our home and live in a shelter.

The Houston Chronicle sat on the counter top, too, and the front page caught my attention. I picked up the paper and read the stark headlines while I fell into a chair at the kitchen table absorbing what I considered a timely warning:

The Women Killed List
The Texas Council on Family Violence reported that an intimate partner killed 136 women in Texas last year. That's an increase of thirty percent over the previous year, the council reports. The youngest woman killed was just a teen-ager-- a fourteen year old shot by her boyfriend, who was a year older. The oldest was seventy-four. Her common-law husband shot her. Eleven children also lost their lives in connection with the 136 crimes, the council reports. There has been "tremendous progress" in areas including creating safe havens and increasing legal protection, said council president Gloria A. Terry, but "there is still much work to do." This year's statistic on domestic violence shelter services: 8,006 adults, who sought shelter, were denied for lack of space this year.

I spotted another article halfway down the page with the same theme, yet rendering for me another warning:
CELEBRITY DOMESTIC VIOLENCE: Orenthal James "O. J." Simpson (born July 9, 1947), nicknamed "The Juice," is a retired American football player, football broadcaster, spokesperson, and actor. He originally attained fame in sports as a running back at the collegiate and professional levels and was the first NFL player to rush for more than 2,000 yards in a season, a mark he set during the 1973 season. The following are excerpts from the two 911 calls Nicole Brown Simpson, O.J. Simpson's wife made to police on Oct. 25, 1993, from her townhouse.

NICOLE: Can you send someone to my house?
DISPATCHER: What's the problem there?
NICOLE: My ex-husband has just broken into my house, and he's ranting and raving outside the front yard.
DISPATCHER: Has he been drinking or anything?
NICOLE: No. But he's crazy.

DISPATCHER: And you said he hasn't been drinking?
NICOLE: No.
DISPATCHER: Did he hit you?
NICOLE: No.
DISPATCHER: Do you have a restraining order against him?
NICOLE: No.
DISPATCHER: What's your name?
NICOLE: Nicole Simpson.
DISPATCHER: And your address?
NICOLE: 325 Gretna Green Way.
DISPATCHER: Okay, we'll send the police out.
NICOLE: Nicole: Thank you.
DISPATCHER: Dispatcher: Uh-huh.
(The dispatcher puts out a domestic violence call for any patrol car to respond to the address at Gretna Green. A short time later, Nicole Simpson called back.
NICOLE: Could you get somebody over here now, to ... Gretna Green. He's back. Please?
DISPATCHER: What does he look like?
NICOLE: He's O.J. Simpson. I think you know his record. Could you just send somebody over here?
DISPATCHER: What is he doing there?
NICOLE: He just drove up again. (She begins to cry) Could you just send somebody over?
DISPATCHER: Dispatcher: Wait a minute. What kind of car is he in?
NICOLE: He's in a white Bronco, but, first, he broke the back door down to get in.
DISPATCHER: Wait a minute. What's your name?
NICOLE: Nicole Simpson.
DISPATCHER: OK, is he the sportscaster or whatever?
NICOLE: Yeah. Thank you.
DISPATCHER: Wait a minute, we're sending police. What is he doing? Is he threatening you?
NICOLE: He's (expletive) going nuts. (Sobs)
DISPATCHER: Has he threatened you in any way or is he just harassing you?

NICOLE: (Sighs) You're going to hear him in a minute. He's about to come in again.
DISPATCHER: OK, just stay on the line...
NICOLE: I don't want to stay on the line. He's going to beat the (expletive) out of me.
DISPATCHER: Wait a minute, just stay on the line so we can know what's going on until the police get there, OK? OK, Nicole?
NICOLE: Uh-huh.
DISPATCHER: Just a moment. Does he have any weapons?
NICOLE: I don't know. He went home, and he came back. The kids are up there sleeping, and I don't want anything to happen.
DISPATCHER: OK, just a moment. Is he on drugs or anything?
NICOLE: No.
DISPATCHER: Just stay on the line. Just in case he comes in, I need to hear what's going on, all right?
NICOLE: Can you hear him outside?
DISPATCHER: Is he yelling?
NICOLE: Yep.
DISPATCHER: OK. Has he been drinking?
NICOLE: No.
DISPATCHER: OK. (speaking over radio to police units) ... All units: additional on domestic violence, 325 South Gretna Green Way, the suspect has returned in a white Bronco. Monitor comments. Incident 48221.
DISPATCHER: OK, Nicole?
NICOLE: Uh-huh.
DISPATCHER: Is he outdoors?
NICOLE: He's in the back yard.
DISPATCHER: He's in the back yard.
NICOLE: Screaming at my roommate about me and at me....

    I cut Nicole's telephone call short and sat the newspaper down on the table while feeling disturbed and staring at a black-and-white print of the celebrity couple—she was now dead. I glanced up at the clock over the utility room doorway while considering that O.J.'s beautiful blonde ex-wife not only looked a lot like me, but was my age with two young children, too. I had a few hours before I was to take my final exam, but I took heed to the warnings I read in the newspaper and considered the news articles an omen. Nicole Brown Simpson and I were both victims of domestic violence, and as she had done, I, too, would divorce my abuser. However, unlike Nicole's situation, I did not believe Seth would kill me in the process.

I opened my class notebook to the first day of class three months earlier, and found my professor's office telephone number. I would call the Asian economist and explain to her that I would not be able to take her final exam that morning because my husband assaulted me and went to jail. I would add for her further consideration, that I had to find and hire a lawyer that morning, too, and get my husband served with a protection order and divorce petition while he was behind bars for the next twenty-four hours. I would then call Marilyn, my next-door neighbor, and ask her if she would babysit my two youngest children while Bella was in school, and I went to see a lawyer.

I dialed the university and got my professor on the phone. She was sympathetic toward my children and me, and agreed *to not fail* me in the course, for not taking the final exam that morning, but, instead, would register a *withdrawal* on my permanent transcript record. She informed me that taking the final exam later was not an option.

I hung up the phone and wiped the tears of disappointment and hurt off my cheeks, and angrily began searching through the Montgomery County phone book for a divorce lawyer. I was done with this creep from hell!

10
A FREE PASS OUT OF JAIL

DAYS LATER and my kitchen phone rang late evening. I picked up the receiver while wondering if the caller was my angry husband, after a civil process server gave him court papers while he was behind bars, prohibiting Seth from returning to the marital home. I also petitioned him for a divorce with notice of a hearing for temporary orders. I figured Seth was out of jail by now and probably was staying over at Pete's or his mother's house. I reluctantly picked up the receiver and said, "Hello."

    A confident voice answered, "Well, hello, Jean! This is George Harmsworth."

    I felt delight and instantly perked up. "Hey, the handsome Connecticut boy! How are you?"

    "I'm good," he tittered as if embarrassed by my complement. "I was wondering if your old man is around."

    "He's not free to come to the phone right now," I enlightened.

    "Okay, no problem; tell him to give me a call."

    "I won't see him until we go to court."

    "What?" George acted startled by my revelation.

    "Seth and I are now separated. He doesn't live here anymore. I put a restraining order on him because he attacked me."

    "Oh, I'm sorry, Jean. Wow," he replied while digesting the situation. "I never suspected that you two were...well, I thought you guys were living the American dream, to listen to Seth tell it."

    "I guess it looked that way to you," I sadly acknowledged.

    "Are you okay?" George asked me.

    "No, I'm not okay. He, ah...he attacked me one morning," I said while holding back my tears of indignation. "I'm not going to put up with him kicking me or strangulating me anymore. I called the cops on him. He prevented me from finishing my semester at the university--again. I have a *D* on my transcript, in accounting, because I did not take the final; and my professor in my microeconomics class gave me a *W*. Seth's whole point is to stop me, and he's winning. He's crazy like he's on drugs. I got up early to study for a final, and ah...Well, it's hard for me to talk about it, without falling apart. I called the cops after he attacked me."

    "Does he do drugs?" George sounded disturbed.

    "I think so. I'm going to level with you, George. Seth hides behind a smoke screen. He doesn't manage a bunch of accounts. He closed one deal, in our entire relationship, and he doesn't manage that account. He doesn't do anything for the income he makes, and I don't understand why he gets a check in the mail every month. In addition, Seth is obsessed with the yard. He goes outside in the morning, comes in around midnight every day, and has for years. I think he's paranoid to go out into the world."

"Well, I wondered about him and his business when I came to your house. I didn't see an office or a desk top computer."

"He doesn't have an office. I bought myself a word processor when I was taking a writing class at Rice, but we've never had a computer in our home. Seth throws his unopened mail from his employer into a corner in the garage. There's a mountain of unanswered correspondence in there."

"Wow, that's weird behavior. He's irresponsible." George replied. "I'm sorry he's hurt you, Jean, but I have to tell you something about Seth--he's always been abusive. When Seth and I were in college, he stole my girlfriend, Deb, as you already know--"

"I remember that story," I confirmed. "You and Seth leaked that story to me when you were here in August. Do you realize that visit was already over a year ago?"

"Wow, seems like yesterday. I've called Seth periodically since that visit. We've talked, but he's never admitted any of these things to me about his marriage. I understand why not now."

"I'm sure he's built his case against me to you," I pried.

"He's a snake in the grass," George vented. "When he stole my girlfriend in college, I felt betrayed by him; and then, they got married. I lived in the apartment below them, and I heard their horrible fights, every night, after they wed. Deb told me that Seth stabbed her in the hand with a fork, one night, at a dinner table at a restaurant. He never loved her. Seth just wanted to beat me at something, since he couldn't beat me on the tennis court or basketball court."

"I'm sorry Seth hurt you, George. Seth is still an abusive man. He cares about no one, not even himself really."

"It doesn't appear so," George quipped.

"He doesn't love himself, George, and he can't love me or his kids because that's just spiritual law."

"That's right, Jean."

"I was sitting in the car with my arm resting on the console between the seats, and Seth was sitting behind the steering wheel, and we were arguing, and he took the key in his hand and gouged out my arm that was resting on the console. I now have a three-inch scar on my left arm between my wrist and elbow."

"Jean, I'm so sorry."

"I'm divorcing him, and I have a hearing coming up on Friday."

"This Friday?"

"My lawyer got me an emergency hearing because I need some money."

"Good. What about the ski trip?"

"I'm going skiing!" I confirmed. "Seth won't be there because I am not giving him his airline ticket."

"And are Charley and Fred still going?"

"Yep, and we're going to have even more fun without that bastard," I said while I felt like crying. "Seth and I will be in court Friday morning; and later that evening, Charley and Fred will meet me at my house. They're staying overnight because I live close to Intercontinental Airport, and we're driving together in one car to the airport the following morning."

"I'm glad they're going to be there with you that evening after your hearing."

"Me, too. You guys are good support for me right now."

"Whatever I can do, let me know, Jean."

"Thank you, George." I really liked the man from New England and was looking forward to spending more time with him on our ski trip. "Where and when are we going to meet you, George?"

"You don't need to pick me up when I get to Steamboat. I'm renting a car at the airport and driving over to our condo."

"We might hit the slopes before you get there, but we'll ski in and meet you at the condo. A green trail leads right up to our back porch."

"I figured I'd get there by noon."

"I'm excited about our trip. I've hired a nanny to watch the kids for four days."

"Oh good," George acknowledged.

"This getaway is exactly what I need right now. I was envisioning my holidays to be happy and more relaxed. I didn't expect to be embroiled in a divorce action. I never wanted my family to break apart." I began to sob. "Seth has only been gone two days, George. He went to jail, and I went to the bank. I took all the money out of our account and paid for my lawyer, and I told my lawyer that I didn't have a job and that his fees took almost every dime we had in the bank. That's why he got me an emergency hearing for temporary orders. My lawyer's good. He's asking the court to give me the house, and custody the kids, and my car, of course, and that Seth be ordered to pay me monthly maintenance during the interim of our divorce."

"Good," George acknowledged.

"I'm terrified to go into a court room and face-off with Seth. He's a convincing liar, and I'm afraid that the judge will believe his lies." I wiped the tears off my cheeks.

"Seth wants you to fear him, Jean."

"I do!"

"Don't, Jean! Seth, at most, is arrogant. You have nothing to fear, but fear itself. The judge will see that man for what he is--an abusive loser. You just walk into the court room confident, and hold your head high, and know God is with you."

"But you see, George, Seth has blamed me for everything that's gone wrong in our marriage."

"And you watch, Jean, he'll tell the judge that you provoked him to attack you the other morning."

"That's what I'm afraid of, George."

"That's wrong! The judge is educated; he knows the personality of an abuser is to blame others."

"I hope so, George. I think Seth's abusive personality has really taken a toll on my psychic over the years. I use to be confident. I'm not anymore. He's hit me for years and talked down to me. He's broken my possessions, and he tore up our home. Who does that?"

"A man with no respect for you," George answered.

"He broke my coffee table and my Chinese privacy screen recently; and in our first year together, he broke my $600 white neon sign. I loved that sign, too. My name, *Jean Wynn*, was written in white glass script."

"He's jealous of you and threatened by you."

"He's always competed with me, George."

"That's Seth's nature," George confirmed. "He competes with everybody."

"I was nearly nine months pregnant with Harper, and we were fighting, and Seth pushed me back into a wall out of anger. I fell down on my swollen belly and hurt my baby that day—and he walked away." My tears rolled. "He's always hated me."

"He hates himself, Jean."

"He kicked dents into the side of our car door one night while I was driving out of the driveway without him to go hang out with my girlfriend, Charley."

"He's crazy, Jean, and you've got to get away from Seth before he hurts you more than he already has."

"He's threatened me in the past, George, that if I leave him, no matter what I say against him in court, that he will say the same thing about me. He will twist everything around so that the court will believe him. He says the court will believe him, too, because he graduated from college, then earned his master's degree, and then went to law school. He says that the court will know he earns $100,000 a year, and that I earn nothing, and that the court will see me as a high school graduate with no earning potential. He's right; I haven't held a job in years. I've been home raising my children, and that's why I'm afraid to go to court Friday. He's a convincing liar, and I might lose custody of my two youngest children."

"You're just going to have to be brave, Jean. You're a remarkable woman, and you and your children have to get away from him. I'll pray for you, Jean."

"Thank you. I want to ask you something," I hesitated.

"Okay," he said.

"Do you know Seth to be gay?" I blurted.

There was a lull while George considered my question. "I

don't know, Jean. Do you think he's gay?"

"I don't suspect; I *know* he's gay, George. I've heard and seen too much since our first year together."

"He might be, Jean;" George added, "I really don't know, but you have to understand that I have seen Seth only twice in sixteen years since college, once at your house recently, and about ten years earlier, at Max's wedding, when he was still married to Deb."

"I think he's in love with Runi."

"I've heard him talk about Runi," George affirmed.

"Runi's wife told me that Seth and Runi were lovers. She told me that they were bi-sexual. Seth and I drove up to Springfield, Missouri, just after Harper was born, and stayed with Runi and Joyce. That weekend, Seth left me in the middle of the night and went back over to a man's house who I heard proposition my husband for sex earlier that evening. Do you know Aiden Cooper?"

"Never heard of him," George answered.

"Seth is not in love with me; he's a gay man, and that fact makes him crazy, too."

"Wow," George said as he digested my sad reality.

"And Seth lost his mother's entire life savings recently in the stock market."

"What the hell was he doing with his mother's money?"

"Playing stockbroker, and against my wishes! He never took that Series 7 exam! He didn't have license or the expertise to be playing stockbroker! And the moment that idiotic and guilt-ridden woman gave her firstborn her entire life savings of $85,000, Seth and I began to fight over the possibility of him losing even a small portion of her money. I couldn't get comfortable with him taking a risk like that with her money. He never played the stock market a day in his life; and then, he goes and plays her money on the margin; and then, his stockbroker in New York makes a margin call, and Seth can't come up with the cash."

"Oh, my God!" George droned in complete disbelief. "He was insane to touch his mother's money."

"Right, and he's even more insane, now that he's lost all his mommy's money. This woman won't have a dime in savings when she can no longer work as a secretary. And what now, George? Who's going to take care of the old lady? Not Seth and me! We're getting a divorce due to Seth and his mama's co-dependent relationship! She couldn't say no! And because he has lost all her money, he's crazy angry now, and blames me!"

"I'm so sorry, Jean. How are your children taking all of this?"

"They were sleeping when Daddy was hauled off to jail the other morning. Our two sons are too young to understand what's going on between their parents. I told my boys that Daddy can't live here anymore with us, but they don't understand why not. They love their daddy and miss him. Not Bella though, she's delighted Seth is gone and tells me not to let him back into the house. She's eleven and she's heard enough quarreling. Only once, though, in all the years that he hit me, did one of my children witness him striking me. Harper came between us that day. Seth is careful, and sneaky, and does his crap behind closed doors, including sleeping with my best friend recently."

"What!" George was appalled. "He did what?"

"He screwed my best friend upstairs while I was sleeping downstairs."

"How did you find out?" George asked.

"I busted him coming out of her bedroom, and she turned against me out of her guilt."

"Wow," George replied. "I just want you to know, Jean, that whatever I can do for you, I'm here for you."

"Thank you, George. That means a lot to me."

DREADED FRIDAY ARRIVED TOO SOON. My next door neighbor, Marilyn, agreed to watch my two youngest children while I was in court for what I expected to be all morning. Bella got on the school bus, that morning, before I left for the 9th Judicial District Court of Montgomery County in Conroe, Texas, a few miles north of The Woodlands, Texas. I met my Conroe lawyer, John Pettit, in the hallway, and I briefed him on Seth's less than shining attributes. We entered into the courtroom and sat down at a table next to Seth and his lawyer's table.

"All rise," shouted the bailiff.

Judge Keyshawn, a youthful-looking male in his late thirties, wearing a black robe, walked in and sat on the bench. "Please be seated," the judge instructed all before reading the docket. "Jean Zherneboh versus Seth Zherneboh. Are the lawyers here?"

"We're both present, your Honor," said my lawyer while he and my husband's attorney stood up from where they sat. My lawyer continued, "I'm Attorney John Pettit appearing for Petitioner."

"I'm Attorney Kent Brown, appearing for Respondent," Seth's lawyer added.

I recognized the attorney's name. This man was the same lawyer that Seth had retained to sue the New York brokerage house for losing his mother's money in the stock market.

"Let's get started. Call your first witness," the judge ordered the attorneys while he reviewed the Petition for Divorce.

Seth's attorney sat down, and my lawyer remained standing while he announced, "I call Mrs. Jean Zherneboh as my first witness."

I nervously walked up to the witness stand and cringed at the marital name the court attached to me. Since the cops hauled Seth off to jail, this last time, I no longer used his last name. By my own accord, I took back my first ex-husband's name. I do not need anybody's permission to change my name. I had been Jean Wynn, the American Designer, and my first two children were of the Wynn name, too. My first husband was, and remains an alcoholic, but, nevertheless, Todd Wynn is a good man in his own pitiful way--he loves Bella. I didn't mind sharing the name I had been using since the age of nineteen with Todd.

I sat down in the box, and the bailiff duly swore me in while I adjusted the microphone and then swore to tell the truth, the whole truth, so help me, God.

The courtroom was nearly empty, except for the parties involved in our hearing--my husband, our lawyers, the bailiff, the judge, his clerk, the stenographer, and me.

"Please state your full name for the record," my lawyer instructed.

"Jean Wynn, that's my name now. I took back my old name. Call me Ms. Wynn."

"Okay, *Ms. Wynn*, let's begin."

I informed the court that my three children and I lived in a home in The Woodlands, Texas, within this court's jurisdiction; and I revealed that I had been legally married to the Respondent, since August 1992, only a year and four months earlier. I told the judge that I had two sons with the Respondent--Harper, four years old, and Doren, two years old. What I *did not* mention to the court was that I considered this entire divorce matter a sad state of affairs for everyone and often cried myself to sleep.

"Do you own the home you live in, Ms. Wynn?" My lawyer asked.

"Yes, we bought our home with cash from the efforts of my apparel business."

"And how long have you owned your home?"

"Since late '91, exactly two years ago, we bought the home."

"And what is the value of your home?"

"I would guess we could sell our home for $150,000. We've been updating and remodeling for months now."

"Do you work outside the home, Ms. Wynn?"

"No, I'm a stay-at-home mom."

"What is your education level?"

"I have a few college hours completed."

"Ms. Wynn, let's talk about the time when your husband broke your nose."

I sidestepped around the fact that I had instigated that fight. My lawyer did not launch the abuse that I had suffered by my husband's hand since day one of our sick relationship. My lawyer *did not* give me an opportunity to mention first, all the previous times Seth had assaulted me that had brought me to the brink of insanity, the day Seth broke my nose. My lawyer had not asked about any of the verbal and emotional abuse I suffered throughout the entire relationship. The judge did not understand that the abuse had been such a gradual and progressive pattern in Seth's behavior, that I actually faulted myself for all the unhappiness. The judge did not hear about the emotional, psychological, financial, and sexual abuse I had suffered over the years, or how Seth's abuse escalated over time as I got more determined to do life on my terms. The judge did not understand that Seth's behavior was all about trying to control me.

The events leading up to Seth breaking my nose were taken out of context for my protection, but I confessed that I had a doctor's record to prove my broken nose. I told the court that at the time of my examination, the doctor counseled me to leave my husband after learning of the domestic abuse.

The judge *did not* understand that after I had withdrawn from school that day against my wishes that I had driven home with a mission to kill Seth. The judge did not understand what preceded Seth's assault on me, when this lil' woman barged through the front door and found the rat perched on his throne in the water closet. The judge did not hear that while Seth wiped his ass, I grabbed him by the hair, and threw the bastard to the floor, face down, and held him there with my foot pressed into the back of neck. The judge did not understand that my husband had rendered me an ultimatum, the day before--drop out of school, or else he would hire the lawyer that he had consulted with that day, and divorce me. The judge did not understand that Seth had closed out the bank account that day, too, after I went to school, so that I had no more money for gas. The judge did not understand why we were fighting.

My attorney, Pettit, asked me if my husband broke things, and I spoke of all the occasions, from the beginning, when Seth punched holes in our apartment walls and broke my neon signature sign while I was pregnant with Harper. I revealed how Seth continued to break my things over the next five years, as I had previously described days earlier to George Harmsworth.

My attorney passed the witness, and I felt disappointed by how little of the pertinent information my attorney revealed to this court. I did not feel that the judge was clear that Seth had *never* been in love with me, because he was in love with a man, or that my angry husband had been consistently abusive for five years. I knew Seth had a drug addiction, but because I was honest and had not caught Seth in the act of taking his drugs, I told the court about the times when I witnessed Seth smoking weed with our friends, Pete, Chad, and their girlfriends, while careful not to indict myself as a pot smoker. I did tell the court how I had protested, more than once, that our friends not bring their drugs into our home, or use them on our property. I did tell the court that Seth and company defied my rules. I did not get a chance to tell the court about the crack pipe that I found in my red van after Seth and his boyfriend Runi came home late one evening, ten hours after Seth had picked Runi up from the airport. I also did not tell the court how later that same evening, they drugged this pregnant woman's virgin strawberry daiquiri with sleeping powder so they could have sex on the couch after I had passed out. I did not get a chance to tell the court that in recent days my husband slept with my best friend in our guest bedroom, while I soundly slept in the downstairs bedroom.

Seth's attorney, Kent Brown, then cross-examined me, and attempted to have me admit that I was violent and emotionally unstable, that I was a negligent mother, that I was a drug user and chronic alcoholic, and an unfaithful wife. He asked me about Bella's biological father and told the court after my lawyer objected, that the relevancy of his question was to prove my character and that I had affairs while married to Seth, too. Seth's lawyer told to the court that my parents wanted my first husband, Todd Wynn, to have custody of my first-born child, which explained, for the judge, why Joseph lived with his father. The court gave me no opportunity to explain that I gave Todd custody of my firstborn child out of guilt, and that the presiding family law judge on the bench, during our divorce, said that he would give me custody of my son because he did not feel it was right to split up the children when parents were divorcing.

Seth had coached his attorney, and together, my husband and his legal counsel established plausibility for the court to consider that maybe I was the negligent parent, the abusive spouse, the chronic drug-user, and the unfaithful party. Seth's attorney ended his interrogation by stating that I would not let Seth see his sons and that I was creating parental alienation, while the lawyer failed to reveal to the judge that there was a restraining order in place, since Seth's assault the morning of my economics final, that prohibited Seth from being anywhere near his wife and children.

I was disappointed with my attorney's line of questioning, and felt *he had not made who I was* as a woman, mother, and wife known to the court. The judge did not know of my Godly character of recent years, or of my involvement with my children lives, or of my aspirations to be more and have more in life. The judge did not hear about Jean, the woman who had sacrificed her second husband, Leonardo, to live near her first-born child. The judge did not hear that I had a dream, and believed in my capabilities, and was not a drug-using victim. My attorney did not tell the judge that I had proven myself to be driven and possess ambition, and that these particular characteristics were the very thing that threatened my fear-based husband. My attorney, inadvertently, downplayed my husband's abusive personality with the mention of only a broken nose in five years. When I stepped out of the witness box, I stressed over the fact that the judge did not know my husband had lost his mother's entire life savings in the stock market, which had sent Seth into an angry tailspin that made him even more abusive. The judge did not know that my husband was too paranoid to get out of the yard and go to work, and that instead, he had gambled his mama's life savings.

I felt vulnerable while I watched Seth step into the witness box while I took a seat next to my attorney. Seth sat down; and while I watched the bailiff walk up with a Bible and ask Seth to place his hand on the Good Book, I recalled an evening, before Seth and I came into money, when we entertained in our small apartment, his new boss, Pete, and co-worker, Chad, both from the talent agency:

***

Pete moved the conversation back on track. "According to the Masons, mankind's problem is that he has not been allowed free exercise of his reason by a God who restricts man with a series of do's and don'ts."

"I believe that, too!" *Seth contributed.*

Pete continued, "You don't believe in the God of the Bible, Seth?"

"No, there is no right or wrong--it's one man's opinion against another's."

"And you have a degree in Bible studies?" *Pete challenged.*

"All the more impressive, right?"

"So to murder is not wrong?" I asked Seth.

"Who says it's wrong?" Seth nonchalantly shrugged.

"God," I answered.

Seth snickered as if what I said was ignorant.

Pete continued, *"The Masons believe God is a figment of man's mind."* Seth inserted, *"He doesn't exist. God is a debunked myth."*

Pete considered Seth's words, *"So if God doesn't exist, what mankind calls religion is then fiction?"*

"Yes," Seth affirmed.

Pete shook his head, and I saw that he did not agree with Seth, either. *"I guess you would fit in fine with the Masons."*

"I think so," Seth affirmed. *"That's why I want to join them,"* he said before lowering his voice into a deep sinister sound, *"I want to fit in."*

"You sound like Satan," I chided.

"I am Satan," he replied again in a sinister way.

I turned to Pete, *"He's proud to be a creep."*

***

I returned my attention back to the courtroom just as the bailiff concluded. "Do you swear to tell the whole truth, so help you God?"

"I do," Seth replied.

The bailiff walked away with his Bible, and Seth's lawyer stepped up to the stand. "State your name for the record."

"Seth Boyd Zherneboh."

"How old are you, sir?" the attorney asked.

"I'm 39."

"Will you please tell the court your level of education?"

"I have a BA in Bible Studies; and I'm short a few hours from having a BS in computer science, a MA in ancient near eastern history, and a semester in law school."

"Why did you not finish law school?"

"My wife's constant raging made it impossible for me to study. She was jealous and threatened I was in school, and she wasn't."

Eck! He just described himself!
"Where are you presently living?"
"I'm staying with my sister, Demelza, and her husband, at their home in League City."
"Do they have a guest bedroom for you?"
"Yes."
"Are you asking the Court to award you temporary custody of your two children, Harper and Doren?"
"I am."
"Do you love your children?"
"I love my children as much as any man could ever love their children."

Why did Seth assume that the court believed he loved his children like men who love their wives because they love their children?

"Do you consider yourself a violent person or having a violent temper?"
"I am not a violent person, and I do not have a violent temper."
Judge Keyshawn interrupted, "Mr. Zherneboh, are you presently under charges for family violence?"
"Yes, Class A Assault, your Honor."
Touché!
Seth's attorney continued, "Can you inform the Court of the first occasion when there was some accusation of physical violence on your part toward her?"
"Oh, gosh, she's made a lot of statements. Back in 1989, when Jean was pregnant with our son, Harper..."

I have made a lot of accusations over the years about his assaults on my person. Seth's craftiness with words was that of the cunning snake.

Judge Keyshawn impatiently interrupted, "--I don't care what happened four years ago! We're having a temporary hearing to decide who is going to get which car, and who is going to live where. There is no question in my mind, already, that we're going to have mutual restraining orders against both of these parties. Be brief," he directed to Seth's attorney.

The barrister continued, "Now referring to the broken nose

of your wife, Mrs. Zherneboh, could you enlighten the court on what happened?"

"Jean attacked me on the toilet. She grabbed me off the toilet by the hair on my head and threw me face down to the floor. I reached back and accidentally broke her nose. I could not see where I was reaching."

I noticed the judge glance my way, and I shook my head in pretense of disappointment that what my husband said to the court was a fabrication.

"Do you consider your wife a violent person?"

"She is very violent, very volatile."

"Has she been violent with the children?"

"Yes, she has."

Liar!

"In what respect has she been violent?"

"I've seen her spank Harper and Doren very hard, and I've told her to stop."

I hardly considered swatting a child on the diapered behind child abuse!

"What about any physical or emotional abuse with her daughter, Bella?"

"Yes, emotional abuse. I've heard her scream at Bella at the top of her lungs, using profanity, in a very gross way."

I recalled the afternoon in 1987, when I lived behind Seth and his mother's apartment. I walked up to their front porch and found the door wide open. I saw Seth and his aged mother, face-to-face, standing in the middle of the living room screaming at each other at the top of their lungs, and both using profanity, over her firstborn's need to borrow more money from her because he could not pay his car note, or buy tires, because he did not have a job.

"Has she physically abused you?"

"Yes, she has physically abused me on many occasions, several in particular. She was sitting on the side porch in the slider swing with me, and without provocation, grabbed my hair and pulled my head down; and then, she hit me in the face with her fist and struck me three times. And then I called the police; I had a bruised cheek."

I sat there appalled by his slime ball character while wondering who could ever believe his subterfuge!

"Did she ever physically abuse you in front of the children?"

"Physically abusing me in front of our children was her favorite forum. I would tell her, Jean, don't do this in front of the children; let's go somewhere, but she would insist that they need to see what's going on."

He was Satan's emissary! Again, his testimony made me out to be unstable, and I understood that my husband, the equivocator, whose fear and drug addiction had paralyzed him in our yard for two years, believed that the judge, like himself, had no ability to separate the lies from the fiction anymore. I wanted to jump up and yell out to the judge that when I wasn't in school full-time, or plotting a second apparel business start-up, or writing my novel, or decorating my home, or attending a weekly seminar at Landmark's Center, or taking a writing class at Rice University, then I was cleaning, cooking, and shopping for groceries, clothes, décor. I bathed babies late at night while Seth was still outside obsessing with his yard, ignoring his family, and having private phone conversations with his boyfriend, Runi, in our detached garage. I took my kids to the doctor, my daughter to dance and singing lessons, and myself to the club to workout. This man was a gross deluder; and more than that, he deserved to lose everything that mattered to him! His perjury made me sound emotionally unhinged to this court!

"Has your wife ever destroyed any of your personal property?"

"Yes, she has."

"Very briefly," his lawyer instructed.

"She destroyed--" he hesitated and then blurted, "stereos."

Stereos! Another lie! We had only one stereo, and why would I break our $6,000 stereo? It suddenly dawned on me as to why he hesitated to answer. He was about to admit to the court that I broke his CD in half, but quickly changed his mind. I recalled that time when I stood in our living room in front of our booming speakers and told Seth to stop playing Van Halen's Runnin' with the Devil. I felt the lyrics that blasted that afternoon out into the yard were inappropriate for our young children to hear. Seth would not turn off the music, and I had been requesting for months, that he not play this particular artist. I pulled out the CD from the player and broke it in half—I had made that same request one too many times and had had enough. I recalled the lyrics:

♪*Yeah, yeah, ah, yeah*
I live my life like there's no tomorrow
♪*And all I've got, I had to steal*
Least I don't need to beg or borrow
♪*Yes, I'm livin' at a pace that kills*♪

Ooh, yeah
♪*(Ahh)*
Runnin' with the Devil
♪*Ahh-hah, yeah)*
(Woo-hoo-oo)
♪*Runnin' with the Devil*
Yes I'm, yeah, hoo

♪*Ooh, you know I*
I found the simple life ain't so simple♪

♪*When I jumped out, on that road*
I got no love, no love you'd call real
♪*Ain't got nobody, waitin' at home*♪

(Ah, yeah-ah!)
♪*with the devil*
(god damn it, lady. You know I ain't lyin' to ya)
♪*I'm only gonna tell you one time-ya!)*
Runnin' with the devil
(Yes I am! Yeah! ♪*)*

    I snapped out of that disturbing memory and heard Seth's lawyer ask, "Do you have an opinion whether your wife is emotionally stable?"

    "I do have an opinion; she is very emotionally un-stable when it comes to good judgment."

    Obviously, I married you!

    Seth continued, "She's an unfit mother, even though I feel she loves the children."

    "Pass the witness," Attorney Brown said to the court.

    I seethed while I shot daggers at the arrogant con artist!

My lawyer got up to cross-examine the witness, my husband. "Mr. Zherneboh, did you have a sexual relationship with your wife's best friend, Sabrina Edward?"

"No sir, I did not."

"Is it true that Mrs. Edwards showed you a nude picture of her in your home?"

"No, it is not true," Seth answered.

"Mr. Zherneboh, do you have a relationship with a man named Runi Krieger?"

"Yes, I do; he's one of my best friends."

"Is there a sexual relationship between you and him?"

"That's absurd! Absolutely not! I am not anything other than heterosexual!"

My attorney paused and looked down at the exhibit in his hand. He silently read from the letter Seth wrote to Runi, the letter Seth had written Runi the day before I gave birth to our last child. "Did you write a letter to Mr. Krieger advising him in the following words, 'My god, do you know I love you?'"

"I would have to see the letter that says that, but I could very well have written that, depending on the context, of course, that it was written."

"Mr. Zherneboh, have you been indicted on the recent assault charge?"

"I went to the arraignment yesterday."

"In what court?"

"In Suzanne Stovall's court upstairs. I pled not guilty."

My attorney held a card Seth had written me. "Mr. Zherneboh, you testify that you're not a violent man. Did you ever write your wife a card apologizing for breaking her coffee table?"

"I'll have to see the card, but I don't recall."

"Mr. Zherneboh, you allege that your wife has and continues to abuse alcohol. Is that really true?"

"Yes."

"Does she abuse alcohol before she goes to the university, or after she gets home from a full day of school?"

"She quit her classes and took up drinking. She enrolled into two different semesters and never finished either semester."

He deserved to die! His lies enraged me. His fabrications threatened to be the cause for why I could lose my two youngest babies in this hearing!

"Now, Mr. Zherneboh, you alleged that your wife grabbed you by the hair, and pulled you off the toilet, and threw you face down onto the floor."

"Yes, I did."

"And then you reached back and accidentally broke her nose?"

"Yes sir, I could not see where I was reaching."

"Mr. Zherneboh, do you really expect this court to believe that this slender woman, sitting right here with us, has the strength to pick you up off the toilet and slam you face down to the floor?"

The judged scowled at the witness on the stand.

"Yes sir!" Seth answered with great indignation as if the court did not believe him!

My attorney rolled his eyes in disbelief.

I held all expression off my face. Seth's last statement, that I picked him up off the toilet and slammed him to the floor, and his earlier braggadocios admission of his $100,000 a year income, were the only truthful words he had uttered in court that entire morning! Seth spoke partial truth--I had finally kicked my abuser's ass, after too many years of not retaliating, and I got thirty seconds of gratification, before he jumped to his feet and plowed his fist into my face and broke my nose. I justified my action--even an angel had her breaking point, and I was not sorry that I scooped my body weight off the commode and slammed him face down onto the floor in one single motion! Seth was a 5'9" skinflint!

"Mr. Zherneboh," he lawyer continued, "Tell us about a time when..."

The questioning and answering went on for hours until neither lawyer had any further agenda. Judge Keyshawn then angrily ended the hearing with great irritation. "Anybody can get married and create kids;" he bellowed, "but it takes something special to raise children, and I'm not seeing it here today."

At that moment, I understood that Seth and his lawyer had successfully delivered a plausible argument that I might be the unstable parent and wife. As

Seth had threatened he would do if I ever took him to court, he and his lawyer successfully alleged I did everything that I alleged my husband did to me over the years. The judge did not know whom to believe!

The judge looked at me and then at my husband, "You two need to stop thinking only about yourselves and consider your children right now. Children of divorce, in your children's age group, continue to have fantasies about reconciling their parents. They experience intense grief over the loss of not having one of their parents living with them. Boy and girls tend to react differently to their parents' divorce. Girls become anxious and withdrawn, and boys become more aggressive and disobedient. A child's relationship with his or her parents following a divorce is critical to the child's adjustment. The continuing relationship that children have with their parents is essential to their long-term adjustment. This highlights the importance of not criticizing the other parent in front of the child. Children do best when visits from the non-custodial parent are regular. Children have a fear of change, and their previously secure world is in a state of change. They have a realistic fear that if they lose one parent, they may lose the other parent, and the concept of being alone is a very frightening thing for a child. New surroundings can cause a negative reaction. Many kids withdraw and show signs of depression. Both parents must be involved. Children do best when their divorcing parents treat each other respectfully and civilly. Even if you feel wronged in the divorce, parents must not communicate that to their children. Children are the innocent bystanders and studies have proven that children from divorced families are on average worse off than children who live in intact families. These children have more difficulty in school, more behavior problems, their sense of self-worth is diminished, they are insecure people, and have more problems with peers and more trouble getting along with their parents. A recent study that came out this year found that 90% of adolescents from intact families were within the normal range of behavior, and only 10% of those kids needed professional help. However, 74% of the boys, and 66% of the girls from divorced families fell into the normal range of behavior, and 26% of the boys, and 34% of the girls, were in the problematic range needing professional help."

The judge looked up. "I bet you parents did not know that when our government builds a prison, they use current statistics of boys from fatherless homes, and then the government looks at those same, fatherless boys when they are in the sixth grade, and the portion of that population that falls below national, average reading and math scores, are considered future inmates. Kids living in single-parent homes, or in step-families, report lower educational expectations on the part of their parents, less parental monitoring of school work, and less overall social supervision than children from intact families. 70% of juveniles in state-operated institutions come from fatherless homes. Boys who grow up in father-absent homes are more likely that those in father-present homes to have trouble establishing appropriate sex roles and gender identity. The judge looked up from his notes, "You parents should be ashamed of yourself."

These facts troubled me, and I agreed with the judge--Seth should be ashamed of himself. Seth should have been a better father by first being a loving husband! Did he hate me so much, that he did not care whether his children had a secure home life? Did he hate me so much that he wanted to rip their mother out of their lives? Seth had to be a Godly man to be a stable man, who would honor his vow, till death do we part. I silently prayed. God, my heavenly father, please put Godly men in my sons lives, men who will mentor my sons and show them how to be loving and good men. And, and as far as me and my house, we will serve you, Lord.

The judge continued, "I'm going to grant a mutual restraining order as to property, and as to the violence, and as to the calling and harassment. I'm going to award temporary managing conservatorship to the Petitioner, Mrs. Zherneboh. She will remain in the marital home with the children." He spoke to me, "The father will be allowed to talk to those children once a night, not three or four times a night"; and, then he directed his attention to Seth, "And you're not to call after 9:00 p.m. The father will have standard visitation on the first, third, fifth weekends. Now, concerning the child support and temporary alimony, the father will pay $800 per month temporary child support and $1,200 per month temporary alimony for six months and all interim attorney fees. You prepare the order, Attorney Pettit, and get it to me within the week."

I watched Seth lean over and speak into his lawyer's ear.

"Your Honor," Attorney Brown begged. "I have one more issue that we should have addressed. My client, Mr. Zherneboh, and his wife, have a ski trip planned, and my client requests that his wife give him his airline ticket."

"When is this trip?"

"Their flight leaves in the morning, sir."

"Are you telling me that these two people have a trip planned together?"

Attorney Brown smiled, "Yes sir. They have leased a condo for four days and three nights and have bought two airline tickets."

Judge Keyshawn shook his head in disbelief. "Here's what I'm ordering, attorneys. Mrs. Zherneboh will give her husband his airline ticket, but only if Mrs. Zherneboh agrees to let her husband stay in the condominium, can he stay there. You people are ridiculous! This court is adjourned."

I watched the judge jump up and quickly disappear through a door in the back wall, and then I turned to my attorney. "There's a restraining order, and Seth is not to be anywhere near me!"

"I guess you have even more reason to tell him no," my lawyer answered.

I drove myself back to my Woodland's home from the courthouse and thanked God for his intervention. I had custody of my two youngest children. I could not bear the thought of not raising my babies, or having to feel the sadness and emptiness that I had experienced when I had surrendered custody of my first-born child, Joseph. Moreover, after having watched a vile spirit sit before me all morning, and heinously defame my character with his obscene lies, I was certain that I would die before I surrendered my two youngest sons to the reprobate. The power of evil had terrified me that day in court, while I realized that the presiding judge had bought my husband's lies. Seth, like the legendary Dr. Faustus, who passionately sought power that included the power of rule, money, and knowledge, would realize one day too late that the cost for his bargain with the devil was eternal damnation.

"The hell with you, Seth!" I angrily murmured while I pulled into my driveway.

I got out of my green Volvo station wagon and walked toward my front door. I peered over to the next-door neighbor's house for sight of my children and saw no one outside. I unlocked my door and stepped inside my beautiful home. I worried that in the final hearing, when I went up against *Satan* again, that I risked losing my children and home.

I threw my purse and keys onto the kitchen island, walked over to the phone on the kitchen buffet, and dialed my neighbor. "Hello, Marilyn."

"Hi. How did it go, Jean?"

"I have temporary custody of the children, use of the house, and possession of my car; and the judge gave me child support and alimony for six months."

"Good for you! That's great news! I'll be right over with the kids."

Minutes later, I heard a knock. I swung open the front door and there stood my three smiling children, Bella, Harper, and Doren with Marilyn standing behind them. I squatted down and hugged my children with great appreciation that I still had them in my life. "I love you guys!" I said in delight while I stood back up.

"We love you, too, Mommy!" Harper's glee was contagious while sweet baby Doren hugged me around the legs and adoring Bella around the waistline.

"Did you get custody of the boys?" Bella asked me.

I smiled at my eleven year old, "I sure did! We're all staying together, Bella."

"Yippee," they all cheered while jumping up in joy.

Marilyn stood there smiling with a bouquet of flowers in her hands. I looked at her in question regarding the colorful arrangement.

"These flowers are from a friend," she said while handing me the gift.

"Thank you!"

"No, they're not from me! Read the card!"

I took the small card out of the arrangement and silently read,

I'm thinking about you today. God bless you. George. "Wow," I murmured while surprised. "He's a sweetheart!" I explained further for Marilyn's piqued interest. "George was Seth's college roommate sixteen years ago." I chuckled while stopping short of telling the story about the girlfriend they fought over in college. "George lives in Connecticut; he's divorced and has two daughters. I guess he has reason to like me more than his old college buddy!"

Marilyn laughed. "Obviously."

I chuckled, "Please, come in!" I motioned to the sweet, fifty-something-year old coiffed blonde.

She stepped inside my foyer. "So when are you leaving tomorrow?"

"Our plane leaves at 6:00 a.m." I left the front door open while enjoying the chilly December night air. "My nanny will be here at 5:00 a.m.--I hope."

"Oh, that's an early flight! Is Seth still going?"

"The judge thinks we're insane, and ordered me to give Seth his airline ticket. I have to do that tonight. I have two good friends who will be here shortly, too, Charley and Fred; they're my moral support tonight. They're spending the evening with me; and then, we three are driving to the airport together from here. George, who sent me these flowers, is meeting us in Steamboat." I grinned while considering that the blue-eyed blonde and I might have more fun together than I originally thought.

Marilyn smiled, "Don't move too fast."

"I'm not!" A car pulled into my driveway, and I saw that Charley had arrived. My old friend smiled and waved at us as she pulled up closer.

"I'm not going to stay," Marilyn said as she walked back through the threshold and stepped outside. "I know you have a lot to do before you leave."

"I want to thank you, Marilyn, if I didn't already, for being so good to me and my kids over the last two years."

"You're welcome, Jean. You all have fun tomorrow," she said before she walked off.

"Oh, I will try," I answered while relieved that the court

hearing was over, and that my fun, four-day trip to the beautiful Rocky Mountains was now launched with an unexpected flower arrangement from George, and the arrival of my best girlfriend, Charley. Fred would make the party complete.

 Later that night after Charley and Fred went to bed, I was in my room feeling distraught over the turn of events. My traveling buddies were asleep by 10:00 p.m. in bedrooms upstairs while I sat and fretted on the edge of my bed in the downstairs master bedroom. Bella slept in the bed beside me because we gave Fred her bedroom for the night. I stared at my daughter and assumed she had a sense of peace since having learned from me that day that she would not be separated from her little brothers. I worried, however, that the temporary orders pertaining to custody might change after the final hearing, and that the court would split my children up between parents. I did not want Bella to lose her brothers. I understood that the judge believed the liar in his courtroom that day, and that the judge could not separate the truth from the lies. I could not bear the thought of not living with my two youngest sons. I never wanted to feel again the pain I felt when I lost custody of Joseph ten years earlier.

 I needed reassurance from God that my children's lives were in his hands, and while reaching for the Bible on my nightstand, I whispered, "Father, please give me permanent custody of my two babies. I promise you, that I will raise my children to be God-loving, God-fearing men who do not lie, steal, or cheat."

 I let the pages fall open and read Exodus, chapter 20, and began reading *The Ten Commandments*. I paused on verse 13: *You shall not murder*. God was asking me to recognize where I fell out of grace with him while I recalled the grimmest day of my life—that day in the abortion clinic. I shuddered at what I had done to my unborn child and knew I had to learn the law before I could engender with the spirit and forever lose that which had been controlling my life for thirty-four years. "Forgive me, Father," I sadly whispered, "and forgive me, dear child; I love you."

I wiped the tears off my cheeks while feeling as if I were in hell and read for more clarity, and verse 14 orders: *You shall not commit adultery.* And verse 15 instructs us to not steal, and verse 16 states: *You shall not bear false witness against your neighbor.* And verse 17 says, *You shall not covet your neighbor's house or wife.*

Seth had lied that day in court, and he had coveted his neighbor's wife, too--me. I had committed adultery, and Seth had stolen Leonardo's wife. I murmured, "I am not worthy of your help, Father, for I am a sinner who is no better than this man who threatens to take my children away from you and me."

I read more of God's laws: *You shall not bear a false report; do not join your hand with a wicked man to be a malicious witness.*

I had hurt my sweet and loving Leonardo and made a marital union with a liar. "Oh Jesus," I murmured, "Help me. This mess I created is too big for me; I give it to you."

I pushed forward through Exodus to chapter 23, verse 6 to understand more of what the God of love expected of me while realizing I woke up a day too late. ...*You shall not pervert the justice due to your needy brother in his dispute.* And 23:21 cites: *Keep far from a false charge, and do not kill the innocent, or the righteous, for I will not acquit the guilty. Be on your guard before him and obey his voice; do not be rebellious toward him, for he will not pardon your transgression, since my name is in him. However, if you truly obey his voice, and do all that I say, then I will be an enemy of your enemies, and an adversary to your adversaries.*

I sat the Bible down and chose to believe God's Word: Obey his commandments, and he will be an enemy of my enemy.

I recalled that day in court, and considered, again, how Seth and his lawyer had successfully delivered a plausible argument that I might be the unstable parent and wife. As Seth had threatened he would do, if I ever took him to court, he and his lawyer successfully alleged I did everything that I alleged my husband did to me over the last five years. The judge did not know whom to believe that day, and looked at me, and then at my husband, and said to us, *"You two need to stop thinking only about yourselves and consider your children right now."* I had been thinking only of my children since I had given birth to my last two children; and, on this night, I swore that I would never lie down and give my children to a reprobate.

I had no power to create miracles. I could not give the deaf their hearing, or the blind their sight, as Jesus had done while walking the earth; but, I chose to believe, in my hour of desperation, in the God of the Bible, who told me that if I obeyed His commandments, and believed His Son, Jesus Christ, died for me, to wash me of my past, present, and future sins, then God would take care of my enemies.

I picked up the law book again, turned to Exodus, and began reading chapter 12:12: *I will go through the land of Egypt on that night and will strike down all the firstborn in the land of Egypt, both man and beast, and against all the gods of Egypt, I will execute judgments, for I am the Lord. The blood shall be a sign for you on the houses where you live, and when I see the blood, I will pass over you, and no plague will befall you to destroy you when I strike the land of Egypt. Now, this day will be a memorial to you, and you shall celebrate Passover as a feast to the Lord, and throughout your generations, you are to celebrate Passover as a permanent ordinance. And you shall also observe the Feast of Unleavened Bread, for on this very day, I brought your hosts out of the land of Egypt; therefore, you shall observe this day throughout your generations as a permanent ordinance, too. It shall be a perpetual statute throughout your generations.*

In that moment, I suddenly understood that God's commanded holiday, the Passover, was a reminder that I could choose to be a slave to God and obey his commandments; or I could choose to be a slave of my ego and suffer under the hand of a non-loving slave-master as the Israelites had suffered while in captivity in Egypt. I had not observed God's Holy Days ever in my life, and realized that I was not only in violation of God's commandments, but I also violated God's ordinances and statutes, too.

A knock on the bedroom's sliding patio doors jolted me out of my considerations. I froze in fright while wondering who called at this late hour at the back door. I suspected Seth was on the other side, here to retrieve his airline ticket the judge ordered me to give him that day in court. "Who is it?" I asked through the closed drapes.

"It's me, Jean--Seth."

I slid open the patio door and defensively stood inside the threshold, with my arms folded, while I felt my anger surface and looked at the haggard and disheveled man. "Hold on, let me get your ticket," I grumbled. "Wait here."

"Wait, Jean. I want to talk to you."

"Talk," I spouted while realizing how I detested the liar who attempted to take my children away.

"I'm sorry. I don't want a divorce; I love you."

"Oh yeah, I saw how you *love me* today," I sarcastically shot back.

"I do love you," he defended. "When the judge gave you temporary custody of Harper and Doren, my reality hit me hard. I don't want to separate from my family. I love you and all our children, including Bella. They need their father, too. Can I come back?"

I wanted to believe Seth, and I could believe him when he said that his reality hit him hard. I never forgot the pain I felt when I realized that Joseph, my two-and-a-half year old little boy no longer would live with me. I shrugged while still reeling from Seth's lies that day in court and spewed disgust. "I don't know, Seth."

"Please, Jean. I'm begging you. Forgive me. Let me stay with you in the condo on this trip, and I'll show you that I love you." He smiled while he waited for my reaction.

I felt indignation over what he had said about me that day in court, and my pride stood between me forgiving Seth, and me saying no to his request and making the biggest mistake in my life. How could I *not* forgive this man while knowing the pain he would feel if I continued with the divorce action and won permanent custody of our children? Perhaps, if I did not forgive my husband, and let him come back, and prove something greater to his children and me, then I would lose custody of my two youngest children at the final hearing. The thought that God would punish me *for not forgiving* my husband terrified me into submission. "Okay, Seth, you can come back."

"Wow, Jean!" He replied in delight.

"Stop, Seth!" I angrily ordered. Nothing about this situation felt right logically. "I'm very angry at you for telling lies about me on the witness stand today; and though I saw that you cared only about your agenda, I'm going to give you another chance--this is not just about me."

"Thank you, Jean," he declared while looking as if surprised that I could forgive him. "Can I stay tonight? We have something to celebrate!"

"No!" The idea of me in his arms, again, repelled me. "Go back to wherever you came from." *Hell, I considered.* "We're leaving in the morning at 5:00 a.m. You can meet us here in the driveway."

"Okay, thank you, Jean. Thank you! Thank you!"

"I'm going to bed now," I announced and then began to slide the door closed while feeling damned if I did, and damned if I didn't.

"Wait! Can I have my airline ticket, please?" He kindly begged.

I wondered then, why Seth did not trust me to give him his ticket in the morning, while *he expected me* to trust him to be who he said he was for me--a loving man who wanted another chance to prove his love to me and his children. "Hold on," I impatiently spouted while angry at the conflicting feelings he created within me with his duplicity. I went to my purse on the chest-of-drawers and pulled out his airline ticket. I looked over my shoulder to see Seth step inside my room. He smiled while he looked around our beautiful bedroom. "I love you, Jean. Do you love me?"

I controlled my thoughts, despite my angry feelings and the distrust I held toward him. One minute, he strangulated me, and the next—he tells me that he loves me. He was sick. "I want to love you, Seth, but you make it too hard." I was glad that I had left George's flower arrangement on the bar in the den that evening, and, too, that there was a restraining order in place subjecting Seth to non-violent behavior while in my presence.

"I'm sorry. I'll do better."

"I'm forgiving you," I said while realizing I was in direct violation of the restraining order created before our last hearing. He was to be nowhere near me by order of the court.

THE FOLLOWING MORNING IN DECEMBER OF 1993, Seth met us in the driveway of the home solely awarded to my kids and me by a judge until further ruling at the final divorce and custody hearing. The reception from Charley and Fred was less than cool that morning while they refrained from expressing their shock when I told them, in front of our unexpected traveling companion, that my husband was joining us. My friends were asleep the night before, when the liar came to the patio door, off my bedroom, and negotiated a stay in *my* condominium, as the judge had ordered he must do if he wanted to stay with us. I suspected their thoughts about me accommodating Seth were on hold until they could find alone time with me.

My nineteen-year old nanny pulled up in her old silver jalopy while Fred, Charley, Seth, and I loaded our luggage into the back of my green Volvo station wagon parked in the open two-car detached garage. Her arrival, only minutes after Seth had pulled up into the driveway in his black Mustang, alleviated the pressure I felt to explain to Charley and Fred my idiotic decision.

I gave Lolli, or as my children liked to call their fat babysitter, *Lollipop*, care instructions, emergency cash, and emergency numbers before we all piled into my car and headed to the airport. Our two-and-a-half hour flight to Steamboat, Colorado, departed on time that early morning. I sat between the aisle and Seth with little to say and felt angry while he acted as if everything was back to normal with us. After five years of doing an up-close and personal study of my unstable husband, I now concluded after his last performance in court that Seth had some kind of psychiatric condition, which required therapy. He manipulated me, exploited me, and violated my rights. He often lied to me, and everyone else on the planet, as I had witnessed that previous day in court and over the last five years. He fought with me often and showed no guilt for anything he did to me in the aftermath; and while I felt angry that he sat next to me on this trip, I questioned my own good sense. The bottom line with me--I was deathly afraid of losing custody of my children, my beautiful home, and the $8,000 a month income Seth's commission check afforded us. I feared the smooth-talking liar who touted his annual earnings, master degree, and law school credential in a believable manner as to insinuate his sole efforts, alone, had brought us into a privileged segment of society, could, and would convince even the brightest, that he was a success story, and not the loser I knew him to be in life. Seth was a conman.

Shortly into our long flight, I pulled out an inspirational paperback and flipped open the book to show Seth that I did not care to talk to him on the trip. I read a page and a passage resonated with me: *Watch your thoughts, they become words. Watch your words, they become actions. Watch your actions, they become habits. Watch your habits, they become character. Watch your character, it becomes your destiny. As a man thinks, this is what he is, or so he is.* (Proverbs 23:7)

I looked up and considered that I could not deny my own character while I stared at the reprobate with gouged out sores on his face and realized that my fear was hindering my own good judgment. Was I staying with Seth because I wanted to forgive him and give him an opportunity to not suffer, or was I staying because I lacked courage to leave? Did I really possess faith in God's ability?

Our plane arrived in Denver early that morning by the grace of a time zone, and we connected to Steamboat via puddle hopper. An hour after boarding the ground shuttle that took us from the small airport at the ski resort to our home for the next four days, Fred, Charley, Seth, and I found ourselves sitting in a luxurious living room in a three-bedroom condo, dressed in our ski clothes and drinking red wine while we waited for George's arrival from Connecticut. And as Seth did in any social setting, he dominated the conversation, but on this particular day, he did so with words that did not align with his listeners' reality.

My husband took a sip from his wine glass and excitedly rambled, "I am so happy to be here!" He spoke directly to Charley and Fred. "Life is good! Look at me--I'm sitting here among friends, in a luxurious condo, in Steamboat, and waiting on the arrival of one of my oldest and dearest friends. I'm thrilled I can share George with you guys. He's one of *the inner circle*. He's like a brother to me."

I became aware of the fact that I owned Seth's meaning of the term "inner circle" and now he purposely used the term to distance me from George. His attempted manipulation was ineffective. After flowers and several midnight goodnights over the phone between Houston and Connecticut, I had no reason to believe George was ever a member of the inner circle.

He continued, "...Men come no finer!" Seth took another sip. "I'm drinking from a fine bottle of wine and celebrating my reunion with my wife. How I love that woman!" He said from across the room to Charley and Fred and then shot me a smile. "There is a god after all, and he is good!"

I did not smile back, but, instead, considered his sleek performance as he stood up before us thrilled about the opportunity I gave him to get it right with me and his kids. The actor could convince anyone to give him cash for ocean front property in Arizona. Whatever he needed to create, he just pulled glistening words out of his ass without any regard for truth. Yesterday his Academy Award performance on the witness stand could have cost me custody of my beautiful children. He kicked me in the face one day and celebrated me the very next!

He continued, "I'm having difficulty expressing how grateful I am to be back in the fold. I can't put all my thoughts into words."

"I bet not," Charley spouted in her usual relaxed manner.

I snickered while I realized patience was key for me to keep my faith. I studied the expressions on Charley and Fred's faces—they both looked bewildered. Obviously, they found today's performance odd, too.

Seth continued to plead for my friends' approval. "You can't begin to understand what yesterday was like for me, when my reality hit me that I had lost everything that meant anything to me. When that judge ordered me to stay away from those I love, I, I, I was devastated! My children mean more to me than anything in the world!"

I could see that my girlfriend was using a lot of restraint before she lost control and spouted off, "You're a lucky man, Seth, that Jean would have you back."

Fred casually peered over at me for my reaction.

"That's an understatement," I mumbled to Fred before taking another sip of red wine and feeling angry. I felt like a victim of a cruel head game.

"Oh, she's a doll!" Seth affirmed.

"We've all known that, Seth." Fred confirmed with a gentle smile. "Are you just now figuring out how special your wife is?"

I looked at Fred and considered my friend more special than Seth.

Seth continued, "I know that I'm the luckiest man in the world to have a woman like Jean."

"You are!" Fred acknowledged.

I shook my head in disappointment at the 5'9" gaunt-looking, dark-haired man. "It's not about *luck*, Seth," I spewed while understanding that my words flew right over his self-consumed head.

Charley looked at me and then back at Seth. "I think a person can be too forgiving," she told me. "When I learned Ralph was having an affair with his secretary while I was raising our three kids, I was furious with him. It took me a while to forgive Ralph. He was my ex-husband by the time I found it in my heart to do so—and, by then, I was involved with someone else. I did eventually forgive Ralph;" she nodded, "but I never *forgot* what he did. *I didn't want to forget* how he had no regard for me and our kids, and that truth kept me strong and heading toward divorce court. I could never trust him again."

I internalized my friend's message while I watched her turn her attention back to me. "George should be here soon," she diverted. "It's nearly one o'clock."

"Yeah," I sighed while feeling like an idiot, again, for going against my own feelings and letting Seth back into my life. "Let me call George on his cell and see if he's lost," I suggested as I jumped up off the couch seething over what Seth had done to my sense of security. I now doubted myself! I was not the girl who once believed she could be the next *Donna Karen of New York City*.

Suddenly, the front door blew open, and the golden boy walked in wearing an expensive business suit in tones of silver and black and carrying a black briefcase with a black leather garment bag slung over his shoulder. George flashed us a huge smile when he spotted us gathered in the living room.

Seth screeched, "Hey preacher man, we were just holding a prayer meeting."

A look of confusion flashed across George's face before he blurted, "Pour me one of those, and let the good times begin! I'm here!"

We all chuckled while I watched Seth leap up, before George could drop his luggage, and greet his former college roommate with a warm handshake and slap on the back. "How are you old man?" Seth asked.

"What's this *old* stuff?" George chuckled while he hugged Seth back and peered over Seth's shoulder at me with a warm smile.

"You're still that same guy I knew in college!" Seth cracked while I walked up.

"Not really, Seth," George refuted on a more serious note while turning to embrace me.

"Hey George, you're looking good."

"You, too, Jean. Good to see you again." He stepped back and turned to my husband. "I wasn't expecting to see *you*, Seth." He turned to me for clarification. "You two went to court yesterday, right?"

"We sure did!" Seth happily intervened. "And now, Jean and I are reunited by the mercy of a great god!"

"I wondered if you knew God, Seth," George sneered.

I snickered while noticing George divert his attention back to me for introductions, or for more explanation.

I began to introduce my friends who stood beside me when Seth interrupted, "How you forget we once led church services together!"

"I didn't forget, Seth!" George slammed back as if Seth didn't get his point.

I interrupted their contest. "I want to introduce you to Charley and Fred," I said to our New England gem.

"Hi George," Charley said while she extended her hand.

"It's a pleasure to meet you, Charley. Jean's told me a lot of nice things about you."

"And I've heard nice things about you, too," she replied.

I glanced at my husband for his reaction while assuming Seth could deduce that George and I had been hanging on the phone talking, while he had been in jail for twenty-four hours, and then ordered to stay away from the wife and kids by a restraining order.

"Jean and I go way back," Charley explained, "We lived next door to each other in an apartment complex nearly seven years ago. I had just gotten a divorce after a nearly twenty-year marriage when she and Bella moved into the apartment beside mine."

I contributed more. "Leonardo and I were still married when I moved into the apartment complex; he had just moved to Indiana for a new job."

Charley added, "And Jean's ex-husband, Todd, and their son, Joseph, moved into the apartment on the other side of me," Charley laughed. "It was a real Payton Place back in those days."

I wanted my friends to know that I was a responsible parent. "I didn't want to leave my six-year old son. That debate made me crazy for a while--obviously." I wondered if George could put the pieces together, and then I added, "Seth and his mother and his teenage brother lived directly behind my apartment." I was well aware that Seth did not want me to reveal that detail about his life to everyone in the room, but I wanted George and Fred both to understand how a man like Seth got into my life—by default.

George solemnly nodded and then turned to Fred, "Did you live there, too?"

He smiled, "No, I avoid drama."

We laughed, and I turned to George, "Fred here is one of the sanest men I know."

George shook Fred's hand. "Jean has a lot of nice things to say about you, too, Fred. I hear you're an amazing writer."

Fred chuckled, "Well," he humbly said, "I'm trying."

"Can't blame a man for trying," Seth inserted.

Everyone looked at Seth without any comment and then back at sweet Fred to hear more.

"Fred does more than try;" I boasted, "--he *acts* on his dreams! A director is considering producing his award-winning screenplay in the theatre district downtown."

"Wonderful!" George quipped.

Fred looked at me and then back at the man in the business suit. "Jean and I do a seminar series together. I met Jean about a year ago."

"Fred's my mentor and inspiration," I informed George.

Charley quipped, "Jean's lucky to have Fred! Everyone needs someone *who inspires them.*"

I heard another one of Charley's blows directed at Seth's character and returned George's smile. "Fred inspires me *to write*," I said to my dart-throwing girlfriend in a thick southern drawl, while clarifying specifically for George my relationship with Fred.

George said to the playwright who towered over him, "I've had the privilege of getting to know Jean and she inspires me."

I chuckled while getting that George was letting Fred know he was interested in me, too. I noticed neither one of them was concerned about Seth's feelings.

Fred had seen the bouquet of flowers the night before in my living room and had asked me who had sent the flowers. I told him that George gave me the arrangement and stopped short of explaining my feelings because I was not sure at the moment who I liked more, George or Fred? On one hand, George and I had children and had experienced the same emotional trauma; and, on the other hand, Fred and I both aspired to be writers.

"Let's hit the slopes!" Seth suggested while he glossed over the news that both men had set designs on me.

"Let's go skiing!" Fred encouraged while Charley and I agreed.

Seth took the rivalry in stride and showed no emotion while acting as if he did not understand that neither man had any regard for his position in my life anymore.

"We'll save money," I said. "We'll only have to shell out for half-day lift tickets."

"Half a day is good with me," Charley offered. "I have never skied before;" she told George, "and half a day of falling down a mountain sounds horrible!"

We laughed.

"Drink some more wine!" I said to Charley. "I promise you that you will not get hurt on the bunny slopes. We won't go up to the top until you know how to control your skies, and you'll love skiing! And we'll only go down the easy green trails, or we can take the gondola up to the bar located midway down the mountain and drink instead?"

"I like that idea!" Charley replied.

"I'm taking you to the top first, before we get all liquored up," I said. "The view is breathtaking."

"Just watch out for trees," Fred told Charley, "and you'll be fine!"

"I'm going to step outside and bring my luggage in from my car," George said.

"I'll help you out, padre!" Seth offered.

"I really don't need any help," George insisted.

"Sure you do!" Seth countered while following George outside.

I walked into the kitchen to pour vino for Seth's friend from his Bible college days while guessing my husband needed a cigarette and an opportunity to secure his bond with a man who threatened to take his discarded junk. I felt happy in the company of my friends; and now that George was with us, I felt more alive than ever. I liked George a lot and realized that I had given up a golden opportunity when I agreed to let Seth back into my life.

The men wasted no time outside in the frigid weather and returned quickly with luggage and skies. Fred showed George his sleeping quarters in the bedroom adjacent to the living room and pointed to the twin bed beside his bed. I stood in the threshold of their bedroom with two glasses of wine in hand and watched George drop his luggage on his bed before he walked over to me to take my offering.

The guys followed me back out to the living room while I listened to George, who was an assertive, non-compromising, and a well-informed sales type, sum up his current job for Fred's curiosity. I sat down next to Charley on the couch while the three men stood together before us. "I work for an aerospace company," George informed the stranger. "I'm vice-president of sales and marketing. We sell jet engine parts all over the world."

"That sounds like a profitable gig," Fred replied.

Seth piped in and said to Fred, "I've known George for a long time, and he's always been a master of detail. His determination is impeccable."

George chuckled. "I can teach you a few things, Seth!"

Charley and I laughed while I summed the word *impeccable* did not apply to my husband. And obviously, George had left his wife and children for his secretary, which by no means was the definition of a man who had mastered attention to the details of his marriage. What could George teach Seth? Perhaps George learned, as I did, in the pain found in the aftermath of doing wrong.

Seth retorted, "Hombre, give me your best out there on the slopes. We'll see *who* teaches *who* what!"

George looked at Fred, Charley, and me, and shook his head in disbelief as if Seth's challenge was ridiculous. "I've grown up in the snow and ice, and this arrogant Southerner wants to take me on. You have to be kidding, Seth. You want to challenge me?"

"Oh, George," Seth patronized, "you've got some lessons coming. Haven't you heard? We ol' Texas boys excel at everything."

"That's not what I hear," Charley quipped.

I laughed while I toasted Charley and clanked my glass of wine against her wine stem.

George rolled his eyes at Seth, "Oh, you believe *I* have the lessons coming, huh?" George then spoke to Charley, Fred and me. "There's a major difference between people from the north and people from the south. The north has a work ethic that no matter what the extreme weather conditions, we get it done. A *debrouillard* is what every *plongeur* wants to be called."

"I don't know French," I told George.

George shrugged as if everyone *except me* knew the French expressions. "A person who is skilled at handling any difficulty is a debrouillard." He turned to Seth and added, "...And a plongeur is someone who does menial tasks, like a dishwasher in a restaurant."

Fred piped in, "George Orwell!"

George affirmed with a nod.

"Padre, your memory is short," Seth shot back to George. "I share your reference point, too. A *plongeur* is some boring submarine no one cares about! And, on the contrary, we Southerners are neither dishwashers nor boring."

George chuckled and looked at me; "Seth wants to add an air of romance to cover up the shameful fact that he soon will be hosing down buffet plats in back of the Golden Corral for the next decade if he doesn't close another deal!"

We all heartily laughed including Seth, who became aware, again, that George and I talked intimately when he wasn't around.

"It's all a matter of perspective," Seth said to George with a smile on his face. "In the south, when the heat is on, we intensify our efforts--nothing gets in our way."

I clearly heard Seth and George jockeying for first position. I assumed they had been squaring off since college when the most handsome boy in college, who could have any girl he wanted, stole the Bible thumping geek's only girl. The game remained unfinished between these contenders; and now, seventeen years later, the playing field was finally equitable. George had come into his own, since their college days, and was now a thirty-nine year old businessman with a striking, stoic look, and a history of accomplishments, and big income to match. And Seth, for the last seventeen years, had chased his tail and did not know who he was from one day to the next, though he still had his good looks intact.

Seth had not seen the flower arrangement that George had sent me the day before, while I was in court, and my attraction toward the ambitious, blue-eyed, blonde German remained my secret even to George. I highly suspected George desired me, too, and guessed that he would demonstrate to me who the better man was without a lot of effort over the next four days.

An hour later, after warming up on the bunny slope, a fast-moving chair lift scooped up the five of us. Charley, Fred, George, and I quickly raised high above the pine trees and headed toward the top of the mountain. The lift facilitated only four per chair, and Seth sat alone behind us under stratiform clouds that threatened unfavorable weather.

"I hope it snows today," I said while I peered at snow-covered mountain peaks and pine trees. Other than my voice, we could hear the occasional clank of the chairlift cable, or a clump of snow falling to the ground from a frozen limb, or a lonesome skier zipping down beneath us. "I've dreamed of a white Christmas since I booked this trip last summer," I said to the reticent group. "The last time I saw a winter wonderland, Seth and I were in Aspen two years ago."

"I'd like to see palm trees and feel warmth at Christmas," George countered. "I've considered leaving Connecticut and moving south; the winters are too long in Connecticut."

"It's beautiful here!" Charley added. "But I couldn't live in these frigid conditions six months every year."

"Have you lived in Connecticut your entire life, George?" Fred asked.

"Most of my life," he answered. "When I was first married, I was a youth pastor for a church in Massachusetts for several years; then we moved back to Connecticut. I currently live in my childhood home."

"Wow, that's stable!" Fred answered.

"Yeah, I know. I'm boring," George chuckled. "My grandfather died five years ago, and I was executor of his estate. I bought the old house that he had bought for my mother before I was born. I bought out my siblings when grandpa died. I rented the place to my deadbeat brothers for years; then, when Elizabeth and I split up, I kicked them all out. My younger siblings tore the place up, and I've spent six months restoring, renovating, and repairing the house. I have the old homestead looking good now."

"What's your house look like?" I asked while fantasizing about a life in Connecticut with George and my kids.

"It's a simple, blue, two-story salt box with white gingerbread trim, built in 1825. The home sits on a hill, and the backside of the property rolls down to a pond. I have pear trees growing down to the water."

"That sound like something from a storybook," I replied.

"Are there fish in the pond?"

"Yep, I fish there sometimes."

"It does sound old world," Charley added. "What made you leave the church and go into the corporate world?"

"I wondered about that, too," I added. "Did you have the calling to be a minister?"

George chuckled. "I thought so, that's why I went to Bible College, but my wife wasn't happy living in Massachusetts. She wanted me to make more money, so that we could have children, and she could afford to stay home. So, we moved back to Connecticut, and I got a job driving a truck with this same aerospace company that still employs me today. My wife's parents gave us a parcel of their farm, and I built the home I gave my wife and daughters in the divorce, a two-story Dutch Colonial, with a broad, barn-like roof. That project was quite a feat! I would come home from the plant, and then work on that house until midnight every night of the week. I spent two years of my life building that house; and then, after eight years of trying to have a child, Elizabeth and I finally had two daughters, one after another, close in age."

"How old are your girls again?" I asked.

"Eleven and nine years old," George answered while suddenly looking sad.

I believed George regretted having fallen to temptation and losing everything.

"Sounds like you had it all," Charley said. "Why did you leave?"

"My wife was a workaholic, and *I thought* I wasn't happy."

I was right about, George. He regretted his actions.

He continued, "The grace of the Holy Spirit allows us to rest on the seventh day. She never stopped working."

I considered that perhaps he and his wife had labeled themselves Christians by default—due to education and church affiliation, but that the Holy Spirit did not fill them, and that deep down, they had never truly understood *hope*. Liz did not understand that there was a truth that she did not understand while married to George—a truth that would have set her husband free. If grace lacked in the area of forgiveness, then perhaps it lacked in all aspects of their married life. Had his wife forgiven him, he would have been able to stop feeling guilty and forgive himself, that is, if the Holy Spirit had truly filled George. Had she understood the grace of the Holy Spirit, then she would have understood that her husband had a need to be a protector, and not a predator. His lust for his secretary proved that he did not understand his identity in the Holy Spirit. Also, I considered that maybe Elizabeth had forgiven George for his affair, but that he could not accept her forgiveness?

Charley chuckled, "Maybe you should move to the south. Southern women are not career oriented; they like their homes, luncheons, and freedom to do whatever they want."

"Here! Here!" I confirmed.

George smiled and looked at me in curiosity. "There is a big difference between the women from the north and the women from the south. My best friend, Wells, and I agree southern women are more feminine. The women up north compete with men. That was my wife's issue--she wished she were a man. She was angry that she wasn't a man because she got bypassed for promotions after college."

Charley quipped, "I love being a woman!"

"Me, too," I confirmed.

"That's because you both are beautiful women, and doors open easily for you two," George replied.

Charley and I looked at each other and smiled with a meeting of the mind; George was right.

"But in the south," I defend, "...some men are angry because they're not women!"

Charley and Fred laughed while knowing I was referring to my bi-sexual husband who could not hear us.

George added, "A man has no need to compete with a woman. Men have different roles than women. You southern women appreciate that difference."

"We sure do," Charley acknowledged. "A woman discovers who she is with each accomplishment she attains in her life, and no man has the right to get in her way."

I knew Charley was referring to how Seth had sabotaged my university efforts year after year.

"No, he does not!" George supported. "I believe a woman has the same rights to an education and career as a man, if that is what she wants. I didn't care if my wife went to work or not, after we married, but working is all she ever did! She didn't balance out her life, and she made no time for me."

I read between the lines and heard George justifying his adultery in a trite fashion.

Fred chuckled, "I've never been married. Guess I got comfortable with having no one at home showing me any attention."

We all laughed while I heard Fred illuminating for me *his* strength of character.

Charley quipped and told George and Fred, "My husband gave his attention to his secretary. I discovered my husband was having an affair when I went into his office and announced to his secretary that he and I were having our fourth child. She started crying."

The men tittered.

"And now," I defended, "you can see that his affair was the best thing that happened to you, Charley. You can have any man you want. You're beautiful and smart." I turned to George, "She's got more men chasing her than days in a week."

The middle-age, former college beauty queen giggled. "True."

Upon my introduction to George, I had initially judged his character despicable for his adulterous ways with his secretary, and feared, too, that his influence on my husband's commitment to stay with his children and me detrimental. Now, as our relationship had developed over the phone during Seth's absence, I understood George regretted leaving his Christian wife and two kids, as I, too, regretted having been unfaithful to Leonardo, my second and most loving husband. I assumed George's pain led him to be a wiser man; and like George, I felt I, too, had learned truth the hard way.

I continued to explain to my friends in the chair, "I believe a successful man, made successful by his own determination and effort, and not by a lawsuit or inheritance, is not threatened by any woman on any level."

George continued, "Success breeds more success, and failure breeds contempt."

"Theories should be applied for accuracy," Fred suggested.

I chuckled while hearing Fred challenge George's last statement. George had failed at his marriage, therefore, was he contemptuous?

"Like I said before," Charley reiterated, "Confidence is found in the accomplishment, as well as in the failure of the risk you took."

"Leonardo was always supportive of me." I continued. "I regret that I did not return his love for what he gave me—confidence in me. I got exactly what I deserved when I let Seth into my life."

"You don't deserve to be unhappy, Jean," Charley replied.

"No, I guess not," I answered while I considered the character of the two men on the chair and wondered who the better man truly was? How would I measure a man's character? I recalled that first evening I met George at our home in The Woodlands, Texas. George, newly separated from his wife, and two daughters, had pulled out his wallet, and had shown Seth a photo of the woman who he claimed had changed his life forever. My husband peered at the woman and boasted to his oldest friend, in front of me, that he could take the woman away from him. I sat there with my two youngest children in my lap that night appalled and summed both men to be beastly. Now, nearly a year later, George appeared unhappy to me. I wondered if he still dated his secretary, the woman he destroyed his marriage over? I assumed they were no longer hot and heavy, since he had sent me flowers, the day before, while I was in court with Seth.

"Anyone special, Charley?" George asked my friend of nearly a decade.

"Maybe," she answered. "I'm trying to narrow my life down to one special person."

"Me, too," I joked while wondering what George and Fred thought about my remark.

Everyone tittered as we approached our drop-off point. We got serious and readied ourselves to ski off the fast moving chairlift. We moved to the edge of our seats and aligned our skies, and safely disembarked as soon as we could rest our skies on the snow-covered ground. We skied out of the way of the next approaching chair and over to a white mound and waited for Seth who disembarked right behind us. As far as the eye could see, I saw snow-covered mountaintops that reminded me that our Creator was an awesome God. The freezing wind fiercely blew at the top of the world, and we all covered our faces with wool neck scarves and goggles.

Seth hollered as he skied past the four of us. "Come on, George! Show me what ice man can do!"

George chuckled and looked at us, "Once again, he requires that I put him into second position."

"Go for it!" I recommended. "I'm not playing hot dog; that's your and Seth's game!"

"I'm taking this easy green trail," Fred said to us girls while we watched George ski up to Seth who waited at the top of the hill. "I don't want a broken leg," Fred warned.

"Me, either!" I supported. I saw that my husband did not want to hang with the group, or me, but, instead, Seth demonstrated his need to compete with his old roommate.

I watched George ski up to Seth, and then the two of them disappeared over the slope. I looked at Charley. "Remember to never point your skies straight down the hill."

Fred and I stayed with Charley at the top of the mountain until we were certain that she had adapted her bunny slope techniques to the green trail. And after a couple of hours of slowly progressing down sloping terrain without much falling, the three of us finally spotted the halfway point down the mountain.

"A refuge!" Charley delighted. "I'm tired and ready for a drink!"

"Me, too!" I added.

"Me three," Fred teased.

We skied to the redwood deck covered in snow and began kicking off our skies near the steps when George suddenly appeared out of nowhere and sprayed snow on us.

"You found us!" I said in glee. "Where's Seth?"

"He went back up!" George pointed to the chairlift in the near distance. "He just got on that chair lift." We all looked over at the mid-way mountain lift while George continued, "I'm pooped. Seth doesn't just ski with me; he has to race me the entire time I'm with him. I just want to gently glide down the mountain, not race through the trees at a hundred miles per hour."

"Maybe he's hoping you'll die," I pitched.

Everyone giggled as if they were aware George threatened my husband.

I continued, "He's not much of a team player, George. When we were on our honeymoon, he didn't even snorkel with me."

"That's too bad," he said as if sad for me. "I'm not the spring chicken I use to be," George admitted. "These bones don't mend quickly either, and worse, people do die on these slopes when they hit trees."

"Seth doesn't have enough sense to worry about retribution," I said as I pulled my last ski boot out of my ski.

George considered what I said and then looked away toward the chairlift in the distance. "Well, Jean," he continued, "You got your wish--it's snowing."

"It's perfect," I said to George with a smile.

"So Fred," George began. "Tell me more about this screenplay you have written. I can't say I've ever known a playwright," he said as he placed his skies upright into the ski rack.

"When I get a paycheck, then I'll call myself a playwright," Fred chuckled. "My play is about mistaken identity. An American tourist is mistaken to be the girlfriend of the head of the drug cartel in Bolivia."

George chuckled, "I'm already interested."

Fred continued to talk about his play while we walked inside and went through a serving line. We ordered hot apple cider to warm ourselves, and burgers, fries and chili to fuel ourselves, and then noisily shuffled across the room in our unbuckled hard plastic ski boots, while carrying trays of food and drinks to a round table in the midst of exhilarated skiers doing the same--relaxing and escaping the cold.

We sat and ate, drank, and bantered back and forth for an hour before we left the building. We stepped out onto the snow-covered deck and headed to the nearby ski rack. A snowstorm had rolled in while we were inside. We zipped all the way up and positioned our goggles, toboggans, and neck scarves before clipping our boots into our skies. We then grabbed our poles with an agreement to head to the base of the mountain.

"Do you think we should look for Seth?" George asked me before we skied down.

"Nope!" I retorted. "Seth didn't care if he skied with us or not! He can spend his time in the cold searching for us!"

"I agree with Jean," Charley answered. "The sooner we hit the hot tub, the better."

"I have a bottle of apricot brandy in the condo that's calling us," Fred offered.

"And I stopped at the liquor store, too," George added. "I have a bottle of cognac."

"Let's do it!" I steered as we carefully headed straight down to our ski-in/ski out condominium. As we four slowly meandered down the mountainside, the ski patrol whipped beside us with a man on a gurney.

"Hey Jean!" George blurted. "Isn't that Seth?"

"Where?" I asked while setting my focus on red and white uniforms that flew past us down the mountain.

"On the gurney," Fred answered.

I peered at the skier on the gurney and recognized Seth's toboggan and apparel. "Nope, I don't think so."

Everyone recognized Seth's black and red ski attire, too, and laughed.

"Hey," I defended. "If he broke a bone, then that's his karma--he had it coming."

"I agree," Charley spouted.

"They'll notify us if he dies, right?" I asked.

"Right!" They all spouted.

I continued, "I didn't come here to spend my evening in an emergency room."

"Me, either," Charley acknowledged my attitude with a smile.

Fred inserted as we skied together, "Seth knows where we live."

We skied up to our condo's porch, dropped our skies, and quickly changed out of ski bibs and parkas, and into bikinis and trunks. George took the initiative to fix us elixirs before we headed back outside into the frigid air. Charley threw on her knee-length silver mink over her black bikini and slipped on leather clogs, and I slipped on my suit and heavy mid-calf chestnut brown mink with my ankle-high snow boots. The fair-skinned male Caucasians wore their water-resistant parkas and snow boots in preparation of a brisk walk over ice and snow with sloshing drinks in hand. Fred and George also carried bottles of cognac and brandy, and Charley and I carried towels and an ice bucket. Once we arrived at the resort's courtyard, the freezing temperatures and steaming bubbly water lured us middle-agers to unabashedly unveil our pasty white bodies in front of each other without hesitation. We giggled over the chilling effects experienced between disrobing and immersing into the warm brim.

Charley looked at me and blurted, "Okay, Jean, I can't repress my feelings anymore. What are you doing with Seth?"

I tittered while I noticed Fred and George both seriously wanted an explanation, too. "I've forgiven him."

"Why?" Charley asked.

I shrugged without an answer. "I don't trust him. He's a liar, and he's a good liar, and I fear he will take my children from me."

George interrupted, "Seth hasn't changed since college. He's still arrogant and only about Seth; but, it will be a cold day in hell before he gets custody of those boys."

"I'm not so sure," I replied.

Charley continued, "He only came back because he lost in court. I don't believe you have forgiven him. You fear him."

"Seth wanted to go on this ski trip," Fred reminded.

"And he saw that as an ideal time, and maybe the only time he would have to maneuver himself back into your life," Charley chided. "The court ruled in your favor. You got custody of the kids, child support, maintenance, your car, and the house."

"I know," I agreed.

"That man will leave when the money runs out, too!" Charley added. "Mark my word!"

"I know," I agreed again.

"So if you know all this, then why?" She prompted me.

"Because," I answered, "I fear Seth's capabilities when we go back for the final hearing. I heard his lies yesterday in court. He doesn't flinch when he tells his whoppers, and the judge believed him! At the end of the hearing, the judge admonished *both of us* for being bad parents! I'm not a bad parent, but the judge heard my truth and Seth's lies and didn't know whom to believe. Seth is smart, cunning."

George flashed, "He's cunning like the snake he is, but Seth is *not* smart, or he would *not be doing* what he's doing to you and his children. Seth is a small, arrogant, and pompous *boy!*"

"I want to believe Seth when he says that he doesn't want to lose his family," I admitted. I watched everyone shake their heads in disagreement.

Charley continued, "Something is wrong with that man, Jean."

"But if I forgive him, Charley," I defended, "and *he does become* a better husband, and father, as a result of having learned from his mistake, then I won't lose my children. I believe anything is possible."

"You're not going to lose your children," George insisted.

"I don't know that," I bemoaned.

Charley nodded in disagreement, "I don't trust Seth."

I reiterated, "If I *don't trust* what he says to me, and I *don't forgive* him, and give him another chance to prove otherwise to me and our kids, *then* I might lose my kids. God's says to forgive, and I'm obeying God because I don't want to be punished."

George interrupted, "I don't believe when God told us to forgive one another that he meant you have to take a psychopath back into your home!"

Charley agreed with George.

"Let me get on the same page," I interrupted. "What do you believe a *psychopath* is?" I asked my friends. I had a definition, but I wanted to hear how they described Seth.

Fred piped in, "A psychopath is a personality disorder. The prisons are full of psychopaths and sociopaths."

I looked over at George, "Do you think he's really a psychopath?"

"I don't know, Jean." George answered.

Fred continued, "A psychopath has a deficit of conscience. He feels no remorse."

George added, "Paul told us in Galatians 5:16 to walk in the Spirit, and not fulfill the lust of the flesh, for the flesh lusts against the Spirit, and the Spirit against the flesh, and these are contrary to one another. In other words, Jean, Seth is conflicted, double-minded."

Charley inserted "Seth has no conscience! He is only sorry *now* for his actions because he *lost* his kids, and more importantly to him, he lost his house in yesterday's hearing, too."

"Seth is a confidence trickster," George added for our consideration.

"A what?" I asked George.

"A bunko, a flimflam man, a grifter, a hustler---" George clarified for me.

Fred continued, "--A swindler, a schemer, a con artist."

"--A liar!" Charley blurted.

"He's all that," I confirmed.

George continued, "You're his mark, and Seth is playing to your compassion and naiveté."

I felt confusion, and then Fred blurted, "There is a saying that you can't cheat an honest man."

"I'm honest," I defended.

"I don't think you're honest with yourself," Charley added.

"I'm not, am I?" I surrendered. "I admit that I despise him. I'm outraged by how he has treated me and our children, and I fear him, too."

Charley looked at Fred and then back at me. I felt they all thought I was crazy.

George interrupted, "Trust God, Jean."

"I am trusting in God," I answered with frustration while my fear made me doubt if I truly had faith in God. "What if God expects me to stay put and give Seth another chance? God will give me a second chance, if I forgive Seth. Right?"

Everyone looked perplexed and shrugged.

"Pray," George offered.

"What else can I do?" I replied while I wondered if Seth could cheat me if I was *not* honest with myself. If I wasn't truly walking in faith, but instead, I acted out of my fear? "I appreciate your wise words, George." I wanted to switch gears and take the conversation off me. "Are you still dating your secretary, George?"

His expression switched to a more somber look, and he answered, "No."

"Why not?" I asked while happy to hear he was available.

"Gail wanted to get married."

"Why didn't you want to marry her?" I asked for everyone's curiosity while already aware of the answer. I recalled the last time he was in my home. I had deduced then that he was not in love with the other woman enough to marry her; and now, I knew I was right. He did not leave his wife and kids for his secretary, but, instead, he had left his wife, two daughters, and the beautiful two-story home he had built, out of his guilt. Had George not been feeling guilty over his unfaithfulness to his wife, he might have been able to save his marriage at one point after his affair. Had his wife been able to forgive him for the affair, then she might still be married to him. Neither George, nor his wife, really possessed what it took to be in a committed relationship. Was not love forgiveness? I then advised, "I think you should cool your jets, George."

I was *not* surprised that George would give up his wife, children, and home for a woman that he would *not* marry—guilt was a tool of Satan's to destroy.

George continued, "My best friend, Wells, convinced me that she was a rebound relationship, and that I was making a mistake."

"What exactly is a rebound relationship?" I asked George.

"A rebound relationship is when you are involved in another relationship before you even leave the relationship you are in."

"So George?" I prompted. "You were not in love with your wife?"

"I'm not sure about that anymore," George answered.

"Were you in love with Gail?"

"I thought so," he nodded.

"I don't get it?" I shrugged. I dug deep to understand his depth.

"I just felt that I was moving too quickly into another relationship."

His answer revealed he was not wise, or perhaps, his answer revealed he was not honest. Perhaps, along with his feelings of guilt, he also had too much pride to admit that he felt unworthy of a wife or family, or worse, he possessed too much pride to say, "I am sorry, wife, please forgive me."

Fred added, "A lot of times a rebound is just a distraction from the pain of a broken heart."

George nodded in agreement, "Gail came into my life, and I fell in love with her, or I thought I had, which prompted me to leave my wife and children. Gail then became something else for me, a distraction from, well--." He hesitated and, as if carefully choosing his words, continued, "I realized that she kept me from having to experience the full extent of the emotional pain I felt when my wife served me divorce papers. My wife and I separated, and I was devastated; and then, I stepped away from Gail for a while and concluded that I did not want to marry her because I felt resentment toward her." He sadly shrugged.

Resentment? Did I hear him right? Did he blame Gail for the end of his marriage?

Charley added, "She would always be the *other* woman, too."

"Yeah," George admitted, "and my girls would always see her as the *other* woman--my wife told my daughters I had an affair."

"I'm sure your wife is angry," Charley admitted. "I can relate to her pain."

"She *is* angry;" George confessed, "and she has a right to be angry with me. I'm healing from the pain of my broken relationships, too, and I have discovered that the emotional pain did not kill me. I'm getting through this tough time in my life. Liz will be alright, too."

Charley inserted, "It's what you do with your emotional pain, and what you do to avoid that kind of pain, again, that might kill you."

George nodded, "That's exactly right, Charley. I went to see a psychiatrist during the interim of my divorce. My divorce really messed me up for a while. My doctor put me on Prozac, an antidepressant."

"Are you still taking antidepressants?" I asked while now aware that he bought into the great lie.

"No, I got off Prozac," he smiled. "That pill made me sexually dysfunctional!"

"Permanently?" I asked with great disappointment.

"No, thank God!" He chuckled.

"It's good, George," Charley agreed, "that you deal with the pain of your old relationships, before moving into another one."

"That's what my doctor said," George admitted.

"How did Gail take your breakup?" Charley asked.

"Hard at first," he admitted, "and then, I lost touch with her; and then, something happened to me. I suddenly wanted her back."

"Did you tell her how you feel about her?" Charley asked.

"No," he answered.

"You should have been honest with her; what do you have to lose?"

"Nothing anymore," he said and then smiled at me.

I got that he had been waiting for me to leave Seth. Maybe, though, George did not tell Gail how he felt about her, because he did not feel anything anymore? Maybe he had been caught up in a lie, that what he *thought* he felt for Gail was simply an illusion to destroy his marriage?

Four hours later, Seth showed up with a white plaster orthopedic cast wrapped around his left hand and forearm. He found his wife and friends gathered around the dining table in the condo eating and drinking when he came through the door alone. He appeared happy, but I knew he was upset over our lack of interest. His pride kept him from asking us, if we had attempted to find him, since the park had closed hours ago; and, instead, he volunteered, for our curiosity, that the ski patrol took him off the mountain on a gurney four hours earlier. We did not admit to him that we saw the ski patrol fly past us with him on that gurney.

"An x-ray was taken of my hand" he continued, "and my ring finger is broken."

I did not take pity on him. "Karma," I muttered.

He ignored my comment and talked directly to George. "The x-ray showed a diagonal fracture through the proximal phalanx. This cast is only temporary. The doctor recommended that I have surgery when I get back to Houston and have pins put in my hand, that is, if I want the finger to heal properly, which I do."

I was surprised to hear that a broken finger now required an expensive surgery. "Do these pins stay in forever?"

"No, only for about four to six weeks," Seth answered me.

I nodded while considering that the cost of his upcoming surgery would be thousands of dollars. Normally, we would have the money for such an unexpected fire, but our lawyers had cost us too much. Seth's chaos and mental instability made me angry, and I hurled back, "Great, Seth! We don't have health insurance, so how do you plan on paying for this surgery?"

Seth appeared unmoved by our reality and maintained a calm pretense for our friends; "No problem, Jean," he said cheerily. "I'll come up with the money."

George piped in, "How can you *not* have health insurance, Seth? You sell health insurance, right?"

"I have a license to do so," Seth answered.

I sneered over Seth's word choice while I translated his words to mean, *I don't sell anything because I don't work.*

"But you don't carry health insurance for yourself or wife and three kids?"

"Well, George, ol' boy, I'm not lucky like you to have my employer pick up the tab."

"My employer doesn't pay for my healthcare;" George retorted, "and although I have a divorce decree ordering me to keep my two children insured, I'd have it no other way! What if one of your children, or your wife, was in an auto accident, or needed an appendix removed?"

Seth grinned at George's challenge and remained in control. "Then ol' chap, I guess I'd take them to the emergency room and let the tax payer pick up the tab."

George shook his head in disagreement. "You've admitted to having an annual six-figure salary."

I looked over at Seth with a smirk.

"I sure did," Seth proudly confirmed.

"Tax payers won't pick up your tab!" George huffed. "You'll be forced to sell your house and pay cash for your medical needs. You could lose everything if you, or Jean, or one of your children were in the hospital for months."

"That's what I tell him," I said to George.

Charley added, "You're putting your family at risk, Seth."

I looked over at Seth and solemnly nodded in agreement with our friends.

Seth looked at them and then at me; "I guess I'll have to get on the ball and look into getting us some health insurance, Jean."

I knew better and rolled my eyes out of disgust, while remembering the morning of my economic final--he didn't care about anybody, not even himself. Seth had pinned me against the dining room wall with both his hands wrapped around my neck. He assaulted me with intent to have me fail my semester, and his plan worked. I truly wanted to gouge out his green eyes and match the self-mutilation scars on his face and arms. He had gone to jail that morning, too, and the circumstances forced me to forfeit my economic final, due to having no babysitter and a time constraint, that is, if I intended to serve him a divorce petition while he was in jail. And, instead of successfully wrapping up my semester, I spent money on a lawyer that day, and served him with divorce papers and a restraining order while he was sitting behind bars. The day before we left for this ski trip, I was in court with Seth for a temporary hearing. My lawyer got court orders in my favor that Seth pay me maintenance and child support, only then for the jerk to show up at my bedroom door, hours after that hearing, and tell me that he loved me and wanted another chance. He was a sociopath.

Fred broke up our attack on Seth's obvious irresponsibility. "You missed a good time in the hot tub, Seth. Have a drink, your pain will vanish. Catch up; we're a few drinks ahead of you."

"Is that how I do it?" Seth quipped while he walked into the kitchen and grabbed a highball glass, then some ice, and began pouring from a bottle of vodka.

Hours later, we bundled up, walked outside into the dark, and made our way to the transit center in the heart of the ski resort. We paid seventy dollars a person for that night's entertainment; and along with a dozen other people, we took a gondola ride in the dark, up the Elk River Valley, where horse drawn sleighs waited to take us for a forty-minute ride, under a clear night sky lit up by a full moon. We followed the river through the lower pasture, drifted through the trees, and traversed back down the meadow to the *Bar Lazy L Ranch*. I sat between Seth and George on the backbench of the sleigh, and Charley sat beside Fred in front of us, and the only sounds I heard were the horses trotting through the snow that glistened like diamonds under the moon light, and the bells jingling on the horses' harnesses, and the distant howl of a coyote. I felt relaxed sitting next to George while I cuddle under an oversized wool blanket between him and Seth and stared up at a galaxy of stars.

Twenty minutes into the ride, George burst out in song. "♫*Just hear those sleigh bells jingle-ing; ring-ting tingle-ing, too. Come on, it's lovely weather for a sleigh ride together with you...*♫"

We chuckled and then joined in his merriment; "♪*Outside the snow is falling and friends are calling 'you hoo.' Come on, it's ♪ lovely weather for a sleigh ride together with you. Giddy-yap, giddy-yap, giddy-yap, let's go. Let's look at the snow. We're riding in a wonderland of snow...♪*"

We continued to sing an assortment of Christmas carols until the team of horses pulled up to our destination. We jumped off the sleighs and walked a short distance to an inviting log cabin. Warm drinks and live entertainment was all part of the hospitality while the staff prepared dinner for us. We listened to traditional western music performed by a local band while the smell of grilled beef floated in the air. We ate like royal cowboys that night and had our choice of rib-eye steak, or boneless chicken breast, or seasoned trout, along with a baked potato, corn, cowboy beans, warm dinner rolls, and a choice of brownies, chocolate cherry cake, peach crisp, strawberry-rhubarb dessert, or bread pudding with a vanilla sauce for dessert. After dinner, there was additional entertainment as we relaxed in front of a fire to let dinner settle before bundling back up for the ride home.

I struggled with my angry feelings that night as I had consistently done since I had let Seth back into my life after our court hearing. On the ride back to Steamboat, I sat between Seth and George. I felt squeezed between two persons: one, my ego, which insisted I be withdrawn and indifferent with the father of my two youngest children; and the other person was my other self, my spirit man, which challenged me to be greater in being, and to forgive Seth with the accompaniment of graciousness and empathy. I wanted to forgive the man on my left, and keep him in place, and crown him with respect again; and at the same time, I wanted to acknowledge my ego, and fuel my intrigue with the handsome catch on my right side-- George.

I snuggled under an oversized blanket with my suitors. My heavy mink coat and the tight fit between broad male shoulders under thick wool sufficiently warmed me for the long wintry ride through the plains. George's cologne intoxicated me; and Seth's cologne reminded me who I put first, over and above my feelings, and, too, where my struggle lied. *One time*, I vowed, *one time*, and whether Seth deserved an opportunity to prove his authenticity, or not, was not my call, but I would obey, and be forgiving *one time*.

The wagon pulled up to our origination point after a forty-minute ride through the dark and cold. Seth stepped out of the wagon first, and then reached up for my hand as I stood up from my seat and attempted to step down to the snow-covered ground. Our eyes met as I took his grasp and saw him render to me a loving smile, and while I felt George's breath on my neck as he waited to step out, I smiled back at Seth for the first time in weeks.

George had said very little to me that night over dinner, and I knew by his withdrawal from me that he understood I was not free to choose any differently. George and I were the same, and too much was at stake. We both were trying to achieve goodness in the eyes of God our heavenly father.

Hours later, back at the condo, Seth and I were alone in our bedroom. He told me that he wanted to make love, and I had never felt more obligated than on this night. His sexual overtures felt unfamiliar and wrong, but I dutifully responded with the intention of mending the broken arrow. He stood at the end of the king-size bed holding me. I doubted he truly desired me because he had seldom lusted after me in the five years we had been together, and his refusals had made me feel unattractive. I speculated as to what Seth's agenda was on this night while he undressed me, and I assumed he wanted to make George jealous, and seal the deal with me, that I would drop the divorce and allow him to come back home.

I heard George, Fred, and Charley's muffled voices from the living room, and I promised myself to not utter a sound that night and let any pretense drift to the other side of the door officiating for them that I was crazy and enjoying the company of my husband. I turned off the light.

We both undressed and crawled into bed. He laid his nude self next to me and held me tightly. "I love you, Jean." I refused to respond; and instead, my eyes welled up over his manipulation. Seth had no clue how unhappy I was now. I laid in the dark and felt again as if I was in hell with eyes wide open. I wanted to believe what I read in Exodus 23:21, that if I obeyed God's voice, then my Heavenly

Father would be an enemy of my enemies; and though I felt broken and angry, I had sex with my husband and died that night.

After the four-day ski trip, Seth returned to our Woodlands home to prove to us that he loved us. Our first morning back and I walked into the kitchen looking for the coffee pot. As usual, Seth had risen before the kids and me and had already drunk half a pot of coffee. I grabbed what was left of the hot brew while unsure about what to do with my days, since no longer enrolled at the university. I had taken classes over the last five months. Had Seth not assaulted me, the morning of my economics final, and had a divorce matter not preoccupied me over the last weeks of November, and the early part of December, I would have completed my first semester at the university. Had Seth been a Godly husband and father, we would have enjoyed the holidays, and I would now be heading into another semester, just after my thirty-fifth birthday, while feeling satisfied about my life and accomplishment. Instead, I felt angry that I had not finished either of the two semesters I started at the university because of Seth's insanity. My frustration and anger grew more every day over his selfish need to hurt his children and me.

I had given up on the idea of enrolling into a third semester at the University of Houston, and instead, now plotted to enroll into a paralegal school and complete an eighteen month program which I felt would allow me to go to work sooner and make decent money. I took a sip of my hot coffee and made note to self to interview, this week, with the paralegal school that my neighbor, and relative by marriage, Susan, had attended. Since her graduation, she had boasted of making $50,000 her first year out, while employed by a funeral home corporation. Seth walked through the glass kitchen door and interrupted my thoughts.

"I want you to call the phone company and change our phone number."

"Why?" I asked.

"I don't want our greedy lawyers persuading us to go forward with the divorce."

"You mean *my lawyer*?"

"Yes. I want us to stay together, Jean. You do, too, right?"

I disregarded how I felt and nodded in agreement. I wanted Seth to stay and help me financially with our children, and, too, I had an agreement to forgive him this one time.

"I'll get my lawyer to draw up a motion to dismiss the divorce petition," he informed. "We'll have to both sign the document; and then, he'll notify the court that we're dropping the divorce action."

"You seem so anxious, Seth."

"I am! I'm living here and not paying you as ordered by the court, so until this case is dismissed, I'm in contempt of court!"

"Oh, I forgot," I whispered while wondering why he distrusted me. Did he think I would allow him to come back home; and then, I would file contempt charges on him? "How much did the judge order you to pay me? I forgot."

"I was ordered to pay you $800 per month temporary child support, and $1,200 per month temporary alimony for six months, and all interim attorney fees; so, the sooner we stop our lawyers from doing another day's work, the better off I will be!"

"Of course, you'll be better off. I have to go to the bathroom," I said while I walked out of the kitchen and away from him with my coffee in hand. I felt I was making a huge mistake. Something about his spirit rubbed me wrong. I didn't believe he came back because he suddenly cared about the kids and me, but maybe I was just too angry to see he truly was sorry.

I strolled across the living room and entered into our master bedroom. I stood in the vanity area of my bathroom and looked at the unhappy woman in the mirror. What if he left again? What if he was crazier than I thought? I entered into my walk-in closet and closed the door, and I sat in the back of the closet hoping he would not find me. I had no reason to trust Seth, and I whispered, "I won't walk away, Father. Give me the ability to see what you want me to see, and the ability to hear what it is you want me to hear, and the ability to feel what it is you want me to feel. And give me the wisdom to know what is right, and give me the ability to speak into this world what you want me to speak. And if Seth is not to be in my life, then take him away from me."

11
CHECK MATE

SIX MONTHS LATER, JUNE 1994. The pace of my life felt like a stagnant river on a hot summer day in Texas. My children and I headed out to the mailboxes at the end of the cul-de-sac; and while I pulled out a stack of bills, my two youngest rode their four-wheelers around me. I flipped through an assortment of envelopes and saw that my lawyer, John Pettit, had sent me what I suspected was a copy of the *Motion to Dismiss*. I ripped open the envelope and pulled out what appeared to be an itemized bill for a total of $2,814. My lawyer had continued to bill me at his hourly rate of $200 per hour since our ski trip in December; and now, six months later, he was still working the case via *reviewing the file* each month. "This bill is ridiculous!" I murmured and looked at my sons who rode in circles around me. "Come on, boys, let's go back home."

I bolted back toward our two-story contemporary house with the tin roof, went inside with my kids, and found Seth in the kitchen. I angrily waived the bill in front of Seth for his notice. "My lawyer's billing me as if he never got word from your lawyer that our divorce action was officially dropped. I told him right after our ski trip that we were dropping the divorce—I told him that your lawyer would do the Motion to Dismiss. Now, he wants another $2,814.00! Is he crazy?"

Seth shrugged; "I don't know, call him."

"I will! Better yet, I'll write him!"

"Is that today's mail?" Seth asked me before I walked out of the living room with the stack of utility bills and junk mail in hand.

"Oh, yeah," I said while I walked back over to him and handed him the mail. I was preoccupied with the question as to why my lawyer was still billing me for a case we dropped six months earlier.

Seth took the mail from me, and I watched him thumb through envelopes and find what he was looking for--his monthly commission check.

"I got it!" He said as if relieved and then tore open the envelope.

I watched him take out his commission check and a letter. He studied the familiar pay stub, and I noticed his face turn down. I waited for him to show me his net income while he appeared to be panicking. "How much did they pay you this time?" I asked while I watched him closely read the enclosed letter.

He solemnly looked up at me. "This is the last commission check I'm getting; the company terminated me," he said as if in shock.

"What?" I could not believe they gave Seth such little notice. "Can I see that check and letter?"

He shook his head no. "Not now; I have to discuss this situation with payroll," he said as he walked out the glass kitchen door and headed to the detached two-car garage where he kept his wall phone and the three-foot high rat's nest of unopened mail in the corner of the garage.

I felt my gut tighten over my latest reality, but I was not shocked. I had always known this day would eventually come, and the fact that we had been getting this monthly commission check for as long as we had, since fall 1991, had been amazing. Now, three years later, Seth would finally have to go to work. I knew deep down everything would work out for the best because I knew God was in charge, and he cared about my children and me. Seth had a master's degree and sales experience. We had a gorgeous, 3500 square foot home, with no mortgage, two, fairly new cars, paid for in full, and no credit card debt. God already blessed us. I could take on another child and babysit for money, in our home, and Seth could grab a job until the perfect sales position came his way. I firmly believed we would have no problem putting food on the table, keeping the lights on, and gas in the cars. I took a breath and realized that, without much ado, I could still take out the student loan and go to paralegal school, too. I could take evening classes and babysit during the day! I assumed Seth would work days in whatever job he secured in the near future, but if he had to call on clients in the evening hours, then even better--I'd take day classes, and he could babysit our children while I was in class. The next year-and-a-half would go by fast, and the sacrifice we would make, for me to become a certified paralegal, would be worth the $50,000 a year I would earn in a law office. I had hope and believed all would work out perfectly, and though I was anxious to console my distressed husband, I would wait for Seth to get off the phone with payroll before I would spring our next set of plans on him. Meanwhile, I knew he would get off the phone and be out there in the yard for a while sulking, so I decided to get out the Yellow Pages and locate the number for my paralegal school. I prayed, too, that Seth would give up the drugs I knew he did in secret behind my back and find the courage to come out of hiding.

SIX WEEKS LATER, AUGUST 1994. I had done as I had told Seth I would do. I enrolled into a paralegal school, and a student loan from the U.S. Department of Education paid a hundred percent of my books and tuition costs. I would start classes, designed for student convenience, in a month. Each class was only nine-weeks long, and I could schedule a class either during the day or at night. All classes rotated every semester over the eighteen-month program, so that if I could not fit business law into my first nine-week schedule, then I would be able to take business law during another nine-week session, over the next eighteen months. I loved the idea of working for attorneys, almost as much as I had once loved the idea of being married to an attorney. I still liked the idea of being married to an attorney, too, when I considered my future.

I had bathed my youngest sons and put them into bed, and had settled down in front of the big screen alone—Seth was not home. Had I been busy with studies over the last month, I *could have* appreciated being able to sit and watch late-night TV without any term paper pressing on me, but having *not* been enrolled into any class since last November, I found most television trite, housework mundane, and cooking repetitious. On this night, however, I watched a 1993 legal thriller called *The Firm*. Mitch McDeere, played by Tom Cruise, is a young lawyer. The FBI approach Mitch McDeere and tell him that they are investigating his law firm's mafia connections after two associates are murdered. McDeere makes a deal with the FBI to copy client files and help the FBI bring down the mob, but upon reconsideration, McDeere copies client files and keeps the files for himself, in case the mob wants retribution. McDeere, instead, gives the FBI proof of the law firm overbilling their clients for ten years. In one scene in the movie, attorney McDeere's client complains to McDeere about how his law firm constantly overbills him. McDeere's client reminds his attorney that when the firm puts a stamp on one of their excessive bills, and mails it through the U.S. Postal Service, the act becomes a federal offense, and each instance is punishable by a $1,000 fine and three-to five-years each instance.

I admired how young McDeere told both the law firm's henchman and the FBI that nobody controlled him! Seth had controlled me for years. I felt my husband chained me to the bottom of the barrel where I dwelled in his muck, and more than anything, I wanted to leap up out of the sewage and feel the sun again. The credits rolled across my big screen, and I told myself to get up off the couch, turn off the TV, and go work on my novel, when I suddenly heard Seth come through the glass kitchen door. I looked up to see my husband's unhappy face as he stepped down into the sunken living room.

"You're getting home late," I announced. "Where have you been?"

"Over at Pete's house," he answered. "Chad went to jail."

"Why?"

"The DEA busted him for drugs. I think the Feds have been watching him for a while. Chad was moving kilos to *The Talent House* from the Mexican food restaurant next door when he found himself surrounded by drug enforcement agents pointing guns at him in the parking lot."

"Wow. Did you know Chad was dealing coke?"

"Yeah," he answered.

"Of course you did," I sarcastically replied while sure Chad had been providing Seth powder. "Is Pete involved, too?"

"They put chains on the front door of Pete's business; they closed him down."

"Oh no!" I gasped. "What's he going to do now?"

"I don't know" he shrugged.

"Whoa," I groaned while dismayed over the situation. "Was Pete selling coke, too?"

Seth shrugged as if without an answer. "The DEA closed him down for tax evasion."

"I learned about that tactic at the university," I added. "When the government suspects other parties are involved, the RICO Act allows the law enforcement agency to charge a person, or group of people, with *racketeering*, which is defined as committing multiple violations of certain varieties within a ten-year period. The U.S. Attorney General may designate any department, or agency, to conduct investigations authorized by the RICO statute, and such agencies may use their investigative powers. The IRS has a criminal investigation division, and they look for evidence of money laundering, which is when criminals take the fruits of their crimes and insert into legitimate commerce. I'm guessing Pete's business got locked up because the DEA suspects *The Talent House* is laundering money." I could see Seth withdrew when he realized I knew more than he thought I knew about the situation. On the other hand, did he withdraw because I knew more about the situation than he did? "Are you involved?"

"No," he quickly defended.

"You three hang out together day and night, and you're not involved?"

Seth shook his head no and looked lost in thought. I did not believe the liar. "Well, I guess you won't be running back over there to get your old job back."

"Guess not," he snapped.

"And speaking of jobs, I'm officially enrolled into school again."

He looked at me as if I had lost my mind.

"I'm doing an eighteen-month program *this time*; and then, I'll be a certified paralegal." I watched his expression shift to a look of annoyed and waited for him to start bullying me, but he did not go there. I continued, "I got a student loan, and the cost of tuition and books will be paid for by the loan. And the classes are nine-weeks long. The classes rotate, and the schedule is very flexible, so if you have to work and I have to be home at certain hours while you're gone, then I can arrange to be home. Pretty cool, huh?"

Seth did not react on any level, which I knew to be his *take-away* game. He would not share in any excitement regarding my success. And I knew well, that me working with a law firm in the future threatened him greatly. What if he tried to divorce me again? I would have access to lawyers. His unwillingness to be supportive of me having any kind of career angered me, and I immediately became defensive. "If you had *not* gotten in my way, every time I did a semester at the University of Houston, I'd be more than half-way done with my bachelor's degree by now; but, as it stands today, you are financially busted, and I'm still at the starting gate of my career." I angrily huffed. "You've lost your mother's entire savings account, and you just received your last commission check in the mail, and there is no job on the horizon, because you *never* concerned yourself about our future. I've often told you, over the past six years, that I am *not* going to work some mindless job for minimum wage and put my kids in daycare. That's insane! *I am going* to paralegal school so I can make enough money to support us, if I have to! End of story!" I stood firm and realized that I had just threatened the insecure man once again.

"You don't have to worry about working, Jean," he calmly said. "Go ahead, start paralegal school. I got a job today; everything will be fine. I don't want you to put our children in daycare."

His response surprised me. "What kind of job did you land?"

"I'm doing the same thing I did before I retired."

"Retired!" I mocked while rolling my eyes and recalling how he had chased his tail for too many years. He had put us on poverty row for nearly four years before we got the Florida lawsuit settlement, and then he *retired*.

"I'm selling life and health insurance for a man who has grown his business since 1961. Granville Pike is the name of the owner and business. He's got an upscale insurance business down by the Galleria--Pike Financial. I like Granville. He's a Republican, married with three kids, and he goes to church."

"And that impresses you?" I sarcastically slammed.

"Yeah, Jean," he sneered while apparently not finding my wit funny. "Granville and I bonded today. He told me that he was a Sunday school teacher, and I told him that I had done the same in Bible College."

"You taught? Oh, that's precious! I'm sure you two are two peas in a pod!" I quipped while wondering how Satan and God could ever bond.

"I would think you could say, 'Congratulations, Seth, I'm happy you got a job today," he reprimanded while he got up from the couch as if disgusted and walked through the living room and into the kitchen.

I remained sitting and heard the kitchen door open and then slam shut. The truth was, I did not believe anything this man told me anymore, and the insecurity he created within me caused me to resent his very existence. Did he really have a job? If so, what lies did he tell Granville to get the job? I'd bet the bank that Seth bragged about having completed three years of law school, instead of three weeks! Had my husband been dealing coke all along with Chad and Pete? I believed so, which would explain why he seemed so bi-polar all the years he hid out in the yard and did not work. Was last month's commission check really the last check he would receive? I did not know if he told me the truth, maybe he was cutting me off? I had asked to see his employer's letter of termination that same day he got the bad news in the mail, but he never allowed me to see the document. Seth told me that he misplaced the letter when I asked to see the letter days later. And what about his mother's lost life savings? Seth and I had never talked about how he planned to compensate the old woman in her later years. And what about his relationship with Runi, the man he loved in Springfield? Seth talked to his lover constantly. The phone bills had reflected Seth calling Runi twice a day while I was in class last fall. Were they plotting to run away together? I suspected Seth hid his entire life from me.

I sat there on that couch questioning what was real while wondering if Seth had walked out to the garage to have another late-night private phone conversation with his boyfriend. I calculated that if I sneaked out there, and listened in without his knowledge, I could find out if my husband had a hidden agenda.

I walked into the kitchen and peered through the glass kitchen door. I did not see any sign of Seth. I quietly opened the glass door and stepped out into the dark onto the pebble sidewalk. I took a few steps and sat down on the slider swing under the catwalk. The ceiling fan muffled my breaths. I heard Seth on the phone just inside the garage, and I was right, he was talking to the man in Springfield, Missouri. I instantly felt threatened by their relationship, and my anger flashed again. I was jealous of Runi, the man who had always had my husband's respect and heart. Since Seth had come back from the ski trip eight months earlier, he had returned to his usual disposition--cold and completely disinterested in me. I truly despised him for the game he played with my life. He had lied to me to get back into our home and to do *who knows what* in the future.

He peered out the garage door and saw me sitting nearby. I threw him daggers, but he smiled at me, as if completely checked out on this side of the moon; and his reaction, to my awareness that he did not care that he talked to his lover in front of me, further enraged me. I leaped out of the grounded wooden swing, flew into the garage, and pounced on the phone cradle mounted to the wall. I wanted to rip the damn thing off the wall, but all I managed to do was rile Seth. He pushed me away from the phone with brute force, and I stumbled, face first, into the tool rack hanging on the same wall. I regained my balance and screamed out, "Go to hell! Go back to where you came from!"

He continued to talk into the receiver. "Are you hearing this, brother? Are you clear now, what I'm up against?"

He was performing! My lip felt puffy, and I put my finger up to my top lip and saw I was bleeding. "Get off the phone!" I ordered. "Tell your boyfriend to die!"

Seth laughed into the receiver at whatever Runi said to him. "She needs to get back on her meds," my husband said to his friend.

I lost my sensibility over his cruel and accusatory words and pounced on the insensitive sadist like a wild jungle cat. I grabbed Seth by the hair over his brow and yelled, "I hate you!" I pulled his face down toward his feet. He dropped the phone; and then, I kicked it across the garage floor. I let go of Seth, and we raced for the phone. I won.

"Get the fuck out of here, bitch!" He screamed while trying to pry the phone from my hands.

"No, you get out of here!" I challenged while I ran away from him and down to the end of the driveway while dialing 911. "You tricked me, you son-ov'a-bitch. Go move in with your boyfriend! Why did you come back?" Tears ran down my cheeks while I felt the complicated bitterness I had carried around for too long. I had forgiven him, but had never found peace within myself. I needed to restore the place long ago devastated—my soul. My spiritual being suffered atrophy. I had to be still and let God speak to me. I knew sheep would not drink from fast moving water for fear they would fall in, and I knew to allow the Good Shepherd to lead me to still waters where my fears did not stir.

"911, what's your emergency?"

Seth lunged after me, but I ran into the cul-de-sac to talk to dispatch. "Hurry, I'm being attacked by my husband."

Minutes later, the police showed up, and to avoid boring my listener with our chaotic redundancy, I'll make the story short. The cop split us up, got both our versions of what happened, and because I had a busted lip, Seth went to jail for assaulting me. Simply put, I had had enough, and I felt justified for setting the liar up. He had tricked me since that first court hearing; and now, he could sit behind bars for the next forty-eight hours and seethe over how I now had set *him* up!

The following morning, I heard my telephone ring, and I assumed Seth was calling me. I picked up the phone/fax that sat on the built-in buffet next to the glass kitchen door. "Hello," I unhappily groaned while the top of the phone/fax machine popped open.

"Well, hello, Jean!" The familiar voice happily returned.

"George! Your timing is impeccable." I pressed the top of the phone/fax machine back down.

"I've heard that about me," he chuckled.

I smiled while assuming George was talking about his sexual talents.

"What's going on down there in Texas?"

"Seth went to jail last night," I said with no emotion.

"He did?" He sounded surprised.

"Yes, and I'm expecting he will walk through the door sometime late tonight."

"Why did he go to jail?"

I hesitated to tell the truth. "He came home last night at dark from Pete's house. That's what he said anyway. I don't believe anything he says to me anymore. He just has this chip on his shoulder all the time, and I feel like he hates me." I considered I was talking about myself.

"Why would he hate you, Jean?"

I took a deep breath and considered if I wanted to open up that can of worms, again. "He's gay, George."

"I know you've suspected he's gay. You told me that last year when I called you, just after Seth went to jail for assaulting you the morning of your final."

"I remember telling you. He's in love with Runi, this married guy in Springfield, Missouri."

"I've heard Seth talk about him often."

"Yeah, he refers to Runi as his *brother*. Seth puts a new spin on the term *brotherly love.*"

George chuckled. "Have you asked Seth if he's gay?"

"I'm at the point where I'm not asking anymore; I just know he and Runi want to be together. Runi has always been the reason for why Seth has one foot in the door and the other out."

"Wow, Jean. I'm sorry to hear all this; it must be hard for you."

"Yeah, thank you." I questioned if George was loyal to me, or whether he was Seth's informant? "George, I want to ask you something. Tell me, honestly, did you know Seth to be gay back in college?"

"You've asked me that question before. No, Jean, I've never considered Seth gay, but I haven't spent that much time around Seth over the last ten years. Until recently, I hadn't seen him or talked to him in a decade."

"I heard Seth talking to a guy name Brian one afternoon on the phone. He didn't know I was in the apartment, but I heard him refer to a time back when...well, I don't know exactly when, but he was talking about their college days. I remember, I heard Seth lower his voice and ask Brian, 'Does your wife have any idea, you know, about that time when we--' and then Seth stopped mid-sentence because he realized I was in the apartment."

"Brian?" George prodded while not connecting to the name.

"Yeah, Brian--he was part of the inner-circle during Seth's college days. He's a CFO now for *Bike World*."

"Brian Flannigan!"

"Yeah, that's the name," I confirmed.

"I knew him." George let out a long sigh. "Jean, I'm not gay, and if Seth, or any of those guys were gay, I wasn't paying attention. I was in Bible College learning God's Word! I would have not ever connected that lifestyle to any student going there."

"I wouldn't think so, either."

"The last time I saw Seth, before our ski trip, was at Max's wedding ten years ago. I didn't have much to do with him that night. He showed up with his wife, Deb."

"I see," I said while remembering Deb was George's girlfriend first, before Seth hijacked her. "Did you talk to Deb at the wedding?"

"I did," he answered. "She lives in a small town not far from me here in Connecticut now. She's a registered nurse, and has remarried, and has twin boys."

"How do you know all that, if she was married to Seth the last time you saw her?"

He chuckled, "I ran into her and her family on the beach last summer."

"I'd like to talk to Seth's ex-wife and get her take on what marriage to him was like."

"She lives in New London. Call her. She's probably listed."

"I think I will," I confirmed to myself while believing I had found a golden key.

"I heard Seth and Deb often yelling at each other just after they married. They lived in the apartment above me. She was so unhappy with him."

"He's always been crazy, huh?"

"I think he's always been abusive," George admitted. "That night when I first met you, Jean, I was surprised at how little he had changed since college. He's still arrogant, like he was back then, and I don't understand why, either."

"He makes me crazy with his arrogance. I tried to hang up on him while he was talking to Runi the other night. Everything got out of control."

"I don't want to ever hear he hurt you, Jean."

"Me, either, but it might be me that hurts him before it's over. I can't look at him anymore without seething. I don't trust him. I don't believe anything he says to me anymore."

"What are you going to do?"

"I don't know. He lost his income. Seth got his last commission check a few weeks ago, *so he says*; maybe he's lying. He hasn't worked in years. I can't afford to divorce him; even if the judge orders him to pay me support, he doesn't have an income."

"Will your parents help you?"

"Maybe," I answered. "My sister is getting a divorce and my father is helping her. My mother is terminal, and I, well…I just don't want to burden my father any more than he already is."

"I can understand your position," he confirmed. "Why don't you go back to the lawyer you used the last time you went to court?"

"I could, but there is a pending problem. The lawyer sent me a bill recently. He has been billing me every month since our ski trip. I told my attorney that I was dropping the divorce days after Seth and I got home from the ski trip."

"I don't understand then, why--"

"I never got a copy of the *Motion to Dismiss*. I never got another phone call from my lawyer, after I called him about dropping my case."

"Did you give him your new phone number?" George asked.

I suddenly remembered Seth wanting to change our telephone number after the ski trip, because he did not want my lawyer encouraging me to go forward with the divorce. "No, I didn't give my lawyer my new telephone number," I admitted why slowly putting the pieces together.

"That would explain a few things," George added.

"Seth's lawyer supposedly drew up the *Motion to Dismiss* and had the court drop our divorce case—obviously, he left my lawyer out of the loop. That's right, I remember now—my lawyer said he needed a copy of the Motion to Dismiss. He didn't get one from Seth's lawyer, that's why he kept billing me."

"You ought to call the court and ask them about the status of your case. They should have a *Motion to Dismiss* on record."

"Yeah, I should," I said while aware that Seth and his lawyer manipulated the relationship I had with my lawyer, a man who had won me custody, child support, maintenance, and the house in the hearing for temporary orders. "I'm certain the court would have an executed *Motion to Dismiss*. There's no way Seth will risk being in contempt of court."

"Yep, that's probably what happened, Jean. Your lawyer just kept billing you when he never got the motion from the other lawyer to drop the divorce. Your lawyer could not call you because you had changed your number, and he assumed that you were not crazy enough to take Seth back."

"He assumed wrong. My lawyer billed me for another $2,800."

"Oh no!" George groaned.

"I'm not paying it—I can't afford to." I firmly stood while feeling despair over the situation. I concocted a cheerful attitude while wanting to change the subject and not sound *always angry*. "Enough about me, how are *you*, George?"

"I'm okay; business is way down. I'm wondering if I'll have a job in the near future."

"Oh, wow, that's a jolt."

"Yeah," he said, "but I'm not worried. I'm tired. If my company lays me off, then I'll collect unemployment for six months, finish the renovations on this old house, regroup, and find another job. I'll get severance pay."

"You'll be okay."

"Yeah, I will. Actually, the idea of not getting up to go to work sounds good." He tittered.

"Everyone needs time off."

"You're right, Jean. I understand life changes, that nothing stays the same. There are no guarantees in life, except that life changes. I'm up for whatever is presented to me."

"You've got a great outlook, George. Look, you're a great sales person. You've proven who you are. I'm impressed!"

George chuckled.

"You're the vice-president of sales and marketing. Somebody will hire you. You're polished, seasoned, and highly qualified to get another great job. I'd hire you!"

George laughed, "I'd accept the job!"

I chuckled and heard him telling me to partner up with him.

"I appreciate that you believe in me, Jean."

"What's there *not* to believe in, George?" I challenged.

"Thank you. I'm not worried about my future. I've been with this company for ten years. A change might do me good if the day comes and my company downsizes." He hesitated and then blurted, "Are you going to be okay, Jean? I am worried about you and those kids."

We continued to talk for hours that mid-morning, and I appreciated George's sincerity and expressed concern about *my* well-being. I got off the phone feeling I had a true friend. I considered what my life would be like if I were married to a real friend? George seemed grounded and like the men from my past, like Leonardo, and like my father in some ways, too, a bit of a stoic who strived to be a Godly man. My father had never been unfaithful to my mother, but I believed George sincerely regretted having been unfaithful to his wife and kids; and on some level, I think the Connecticut conservative believed he could find redemption if he rescued me and my three children. I did not hear George encouraging me to leave Seth. I knew, though, that George's religious views maintained that he obey God's commandments and not take another man's wife; but, on the other hand, I believed George wanted to be there for me, and first in line, if Seth and I permanently fell apart.

I called directory assistant next, and got Seth's ex-wife's phone number. George had given me Deb's current married name. I listened to the phone ring in New London, Connecticut; and then, a soft feminine voice answered, "Hello."

"Hi," I hesitated while grasping for the right intro. "You don't know me, but my name is Jean Wynn. I'm married to your ex-husband, Seth Zherneboh."

There was a lull. "What can I do for you?"

She sounded guarded. "I got your number from George Harmsworth. He told me that he had run into you at the beach."

"Yeah, small world."

"I hope you don't mind me calling you, but, well, I need to ask you--" I stopped short of finishing my thought. I felt asking her if her ex-husband was a psycho was too soon. I took a breath and slowed down. "I have two children with Seth--two boys, and they are three and five years old now." I stopped beating around the bush and then blurted, "I wanted to know if Seth was abusive to you."

"Yes, he was," she calmly answered and without any hesitation. "I felt like I was living with a demon."

"I can surely relate," I aligned. "He's in jail...again, as we speak."

"Does he beat you?"

"He kicks me in the shins when he loses his temper. He gouged out my arm with the car key. I have a scar on my left arm now. He assaulted me more than once, and has gone to jail for his crimes," I admitted while I considered that his emotional and verbal abuse felt worse than his physical abuse.

"I suggest you just move on, Jean. I spent years trying to make our relationship work and nothing ever changed with him."

"Did you know him to be gay?"

"No, I didn't, Jean. Is he gay now?"

"He says he's not," I answered.

"I will tell you this, Jean. If you and Seth break up, lock up your car. He stole my car when we broke up."

"He has his own car," I added while understanding he had always been just about himself. "He hurt you, too, right?"

"Yeah, he did," she answered. "He played head games, too. Seth and I spent the night at my parents' home in Massachusetts. The first night there, I specifically remembered placing my diamond engagement set on the hearth before going to bed. No one was in the house except my parents, and Seth and me, and the next morning, my rings were gone. I scoured the house for three days and was frantic; and then, on the third day, my rings were on the hearth, exactly where I had left them. He took them and wanted to make me think I was crazy. I suspect he might have considered hawking them and then got a conscience."

"Wow, Deb. He talks in front of me to his friends about things a husband would never admit to his wife, and then dares me to think I am hearing what I am hearing. And I've gotten to the place where I actually question what I see and hear anymore. I have a hard time trusting *me* now."

"I think he's evil," she answered. "He stabbed me in the hand with his fork one night while we were at a restaurant."

"I heard that insane story from George."

"Seth would flip between personalities like he suffered from extreme mood swings. I'm a registered nurse, and I'm familiar with mental illness like bi-polar disorder. I think he's bi-polar. I'm sorry you have kids with him."

"Me, too," I answered while the heaviness of her words weighed me down. "He talked about getting into law school for a year. I thought the idea was great! I wanted to be married to an attorney. So, long story short, he takes the LSAT twice, wins an interview with the dean of the law school, and persuades the school to accept him! And in the first week of classes, I noticed he barely studied, and by the second week he had stopped studying all together, and by the third week, he dropped out."

"That's the man I knew! I can tell you that I *do not* regret having divorced Seth. I have a kind and loving husband now, Jean. I call him Mr. Stable!"

Deb and I talked for hours, and I heard about the old, and the new and improved. I concluded she was happily married, but more importantly, I heard again, there was light at the end of the tunnel.

I got off the phone with Deb and immediately dialed my father. I was suddenly fearless and motivated to lose this sick relationship. My father had retired a year earlier, in 1993, from the paper mill, and after having sat in a cubicle for thirty-five years and doing the same accounting responsibilities, month after month, and year after year, he now faithfully stood at his terminal wife's side caring for her around the clock. He answered the only telephone I knew them to have in their home. "Hello."

"Hi, Dad. How are you?"

"I'm fine, Jean Ellen. I took your mother to see her doctor earlier this morning. She had to have some blood work done."

"How is Mom doing?"

"Oh, she has her good days and bad. All the traveling this morning wore her out. She's back there in the bedroom sleeping now."

"That's good," I said while I hesitated to say why I was calling. "Seth is in jail and--"

"Again?" He groaned with great disappointment.

"Yeah," I admitted while grasping for an approach as to how to ask him for money. "Seth didn't change for the better. He said he would change, but he didn't come back home and do anything differently. I'm sorry I dropped the divorce action last December. He told me that he loved me and his kids, but he's in love with Runi—Joyce's husband."

My father was a man of few words, and there was a silence while he digested what I just told him. "Are you telling me that he's a homosexual?"

"Yes. I've suspected he was gay since the very beginning. I was already pregnant when I learned the truth."

"Gosh," the elderly German groaned in disgust.

"I want to start another divorce action, but I don't have any money."

"I don't understand why you are broke, Jean Ellen?"

"Seth lost his income in June. His company terminated him. He got his last big commission check in the mail six weeks ago."

"How are yall making it over there?"

"We don't have much money in the bank anymore, a couple hundred dollars for food. Seth got a job recently selling life insurance and health insurance for a company over at the Galleria. He hasn't sold anything yet, and I don't suspect he'll do any better this time in the business, than he did the first three years of our relationship when he was in the business. We lived on Poverty Lane back then."

"Oh, gosh, Jean Ellen," he said as if in despair.

"I'm starting paralegal school soon."

"Oh, Jean Ellen," he grumbled. "You have all this chaos because you disobeyed God's laws."

I interrupted, "I know, Dad!"

"How do you know, unless you read the Bible?" He angrily questioned.

"I'm reading God's Word *now*, and I'm really sorry for not having good sense."

"Tell God you're sorry, not me; although I have to pay *now* for your sins."

"I'm sorry, Dad, and I have already asked God to forgive me."

"And now you have to walk in God's Word, Jean Ellen. That means obey His Word. You have to know what the Word is before you can obey His Word."

"I know, Dad," I said with the greatest of patience while I considered that forgiving Seth was the biggest mistake I had made in recent times. I trusted God was in control, but his ways were not clear. "I'm trying to be right with God, but it's hard to know if what I think is right is actually right. I forgave Seth after we went to court last time—I thought that was the right thing to do. I have no peace of mind with this man living with me under the same roof. I don't expect Seth to have any more success in the insurance field than he did when he was trying to make money the first three years of our relationship—he has no blessings coming, and I don't want to be there again, living in extreme poverty with a man that cares nothing about me or God."

"He acts like a man on drugs. Are yall doing drugs over there?"

"I'm not, Dad, but Seth's crazy ways make me believe he's doing something behind my back. The Drug Enforcement Agency busted Seth's best friend, Chad, for dealing cocaine, and the DEA closed down Pete's business for tax evasion—that's Seth's other best friend. I have reason to believe Seth and his buddies have used coke for years. He's been hiding out from his responsibilities out there in that damn yard! I believe he's high most days." I kept my new revelation that he was bi-polar to myself.

"You just need to forget about going to school and get yourself a job so you can take care of yourself and those kids."

"I know, Dad." I agreed with him; but deep down, I did not want to be one of those women who worked for minimum wage and did not have enough to pay the monthly bills. "I want to go back to my attorney and have him pick up where he left off last December. He did a good job the first time we went to court."

"How much do you need to get him started again?"

"I don't know. I have to go talk to Mr. Pettit and straighten out what I owe him from the first time he handled my case."

"Have him call me, Jean Ellen. I'll write him a check."

"Okay, Dad. I appreciate your help."

"I just want to see you get on your feet. I want to know my grandkids are okay."

"I'll find a job, Dad," I said while wondering how I would do paralegal school and work, too, with three young children at home. "I'll make you proud of me. I promise I won't let you down."

"Make your children proud of you, and don't let them down."

"Of course, Dad. Thank you for helping me. I love you."

"Okay," he said as if those words *I love you* made him uncomfortable. "Have your lawyer call me. Bye."

"Bye," I said while wondering why he could not say he loved me, too.

I called my Conroe, Texas attorney, after I hung up from my father, and told his secretary that I wanted to talk to her boss about filing another divorce petition, and that I needed to do so before Seth got out of jail that day. She set an appointment for me that afternoon.

Hours later, I looked across a shiny, walnut-colored desk at Attorney Pettit, who sat back in his brown leather office chair and spoke to me as if we were old friends. "I'll be happy to file another divorce petition for you, Jean, but, first, you're going to have to pay me what you owe me for the work I did for you the first time."

"But I did," I said with confusion. "I gave you all the money you wanted, before we went to court in December; and then, Seth and I left for the ski trip the very next day, after that court hearing, and four days later, when I got back from that trip, I called you and told you that we were reuniting."

"Did you expect me to file that motion to dismiss your divorce free of charge?"

"No, but Seth's attorney had agreed to file that motion. Seth paid him."

"I didn't hear from the other attorney, and you changed your telephone number. I sent you bills and you never responded."

"I only got *one bill* from you, and that came just recently."

"Well, I sent a bill to you every month!" He declared. "I'll show you copies of those bills."

"I believe you," I said while understanding Seth had confiscated my attorney's bills out of the mailbox.

"I'll make you a deal, Jean. You get your daddy to give me $5,000 and I'll take you to court, and I'll get you the house, and your car, and child support and maintenance for six months, like I did the first time."

"Alright, that's what I want. My father wants you to call him. He'll pay you."

"I'll be happy to call your father, and I'll draw up the petition today and serve that bum in jail, right away, with a protective order keeping him away from you and your children."

"What if Seth gets out of jail before we can serve him?"

"If he shows back up at the house, or calls you, then tell him that you want to go off and talk in private. Act like everything is okay, like you're not divorcing him; then, call my office, and tell them where you're going, and we'll have a civil processor serve him right there in the restaurant, or in the parking lot."

"Okay."

My attorney stood up. "My secretary will call you when she needs a signature for your supporting affidavit for the protective order. She'll fax it to you. And, I'll call your father and get payment from him."

I stood up and shook my attorney's hand goodbye, while feeling I was putting myself into a risky position because Seth currently had no income. I was electing to go it alone with three kids without any guarantee Seth would ever be able to pay me per any court order. I had not worked outside the home in corporate world in over a decade. Even if I got court orders instructing him to pay me monthly maintenance and child support for the next six months, how would I afford a fulltime babysitter, for two young children, and all the household expenses if Seth has no income, or is found in contempt of court and put in jail for nonpayment?

I had barely walked into my house through the glass kitchen door after driving back from the Conroe attorney's office when I heard my kitchen phone/fax machine ringing. I grabbed the receiver just as I heard a knock on the front door. I heard my father speak through the receiver, "Hello."

"Hi, Dad! Hold on," I said to the sixty-one year old man and then rushed to the front door and swung it open. Marilyn stood there on the front porch smiling with Harper and Doren at her side. They all appeared happy to see me. "Hi, Marilyn; hey guys," I squatted down and greeted my boys with hugs before they crossed the threshold. I stood up and spoke to my neighbor. "My father is waiting on the phone."

"I'm going to run," Marilyn replied. "I enjoyed the time with your sons."

"Thank you so much for watching them for me," I said as she headed back home.

"You're welcome." She smiled.

I shut the door and spoke to my babies who had drifted to the toys on the den floor. "I'll be off the phone in just a moment, boys. I'm talking to Grandpa."

"Okay, Mommy," Harper said while he turned on the big screen TV to watch Sesame Street. I turned my attention back to my phone call in the adjacent room. "I'm back, Dad."

"I talked to your attorney, Jean Ellen, and I agreed to give him a $1,000 payment to get started before I talked to my buddy Jerry Hoppas. I want you to use Hoppas for your divorce. Call up Pettit and cancel your business with him. Jerry will do what that other attorney says he'll do for you, and he's costing me a lot less money."

"Okay." I felt uncomfortable with the change of lawyers.

"After you cancel with Pettit, then call Hoppas. He told me that he'll get your case going as soon as possible."

I felt an urgency to call my dad's friend and tell him that we had to serve Seth quickly, before he got out of jail that day and came back home. I needed to instruct Attorney Hoppas to have Seth served while he was behind bars; and if not possible, then I would go out to dinner with Seth, under the pretense that he and I had to talk about the terms of our marriage. A civil process server would hand Seth, in a parking lot, the second divorce petition, along with another restraining order keeping him away from the marital home.

I got off the phone with my father while dreading having to make that phone call to Conroe, Texas. Attorney Pettit did not take the news well that my father's best friend replaced him. The angry attorney informed me that I had wasted his time, and that I still owed him $2,800 for the work he did on my case from January through the present. I informed him that I had called him just after the ski trip in December and had informed him that I dropped the divorce. He said that he received no notice from Seth's attorney that the court dismissed my divorce petition. I argued that whether or not he got a copy of the Motion to Dismiss, he knew we were dropping the divorce action. He insisted that I owed him more money, until I had enough and hung up on him. I felt mistreated and abused by the crook, and frankly, I had enough of abusive men. I sat down at my word processor and typed a letter to Pettit that afternoon informing him that our business was officially over, and as far as I was concerned, I owed him no more money. I also pulled knowledge from the Tom Cruise movie, *The Firm*, and told the attorney that I had dropped the case back in December, and when his law firm put stamps on his excessive bills, every month thereafter, and mailed those phony bills through the U.S. Postal Service, the acts became a federal offense. Furthermore, I reminded the crook, each instance was punishable by a $1,000 fine, and three to five years in jail. I added a postscript, too. I prayed he would get some integrity.

Two days later, on August 4, I got an envelope stamped **Final Bill** in the mail from the Conroe attorney and a corresponding letter. I began to read:

Dear Jean: I am in receipt of your letter of August 2, 1994. Since you requested all further communications be in writing, I am complying with your request. I know that what you are going through, either must be terrifying for you, or is the result of cold, malicious calculation. I regret you feel toward me as expressed in your letter. I have only tried to give you the advice that I thought you needed. You have very serious problems, not only with the legal side of your divorce, but also emotionally. You need to get something done about both matters."

I scanned over the next two paragraphs wherein he defined what he had done for me to get me the court orders in December; and then, I stopped and slowly re-read the following:

...*Jean, I realize that your mental state is not the best, but you are just way out of bounds. You act as though you, as well as Seth, are on drugs. If you want your file, you are free to come get it. I will release it to you and settle my claim against you for $1,500. That's more than generous. You really don't need to pray for me; I request that you don't. From your life's sick, sad history, and the way you live, and are raising your poor children, you don't know how to pray to any deity that I am at all interested in receiving anything from. If you are interested in settling our differences, please contact my office. If not, I assure you that I will pursue all legal remedies to collect my fees.*

Very truly yours,
John F. Pettit

His letter infuriated me while I clearly heard him retaliating for my attack on his character. He wrote lies, as if he expected to enter his letter into a court of law as an exhibit. He threatened to testify against me, and tell a court that I was an emotionally unstable drug user. I saw beneath his lies his motive to intimidate me. I considered ripping up Pettit's letter so Seth would never get his hands on the incriminating instrument, but upon reconsideration, I decided to keep the man's written attack on me and show my dad's best friend, Jerry Hoppas, the letter. My new attorney would tell me where I stood with this creep. I filed Pettit's letter away in my two-drawer filing cabinet next to my office desk in my bedroom--my sanctuary where I worked on my novel, the instrument I believed would, one day, allow me to run away with my kids and live comfortably.

SEVENTY-TWO HOURS AFTER SETH WAS ARRESTED, he waltzed back into the house. Seth had the legal right to come back home if he chose because I had not filed any restraining order against him over the last three days. Maybe I felt too guilty, over the attack that caused him to go to jail, to permanently shut him out? But, more honestly, I did not have the money in our bank account for a lawyer, and I did not have any option, except to sit still until Attorney Hoppas and I got together on this divorce matter. My father's oldest friend was taking his time.

I assumed Seth took a cab home from jail that evening because I did not hear him drive up into the driveway, and into the garage, when he suddenly walked into the kitchen through the glass door. I sat eating dinner with Bella, Harper, and Doren at our kitchen table.

Harper yelled out, "Daddy!"

Doren smiled and held up his spaghetti noodle for his father's view.

"Doren is eating spaghetti! Mama's cooking is good, isn't it, son?" Seth walked over and hugged the boy covered in red sauce while Doren sat in his high chair grinning.

"Yummy, Daddy!" The three-year old kicked his chair in delight and took another bite of his noodle.

"How are my boys?" Seth asked as he walked over and hugged Harper, his five year old who sat on a booster seat at the table.

"Good, Daddy!" Harper answered.

Seth planted a big kiss on his firstborn's cheek. He looked at my eleven-year-old daughter, smiled, and with a nod asked, "How are you, Bella?"

She had the scoop from me and snubbed him.

Harper continued, "You know what, Daddy?"

"What son?" Seth patiently asked before letting out a long sigh.

I watched my husband's interaction with his child, and knew, by Seth's expression, that he had no patience for his parental role, while his piercing green eyes darted over at me for my attention.

"Mommy says when I turn five I can play baseball," Harper happily informed him.

"You are already five," Seth patronized.

"I know!" Harper defended. "And I'm going to play baseball soon."

I added, "You'll play T-ball in the spring, Harper."

"What's T-Ball?" He asked me.

"You'll hit the ball on a stick when you're at home plate," I answered.

"Oh!" He hesitated while he considered his next question. "When is spring?"

"Spring is after Christmas."

"When is Christmas?"

"In about four months," I answered.

Seth interrupted while still standing before us at the table; "We need to talk, Jean." He turned to Bella and instructed, "Watch your brothers. I need to talk to Mom alone."

Bella looked at me for my reaction.

"I'll be back in a minute," I said as I got up and followed Seth through the heart of the house and into our bedroom. He closed the bedroom door while I sat down on the end of the bed. He remained standing before me and blurted as if irritated, "It wasn't supposed to go that way! I'm sorry. I want to do it right."

I was surprised to hear those words. "No, it wasn't supposed to go *that way!*" I angrily blurted.

"I'll get it right, Jean. I promise."

I debated whether I owed him an apology, or not, for attacking him while he was on the phone with Runi, but my angry feelings surfaced, and I did not feel I could forgive him. "You carry on with your boyfriend right in front of me!" I reminded myself. "How do you expect me to react? You are *in love* with Runi!"

"No, I'm not!" He insisted. "I'm honest, Jean, when I tell you Runi is *not* my boyfriend. Yes, he's my best friend, but no, he and I are *not* lovers."

I didn't believe him. I had no reference from my past where any man I knew talked to his so-called *best friend* twice a day for months. Not my father, nor either one of my brothers, nor Todd, nor Leonardo, ever made declarations of their love to their bud on the phone in front of me, nor, I suspected, behind my back, either. I had never found any love letter written by any of those men to their bud, further supporting their adoration and allegiance. My unfaithful husband had written Runi of their fantasy trip to Greece only days before I gave birth to Doren. And then, there was Sabrina, my best friend. Seth assumed I did not know which way was up! "This relationship will not work if you keep Runi in the picture." The conversation at hand reminded I would never talk to *my* so-called *best friend* again! Sabrina and I had been like sisters since fifth grade; and now, due to Seth's evil games, we were done!

"You're asking me to stop talking to my best friend, Jean! You are insane!"

I angrily stood up to him face-to-face and blasted, "I supposed I was your *best friend!*" I seethed while I considered how he had intentionally sunk my relationship with Sabrina, my confidant. I headed out the bedroom door to spend time with my children around the dinner table.

Seth grabbed me by the arm before I could walk out of the room. "You are my best friend. I love you and our children. I want to do this right, Jean. I want you to go to school. Look, we can make it as a family. I want you to take your paralegal classes, and I'll continue to earn the money, okay?"

"You have such audacity to stand in front of me and look me in the eyes while you lie about how much you love me!"

"I'm not lying! I want you to stay home with our children and give me an opportunity to get it right. Okay?"

I shook my head *okay* while realizing I did not want to cut off my nose to spite my face, either. I wanted to be a well-paid, certified paralegal, and at this point, I needed Seth to stay and help me with three children, even if babysitting was all he could contribute.

"Are you going to give me a chance to do it right?"

"Yes," I answered. I could not stand the sight of him.

"Did you go see an attorney while I was in jail?"

"No," I lied.

"Good." He forced a smile. "I love you, Jean. You'll see; I can get this right."

I had nothing more to say because I simply felt he was full of crap. "Do you want some dinner?" I asked with glacial indifference.

"I do! I'm starving!" He favorably replied while heading out the bedroom door in front of me. I lagged behind to look at the pitiful woman in the vanity mirror, and while doing so, I heard him joyfully shout from the living area as if relieved he was once again allowed back into the fold by me. "Daddy's home! And Daddy is hungry!"

The phone rang beside the bed. I picked up and answered, "Hello."

"Jean Ellen, this is your daddy's friend, Jerry Hoppas."

"Hello Jerry. How are you?"

"I'm fine. I hear you need a divorce."

"Uh, well, I guess not right now, Jerry. I appreciate you wanting to help me, but since you and my father have talked, Seth has come back home, and he wants me to give him another chance *to get it right*. So, I'm not going to file for a divorce."

"From what I hear from your father, Jean Ellen, I might disagree with that decision."

"I can understand your feelings. I'm sounding and looking like a fool with all my indecisiveness." Or better said, I thought, *Seth's indecisiveness!* "I don't feel now is a good time to start a war with him. I need Seth's help with these kids. I haven't worked in years, and he's got a job now, and--"

The attorney interrupted, "--I understand, Jean Ellen. You two have kids. I hope you can work it out. Your father and I are of the belief that families should stay together."

"Me, too," I said while recalling the time in 1988 when Seth and I sat in front of this same man in his downtown Houston law office. I was inappropriate that day when I brought Seth with me to seek a divorce from my husband, Leonardo; and I remembered Seth attempting to tell Hoppas that my former husband Leonardo was gay. I stopped Seth in mid-lie that day, and set the record straight that Leonardo was *not* gay! Now, I understood why Seth had tried to tell Hoppas that lie. Seth knew that eventually I would discover he was bi-sexual, and he plotted then how he would exit from our marriage. Had I supported my boyfriend's invention, then Seth would be able to tell the judge in our divorce that I accuse all my husbands of being gay.

"It was my opinion back in the 70's when you graduated from high school, and I shared my opinion with your father back then, too, when I told him that he should have sent you to college. I have three daughters myself, and would have *not* ever considered *not sending them* to college. I wanted to ensure they could stand on their own two feet if they ever found themselves in your position."

"I wholeheartedly agree with you, Jerry. My pot smoking was a lame excuse for him to take back the $10,000 savings bond he had saved for my college education. But, that's all in the past now—and I've forgiven him."

"And what he's spending now on legal fees for you and your sister, he could have paid for both your college tuitions."

"I've considered that, too. Well, Jerry, I appreciate your support and kindness. I'm going to get off and finish my dinner with my family."

"Okay Jean Ellen, you take care."

"Thank you, Jerry."

We ended our telephone conversation on a good note, and I was certain I would use his services in the future.

While I walked into the kitchen to join my family at the dinner table, I calculated Seth had been missing for three full days. I knew, as fact, that the jail released him two days ago because I called the jail to check on his status. I sauntered into the kitchen, sat down at the head of the table, and asked the man who stood at the stovetop loading his plate with seconds, "Where did you go after you were released?"

He stopped piling pasta onto his plate, turned around, and looked me straight into the eyes while I knew he questioned whether I had called the jail. I had called the jail trying to find out where he was so I could have him served with divorce petition number two and another protective order.

He played safe. "I called my mother. She came and picked me up, and I stayed with her to cool down."

I rendered no commentary and wondered if he told his mother that he was leaving me. I questioned if Ma encouraged him to leave the kids and me. I was certain Wilma had to be angry with her firstborn for having lost her life savings, and I assumed she encouraged her son to leave me and move back in with her. After all, who should take care of the old woman, but the man who lost every cent she had to her name. "What's the status of your lawsuit against the New York stockbroker?" I asked.

"We're still waiting for an arbitration date," he answered while continuing to stand over the stove and heap spaghetti noodles on his plate.

I wondered if he would leave me when he settled out of court. "Exactly what is arbitration?"

"A third party comes in and a decision is issued after a hearing. The parties agree in advance to comply with the award."

"Do you do this arbitration in a court?"

"No."

"Do you get to present evidence and testimony?"

"Yes," he answered.

He seemed unwilling to discuss the case in detail. I figured this event was just one more of his secrets. "Does your attorney feel you have a strong case?"

"He feels I have a very strong case."

"When do you think you'll have your arbitration?"

"Like I said before, I don't know."

Seth walked up to the table and looked at Doren; "I think you're going to need a bath, kiddo. You're covered in more spaghetti than you ate."

All heads turned to the youngest member in the family covered in red sauce from top to bottom, and we laughed at the site of the grinning three year old who sat in his high chair with a bowl of spaghetti turned over on top his head. Doren attempted to be the family jokester, the funny guy, and perhaps the boy in a diaper did so to bring happiness to his unhappy family.

Seth changed direction of the conversation and confirmed what I thought--he did not want to talk to me about his arbitration. "Please," I offered, "do the honors. You may bathe *both* your sons tonight. I feel like writing tonight. I haven't relaxed in eons," I admitted while feeling as if all I did was handle legal issues anymore. I had the full load of caring for the kids in Seth's absences and I felt emotionally exhausted.

"I would love to give my sons a bath," he declared. "You guys are getting a bubble bath tonight!"

"Daddy," Harper interrupted.

"What son?" Seth responded.

"Are you moving out again? I thought you moved out."

Seth looked at me in question, and I shook my head *no* to indicate I had said nothing to his sons. "No, Harper. Daddy is never going to leave you guys again! I'm home and here to stay! I love my family!" He unabashedly declared.

Harper continued, "Then where did you go?"

I snickered while watching Seth squirm.

"Daddy went on a business trip," he lied.

"Mommy said you were at Granny's house."

"I went there, too," he confirmed for his firstborn.

Bella flashed me a confused look while she questioned his sincerity. I had told my daughter during Seth's recent three-day absence that I wanted to divorce him and serve him papers while he was in jail.

Life continued in its familiar way. Seth worked in the yard that weekend and seemed to avoid me even when I was outside with our children. I recalled my childhood days living at home, and remembered how I loved climbing the huge oak tree in our backyard. My siblings and I moved into that homestead, with both our parents, when I was in the first grade; and the oak tree, with its four rungs hammered into its wide trunk, and a plywood platform that lay across the branches, high above the ground, was my happy place. The neighborhood kids liked to climb the tree with me, too.

Harper was going into kindergarten in a month, and I felt he needed a tree to climb, too. I had taken some wooden planks left over from our remodeling job, and laid out a floor across two, v-shaped limbs, high up over my child's head in a tree that grew next to our two-story house in the backyard. I stood on a ladder that leaned against the tree trunk and placed the planks in place while Harper stood below and supervised my work. I, however, had to stop short of completing the building project and go buy nails, much to Harper's disappointment. I promised him that when I bought the nails, I would then hammer the planks in place, and then, hammer rungs up the side of the tree, too, so he could climb up to the high wooden deck. I recalled, too, the day when my baby brother fell off our plank at home and broke his arm, and the memory caused me to re-think my own child's safety. The planks I placed across the limbs, under Harper's supervision, were at least twenty feet high off the ground, and I felt I needed to buy more lumber for walls and told Harper of my plans, too. Money was a problem though, and affording wood for tree house walls was not a priority. I climbed down and told Harper that I would try to find a rope and tire and make him a tire swing, until I could buy more wood and nails and finish his tree house.

I stayed in the house caring for the kids when they played inside. I cooked, cleaned, and tended to my children, and when they headed outside to be around Daddy, I wrote my novel to take my mind off my agonizing thoughts over my grim marital situation.

Seth walked in through the glass kitchen door while I prepared dinner that Saturday evening. He headed toward the refrigerator while grabbing his forehead. "Oh shit that hurt!"

"What's the matter?" I asked while chopping tomatoes. I watched him grab a zip lock baggy out of a drawer.

"I ran into the garage door," he said while he filled the bag with ice from the freezer bucket.

"Ouch," I groaned for him. "Let me see your head."

He turned and showed me a golf-ball-size bump, smack dab in the middle of his forehead. "You've got an egg, alright! How did you run into the garage door?"

"The door won't go all the way up anymore," he answered. "It's off the track."

"How did that happen?" I asked.

"I don't know," he said.

"Well, I hope you can fix that door; I don't like leaving our garage open at night."

"We need a new garage door," he said, "...and we don't have money for that right now."

"If the door is off the track, why do we need a whole new door?"

"The door itself is broken," he answered.

"Oh," I replied while understanding that unless he closed a deal, we were going to get further and further behind financially. Seth had never been much of a handyman either, except for the time when he bought a wet saw and cut Saltillo. I was impressed, and would have been even more impressed had he finished the flooring job. "When are you going to finish laying the tile?" I was referring to the kitchen and den floor that had been unfinished since before Seth went to jail last year during my finals."

"One day, Jean," he answered with no enthusiasm just before exiting back out into the yard.

"One day, some day," I mumbled to myself.

LATE INTO THE NIGHT, I lay in my king-size bed alone. I woke up and wondered where Seth was that night. I spotted an illuminated red light on the phone indicating another line in the house was in use. I looked at the clock on the nightstand and saw the hour was 3:00 a.m. I wondered whom he was talking to in the middle of the night. If not Runi, then who? I quietly picked up the phone and instantly recognized Seth's voice. His breathy words labored to express his emotions. "You're the source of my wisdom and virtue, man. You are less mortal than human seed."

A sultry, deep male voice replied, "You're my aphrodisiac, my proclivity, the soldier who stands next to me on the battlefield."

I recognized Runi's voice, but he sounded as if he responded in the act of masturbation. He encased spurts of words with hot desire.

"I own you, man" Seth dominated. "You were just a boy when I found you on the Dorian Island of Crete. You were my eromenos."

"I was, and I never pretended to not enjoy my erastes;" Runi admitted, "and I still long for your cock."

Seth moaned harder. "There's no shame to love you in all our maturity and manhood. I love the reciprocity."

"No fickleness here," Runi vowed. "Your beauty is what enthralls me--your broad shoulders, large chest, your wasp's waist, your protruding buttocks, and your small penis."

Seth humorously snorted, "You are an aristocratic phenomenon."

"I thank the god Eros every day for you, Seth," Runi reaffirmed.

"You cause me to lose my senses, brother," Seth said as if intoxicated. "Some sort of mania, a divine madness takes possession of me. I am unable to resist you, and I cannot sublimate this passion of mine for *primitive pretense*."

My anger surfaced. He referred to our relationship as a primitive pretense. I listened for more truth.

Runi blissfully moaned while sounding as if he had frothed his cream. "The true erastes will prefer the beauty of the soul above that of the body. Virtue and knowledge is found within you, brother, and I am a slave to my passion."

I clearly heard Runi making reference to me when he reminded Seth that his sexual preference was a man over that of *the body*--me. I recalled the night Seth and I were in Springfield, Missouri, when our firstborn was six weeks old, and when the golden boy, Aiden Cooper, said to my husband in front of me, "Why would you want that, Seth," Aiden pointed toward me, "...when you can have this?" Aiden pointed to himself. I was shocked that night.

Seth declared in ecstasy to Runi, "Let's not let what Zeus split in half be reason why such carnal union with the opposite sex fails to satisfy the spiritual affection I crave with you." Seth's moan was that of a man who was having an orgasm.

I had heard enough erotica between the thespians and quietly hung up the phone while feeling right—I had always been right about them. I was aware that neither ever knew I was listening. I lost no sleep over what I had suspected since the very beginning of this horrid relationship. Their renewal of vows proved they joined at the hip, and before I drifted off that night, I shifted gears. Seth had deceived me since the beginning, and as that truth took root, I was furious; and now, payback would be hell.

The following day, I called my best friend, Charley, in Galveston, Texas. She lived an hour-and-a-half from The Woodlands, Texas, and the long drive back home, and too many drinks while out with her, would be reason for me to stay overnight. I told her briefly over the phone what I had confirmed about Seth and Runi.

As the Texas sun began to sink in the west and without any announcement of my evening plans to Seth, I headed into the master bathroom and showered. I stepped out of the stall to dry off and saw Seth had bathed upstairs when he entered into the room wearing only a white towel wrapped around his waist. He leaned over the sink and began to shave. I walked over to my sink on the opposite wall wearing only a white towel, too, and quickly brushed my teeth before applying my makeup. Neither one of us had expressed any plans, to the other, about leaving that night. I figured Seth was trying to get out the door first while I nonchalantly strolled into my closet. I stood there looking for the hottest outfit I could muster up. Seth met me inside the walk-in closet wearing only his white bikini brief and black socks. I watched him step into his best dress jeans and then slip into his snakeskin boots.

I pulled my one-piece, clinging body suit off the rack and grabbed my black leather belt and knee-high boots before walking back over to the bed. I dropped the towel and began to dress. Seth came out of the closet while slipping on his long-sleeve, black silk shirt. He threw me a smirk while he buttoned up.

"Where are you going?" I questioned while slipping into a sexy black bra and panty.

"I'm meeting Pete and Chad tonight. Where are you going?"

"I'm meeting Charley," I answered while stepping into my red and black clinging cat suit. I walked over to Seth and turned my back to him; "Please zip me up."

Seth accommodated, and I returned with a thank you. I then snapped on my hip-hugging, black leather belt, with pewter studs that matched the pewter chains on my black leather bootstraps. I sat down on the edge of the bed and slipped on my knee-high boots while I noticed Seth looked a bit uncomfortable. I then jumped up, looked into the mirror on the back of the bedroom door, and grinned--I looked hot! I looked over at Seth and declared to my insecure-looking husband while I pretended to throw a lasso, "Let's rodeo!"

"Where's the rodeo?" He calmly asked just as the phone on the nightstand rang.

I knew he had no clue where Charley had recently moved to in Galveston. "You better answer it," I insisted as I walked back into the bathroom. "Maybe Chad is moving the party to his drug dealer's house?"

Seth hesitated to answer the phone, but then, acquiesced on second thought. "Hello," he said while I watched him watch me put my make-up into my cosmetic bag. I then grabbed my bag off the vanity, while I concluded Pete was on the other end, and hastily headed out of the bedroom and into the heart of the house. I had already given Bella her babysitting orders with Charley's telephone number, and was making mental note of everything I needed for an overnight stay in Galveston--toothbrush, a change of clothing, flip flops, something to sleep in. My suitcase was packed and stowed in the garage. Bella and her two younger brothers were upstairs playing video games while I stood in the middle of the family room contemplating going upstairs. I was questioning if Seth would leave the eleven-year old to babysit all night long, when he suddenly ran past me for the exit. I saw he was missing an accessory as he stepped up out of the sunken den and into the kitchen. "You forgot your belt!" I shouted as he headed toward the glass kitchen door in effort to beat me out the door.

He stopped dead in his tracks, looked down at his waistline, and with great disgust shouted, "Oh, shit!" He instantly turned around and trotted back into the bedroom to retrieve his studded, black leather designer belt.

I laughed and sprinted out the kitchen door for the hot car that matched my hot look. I grabbed my suitcase out of the open garage, jumped into Seth's muscle car with two pieces of luggage, turned on the ignition, locked both doors, blasted the rock music, and waited in the driveway to see the disappointment on my husband's face when he saw I had possession of his bad boy machine. Seconds later, the dark-haired man stumbled out onto the driveway while still buckling up his belt to see me sitting behind his wheel. I smiled when I saw his mouth turn down. I waved goodbye and slowly backed out into the cul-de-sac with sexy lyrics from The Eagles' *Life In The Fast Lane* blasting out the cracked window:

♫*He was a hard-headed man*
He was brutally handsome, and she was terminally pretty♫
♫*She held him up, and he held her for ransom in the heart of the cold, cold city* ♫
♫*He had a nasty reputation as a cruel dude*
They said he was ruthless, they said he was crude ♫
♫*They had one thing in common, they were good in bed*
She'd say, 'Faster, faster. The lights are turnin' red.'♫
♫*Life in the fast lane*
Surely make you lose your mind...♫

    My husband was tagged the babysitter that night, and as far as I was concerned, Pete, his good bud, who lived only a few blocks away, could keep him company at our home if phone sex bored Seth that night, and I, well, I was ready for *the fast lane* as Henley sang. Like I said the night before, I shifted gears--I wanted revenge.

    I moseyed out of The Woodlands in the black five-speed Mustang and rolled onto the on-ramp of I-45 for an eighty-five mile drive south. I had not been on the freeway more than a few minutes when I caught sight of Seth in my rear view mirror driving the mommy mobile. He caught up beside me and rolled down his front passenger window of the Volvo station wagon. I rolled my window down to hear if he had something important to say concerning our kids, and he yelled, "I'm following you wherever you're going!"

    I smiled at him while I replayed in my mind the phone sex I heard the night before on the telephone and then rolled my window back up with no regard for his wish. I stepped on the accelerator, shifted into fifth speed, and began zigzagging over four lanes of heavy traffic with the intent to lose him. I watched him in the rear view mirror keep up with me in the green turbo machine. I raced ahead even faster and saw him fall behind as I intended he do, and when I was sure he had lost sight of me, and I could no longer see him in my rear view mirror, I then shifted down and abruptly pulled over to the shoulder and idled. When he finally spotted me from three lanes over, while he flew pass me at 80 MPH, I waved bye-bye. His expression was worthy of a belly laugh, and as he sailed pass me with the fast-moving traffic, I then took the exit ramp only a few yards in front of me and several yards behind him, and ventured toward my destination without the creep from hell following me. I chuckled at my brilliance and realized I enjoyed winning at something, at anything! I figured if Seth wanted to prevent me from feeling like a winner with his attempts to sabotage my education and marriage, then so be it. I'd win at beating him at his loser game!

    I agreed to meet my friend at her *Pepto Bismol* pink, one-story shotgun built in the late 1800's. The architecture of Charley's Galveston, Texas rental stemmed from the Greek revival. Modern day architects called her house, with its corrugated metal roof, a shotgun because a person could shoot a shotgun shell from the front door and out the back door without hitting a wall. The historic Galveston home was flush with the sidewalk and located in a working man's neighborhood with a corner store only a few blocks from the Gulf of Mexico. Charley, of course, turned the old house into a dollhouse with her good taste, a little paint, and some lace; and I was impressed with the warmth she could create on a beer budget. She was divorced, 46 years of age, beautiful, had four wonderful children--one still living at home, and had a self-employed, ex-husband, who remarried, was financially set, and who was also a game player with the small amount of monthly child support he paid her every month. She had lots of male admirers who bestowed gifts upon her, and she was my role model for strength. She gave me the twenty-five cent tour of her latest rental property while I gave her the vivid details regarding homosexual phone sex.

    "It seems having a small penis is desirable among them," I said as fact.

Charley laughed, but shook her head in disagreement over her struggle to understand me. "You know, he will leave you when the money runs out!"

"The money has run out," I declared. "He lost all of his mother's money in the stock market; and now, he's lost his hefty monthly commission, too."

"You'll see; he's on his way out, Jean. He doesn't care about you or those kids. Seth is just about Seth."

"Then why did he come back after the ski trip?" I pleaded.

"Because he doesn't want to have to pay you child support right now, and he's got a home to live in with no mortgage, but when he gets financially back on his feet, he'll leave you."

"I know you're right, Charley," I sadly grieved. "I have this fear he might disappear in the middle of the night with my kids."

"He might disappear with them," she affirmed.

I took a deep breath. "I wonder if he will be there with my kids in the morning when I go back home?"

"Don't worry about him running away tonight. Seth isn't going to leave without all his valuable possessions, and I don't mean the kids! He wants everything in the house, and I'd suspect the house, too. You guys don't have any money, and he can't afford to move right now, and he's not *that* stupid. And as long as he doesn't have the means to support himself and two kids, he's going to stay in that beautiful paid-for home with you."

"He gets a $400 a week draw for the first three months with this new insurance company."

"That job will keep him put for now. He isn't going anywhere on that chicken feed," Charley confirmed. "He wouldn't be able to feed his kids, or pay a babysitter on $400 a week, and just like your first three years together, before your apparel business lawsuit was settled, he probably won't close any deals in the insurance business *this time*, either!"

"Yeah, you're probably right," I sighed while finding a bit of relief in her depressing logic. "I pray all the time God keeps me and my children safe."

"Good, keep praying, and pray you get a job soon, too."

"I don't know how to do that work thing when he's gone all day and all night," I said with frustration.

"Get a babysitter."

"I could," I nodded while doubting I would make enough money to pay a babysitter and all the household necessities, too, on minimum wage when Seth finally flew the coop. "I'm determined to go to paralegal school," I reminded her.

"He will leave you before you complete that certification," she coolly warned.

"Probably," I agreed. "He followed me tonight. I lost him, but before I left him in the dust on the freeway, he told me that he wanted to go with me."

"I thought he was going out with the boys tonight?"

"He was, and then," I shrugged, "he changed his mind, I guess."

"He has a need to control you, Jean. He's paranoid you might leave him before he leaves you! You're beautiful, and there are a lot of guys who would love to be your man."

"I see how the heads turn, and Seth is right to feel paranoid!" I spewed. "He's got it coming!"

"My mama use to say," Charley continued, "'what goes around comes around.'"

"That's a universal law," I affirmed. "What we put out there, good or bad, comes back to us. I've rolled that truth around for years while questioning how I ended up with Seth. I did Leonardo wrong, and Seth was and still is my punishment," I solemnly admitted.

"Live and learn! Treat others as you would want them to treat you."

"Well, Seth treats me like I'm an idiot, so I guess it's time for me to treat him like an idiot! Let's go have some fun with your friends."

"You'll like these guys." Charley encouraged. "Forget about that loser for a night. It's time for you to enjoy life. I want to introduce you to Jerry."

"I'd like nothing more!" I answered.

We spent the evening at the bar/lounge at the Holiday Inn on Seawall Boulevard. Charley, and her tall boyfriend, Jerry, and his group of friends, prominent businessmen who ran Galveston, were regulars every week at the club. The network received us and gifted us with free cocktails and appetizers throughout the night. Jerry owned most of the real estate in Galveston, and his friends were doctors from the University of Texas Medical Branch in Galveston, and lawyers whose clients lived on the island, or across the causeway on the Mainland.

Half way through the evening, I sat at the bar with Charley and a lawyer named Adelmaro, while Charley's handsome boyfriend, Jerry, with the thick silver hair, confidently stood in a circle on the other side of the small, dark room chatting with his buddies. Adelmaro, coincidentally, was a Greek, and he told me his name meant *distinguished because of his lineage*. While I sat there and noted my girlfriend talked to two male tourists on her left side, I immediately tuned in to the cultural historian, and asked Adelmaro to enlighten me about the Greek society, while I worked the conversation to get an answer to the questions I had after listening to a 3:00 a.m. telephone call the night before. What I learned, from the lawyer, allowed me to connect the dots.

"Plato argued that since human beings are unequal in virtue, virtue must be something that varies among people," he impressed upon me. "Since no human being ever knowingly desires what is bad, differences in their conduct must be consequence of differences in what *they know*."

I refuted, "Weakness of will interferes with moral conduct! I was taught early on what was right and wrong--most of us were."

"Based on what code?" He challenged.

"Pardon me?"

"From what source did your sense of right and wrong come from?"

"My parents, they told me about God's laws," I answered.

"Did they have it right?"

I considered his question. We were Catholic and the oversized Bible in our home had sat on the coffee table for years as a foot prop. "I don't know," I shrugged. "My parents expected the Catholic school to teach us."

"What if you don't really know God's laws?" He asked.

"Then I guess one might make bad choices. I suppose you have to read the Bible to know God's laws."

He smiled. "Which one?"

"Is there more than one?"

"Christianity is based entirely on the Bible. Judaism's Bible is called the Tanach. The Christian Old Testament was based on the Tanach, but was altered to support the teachings of Christianity. Islam considers the Bible to be an important historical and religious book, but considers the Quran to be more important, and more accurate. Mormonism, or better known as "The Church of Jesus Christ of Latter-day Saints" believes that the Bible was correct when it was written, but that the versions we have today have been corrupted over the years. Mormonism considers the Book of Mormon to be superior to the Bible. Jehovah's Witnesses use "The New World Translation of the Holy Scriptures" Bible. Contrary to common belief, it hardly differs from other translations. In fact, the only major difference is that this translation has kept God's personal name-- Jehovah, whereas other translations have removed this name."

"I suppose many people have never read any of these books."

"You're right. So the question really at stake is, 'What is virtue, if you don't know God's Word?'"

I took a drink and considered his question. "Virtue is moral excellence; a character trait valued as being always good, in, and of itself. Do you really have to read the Bible to know it's wrong to murder?" My own question challenged me. I had not read the Bible until recent years, but I had always believed, since childhood, that murder was wrong, yet I had justified murder when I had an abortion.

"What if all the men in your family think going to jail is just a passage in life?" He challenged.

"You have a point," I replied.

"The opposite of virtue is vice," the lawyer added.

"Vice, huh?" I pondered.

"Vice is a defect in thinking. What we call immorality."

"And to be a man married with children, and to keep a lover on the side is up for debate?" I challenged. "It's a no brainer--it's wrong. It's a vice!"

He shrugged. "If you and your husband were to agree to the terms, is it still wrong?"

"I would never agree! Certain things are wrong, like when a man is involved with a woman, and he has another woman on the side; or like when a married man with children takes a lover, or worse, he takes a male lover! Homosexuality is a vice."

He chuckled. "There was no word for *homosexual* or *heterosexual* in ancient Greece; all that existed was various types of love. There was acceptance in loving relationships between a mature man and slave boy, or man and prostitute, or man and woman. An older, mature male, commonly took a young beardless boy into his arms, but when the boy grew facial hair, the culture looked down upon the union. Male love between two mature men was problematic, and whether in Greece, or Rome, the passive partner, in such a relationship, was universally the butt of contemptuous jokes. Society considered a mature man weak, if he allowed another male to manhandle him, and force him into the passive role; and for a man who faced this struggle, to have sex with a woman was preferred over a mature male submitting to a male aggressor. Three thousand years ago, passive adult males were believed to be effeminate and driven into such forbidden relationships through irrational lust, but such relationships became common during the Roman period when true love was proven to be lifelong and supported an evolution of belief that the love of a boy did not suddenly end when he was grown."

I wondered how Runi and Seth related to each other. Boy, man, or man-to-man? Did my husband feel some type of self-hate for enjoying the passive part? Did he feel that enjoying the passive part enrolled him into the lowest depth of vice? Did Seth feel worthy of my love? Worse, perhaps Seth felt the only stable love was the love between two males, and I, once necessary for begetting heirs, was but now a terrible vice.

The lawyer continued, "A Greek named Lycinus said all men should marry, but let only the wise man be permitted to love boys, for perfect virtue grows least of all among women."

"That's how that culture felt about women?" I asked with great indignation.

"Socrates believed there were two types of men: those who marry a woman to continue their lineage and who are faithful to her; and then, there are those who marry a woman to continue their lineage, but who retain a male lover. Socrates said these men with lovers on the side conceive and bear the things of the spirit, like wisdom and virtue."

I noted Charley tuned in to our conversation.

"How does a man find *wisdom* and *virtue* when his premise is woman has little virtue?" I argued. "Virtue is strength of character; conformity to a standard of right--morality! What did Socrates know about woman or morality? Nothing, I would assume! He proposes that while a man is married and has children, that he keep a male lover. I think as a woman married to such a devil, I would teach that man a hard lesson." I declared to the lawyer while wondering if he was gay, too. "He will get some wisdom alright! I think Socrates was a dick sucking idiot!"

Adelmaro laughed along with Charley while I knew the lawyer did not understand I had a bisexual husband. I turned my attention to my friend on the other side of me and rolled my eyes at her over the subject matter. I continued to blast my opinion Charley's way, "Woman prohibited man's spiritual growth?!!! I've always longed for an intelligent argument with a man. Long ago, my search criteria entailed a familiar set of male character flaws. I'm now ready to compete in the hurdle event at the Olympics."

Charley laughed.

I shot back to the lawyer, "And no, I'm not a gold digger—I never married anyone for their money, unfortunately. And I learned late in life that arrogance does not equate to intelligence." I was referring to Seth.

Adelmaro's grim expression was followed by, "Excuse me, Jean, but I have to find the men's room."

"Sure," I acknowledged while he got up and walked away.

I turned to Charley and joked, "I'm too militant; I drove him away!"

She laughed when the club's bouncer walked up and interrupted us. He stood between our barstools and whispered to Charley and me, "I don't want to alarm you girls, but there's a guy over there hiding behind the palm trees along the wall at the entrance. He's been watching you two all night. Just be careful."

Charley and I peered behind ourselves and spotted a pair of black and white snakeskin boots underneath leafy palm fronds. She looked at me in question, and I whispered, "That's Seth. Tell the security guard to not be alarmed."

Charley smiled and whispered back to me, "He's so weird."

"He tells me all the time he's not normal."

We looked at the bouncer with big grins. I admitted to the big man, "That's just my husband, but thanks for the heads up."

"Is he dangerous?" The bouncer inquired.

"Only to himself," I replied.

Charley laughed.

"Don't walk out to the parking lot alone," the grinning man said as he walked off.

Charley smiled and yelled back, "I never walk out to the parking lot *alone*."

"Me, either!" I quipped.

After the bouncer walked away Charley turned back to me and said, "These two guys sitting right here," she pointed to two middle-aged male tourists who sat on her left side, "...are staying here in the hotel. They're photographers from Oklahoma, and they want us to come up and see their photos." She smiled and waited for me to compute the humor.

I chuckled. "You gotta be kidding."

"Yep, it's fun to kid!" She nodded toward the palm trees.

I chuckled at the possibility. "I'd like to see their photography."

Charley then turned and spoke to the two out-of-towners, "This is my friend, Jean."

They both shot smiles over at me. I leaned over Charley and shook the nearest hand of the man with dishwater blonde hair, a fallen jaw line, and smiling blue eyes, "Hi," I said. "And you are?"

"I'm Tim Raction," he answered for both of us girls.

"Hi, Tim," I returned and then looked over at his peer who waited his turn and stuck my hand out for an introduction, "I'm Jean." He was another average-looking, balding, gray-haired man with a good-humored expression.

"Mike Marlow."

"Hi Mike," I said as if sincerely interested while wanting to screw with Seth. "Charley says you're both professional photographers?"

"Yeah," Mike confirmed while I continued to hold his hand and throw him a flirtatious smile. "We work for the same company--Kodako."

"I love good photography," I said while I released my grasp and avoided glancing at the palm trees. "Do you guys have an exhibit here in Galveston?"

Charley smiled while we watched the two males light up over our sudden interest in them. They were both in their early- to mid-forties, and the least of the two in looks, Mike, the balding guy, gladly explained, "Oh no, we don't have a showing anywhere, but we have pictures upstairs if you girls would like to come up and see our work?"

I was not sure what their intentions were, and maybe they wanted to take nude pictures of us, but whatever they intended, my agenda was all that mattered! "Oh yeah, I would love to see your Polaroids!" I quickly offered.

Charley chuckled while sliding off her barstool and enthusiastically replied, "That sounds like merriment! Let's go play!" She tapped me on the arm and whispered, "Wait a minute, let me talk to Jerry for thirty seconds."

I watched Charley quickly walk over to her boyfriend and whisper something into his ear; they laughed; and then she strolled back over to our party. We headed out of the dark club with the two conservatively dressed photographers and toward the brightly lit lobby of the hotel. She and I smiled at each other as we passed a pair of snakeskin boots that froze as we approached the palm tree area to exit the nightclub. The photographers remained unaware of the stalker. We giggled as we followed the two men through the lobby toward the elevator and did not look back to see if the boots were watching us from the club door. Tim Raction, our lead man, hit the button on the lobby wall and the elevator doors abruptly slid open. We four stepped into an empty elevator without any discussion. I felt the men were scared to death of us as we prepared to move up to their room on the fifth floor, and rightly so that they fear two strange women! Nor did we know them, but the truth remained, Seth was the butt of our joke currently in play.

Just as the doors were about to seal us into the box and go up to who knows where, an arm reached in from outside and pried the elevator doors back open. Seth stepped into the elevator wearing a long, double-breasted black leather coat and black leather gloves with the ten fingertips cut out. I refrained from any show of emotion while I heard Charley calmly say, "Hi Seth."

"Charley," he muttered while he gave me an angry look to indicate he felt he had busted me. The green egg in the center of his forehead, caused from him hitting the garage door, protruded like a horn.

I said nothing to our new guest and pretended to not know the pimp in the snakeskin boots when Mike Marlow curiously asked Charley and me, "Who is this?"

My girlfriend nonchalantly answered, "Jean's husband."

Mike and Tim exchanged an *uh-oh* look and immediately froze up in expression. They said not another word to us while their eyes remained fixed on the floor for the ride up. The elevator dinged and opened up to the fifth floor. We all got off the elevator, Seth included, and without any further words spoken, we quietly followed the two photographers to their room, located halfway down the long hotel corridor. Seth did not have a clue what we were up to, but he waited quietly with us in the hallway while Mike dug in his trouser pocket for his room key and unlocked the door. The photographer swung the door wide open, and we all walked into a typical hotel room with two queen-size beds. The other photographer, Tim, walked over to the desk and picked up a photo album and brought it back over to where Charley and I stood in a half moon at the end of the first bed with his friend, Mike. Tim opened up the book to the first page, and we all looked over his shoulder while Seth stood at the door watching the performance.

"Oh, that's a really good shot," Charley commented.

"I took that picture in Niagara Falls," the photographer proudly replied.

"I've been to Niagara Falls," I revealed. "I went in the 80's."

"Oh, shiiiiiiiiiiiiiiiiiiiiiiiiiiiiiiiii...t!" Seth loudly groaned in disbelief that we girls ventured up with these men to their room *to look at pictures*.

I smiled and then looked up at Seth along with the rest of the gang to watch him make a quick exit out the door. The door slammed shut behind him. My eyes met Charley's, and we began to laugh, and we laughed harder, and then even harder, until I grabbed my side, as she did hers, and we both fell backwards onto beds with tears from uncontrollable laughter streaming down our faces. The photographers expressions remained serious over the fact that hubby hung outside the door somewhere nearby. They stood at the end of the beds in bewilderment while watching us crack a rib.

Suddenly, there was a hard knock on the door, and Charley and I instantly stopped laughing and jumped up off the beds, both in expectation that Seth came back for more torture. Mike Marlow sat the photo album down on the desk while Tim carefully opened up the door. Charley and I stood behind them and curiously peered out the door.

"Hello. I'm sorry to bother you folks," the hotel security guard kindly said to us. None of us responded, and the guard continued, "I've been watching this man right here loiter around the hotel all night, and he says he's married to one of you women?"

Charley and I understood, before we left the dark nightclub, that the bouncer informed the hotel security guard that the man hiding in the palm trees was my husband. Seth paced in the background of the hallway while the security guard carried the joke further along.

I looked at Charley and shrugged, as if confused by the security guard's words, and she shrugged in like manner, as if she too had no clue as to whom the pacing stranger in the trench coat was either. I solemnly answered, "We don't know him."

"They are lying, officer!" Seth angrily protested.

The security guard glanced at Seth, but did not respond. He looked back at us and continued, "Okay, well, I'm sorry to have bothered you."

"No problem," I eased. Most likely Charley's boyfriend, Jerry, had help set up the joke with the hotel staff. I looked at Charley and she continued the serious game called *we are confused as to who this strange man is*.

The security guard continued, "I am going to escort this man out of the building tonight, and he won't be allowed back into the hotel. I suggest you girls not go out into the parking lot alone."

Charley added, "We have no plans to leave the hotel tonight."

"Good," the officer said while Seth watched us in all seriousness from the hallway and did not say another word in his defense.

The photographers, who knew the man to be my husband, went along with the gag, too. Of course, they wanted my husband thrown out of the hotel.

"Goodnight," the officer said to the party of four at the door.

"Goodnight, sir," Tim said as he closed the room door. Charley and I fell back into the beds again and laughed over our denial of knowing the creep from hell. In between laughs, I asked Charley, "Why does he care?"

"He doesn't, Jean. And what's up with that bump on his forehead?"

"He ran into the garage door the other day."

"He looks like a green-eyed monster," she huffed. "Let's go downstairs and find Jerry."

"Let's go!" I answered. "Guys, you're welcome to join us."

"That's alright, ladies," Mike nervously answered. "I think Tim and I have had enough excitement for one night."

The other photographer added, "We've got an early morning."

"Okay, we understand," Charley replied. "Nice meeting you guys."

"You, too," they both answered while standing at the end of the beds and watching us dash out of the room.

"Thank you," I said to them as I followed Charley out the door. I felt I had taken revenge on Seth for screwing my best friend, Sabrina, and for keeping a boyfriend in the picture during the entire marriage!

The following morning around 10:00 a.m., I woke up in Charley's bed beside her, told her goodbye, and groggily drove myself back home to The Woodlands, Texas. I feared Seth would be more determined to disappear with my two youngest children after last night's joke. Charley and I had gone out to breakfast with her boyfriend and some of his friends, well after midnight, and she and I had fallen asleep just before the sun came up; but regardless of having too little rest, I anxiously drove home. I pulled into the cul-de-sac just before noon and found relief the moment I spotted my two youngest, Harper and Doren, at the foot of the driveway on their four wheelers. Seth was digging into one of the rectangular planter boxes beside our driveway with a long-handled shovel. I assumed Bella was in the house, or hanging out with her good friends, James and Jo Ann, who lived around the corner of the cul-de-sac.

James and Jo Ann, twins, would start the fifth grade with Bella after the summer break was over, along with another neighbor of the same age, Elizabeth. My daughter had three very close friends within walking distance to play with all summer long, and more often than not, she spent time at their homes and avoided the daily arguments between her stepfather and me. We had bought our home at the end of 1991; and now, August 1994, three years later, I felt we were about to lose everything due to Seth's insanity; and that fact made me unhappy and angry, and I assumed, had left my children feeling insecure, too.

IN HELL WITH EYES WIDE OPEN

Seth was dressed in his landscaping uniform--safari khaki green shorts, dirty tennis shoes, a navy and orange *Houston Astros* T-shirt, and a layer of dirt. I saw Harper and Doren in my rear view mirror happily pedaling their wheels toward me while I slowly pulled into the driveway. Their father rendered to me a grim expression as a forewarning before I turned off the ignition. I defensively stepped out of his black Mustang, and he angrily announced to all the neighbors, "Oh, the slut is home! I had to go to work today, and you weren't here! What was I supposed to do with these kids?"

"More worthy of discussion, Seth, what am I supposed to tell these kids, after you run off with your boyfriend?" I angrily challenged and then shifted into mockery. "You're such a poor sport!" I arrogantly chided while I stood by the black Mustang and shook my head in disgust over the audacity he had to get angry *with me?!* "I saw you standing behind the palm trees in the night club, chump! You got played by everybody in the club!"

Seth chuckled with an arrogant pride and rolled his eyes at me as if to indicate I was inventing a convenient lie to cover *my unfaithful self* while I continued to blast, "I'm clear who you are for me, Seth. And I want you to know that since your focus is to sabotage our marriage and family, and my career, and my education, too, simply because you lack having a brain, I've decided to play your *lowlife* game, too. As you have informed me in the past, and have proven to be your word in court, that you will charge me with *whatever* allegations I make about you, I am here to tell you that I am now giving you something to work with, Seth! And, you should know, the war is officially on between us," I replied at the same volume he announced to the neighborhood his opinion of me. "And know this, jerk off, whatever you do to hurt me, *I'll one up you!* I swear to God--count on it! I've had enough of your deception! I am no longer a nice person! I am now your nightmare."

He returned a laugh, acting as if my threat did not bother him in the least.

I ignored him while I grabbed my luggage out of his black Mustang, slammed the door shut, and walked up the driveway past the dirty man. I spotted my green Volvo station wagon parked inside the garage. I stood at the entrance of the garage and looked up to inspect the two-car wide garage door. Seth had told me the door was not only off the tracks, but also broken. "This garage door looks perfectly fine to me, Seth!" I huffed. "It fell off the right-side track. Put the door back on the track so we can close our garage at night!"

He ignored my order while he dug a deep hole in the planter box for a palm that sat nearby. I figured he wished he could bury me in that hole!

My two sons pedaled up to me on their wheels. "Hi boys," I said with a smile trying to hide my angry feelings toward their father. My five-year old, Harper, had obviously dressed himself that morning because his shirt was inside out. His younger brother, Doren, rode up closer and rammed his four-wheeler into Harper's *Big Wheel* and the two little boys laughed.

"Where have you been, Mommy?" Harper asked between giggles.

"I spent the night with my friend, Charley. Do you guys want to come in the house and eat breakfast with me?" I looked at my youngest, Doren, and saw he wore only a dirt bead necklace and a soiled diaper. I had been trying to toilet train my three-year old in between all the marital chaos, but Doren seemed resistant to growing up, and I wondered if he was rebelling against his parents' chronic unhappiness.

Harper was quick to get off his *Big Wheel* and follow me into the house for a meal. Doren seemed to want to stay outside and sat firmly on his battery-operated four-wheeler. "You need a bath, Doren, and some clean clothes," I persuaded.

"No bath," he angrily ordered, "...and no breakfast!"

"It's lunch time, Jean," Seth grumbled. "I fed them breakfast hours ago."

"I want lunch, Mommy!" Harper enthusiastically aligned.

"Oka, let's go eat lunch!" I happily said to my five-year old while picking up on the angry attitude from my youngest. "We have to change you, Doren."

"No, I want to stay with Daddy."

Seth had been listening to us from a short distance, "That's Daddy's boy!"

I shot Seth a dirty look; "Okay, then *you* change Doren's diaper before he gets a rash! Take his diaper off out here and hose him down!" I said to Seth before I went inside with only Harper. I was clear Seth was creating camps with our children.

The following morning, Seth got up early to go to his new sales job at the Galleria because I was home to babysit on this Tuesday morning. He drove his black Mustang into the city, and I stayed home still tired from the late night out with Charley. I was eager for the fall semester of paralegal school to begin.

Harper would start kindergarten in the fall, too, and I took my son's shot records to the registrar that morning to complete his registration at the neighborhood elementary school. Coincidentally, the registrar at Harper's school recognized the name of my emergency contact, Harper's grandparents, told me that she was one of my mother's oldest friends, and introduced herself as Mrs. Fox. I didn't know the woman, but I was thrilled Harper would stand out from the crowd of kindergarteners, and felt, too, that with Mrs. Fox's help, my five-year olds' transition into half-day kindergarten would be smooth.

"I'd be delighted to keep a special eye out on Patti's grandson!" Mrs. Fox happily informed me from behind the counter in the school's front office. "Your children are beautiful," she said while she studied the two boys who played together across the room.

"Thank you."

"I bet Patti adores them."

"Yes."

"How is your mother doing?"

"Not well," I revealed to the woman whom I knew had no clue about my mother's setback.

"Oh, what's the matter with Patti?"

"My mother has Hepatitis C of the liver, and she's terminal."

"Oh no! I'm sorry; I had no idea, Jean Ellen."

"She's not broadcasting her illness," I comforted her old friend. "I'm sure though, she would love to hear from you."

"I haven't talked to Patti in years, but I will call her right away! Give me her number just in case I have something different," Mrs. Fox requested while she slid a piece of paper across the countertop.

"They've lived in the same house since I was in the first grade, and they've had the same telephone number, too."

"They are stable people," she commented.

"That's an understatement!" I jotted down my parents' telephone number they had kept for twenty-nine years. "She'll be happy to hear you are keeping a safe eye on my son. She doesn't trust my husband."

"Why not?" The woman asked.

I hesitated to dump too much information on the stranger. "Life is not good at home these days. My husband is really unhappy and--" I stopped out of embarrassment and shrugged off any further explanation.

"Harper will like kindergarten," the woman comforted.

I whispered, "My husband and I had a temporary divorce hearing last Christmas, but we dropped the divorce. I wish I hadn't dropped the divorce--biggest mistake I made in a long time. My parents are disappointed, too, that I am still married to him."

"How are your children holding up?"

"Not well, their parents fight too much. They've been caught in the middle for years, and I would guess they hate us by now."

"I'm so sorry," she offered.

"We'll get through this somehow. I'm going to paralegal school when Harper starts kindergarten."

"Oh, good for you!" She smiled.

"Yeah," I said while doubting I would ever see the first class. "I've been a stay-at-home mom since my last two children were born; and now I feel penalized. My husband lost his income in June and just started a new sales job. He's selling health and life insurance. Maybe things will smooth out for us; that's what I'm hoping for."

"I'll pray for you," Mrs. Fox offered. "Call me if I can help you in anyway."

"I certainly will, thank you. I need your prayers." I said as I left the registrar's office with my two youngest children and headed back to my green Volvo station wagon parked in front of the elementary school built in the woods, and only a mile from my home. Harper would take the school bus to kindergarten each morning and come home at noon on the bus, too, or vice versa. I wasn't sure at this point if he would be in morning or afternoon kindergarten. I was thankful that Mrs. Fox was manning the front desk at his school.

Until school began for Harper and me in a few weeks, I would continue to write my novel and care for my children while Seth worked all day at his new sales job. My novel in progress took my mind off my worries that Seth would leave me again as soon as I began paralegal classes, or more likely, as soon as he got the award from the arbitration hearing. I lost myself in characters based on other people I knew, and what I noted most interesting about my storytelling, over the past year, was that I still had problems writing about me. I did not feel comfortable revealing my life on paper, and even less capable of explaining my sad pitiful life. What did I not know that I did not know about me?

The upcoming arbitration hearing was about Seth getting his mother's $85,000 back that he lost in the stock market, plus a lot more, according to my husband. I was never clear as to how much he hoped to win in the arbitration hearing, but part of me secretly wanted Seth to lose his arbitration because I suspected he would leave us if he had enough money. I did not go look for a job as my father and Charley advised I do; but, instead, I continued to be a stay-at-home mom and wait for Seth to bring home the bacon as he had promised me that he would do for us. Besides, I could not really hold down a job because Seth left at 6:00 a.m. and sometimes did not come home until nearly 10:00 p.m.

Money was scarce, since his last commission check in June, two months earlier, and we had just enough to pay our utilities and buy groceries on his measly, weekly, base pay of $400. I had also received an annual tax bill for $3,200 and did not know how Seth and I were going to pay our property taxes due in one lump sum at the beginning of the year. I understood that the bank foreclosed on homeowners who did not pay their property taxes, but I did not know how long of a grace period I had before the bank would start foreclosure. Our entertainment was limited to Pete, Chad, and their girlfriends dropping over occasionally. Seth ignored my frequent requests that our friends not bring drugs to our home; and often, Pete and Chad pulled weed out of their shirt pockets. I stayed angry about everything.

Barely a week had passed since Seth's most recent release from jail; and since his release, I chose *to not use* my father's lawyer friend, Jerry Hoppas, to file a second divorce petition. The kitchen phone rang, shortly after the sun went down, and I picked up to find Seth on the other end of the receiver. "Jean," he blurted, "I'm in the emergency room."

His announcement startled me. "Are you okay?"

"I was in a car wreck. Give me our medical insurance information."

"What are you talking about?"

"What's the policy number?"

"Are you crazy, Seth? You know we've never had any medical insurance *ever.*"

"Okay," he said and then abruptly hung up.

An hour later, he entered through the glass kitchen door wearing a white, long-sleeve dress shirt, and crisp dress slacks and acting as if everything was fine. I was alone downstairs, at this late night hour, sitting in front of the TV. He seemed to be okay and cheerfully greeted me with a hello.

"What was up with that phone call?" I asked.

"I totaled my car," he said. "I was hauled off from the crash site by an ambulance."

"Oh no," I groaned while aware the only car insurance we ever had bought was liability, and the coverage had long ago expired for lack of payment. "Where is the car?"

"The car was towed away at the crash site."

"Will you be able to repair it?"

"No, Jean. I totaled the car," he said nonchalantly.

"Whose fault was it?"

"Not mine," he quickly defended. "This guy behind me plowed into me. He has insurance, and I'm suing him for bodily injury."

"Oh," I said while digesting the situation. "But you don't seem to be hurt," I questioned.

"I suffered a concussion."

"You did?"

"The ER room took x-rays. They confirmed I suffered a concussion."

"What exactly is a concussion?"

"A concussion is a blow to the head that shakes up the brain, which temporarily prevents the brain from working normally."

"But your brain never worked normally," I dryly reminded.

"They don't know that," he retorted in good humor.

"So now you're going to take my car every day to work?"

"No, you can take me to work."

"That's a thirty-mile trip one way!"

"Look, Jean. Until I close some deals, we don't have an option. I need a ride tomorrow."

"How do you call on clients if you don't have a car?"

"I'm not calling on clients tomorrow. I'm in a product class all day."

"Okay. I'll take you to work. I promised Harper to buy him some new shoes for kindergarten."

"We don't have money for shoes," He groaned.

"He needs shoes, Seth. His feet have outgrown his only pair of shoes. I can't put it off a day longer. Doren can wear Harper's outgrown shoes, but Harper needs shoes for school."

"Alright then, buy our son some new shoes." He walked out of the den and went into our master bedroom, and minutes later, returned shirtless and carrying his white dress shirt, a needle, and a spool of white thread. He plopped himself next to me on the sofa and threaded the needle.

"I'm glad you didn't get hurt today," I said while I watched him sew.

"I did--a button came off my shirt," he teased.

"I have a box of loose buttons if you need one," I offered.

"I still have the button," he said while he cut the thread off the spool.

I sat there with little to say while feeling bummed he had lost *his* car. Now his negligence tied me to the home without transportation because he would take *my* car into the city to earn us a living. "When do you think you'll get your insurance settlement for *the concussion?*"

"I don't know," he answered. "I suspect we'll settle in a couple of months. I have an attorney on the case already, the same one who is handling my arbitration. He called *State Farm* today and began a bodily injury suit."

I considered two or three months too long to not have cash for a car, and wondered how not having a car would interfere with my school plans. "Do you think you'll close a client anytime soon?" I asked while understanding we had just enough money to buy groceries and pay for utilities on the $400 a week base pay his new employer was paying him.

"I don't know; I've got some things on the burner." He whipped the small button onto the front of his white dress shirt; and then, with a snip, he cut his thread and declared, "I've got it all sewn up, Jean. There is nothing this man can't do!"

I smiled, but I lacked the confidence in his ability to close any deal, and sensed something no good was up with him, especially after he called me from the hospital, knowing well, we had never had health insurance a single day in our relationship. He did not seem to have too much remorse over the loss of his bad boy car, either. "That bump on your forehead has not gone down too much."

"Nope," he confirmed.

"It changed colors, does it still hurt?"

"Not anymore."

I suddenly put the pieces together. He told the hospital that he got the bump in the car wreck, instead of the truth—that he bumped his head on the garage door that hung a quarter of the way down because the door was off the track. The hospital evaluated the bump and told him that he suffered from a concussion. "Did you hit the windshield today when that man hit you from behind?"

"I sure did," he said with great conviction.

I didn't believe him.

The following morning, the children and I jumped into my green Volvo station wagon and drove Seth into the city to drop him off at Grandville Pike's impressive office suite in a glass tower. This was the day he had no sales calls because he had product class all day, and the day I would buy Harper new shoes for kindergarten. Harper was excited about being a big boy and going to school, but I had mixed emotions about my little boy going off to school and leaving me.

After dropping Seth off at work earlier that morning, and after our very limited shopping spree, I returned home with the three kids. Harper was very proud of his new canvas shoes and jumped out of the car carrying his old shoes in a shoebox in a store bag. "These are you shoes, Doren," he informed his brother. "You can pretend they are new!" He advised as he jumped out my green Volvo station wagon and raced toward the front porch to test his new running shoes for speed. Harper's statement had little impact on his younger brother who happily followed him and Bella to the front door. My daughter, Bella, had a house key in her purse, unlocked the door while I drove my station wagon into our open garage and unloaded a sack of groceries. Seth had still not put the garage door back on track, and I felt it was just a matter of time before a thief stole something of value out of our garage, such as our expensive bikes, lawn tools, or even our only car.

I pulled my groceries out of the back of my station wagon and slammed the rear end shut while I watched my children race into the house. I suddenly heard my four-year old yelling from the front porch, "Mommy! Come see. Something happened to our house!"

"What?" I asked in confusion and saw Bella run out toward me with a disturbed look. My heart leaped and I raced inside expecting to see my greatest fear manifested.

"Sissy, we've been robbed!" Harper said as we all walked into the house together.

I stood in the foyer of my once beautiful home and sadly shook my head. Seth had gutted our home. There was nothing but the old worn sofa left in the family room. He had tricked me that morning, when he asked me to drop him off at the office and take the kids shopping. "Oh, my Lord," I groaned while I got the reality of my life. "What has he done?" I walked into the center of my plundered family room and fell down into the sandy-colored velveteen sectional. I was speechless and in shock, again.

Harper and Bella sat down beside me on the oversized Ottoman and said nothing while we watched Doren walked from empty room to empty room as if he were looking for something in particular--his daddy.

I digested what Seth had done. He had taken all our expensive electronics, paintings, the nicest artwork from shelves, even my favorite blue leather tufted Queen Anne-style chair that I had bought during my marriage to Leonardo. He had moved out just before his son started kindergarten, and of course, before I started school, too. His departure would have a huge impact on our son's first year of school. How could Seth be so selfish and not realize the pain he caused his babies? "Oh, my God, what has he done?" I moaned while realizing our children would not feel secure in their lives, again, because the home life they trusted was now just a memory. I was sure my young sons would now worry I would run away one day, too. Why would they ever feel secure, and for whatever reason Seth could justify for leaving us, our sons would always feel they were not important enough for Daddy to stay home.

Harper interrupted my sad thoughts, "Mommy, did Daddy move out?"

I shook my head and replied, "Yes." I saw Harper's face instantly turn down and become sad looking. How long would this child stay sad?

"Daddy don't love us anymore?" My son asked me.

Tears welled up in my eyes, and I tightly hugged my five-year old son. I did not answer Harper while my tears ran down my cheeks out of his view, and while I watched my youngest child frantically search the house for a sign of Daddy. Doren ran from my bedroom, to the kitchen, to my bedroom again, like a crazy person, asking us all the while, "Where's Daddy? Where's Daddy? Where's Daddy?" He was brokenhearted and unwilling to accept his latest reality.

I hated Seth in that moment when I spotted Harper looking up at me and noting my tears. "Don't cry, Mommy. I still love you."

"I love you, too. I love all of you, and I swear I will never ever leave you guys."

Bella wrapped her arms around Harper and me and hugged us tightly. Doren saw us hugging and stopped dead in his frantic tracks. He ran up to us, threw himself face down into the Ottoman, and wailed. He could not express his sadness in words, but he felt the sadness his father made him feel again, with his second departure.

I stroked my baby's blond head and then reached over to pick up the crying child and put him in my lap. "I swear, I love you guys with all my heart," I said while I held Doren tightly. "I will always be here for you. I will not ever leave you."

Bella got up from the Ottoman and walked into the adjoining master bedroom, and quickly came back out. "He took your bed, Mom, and your desk and word processor, too."

"My word processor?" My book was on that word processor. "He took my book?!" I could not believe how little he cared about any of us.

The phone rang, and I guessed Seth was calling to gloat. I walked across the room carrying Doren on my hip to answer the phone on the wet bar. I looked at my Caller I.D. before I answered and read *anonymous* on the box. I picked up the receiver and said hello.

"I guess you now clearly understand our marriage is over!" He growled.

I refrained from calling him every name in the book because I held Doren on my hip. "Great, Seth! You're a wonderful husband and father. You make your children sad."

"And you're a bitch, and I've had enough of your crap."

I did not recognize his intensity; he had to try so hard to justify hurting his children that he sounded demonic. He continued,

"This is just the beginning. I have two lawsuits in the works--an arbitration that will settle, in my favor, for no less than half-a-mil, and of course, my bodily injury case. That suit will be a quick ten grand. And when I get all this money together, I'm coming after those boys. There is no way in hell you're going to take my sons away from me! You don't have a dime, bitch, to fight for custody! Good luck trying!"

His threat was too hard to listen to, and I felt I would lose my kids because he was right--he had all the money in the world, and I had not a dime or job. My greatest fear surfaced in that moment, and in my panic, I slammed down the receiver as if I held a poisonous snake next to my ear. I looked at the teary-eyed child on my hip, and then across the room at my five-year old sweetheart who was so disheartened by the turn of events. My reality sunk in, and I whispered, "Oh my God, he's going to take my beloved children away from me!" I knew I had to stop him, but how?

I had to stop him from winning that arbitration! How could I do that? I knew nothing about that big lawsuit while realizing he had purposely devised around my ignorance. "Bella," I pleaded, "Please, be with your brothers for a while. I have to search for something out in the garage."

"Okay," she said while she hugged Harper. "What are you looking for?"

"I don't know yet," I said while I brought Doren over to her side. I sat my baby on the couch nearby his brother and sister. "Seth might have left something useful out there in the garage. That was Seth on the phone, and he was bragging that he was coming after your brothers next."

"He's can't take them, Mommy!" She sternly advised.

Harper loudly protested, "Don't let Daddy take us, Mommy!"

"No, I won't. He's not splitting you three up!" I confirmed as I walked out toward the garage; and then, I angrily added under my breath for my ears only, "It will be a cold day in hell before you get custody of my two babies, you bastard!"

I walked under the catwalk on the pebble sidewalk and stepped into the side door of the two-car garage. Due to the fact that the big, wooden, two-car garage door was off the track and wide open, there was a lot of sun light streaming into the room. I searched through the three-foot tall stack of unopened mail in the corner of the garage Seth had called his office. I then searched through the blue and yellow drawers of a chest once used in the boys' nursery and found nothing of any use. I felt there was something in the garage that would provide me an answer to my dilemma. I then spotted the wall phone and next to the wall phone was the built-in wall ladder that went up to a storage area above the rafters. I peered up at the opening in the ceiling and considered Seth might have hidden something up there. I then climbed up the rungs until I could see what was above the rafters. I climbed up and looked around. The baby bed was lying across the plywood and several boxes of Christmas decorations sat up there, too, all outside of my reach. I considered crawling across the plywood to look into those seasonal storage boxes; but, instead, I peered straight down at the rafter flooring and noticed a thick batting peeking out, about eight inches from underneath the plywood, that served as insulation between the garage and the overhead storage space. I lifted up the blanket insulation just around the attic opening and there were the hidden documents. "Oh, thank you, God!" I pulled out a thick bundle of papers and read the top heading of the first page:

IN THE UNITED STATES DISTRICT COURT
FOR THE SOUTHERN DISTRICT OF TEXAS
HOUSTON DIVISION

SETH ZHERNEBOH
VS.
PRUDENTIAL SECURITIES
INCORPORATED, GEORGE SHELLER
AND TAMARA ZELESKY

<u>PLAINTIFF'S ORIGINAL COMPLAINT</u>...

I scanned the legal document reading for the basis for the suit, and there it was: *This is an action by an investor seeking redress for the fraud perpetrated upon him through an account....* My eyes scanned over account numbers and searched for the key words:

...the bases of this suit concern the offer and sale of investment advice and counsel and the outright fraud and misrepresentation of a registered representative of Prudential....

I continued scanning the lengthy legal document, page after page, until my eyes caught a dollar amount: *Plaintiff seeks no less than $500,000 in damages....* There was Seth's *half-a-mil* right there that he claimed he would win in his arbitration and then use to get custody of my beautiful children!

I needed to know when the lawyer and stockbroker were holding the arbitration. I continued to flip through the thick bundle of legal documents until I found a recent letter from the *National Association of Securities Dealers (NASD)* addressed to all parties including Seth's attorney at the powerful law firm in downtown Houston: *Re: Zherneboh Investments v. Prudential Securities, Inc.*

I continued to read for the meat, and there was the information I needed to know: *The Midwest Regional Office of the NASD Arbitration Department will be conducting its hearing in Houston, Texas August 21, 1994.*

I considered the date of Seth's arbitration, and August 21st was tomorrow! "Y-o-u...bastard!" I yelled while climbing down the wall-stair and realizing how greedy he truly was! "You move out the day before your arbitration so you do not have to share the cash settlement with me! You are going to leave me destitute, and you think you're going to come after my kids, too? I think not!"

I stared at the phone on the garage wall while seething and considering how he had taken everything from me since the beginning of our relationship. In 1988, he had dared me to take any further action with my fashion design, manufacturing and wholesale business after the crash in Florida. He stood before me and called my apparel dream silly, and told me he had been insane to believe for one second that I could be the next *Donna Karan of New York!* In addition, he entered into my productive and creative life under pretense—he had a secret lover, a man he loved. And Seth brought into our relationship a drug addiction, too. I had found a crack pipe in my red van while pregnant with Doren after he and Runi had spent the entire day together. They then came home late that day and drugged me, a very pregnant woman, with sleeping powder they put in a strawberry blender drink they made for me so they could have more sex!

My anger exploded with the gall of Seth! Since the beginning of my vacation in hell, Seth had always had delusions about how the grass was greener down the Nile River. I recalled the letter he wrote his boyfriend the day before I gave birth to his second son; Seth detailed some fantasy trip he planned for them to take down the Nile. Seth resented me for trapping him, and as a result, he often assaulted me because he hated me. I was clear, now, that when Seth met me, he thought I was going to be rich and famous, and that I would rescue him from his self-imposed poverty. The thirty-two year old jumped on my bandwagon for no reason other than to escape living with his angry mother and teenage brother, and when my apparel business crashed in Florida, and I was already pregnant with Harper, his hate for me began to fester. Seth prevented me from having the family I dreamed of having which included a loving husband and happy children! I left Leonardo for his con! Seth stole my opportunity to go to school, and to finish my degree, and then be able to fly financially when this predictable day came. Moreover, he stole my novel, my latest dream, and all the hard work I put into that writing project over the last two years while I was under his dictatorship. That book was my escape out of poverty! And now he wanted my two youngest children! He needed to die!

I picked up the receiver and dialed information. "Operator, give me Prudential in New York, New York."

I held on and went through several people at the brokerage before I found myself talking to their Legal Department. "This is Attorney Zelman, Lead Counsel for Prudential. How may I help you?" The professional kindly inquired.

I angrily blurted, "My husband is suing Prudential for no less than a half-million dollars. I have the legal doc in front of me, which indicates he has arbitration tomorrow! I hate him, and I would like to help you stop him from getting a penny."

The woman laughed. "Wow! I can't refuse that offer. What's your husband's name?"

"Seth Zherneboh," I answered, "...and his legal team is Spencer and Associates in Houston, Texas."

"I'm very familiar with this case," she confirmed. "What's your name?"

"Jean Wynn. I'm Seth Zherneboh's very angry and soon-to-be ex-wife! And I no longer use his name, effective today!"

The woman chuckled; "He really pissed you off!"

"This man has taken me past the point of no return. Now, I'm out for his blood. I'll stop short of killing him!"

The attorney laughed. "I agree; sometimes a man can take you pass your breaking point. I had one like that once," she admitted.

"What are his grounds for suing you?" I asked the attorney.

"He says Prudential took advantage of him, that he was naïve about investing money."

"Yeah, I read the legal document, too. He's *not* naïve about investing money. He worked as an investment advisor for decades. He counseled wealthy Jews in Houston a decade ago; he told me so. He held financial seminars at their uptown community center and told them how to invest their millions."

"Can you prove that?" She asked me.

"I don't know; let me do some research. He's taken everything out of our home, but I have an idea."

"Let me give you a fax number. Do you have a fax machine?"

I wondered whether I still had one. "Hold on!" I said to Prudential's attorney, and then sat the receiver down and walked back into the house, through the glass kitchen door, and peered around the door to see that Seth had left the broken fax machine with the sprung top on the buffet in the breakfast room. I hurried back into the garage and picked up the receiver. "I do have a fax machine!" I happily confirmed.

"Great! Fax to me at this number any document you can find that proves he worked as an investment advisor or financial counselor."

"I'll be happy, too," I said while I jotted her New York City fax number down, "...that is, I will fax to you documents, if I can find the proof! He gutted out my house earlier today. I'm not sure if he's taken everything; I'll have to investigate."

"Okay," she agreed. "I'll be waiting to hear from you. Good luck."

"Wait!"

"Yes?"

"I want you to compensate me. I don't want money. I want a favor."

"And what's that?"

"I want you to buy me the transcripts from my past hearings and my future hearings. I want the exact words of all the witnesses because he and his witnesses lie, and I will show them up to be liars in our next divorce hearing." I considered, too, that one day I would write a novel about this horrid life of mine while married to Seth, and set the record straight, and I would use the transcripts to tell the truth.

The lawyer laughed. "Sure, no problem."

"Thank you," I said. "He's a liar, a huge liar, and I don't want this man raising my sons."

"I will be more than happy to help you break him."

"Thank you."

I got off the phone trembling with fear. If I could not prove my allegations, I would lose my babies. I walked back into the kitchen, through the near-empty den, and into my bedroom. Bella was right; Seth had taken my king-size bed. He had also taken my small desk, chair, word processor, and filing cabinet. He had all my floppy discs and my entire novel! He stole my dream, my writing project, and my hope for a better future. He had every important document pertaining to this family, and to our estate, in that filing cabinet, too; and worse than possessing everyone's birth certificates and social security cards, he had the angry letter from Attorney Pettit wherein my own attorney wrote I acted as if I were on drugs! Seth could and would use that letter against me in court, and what better evidence than my former attorney calling me crazy!

I breezed through the vanity area of the bathroom, and then entered into my over-sized walk-in closet, to discover that Seth took everything out, except for my clothes and shoes. Suddenly, I remembered where I stored his old archives!

I flew upstairs, and at the top of the landing was the cedar closet. I swung open the door to another large, walk-in closet and found our cedar closet still filled with winter sweaters, ski clothes, old skies, boogie boards, ice chests, and other seasonal junk. Seth had not wanted any of it! I dug my way toward the back corner where I knew I had stacked Seth's boxes of old files from a decade earlier, from the time when he worked as an investment advisor. There was the box I was looking for, dated 1984 in bold marker on the side, and holding ten-year-old files!

I flipped through fifty green hanging folders and found one document after another that I felt would serve to put his arbitration in the trash. And right there, too, in that same box, was the invitation to Seth's financial seminar held at the Jewish Community Center in Houston. Oh, how well my memory served me! I did not even know him back then!

I excitedly dashed back downstairs, trotted through our sunken den, and entered into my designer kitchen to where my fax machine waited for my act of destruction. I held the broken top down on the fax machine with one hand, and inserted each document, one at a time, into the machine with the other hand. And while I considered that this evidence went straight to the lead counsel for Prudential Securities in New York City, my heart leaped and I rejoiced. I whispered with each fax confirmation, "Fuck you, Seth! Fuck you, Seth!" I danced around the kitchen between fax confirmations, and when done proving that he was a liar, I felt the greatest satisfaction; and, with much zeal, I shrieked, "Thank you, Lord! Thank you, Lord!"

When I finished helping Prudential's Legal Department gather evidence to use against Seth, I then called information again. "Please give me the number to *State Farm Insurance Company* in Houston, Texas."

I immediately connected to the insurance company, and as I did for Prudential, I offered my services to help them *not* pay Seth a dime, either. I added for the claim agent's knowledge, "That car wreck did not put that bump on his forehead. Our garage door doesn't go all the way up, and my husband walked into the door." I told the agent in the Claims Department. "He's a liar and a scumbag, and he was not hurt in that car wreck at all—he moved out the following day. He had the strength of Hercules to move out all our household possessions the very next day after the car wreck. He had a concussion *the day before* the car wreck, when he ran into our partially closed garage door. He waltzed into our home just fine after the car wreck, after he left the hospital, and bragged to me about how he was going to sue you guys for bodily injury."

"Oh yeah?" The claims agent delighted in my information.

"Yeah! Don't pay him a dime, and I'll be your witness if you need me to be!"

And when I was finished ruining Seth's position in each one of his lawsuits, then I called Grandville Pike, his conservative, Republican, churchgoing, married employer, and burned his ear in hopes I would cause the good man, who loved his wife, kids, and grandkids, to not trust his new employee and send Seth right back out the door.

"For your information, Mr. Pike," I added after our brief introduction over the phone, "Seth collected commission checks out of our mail box for the last three years and did not work that investment business a single day. He doesn't even own a computer, and his unopened mail is stacked three-feet high in a corner of our garage. That corner is what he calls his office. I suspect his former employer realized he wasn't turning over any business and fired the drug-using bum."

"Does he do drugs?"

I recalled the lies Seth told on the witness stand about me, and I felt motivated to write the best seller. "Yes, he does drugs! Since 1991, when we bought our Woodland's home with a lawsuit settlement from my apparel business, Seth has spent every day, from sunrise until dark, landscaping our yard, snorting coke, smoking marijuana, and drinking coffee spiked with expensive liquors. Who does that when they have three children? I found his crack pipe years ago after he and his boyfriend spent the day in my van screwing each other; and since, I have frequently witnessed Seth smoking pot with the guys he formerly worked with at the Talent House."

"What is the Talent House?"

"It was a business that Seth worked at, which is no longer in business because the Drug Enforcement Agency put them out of business, and the IRS put chains on the front door. Seth worked at the Talent House just before he started law school. Did he tell you that he dropped out of law school after only three weeks?"

"He said he attended law school for a couple of years."

"No, three weeks was the total effort. He's neurotic—he can't focus. His ex-wife is a nurse, and she told me that he is bi-polar. The drugs cause him to sit in the mirror for hours while he gouges out holes on his face and body—probably the meth. Anyway, the drug bust over at the Talent House, where Seth and his two closest friends worked, made the six o'clock local news—I saw the segment. The DEA arrested one of them for trafficking cocaine; they caught Seth's best friend moving kilos from the Mexican food restaurant next door over to the Talent House. The DEA put chains on the front doors of The Talent House. Seth and his friends were all in on the drug deal together—Seth just didn't get caught."

"I don't tolerate drugs in my workplace," Grandville Pike contributed.

"And you shouldn't! I have asked Seth and his friends not to do drugs in front of our kids for years, but they don't listen to me. And Seth's previous employer sent him his last commission check in June, two months ago. I'm sure his employer *did know* he was a drug addict. His former boss certainly knew Seth did not perform. Seth admitted to me that his former boss called him into his office and accused him of doing drugs." I was referring to the anonymous letter I sent to Seth's boss telling the man that his employees were not performing because of drug use. "We barely make our bills on the $400 base pay you pay him every week; but now, he's abandoned me and his three children for the second time. Well, the first time he was gone, he was in jail for assaulting me while I studied for a final I had that morning at the University of Houston. I served him a divorce petition behind bars later that day; so technically, he didn't *abandon* his family *that time.*"

"Are you now divorced?"

"No, I dropped the divorce; he talked me into taking him back after he lost the house and kids in the last hearing for temporary orders. I did the Christian thing and forgave him. The court ordered Seth to pay me child support and maintenance each month, but because he doesn't work for a living, and because he would rather file a lawsuit, than labor for money, he felt he would find himself in contempt of court. Therefore, he convinced me that he loved his kids and me, and that he was sorry for what he did, and I wanted to believe him because I needed his help with the kids and this big house. I'm a stay-at-home mom, and I haven't worked in years. I think Seth is a sociopath with no conscience whatsoever. He's quite the talker, as you know--he can sell ocean front property in Arizona. You don't know the man as I do, but he lost his mother's lifesavings in the stock market here recently. He didn't know anything about playing the stock market, but he convinced his poor, single and aged mother, that if she withdrew her investments, and paid the penalties for early withdrawal, and gave him all her money, then he would make her rich--and mostly himself, that was his point. Seth then played the margins with her entire savings of $85,000, lost everything in one single play, and then blamed Prudential for taking advantage of his naiveté. He's suing them now."

"He's suing his stockbroker for losing his money in the stock market?" He sounded as if what I said about Seth was not credulous.

"Well, technically, his mommy's money--all $85,000. He didn't have any of his own money. And he has arbitration tomorrow--he's asking for *half-a-mil* from Prudential! And he's very greedy; he gutted out my house today after I dropped him off at your office, and then he called me and threatened to do worse to my life. My kids and I came home, and they learned they could not trust, again. They were devastated to learn that daddy moved out for the second time. Seth had told them that he would never leave them when he came back the other times. Seth called while they were still crying and in shock. I answer the phone, with our sad baby on my hip, and he brags to me, over the phone, that he has all the money in the world to screw me even worse, and that he's leaving me in a no-win position, and taking my kids to boot. Seth says that when he wins his arbitration, then he's going to sue me for custody of our two youngest kids. He says I won't be able to fight him because he's left me without a dime in the bank. So, to be honest with you, Mr. Pike, I'm trying to bury him six feet under so he won't ruin my life and the lives of my two sons."

"I'm so sorry," the man replied with the greatest of compassion.

"Thank you, I appreciate your sympathies. Seth is only out for himself, sir. He *used me up*, that is the term he and his friend Chad call a woman my age—*a used up woman*; and now, he wants my kids so he can keep the marital home which is paid for in full. I suspect if he were to win custody of our children, and get the marital home in our divorce, then he would move his mommy into our home since he has lost her entire life savings. She will care for the children while he is off at work—that's perfect for him. I also suspect he will come out of the closet and move his boyfriend into my home, too, and they will all raise my two youngest children."

"Are you saying he's married to you, but he has a *boyfriend*, too?"

"I heard them masturbating the other night in the middle of the night; they were on the phone together."

"Oh, I'm so sorry, Ms. Zherneboh, for you and your children," he said with disgust. "This must be hard for all of you."

"It's nauseating. My name is Jean Wynn. I changed it. I'm not using the creep's name anymore. All this chaos is more than anyone would want to endure in a single life, but my purpose for calling you is to give you some insight as to the character of this man you just recently hired and brought into your company."

"I appreciate the courage it took for you to share these intimacies, Ms. Wynn. Thank you. I'll keep you and your children in my prayers."

"Thank you, Mr. Pike."

I sat the receiver back on the wall mount and wondered if that maneuver was over the top; after all, Seth needed a job to pay me child support! Perhaps I just cut off my own nose to spite my face? Oh well, I felt God would show me a better way, and the creep deserved to live in hell.

I stood there trembling and felt exhilarated over having destroyed Seth's life. I had taken control! Again, I found myself staring at his three-foot stack of mail in the corner of the garage next to the small yellow and blue chest-of-drawers. This corner of the garage had been his office for the last three years, and a force lured me to look closer. What was inside all those envelopes? I picked up a large, already opened, gold envelope from the top of the stack, and examined the postmark--June 1994--two months ago. I pulled out the contents and found his June paycheck stub, from his last commissions check. I pulled out another opened envelope off the stack and noted the postmark--July 1994, a month later. I pulled out a July statement from his employer and studied the dollar amounts. Seth had received a *$900 advance* on July 1, and then a *$914 commission check* on July 15. I then snapped Seth had lied to me; his June commission check was *not* the last commission check he would receive from his employer. I questioned what he had done with the *$900 advance* he received on July 1st? I had no answer...yet.

I continued to search for my answer and discovered a copy of a letter Seth wrote to his employer only a few days earlier:

August 6, 1994

Attention Beth McKinney, Payroll

Dear Beth:
 Thank you so much for your kind attention and assistance during my personal crisis. My new residence is 16200 El Camino Real, Apt. A, Houston, Texas 77062, and my office is 1513 Green Emerald Plaza, Ste 9060, Houston, Texas. Please send my last commission checks to my apartment; this is my new home address.

Seth had plotted to move out months ago! He had lied to me about his commission checks, and he had taken the July check and rented an apartment! He had used the $900 advance as a deposit on an apartment he reserved for an August move in date! My bed, desk, word processor, and novel were in his new apartment!

I opened up another envelope from the top of the rat's nest and found another statement summarizing his last six months of pay. July, not June, was his last sizable paycheck; and he received his final paycheck for $298 in August! He was without an income now, but only since this month!

I was furious Seth played me. The $900 he paid for rent would have bought us a lot of groceries. I suddenly recalled Deb, his ex-wife's words to me over the phone, *"I will tell you this, Jean,"* she said to me. *"If you and Seth break up, lock up your car. He stole my car when we broke up."*

"He has his own car," I added for her understanding while understanding that he had always been just about himself.

I peered at the mommy mobile parked in the garage and knew he would come back for my Volvo station wagon, now that he had totaled his Mustang. I ran into the house and found Bella, with her brothers, upstairs playing with their video games and toys in the playroom. "I'm running up to Wal-Mart to buy a security club for my steering wheel, Bella. I don't want Seth stealing my car because he doesn't have a car anymore. Watch your brothers; I won't be gone long."

"Okay," she said while I raced downstairs thinking of how I could get my garage door back on its track before the sun went down. I thought about Linda, a new friend that I met in my weekly seminars. She lived about ten miles away, and I needed her moral support and help. I ran into my bedroom closet and pulled out the only stashed cash I had to my name, from a pocket of a winter coat. I figured the security device that I would buy would cost less than the hundred dollars I had in my hand, and though I needed that cash to buy my children food, without a car, I would not be able to get a job and support them in the long run. I then stopped at the kitchen phone, before heading out the door for Wal-Mart. I dialed Linda and she answered. She gladly agreed to come over and help me.

I drove up to the neighborhood Wal-Mart and bought *The Club* for sixty-dollars, an expensive security device that locked up my steering wheel. My adrenalin worked overtime, and the more I thought about Seth and what he had done to his children and me, the more I despised that man.

Thirty minutes later, I securely locked *The Club* onto the steering wheel of my Volvo station wagon parked in my garage. Linda stood on a ladder inside the garage, and I stood close to her on a solid, five-gallon paint bucket; and together, we managed to get the heavy, wooden, two-car wide door back on its track.

She climbed down off the ladder and pressed the garage door opener, which was mounted nearby over the telephone, and we watched the door rise all the way up and then go all the way back down. "What would I do without you, Linda?"

"I don't know," she chuckled.

I grinned while I looked into the pretty, blue-eyed blonde's twinkling eyes. "Thank you so much for coming over here. I feel safer now knowing he can't get to my car."

Linda shook her head in disgust. "It's men like him that have made me run whenever somebody gets close to me."

"Not all men are like, Seth."

"Thank God! Where did you find that bastard?" She asked.

"I took a trip to hell and let him pick me up," I somberly replied.

She chuckled, "And from what you've told me, he's the devil, alright. Do you fear his retribution?"

"What do you mean?"

"If you did manage to stop him from winning the arbitration, he's going to be very pissed, and what if--?"

"What if what?" I challenged. "What more can he do to me?"

"He can kill you!"

I blew off her ridiculous suggestion that Seth would ever kill the mother of his two children. "Seth will probably come back home, like he always does, when he discovers he doesn't have a *half-a-mil* coming to him from his arbitration, or $10,000 coming to him from his recent car wreck, or a $400 a week base pay job anymore!"

"Oh, I'm worried for you," Linda groaned. "He will kill you!"

I smiled and echoed what I saw in my mind's eye. "I would love to be there when his lawyer tells him he doesn't have a case anymore against Prudential, and then, even better, I would love to be able to watch him over the next several days when he realizes what I've done to his entire life. I warned him. I told him I would do worse to him every time he hurt me."

"And you take pure satisfaction out of messing up his mother's life, too?" Linda cautioned.

"No," I said while feeling conflicted. "She has always resented me. Now she has a reason to war with me."

"She will be your enemy because she is not going to recoup her life savings, and she'll be out for revenge, and she's going to encourage her son to live with her and not return to you. I don't think Seth will ever come back home. You've gone too far. I think you ought to get a restraining order for your own safety."

"He's clever, Linda, but I'm staying three steps ahead of him."

"I don't know, Jean. I think he's devious--evil to the bone."

"His ex-wife said that about him, too," I confirmed.

"We're right about him. I think he totaled his Mustang with every intention of taking *your* car and moving into his apartment on the other side of town with his two sons, and all your household possessions. He knew that if he could leave you without a penny or a car, he would cripple you. He calculated that you would not be able to get a job without a car, and that the next time you two went to court, he would get the kids because he had the job--the income, and the car, and the $500,000 nest egg in the bank! And he figured the court would see that you don't have what is necessary to provide a good life for your children. Seth figured, too, the court would order you to pay him child support! And he planned all of this since last December, after he got you to drop the first divorce wherein *you* had everything given to you by the judge."

"I know you're right! The last time he got out of jail, he didn't come home. He was gone for two days after his release. He told me that he was with his mother cooling off."

"Or setting up his apartment," Linda suggested.

"He played me for a fool. I shook my head for his lack of compassion toward me. "I am a woman who gave him two children—the most beautiful gifts he has ever received in his life. Now he devises methods as to how to rob his children of their mother?"

"He's a psychopath, Jean." She nodded and patiently listened.

Seth exasperated me. "And when he finally came home from his mother's place, he needed to know if I had hired a lawyer. I lied to him and said no, but my father's friend, Jerry Hoppas, was waiting in the background. We were about to serve him with another divorce petition. I put my lawyer on hold because Seth pulled me into the bedroom and told me that *he wanted to do it right.*"

"Do it right?" Linda chuckled.

I shook my head and rolled my eyes over my own stupidity. "Exactly! I assumed that he wanted to do *our relationship* right!"

"Well, if it matters, what you did to Seth today made up for any confusion he may have had about taking advantage of your gullibility."

I smiled. "I wish I could see the look on his face when his law firm tells him, what I hope they will tell him, in the next few days!"

"You need protection," Linda advised.

"Like what?"

"Like a gun!" She answered.

"I'd like him to put me in a position so that I would have to shoot him to defend myself."

"Be careful."

"I have changed my thinking about this man. I suspect he would kill me, if given the chance, and if he could get away with it."

"No doubt! He's evil to the bone."

I bought a new door lock for this door on the side of the garage. Will you help me install the lock?"

"Of course, Jean!" She happily agreed.

12
LEVELING THE PLAYING FIELD

AUGUST 1994. I went to bed that night with my three young children sleeping in the master bedroom next to me. Seth had taken my king-size bed when he pillaged our quaint village. He had stolen every tangible valuable in our marital home and our sense of security, too, and he had warned me earlier that day, on the phone, after the kids and I came home to a gutted house, that he was coming after his sons next. I knew Daddy would climb up into the tree next to the house, and crawl onto the first-floor roof, and try to pry open an upstairs window in the middle of the night. I feared waking up and finding my two youngest children gone, and I told them so that evening. My five-year old, Harper, ordered me to not let Daddy take him after I instilled such fear. I ensured for both Harper and Doren's understanding, that I would not let Daddy *kidnap* them, a word I quickly introduced into their young lives. I explained to my concerned sons that Daddy might take them to Arizona, or to another state far away, and hide for a very long time, and that they might not ever see me again.

I recalled Seth casually mentioning to me in the past year that Runi was planning to do an archeology dig in the great Southwest. I suspected that when Daddy's boyfriend left his wife, Joyce, in Springfield, Missouri, in the near future, then Seth would meet so-called *Uncle Runi* in the desert with my two youngest children. I needed for my own protection a court order making Daddy a criminal if he violated the custody arrangement making me custodial parent; then I could at least get the FBI on my case if my children turned up missing. Seth had just as many rights to live with his kids as I did at this point, and the law school dropout knew that the court could not press kidnapping charges against him if he moved away with his two sons before we went to court and got orders.

He had lost temporary custody of his two sons, and the use of the marital home, in our first court hearing in December of 1993; and, the court ordered him to pay me $2,000 a month for six months, or until the court granted the final divorce. Now, eight months later, I regretted having ever dropped that divorce action, and losing those temporary orders made in my favor, while recalling how Seth had recently stood in front of me, in our bedroom, just after having spent a night in jail, and told me straight up *that he would get it right*.

If he executed a plan to kidnap his two children, as I suspected he might do, out of retaliation for what I did to his financial future, then I would have to spend money that I did not have, on an investigator, and on a lawyer to get custody of my children again. And, whether he took them to his apartment, on the opposite side of the city, or completely disappeared with them, such a criminal act would cost me tens of thousands, if not hundreds of thousands of dollars, and maybe even a decade, or a lifetime, without my sons.

Early in my relationship with Seth, before I knew he could not be trusted with our children, I had revealed to him *how* my first husband, Todd, had picked up Joseph and Bella for a weekend visitation, *after* we separated, and *before* we went to court in 1983. I told Seth *how* Todd had returned only baby Bella to me after his weekend visitation, and *how* Todd had refused to let me see my firstborn again until we went to court months later and got legal orders pertaining to custody. Todd had managed to take custody of our son through intimidation and trickery, while somehow understanding I hung my head low and felt what I had done reprehensible. The difference between now and then was twelve years of wisdom. I was no longer dealing with blameworthiness over having had a child outside of my marriage. My Catholic guilt, at the tender age of twenty-four, made me feel ashamed, and unworthy, to parent my first-born son to the degree that I surrendered Joseph to a drunk due to my own self-reproach. I had regretted that life-altering decision since that day when I stood in that divorce court and told that wise judge that I thought *it fair* that Todd raise Joseph and I raise Bella, after the elderly magistrate objected to me splitting up my two children. That judge had told me that he would give me legal custody of both my children, and had expressed his opinion to me that breaking up the parents was too hard on children, but to separate the siblings was an even worse act. I had too much remorse over my sin to understand anything but the stigma of what I had done. I felt too guilty. I learned in hindsight to say screw guilt when I finally could see that Todd was first unfaithful to me, when he refused to stop drinking every night during our marriage. I had never agreed to marry an alcoholic, and while I had unfaithfully wandered off one night, out of anger and disrespect for the marital dysfunction, screwing my high school crush was a natural reaction on my part for wanting something more than living with the walking dead.

  No circumstance would now come between these last two children and me. I would fight for them and leave the impression, with any onlooker, that I was a crazy bitch, who would stop at nothing to give my children an opportunity to grow up with a parent who had a heart for a loving God and for his son and our Lord, Jesus Christ. And any thought, on Seth's part, that I could be intimidated again, like that scared twenty-four year old woman, was just delusion. I weighed Seth's belief system, too, and could see that my husband bought his own press about me being fearful of him, and too uneducated, to provide a good life for my children; and until recently, he had been right to believe such hype. I had been fearful of fighting Seth in court, and more enlightening, I had been uneducated about the difference between Seth and me. His flaw in his strategy to beat me was that he considered himself god. He believed we were on the same playing field, both carnal men, with him having the advantage of having a college degree and a recent history of having earned an income. I saw differently; and unbeknown to the selfish airbag, I was now fearless because in faith, I walked with God the Father and his son Jesus Christ, and Satan could not overcome us. I would maintain custody of these two kids because God loved me. A reprobate was not raising my children! I did not care how many degrees Seth had earned in a lifetime, or how he flaunted his *intellectual superiority* in front of me and every other unsuspecting fool, this custody fight was now an official declared war between Satan and God. Let the game begin, Seth had a new lesson to learn. He could never win because he was on the wrong team. This game was about my children's well-being, and a promise I made to God to raise them in His Word.

    I spread sheets and blankets out on the bedroom carpeting for us to lie down on that night after Seth gutted our home. I propped a stack of white patio chairs under the doorknob of the master bedroom. The plastic chairs would rattle if he tried to push open the door. I plugged a phone in next to me on the floor and went to sleep beside my children feeling the heavy burden of a threat. I had to get my father's friend on board as soon as possible. I would tell Attorney Hoppas this situation was an emergency while I considered disappearing with my kids for a while, until we went to court. Bella was on summer break, and we could leave town.

    The next morning, I rose with the first crack of daylight and got up to check the damage. My children were still asleep next to me. I moved the stack of white patio chairs from under the doorknob and quietly ventured out into the heart of the house. I walked into the family room and peered at the wall of windows. I saw nothing out of place. I trotted upstairs to investigate, and saw no indication of a broken screen or pried open window. I dashed back downstairs and headed into the kitchen. I grabbed the coffee pot off the counter, next to the kitchen sink, and began to fill up the decanter with water. I glanced out the kitchen window, over the sink, while the water ran into the carafe, and saw the garage door raised up, and my car missing. He had broken into the locked garage and somehow had removed the sixty-dollar security device I had placed on the steering wheel.

    I turned off the water and exited out the glass kitchen door. I walked out under the catwalk and went into the open side door of the detached garage—he had managed to open all the doors. There was no indication of the thief ever having been there in the middle of the night--his escape with our only car was clean. I walked out of the empty two-car garage, and then around to the back of the house, while looking up at the tall tree that grew next to the wall of windows. I had laid ten heavy planks across two limbs with the intention of buying nails someday in the near future and securing the deck onto those two v-shaped limbs. The floor of what was to be a tree house with walls one day was missing. I looked down to see the boards strewn on the ground. I chuckled at my vision of Seth falling to the ground in the middle of the night--the drop was at least twenty feet. Obviously, as I suspected, Seth had planned to kidnap the kids last night just before he drove away in my Volvo station wagon, but he never made it to their bedroom window. I hoped he had broken a leg.

  I grabbed my keys from inside the house and walked down to the mailboxes at the mouth of the cul-de-sac, unlocked my box, and grabbed yesterday's mail. I flipped through the envelopes and flyers while I walked back toward my home and opened something from *Emergency Physician Statement*. I pulled out a two-page document. He owed $256.00 for services rendered. The second page was a copy of a *Health Insurance Claim Form* that he had filled out in the emergency room, only a few days earlier, when he totaled his black Mustang. I studied the form and in the *Patient Status* box, wherein the hospital asked Seth to indicate whether he was *Single*, *Married*, or *Other*, Seth checked *Other*. His answer confirmed, again, that he had planned this separation way in advance of when he actually left. He moved out of our marital home the day before, the day after he totaled his Mustang. I saw another lie on the *Health Insurance Claim Form* where he indicated he had a *Group Health Plan*. We had never had medical insurance a single day in our six years together, but this lie, he told the emergency room, supported why he called me that night from the hospital and asked me for our policy number. I suspected he intended to show this insurance claim form to the judge in our next court hearing and appear as if he was a responsible, but estranged husband, who carried health insurance on his family. Seth would consistently lie, and no one would be able to separate the truth from the fiction. I really believed Seth purposely wrecked his Mustang the day before he moved out of our home, so that I would have no car, and, because I had no car, I would not be able to get a job, after he left me without a dime in the bank. I felt instant outrage. I firmly believed he purposely caused another driver to slam into the back of his car, so that he could sue for bodily injury--the icing on the cake, and a minor award, in the range of $10,000 minimum, for disabling me, and losing his beloved hot rod. His personal injury suit would settle in two or three months, and by then, he would have the $10,000 from his car wreck, and the $500,000 or more from his arbitration settlement, when his measly $400 weekly base pay stopped after his three-month probationary period at Grandville Pike's office. If everything went his way, he would pay his mother back her $85,000, stick $400,000 into a savings account, and have a court order in place requiring me to pay him child support for the next fifteen years.

I could see clearly how his wicked mind worked: He intentionally wrecked his prized possession, his muscle car, just after he landed a sales position with Grandville Pike. He knew that when he totaled his sports car, that he would not be personally inconvenienced. He would drive my car, and I'd be stuck at home with children. He totaled his Mustang *two days* before his arbitration with the New York City stockbroker. His high-powered Houston law firm told him that he had a strong case and would settle outside of court for no less than $500,000. He played me like a chess game. He wrecked his car with the intention that the children and I would take him to work the very next day. He knew that we would drop him off at his office, and that we would spend several hours that morning, eating breakfast and shopping for shoes, long enough for him to immediately return to our home in The Woodlands and heist all the fine furnishings, electronics, and art work. He looted our valuables yesterday, and moved into an apartment on the opposite side of the city, an apartment he had reserved months earlier with a $900 deposit and an August move-in date. He moved out of our marital home, one day before the arbitration, so that he would not have to share his award money with me. I would not have the details of how much he won, if he left before I could ask. He looted my home, the day before his arbitration, and then arrogantly called me minutes after the kids and I discovered his devastation, to threaten me. He told me, in that telephone call, that he had a half mil coming his way, and when he got his arbitration settlement, he would fight me for custody. He informed me that I would lose custody of my children because I was too broke to fight him, and I could not support my children because I had no car, job, or money. Seth even alienated me from my good attorney, who had managed to win me temporary custody of my children, temporary possession of the marital home, and monthly maintenance for the interim of our last divorce action. Seth had told me, months earlier, that his June commission check was his last check, when in reality, he had collected money in July, and in August, too. He spent our grocery money on an apartment deposit. He executed all the strategies needed to put me in a position to lose. He planned all these devices to ruin me since the day I dropped our first divorce action, just after our December ski trip--and this time, eight months later, *he did do it right*. And when we went to court, in the near future, he would be able to say, that I had no ability to care for our children. I had no car, no job, no money, or college education. He would further emphasize to the court that I was not capable of earning a substantial income and giving our children the lifestyle he could afford them. He challenged me when he had asked in the past, "And what makes you think a court would give you custody of the kids, if you left me? Without me, you don't have any economically viable opportunities!" I had to agree with him; I did not have any economically viable opportunities. I had been a stay-at-home mom for years, and I was not a *viable commodity* in the work place! He would tell the court that I was not in the children's best interest! I considered that I had given Seth another chance, after the ski trip, to prove himself a good father and husband because I believed God wanted me to forgive him one time. I had heard God's voice and obeyed. I did not have a job, money, or a car, but I had something greater. I had peace of mind, that in the end, my Heavenly Father would have the final say.

    I hurried up the long driveway and headed straight for his rat's nest in the corner of the garage again. I pulled off the top envelope with a recent postmark, which I knew already contained in his own writing, instruction to his employer as to where to send his last payroll check. I re-read his message:

August 6, 1994,

Attention Beth McKinney, Payroll.

Dear Beth:

Thank you so much for your kind attention and assistance during my personal crisis. My new residence is 16200 El Camino Real, Apt. A, Houston, Texas 77062, and my office is 1513 Green Emerald Plaza, Suite 9060, Houston, Texas. Please send my last commission checks to my apartment; this is my new home address.

"You're going to have a *personal crisis* when I get finished with you!" I opened the thick, Houston *Yellow Pages,* that lay on top of our sons' former nursery chest-of-drawers, that sat right next to Seth's three-foot tall rat's nest, and turned to *Wrecker Service.* "I'm going to wreck your life alright!" I angrily mumbled to myself. "Let's turn the table on you *one more time.* How many times will you have to go around this mountain, Seth? You are *not* going to win this war, Satan!" I mumbled to myself while I dialed the wrecker service number on the nearby wall phone. I listened to the rings while I studied the biggest picture ad on the page and wondered how I would retrieve my car without any money. "Roy's Wrecker," the male voice answered.

"I want you to go pick up my green Volvo station wagon from my husband's apartment at 16200 El Camino Real, Apt. A, Houston, Texas 77062, or you might find his car at his office at 1513 Green Emerald Plaza, Suite 9060, Houston, Texas." *I figured he would drive to his office at least one more time.*

"Do you own the car?"

"I am the rightful owner."

"Is your name on the title?"

"Texas is a community property state, right?"

"Yeah," he dragged, "but I don't want to be arrested for car theft."

"You won't. My name is solely on the title." I lied. "My husband stole my car out of my garage last night. He wrecked his car two days ago, and then came after my car. I have three children here to care for and no car! Isn't he precious?"

"So it's your turn now, huh?" A gruff voice asked.

"How much will this last laugh cost me?"

"$65 for the first 10 miles we drive to pick up your car, and $2.50 for each additional mile to bring it back here."

"Where's here?" I asked, but then interrupted, "No, never mind! Don't tell me where my car will be stored. I want you to keep the car in storage. If you bring it back here to my home, he'll steal it again. I want him to pay out the ass to drive my car."

"Our storage fees are on a per day basis."

"Good!" I replied. "How much to store the car? $100 a day? $50?"

"Something like that," he answered.

"I want you to store the car for me until I know how the judge rules, and who gets this car. If the judge rules I get to keep my car, then give me a break--don't charge me anything, but towing. However, if the court awards Seth my car, in the next hearing, rack up daily storage fees, and pad the towing charges. If I can't have the car, then neither can he!"

The repo man chuckled. "I take he's really pissed you off?"

"Let me put it this way. I wouldn't cry, if he conveniently died."

"When will the judge rule on who gets the car?"

"I don't know, yet--could be a month, or longer, before we go to court again."

"Okay. Do you know when your husband will be at that address you gave me?"

"Not really. I assume he has already taken off this morning for arbitration, and if I'm right, then he will be in a hearing until late this evening. If the arbitrator settles in his favor today, you should know he is very wealthy. Charge him hefty storage fees. I guess you might find my car at his apartment after the sun goes down."

"Yes ma'am, we'll get your car back."

"Keep it safe for me; it might be two or three weeks before I get it back from you. It all depends on when I go to court and on what the judge rules, and if I lose possession of the car, and if Seth cannot pay you to get it out of storage, then you can have the car in lieu of services rendered, right? I have copy of clear title."

"Yes ma'am. We'll need you to fax a copy of the car title, and I need a letter from you with your signature giving us instruction to pick up your car."

"No problem, give me your fax number." I had nothing to lose by telling the repo man that my husband's name was not on the title. He would exercise his own judgment when he got a fax of my car title and saw differently. I prayed he had compassion for me.

I hung up and smiled. Payback felt good. I believed I had a duty to give Seth a taste of his own medicine and to stop him at every juncture. I picked up the mail I had sat down on my children's old chest of drawers, flipped through the stack of unopened mail again, and saw correspondence from the *Montgomery County Sheriff's Department* addressed to me. I suspected this correspondence related to Seth's most recent arrest in the driveway, the night I assaulted the telephone on general principle while he was on the phone with his boyfriend.

I pulled out a copy of a complaint Seth filed dated 8/1/1994, an *Offense Report*. Seth had filed a counter-complaint regarding that night:

COMPLAINANT, SETH ZHERNEBOH ADVISED THAT ON 08-01-94 AT APPROXIMATELY 00:39 hours he was on the telephone with a friend, when his wife got verbally irate with him because he was on the phone. She then walked up to him, grabbed his hair and forcefully pulled Mr. Zherneboh's head down toward his feet and struck him in the face with a closed fist three times. His wife then began telling him to leave or she would call the police, so he dialed 911. Upon arrival of police, Mr. Zherneboh was arrested for family violence. At 12:00 hours on the following day, Mr. Zherneboh states that upon entering the marital home, suspect [wife] told him to leave and he said he would as soon as he gets a few items. She threatened to call the police. Mr. Zherneboh then got on the phone to call his attorney for advice, and in the process, suspect struck him, open handed, approximately four times to the head area. Mr. Zherneboh states he then fell to his knees and she kicked him until he felt pain.

Another lie! I disconnected his phone call that night, after becoming incensed by the conversation he had with his boyfriend, right in front of me; and when I went after the receiver, he slammed me into the wall. I hit the tool rack, face first, and busted my lip, and our fight spun out of control from there. He now made himself out to be the victim of domestic violence in this relationship. Seth manufactured more evidence to enter into our next court hearing, in order to defend his character, while he knew that my lawyer would inform the court that Seth faced *Assault A* charges on a previous assault.

    I asked the detective, on the previous assault case, when Seth attacked me, one early morning, when I got up to study for my economics final, if I could drop the charges. The detective told me that the District Attorney's Office would investigate the case, and then make the determination over whether to prosecute Seth, or drop the charges. I had no more say in the matter. The detective explained, "The DA will appear against the accused in a court of law, but first, they gather and analyze evidence to see if there is a case. The court understands that the abusive spouse often threatens the victim with more abuse, if she does not drop the charges against him. Most likely," the detective continued, "Seth will be ordered to take an Anger Management class and get required counseling."

    "Great!" I retorted. "What's a class going to teach him? Seth needs years of counseling!"

    I put the memory of that phone conversation behind me. I held the *Offense Report* at my side and considered the ramification of Seth's charges against me. He was being true to form--a consistent liar. He was out to confuse the District Attorney's office, just as he confused the judge on the bench in our last divorce hearing. As he had promised me--whatever I did to him, he would do to me, and whatever I charged him with, he would charge me with the same. All of his energy went into devising pretense for an unsuspecting court that would not be able see the forest for the trees, or, in other words, the court would be overly concerned with detail while not understanding the whole situation. The court would focus too much on specific problems and miss the point. Had Seth learned these calculating and manipulative measures in three weeks of law school? My lawyer would have to be able to explain the relevant parts without

Seth catching him up in his psychological game. I feared Seth's intelligence.

George had called the house again that evening, pretending to be looking for Seth when I answered. I assumed Seth had called George, his buddy in Connecticut, after Seth had moved out of our marital home and into his new apartment on the other side of town. I did not trust George because I knew Seth was working every angle, and George was not a detail Seth would ignore. George had access to my mind and its ever evolving considerations. Seth knew that in the past year George and I had talked for hours in his absence. Now, I assumed Seth maintained steady contact with George since the ski trip we all took together to Steamboat, Colorado.

"I'm going to hide out until I get to court," I said to George. "Don't tell Seth where I'm going."

"I don't know where you're going, Jean."

"I'm going to a place Seth has never been to."

"Where's that?" George asked.

"Where there are no modern day conveniences," I answered. "It's better you don't know; then you don't have to lie to Seth."

"I don't need to know."

"I might or might not go there, not certain yet." I was thinking about my grandmother's home two hours away in the Texas Hill Country. She had been in a convalescent home for years, and her home sat empty in a small German town. "My friend, Linda, says I need to buy a gun."

"I have a bow and arrow," George offered. "It's quieter."

"Do you have a horse, too?" I asked him.

He laughed. "Do you need a gun?"

"I do," I tittered. "I'm having the most fun with Seth that I've had in years."

"You are?" He asked as if confused.

"No, not really, but I'm getting more and more fierce, George."

"I like your fighting spirit, Jean."

"I'm fighting for my kids," I answered.

"Seth doesn't deserve you."

"Oh yeah, he does," I argued.

George chuckled. "Seth calls me, but he doesn't ask me if I am talking to you. I think he suspects we are talking."

"He knows we're talking!" I spouted while certain Seth had seen the chemistry between George and me on the ski trip. "He is so pompous--so arrogant."

"I hope everything goes as you expect, Jean."

"Me, too," I groaned. "Me, too."

"When will you know about the arbitration?" George asked.

"You mean, when will I know he has crashed and burned?"

"Yes."

"When a bullet speeds past my head," I said with some seriousness.

"So you think he will miss?"

"He's not that stupid. He wouldn't resort to killing me."

"I don't know, Jean. What you've done is pretty impressive."

"Isn't it?" I tittered while taking great satisfaction over the work I had done over the last two days. "You know, it's a sad state of affairs I have to operate at this level to be impressive."

"He has no clue as to what he has started with you," George solemnly admitted.

"Seth will see what he walked away from a day too late. Seth is stupid; he hasn't figured out that he can't screw with me. I know too much about him."

George chuckled.

"For starters, Seth sits down to pee. He pees like a girl."

George laughed again. "There's never a dull moment with you, Jean."

"I'm just warming up." I clarified. "Haven't you heard, George? According to Seth, my conversation is good for the length of one drink at a bar."

"I didn't know that," he affirmed.

"Ask Seth about that, the next time he calls you. Seth buys his own press about me, but that works in my advantage. He doesn't expect what he's got coming. This is now *The War of the Roses*." I referred to the 1989 movie starring Michael Douglas and Kathleen Turner.

"You know they die at the end of that black comedy," George reminded.

"That's a grim thought." I stood in the kitchen talking to George on the telephone/fax machine, with the sprung top that sat on the built-in dining buffet, right next to the glass kitchen door. I stepped toward the family room to see what my quiet sons were doing and felt the restraint of my short cord. I peered into the family room from the kitchen and saw Harper and Doren sitting at a small child's coloring table. Harper was cutting from a hot rod magazine with a pair of child scissors and Doren was scribbling. Doren suddenly threw down his crayon and reached for Harper's cutting device. Harper flung his scissors away from Doren's grasping hand, and the scissors struck his younger brother's face. I heard Doren instantly cry out and reach for his lip. My injured child turned to face me with blood running down his chin, with his arms stretched out for me.

"I have an emergency, gotta go, George." I hung up the phone without his response and raced to my bloody child. I squatted down next to the crying three-year old and saw he had a wide gash on his top lip.

Calmly, I informed, "That's a deep cut, Doren. Harper didn't mean to hurt you; it was an accident." I looked over at my five-year old. "Right, Harper?"

Harper appeared upset and nodded while Doren's tears simmered.

"I'm going to take you to the doctor; you need stitches," I said while I picked up my youngest to carry him to the kitchen sink where I could wash away the blood.

"What are stitches?" Harper asked while he followed Doren and me into the adjacent room for water and a clean paper towel.

"The doctor will band aide his skin together so he will heal without a big scar."

"Oh," he said. "I'm sorry, Doren."

Doren whimpered while he viewed the blood on his fingers, "My lip bleed."

"It's bleeding, Doren, but it will stop soon." I suddenly remembered I did not have a car and panicked while I wondered who would be home in the middle of the day. I grabbed my purse and keys while I held Doren in my arms and Harper followed us out the front door. We went to Marilyn's house next door, and fortunately, she answered when I knocked on the kitchen door. "Can you take me to the emergency room? His lip needs stitches."

"Of course," she said with great empathy and grabbed her keys and purse.

Hours later, after Doren was stitched up, we drove back home. Marilyn came over to my house so she and I could talk outside young ears. Doren slept off his anesthesia on the old couch in the family room, and Harper had fallen asleep on the other end of that same couch. I sat in the adjacent room at the kitchen table drinking tea with my cherished neighbor and advisor. I explained to her what Seth had done to me in recent days and began to cry.

"Look around, Jean--he's not here. He's not here for you because he doesn't care about you, or his kids. Why shed tears over him?"

"What am I going to do? I fear losing my babies to that liar."

"You're not going to lose them. I'll testify for you and tell them you're a good mother. I've also watched Seth out there in the yard for years—I know him, too."

"Thank you."

"You've got to get another lawyer and go to court again. The sooner you end this nightmare, the better off you and your children will be. You've got to have a car and money, Jean."

"I know," I sobbed.

"Call your father; he had agreed to pay for your next lawyer. Tell him it's time now to move forward with a divorce action."

"I will," I answered.

"Your freedom starts when you stop denying the issues that truly exist. You are not going to change Seth, and until he realizes he lost everything that mattered—you and his kids, he will never change."

"I'm scared."

"That's okay. Your first lesson is to be courageous in the midst of your fears. You and your children are entitled to have peace."

Hours after the emergency room, and after Marilyn went home, I called my best girlfriend, Charley, and asked her if she would be my witness the next time I took Seth to divorce court. I calculated Marilyn and Charley would be credible witnesses. Charley did not hesitate to help me. I told her how devious Seth had been of recent days, and how he had left me without a car, and before that evening's sunset, Charley drove up into my driveway with a car for my temporary use.

We stood in the driveway next to her black ten-year old Chrysler. "Walter bought me a convertible recently; he didn't want me driving this car anymore because it was gift from my last boyfriend. I was going to give this car to my youngest son, but Ken left town in a huff on a bus."

"I am so grateful. Thank you, Charley. You're a lucky woman to have so many men who truly care about you."

"I am grateful, and I want to pay my good fortune forward. Take this car for a while. I want it back at a later date. My youngest will come back to Houston broke in the near future, and by then, maybe you'll have a car again. I'll have to give my son this car so he can get a job and pay rent, if he wants to live at home."

"I understand," I nodded while I heard the phone ringing inside the garage. "And speaking of nice men--this caller might be George. I abruptly hung up on him earlier today, when I had to race off to the emergency room. I have really grown fond of this Yankee," I said to Charley while I walked up to the phone on the garage wall. "Hello," I answered with a smile on my face.

"You fucking, bitch!" Seth angrily roared. "You have cost me everything!"

I continued to smile and sweetly poured out, "Hi, Seth. How are you?" I knew in that exact moment he had lost his arbitration, and I felt ecstatic. I did not say another word, but let him continue to rage.

"How the fuck am I suppose to pay Ma back?" He yelled.

"What are you talking about, Seth?" I played dumb while maintaining a caring sound.

"You know exactly what I'm talking about, bitch! I showed up for my arbitration this morning, and my lawyer said I didn't have a case. I was stunned and asked why not, and he said *because her name is Jean Wynn.*"

"What?" I toyed.

"Don't *what* me, bitch! And how do you expect me to go to work tomorrow when I don't have a car?"

I was surprised to hear the wrecker service had already nabbed my car. "Where is *my* car?" I asked. Apparently, he had returned to his apartment, earlier than I had expected he would that day, because the lawyers cancelled his arbitration that morning.

"I suspect the Volvo is sitting in your garage!"

I would not confirm whether my car was in the garage or not. He would have to drive thirty-five miles across Houston to see for himself that he could not steal my car twice. "I'm sorry for your misfortune, Seth." I remained cool while thrilled I had put him out of commission. "I guess I don't have to worry about you having all the money in the world to fight me for custody of my babies now. Maybe *character* will be all that matters when we go to court this time?"

"Fuck you!" He yelled. "Those are my children, too."

"No," I sweetly replied as if talking to a kindergartner, "Fuck *you*. I have to go now. Charley is standing here in my driveway. Her boyfriend just bought her a new car, and she gave me her old car. I hope you can find your car, Seth. Have a good evening now."

"Wait, Jean, I--"

I hung up on him with no interest in hearing anything else he had to say. We were ready to go to court now. I let out a shrill of great delight while I danced around the garage as if I just won the lottery! "Oh, thank you, God!" I yelled to the heavens. I turned to Charley in glee, "Seth did not have arbitration today. His lawyer told him, when he showed up for arbitration this morning, that he no longer had a case because of a woman named Jean Wynn! I beat that snake!"

Charley smiled. "I'm so happy for you, and relieved, too."

"Seth asked me how I expected him to go to work without a car." I shook my head over his audacity. "Why does he think I care?"

"He's completely insane right now."

"I will assume he hasn't talked to his employer yet, because he still believes he has a job."

"Oh, that's right; you updated his boss on his true character. I bet he will get fired in the morning."

"I bet he will, too, Charley, but most likely, he won't tell me if he gets fired."

"He won't give you the satisfaction," Charley added.

"No, he won't, and he'll go to court and pretend he still has a job, even if he doesn't."

"Probably, he lies about everything," My friend confirmed.

THE FOLLOWING DAY, my father sat at the end of my kitchen table with his grandkids playing around his legs and showing Grandpa how fast their cars could scream across the kitchen floor. Dad had his checkbook out and was paying a stack of my utility bills, while I put the groceries away he brought through the front door out of his car.

"Thank you, Dad, for everything. I don't know what I'd do without you," I said as I put a gallon of milk into my black side-by-side.

"I paid Jerry Hoppas yesterday, too."

"Thank you, again. I talked to your friend this morning. I told Jerry I needed a protective order to keep Seth in his place. I think Seth wants to get hold of these kids before we go to court. I don't know what I'll do if Jerry can't get a hearing set on the docket before school starts in a few weeks. I fear Seth will nab Harper out of kindergarten."

The sixty-one year old appeared worried. "Jerry will schedule you a hearing soon. He's aware of the urgency."

"That's what he told me, too," I said while not sure if my dad's oldest friend took me seriously, when I told him of the danger that lurked, as long as the court did not place Seth under orders.

My father continued, "I think you ought to sell this house before you get caught up in a lengthy divorce action," he suggested. "Jerry thinks so, too."

"I'm ready to sell this house. I can't depend on Seth anymore, and I need some money in the bank. I need a car."

"You have one now," he said.

"Charley loaned me that car; she has plans to give it to her son when he comes back home broke."

He nodded while getting more of my grim reality.

"Will you buy me a car, Dad? It doesn't have to be new. I'll pay you back in monthly installments, as if you're the bank."

He chuckled. "But you don't work."

"I'll get a job when I get a car."

"Hopefully the court will award you the Volvo."

"And if Seth gets my car?"

"Sell the house, Jean Ellen, and then buy yourself a car, and put the car in your brother's name so Seth won't steal it."

"That's a smart idea," I answered while doubting Seth would agree to sell our home.

"Seth is broke now," my father continued, "and I'm certain he'll agree to sell this house right away. A long and drawn out court battle could last for years, if you're fighting over this property and the kids. Seth might not fight you, if there is no equity to take. Split the equity with him."

"Maybe he'll agree to sell our home; maybe he won't." I shrugged in disgust. "Either way, I'm taking him to court. I'm not certain he wants to split the proceeds from the sale of this house with me."

My father looked at me in question.

I continued, "Seth owes his *ma* $85,000, and he doesn't have a dime to his name now. As you know, I blew up his arbitration after he threatened to take my children away from me. He also attempted to sue *State Farm* for bodily injury, but I called the insurance company and told them he wasn't hurt in that car wreck, and that I'd testify on their behalf that my husband is a fraud. And I suspect his boss fired him, too. Seth is broke now, and he doesn't have any way to pay his mother back her life savings. *If* Seth gets sole custody of our children, then the court will most likely award him this house, too—that's how he sees it. And *if* the court gives Seth our marital home, then he can sell this house later when its market value doubles, and then pay back his mother her $85,000, or he can take out a second lien against the current $125,000 equity--an equity that will double in ten years. I firmly believe his mother supports him divorcing me and getting the kids, especially now that I've ruined her financially. If he doesn't divorce me, then he won't be able to pay her back. He plans to move his mother into this house, and if he doesn't sell the house right away, which he won't, then Seth will work, and she'll be the live-in granny who babysits, cooks, and cleans, until he does sell the house and pays her back. Seth can live with his conscience again, if his plan goes as he desires. However, *if* he and I sell the house before we divorce and split the proceeds 50/50, then he won't have more than $50,000 at the very most, and he owes his ma $85,000—so there won't be anything left for him."

My father shook his head is disappointment, "Gosh, he's greedy—that apparel business was your business started with Leonardo."

"Yes it was, but Seth wants everything. He and I can sell this house for at least what we paid for it three years ago, or for a bit more. *If* Seth is awarded this house and holds on to this house for ten years, then, most likely, this house will appreciate, maybe even double in value."

My father internalized what I had been looking at since Seth's New York broker made that margin call. "I believe Seth will agree to sell the house with you, because the last time you two went to court, you were awarded the house and the kids. He knows he can't win."

"Does he?" I asked while doubting Seth could see past his own arrogance.

"I'm going to give you some cash, and you can go to the grocery store and to the post office and mail these utility payments. I paid all your bills in full for this month. I'll stay here with my grandkids." The German stoic had no use for frills. He made his point and moved on to another topic. Once he had the bottom line, the accountant had no use for excessive data--end of discussion.

"Thank you, Dad." I said while I took the stack of bills from the man with silver hair.

"I'm glad I can help." He shot me a crooked toothy grin.

"I wish Mom could have come over with you today. I miss her."

"She started to come with me, but decided she wasn't up to it. I'm taking her to her doctor tomorrow."

"How is she doing?"

"Not well," he sadly replied. "She suffers from a lot of pain."

"How are you holding up?" His news about my mother's failing health hit me hard; and I became aware I was not emotionally available for Mom because Seth trapped me in his constant chaos.

"I never dreamed when I retired my life would be this hard. Between your mother, and you, and Holly, and all this divorce stuff between you girls--" he stopped and shook his head in disappointment, "Well, I envisioned these years differently."

"I'm sorry." I felt guilty.

"Holly is not working. She can't hold a job anymore. I guess her divorce affected her work. She's missed the mortgage payments. She calls me up crying and tells me that Don won't send her and the kids any money. The bank is about to foreclose on her. I might have to go buy her house off the auction block. If I don't, my grandkids might be on the street."

"Both Seth and Don are sorry excuses for men. I'm sorry I'm part of your stress. Everything could have been done differently, Dad!" I spewed. "Seth and I could have given our children a happy home life, and a sense of security, but, instead, the children and I now discuss issues like *parental kidnapping*. Seth and I could have finished our remodeling project instead of shelling out thousands of dollars on two attorneys and contemplating the sale of our beautiful home. We can't even pay this year's taxes because all our money has gone to these lawyers. My kids and I could have been enjoying my mother's last years here on earth, and had more time to spend with her while she can still get up out of bed and go to lunch with us; but, instead, I find myself spending emotional energy to care for three children without a car or money. Seth could have finished his law degree! I could be finishing my bachelor's degree these years; instead, Seth ensnares me in his idiotic and non-productive chaos. The kids and I could have enjoyed the half-a-mil award settlement *with Seth*, but instead, I had to destroy his settlement opportunity in order to secure my children in my life. His mother could have had her life savings restored! Why didn't Seth want to bring love and peace into his family, instead of giving his wife and children all this heavy, debilitating crap?"

"Greed is Seth's sole focus, and his having the understanding of Christ darkened, is a result of him being alienated from the life of God. He has chosen to give himself over to lasciviousness, and to work all uncleanness with greediness." He stopped and pulled out of his memory, "Ephesians 4:18."

I nodded. "Seth originally felt torn between me and his children, and the man he truly loves--Runi."

"Seth loves no one!" My father spewed.

"—No one, not even himself!" I reminded myself. "But now, his ma is part of this tangled web he weaved when he practiced to deceive. He cannot find peace in leaving the old woman alone *and* broke, and the children and I come after his mother, and we now pay the price for *my lack of knowing* what was right and wrong from the very beginning."

"We're all paying the price. It's dangerous to allow your feelings to govern your life, Jean Ellen. Choose, instead, the Word of God to govern your life, and stay sober because a sober mind will transform you to choose God and not the ways of the flesh. All this stuff--your divorce, Holly's divorce, and your mother's illness is a test for me, too. I didn't believe I'd have this kind of challenge when I was this age; and yet, if I elect to feel all of this is *a burden*, then I separate myself from God and my burden is too heavy."

"Walk in faith that God loves you," I said as a reminder to myself. "God hears your prayers, and God promises he will answer."

"Yep," he smiled.

"All these years I called you *a stoic* as if that way of being was a bad thing. I see differently now; you don't seem to let your emotions run you. In contrast, I realize Seth never loved me, or apparently, loved what God gave him--his wife, children, a family, a home. He has no relationship with God. Seth feels he creates everything in his life, and in some ways, he does. He's created all this sadness." My anger dissipated and I took a long breath. "I'm w-a-y overdue to find someone who can love me!" George flashed to the forefront of my mind. "I've had too many years of Seth's chaos."

"God loves you, Jean. You'll be better off without *Seth*. What kind of man is he?!!!" My father angrily asked.

"A man with no love to give. A man of God loves his wife if he loves his kids."

"Seth is no example of what a Godly man is! Seth has a lot of nerve while he plunders you and his children's lives. He has no boundaries. Respecting boundaries doesn't complicate life--boundaries simplify life."

I asked my father to stay overnight and he agreed to stay, because my brother Henry, my parents' third child, and the confirmed bachelor in the family, still lived at home and would be there for Mom.

I needed Dad to stay with my three children for a few hours this evening while I hunted for a man with a job offer. I drove my car to Chase's Night Club after sunset. I had not been to the local watering hole since Sabrina and I were last there--the same night she slept with Seth. I pulled into the parking lot in front of the club's front door on this Friday night. The music blared into the parking lot, and upon my entrance, I saw hundreds of people crammed into a medium-size room. I scanned the well-dressed crowd for an out-of-shape man nearing forty, with thick blonde hair, green eyes, and shaggy brows. I meandered around the room and spotted the tall and heavy-set man, as I suspected I would--he practically lived in the place. Jay spotted me from the couch where he sat and instantly leaped up with a grin and headed toward me.

I stood with open arms and hugged him. "Welcome, Jay Stephens!"

"Jean Wynn! Where have you been?"

"Vietnam."

He looked confused.

"It doesn't matter--" I chuckled while waving off my lame joke and continued to enlighten him. "I'm back. There's a temporary cease-fire. I came in here tonight specifically looking for you."

"My lucky night."

"No, it's my lucky night that I found you. My husband is gone, and I need a job."

"It is your lucky night and mine! I'm thrilled your husband is gone! But curious, how are you handling his departure?"

"Not as well as I would like. I need to make some money and buy a car; and then, my world will be almost perfect."

"Good attitude! I still have Weekday Magazine, but you need a car to do the sales job."

"I have a car for now. Give me the job and come over tomorrow night for dinner. I want to talk to you about some ideas I have for your TV show."

"I would love to come over, Jean."

"Perfect. We'll talk tomorrow night; I can't stay tonight. My daddy is watching my kids."

"I'll be over about 7:00 p.m.?"

"Perfect!"

"Give me your number, Jean."

The following morning, I cooked my father breakfast and made him coffee. My brother, Henry, had plans on this Saturday, and my father had to return home as soon as possible. I was loading up the dishwasher with breakfast dishes just after he departed when I heard the doorbell. I walked to the front room and peered out the window—Pete, Seth's best friend, and former owner of the Talent House, stood on my front porch with a smile. I smiled back, but my guard went up instantly.

I swung the door open. "What are you doing here, friend?"

"Checking on you, Jean. Are you alright?"

"I'm okay--my father just left."

"Do you have company?" He asked while pointing to the unfamiliar car in the driveway that Charley loaned me.

"No, that's my car."

"Can I come in?"

"Certainly." I stepped out of the threshold and walked toward the kitchen. "How about a cup of coffee?"

"I would love a mug," he said as he followed me through the sitting room and into the gourmet kitchen.

"Seth moved in with me," he stated without any emotion.

I was startled by the revelation and confused because I knew the wrecker service had confiscated my Volvo from his Clear Lake City apartment on the other side of Houston. "Why is he living with you?"

"He needs a place to stay until he can get financially ahead."

"Oh," I quipped while feeling uncomfortable that Seth was now living within walking distance from me. I suspected that without a car, job, or half-a-mil, Seth couldn't fulfill his Clear Lake City lease and moved out just after he moved in. "Where's all his furniture?"

"I think he put his stuff in his sister's garage."

I considered my word processor and novel was being stored at Demelza's house in League City, Texas, fifty-five miles away from my home. "What's he driving?"

"He isn't driving anything--that's partly why he's living with me. I'm driving him when he needs to go somewhere."

Pete had bought a smaller one-story home in The Woodlands shortly after Seth and I had purchased our two-story in October 1991. Seth would be conveniently close now to commit his crimes on me. "He took my car, Pete! He doesn't have any concerns about how I feed my children without money, or how I could get a job without a car."

"I'm worried about you, Jean. I told Seth that you were my friend. He wants me to go to court and testify against you. I won't do it."

"What lies does he want you to tell the court about me? That I demanded that you guys not do your drugs in my home. That I'm the irresponsible parent?"

"I told Seth you were a good mother. I'm not taking sides here."

"Thank you, Pete," I said while I tried to calm down.

"You need to watch your back, Jean."

"You told me that before, what do you mean?"

"I mean, don't jump out of an airplane with a parachute, and don't go snorkeling. You know what I mean."

"No, I don't! Elaborate!"

"He's pissed that you financially ruined him."

"Oh, boo hoo," I retorted. "He's abandoned me and his children. He doesn't care whether we eat or die! Doren had an accident the other day, and I had to race him to the emergency room, but I didn't have money or a car. I had to knock on the neighbor's door, Pete! And thank God she was home!"

"I don't agree with anything he has done. He's gone off the deep end, Jean."

"I won't lie down! If Seth wants to take me on, then I will put him under."

"This war is getting out of hand, Jean."

"He's not taking my kids away from me!"

"He thinks because you haven't worked in years that you won't win custody of your children. He will argue that he's the better provider."

"Oh right!" I challenged. "I bet he doesn't have a job?"

Pete did not answer.

"You're protecting Seth."

"He asked me to not give you any details about his life."

"I know he has no job! Seth underestimates me. I have a friend who is a TV producer, and he wants me to work for him."

"Oh yeah? What does he produce?"

"He has a weekly TV show, and he features local Houston businesses in ten-minute segments. I will find the business and sell them on the idea of being featured on his TV show."

"Very cool," he nodded as if considering the idea for himself.

"What are you doing these days for money?"

"I'm not working," he answered. "Might sell the house, and go back to Italy."

"Did the DEA put Chad away?"

"They tried, but Chad's daddy seemed to have some pull with the judge and enough money to keep his son out of prison. Chad's a lucky son-ov'a-bitch. He got probation and community service."

"That's it?"

"That's it," Pete confirmed. "I lost my business, but I'm not implicated since Chad squeezed out of his jam."

"Will the IRS take the chains off your business?"

"Nope, not unless I pay off back taxes. I think I'm done there."

"Are you able to make your mortgage?"

"Not this month. I thought Seth might help me, but he's broke, too. In addition, Karen is threatening to leave. She grew unhappy with me after the IRS chained up the front doors of my business. She's about to walk out."

"I'm surprised she's still around," I added while reserving my feelings about the gold digger.

"Me, too," he nodded. "My mother is still living in Italy with her husband. I could help them run their construction company. I'm not sure what I'm doing yet. I have my daughter here to think about, too."

"I don't blame you if you leave. I'll miss you."

"I'll miss you, too, Jean. You're a good friend."

AUGUST 1994. THE SECOND DIVORCE ACTION AND THE FIRST HEARING FOR TEMPORARY ORDERS. My next-door neighbor, Marilyn, agreed to be my witness, as well as did my best friend, Charley. The girls would meet me at the courthouse this morning. My brother, Henry, drove over to my home to watch my two youngest children while I was in court for what I expected to be all day. Uncle Henry would ensure that Harper got on the kindergarten bus that day, too. Bella skipped school, this time, and drove with me over to the courthouse. I hoped the judge would take my eleven-year-old daughter into his chambers and ask her questions about her mother and stepfather. My lawyer had agreed with me that Bella would make a good witness, but felt the judge might object to a child her age being involved at all.

My daughter and I drove toward the familiar court, the 9th Judicial District Court of Montgomery County in Conroe, Texas, just a few miles north of The Woodlands in the car Charley had loaned me. Bella and I both had hopes of getting temporary orders and beginning what would be the end of my horrid marriage to Seth. And this time, instead of meeting Attorney John Pettit, my first attorney, in the hallway, I met my father's oldest friend, Attorney Jerry Hoppas, in the back of the courtroom. We shook hands and stepped out into the hallway. Bella sat nearby and listened while we talked. I briefed my new attorney on Seth's less than shining attributes and prayed Attorney Hoppas could get me the same temporary orders I got the first time with Attorney Pettit's help--custody of Harper and Doren, control over the house, and use of my car, along with child support and maintenance for the interim of the divorce.

My attorney and I returned to the courtroom minutes before the hearing was to begin. We sat down in the center of the room at the lawyers' table next to Seth and his lawyer. I instructed Bella to sit in the audience. I recognized Seth's attorney. He was the same man Seth used in our previous hearing, the day before we left for our December ski trip to Steamboat, Colorado in 1993—six months earlier.

I looked around to check on Bella, and to my surprise, spotted Seth's sister, Demelza, sitting in the front bench beside my daughter. I assumed my estranged husband had rehearsed his younger sister as to what lies to say about me. Our eyes met, but she gave me a blank stare rendering no sign of having taken any position with me.

"All rise," shouted the bailiff.

Judge Kelsey, a handsome male in his late forties, or early fifties, with thick, silver hair and wearing a black robe, walked up to the bench looking grim. I did not recognize the judge as the same judge we had the first time we were in this court and found no relief.

"Please be seated," the judge instructed before sitting down and reading the docket. He announced his first case. "Jean Wynn versus Seth Zherneboh. Are the lawyers here?"

My lawyer stood up and loudly answered, "We're both present, your Honor,"

I watched my husband's attorney stand up from where he sat, while my lawyer continued to talk to the judge, "I'm Attorney Jerry Hoppas appearing for Petitioner, Ms. Jean Wynn."

Seth's lawyer then introduced himself. "I'm Attorney Kent Brown, appearing for Respondent Seth Zherneboh."

I not only recognized Seth's attorney by face, but I knew the name, too. Seth had retained Attorney Brown to sue the New York City brokerage firm for losing his mother's money in the stock market. I was certain Attorney Brown and Seth would bring up for the judge's understanding that I had ruined Seth's opportunity to win *half-a-mil*. Would the judge care that I sabotaged my husband's lawsuit? I didn't know. Would a judge take offense that Seth would sue his brokerage house for losing his ma's money in the stock market? Perhaps he would believe Seth's suit to have been frivolous if I could ruin his opportunity to sue Prudential.

I heard a woman's voice in the back of the room talking to the bailiff and turned to see, to my shock, that Sabrina had come to the hearing and obviously on behalf of my husband. I had not seen her since the end of November, ten months past. She caught my stare and threw back a smug, holier-than-thou look, as she sashayed toward me; and very arrogantly, while passing in front of the lawyers' table where Seth and I sat, she threw my husband a sassy smirk, and then proceeded to sit down next to Seth's sister, Demelza, in the first row of benches in the courtroom. I did not know the two women knew each other, but they appeared to be intimate with one another. My oldest friend and my sister-in-law whispered to each other and threw tormenting glances at me for my worry. Both appeared delighted they were there together in court that day to help take my children away from me. My eleven-year old daughter who sat on the other side of

Demelza appeared disturbed while she watched the two women whisper. I could not believe Sabrina had no regard for me, or for my daughter.

I threw my head into my hands and over-dramatized how sad I felt for Sabrina's benefit. I had hoped to remind the overweight woman that we had been friends since the fifth grade. I silently prayed, *Protect my children and me, Father, from these vipers. I ask you in your son's name, Jesus Christ.* I then lifted my head up out of my hands and smirked back while sending back a message to my so-called *sister* that she ought to fear me! I had just as much garbage on her as she had on me, and she knew it! Had Sabrina forgotten that she had told me that her daughter was the child of a fellow student in her art class--an art class she took while married to Goose. That a man named Jack had fathered her only child. I figured my ruthless husband had threatened Sabrina by telling her that I intended to talk to her husband about their sexual interlude. Sabrina's strategy here today was to ensure that if I were to ever reveal to Goose, that his wife slept with my husband, then Sabrina would defend herself by explaining to her lawyer husband that I was trying to destroy her marriage because she had testified today on Seth's behalf in an effort he win custody. If not that explanation, then she would tell Goose that I was jealous of her life, and that I wanted to take her life. I recalled Sabrina telling me that her husband had her sign a prenuptial contract eleven years earlier, and I knew she had not held a paying job a single day since she married at the age of twenty-three. Sabrina would cut my head off if it meant her survival.

The judge asked, "Are the children here?"

I turned my eyes back to the bench while I feared what Sabrina might say about me. She had been my lifetime confidant. We were always two peas in a pod who saw eye-to-eye on everything, that was, until Seth seduced the fat egomaniac who thrived on male attention.

My lawyer replied, "The two children of the marriage are not here, Judge. There's one child by a previous marriage that's here, but I'm going to invoke the rule."

"Do you intend to call the eleven-year old as a witness?" The judge asked the lawyers while looking down at a legal document I assumed listed our children's ages.

Seth's lawyer answered, "No sir."

My lawyer followed with, "I would like to reserve that privilege."

The judge replied, "I'm not real keen on having little children testify in family law domestic quarrels. If I am going to interview the witness, I'll do so with the court reporter present, but I'm not going to put a child on that stand. I don't want her in the courtroom hearing this matter, either. I take it the child's been with this family for a while?" The judge then looked up and at Seth and asked, "Mom's been living with the stepfather of this child approximately how long?"

Seth answered, "We've been married since 1992."

"You've had a relationship with this child for the last two years?" The judge questioned my husband.

"I've had a relationship with her a little over seven years."

I considered Seth's phrasing and wondered if the judge clued in to the snake's craftiness right then at that moment?

The judge looked at my attorney, "I will interview the child in chambers, if you request I do."

My attorney spoke, "Judge, the Petitioner invokes the rule."

Was that a yes, or a no, regarding whether Bella would talk to the judge? My attorney had better take the opportunity!

The judge spoke to my daughter and to the rest of our witnesses that sat in the front bench of the courtroom. "The rule has been invoked," he reminded. "What the rule means is you're not permitted to remain in the courtroom. After you testify, you are to remain outside the courtroom, unless you are dismissed."

I turned to see that my witnesses, Marilyn and Charley stood in the back near the door listening to the judge's instructions. I smiled at my friends, and they acknowledged me with caring expressions.

The judge continued while I turned to see Bella, Demelza, and Sabrina move toward the exit. I smiled at Bella.

"Call your first witness," the judge ordered while he reviewed the Petition for Divorce.

Seth's attorney sat down, and my lawyer remained standing while he announced, "I call the Petitioner, Jean Wynn, as my first witness."

I walked up to the front, sat down in the witness box, and then the bailiff duly swore me in. I adjusted the microphone and swore to tell the truth, the whole truth, so help me God. I had a sufficient amount of bad stuff on my husband and had no need to lie about anything.

The courtroom was nearly empty except for the parties involved in our hearing--my husband, our lawyers, the bailiff, the judge, his clerk, the stenographer, and me. Our witnesses were outside the courtroom door, in the hallway, and waited for the bailiff to call them to the stand. I prayed Charley and Marilyn would take Bella under their wing.

"Please state your full name for the record," my lawyer instructed.

"Jean Wynn."

"Okay, Ms. Wynn, let's begin."

I informed the court that my three children and I lived in a home in The Woodlands. "I have been legally married to the Respondent since August 1992--two years to be exact." I turned to the judge and said, "I have two sons born of the marriage, Harper, five years old, and Doren, three years old."

"Do you own the home you live in, Ms. Wynn?" My lawyer asked.

"Yes, since October of '91--three years ago. We bought our home with cash from the efforts of my apparel business." I answered while reminding self that I had to reveal, before I got off this witness stand, Seth's abusive personality; his drug addiction since the beginning of our relationship; his *eromenos--Zeus's other half*, a name Seth called his boyfriend during phone sex; and Seth's unwillingness to get out of the yard and work for a living. I would also tell the court that Seth and I were flat broke because my husband had refused to work for the last three years, and that he lost his ma's life savings in the stock market and--

My lawyer interrupted my thoughts, "Do you work?"

"No, I stay home with my three children. I want to go back to school. I've enrolled twice at the University of Houston; well, actually, I enrolled three times into school. This last time, I was going to a paralegal school. Every time I took classes at the university, with a goal to earn a bachelor's degree, Seth did whatever he had to do to cause me to drop out of the university. I was about to start paralegal school before he moved out this last time. He's threatened I might leave him if I get a degree."

My lawyer continued, "Have you ever held a job?"

"Yes, before our marriage. I worked for the oil companies for ten years, and then I started an apparel manufacturing and wholesale business--that's when Seth jumped on my bandwagon. He wasn't working when I met him. The bank had just repossessed his car when he came into my life. I saw the repo man haul his car away when we lived in the same apartment complex. He was smoking weed that day, sitting on his mother's apartment patio, when I walked by and saw the tow truck drive off with his car. I guess I looked like a meal ticket. I was rich, by his terms, and I lived in their apartment building. He was fighting with his mother, back then, too, because he constantly bummed money from her. I saw them fighting one day when I walked up to their apartment. Their front door was wide open, and I just stood there embarrassed while listening to profanity fly between both of them. The day he lost his car, I invited Seth over for dinner, and that's all I have ever been for him since--a meal ticket and a baby machine. He's always been in love with his best friend, Runi." I stopped talking. I had given the court the broad strokes in one breath.

"Did your husband work during the marriage?"

"He closed one deal after he met me. It took him three years to close his first deal, and he collected a commission check from that one deal every month, for the last two years. He did not work his one and only account, and the company got rid of him recently. And he has spent the last three years landscaping our home and doing drugs. He created no backup plan in case we suffered a loss of income. His idea of working was to talk his mother out of her life savings and play her money in the stock market. And he lost the entire amount in one day."

"Do you feel Seth is a responsible father?"

"No, not at all. His kids are not his priority. I've seen the children playing in the street when I drive up."

"Ms. Wynn, do you currently hold a job?"

"No, I'm a stay-at-home mom. I have always been home with my children."

My lawyer stopped questioning me right there. "I pass my witness."

I objected! I didn't want my lawyer to stop there because I wanted to elaborate on why Seth had a need to get permanent custody of our children. I wanted to explain to the court that if he got custody of his two sons, then he would get possession of our marital home, and then he would be able to sell the house down the road, or take out a lien against the equity, and pay his mother back.

Seth's lawyer got up and walked up to the witness stand. "Ms. Wynn, when you observed the children in the yard, or in the street, and unattended, in your opinion, you don't know if, on any of those occasions, Seth was around the corner, on the side of the house, or in the garage, do you?"

"I never observed him. I'd guess he might be on the phone in the garage. That's the phone he uses when he--"

He interrupted, "You don't know exactly where Seth was, if you couldn't see him. You don't know--it could have been possible he had been there?"

I was about to tell the court that he liked to masturbate on that garage phone with his boyfriend, when Seth's attorney interrupted me with his stupid question. "I guess so," I impatiently answered.

"Nothing further, your Honor." Seth's attorney stepped away, and my attorney stood up from his seat and called my best girlfriend as his next witness.

I was surprised that Seth's lawyer quit asking me questions so quickly while Charley walked up to the stand looking nervous. I sat back down at the lawyer table and watched the bailiff swear my witness in.

My lawyer began, "State your full name?"

"Charley Benson."

"Ms. Benson, are you acquainted with the parties of this matter, Seth and Jean?"

"I've known both of them about eight or nine years."

"Have you had occasion to visit with them in their home?"

"Oh, yes."

"On more than one occasion?"

"On many, many--I spend the night."

"How frequently would you say, over a period of time, you have visited in their home?"

"Sometimes, once a month, when the kids get together. They are all friends."

"During the visits to the home, have you had an occasion to observe the behavior of the children and of the parents toward the children?"

"Yes, sir."

"Between the two parents, who was the primary caretaker of the children?"

"Very definitely, Jean."

Seth's attorney interrupted, "Objection, your Honor, if he's asking for some kind of legal conclusion."

The judge responded, "Overruled. That's not a question of legal conclusion."

My attorney continued, "In what way would you say Jean cared for the children more than their father?"

"Well, there were times when they were having financial problems, and Seth wasn't working, I'd say that she was the one trying to figure out how to make ends meet."

"I'm talking about with regard to the personal care of the children?"

"Jean did everything. She changed their diapers, bathed her boys, prepared the meals for her family, dressed her children, and sent them to school. I've never seen Seth dress his children."

"Did you have an occasion to ever observe the father's conduct toward his children?"

"Yes, it's just the typical acknowledgement of his kids--you know, he'd be out doing something like most fathers."

"Did he hug and kiss the children?"

"I don't know. I guess if Jean and the kids left or went somewhere."

"Did you ever observe either one of the parents disciplining the children?"

"Yes."

"Who normally did that?"

"Both of them."

"Ms. Benson, have you ever had an occasion, or have you had any occasions to observe wounds or bruises or injuries to the body of Ms. Wynn?"

"Yes, sir, every time--on many occasions."

I recalled the afternoon at Fred's picnic and how the four of us--Charley, Sabrina, Linda, and I sat out on the grass in Fred's backyard, in front of the ocean, eating and talking. Sabrina had embarrassed me that day by pointing out to the girls the bruises on my legs, and she and Charley were on the same page with their opinion about my abusive husband.

Charley continued, "She calls me up, and I come over there when she's going through a hard time. She often has bruises on her arms, legs. She doesn't really want to talk about it, but she will."

"Did you observe her with a broken nose in September of 1992?" My lawyer referred to the doctor report I had given him.

"She told me about that occasion--when he forced her out of school."

I knew Charley would stop there and not admit to the court the funniest part of the incident when I swooped Seth off the commode while he was wiping his ass. She and I had shared laughs over that story.

"Did you have an occasion to observe a cut on Ms. Wynn's arm?"

"Yes. She got to the point where she didn't want to say anything. I'd come over there, see her bruises, and say to her, 'Don't tell me it happened again. Why do you put up with that?'"

Mrs. Benson, do you have an opinion as to in whose care and control the children's best interest would be served, as between Mr. Zherneboh and Ms. Wynn?"

Seth's lawyer interrupted. "Objection, your Honor, no foundation, calls for speculation."

The court overruled the objection and replied, "This is a fact witness. She can give an opinion."

Charley continued, "My opinion is Jean is a very good mother to those boys. She's given them a good Christian background. I just feel like, even if Seth did get visitation rights, she'd be controlled because I don't think--"

My lawyer interrupted, "Why do you say that?"

"I just don't feel like--if he's not--I just don't feel like he'd be a good father, period. I'd rather see them with anybody, but with Seth."

"You have animosity?"

"No. We've always got along. It's just that I've seen through the years what has happened, and how he's been toward Jean, and I just don't see how he could be a good father."

My attorney looked at the judge. "Pass the witness, your Honor."

Seth's attorney walked up to question Charley. "Ma'am, have you ever been treated for alcoholism?"

"No, sir."

"Do you ever go a day without missing a drink?" Seth's attorney asked.

"Sure do."

"You consider yourself an alcoholic?"

"No sir."

"Do you barhop with Jean?"

"We've been out about twice every six months. It's not barhopping; it's having a drink at a social event, or when we're having dinner."

"Have you ever been in the company of Ms. Wynn where she has yelled at her children?"

"I wouldn't say she yelled. She disciplines them."

"When she disciplines them, she uses profanity, does she not?"

"Oh, no, sir," Charley answered. "I've never heard profanity. I've heard Seth use profanity, but not Jean."

Seth's lawyer stopped the questioning. "Pass the witness."

The judge asked, "Is this witness released?"

My lawyer agreed, "Yes, sir."

The judge looked at Charley, "You're excused. You may return to your duties. Call your next witness."

My lawyer called my next-door neighbor.

I watched Marilyn walk up to the witness stand while I felt good about my girlfriend's testimony--Charley had no need to lie. She knew exactly what had been going on between me and Seth for years. On the other hand, I had no clue how effective my next-door neighbor would be as far as persuading the judge to see me as the one with the integrity. I sat in bewilderment while I watched the bailiff first duly swear in Marilyn. She had written her testimony on paper at my kitchen table, and had requested I submit the document to the court in lieu of her showing up in person today, but after having given her a heads up that her written affidavit would not be admitted into this hearing, she agreed to appear in person. I gave her credit for having courage. She had been married to a good man for twenty-five years, and I was certain Marilyn was naïve about breaking down Seth's bad character--even if she did volunteer at the center for abused women in The Woodlands.

Seth's lawyer asked my friend, "Did you ever observe any family violence directed toward the children by either one of these two parties?"

"Doren, the youngest, had bruises on occasion from falling, I was told from being clumsy, but I never observed any family violence directed toward the children."

"Have you ever seen family violence between the two parents?" Seth's lawyer pointed to Seth and me.

"Yes."

"When was that?"

"That was probably six or eight months ago. They were fighting and chasing each other around the outside of the house."

"And the family violence you observed--Was this mutual between the two, or one-sided?"

"It was a fight, a very loud fight."

"And have you seen this happen very often?"

"That was the only time I had seen anything outside. And then the two times when I saw the police come to their house."

"Has either party ever made any outcries to you about family violence? Have either one of these two people come to your house and said, he beat me up, or she beat me up, or look at this scar or bruise?"

"No. After the police came the second time and took Seth to jail, I went over and talked with Jean. She was quite upset and her clothing was torn."

I did not call the police when Seth broke my nose after I first swooped him off the toilet because I felt guilty--even if he did force me out of school my first semester. I did not call the police when Seth took his car key and gouged out my arm that rested on the car's console, or when he periodically kicked me in the shins—in private or in front of Harper; but I did call the police in August of 1992, after a night out with Seth, Pete, Chad and their girlfriends. Pete drove over 100 MPH while under the influence, and when Seth and I got home that night, we fought over what I called our "loser" friends and their drugs. Seth broke my coffee table out of anger during that argument, and in turn, I threw his prized 5,000-year old clay bowl into the brick fireplace and watched it return to dust. Seth then retaliated and broke my rice paper privacy screen. I called the police to stop the destruction. Seth was forced to leave that night, but he did not go to jail. Then, sixteen months later, in December of 1993, after he attacked me while I attempted to study for my economics final, one early morning, I called the police and he went to jail. And I called the police again eight months later, in August of 1994-- just recently. I called the police because he was on the phone with his boyfriend, whom he had phone sex with while believing I was asleep. My patience was gone, and my ways were becoming violent like Seth's ways.

Seth's attorney suddenly stopped and looked at my attorney who sat quietly next to me and asked him, "Is this witness released and allowed to return to her duties?"

My lawyer had no more questions for Marilyn?

The judge interrupted and asked my attorney, "I believe that is your two witnesses. Do you rest?"

Attorney Hoppas answered. "Yes, your Honor, I rest. We have nothing further. She may return to her duties."

The judge spoke to Marilyn, "You're released. You may go home." The judge then looked to Seth's attorney. "Call your first witness."

Attorney Brown beckoned Seth who had anxiously stood up prematurely. Seth walked up to the stand while I watched Marilyn exit the courtroom. My neighbor friend did not turn around and look at me, and I wondered who would shield my daughter from Sabrina and Demelza's viciousness out there in the hallway now that Charley and Marilyn had left the building?

"I call Mr. Seth Zherneboh," Attorney Kent Brown announced.

I turned my attention back to see Seth sit down in the witness stand. My husband wore a gray conservative suit with a crisp white shirt and blue silk tie--he looked like a dog to me. I watched him coolly adjust the microphone, and then the bailiff asked Seth to tell the truth, so help him God. He swore that he would tell the truth, and the bailiff departed while his lawyer casually walked up to the stand and asked the witness to state his full name.

I wondered how 'the swearing in' made any difference? Seth was a man who declared, long ago, that he had no god—he was god; and, as far as telling the truth, well, he consistently lied about everything. Charley, Fred, and George had labeled Seth a sociopath that day in the hot tub at the Steamboat ski resort. I believed Seth to be a pathological liar, like Brini, but maybe they were sociopaths, too—not only did they both chronically lie, but also, they did not know right from wrong. Simply put, they were both amoral.

"Are you presently employed?"

"I am."

"What is your--" his attorney began when the judge interrupted.

"Is this El Camino apartment address in Clear Lake City on the Petition where he is living?" The judge asked Seth's attorney.

"No, it's not," Seth answered for his attorney. "I stayed there briefly, your Honor."

"Go ahead," the judge continued.

Pete, our mutual friend, and Seth's former boss from The Talent House, had indicated Seth had moved into the El Camino apartment and then moved right back out after he discovered the havoc I wrecked on his life.

What is your present employment prospect?"

Prospect? I was thrilled to hear Seth had no actual job!

"I am employed by *Outside Houston Show* as a segment producer."

My mouth fell agape while he contradicted his lawyer's use of the term 'prospect' and revealed that indeed he held a job. He had a job exactly like the sales job Jay Stevens offered me! Seth told me that he would match me, when we went to court, and he proved to be good for his word. Had I accepted Jay's job offer, and took the segment producer job at the Weekday Magazine TV show, the judge would be even more confused. Seth mirrored me. He made the same allegations about me that I made about him, and though his accusations were lies, the judge did not know the difference. I quickly put two and two together. I had recently told our mutual friend, Pete, from the Talent House, that a friend of mine from Chases' Night Club wanted to hire me to be his sales rep for his weekly TV show, and that I would sell segments of airtime to businesses around the city. Pete had taken my job opportunity back to Seth. What Pete did not know was that Jay Stevens had come over to my house for dinner. After dinner, Jay had gone into the front room of my home and banged out beautiful notes on my white piano and sang romantic songs to me. He kissed me that night, too, and I instantly closed down and sent him home. I questioned that night, after listening to Jay, whether he was bi-sexual, because he talked all night long about his drag queen friends, and caused me to doubt his orientation, which then caused me to step way, way, way back. I refused to go to work for the TV producer--it felt too familiar.

"When do you begin work?" Seth's lawyer asked.

"Actually, I began! I was supposed to begin work Wednesday, but I was unable to because of--"

His lawyer stopped him short. "--this proceeding?"

"Yeah," Seth nodded as if confused. "So I'll begin work Monday."

His lawyer stopped Seth from telling the court that he had no car, and that I had a tow truck repossess my car, after he left the kids and me without any form of transportation.

"What are you going to be doing for *Outside Houston?*"

"I am going to be a segment producer doing outside sales, going to different businesses, and selling air time on the program."

"Does that job description require the use of a vehicle?"

"It absolutely requires the use of a vehicle."

"Do you have a vehicle presently?"

"No, I do not."

"What about this Mustang? You were involved in a car wreck?"

"Yes, I was."

"What happened to that car?"

"That car sustained rear-end damage of about $4,500."

"Where is it now?"

"It's was towed to Charlie Thomas Chevrolet."

"Is it being repaired?"

"No, it is not."

"Why not?"

"Because we are not insured, and I don't have the funds to do it."

"Why are you not insured?"

"I called my wife after I had the accident, and she told me that we weren't insured. I asked her why not, told her that I had the statement in front of me that says we are insured, and she says, "Well, they sent us that statement, but I didn't pay the insurance premium.""

A lie! He called me from the hospital and asked me if we had medical insurance, not car insurance. We had never bought medical insurance even though Seth had license to sell medical insurance products!

"Are you asking the court to award you possession of the Volvo?"

"I am as a necessity. I need the Volvo to do my job in order to bring in an income to support my children and myself."

I fumed. He intentionally wrecked his car; and now, he wanted mine! He told the court that I didn't pay the insurance premium on the car?! We had carried only liability as required by law, but liability would not cover any damage to our car if Seth were in a car wreck. Our insurance company cancelled our policy, months ago, when I stopped paying the monthly premium because Seth no longer had a monthly income.

"Is the Volvo paid for?"

"Yes."

"Are you also asking the court to award you temporary custody of your two children, Harper and Doren?"

"I am."

"Have you spoken to either one of your children on the phone in the last few weeks?"

"I guess it's been two days ago. After much rhetoric on Jean's part, she finally put each one of them on the phone. And after thirty seconds, she took the phone away from each child. She's creating parental alienation!" He said with great zeal.

Parental Alienation?!!! The truth was he had moved away, and the only phone call he ever made to the house was to threaten to take my children away after the children and I walked into a half-empty house one day after dropping Seth off at work. After that threatening phone call, I got a restraining order placed against daddy. The court ordered him to not contact us, and prevented him from breaking into the house while we slept, or coming anywhere near us.

"Please tell the Court what happened yesterday at Harper's school."

"After carefully reading the protective order that I had been served with, I drove over to the school. I did not know when Harper was in school. I went into the school dressed in a suit. I went into the office, and I asked the woman if Harper was in school now. They said he went to afternoon kindergarten. I said, "I'm his father, Seth Zherneboh, and showed them I.D. I said I would like to see him briefly for about five minutes. They said I'd have to come back. I came back at 12:30, and Officer Thompson met me in front of the school. This officer stated I could not see my son. I told him, 'Officer, are you telling me now, so that I am clear, that if I walk in there, and ask the administrators of the school, to bring my son out to me, so that I could visit with him in their presence, for five minutes, that you'll take me to jail?'"

My attorney stood up and objected. "Hearsay, self-serving. It has nothing to do with--"

"It's not question and answer," the judge reminded Seth's lawyer. "Let's resume with question and answer."

Seth finished his story anyway. "And the officer said, 'Yes, I will take you to jail.' So, I turned around and left, and that was it."

Seth was trying to kidnap Harper before this hearing! Thank God, my mother's old friend worked the front office of my son's school and had alarmed the school administration of the situation that day.

Attorney Brown asked, "Mr. Zherneboh, did your wife call your work recently?"

"Yes, she did. She talked with the general agent who is in charge of the office."

"Did you find out what was said by her?"

"He told me. His name is--."

My attorney stood up and yelled, "Your Honor, I will object to what somebody told him as hearsay."

The judge angrily replied, "Well, we're going to have an order that is not going to permit that type of behavior to occur. All right, we're not going to have phone calls going to each other's place of employment. All that is going to stop--A lot of your behavior is about to stop. Go ahead," he said to Seth's lawyer.

Attorney Brown continued, "As a result of those phone calls, or that phone call from your wife to your work, did that damage you any?"

"Yes, the very next day."

"Is this the new job or old job?"

"I have been a career financial advisor, and I guess, in a sense, it's my *old* job, because my boss told me that I could no longer have the office the next day, as a result of her phone call."

His old job? He had been there less than a month! Seth just confirmed for me that Grandville Pike fired him due to the phone call I made to his boss!

The judge asked Seth, "What is your pay going to be on this segment producer job?"

"This job is commission only. I'll be working both as a licensed producer in field sales, and financial advisor."

Producer in field sales? Financial Advisor? Was Seth talking about his investment advisor job that Grandville Pike had just fired him from, or was Seth talking about his new segment producer job?

"I may be able to get another office," Seth continued.

Another office where? I clearly heard Seth's deliberate phrasing to confuse the court. Was he trying to tell the court that he would work in two capacities? He didn't even like to work!

"Are you going to be getting a draw in your new job?" His lawyer asked.

"A draw against commission?" Seth asked for clarification.

"A draw against commission." His lawyer reiterated.

"No."

"How are you going to be paid on your commissions?"

"Weekly."

"What is your estimate? What can you earn doing this job?"

"They are not specific, and they tell me that this may not be for me. Up to possibly fifty or sixty thousand dollars."

May not be for him? Was he saying that he doubted he could sell airtime, or that he doubted he would earn sixty thousand dollars a year?

Are you still receiving any income from your previous business ventures?"

"No, I am not," he answered and continued, "I feel I am fit for this job, tailor-fit, the potential would be anywhere from *thirty* to fifty thousand dollars a year."

He now reduced the annual income from $50,000 to $60,000, down to $30,000 a year for the segment producer job. Obviously, after Seth gave his position second thought, Seth decided to give the judge a conservative annual figure of $30,000 because he might have to pay too much child support and alimony if things did not go his way in this hearing!

"Do you know if your wife's been faithful to you during your marriage?"

"I know that she has not."

"Briefly, give the court an example," his attorney requested.

"I caught her at the hotel in Galveston, the Holiday Inn. I observed her and her friend Charley at a bar talking with two men, and I observed them going to the elevator, upon which I entered and rode up to the floor with them. They got off, and the four of them walked into the two men's hotel room and closed the door. I left."

The judge looked at me for a reaction, and I rolled my eyes as if Seth's accusation was as ridiculous as it sounded. I assumed this incident Seth spoke about was to mirror my allegation that Seth had a boyfriend.

Seth continued, "And I also know when I was working as a talent agent across the street from our apartment, that a male dancer that lived in the same apartment complex that Jean and I lived in, would come over and spend at least every other day with Jean while I was at work."

I remembered the sexy male stripper around the pool. He danced for the boys in a gay bar every night. I was nine months pregnant, too, with a two-year old at my side, when I would sit around the pool with my two children and talk to the twenty-five year old male. Most likely Seth knew him better than I did. There were so many details that I had forgotten, like the time when Seth worked for the Talent House. I recalled that day in 1991, when I went to the mailbox and pulled out Seth's acceptance letter from a law school, and with great excitement, I took the letter, and my very pregnant self, and pushed our two-year old Harper down the street in his stroller over to Seth's work place. I wanted to give Seth the good news, but I got the bad news when I found Seth and one of his beautiful young models getting off the unfinished floor of his office building. I wondered if the judge would find relevancy in deciding the custody matter, if he heard that Seth's former employer, and best friend, Pete, and his business, the Talent House, was shut down by the IRS, the same day the DEA busted Seth's other best friend in the parking lot of Pete's business for dealing kilos of coke? I realized then, no attorney that cost less than $50,000 would be able to stack up all the evidence I had against Seth for the court to clearly understand I was not the bad guy here. I was getting what my father paid for--an attorney who specialized in business contracts!

"Mr. Zherneboh, please tell the Court where you are living now?" Seth's attorney continued.

"I'm living in League City, Texas, with my sister and her husband and two children."

"What kind of home is that?"

"It's a four-bedroom home."

"Is your sister here on your behalf today?"

"Yes, she is here to testify."

The judge interrupted, "How long does he plan on living there if he doesn't get the exclusive use of the marital home?"

Seth answered, "I can stay as long as I need to."

"Go ahead," the judge instructed.

"Do you have an opinion whether your wife is emotionally stable?"

"I do have an opinion. Jean is very emotionally *unstable*, and her mental judgment is poor...."

My heart sank to the pit of my stomach while I heard the drug-using, bisexual bum tell the court that I was unstable. Seth had made himself crazy over having a wife and kids, when in fact, he was in love with a man.

The morning felt long, and we took a lunch recess, and after lunch, my lawyer cross-examined the liar.

My attorney asked, "Mr. Zherneboh, the testimony that you gave with regard to the infidelities of Mrs. Wynn."

"Yes."

"Is absolutely false, is it not?"

"No, that is absolutely incorrect, sir," he insisted.

"Mr. Zherneboh, do you have one witness to any of those occasions?"

"Yes, I do, sir."

"Who?"

"Sabrina Edward."

"Is that the woman you had the relationship with, that's here today?"

"What relationship are you talking about?"

"Is she the lady with whom you allegedly were passing back and forth nude pictures of her?"

"I'm sorry. I don't understand what you are talking about, sir?"

"Is she the lady with whom you were recently seen by Ms. Wynn as smoking pot with?"

"If my wife said Sabrina Edward, then that Sabrina Edward is here."

"Do you have another witness to these 'infidelities'?"

"Yes, I do. Charley Benson, but I doubt she would testify."

"I doubt it, too," my lawyer enforced. "Mr. Zherneboh, you have a relationship with a man by the name of Runi Krieger?"

"Yes, I do."

"What kind of relationship is that?"

"He's one of my best friends."

"Is there any sexual relationship between you and him?"

"That's absurd. Absolutely not! I am not anything other than heterosexual."

Denial was Seth's standard defense. He had said that exact thing in the previous hearing, the only difference now, was that since that last hearing, I had heard Seth and Runi masturbate on the telephone one night, and I knew better.

"Do you write letters to Mr. Krieger?"

"On occasion."

"Have you visited his home with your wife?"

I recalled that evening after dinner when Joyce and I sat in her basement. She confided in me and revealed our husbands were gay, and much later that same night, Seth left in the middle of the night to return to Aiden Cooper's house, after I heard Aiden solicit my husband for sex earlier that evening.

"Which home?"

"Any home?"

"Yes."

"Did you write a letter to Mr. Krieger advising him in the following words: *My God, do you know I love you?*" My lawyer looked up from the letter Seth had written Runi the day before I gave birth to our last child.

"I would have to see the letter, but I could very well have written those words, depending on the context, of course, that it was written."

"Mr. Zherneboh, you testified a while ago, I believe, that the assault charge pending against you is a misdemeanor?"

"I believe it's a misdemeanor."

"You know, in fact, it's a felony, don't you?"

"No sir, I do not."

"Have you been in court on it?"

The judge interrupted, "How do you know it's a felony?" He asked my lawyer.

"I don't know that it is."

The judge continued to speak to my lawyer, "We can't pick his assault up on the computer. This court ties into the felony court, to only felony charges. There's no indictment pending."

The judge looked at my husband. "Have you been indicted? Have you had a court date yet?"

"The arraignment was yesterday," Seth answered.

"In what court did you go for arraignment?" The judge asked Seth.

"Upstairs, I believe it's Suzanne Stovall's courtroom."

"It's a misdemeanor," the judge concluded.

"That's the second time that you have been charged with assault, is it not?" My lawyer asked.

"Yes, that is correct," Seth confirmed.

"What happened on the first charges?"

"They were dismissed."

"Were you required to get counseling?"

"Yes, I did. "

"Do you have a counselor?"

"I went three times, which is what the Assistant District Attorney requested; and then, I went four more times on my own."

"You've testified that you're not violent?"

"$65 an hour."

What kind of answer was that! I questioned while my lawyer skimmed over his non-responsiveness answer. Did Seth's counselor tell him that he was not violent for $65 an hour?

"Did you ever give Ms. Wynn a card wherein you apologized for breaking her coffee table?"

"I'll have to see that card."

"You don't recall doing that?"

"I don't recall it."

"Do you, in fact, recall breaking a coffee table?" My lawyer asked while he peered at the apology card in his hands.

"No, I don't."

"Do you recall--"

Seth interrupted, "Although I've broken things, to answer your question, I've broken things."

"Endangering--"

Seth interrupted again, "I don't know if you're asking if I did it on purpose, on anger--no, sir."

"Did you throw Jean's answering machine? Did you tear up her answering machine?"

"No, sir, she tore that up."

"Did she?"

"Yes."

"Did you poke holes in the walls in the apartment?"

"No, I did not."

"Who did that?"

"I don't know that any holes were poked in the apartment walls."

"Did you tear up her Jean Wynn neon sign?"

"No sir, I did not."

"Why did you not pay the car insurance on the car that you say was not insured?"

"I made the mistake of allowing my wife, who demanded to be in full charge of the record-keeping, of the bill paying, of the check writing. That is why, sir."

He allowed me?

"Did you give her the money to pay for it?"

"Yes, she had full access to the checking account."

"What's in the checking account?"

"She closed the checking account after she had me thrown in jail, sir."

"What money have you given her since July of 1994--two months ago?"

"Oh gosh, I believe my last check was for $17."

"So you gave her $17 since July?"

"I can't say for sure."

"Did you give that money to her?"

"What do you mean, did I hand it over to her?"

"Yes," my attorney answered.

"It went for our daily living necessities."
"You just testified she was supposed to pay the insurance. How would she pay it, if she didn't have any money?"
"The insurance was due before my payroll check ended."
"Mr. Zherneboh, do you use drugs?"
"No, I do not--"

Seth finally left the stand, and Demelza came up to testify.

I had not been around Seth's sister, but once in three years since we had moved to The Woodlands, Texas; and that time was when Seth's mother had driven to our house with Demelza and her two granddaughters in her car. Demelza had not attended our wedding. I suspected that Demelza's sudden lack of interest in our little family was due to her having grown pea green with envy after Seth and I got the $300,000 settlement from my apparel business lawsuit. Demelza had refused to have any kind of relationship with Seth or me after we came into our money and bought a beautiful custom home near The Woodland's Country Club. I suspected, too, that Seth's insecure sister, who carried forty pounds of lard on her ass, was not about to bring her fairly new and handsome husband around her sister-in-law, who had the height and body of a model after bearing four children. I had played tennis with Seth's sister when we lived near her during the days just after Seth and I had crashed and burned in Florida, and when she was a single mother struggling to get through school. She had come over to our apartment several times with her two daughters, who were near Bella's age, and they had visited with my daughter, Harper, and me while Seth was off at work. Back then, I was looking forward to Bella having close cousins to play with while growing up near Seth's family. I liked the idea of having a sister-in-law and close friend.

Seth's attorney, Kent Brown, began. "For the record, state your full name."
"Demelza Bransford."
"Where do you reside?"
"In League City, Texas, at 218 Green Shore Drive."
"What type of neighborhood is that?"
"It's in middle-class suburbia. Nice yards. The park is in our back yard, so we have a swimming pool, tennis courts, and basketball courts."

I knew of her neighborhood in League City, and her home was an ugly track home valued in the range of $55,000 with a barren front yard.

"Are you married?"

"Yes, to Gregory Bransford."

"What does he do for a living?"

"He's a probation officer."

"And where do you work?"

"I'm a counselor for Harris County."

"What type of counselor?"

"Drug and alcohol. I'm a clinical psychologist."

The judge interrupted and asked Demelza, "Are you licensed by the State of Texas?"

"I'm working on my MLPC."

"Briefly what is your husband's education?" Seth's lawyer asked.

"He has a Master's in Psychology."

"Have you observed Seth and Jean over the years since they have been married?"

"Yes."

"And while they were together prior to the marriage?"

"Yes. I lived in the same neighborhood during those years."

We lived three miles apart during those years when Demelza and I played tennis together, when she lived in a rent-subsidized apartment complex, went to school, and supported her two daughters on food stamps and welfare.

"Are you able to aid and assist your brother, Seth, while he gets back on his feet?"

"Yes, we are a two-income family. We're doing quite well."

"And do you have room available in your home to take on Seth and his two boys?"

"Yes, we have four bedrooms."

"Are you willing to do that if the court so awards custody temporarily to Seth?"

"Yes, that's family."

"Now, over the years, since you've known Ms. Wynn, would you consider your brother, Seth, or Ms. Wynn, the primary caretaker of Harper and Doren?"

"Without a doubt, Seth is the more nurturing."

My lawyer interrupted. "May I have this witness on *voir dire?*"

"For what purpose?" The judge asked Attorney Hoppas.

"To establish the fact that she hasn't been around these people."

"That's cross-examination," the judge answered, "not *voir dire.*"

Seth's lawyer continued, "On what information and knowledge do you base that opinion?"

"Personal observation," Demelza answered.

"What observations have you made to support your belief?"

"Well--" she began, "I lived right behind Jean, and I've seen her interact with her children. I've seen her unresponsive, not even observing where they're going. In addition, she has small children. I've seen her physically and verbally abuse the children."

"In what way?"

"I've seen her hit the children, grab them by the arm, and pull them, which could dislocate their arm sockets. I've seen her degrade them."

I wondered how it could be that my daughter made straight A's if I had truly degraded her. I then recalled Seth and his mother standing eye-to-eye in his mother's apartment, behind my apartment, back in the 80's, fighting—both of them flinging the f-word at each other. Obviously, Demelza was describing her family's abusive ways with one another.

My attorney sprung to his feet and interrupted, "I object to this, unless this witness can establish a time and place for those incidents."

"Yes, I can," Demelza supported.

The judge instructed her, "Alright, do so, please."

Demelza continued, "I was over at their Woodlands home, visiting them. This was in the morning, she--"

Seth's attorney interrupted his witness, "All these events occurred at one time?"

"No."

"This is the verbal and physical time, where Ms. Wynn had struck the child? Or said things, because the child had soiled his diaper, which was appropriate for that age level?"

My lawyer angrily sprung to his feet and interrupted, "Your Honor, my understanding was the court ordered this witness to establish a time."

Demelza continued, "On 'the visit' to The Woodlands."

The judge angrily turned to Demelza, "You be quiet! Now we're going to do this by question and answer;" the judge continued, "and we're going to do this in a proper method. You are to answer the question, and don't volunteer answers. Now answer this lawyer!"

The judged turned to Seth's lawyer, "Now Attorney Brown, ask her a question."

The judge looked at Seth's sister again, "And you answer it! I already instructed you to put your observations into time and place."

"I'm sorry, your Honor," Demelza meekly replied.

"What month and year did you make your observations?" Seth's lawyer asked.

"I think it was around February 1993, last year."

That date put her in our home before I filed the first divorce at the end of 1993.

"I drove up with my mother. Seth was not home, just Jean. And the kids were soiled. One of them, the youngest was soiled, smelling, reeking, so it was obvious the baby had been that way for a while. It's just that Jean got very upset that the baby was 'that way', and he was two. And she pulled him up, hit him, and struck him on the head, which concerned me because you shouldn't strike, and the verbal--the yelling and screaming--was totally inappropriate for what I saw. And then, she disrobed him, yanked him up by the arm, took him outside, and cleaned him off with the garden hose. It was degrading, and I thought totally inappropriate."

"Did you see similar behavior by Ms. Wynn towards her children on any other occasion, and if so, when?"

"This time was when they lived on my side of town, and it was with the oldest son, Harper. He was little, and we were around the pool. In addition, it was quite dangerous for a toddler because--, well--, she wasn't even watching him. She was off doing--, she was just talking, wasn't observing. And I observed him with some cigarettes in his mouth, and I instructed--, I told her what I saw. She didn't care less; and then, I had to go over there--, get the cigarettes out. And then, the next time, he had put pebbles in his mouth. She was unresponsive to his needs and his wants. And that day that--, she paused and continued, "If he was going to get changed, it was obvious I had to do it; otherwise, he would be left with feces."

I cringed at the lies they all told. She and Seth made me out to be negligent, and somewhat retarded, as if I sat around drooling on myself and remained constantly 'unresponsive.' I swore right then, that I'd carry forward my memory of this day for my children's eventual understanding of their Aunt Demelza. This deluder had it coming along with Seth!

"Were there any other observations?" Seth's lawyer asked.

"I saw some verbal and physical abuse with Bella."

"What did you see?"

"I saw neglect. I saw her leaving Bella alone."

I considered myself either a pushy Jewish mama, or a pushy stage mom, but neither personality was neglectful.

My attorney interrupted, "Again, I'm going to object."

Demelza responded, "Okay, time. Sorry."

"The dates--, oh--, it was around--, let's see--" she paused and continued, "This is tenuous, but, if you need a specific date, I remember when I was--; they were living--; she was living behind me in the apartments; so it had to be about seven years ago with Bella."

Demelza was referring to the time when I lived in the apartment with Bella, while still married to Leonardo. I lived behind Seth's mother's apartment. Seth's mother shared her apartment with Seth and his teenage brother--not Demelza. I remembered Demelza came over to her ma's apartment and swapped food stamps with her brother, if he would write her term papers for her undergrad degree.

"Bella, at the time, had to be about four. It was summer because we were in the pool. I asked Bella how long her mother had been gone. She said all morning. I asked Bella if she had eaten. She hadn't eaten. I know that behavior was consistent--, that Jean would leave Bella alone."

"Do you have an opinion whether or not Ms. Wynn would leave her two boys unattended and neglect them?"

My lawyer interrupted, "Your Honor, that would call for pure conjecture."

"It's late. I'm tired," the judge moaned. "Let's move this along as quickly as we can. I know when it's seemingly just a form of observation. Let's try to be a little bit patient."

Demelza continued, "I called up and asked to speak to Seth or Jean. Bella said they weren't home, and the boys were left in her care which I thought was totally inappropriate."

"Is there any question in your mind that the children love their father?"

"No, they are very responsive to him and cooperative. When he asks them to do things, you can just see the love, when he runs up and gives them hugs and kisses."

"Do you see the same nurturing love when the children are with their mother?"

"I've known her for seven years, and I've never actually seen her go up and hug them--never. And that just disturbs me."

She disturbed me with her lies! And I was going to give her something one day to be responsive about! These were my children she was screwing with!

Seth's attorney stopped and looked at the judge. "Pass the witness, your Honor."

My attorney got up and asked, "How long has it been since you've been in the home of your brother, Seth Zherneboh, and his wife, Jean?"

"Since they moved to The Woodlands?"

"That's over a period of three years, is that not correct?"

"Correct."

"How many times have you been there?"

"Once."

And she did not come over for our wedding either.

"So you don't know what has taken place in the home during the period of three years, do you?"

"I have kept in contact. I've called. I've kept in contact with, with--" She stuttered for an answer.

"How many times have you called?"

The judge angrily interrupted my lawyer. "Stop interrupting the witness. This court reporter is great, but she can't take down two people talking at once. You allow the witness to finish answering the question, please. Go ahead. Ask the question."

My lawyer continued, "How often have you called?"

"Several times."

"And the last time was?"

"I called when she put him in jail, and I called to see if they were okay."

Another lie! Demelza and I did not speak to each other, ever. We were not friends.

"During the past three years, other than the one occasion that you spoke of earlier, have you--"

Demelza interrupted, "The boys have been over with Seth."

"Have they been in your home?"

"Yes."

Another lie. Seth had no use for his nutcase sister until this hearing.

"Has Ms. Wynn been in your home?"

"No."

"So you have really never seen Ms. Wynn around her children, but on one occasion, during the past three years?"

"I saw her interact with her children during the holidays."

The judge spouted, "Move on to something else, counselor. I know how many times she's seen the kids. I am listening."

"You don't like Ms. Wynn do you?"

"I like her. She's a nice person. It's hard not to like her."

That reason was exactly why Demelza stopped coming around me when she married Greg. The fat slob feared her husband would find it hard to not like me!

Demelza continued, "As a mother, that's a different story. Just as the clinical observations that I've made; it did concern me."

Ironically, the woman I had early on determined to have multiple personalities was now doing 'clinical observations' on me! The court had already established that she was not a licensed psychologist. I knew her to be barely out of her bachelor's program, and working on her admission into a master's program

when we last had contact. She was fat, and insecure, and our friendship ceased the minute she met her future husband who married beneath himself.
"You say you are a clinical psychologist?" My lawyer asked.
"Correct, master level. Working on the MLPC."
"Are you licensed?"
"I'm working on my MLPC."
"You're not licensed?"
The judge blasted, "She's not licensed!"
Demelza continued, "No sir."
My lawyer stopped and said to the judge. "Pass the witness."
Seth's lawyer responded, "Nothing further."

Sabrina Edward came up next. Seth and Demelza's testimony disturbed me, and I feared losing custody of my two youngest children due to their gross lies. I refrained from showing my angst on my face. Sabrina now prepared to testify against me, and without a doubt, she intended to lie and betray me to simply cover her ass. She did not care if Seth got custody of his two young sons; however, if I were to tell her husband, in the future, that she slept with my husband, then she would be able to deny the accusation. She would render to Goose a plausible explanation. She would plant doubt in her husband's mind with her tale, too, because he would question why she would turn on her lifelong friend. She would add to his confusion, that I was just trying to hurt her marriage, when I told her husband that she slept with my husband. She would remind her husband that she testified against me this day in court, and helped Seth get custody of my children. I knew she and Seth were both sociopathic liars, and whatever line of crap Seth gave her, to make her turn against her so-called *sister*, it worked in his favor. I felt sure that he seduced her with the illusion he would soon have *half-a-mil.* I had given Seth the formulae to her heart—I told him outright, early on, that she was a gold digger, and had never been faithful to her husband since day one of their marriage. The bottom line, Sabrina never worked in the eleven years she had been married to Goose; and she would do whatever she had to do to preserve her pre-nupt marriage, and not give Goose an opportunity to throw his unfaithful wife to the curb. But then again, maybe the prenuptial agreement she admitted to signing prior to marriage was just a fabrication on her part, so we would believe Goose was very wealthy.

    Seth's lawyer began. "State your full name, please."

    "Sabrina Edward."

    "Where do you reside?"

    "In Port Neches, Texas."

    "Did you travel from Port Neches to appear here today?"

    "Yes, very early this morning."

    "How are you employed, if you are employed?"

    "I'm a homemaker, and I do volunteer work in my community."

    "How many years have you been a friend of Ms. Wynn's?"

    "We grew up together, twenty-five years."

    "Would you consider yourself best friends at any time?"

    "Yes."

    "Recently, do you still stay in touch as friends?"

    "Not at this moment, but that's been in light of last--, this past year--, we're not seeing eye-to-eye on many, many--, a great many things, namely our child rearing."

    Seth's lawyer continued, while I showed no reaction to any lie she created. "In reference to Ms. Wynn as a mother, how long have you known her and been a friend of hers? As long as she has had children?"

    "Yes, I knew her first husband--, and her firstborn. Her second-born child. Her second husband, and of course, I know Seth, and I know her two children from this marriage. We go back very far."

    "Do you have an opinion, based on those observations, of whether Seth is the nurturing, primary caregiver, or whether his wife, Jean, is that for their children?"

    "Seth is the primary caretaker of not only her children, but mine when I visit. I trust him implicitly with them. He gives them great attention. And he is the primary caregiver, in my opinion. I've been around their household and all of *her households* for a very, very long time."

"What attention have you seen Seth give to his two boys?"

"He comes in; he throws down the briefcase; he wants a big hug, a big kiss and asks, 'How are my boys?'"

Comes in with a briefcase from where?! She had never been to my house and experienced Seth anywhere but in the yard stoned!

She continued, "He says, 'Hi, Bella.' He loves those children."

"Is he someone who would just simply pour them a bowl of cereal in the morning and neglect them the rest of the day?"

"No, I've spent many a night over there, and the next morning, I'm usually up with the kids because I sleep upstairs with them. Jean saunters in at 11:30, 12:30, noon, even if I'm visiting. You would think you would want to get up for your children, much less get up for the guests. That's hasn't been the case. Seth has always gotten up."

"Do you feel that, or believe that Ms. Wynn is a fit or unfit mother?"

"I think she's an unfit mother at this point, yes."

"For what reasons?"

"Well, for one thing, we both have three-year olds right now. I was appalled at the fact that she told me on our last visit, she said, 'Oh, you still got her in pull-ups?' I said yeah, and she admitted to having had enough of that stuff. She said, 'I gave him a beating every day for weeks solid, until he quit messing in his pants. She said he would say, 'No, Mommy. I don't want a spanking. Don't.' She said, 'I got tired of it. That's how I broke him of it. It's not brain surgery.' I may not be--, you know--, I'm no expert, but of all of the literature I've read, and me personally going through it with my daughter, that's not the way to handle that. That's her own anger with her situation and her life, and she's taken it out on those children."

"Have you ever seen her take out that anger on her children, in any other manner, on any occasion?"

"She's been ranting and raving around the house, unhappy with Seth, unhappy with everybody, and Doren and Harper would be there. I'd say, 'You better calm down.' And she'd say, 'Oh, they know what's going on, and if they don't, they need to know. They need to know what kind of man their daddy is, and what I have to put up with.' This is a three- and five-year old, and an eleven-year old, as we speak, sitting outside, rather than being in school."

I sat there while my anger hit the ceiling but refrained from any show of expression, but I swore that one day, I would get Sabrina back, too, right along with Demelza and Seth.

"Do you have any knowledge of whether she has left her children unattended at home?"

"Yes. I tried to call her after my last visit, and Bella answered the phone. 'Mom's not here. She went to get the Volvo repaired.' I said, 'Well, when is she going to be back?' The child said, 'I don't know.' She tells me that she's alone. This is an eleven-year old."

"Have you ever seen Jean act out in a violent rage toward her husband, Seth?"

"Yes."

"When?"

"The last visit--all the visits. She cries on my shoulder on the phone and tells me how much she's doing--, all this; but then, when I get there, she's raging at him, and hitting him, and flipping his hair up, walking by, and doing this business, saying you're nothing but a bald so-and-so. This is--, you know--, we're--, one minute, we want to reconcile; he is the best thing since sliced bread. She can't seem to make up her mind. She runs hot and cold, completely unstable. Nothing you can count on as a life partner, much less as a mother at this point."

I wondered if the woman, who slept with a collection of other men, since the beginning of her marriage, felt her husband could count on her?

Seth's attorney stopped and said to the judge, "I pass the witness, your Honor."

My attorney got up to cross-examine Sabrina. "Where do you live again, in Beaumont?"

"No sir, I live in Port Neches."

"Are you married?"

"Yes, I am."

"To who?"

"For eleven years."

Sabrina's answer was non-responsive. She did not want to indicate she was married to an attorney, much less put his name on record. I knew that any of her testimony on record threatened her sense of security.

"Do you have children?" My attorney asked.

"One husband, one child--a three-year old, and I have a stepson, twenty-three, recently married, in the United States Army."

"Do you work, Mrs. Edward?"

"Yes, I work within my home and within my community."

"Do you have a place of employment?"

"No, I do not. I work in my home."

"Did you ever apply for a job at a store called *Casual Corner?*"

"Yes. Jean's sister, Holly, who is the same age as me, worked there with me. I couldn't keep my job because I didn't have transportation."

"Did you apprise the store manager that ran *Casual Corner* that you were Holly's friend to get the job?"

Sabrina objected. "Sir, you're talking when we were fifteen, sixteen years old!"

"Did you or not?"

"I can't recall. I doubt it. We're like sisters."

The judge interrupted. "What is this about? Why are we going into something that happened when she was fifteen years old?"

My lawyer answered, "The lady's voracity, judge."

I assumed my lawyer was talking about Sabrina's ravenous lust for territorial expansion when he emphasized her voracity! She indeed had a voracious appetite for sexual interludes with men other than her own husband.

Sabrina interrupted my lawyer and judge's exchange. "Sixteen. Voracity. We were all voracious back then."

Obviously, Sabrina did not understand the definition of voracity— Sabrina was the child molested by her father and brother, not me.

"We were like *The Three Musketeers*, sir. If we want to pile little stones and throw them, well, then Jean, and Holly, and I can have the biggest rock fight, catfight, clash of the Titans, you have ever seen. Now, I don't recall, sir, what I did at sixteen."

The judge interrupted Sabrina, "Be quiet!" He then spoke to my attorney, "Just ask the question and move on."

My lawyer had just told the judge that he was leading up to the lady's voracity? Obviously, the male judge wanted to hear about Sabrina's ravenous and insatiable appetite for sex. I knew the judge questioned why, after all these years, Sabrina turned against her oldest friend? There was only one answer to the half-a-mil question.

My lawyer began, again. "Mrs. Edward, did you have occasion to recently visit in the home of Mrs. Wynn and smoke marijuana with her husband?"

"No, not recently."

"Then how long ago did you smoke marijuana with her husband?"

"I couldn't tell you."

"Were you in their home in July of last year?"

"I've been in their home almost every month, for the last year-and-a-half."

"You're a great friend of Mr. Zherneboh, are you not?"

"Mister?"

"Mr. Zherneboh," My lawyer clarified.

"I've only known him through his wife. Seth and I are good friends, but I am *her* friend. That's one reason why this is so painful for me."

"Mrs. Edward, have you had an affair with Mr. Zherneboh?"

"No, sir, your Honor, Counselor, Counselor, stenographer, no!"

"Mrs. Edward, did you happen to display a picture of yourself in the nude to Mr. Zherneboh, and his wife, in November of last year?"

"When was it?"

"Your last trip to their home," my lawyer clarified for the court.

"Jean had told me that Seth couldn't believe that I was ever in good shape because--, you see--, when we have an occasion to go out, I am *the little fat girl* who stays and watches the purses at the table because I'm the married one, while they go off and do their thing. So, in my defense, I showed Jean the picture before I ever showed Seth. I said to her, 'You remember the picture you shared with me--the photo

Seth took of you in the pool wearing a wet t-shirt?' I said to her, 'Look at this picture that Goose, my husband, took of me in our backyard, in our swimming pool.' I'm on a float halfway submerged in the water, your Honor. And I said to her, 'See, I'm in shape here. Do you think Seth would believe it, if he saw me back then?' And I asked Jean, 'Can I show it to him?' In my defense of--, you know--, once, I've--," she paused and then looked my way and said to me. "One time, I was in shape like the rest of you girls." She sneered and then turned back to the questioning lawyer, "Jean didn't have a problem with me showing her husband the picture. All of a sudden, now, she has a problem with it? I cleared that with her before he ever saw that picture."

Sabrina seemed to stumble over her usual, smooth-talking self, and I figured she felt fat and stupid, right about now. I enjoyed watching the whore squirm in her lie.

The judge interrupted, "That's enough about the nude picture. Go on to something else."

My attorney replied, "I have no further questions."

Seth's attorney responded, "Nothing, your Honor."

My attorney concluded, "We rest, your Honor."

The judge spoke to Sabrina, and then to all of us, "Your witnesses can remain in the courtroom."

I locked eyes with the con woman, but refrained from any expression while she stepped out of the witness stand and moseyed over to the back door to listen to the finale. I turned my attention back to my lawyer while aware he did not request that the judge interview Bella. I wanted to say something to Attorney Hoppas, but did not get a chance to insist that he make that interview with my daughter happen, because the judge was in a hurry to wrap up what had been a long day, and continued to hold court.

I was beyond worried over the lies that Seth, Sabrina, and Demelza told the court, and silently prayed again, while the judge examined his notes. *Please, Father, protect me and my children from these liars. Don't let these snakes take my beautiful children away. Protect the innocent from their corrupt influence.*

The judge interrupted my prayers when he sounded off to the court. "The orders I'm going to set are in the best interest of the children. I have some very odd circumstances involving residences, income, that makes this decision *fairly difficult*. I'm not going to make a final temporary order here, and I will reset this case for thirty days, and order both of yall to appear in front of Dr. Carey in The Woodlands, a forensic psychologist. He's going to do a court-ordered evaluation. Both of you will pay for the evaluations. Ya'll arrange to pay him. You're under a court order to be completely evaluated by this doctor. Make the children available for that evaluation, too, including the stepchild from the prior marriage. I'm not going to remove the children out of their home, or disrupt their school. They are to remain at the house. I'm going to find out if there is family violence. Now, when I make that discovery, your lawyers will explain that I *cannot* make a joint managing conservatorship. I have to make it one way, or the other, if I feel there is violence."

I was terrified that we had to go to court again in thirty days. Seth and I did not have any money for anything; much less could we afford a court-ordered forensic psychologist to evaluate all five of us. I was already in contempt of court with such an order in place! And I feared Seth would sway the court-ordered psychologist with his grandiose lies, and then be given sole managing conservatorship by the judge in thirty days because the judge believed I was violent. I feared I would lose custody my children. The judge's words interrupted my worries.

"I'm going to award temporary managing conservatorship to the Petitioner, Ms. Wynn, and temporary possessory conservatorship to the Respondent, Mr. Zherneboh, giving him first, third, and fifth weekend visitations with the children, but the children's visitation can only occur in the home of the sister, Demelza Bransford, *who is present* during all visitations. Forget the one day in the middle of the week-- that's too disruptive. And these kids are not to be removed outside the county, except for the purpose of the visitation."

The judge looked at Seth. "You are not to remove these kids from school, or daycare. While the visitation is going on, there will be no other persons there--male or female, except for your sister and her family. No drugs, or alcohol, while you have possession of the children."

The judge looked at me, "That applies to you, too, ma'am, while you have these children. No alcohol or drugs in your home, either. You will not have any persons of the opposite sex at your home."

He looked back at Seth. "Neither will you, sir--no persons *of any interest*, whatsoever, until I get this thing sorted out. From what yall have presented to me, the Volvo is to be turned over to the husband. I need somebody with a job, and with an income, and he is the only one providing that, right now. I only have one car, and I got a guy at least who has a job."

He looked at me, "She's not going to get a job, unless she has transportation. We're only going to do this for thirty days."

Now regarding child support and temporary alimony," he turned his attention again to Seth, "You're to pay her $500 by the 16th. She has to have money to live off. I want another $500 paid to her by the 30th. I don't care where you get it, as long as it's legal, but you have to give her some money to live off of while she's got these children. I'm going to grant a mutual restraining order as to property, and as to the violence, and as to the calling, harassment. You'll be allowed to talk to those children, and you're to make only one phone call a night, sir."

"Now, I'm tired," he continued. "It's a long day, and I do not grasp from yall, that yall are sitting here with any type of long-term plan, as to what's going to happen with your lives, with these children. Now you made a foul-up of your marriage, a foul-up of your relationship with your friends and family, and with each other. I'm going to impose the orders that I think are necessary to prevent you from fouling up these kids' lives. I want a complete forensic analysis of the children. You're going to figure out some way to pay for that. And I want yall back in here in thirty days, or at least, in here when I get the results back from the doctor; then, we'll continue this hearing. He is a forensic psychologist. He's to do a court-ordered evaluation. His report only goes to me, and I will review the report; then, I will make changes I feel are necessary in these temporary orders, which may involve changing custody. It may involve appointing Children's Protective Service to these kids; but by God, I'm going to take care of these children. Do I make myself clear?"

"Yes your Honor," Seth and I simultaneously replied.

He looked at me. "There's nothing I can do about the Volvo. Maybe in the next thirty days, yall can arrange something. Maybe he'll get a commission. We're going to find transportation for you, too."

I sat there and quietly prayed that Charley would let me continue using her car for a while, so I could find a job and appear in the best interest of these kids, in thirty days.

"I know that I sound angry," the judge spouted, and then turned to Seth, "If you strike this woman, I will put you in jail for six months. I will see to it that this court prosecutes you. I'm also going to contact Suzanne Stovall upstairs concerning the Class A misdemeanor case, and see what the conditions of the bond that you are out on. I got you in here, and I got you over there. If you foul up, you get drunk, you go over to this woman's house, then you're gone."

He turned to me, "If you violate this order, then you're gone, too."

My lawyer interrupted, "Your Honor, I have one question. You made provision for two payments of $500 each. Is there a payment due beyond that?"

The judge shook his head yes. "He pays her $500, every two weeks, until we get the evaluation done. You prepare the order, Attorney Hoppas. Get it to me soon."

I sat there in the courtroom with Seth, Demelza, and Sabrina. My friends, Charley and Marilyn, had left earlier in the day. I looked at my sweet daughter, Bella, who had entered into the courtroom and sat with the enemies. I held back my tears and fright. Seth had thirty days to tighten up his act, and I feared the worst.

Bella walked over to the lawyer's table. "Can we go now, Mom?"

My lawyer interrupted my daughter, "Just a few things before you and Bella go home. I'll have a copy of your orders in a couple of days. Call my office. They'll have Dr. Carey's office number, too."

"Okay," I nodded while he extended his hand.

I shook his hand goodbye and said thank you while not impressed with his performance.

"You did alright today," he advised. "I'm sure your father will be pleased to hear you have the house and kids."

"Only for thirty days," I said with great dismay.

"Get that forensic psychologist's evaluation scheduled as soon as possible. The sooner we get that evaluation done, the sooner we can go back to court."

"Alright," I answered while fearful of the outcome when we did go back to court. I watched him lock up his briefcase.

He nodded, "Have a good evening, Jean Ellen, Bella."

"Thank you, again."

"You're welcome." He then walked out of the courtroom.

I looked at Bella. "Let's go."

I stopped worrying about the upcoming evaluation, and tuned in to my daughter while we headed out of the courtroom. "Thank you, Bella, for coming with me today. I know it was a very long day. You were supposed to talk to the judge."

"Why didn't I?"

"Judge Kelsey was too tired. Next time, okay?"

"Okay," she sighed as we walked down the hallway.

"Thank you for being so patient," I added. "I know it was a long and boring day for you."

"Mama, I have a secret to tell you." She grinned like Garfield who had swallowed the canary.

"You do?" Her secret worried me because I assumed Bella heard something from one of my enemies. Seth suddenly walked up to us in the court hallway and broke through my considerations.

"So where's the Volvo, Jean?" He snarled.

I grinned at the tired-looking man in the worn gray suit. "It's in storage at the wrecker service yard."

"It's not in our garage?"

"Nope! It's not in *my* garage." I said flippantly. "I didn't want you to steal it, and I figured if you insisted on stealing *my car*, like you did before, then you could pay to get it out of storage, if the judge awarded you *my* car."

"How much is storage going to cost me?"

"A lot!" I answered while taking complete pleasure in the conversation.

"What's a lot?" He growled while he got the reality.

"Probably $1200, $1500--something like that!" I nonchalantly shrugged as if he, or I, had more than twenty dollars to our name.

His lawyer walked by, and Seth stopped him, and in a shrill voice, blasted his level of upset for the man's consideration. "Hey, my wife here is telling me that I have to pay $1200 to get the Volvo out of storage! Unbelievable!"

His lawyer looked over at me, and then back at his client with no expression.

I smiled.

"Good luck with that," Attorney Brown nonchalantly answered as he walked off. "I'm sorry, I have to hustle. I have a dinner date," he said to us over his shoulder as he continued to head down the hallway.

I felt his lawyer's disinterest, and assumed Seth owed his lawyer money, but could not pay him. I knew Attorney Brown had initially come on board and worked for Seth on contingency, based on the premise that they would both win a portion of that *half-a-mil* from the New York brokerage house.

I looked at Seth and quipped, "I've a dinner date, too, with my children! I have to go."

He grimaced and blasted, "Wait! Where the hell is this storage unit?"

"They're in the *Yellow Pages--Roy's Wrecker Service*. They're on my side of town. They charged a lot, to drive over to your apartment, way, way, way on the other side of town, but I told them to put it on your tab. And then there are storage fees, too. I told Roy that day, when they got my car back from you, that you had won a *half-a-mil*. I informed them that you had a lot of money, and that if you were not so lucky to win your arbitration, then they could keep the car. They couldn't see how they could lose!" I smiled while I knew this was one more knife that I inserted and twisted. "Good thing you have a job. You do, don't you?"

He shook his head in disbelief and growled. "You are a fu--"

"A what, Seth?" I sweetly interrupted, as if I didn't know what he was going to call me for the one-millionth time. I watched him look around while I reconsidered his name-calling. "I am everything you allege I am, plus more, Seth. I'm just getting started." I took Bella by the hand. "Don't mess with me, Seth. Remember what you and your lying witnesses allege about me? I'm unstable and dangerous," I said under my breath before I walked away. I did not have an ounce of respect left in my being for this man.

Bella sat in the passenger seat next to me while we drove back to our Woodlands home to relieve Uncle Henry. The sky was dark, and I felt traumatized by the day's events, by the lies told about me by people who supposedly once loved me.

I flipped on some easy listening music for the drive home, when Bella began telling me what she had tried to tell me in the courthouse. "Mom, I was sitting in the hallway, listening to Sabrina and Demelza. They said a bunch of bad things about you, Mom. They were talking to me."

"They were rehearsing their lies that they told on the witness stand today, Bella. And they're threatened by me, too--both of them."

"Why are they threatened by you?" Bella asked

"They each have their reasons."

"Mom, I heard--" Bella hesitated and grinned at me. "I was sitting beside them on the bench in the hallway."

"What did you hear?" I feared what she may have heard.

"Sabrina told Demelza that Todd was not my real father."

Whoa, I couldn't believe what I heard from my young daughter. Sabrina had no boundaries. I wondered how she would feel if I told her daughter, one day, of her mother's affairs with other men. "Todd loves you, Bella."

Bella continued, "Who is Mario, Mom?"

13

MAKING A DEAL WITH THE DEVIL

AN HOUR LATER and I sat down in Bella's bedroom and told my eleven-year-old daughter about Mario. I was just going to give her the unrestrained truth and leave no err for fairytale. "I've known your biological father since childhood. We went to the same Catholic school for twelve years. We attended the same Catholic church every Sunday. He grew up with both his parents under the same roof like me, and he lived only a few blocks from where I grew up, his entire childhood, too. His parents still live in that same neighborhood where Grandma and Grandpa live. Mario and I noticed each other in high school. First, I noticed him. I had a crush on him, but he glued his eyes on the head cheerleader, Fran, for years, until they graduated. They parted after high school graduation. After Mario graduated, I still had two more years of high school, and for the most part, I forgot about him. When I was a senior, he and his friend Steve came driving around my parents' house in Steve's big orange pickup trying to see if they could catch me in the front yard. I had previously run into Mario and his best friend Steve in front of the grocery store, and I knew Mario was still hanging around the old neighborhood after high school graduation. So, Mario and Steve spotted me washing my car one Sunday in my parents' driveway. They stopped and came into my parents' house and visited with me, while Mom and Dad, and my sister, and two brothers, were at church--we just talked. They left before the family got home. I think those boys were scared of my parents. Mario sat on the end of my twin bed, and I remember just staring at him and feeling surprised by his visit. I had a bright yellow headboard and footboard, and lime green walls. I liked to show off my cool hippie décor. I was proud of where I lived."

Bella's eyes popped. "Lime green walls!"

"And Holly painted a fluorescent peace sign and the word *Love* in pinks and oranges. My mother said she would paint our room any color we picked out, and she did! She went all out, too. She bought lime green, white, and silver sticky vinyl shelving paper, with these mod geometric designs, and covered the ugly, sliding closet doors with the tacky paper, after she painted the walls lime green, and the chest-of-drawers, desk, chair, and headboards bright sunny yellow--the brightest yellow she could buy. Holly and I thought our room was the coolest room."

"Can I have a lime green room?" Bella asked.

"Absolutely not!" I said in all seriousness.

Bella chuckled. "Purple?"

"Better!" I chuckled. "Back to the Mario story. After he graduated from high school, and disappeared for nearly two years, I felt differently about him—I forgot about him. In my senior year, I was in fascinated with a handsome nineteen-year old Cuban named Kevin Negron. My mother was crazy about Kevin, too, even though he was Cuban. She was making strides with her bigotry.

"She liked him?"

"Well, yeah, she did. He'd come over to my house and flirt with my mother. He was tall, dark, and handsome, and she was sorry he stopped coming around me. I think she wanted me to have a boyfriend in my senior year. Kevin liked me for about five minutes before he ran back to his former cheerleader girlfriend."

"He had a cheerleader girlfriend, too?"

"Yep," I sadly nodded. I reserved not telling my young daughter that Kevin was the second boy I had sex with, the first one was Dennis, who yelled out *Sarah* at the peak of his orgasm. Kevin, the long and lanky Cuban broke up with me the day after our first sexual interlude, when his cheerleader seduced him back into her life. Back then, I was batting zero and feeling hurt by the loss of something I interpreted as love.

"Mama," Bella searched for the perfect words, "Why do you love men who don't love you back?"

"Good question, Bella." I nodded. "I'm going to look at that question closer. I can tell you now, that back then, I didn't know what love was."

"Why not?"

I shrugged. "I think I had to first figure out what love wasn't, before I could know what love was."

Bella digested my words.

"But I will tell you this, Bella. There is no such thing as meaningless sex, and having casual sex outside of love creates a false hope and ultimate heartache."

"I'm never going to have sex!" She declared.

"Wait until you're mature. Any male, before the age of thirty, usually wants sex and not marriage. Too many girls buy into the fairytale. I wasn't smart about those things when I was young. I think I was looking for acceptance when I first had sex. I didn't love myself. I had no standard of perfection—no God in my life, and somehow, these guys were supposed to make me feel complete. They never did, though; on the contrary, I felt rejected. I guess my poor self-esteem stemmed from me believing that my father didn't care about me. Be careful, Bella, that you don't think the same."

"I won't."

"So fast forward, four years later--I'm twenty-two years old. I'm married to Todd. Joseph is almost two. I work at the Shell refinery as a clerk typist in the Purchasing Department. I'm bored with my life. Todd drinks every night of the week and watches every sport event on TV. I'm bored with his perspective, too. I shop with credit cards and buy stuff I don't need while trying to fill a void. I can't afford to quit working because I've accrued too much debt, and a stranger in a daycare facility raises Joseph. I'm too tired at night, when I get home from work, to be any good to anyone. I am also busy trying to take classes, and going to the gym in the evenings, to be more, and to have more. Todd and I fight all the time, over his drinking, and over my spending, and I'm contemplating a divorce. Todd and I worked at the same refinery, too. We ride to work together, and home together. Todd and your two-year old brother are out-of-town, for a long-weekend, visiting Todd's parents in New Orleans. And I'm out with Sabrina, one of those nights, for the first time in many years, and Mario walks up to us in that Houston nightclub. I hadn't seen him in four years. It's the *Urban Cowboy* movie era, too. Hollywood filmed *Urban Cowboy* in Pasadena, Texas, at the Gilley's Night Club, a place where hardhats go to play, after they have worked all day in refineries along the Houston Ship Channel. All of Houston sported western wear, hats, and boots, during this time, and everyone wanted to be a cowboy, or a cowgirl. And your biological father, twenty-seven year old Mario, came waltzing up to Sabrina and me, in a Houston nightclub, looking exactly like John Travolta in *Urban Cowboy*. I had seen him since high school. There is a scene in Urban Cowboy where the camera slowly pans up from Travolta's boots, and the viewer finally sees him leaning against the bar in the noisy Gilley's Night Club, holding a beer bottle with one hand, his other hand resting at his belt. Travolta's wearing a dark blue, western shirt with white pearl snaps. The camera stops at Travolta's newly shaved and dimpled-chin face, and there he is--this beautiful work of Italian art, wearing a black cowboy hat. He was the best-looking man in Hollywood. Travolta had these beautiful, full, kissy lips, and sultry blues eyes that melted me. I was in love with the movie star. And Mario was Travolta's twin, but Mexican flavor, still with a beard. I couldn't resist Mario. He was more than just a high school crush; I was now with a movie star! And, coincidentally, I looked a lot like Sissy, too. I was a cute thing, when I was twenty-four. Debra Winger played the character of Sissy in the movie *Urban Cowboy*. I had this long, dark brown, curly hair, and round, youthful, pretty face, too. I danced with the cowboy that night, drank too much, didn't keep a sober mind, and went home with Mario to fulfill my high school fantasy. I guess he did, too. We conceived you.

"The first time you were together?" She asked with a smile.

"Yep! In hindsight, it was perfect. *When* you came into my life, *how* you got here, and *why* you got here was all perfect."

"Does Todd know?"

"Oh yeah, you came out looking like a dark-skinned Latino baby with these huge, coal-black eyes, just like Mario's--except your eyes have warmth. You had thick, black hair, and as much hair as a one-year old child when you were born." I chuckled. "Todd's mother took one look at you, and set Todd straight, after he and I separated, as if that blue-eyed, red-head, with milky white skin and freckles couldn't figure it out on his own! But he told me that his mother told him."

Bella laughed.

"I will admit, Bella, I had a hard time with my dishonesty back then; I felt guilty after you were born. I didn't know for sure whose child you were until you were born, and I didn't say a word, either, while I was pregnant. But, as the years passed, I came to understand, that the how, the when, and the why, was perfect. Your purpose for coming to the earth was way bigger than allowing others to stigmatize you, or me, or us taking their judgments personally."

"What's stigmatize?"

"Smallness, judgment. Oh, one might say, behind our backs," I changed the tonality of my voice to dramatize that of a gossipy woman, "'Did you know Jean had that child outside of her marriage to Todd?' And the response might be, 'That's not Todd's child! Oh, no! What a harlot!'"

Bella laughed. "You're funny, Mom."

"I try to be. It's as simple as this, Bella. I didn't want to partner with a drinker. I told Todd to quit, and he didn't, and the anger and hurt spiraled out of controlled."

"He still drinks, Mama."

"I know he does," I replied while sad for Joseph. "Your purpose is way bigger than you might understand, Bella. You're like an immunization, like a flu shot."

Bella grinned, but her expression clearly indicated she did not understand me. "What?"

"When you get a flu shot, supposedly your body then builds up toleration to the influenza; and then, supposedly you don't get sick. Some people still get sick, but most don't. You, Bella, are to teach unconditional love, and when you do, people will stop getting sick, too. Their fears and judgment break down their minds, and then their bodies. Their thoughts are either a high frequency—or, what we call a love frequency; or their thoughts have a negative frequency--a low-frequency light wave. A low frequency light wave is a fearful and judgmental mind, and such negative thoughts connect to the influenza, or virus light waves, which are of the same low frequency. Your thoughts are projected light waves, and you receive light waves, what we call the atmospheric light waves. Light waves move in both directions--to you and from you, and DNA is carried by light waves, and DNA is what causes life to grow everywhere because light waves go everywhere."

Bella smiled. "So sickness is caused by the mind?"

"Yes, light waves are receptive to other light waves, and your negative thoughts connect with negative atmospheric light waves." I continued, "You were God's idea--not mine, Bella, and you do have a big job here on earth. Todd and his family, and my bigot parents, and my judgmental extended family, and Leonardo and his family, and Mario and his family, all needed your presence in their lives so they would choose."

"Choose what?"

"Well, that depends on who we are talking about. You see, when one lacks something, like the ability to love unconditionally, then God sends in something like Bella, to help all those who are weak grow stronger in God's light."

Bella smiled.

"I know one day you'll find Mario and give him a choice. And, hopefully, through your bigness, he'll learn how to love. Your very presence is profound with God. You've impacted everyone in this family--Todd's family, and my family, too, in ways that only you could teach because of the when, the how, and the why."

"Does Mario know about me?"

"Yes. He met you at Sabrina's house when you were three months old; and then, again, when you were two years old. I brought you over to his apartment and laid you down in his bed."

"What did he say about me?"

"The necessary thoughts went unspoken, and I wasn't going to force him to be anything. He had the right to choose."

"Did he know I was his child?"

"Yes. When he met you at Sabrina's house, he took one look at you and knew you were his child. He was so shook that he scrambled out of the house. I was at a place, that weekend, where I would choose either Mario, or Leonardo. Mario made my choice easy.

I began a life with Leonardo. You and I moved into Leonardo's house, and he called himself Daddy. Leonardo loved you. Todd loves you, too."

"Can I meet Mario?"

"One day you can go find him, but not now. I don't want Mario around while I go through this divorce. The other side will use him to smear my character."

"Okay."

"How do you feel, Bella?"

"I'm okay, but I want to know why Leonardo went away and never talked to me again?"

"I guess the amount of love he has to give is small like Mario's."

Bella smiled. "I'm always going to have huge, huge, huge amounts of love to give everyone."

"You were born blessed, Bella." I smiled. "You were in court yesterday, and you heard vicious stuff out there in the hallway from Sabrina and Demelza, that you may not understand, but I feel compelled to read something to you, okay?"

"Okay."

"I'll be right back."

"I'll be here" Bella chuckled while I raced out of her bedroom and downstairs to retrieve the book on my nightstand. I hurried back before my daughter got distracted, and I sat down on her bed. I opened the pages of the Bible to a story of betrayal. "This passage is the last supper."

Jesus said, 'You will all fall away for it is written: I will strike the shepherd, and the sheep will be scattered, but after I have risen, I will go ahead of you into Galilee.'

Peter declared, 'Even if all fall away, I will not.'

Jesus said, 'I tell you the truth, today--yes. Tonight, before the rooster crows twice you, yourself, will disown me three times.'

Peter insisted emphatically, 'Even if I have to die with you, I will never disown you.' And all of the others said the same.

Before the Sanhedrin

They took Jesus to the high priest, and all the chief priests, elders and teachers of the law came together. Peter followed him at a distance, right into the courtyard of the high priest. There he sat with the guards and warmed himself at the fire.

The chief priests and the whole Sanhedrin were looking for evidence against Jesus so they could put him to death, but they did not find any. Many testified falsely against him, but their statements did not agree.

Then some stood up and gave this false testimony against him: "We heard him say, 'I will destroy this man-made temple, and in three days will build another, not made by man.'" Yet even then, their testimony did not agree.

Then the high priest stood up before them and asked Jesus, "Are you not going to answer? What is this testimony that these men are bringing against you?" But Jesus remained silent and gave no answer.

Again, the high priest asked him, "Are you the Christ, the Son of the Blessed One?"

"I am," said Jesus. "And you will see the Son of Man sitting at the right hand of the Mighty One and coming on the clouds of heaven."

The high priest tore his clothes. "Why do we need any more witnesses?" he asked. "You have heard the blasphemy. What do you think?"

They all condemned him as worthy of death. Then some began to spit at him; they blindfolded him, struck him with their fists, and said, "Prophesy!" And the guards took him and beat him.

Peter Disowns Jesus

While Peter was below in the courtyard, one of the servant girls of the high priest came by. When she saw Peter warming himself, she looked closely at him.

"You also were with that Nazarene, Jesus," she said.

But he denied it. "I don't know, or understand, what you're talking about," he said and went out into the entryway.

When the servant girl saw him there, she said again, to those standing around, "This fellow is one of them."

Again, he denied it.

After a little while, those standing near, said to Peter, "Surely you are one of them, for you are a Galilean."

Peter began to call down curses on himself, and he swore to them, "I don't know this man you're talking about."

Immediately the rooster crowed the second time. Then Peter remembered the word Jesus had spoken to him: "Before the rooster crows twice, you will disown me three times." And he broke down and wept.

Later that evening, Seth showed up at my front door to pick up his two sons for his court-ordered visitation. I peered through the wall of windows and spotted Pete sitting in his white Mustang in the driveway before I angrily flung the door open and found Seth. The very sight of the man, who threatened to permanently take my children away from me, repulsed me. I did not make eye contact with the liar, but, instead, hugged and kissed my sons goodbye in the threshold before they happily walked away with their father toward Pete's car. Obviously, Seth did not have the funds to get the Volvo out of storage yet. "Have them back here by 6:00 p.m. Sunday evening," I reminded. I glanced over at Pete who had remained behind the steering wheel. He threw me a smile and waved. I did not return the gesture and closed and locked the front door.

I heard my phone ring and raced through the den toward the kitchen. I looked at the Caller ID before I answered the phone.

"Hi, George," I solemnly answered.

"How are you, Jean?" He said without his usual glee.

I hesitated not knowing whether to be honest; I still did not completely trust him, or Pete, for that matter, any longer. Was George a spy for Seth? I chose to believe George cared for me. "I just spent the entire day in court, and I'm shell shocked."

"How did that all go?" He pried.

I heard sincerity in his voice and my tears welled up. "Not good, George." I stopped speaking to hold back my tears.

"I'm sorry, Jean," he tenderly replied.

I figured he thought I was about to tell him I lost custody of my children. The very idea broke me at the seams, and I began to wail. "I got temporary custody of Harper and Doren again, but that's not why I'm crying."

"Good," he said while he digested my news.

"Seth just left with the kids. He's got every other weekend visitation."

"Okay, but his having weekend visitation is all part of divorce." George carefully reminded me while waiting on me to pull myself together.

"I'm sorry, George. I've never been this afraid in my entire life."

"What happened, Jean?"

"We have to go to court again in thirty days. Seth got my Volvo. The judge gave him my car because Seth said he has a job."

"Does he really have a job?"

"I don't think so, George. He told the judge that he had a segment producer job, but that he hadn't started the job yet. He needed a car."

"You think he's lying, Jean?"

"Yes, I do because I had a job offer as a segment producer first."

"You did?"

"Yeah, a friend offered me the position, but I decided against taking the job. I told Pete, who is Seth's friend and former employer, about the job offer, and he told Seth."

"Wow," George said while contemplating the deviousness of his old roommate.

"Whatever I charge Seth with in court, he makes the same allegations about me. He thought when we went to court, that I'd have a job; so he plotted that we would both have the same job when we went to court!"

"He is truly the snake I've considered him to always be--I can't believe him."

"He brought in Sabrina, and his sister Demelza, today, too-- they all lied. I'm scared George," I began to cry again.

"Jean, you got temporary custody of your children today. Obviously, the judge did not believe those liars."

"The judge doesn't know what to believe, George! The judge ordered Seth and I to pay a forensic psychologist to examine the parents and kids. We can't afford that expense! I'm in contempt of court if I can't come up with the money for the doctor to evaluate the kids and me in the next thirty days. The judge will be angry with me. I don't have a job. Charley has loaned me a car for a while. I don't know how long I can keep her car. If I get a job, then how will I afford to pay for a daycare, or for gas, food, and household expenses, and save enough money to buy another car, too?"

"Seth's been ordered to pay you alimony and child support, right?"

"Until we go back to court again. The judge says he might make changes to his custody orders after he gets the report from the court-ordered psychiatrist."

""Keep the faith, Jean."

"George, I haven't worked in nearly a decade. I don't have knowledge of the latest computer skills. I am not qualified to do anything! I'm a stay-at-home mom!"

"Jean, you have skills and a brain. Don't underestimate who you are."

"If I go to court without a car or a job, Seth is going to get custody of these children because he will look like the better provider."

"I wish I could do something for you, Jean."

"It's all about money, George."

"And speaking of money," George sadly blurted, "I got laid off, Jean."

"Oh no," I sympathetically replied while wishing I could run into his arms and hold him.

"I was expecting to be laid off, and it's okay. I got a good severance package. I'm going to enjoy my time off without a job. I'm still working on this old house; and now, I'll have plenty of time to do what I need to do to finish up."

"Well, you're taking it well."

"I have, too, Jean."

"I'm not feeling strong right now, George."

"I know. You've been through a lot today."

"I heard my oldest friend, Sabrina, betray me again. She was in court today and on the witness stand testifying against me."

"I'm sorry. Why did Sabrina testify against you?"

"Because she slept with my husband, and Sabrina calculates that if I tell her husband about her and Seth, then she will counter by telling Goose that I'm lying because I'm angry at her because she helped Seth get custody of my children."

"Not much of a friend," George summed.

"No, she's not," I responded while feeling hurt. "I don't want to go back to court, George. I'm frightened I'll lose my kids. Seth is such a convincing liar, and the judge appears to believe everything he says." I wailed again while I considered not raising my sons. "The judge made orders that I cannot have alcohol in my house because he believes I'm an alcoholic!"

"What?!!!" George exclaimed.

"And I can't have anyone of the opposite sex over, either, because between Seth's, Demelza's, and Sabrina's lies, the judge is convinced I am an *unresponsive* whore." I was referring to Demelza's overly used term to describe for the court how she saw me as a mother—*unresponsive*.

"Unresponsive whore!—that sounds like a woman working in a burned out profession."

I laughed.

"I'm trying to make you smile."

"Thank you, George. Seth's sister, Demelza, used the word 'unresponsive' often today to describe my interaction with my children."

"Oh, Jean, I'm sorry you have to go through all this." George supported. "God is omniscient and omnipotent. He knows your heart, and he is not going to let that snake win custody of those kids."

"I want to believe that to be true, George, but every time we are in court, the judge talks to me like I'm the neglectful and unstable parent, and the abusive and drug-using spouse. Seth and the liars paint me that negative way, and the judge is buying their tales about me!" I wiped the tears off my cheeks.

"Look Jean, Seth has been ordered to pay you support, right?"

"Yes," I replied in between my tears.

"He won't have enough money to pay you, Jean. I don't believe he's going to be blessed with any kind of financial gain."

"I do believe that will be the case. God must be angry with the liars. This courtroom is a den of evil, George!"

"You're a good woman, Jean. People see that quality about you."

"The judge believes Seth is an ambitious, hard-working man! Nobody sees truth in these courtrooms! It's all about the lawyers' gain. Seth's lawyer was much better than my lawyer was today--my witnesses were honest. Seth's witnesses lied."

"God still presides over evil! Just pray, Jean, and believe God will take care of the liars in the court. Hold on. I want to read you something in my Bible," he said while he flipped open his book. "In Exodus 23 we are told: *Do not spread false reports. Do not help a wicked man by being a malicious witness…Do not deny justice to your poor people in their lawsuits. Have nothing to do with a false charge, and do not put an innocent or honest person to death, for I will not acquit the guilty.*" George paused. "Seth and his witnesses will suffer God's wrath. God says so right here."

"Seth doesn't worry about God's wrath because he believes he is god!" I continued, "The essence of God is love. Seth is not love. What choice do I have, but to believe God will set the record straight?"

"He will, Jean. Have faith and believe God's Word to be true."

At the moment, I doubted I was worthy of God's help anymore than Seth was worthy of God's help. Those nagging feelings, that stemmed from a long ago abortion, and from my past infidelities, crept back to the forefront of my thoughts, and I felt unworthy of God's love. I heard the little voice telling me to have no hope for anything greater because I had sinned, and had been an unfaithful wife to my loving Leonardo, and that I deserved what I got from Seth. I believed that I was responsible for the abuse that I got from Seth, and unworthy of being loved by him, or by any man. I snapped out of my self-deprecating mode; those negative thoughts belonged to Satan. I reminded myself that I had asked God to forgive me in the past, and he had forgiven me, and Jesus renewed my spirit when he died on the cross. Now, I had to stay faithful and move forward as a child made in the image of God the Father, Jesus Christ, and the Holy Spirit. I dismissed the voice of Satan—he had no place in my life, or authority over God. I reclaimed my place in the Kingdom as a child of God's and found my peace again. I was not warring with God—I was warring with Satan and his emissaries. I silently prayed, *Help me Holy Spirit to not live deceived by lies.* "Strangers are going to decide my children's fate? Really?"

"You can always take Seth back;" George answered while reflecting my consideration, "and I'm guessing because he lost custody of his kids today, that he will want to come back home, again. When he lost last time, he wanted to come back, right?"

"He came back to take that Steamboat ski trip with us;" I said with a great amount of resentment. "And he came back last time to implement his new and improved strategy that he would use to beat me for the next time we went to court, which was today."

"I'm guessing, Jean, that if he can't pay you the child support and monthly maintenance that the judge ordered him to pay today, then he'll beg to come back for the second time, rather than find himself in contempt of court. I wouldn't let him come back, Jean. You and the children have been put through too much, with that man."

George was reminding me that if I allowed Seth to come back, then we all would suffer more. Seth would only leave again, and each time we went to court, Seth would put me in a more disadvantaged position. What would he plot to do the next time? "I agree, George. The children and I have already suffered through too many years of chaos. My father is paying my bills right now—my burden is now my father's burden. Dad tells me to sell this house before Seth and I get stuck in a lengthy divorce. I want to sell this house right away. I don't have any money in the bank, and I need to buy a car before I find myself without a car again. If I had money, then I could get on my feet. Maybe I could afford a nanny, too." My anger surfaced over my reality. "My mother was so right about Seth. She said he would suck me up like a vacuum. He is a reprobate, or better, to use his favorite term for himself—'a piece of shit!'"

"Oh, Jean, I don't think you should take Seth back, not even to sell the house. The court will award you the house and the kids in the end."

"I don't know," I answered while realizing my faith in God waivered with my doubts.

"The forensic psychologist will get to the bottom line, Jean, and report back to the judge the truth about Seth, that he's an over-educated bum."

"And what if he doesn't see me as the better parent? And what if Seth convinces this court-ordered fool that I am the bi-polar and drug-using parent, that I am an emotionally unstable alcoholic and unresponsive whore? What if Seth and his lawyer buy off the forensic psychologist? I cost Seth and his lawyer their arbitration. The arbitrators threw out Seth's half-a-million dollar court case against the New York brokerage, due to my efforts. Seth's lawyer *did not get* his 33-1/3% cut of that half-a-million dollar settlement, either. I figured the lawyer lost at least $166,000 if they had settled for the minimum of $500,000."

"Congratulations, Jean--good work."

"Thank you," I said while realizing it was not me who had destroyed that opportunity. "I give credit to God."

"God is good."

"I cost Seth his job, too. He and his lawyer both hate me. Seth hates me with a vengeance, and I suspect his ma does, too, now. She never did like me; but now, she's got a reason. Seth came in the middle of the night and took my car out of the garage, just as his ex-wife said he would do. That same night he climbed up the tree next to my sons' upstairs bedroom and stepped onto a wooden platform I laid up there across two v-shaped limbs. I was building my sons a tree house. I hadn't nailed the wood planks into the tree limbs yet, and had second thoughts about the structure, thinking the tree house was too high and too dangerous for my children. Seth stepped onto that wooden deck, to get onto the first-story roof, to pry open my sons' bedroom window, that same night he broke into the garage to get my car, and when he did, he fell about twenty feet to the ground."

George chuckled, "I would have liked to have seen that!"

"Me, too!" I giggled. "I had my kids sleeping next to me on the floor in my bedroom that night—he took my bed. I propped chairs up next to the door knob of my bedroom. I had the phone next to me, too. I was ready to call 911 if I heard him in the house."

"Wow, I'm sorry, Jean, that you and your children have to go through all this. The hell with that man! Doesn't he even consider his kids' well-being?"

"No," I answered. "Seth, and I assume, his lawyer, would like to beat me in court. I don't know how Seth paid his lawyer this last time we went to court. He doesn't have a dime to his name. And he hasn't started his segment producer job yet. I'd guess that Seth's lawyer worked free this last time we went to court, that he wanted vengeance for me costing him and his client the arbitration award from the New York brokerage house. Seth's lawyer is good in court—he's very good; and my lawyer is not a divorce lawyer, and he doesn't really grasp the magnitude of this situation. He's my father's oldest friend—they were friends in college. My father is paying Jerry."

"Faith is when there is nothing else to hang on to but God's promises, Jean."

"I know. The allegations I make about Seth in court roll off their ears like water on a duck's back. The court is not bothered that my husband has a boyfriend because they believe I have a boyfriend, too! I did not even get a chance to tell the court that I heard Seth masturbating on the phone in the middle of the night, but I don't think the court cares that my husband is gay."

"With who?" George asked as if shocked.

"Runi was on the other end of the phone…"

George's interest in my well-being continued after that call, and I began to look forward to our nightly phone calls, again. He had sent flowers before the first hearing, before we went to Steamboat;

and it was then, that I knew we could be more. He had not sent any more floral arrangements to me since our ski trip. We did not have any more phone conversations since I had allowed Seth to come back home and try again, after the first court hearing. However, since I had filed the second divorce petition, less than a year after the Steamboat ski trip, and since I had taken Seth back to court for the second time, our nightly phone calls were frequent again. Our ongoing conversation evolved, and we drafted terms for a partnership. We began to dream what was possible for us. We discussed what had been right, and what had been wrong in our previous relationships, and for us, a relationship that put God, and His Word first, was mandatory. Anything else was an illusion, which would lead to another shattered dream.

I recalled that George had claimed that he and his wife had put God first in their relationship. They were now divorced, and he had been a youth pastor at a church when they first set out as a couple! I recalled the night I first met George. He stood in my living room talking to Seth and me about his divorce:

...George stepped back into our adult conversation and whispered, "I never expected everything to be as hard as this divorce has been for all of us." George turned to Seth, "Liz is so angry at me, and the kids are suffering, too. She's filling their heads with negative stuff about me, telling them I was unfaithful. I hate the whole thing, but I couldn't breathe anymore. I had to get out of there."

"You have to do what you have to do," Seth retorted. "I remember Liz. She was pretty straight laced, a good Christian woman, George."

George rolled his eyes. "The woman is rigid. She works day and night—she's a workaholic."

That night, not even a year ago, I sat there in my living room with two babies in my lap. I heard George brag about his beautiful secretary to Seth. He held out a picture of the woman for Seth's consideration, and my arrogant husband, after looking at the prize, told George, in front of his two children and me, that he could take George's new girl away from him, just as he had proven to do in their college days with Deb. I did not like Seth or George's character that night. I felt threatened my husband would follow George's lead and leave me, too. I snapped out of that uncomfortable memory while wanting to believe George had since grown out of his pain. How could I know George would not leave me for another woman? In recent days, George had told me that he was lonely, and he admitted to me that he regretted doing what he had done to his wife and two daughters. He seemed to be remorseful. Maybe the sinner wanted to redeem his character in the eyes of God by loving my children and me?

    Seth's first and third weekend visitations came and went, and when he brought our children back to me on Sunday evening, three weeks after our last court hearing, he gave me what I had been praying for--an opportunity to let him beg his way back into our life. I pretended to not be angry with him, when he showed up at my front door. I acted as if I were genuinely interested in him. I was learning about the dimensions of forgiveness in my pretense—there were limitations. When the respect is gone, the relationship is over.

    I looked past Seth, and spotted my green station wagon in our driveway. "So I see you got *my* Volvo out of storage," I snidely prodded. "That cost you a small fortune."

    "I borrowed money from Ma," he said as if piqued. "Roy charged me an arm and a leg, as if he thought I was a millionaire."

    "A half-a-mil is almost a mil, right?" I smiled.

    He refrained from any kind of expression, and I continued, "You've been on the segment producer job for two weeks now, right? You having *that job* was why you were awarded *my* car."

    "Yeah, well, *that job* is not what they made it out to be," he excused.

    That was what I wanted to hear! "No? Too bad," I spouted while feeling not the least bothered that his life was not working for him. "I figured at fifty, sixty thousand dollars a year, you would be raking in at least four thousand dollars a month?" I chided while knowing, without a doubt, that no one bought anything from him because he had the spirit of a con man.

He shook his head in despair, "No. I'm not making even a hundred dollars a month, Jean. I haven't been able to sell a segment of air time to any Houston area business that I've called on yet."

"Well, your sales abilities have slipped. Is that my fault, too?" I recalled the last time we were in court. When asked about law school, he lied on the witness stand, and blamed me for his inability to commit to anything: *My wife's constant raging made it impossible for me to study. She was jealous and threatened I was in school and she wasn't.*

Seth did not say a word.

I continued, "Wait a minute! I apologize to me. Your karma is not my fault! You always sucked as a salesman." My jabs flowed out easily because I truly despised the weasel. I felt a need to hurt him. "You have *my* car, Seth. I can't go get a job without *my* car, and I'm broke, dead broke. I'm really expecting you to pay me what the court ordered you to pay me. If you don't pay me, you'll be in contempt of court," I threatened. "I want my money now, and I'll take you to court if you don't pay me soon. Daddy keeps a lawyer on retainer for me."

"I know he does, I know, I know," he angrily pleaded and then took a breath and calmed down. "I really want you and the children to have money."

"Sure you do," I said with no authenticity. "I think we should sell this house, Seth. We'll split the proceeds fifty/fifty. That's at least fifty grand to you, and fifty grand to me, after we pay Realtor commissions."

He looked at me as if contemplating the 50/50 split another way and then blurted, "We can't afford any forensic psychologist. Will you drop the divorce?"

"I can't drop a loaf of bread into my grocery basket until you pay me the child support and monthly maintenance the court ordered you to pay me three weeks ago. And we're not going back to court until the court-ordered forensic psychologist evaluates us, and the judge gets that report. So, if you can't pay for these court-ordered things, Seth, then, I guess we won't go back to court. If it's a year before we go to court, then fine with me because you have orders to keep paying me until we do go back to court. Daddy's paying my bills. Charley loaned me a car."

"Let's drop the divorce and make our marriage work, Jean. I'll agree to sell the house, if you drop the divorce and let me come back home."

"Maybe," I calmly answered while not surprised, in the least, that the deadbeat wanted me to drop our second divorce action because he was broke and found himself in contempt of court, again. The bottom line with me was there was no way I was going to chance losing my two youngest children by the orders of a judge made confused by Seth and his lying witnesses' deceptions. "We've spent so much money on all this legal chaos, Seth!" I angrily spouted. "Good thing you dropped out of law school so you could tear your family apart instead!"

"I've screwed up," he admitted with the greatest of patience.

"You think? Dumbass! Now, what? You want to come back and *'get it right'* one more time?"

Seth looked at me as if he did not understand me and dared not to reply.

"Don't play games with me," I sneered. "I'm clear that after our ski trip you came back just to screw me big time--you never intended to stay. You plotted out so meticulously how you would disadvantage me for the next time we went to court. Your game plan backfired though, didn't it?" I angrily asserted. "You didn't pass go and collect *a half-a-mil*, did you? And neither did Sabrina! And, I'm not un-stable, or bi-polar, or violent, or an alcoholic, Seth! I got the kids, after it was all said and done! You bought your own press believing I was stupid. What do you have to say now?"

"I'm sorry," he humbly responded.

I huffed over the idiot's admission and was clear he wanted to come back home out of his own selfish need and greed, and not because he cared about his children or me. I continued, "I am sure you are sorry that you lost so big; and now, you find yourself in contempt of court, and at my mercy again. And I'm clear, too, that I dislike you more than you dislike me now."

"I don't dislike you, Jean."

"Surely you jest, Seth, because I truly, truly dislike you," I growled without an ounce of toleration for him.

"Maybe I can change that," he suggested with a grin.

I snarled while I looked at him as if he was out of his mind, and angrily shook my head over his audacity to think for a second that I was still attracted to him.

"Let's stop all this nonsense, Jean, and be a family again--our kids need us."

I shook my head in disgust. "Spare me any more of your lies. I will drop the divorce, and we will sell this house. And you will bring back *my* car."

"Of course!" he said as if suddenly relieved. "I don't want us to divorce any longer--"

"Whatever," I interrupted while wondering what his angle was now. I felt my emotional burden dissipate the minute he agreed to drop our divorce and sell the house. I recalled the last time my father came over with groceries and paid my monthly bills.

***

"Seth is broke now;" my father continued, "and I'm certain he'll agree to sell this house right away. A long and drawn out court battle could last for years if you're fighting over this property and the kids. Seth might not fight you, if there is no equity to take. Split the equity with him."

***

My father's request was more like a demand, if I wanted him to continue to pay my lawyer fees and help me out with the monthly bills until I got back on my feet; but then again, my father was the accountant by profession. He knew that if I had my portion of the equity, then I would not need him to pay for my lawyer and household expenses, once I sold the house. The upside of my father's demand, was that if I did take Seth back, for the second time, then I would no longer fear losing my two children in thirty days, or whenever Seth and I finally went back to court, when the judge would hear more of Seth's inventions, and how I still had no car, job, or money. If I accommodated my father's wishes, and sold the marital home, then I would have fifty thousand dollars in my sole bank account. I would then buy a car in my brother's name, get a job, and file for a third divorce action.

I continued, "We'll sell the house under market value, Seth. If we price our house low, then we'll sell it fast. There's a lot of competition in the neighborhood. Newer homes are going up as fast as the builders can build them in the back of The Woodlands. We can't ask the same price for our twenty-year old home as the builders are asking for their new construction."

"Okay," he nodded. "Call up a Realtor right away."

"I will schedule a Realtor to come over here tomorrow and list our home on the MLS. Be here tomorrow so we can sign the listing contract together," I sternly instructed. I knew my father would be happy to hear Seth had agreed to sell the house, too. The equity in our house was the reason why Seth would fight for custody of his two children. Whether my father would be happy, that I allowed Seth back into our home, was another issue. I figured Dad would feel I had wasted his hard-earned dollars on his attorney friend, and on that expensive, all-day court hearing. In my defense, for making a deal with the devil, and letting the devil move back into my bed, I would remind my father that if Seth and I continued with our divorce, then we would have to go to court again, in thirty days, after we first paid a forensic psychologist to evaluate our family. Dad would have to pay for the forensic psychologist, as well as for that next court hearing, too—a hearing I feared I could lose custody of my children over, if I did not have a car and a job. So, I would reason for my father's logic, that I was saving him money, in the long run, by taking Seth back and selling our house first, before we divorced, while also ensuring I would not lose custody of my children because I could not provide for them.

Seth moved back into the marital home immediately, and we executed our agreements. I dropped the second divorce action that I had initiated, and he, once again, happily signed off on the agreement to drop the divorce action. Also, as he agreed, we listed our two-story 3500 square foot home on the real estate market with *Century 21* for $115,000 which was a steal, and Seth drove my Volvo station wagon back into the garage, and put our fine furniture, electronics, my unfinished novel, my word processor, and our expensive artwork back into our home.

The weeks passed, and my husband did not have any successes with the segment producer job. He brought home an all-in-one TV/video tape player and showed me examples of TV segments already produced by his employer, which included a gamut of interesting Houston businesses; but, nonetheless, Seth's karma was back in his face, as if he had breathed life into negative spirits that now wrecked havoc on his career.

I firmly believed the negativity he previously created, now worked against him, confirming for me that what goes around *will* come back around. Seth's failures were the direct result of his devious mindset. I had studied light waves. I knew light waves were energy, that light waves traveled in *both* directions. Life grew wherever light waves existed. Light waves could penetrate anything, and where light waves penetrated, life could and would exist. Seth was dark energy and not of the light.

In the meantime, I took on a babysitting job in our home and earned a hundred dollars a week, enough to pay the light bill and buy a gallon of milk. My girlfriend, Charley, called me with concerns over how I was doing since the hearing, and I surprised her with the news that Seth had moved back home, and that I had dropped our second divorce action. She responded by telling me that I was crazy to take Seth back in, and thought I should have let him be in contempt of court for nonpayment. She thought he belonged in jail. I told her that I was not interested in helping Seth at all, but that I was helping my children and me. She disagreed with my strategy to sell the house and split the proceeds 50/50 with Seth, and believed that the court, in the end, would give me the house along with the kids. I argued that I was not certain about that, and further stated that being *not certain* was too risky. Right after that phone call, Charley quickly drove over with her youngest son, and he took back the car she loaned me. I was grateful for her kindness, and did not expect my dear friend, or anyone, for that matter, to understand that I was doing *what I had to do*, to get on my feet, and keep my kids without the slightest risk of losing them permanently to a reprobate.

My family and I headed toward the holidays. Seth and I were broke for the most part, and I felt angry over having to stay stuck in my situation until we sold our home. I despised my husband and could not forgive the liar, drug addict in love with another man, and when we talked, he pushed all my buttons without much effort. I had no patience for him; and more often than not, I found myself telling him off. I seethed in his presence and fought with him almost every day since his return home. I was angry all the time, and felt the world would be better off if he died!

One quiet afternoon while Seth was working at the grocery store, my kindergartener excitedly ran through the front door, after just getting off the school bus, and shouted, "Mom! Mom! Where are you?"

"I'm in the kitchen, Harper," I answered from the kitchen while I walked toward the living room and met him halfway. The five-year old was out of breath and handed me an announcement.

I quickly noted what excited him--T-ball registration. I looked down at the short boy and smiled. "Harper, this is the day you've been waiting for, huh?"

He nodded yes. "My teacher says boys and girls can play T-ball. It's not like Joseph's team."

"Because your brother's team is just boys, right?" I prompted.

Harper nodded in agreement while he waited for me to read the rest of his flyer. "This announcement says we have to sign you up this weekend."

"Do I start playing baseball games this weekend?" Harper eagerly asked.

"No, we only sign you up this weekend. When everyone signs up, then they'll put the boys and girls on teams; and, after you get on a team, then you'll have to go to practices first, before you start playing games."

"Yeah!" He excitedly jumped up.

"You are a serious about playing ball, aren't you?"

He grinned. "I want to hit balls like Joseph does and run to bases!"

"Oh!" I had not realized that taking Harper to Joseph's little league games had such an impact on my third child. "I'm so excited for you, Harper! I can't wait to watch you play T-ball. Daddy and I will sit in the stands, and cheer you on, when you get up to bat, or when you race across the field to catch a ball!"

"Wow!" The child relished the idea of being a star player. "I'm going to go tell Doren and Bella!" He skipped out of the room excited about his life and ran upstairs.

Seth walked through the glass kitchen door in his grocery store uniform--a white, short-sleeve dress shirt, with a black bowtie, black slacks, and black leather shoes. He carried a plastic grocery bag in with him.

I smiled and asked, "How was your day?"

He grumbled while he pulled off his nametag and threw it onto the kitchen counter. "Hey, what can I say--I'm a forty-year old stock boy."

"What's in the bag?" I asked.

Toiletries," he dryly answered as he headed toward the master quarters to drop the items.

"Like what?"

"Cold medicine and razors."

"Nobody is sick around here," I retorted while wondering why he kept spending what little money he made as a store clerk, and what I made as a babysitter, each week, on superfluous toiletries. He brought in a bag of toiletries every evening when he came home from work. I questioned whether he was actually purchasing the items, and chose not to question his integrity in lieu of keeping the peace.

After he pulled off his monkey suit, as he called his grocery store uniform, he came back into the kitchen. "I find this situation humiliating, Jean. Our neighbors come into the store and see me working as a stock boy--I'm embarrassed."

"Nothing to be embarrassed about, Seth! You're doing an honest day's work."

"Oh shit," he groaned.

"Hey, welcome to the grown-up world. *You have to do what you have to do.*"

"We'll, I've been thinking about doing something else."

"What?"

"I'm thinking about running a TV commercial, advertising for lawyers."

"That's interesting. I haven't seen any commercials for lawyers now that I think about it. Is it legal to advertise for lawyers?"

"Hold on, Jean. I left something in the car I want to show you." He walked out through the glass kitchen door and came back into the room a minute later with a manila folder. He pulled out a legal-size pad with his handwriting. "Well, I didn't know if it was legal, so I went over to the law library and did some research this morning before I went to work." He referred to his notes. "I found that The State Bar of Texas first began trying to regulate ads under disciplinary rules approved by its membership and adopted by the Texas Supreme Court in 1982. Then I read that the rules changed in 1990; and then, again in 1993, when the State Bar sought passage of a referendum to amend the advertising provisions in the 1990 version of the Texas Disciplinary Rules of Professional Conduct. The State Bar believed that there were abuses in lawyer advertising that could be restricted by the rules. Then in 1993, the Legislature passed SIB 1227, which included instructions for the Bar to adopt rules and regulations regarding advertising and solicitations by June 1, 1994."

"That was just this past summer," I confirmed.

"Yeah, so State Bar members approved advertising rules in May of this year, rules that required lawyers to get pre-approval for ads and written solicitations from a newly created Advertising Review Committee. However, the rules drew a constitutional challenge. Jim Adler of Houston-based Jim S. Adler & Associates led *Texans Against Censorship*, which filed suit in the U.S. District Court for the Eastern District of Texas, alleging the advertising rules violated the First Amendment right to free speech. Adler says he began advertising his legal services in the late 1970's or early 1980's, even though he had been taught at the University of Texas, School of Law that, 'It was unseemly to advertise.' The reality was that he had to have a way to attract his clients, who were mostly blue-collar workers. Adler said he had to have a way to feed his family." Seth looked up and smiled at me.

"And what did Attorney Adler achieve in court?"

"The established advertising rules were overturned. I can run my commercial now."

I nodded, "Wow, that's great--and that door has barely been opened."

"Yeah, there is no referral service being advertised on TV. I'm ahead of the geniuses. I figure I will scroll attorneys' names down a TV screen for thirty-seconds. I'll call my referral service *Legal Stop*. Do you like that name?"

"It's catchy. How will you afford to produce and run a TV commercial?"

"That's the best part about this scheme, Jean. I'll collect $3,000 from each attorney up front, and then add their name to the scrolling list of attorneys on the TV commercial. I figured if I scrolled sixty attorneys, I'll have more than enough money to produce my commercial and run the ad on several networks."

I did the math. "Sixty attorneys times $3,000 each is $180,000!"

"Yep," Seth proudly beamed. "...and, the networks have told me that I can run a series of thirty-second commercials morning, noon, and night."

"What will a network charge you to run your commercial for a month?"

"I don't know, yet--I have to meet with their account reps."

I digested what Seth was telling me. "$180,000 is good money, Seth," I said while getting excited with him over his idea. "It sounds too easy."

"It is. I just need to call on clients. I have found all the statutes in the law books that I need to convince the attorneys that my commercial is legal."

"And when I call *Legal Stop* looking for an attorney, then what happens?" I asked.

"You get a live voice from a message center that will have the right attorney call you back. And I'm going to put together a call center and have my people set appointments for me to meet with these attorneys. I'll sign attorneys up to be part of my network."

"A call center?"

"Yeah, like a telemarketing group. I found an office space here in The Woodlands that I want to rent."

"You did?"

"I just looked at the property today. It's cheap, too. It's a small office complex that houses only four businesses. I'd be the fourth business in there."

"And what would you do there?"

"I'd set up my call center."

"Call center? Sounds like a lot of overhead."

"I'm excited," Seth said while he looked for something to eat in the refrigerator.

"There's pasta in there," I suggested. "...And, to change the subject, Seth--the big excitement around here today was when Harper brought home his T-ball registration. He was so excited he could barely contain himself. So this weekend, you and I and the boys will go register Harper."

Seth smiled, "Okay."

"Why don't you consider coaching?"

"I like that idea," he said.

"Todd's been coaching Joseph on his little league teams for years," I said while hoping Todd's involvement with Joseph would influence Seth to have more interaction with his sons. Seth had lied on his law school application when he wrote, "NASA Area Little League volunteer coach for daughter's seven-year old slow pitch team in 1990." Perhaps he deeply wanted to be an involved parent?

"Where are my sons?"

"I suspect they're upstairs playing video games."

He started to race out of the room, but I blurted, "Wait, there's more, Seth."

He turned and waited.

"I lost the babysitting job today. She walked up to the door this evening to pick up her kids, and without any explanation told me that she would not be coming back with them."

"Why not?"

"I have my suspicions she heard about our loud arguments, either from Marilyn next door, or from her child."

"Too bad, but you don't need to worry about making any money, Jean. Let me take care of you and the kids. I'm starting this business right away. I quit my job at the grocery store today. Tomorrow I'm talking to my first attorney."

"Don't you think you should hold on to your grocery store job for a while?"

"I'm not going back again," he answered.

I found no solace in his words, but felt threatened. He was talking to an attorney tomorrow, and I suspected he would leave again when he collected his projected $180,000 from sixty attorneys. He would probably give an attorney a sweet deal on his television commercial, if he filed a third divorce petition on his behalf. "I'm going to look for a job," I countered. "I wouldn't mind getting a job at the bakery at the Grogan's Mill shopping center"

"You stay home, Jean--take care of the kids while I start up this company."

"Hey," I said just as the idea clicked in my own head, "Why don't I help you start up the business like George and his wife, Elizabeth, did together when they built their Connecticut shipping business."

"Now his ex-wife," Seth reminded.

"He told me that she brought the kids to work with her before they were in school. That would be perfect for us."

"No, Jean--you just stay home with the kids. Harper's in kindergarten for half a day and Bella has to get on the school bus every morning, too. They need to be here at home, and they need you at home, too. I need you at home."

I stared at Seth while knowing he did not intend to have me on board his new start-up because he had no intention of staying married to me. Since when did he care about his kids? I impatiently snapped, "Okay, I'll stay home, and spend all the money you make."

His expression shifted to disapproval for a few seconds; and then, as if to comfort me, he threw me a pretentious smile as if he could reassure me that I had no financial worries, or more accurately, he had no financial worries. I would never get my hands on his money. "Yeah, stay home, Jean, and write your book if you need a creative outlet."

"Maybe I will write that best seller," I shrugged while feeling like a sitting duck. I had no control over my life. I recalled how he had taken my word processor, and my novel in progress, when he moved out the last time, and how he had stored everything of mine on the other side of Houston, in Demelza's garage. My novel was all I had to call my own. I was certain this man, who cared nothing about my well-being, would never dictate anything to me again. I felt threatened and maintained a defensive posture with the thief. "I saw a *help wanted* sign at the bakery today. I think learning how to decorate cakes would be fun and creative. And I need something to do outside the home. I'm going to get that job, Seth."

"I don't think you should bother, Jean."

"Seth," I impatiently advised, "you do your thing, with or without me. I need the car right now, watch the kids. I'm going up to the store to get an application. I am not looking for your permission."

"Okay, go get a job, if you so desire," he said with disgust while he threw his hands up in frustration. "Any news from our Realtor yet?"

He was so transparent. "Yes, he called today and said that those interested buyers went with new construction. They probably figured they would have to do an exorcism if they bought this place," I answered as I walked away and headed for the master bedroom to get ready to see a store manager. I mumbled, "Please, Father God, sell this house quickly." I felt Seth was plotting to leave me, before we sold the house, so he could go to court with the advantage of money, car, and job. This *Legal Spot* business would provide him that opportunity.

I freshened up, changed, and within thirty minutes was driving my Volvo to my future employer's business. I fretted over my grim situation—I needed a job and a car fast, and I knew better to believe, for one second, that Seth had my best interest in mind. My window of opportunity would shut again when Seth walked out the door for the third time. "Please, God, I can't do this without you. Help me, help me, help me," I pleaded while I drove through The Woodlands.

I determined that I could work at the local grocery store, especially now since Seth was working for himself, calling his own hours, and keeping an office nearby in The Woodlands. I could use the car, or he could drop me off at work, or I could ride my bicycle to work, if the worse occurred--that he left again, and that is, if I could find a babysitter that would not break the bank on a bakery income. The heavy traffic in The Woodlands snapped me out of worry and reminded me that I was not wearing my seatbelt. I struggled with trying to snap the ends together while I drove and suddenly became aware that my right hand was numb. My index finger and thumb had no dexterity. My hand suffered paralysis. I had never experienced any loss of feeling in my hand, and did not understand why I did not have the strength to snap on my seatbelt. I questioned if Seth was poisoning me. I did not trust the bastard.

Minutes later, I found myself sitting in the deli area of my favorite grocery store and filling out an application for the bakery position I saw on the door earlier that day. I wrote with my left hand, but my fingers could barely grasp the pen. I wondered how I would decorate cakes if I could not hold on tightly to a frosting bag. I was hoping that the numbness was temporary, that I had pinched a nerve somehow, and that by the time I started the bakery job, my hand would be back to normal.

I firmly shook the manager of the bakery department's hand with my right hand. I felt confident and collected before I sat down and interviewed with the fat elderly woman. She liked me and agreed to train me, and when the bakery manager asked me when I could start work, I suggested a week from this day, hoping by then that I would have the feeling back in my left hand. She agreed to wait a week.

I raced home excited to tell my kids about my job offer at the grocery store while feeling proud about securing the job. I pulled into the driveway and heard my phone ringing just as I stepped through the glass kitchen door. I saw Seth and the kids in the den watching TV and yelled at them before I picked up the phone, "I got the bakery job!"

"Where I worked?" Seth asked as if instantly annoyed.

"No, I got a job with your store's competitor. Aren't you happy for me?"

No response from my husband, but all my children cheered.

I picked up the receiver off the broken fax/phone machine that sat on the breakfast room's built-in buffet and said hello.

"Jean, this is Joyce. Don't say my name, just listen," she urged.

"Okay," I said barely above a whisper. I peered into the den and saw Seth watching TV, but I knew he was listening.

"I don't want Seth hearing what I am about to say to you."

"Okay," I assured her while changing hands because I could not hold the receiver with my numb left hand.

"Runi and I have finally split up. He walked out the door two days ago."

"I was wondering about yall, just the other day," I replied while now aware Seth and Runi probably were plotting to live together in my home.

"Yeah, he walked out with his clothes, said he didn't want the house anymore, that I could have it all."

"That's decent. How are you?" I whispered.

"It's hard, but I'm ready. I really feel Runi and Seth want to come out of the closet."

I did not respond.

"Seth needs to come to Christ"; she added. "…and, until he does, you can't trust him, Jean."

"I'm quite aware of that," I affirmed.

"I'm going into the hospital tomorrow."

"Why?"

"I'm having black outs, seizures."

"Has that happened before?" I maintained separation between what Joyce was saying to me, and what Seth was hearing me say in response.

"Never," she answered. "My doctor doesn't know what's causing these seizures, either, so he scheduled me for some diagnostic testing. He suspects there is an uncontrolled discharge of central nervous system neurons leading to neurologic dysfunction."

My heart fell into my stomach while I pulled up my dysfunctional hand and tried to feel sensation by squeezing my two fingers together. I still had no strength to press my fingers together. I whispered, "Do you have any history of any condition, like diabetes?"

"Nothing, Jean. I've always been healthy--never been sick a day in my life. And now, I'm having these seizures to the point of blacking out."

"Please call me as soon as you know something." I peered into the den and saw Seth still pretending to watch TV. I didn't want Seth to hear that I had neurologic dysfunction in my hand, or that Joyce was sick. I would tell Joyce later about the numbness in my hand.

"I will call you, Jean. I want you to be careful over there. I don't trust Seth, or Runi, for that matter."

"We'll talk later, girlfriend."

"I'll call you when I get my test results back. Bye, Jean."

I hung up the phone and walked around the kitchen stunned by Joyce's confirmation of my suspicions. I walked over to the coffee pot and stared at what was a full pot of coffee. I stepped into the threshold between the kitchen and den, stared at the man watching TV, and questioned if he would kill me? I blurted, "How old is this coffee, Seth?"

I watched Seth turn his attention to me. "I just made the coffee, Jean."

"Do you want a cup, Seth?"

"Already had a cup," he answered. "Who was on the phone?"

"Charley," I lied.

I walked over to the near-full pot of coffee, picked up the decanter, and poured the brown liquid down the sink while looking closely for some kind of unusual residual. I did not notice anything unusual, but I swore right then, that I would never drink any more coffee that I did not personally brew.

    Two weeks passed without any chaos. Seth did initially sign up as head coach on Harper's T-ball team, and I was thrilled he was involved in his son's life. Harper was proud, too, that his daddy went to practice with him and coached his team; but, soon thereafter, I saw Seth's ego get in the way of his relationship with his son. The assistant coaches quickly discovered that Seth came late for his own practices, and they reprimanded their head coach. Seth quickly learned he did not know the T-ball rules. The assistant coaches took their child's little league start seriously, and they had no patience with a coach who did not know league rules, nor was interested in learning them; and after the second week of practice, Seth came home feeling angry, and inferior, and quit coaching his son's team all together. He turned all his attention to his work from that day forward.

    After Seth resigned as head coach, I took Harper to his weekly T-ball practices, in the evenings, after kindergarten, while Seth built his new company from the ground up. He leased the cheap office space he had told me about, and hired telemarketers to make him appointments with attorneys, and over the first four weeks, he collected $3,000 from attorneys every single day. He hired a video company to make him a thirty-second spot, and then paid his first TV station to run his commercial throughout the day for $10,000 a month.

    My left hand remained paralyzed, and my condition forced me to decline the cake-decorating job at the bakery. I spent my time at home with the kids. Seth ensured me that he would not schedule meetings with attorneys when I needed the car to take Harper to his T-ball practice. Seth promised to attend Harper's practices and to support his oldest son in his T-ball activity; but, as the first month of practices ended, Seth was too tired, from his hectic work schedule, to join us on the baseball field three times a week.

    Seth quickly became secretive with his new lawyer referral business, and after the first two weeks, I knew less and less about his operation. The only way I had any idea of the kind of money Seth was making was to wait for one of his 30-second spots to appear on the TV station, and then count how many attorneys scrolled down the screen. I counted thirty attorneys and calculated that Seth had already collected $90,000 in the last month, and I knew then that he would leave soon. He had not given me any money, either, in the last month; but, instead, came home with bags of groceries and wrote bills for the utilities. I knew he was not staying much longer by how much distance he had put between him, his new business, and me. He paid little attention to anyone under his roof, and his business with attorneys and his employees consumed him.

One night when we had no T-ball practice, Seth came home around 8:30 p.m. from his office. Harper had been waiting for his father to come home all night to surprise him. One of the T-ball coaches had dropped off Harper's new uniform earlier that evening, and the five-year old was thrilled. He immediately put on his Cub's uniform and grabbed his over-sized plastic bat and big plastic ball. We went outside, and I pitched balls to my son in the driveway for an hour. When the sunk sank, and we stopped playing, and went inside, we made a plan that when we heard Daddy drive up into the driveway Harper would run upstairs and hide until he heard Daddy, or me, call him back downstairs. He wanted to surprise his daddy in his new uniform.

Seth came into the house and found me sitting by myself in front of the TV in the den. "Hi, Jean," he smiled.

I smiled back. "Hi Seth."

"Where are the kids?"

I winked to clue him in on what I was about to say. "I don't know. Why don't you yell for them?"

Seth turned and looked up the stairs and yelled, "Harper, Doren! Come down here and say hello to your daddy!"

Harper came proudly trotting down the stairs in his new blue and white uniform, striped socks, black cleats, baseball cap, and carrying his big red plastic baseball bat

"Wow, look at you!" Seth exclaimed.

"I'm a Cub, Daddy!" The five-year old said so proudly with a wide smile. He then stood like a batter, in the middle of the room, with his bat over his shoulder, and in position to hit the ball.

"You sure are!" Seth retorted as he picked up his son and

squeezed him in delight.

I added, "You're an All-star, Harper. I can't wait to see you on the field playing a ball game. We're going to sit in the bleachers and yell, 'Run Harper, go faster!'"

"Or stop on base!" Seth added. "Do you know to run when the boys are chasing the ball around the field?"

Harper nodded yes and beamed, "When I bat, I run!"

Seth and I chuckled. Harper had experienced me, Bella, and Todd sitting in the stands and cheering on his big brother, Joseph, and knew what was to be expected.

Harper continued, "I'm the best player on the team, Daddy!"

"I bet you are," Seth replied.

Bella came down and smiled at her little brother. "You look cute, Harper."

"Thanks," He proudly said to his sister.

"Where's Doren?" Seth asked.

Bella replied, "He's asleep up there."

I noticed Harper's new baseball cleats were untied. "When will you learn how to tie your shoes? Bring them over here. I'll show you one more time." I demonstrated once again how to loop his laces, and when I was done, I untied his strings. "Now you try to tie your own shoe laces."

I watched Harper sit down and enthusiastically loop the string around his finger and make a loose bow. "Good job!" I said while I pulled his loop tighter. I looked at Seth. "I have a doctor's appointment tomorrow for Doren. I think he's got a hearing problem."

"Good, his speech is not right."

I speculated over whether our arguments were so loud that my baby made himself deaf. "I'll need the car in the morning, so I'll drop you off at your office." I had never been inside Seth's office since he had signed the lease and moved into the building. I knew he would never invite me in, or introduced me to the staff. I had no way of getting to his office most days because I was home without a car, and Seth liked it that way. "Can the children and I come in and meet everyone?"

"What time is your doctor's appointment?"

"10:00 a.m."

"I don't have to go to the office until you get back," he responded. "I'll stay home and ensure Harper gets on the noon-day bus."

"Okay," I answered while aware of how he had evaded my question.

A MONTH LATER. Joyce called me from Springfield, Missouri, as she promised she would after she got her tests back from the diagnostic center. Her timing was perfect when she called because Seth was at still at his office.

"They don't know why I'm having seizures;" she continued, "and, actually, I haven't had a seizure in a while. Not since Runi left."

Her admission had more impact on me than she understood. "Joyce, I'm having numbness in my left hand. I wanted to tell you about my paralysis when you called several weeks ago, but Seth sat near and listened. I got a job offer at the bakery at the local grocery store, but I had to decline the job because I have no grasp in my left hand, and I'm left handed."

"Have you had a problem with your hand before?"

"No, I'm fit and healthy. I don't think it's a coincidence we both have neurological dysfunction right now."

"I don't think so, either, Jean!" Her anger surfaced. "I think Seth and Runi are evil."

"I have a very hard time believing Seth would hurt the mother of his children."

"Do you really?" She asked. "After all you've seen, you still question his character to be anything less than depraved."

"You know, Joyce, to be honest, I don't have a hard time believing he would hurt me at all." There was a time when Pete and I challenged his position with God, just before Seth went to law school. Pete asked Seth if he believed in our Heavenly Father of the Bible, and Seth answered, 'Sure I do, brother, but there is no right or wrong--it's one man's opinion against another's.' I clearly remember that I was disturbed that night by what I heard from the father of my children."

"You should feel disturbed, Jean. You have a demon living in your home."

I remembered the rest of what had disturbed me:

... "And you have a degree in Bible Studies?" Pete challenged.
Seth quipped, "All the more impressive, right?"
"So to murder is not wrong?" I challenged.
"Who says it's wrong?" Seth nonchalantly shrugged.
"God!" I answered while clear on that subject after much self-inflicted torment.
Seth snickered as if what I said was ignorant.
Pete continued, "The Masons believe God is a figment of man's mind."
Seth inserted, "They are right, he doesn't exist. That so-called God in the Bible is a debunked myth."

I validated my reason to believe Seth would kill me. Indifference was a tool of Satan's. "I don't trust him, Joyce. I pour the coffee out every morning when I first walk into the kitchen. He gets up hours before me and makes coffee. There's always a full pot of coffee in the kitchen when I rise. My gut instinct tells me to not drink it."

"God might be talking to you. You need to get out of there, Jean, before you end up dead, or with HIV."

I suddenly remembered how Seth and Joyce's husband, Runi, had drugged me with sleeping pills when I was pregnant with Doren. I was jolted out of that memory when Seth barged through the glass kitchen door. I was surprised to see him because I did not hear him drive up into the driveway. "Seth is here," I said to Joyce. "I'm taking Doren to the ear specialist again today. I'll talk to you later."

"Wait! What did the specialist tell you the first time?" She asked.

"He's had a number of earaches, and the doctor says he's partially deaf which is why his pronunciation is off. He can't hear all the sounds."

"Oh no, Jean. Well, maybe they'll give him a hearing aide."

"I don't know yet, but I was heartbroken to hear Doren was

partially deaf in one ear."

"You have to hang on, Jean."

"I am; I'm praying every day."

"Remember, acknowledge God in all his glory, and thank him for your circumstances."

I disagreed, but kept my thoughts to myself because Seth was listening. *Thank him?! I pray every day that God will change my circumstances.*

"You might go around this same mountain again, if you do not understand that until you thank God for your circumstances, you will encounter this lesson again."

"Really?" I wanted to say so much more.

"Don't try to run from your circumstances, embrace them. Acknowledge that where you are is the perfect place because God has you in his palm, and he wants you to believe in him when you have nothing else but faith."

"I get it," I said to her, but the truth was that I hated everything about my life and desperately wanted the circumstances to change.

"Long suffering is a fruit of the Holy Spirit, Jean."

"I'm over it."

"Let me read you something from this morning's read. Galatians 5:22. *But the fruit of the Spirit is love, joy, peace, longsuffering, kindness, goodness, faithfulness, gentleness, self-control. Against such there is no law.'* The Hebrew translation for "long-suffering" literally means "long of nose." The idea is simple. If God takes a long breath, His anger is delayed. The longer His nose, the longer it takes for Him to come to judgment, rather than mercy. And God has a very long nose! Scripture says *erech apayim*, which translated, literally means "long noses." The rabbis explain this apparent error by noting that God is equally long-suffering with the righteous *and* with the wicked. He is long-nosed toward both. God is gracious toward the righteous *and* the wicked. His attribute of mercy is not limited to those who have accepted His covenant. It extends to all. When we are living in covenant relationship with God, we have but one goal--to imitate the character of God in life. His character is our standard. We are to emulate His compassion, His graciousness, His goodness, His mercy and His *long-suffering*. We are to exhibit double-breathing. Our forbearance must extend to the righteous and the wicked *in equal measure*. If God can breathe twice, so must we. Who do you *tolerate*? Who do you *put up with*? How do you act toward those who drive you crazy, or who are morally repugnant?"

"I'm looking at him," I said while I watched Seth make another pot of coffee.

Joyce giggled. "Keep the faith and keep me in touch. I love you. Be careful."

"I will, and I love you, too." I hung up the phone and looked at Seth. I felt I was living with a stranger. Who was this man? Would he really harm me to get custody of his children?

"Who was that?" He asked.

"Joyce. She told me Runi walked out for good."

"He did," Seth confirmed, and then handed me the car keys to our only car.

What Seth did not understand was that I had learned from Runi's wife, four weeks earlier, that her husband had walked out; Seth had never revealed such fact. I agreed with Joyce, too--Seth and Runi were up to no good. Runi left Joyce the house because he expected to move into mine. I then questioned if Seth intended to sell our house if we did get an interested buyer.

HARPER'S OPENING DAY WEEKEND. Friday night and no sign of Seth--he did not come home. I called his office, but there was no answer. I was furious. I figured he was having an affair. The following morning, he came waltzing through the glass kitchen door at sunrise still donning the clothes he had worn the day before to work. He wore gray suit slacks, had lost his tie, and the long-sleeves of his white dress shirt were rolled up.

I sat on the couch that early morning and watched him step down into the den and pass in front of me on his way to the master bedroom.

"I left you a couple of messages at your office last night. Where have you been all night?"

"I'm leaving," he said coldly as he headed out of the room.

"You're moving out?" Surprisingly, I felt stunned.

"Yep," he confirmed without any show of emotion while not stopping to talk to me.

My anger surfaced and I wanted to kill him. "Your son's Opening Day is today," I reminded.

He stopped dead in his tracks as if reconsidering his departure. I stared at his backside. He did not turn around to look back at me, but, instead, peered down at the floor while frozen in place, and appeared to be debating his choices. He then walked out of the living area and into our bedroom. I got up and found him in our walk-in closet taking his suits off the dowel.

"You are such a low-life," I grumbled while still feeling numb. I was glad the children were still asleep upstairs. "And I suppose you're taking *my* car, too?"

"I sure am," he smugly snipped.

He walked out of our closet with an armful of clothes on hangers and headed through the house. I stood there in our closet stunned and outraged by his insensitivity. I grabbed an armful of his clothes off the rack and headed toward the car, too. He went out the glass kitchen door ahead of me. I stood in the threshold watching him place his suits into the back of my green Volvo station wagon in total disbelief he would leave his kids again, but especially on this most special day. I wanted to gouge out his eyes; but, instead, I threw his clothes out the kitchen door; they fell onto the pebble walk. I raced back to our closet and grabbed more of his clothes, and as I headed toward the open kitchen door, he stepped inside the house and spewed in a low voice, "Don't throw my fucking clothes on the ground, bitch!" He was being careful not to let the next-door neighbors hear him while he picked up his clothes off the dirty landscaping chips. I suspected he thought one of our neighbors might appear as a witness in the next divorce action, as I had previously done when I put Marilyn on the stand in our second divorce action.

I raced back to our closet and grabbed more of his clothes. I wanted him out of my life, once, and for all—he made me crazy. I hurried back to the glass kitchen door and threw the second armful into the yard, and loudly yelled for everyone to hear, "Oh, you worry about your clothes, but not about your family, you scumbag!" I was furious he was taking my car again--our only car, and the big money he was earning these days with *Legal Spot*, and leaving the children and me to fend for ourselves, again. "You deserve to die!" I yelled while I thought, *God, how do you ever expect me to embrace such circumstances?*

"No, you should die, bitch!" he grumbled under his breath while picking up his clothes off the ground.

"Your son has been waiting for this day--it's Harper's Opening Day Parade and first ball game. You *were* the head coach!"

"I quit, remember?!!!" He growled under his breath.

"You quit your son, sons? You are the lowest form of man." I studied the angry expression on his hard face. A demon possessed Seth. "How are we to get to Harper's games and practices if you leave and take our only car?" I challenged.

"Call your daddy...or Charley!" He picked up the last of his clothes off the ground and threw them into the back seat, then jumped into my car, started the ignition, and backed out. I stood in the driveway in disbelief and watched him leave his family for the third time. The pain I felt sat like a rock in my gut. There had been too many goodbyes. I felt numb and limp as I walked back into the house through the glass kitchen door not wanting to tell my children, one more time, that their father had walked out on them. I heard the familiar thumps of a child trotting down the stairs and looked into the den to see my five-year old, Harper, happily coming down the stairs in his baseball uniform.

He spotted me standing in the kitchen. "Mommy! I dressed myself! Is it time for the parade?" He ran across the den and abruptly stopped in the threshold of the kitchen with his brand new uniform on and wearing an ear-to-ear grin. I studied the short little man dressed in his cardinal blue baseball cap and *Cubs* T-shirt tucked into a pair of white knickers. His navy striped, knee-high socks were pulled high over the top of his knickers and stopped mid-thigh. He skipped a belt loop, too, but he stood proud and was ready for his big day. I smiled while a tear ran down my cheek.

"Wow, you look so cool! I think those socks are too high, Harper." I walked over to him and squatted down. I folded down the tops of his socks and put them underneath the knickers. I looked into his smiling face, and then pulled him in for a tight hug.

"Why are you sad, Mommy?" He asked while I hugged him.

I tried to hold back my tears, but the more I considered how I would tell my son that his father walked out, the sadder I became at the thought of breaking his heart. I hugged him and began to cry uncontrollably, and in between my tears, I softly blurted, "Daddy left us again."

Harper's face instantly turned down, and he acted as if stunned. He kept a strong composure and bled no tears, nor did he speak a word, and upon that sight, I held him tighter and cried for him, too.

Later that same day in the midst of the biggest event in my kindergartener's life, the Opening Day Parade and his first game, my little leaguer ever so slowly passed in front of Bella, Doren, Uncle Henry, and me. He rode in the back of Coach William's pick-up truck filled with eleven other five- and six-year old baseball players. The team parents decorated the truck with blue and red streamers and balloons. Bales of hay filled the bed of the truck and a large banner displayed on the side introduced the Cubs. I stood on the curb hand-in-hand with Doren, and with Bella and Uncle Henry standing on the other side of me. Everyone but Doren, hooted and hollered and cheered-on Harper's team as their coach's pickup crawled passed us in a slow-moving line of other baseball trucks filled with little league teams. I threw my little baseball player a kiss from the curb, but he did not react. He sat on a bale of hay, in the back of the truck, by himself, looking as if he was lost in thought, while the other boys and girls in the bed of the truck threw candy, cheerfully jumped up and down, and waved to the crowd. I was not certain he saw his family standing on the curbside and waving at him and his teammates, as they passed by us in the parade. I studied the little man, in his first baseball uniform, in the back of that truck, where gaiety surrounded him. I clearly saw, that unlike the others his age, the mournful-looking boy did not smile, or laugh, nor stand that day and wave to the crowd; but, instead, he sat lifeless, and alone, as if he just discovered his father died. Again, a tear fell down my cheek, as my son headed down the street in the back of the pick-up truck, believing his father did not love him.

I rode home with my kids in Uncle Henry's car after the baseball game. Harper played outfield that day, but could not focus on the game--he had lost his heart to play.

My brother pulled into my driveway that late afternoon with me and my children in his car, and for the first time, I noticed the *Century 21* sign was missing in the yard. "Seth took down the For Sale sign!" I said to Henry while feeling confused. "Why would he do that?"

My brother shrugged and turned off his ignition. I got out of his car to look for the whereabouts of the sign. The signpost was heavy and tall, and I couldn't imagine Seth having carried it too far. I searched around the back yard, looked beside the detached garage, and found no sign. I walked into my garage and look for the For Sale sign there. I stood in the threshold of the side entrance of the garage, looked up, and considered whether Seth had placed that heavy sign and post in the rafters over the garage. I climbed up the rails on the garage wall and peered up over the rafters, and sure enough, he had laid that heavy sign up there. Why did he want to take the house off the market when we had no contract yet? Why would he not want to split the proceeds 50/50 with me? We had gone to court already twice, and both times, he lost the kids and the house to me in the hearings for temporary orders. Why would he rather risk not getting the house at all by court order, instead of volunteering to sell the house with me and splitting the proceeds 50/50? Nothing made sense to me these days. I recalled Joyce telling me that Runi no longer cared anything about their house when he left her for good. How did these pieces fit together?

14
THE UNIMAGINABLE

A phone call and a week later, in this dreary year of 1995, my father drove over to my home with groceries and a willingness to help me and his three grandchildren out, again. I knew that I had given my father every reason *to not help* me anymore. I had gone to divorce court twice, after filing two, different divorce petitions, and both times, I dropped the pending divorce action wherein the court rendered temporary orders in my favor. My father had paid my bills for the months preceding the last court hearing, too; and now, he sat in my breakfast room paying more bills because Seth had left me and the kids, for the third time, and without a dime, again. Since the age of sixteen, I had turned my back on all my father's spiritual teachings in support of the anger I held toward him for nearly a lifetime; and now, he stepped up to the plate to help me and my three children. My disobedience to God's Word was now costing this man thousands of dollars. I stood at the opposite end of the kitchen, watched the stoic stash his personal check with my gas bill into an envelope, and place a stamp on the outside. I saw his unconditional love, and promised God to obey his commandment and honor my father for the first time in my life. At the age of thirty-six, I no longer questioned whether this flawed man loved me or not. My father had always loved God, and as a condition of his relationship with God, my biological father always cared for his wife and children.

I held a stack of Seth's mail that I had grabbed off the wet bar and said to the elderly man, "In the week Seth has been gone, he has purchased a $3,000 phone system for his office. He's paying salaries, too! His bank statements still come here. He's raking in the money from attorneys. His deposits reflect so!"

"How many employees does he have?" The elderly man asked.

"I don't know; I've never been privy to such information. Here are three bills from three TV stations, and he owes each of them $10,000. He has an office lease and utility bills. How is he affording all these expenses?"

"He's not paying the IRS," my father answered.

I threw up my hands. "Seth has never been concerned with the IRS! He's making a lot of money. I've counted over thirty attorney names on his TV commercial. I should be his competition! He hasn't given me the first dime he made with this business. He doesn't care how the kids and I get along."

"That's because he expects your father to come up with money to feed his kids," my father angrily retorted. "I'll give him three months before he's crawling back here broke, again."

"I'm not sure he's going to crash this time," I argued. "I need a car, Dad. I can't start up a business, or get a job without a car. Part of the reason I took Seth back the last time was because he had *my* car. He wasn't making any money, and couldn't pay me the court-ordered maintenance and child support, either. I thought it would be easier for Seth and me if we worked together to support this family."

My father shook his head in disgust over Seth's character. "He will crash and come crawling back because he's too greedy."

"I am *not certain* about that, Dad."

"I am! You two need to sell this house!" He grumbled. "I've got your sister pulling at my pocket book for attorney fees, and your mother's illness is costing me a fortune. I'm drawing money out of my retirement accounts these days."

"We *had* a For Sale sign in the front yard, but now that Seth is rolling in the money from *Legal Spot*, he doesn't want to sell the house. He took the For Sale sign down just before he left for the *third* time."

"I don't understand why he did that, Jean Ellen? Both times the court gave you the house and the kids. I would think Seth would want to sell the house, and split the equity 50/50 with you, before the court makes final orders that you and the children have sole possession of the house? You're being more than fair with him; after all, you and Seth bought this home as a result of your and Leonardo's apparel business. That apparel business was never Seth's business in the first place," the man angrily shot back. "When a judge figures that out, then you'll be awarded the house."

My father was putting my lack of integrity back in my face, but I chose not to comment. "No, Seth doesn't want to split the equity with me; he wants the whole kit and caboodle. He still owes his mother her life savings of $85,000. If he splits the house equity with me, then, at the most, he'll receive $50,000 in the split--that is, if we sell the house for $120,000—we have to pay the Realtor commissions and closing costs. How will he pay off his mother and have any money for himself, if he doesn't get the whole house?"

My father shook his head in disgust.

"He is really pissed off that I screwed up his arbitration, too. He was sure he would win *half-a-mil* in that hearing. That arbitration was schedule the day after he left us the last time."

I watched my father suck on his pipe and contemplate what I was saying. "Gosh, Jean Ellen," he said in pure disgust, "That man's not right with God, or his family."

"That's an understatement! Seth stuck that heavy For Sale sign up in the garage rafters so I wouldn't be able to put the sign back up in the yard. He doesn't give our children's future, or mine, any consideration. He wants me broke and without a car. I guess he thinks three times is the charm for him, if we go back to court."

"Your house is still listed on the MLS, right?"

"It's still under contract."

"Okay, your Realtor will still show the house, with or without a sign in the yard."

"I guess so."

"Your husband has all these hair-brain, get-rich-quick schemes. Gosh, Jean Ellen, first he gambles his mother's money; then, he starts this lawyer referral business, without looking at the bottom line. He'll be broke in a month, and crawling back home, and I'm not going to afford another lawyer for you, either. When he comes back broke, take him back for the last time, and you two sell this home. And then you'll both have money to afford your own lawyers, and you can buy your own car, and, as I've suggested in the past, put the car in your brother's name."

I doubted Seth would be crawling back home broke, and I felt threatened he would file a third divorce petition soon, with one of his *Legal Spot* attorneys. "I feel like a sitting duck," I argued. "Seth is gaining momentum in creating the illusion of being successful for his next court case against me, while I sit here broke, and without a car, one more time. I tried to get a job before he left this last time, and I did! It was a good job at the bakery."

"The grocery stores pay good hourly wages, Jean Ellen—they're union. And they have good benefits and retirement plans."

"But I couldn't take the job!"

"Why not?" The skeptic asked.

"Because my left hand was paralyzed for a while. Just in the last week, I started getting sensation back in my fingers, but it's too late to take the job now. Someone else took that job."

"What do you think caused your hand to go numb?"

I reserved my answer. I would not tell this elderly man, who had the burden of a dying wife, and two daughters who both endured nasty and expensive divorces, that I thought Seth poisoned the mother of his two children. I did not want to worry my father, or my terminal mother, with such wickedness mainly because I gave Seth the benefit of the doubt. I had no proof. "I don't know why my hand went numb," I answered while remembering Joyce had admitted to me that her seizures and blackouts had stopped since Runi had left her, too. "...And, I don't know *why* Seth doesn't want to sell the house, either!"

"I understand all this divorce stuff is a heavy burden for you, Jean Ellen; it is for me, too. You have two choices, though--you can carry your burden and have it crush you, or you can cast your burden upon the Lord."

I instantly balked at his belief that I should just wait around for a miracle, while I felt my threat was bigger than my trust in God to provide me a car or lawyer. I reserved my argument while I worried about not having the essentials in life and losing my kids to Seth--the successful ad man.

"You'll have to come under the authority of someone, Jean Ellen. Jesus told us that submission is required to enjoy His rest."

I wiggled my fingers and summed that my hand was back to normal, now that Seth had been gone a while, too. At the moment, I had a hard time with trusting in the Lord. I feared the circumstances would dictate who would get custody of the kids.

"Go mail these bills," he said while stacking them on the end of the kitchen table. He took cash out of his wallet and sat a hundred dollars next to the bills along with his car keys. "Go get Doren's ear medicine, too. And take my car. I'll stay here with Doren and make sure Harper gets on the school bus."

"Thank you."

He nodded okay.

"Doctor Nair, Doren's audiologist, said that Doren's audiogram was normal. The examination revealed mild right, middle ear fluid. And the doctor recommends observation for the time being. If the fluid does not clear in three months, or so, then he will arrange to drain it with surgery. He'll insert tubes like we did with Bella."

My father digested what I said just as the phone rang. I stepped down into the sunken den and walked over to the wet bar and looked at the Caller I.D. box. *Legal Spot* was calling. I picked up and barked, "What do you want, Seth?"

"What are you doing, Jean?" He asked as if all was lovely in our world.

I worried Seth would kidnap his kids now that there was no protective order in place, and prayed he would not disrupt Harper's first year in school and make his son even unhappier. "My father is here visiting with me and his grandkids."

Seth harangued, "Guess you didn't start paralegal classes after all?" He tittered as if amused.

His words enraged me, but I remained calm. "Nope, once again you foiled my attempts to provide a better life for my children."

"You won't get custody of your children because you cannot give them the life they deserve."

I raged on the inside, but reminded myself to remain calm and not show him any fear. "You'll be in jail, Seth. I will have total custody of these children." Then I played my trump card. "I'm going to collect all the stolen merchandise you stole, while you worked in the drug department at the grocery store, and take it back to that store manager today. Think about that, Seth. Ha!"

A sinister laugh echoed in his effort to tell me that my threat did not bother him, but I didn't believe him. I continued, "You're too stupid to worry. Let me give it to you straight--your theft is not a misdemeanor. This amount of stolen merchandise is a felony. You're a felonious thief! You have stolen more than a hundred dollars' worth of merchandise. I'd say you must have looted somewhere in the neighborhood of five hundred dollars? Wouldn't you agree, Seth?"

"I don't know what you're talking about." He remained calm

and listened for more detail.

"Well, Seth, maybe you have some money for me? I'll take the five hundred dollars. I need to feed my children. And I might be persuaded to not turn in all those bottles of stolen cologne, if you act responsible."

"Fuck you, bitch!" He retorted while he realized I had found his stashed colognes in the garage rafters, where he had also stashed his legal information about his lawsuit against Prudential.

I chuckled. I was getting the best of my husband, and then calmly continued, "No, fuck *you*, Seth. You're collecting thousands of dollars from lawyers. You're paying a staff of employees each week--a telemarketing crew, and you're running tens of thousands of dollars of TV commercials each month on several networks, and you leave me without a single dime to care for our children! I have all your bills here!"

"Guess you better get used to your new lifestyle," he growled. "If you can't care for *my* children, then the courts should hear about it."

"Oh, I can take care of my children," I yelled. "I'm going to the welfare office this morning, and I'm getting on food stamps. I have an appointment at 10:00 a.m. at the Attorney General's Office in Conroe to see about child support, too, and my daddy is here to watch my children...so don't bother trying to break into my house while I am gone."

He exulted, "It's your house for a short while."

"No, Seth," I angrily replied, "When the court hears I had to get food stamps to feed my children, they'll straighten it all out."

"Yeah, sure they will," he laughed, "and how are you going to take me to court, on your good looks? That sure won't buy you an attorney!"

"Count on it!" I yelled while realizing he had calculated that my daddy would not pay for a third divorce action, after I got everything I wanted both times in both hearings, and then dropped the divorce action, and let the bum back in. "Do you ever think how God our Heavenly Father might feel about you right now?"

He laughed and I continued, "You're going straight to hell,

and everything you do to me, and to your kids, you will be held accountable."

"Oh, I'm worried--" He mocked.

"And you should know, Seth, I am going to the welfare office today to get on food stamps. And the next time we go to court, I will tell the judge that you abandoned your wife and children, and that out of the $90,000 you made just in the first month with *Legal Spot*, you gave us not a single dime of support."

"When are you going to the welfare office?"

"Right now, Seth!"

"Are you going to the agency in Conroe?"

"Why?" I asked while wondering if he considered giving me money.

He did not respond.

"I'll be at that same Conroe office where we went before, when you kept us at poverty level for the first three years of this shit relationship. If you want to bring me some cash today, I have a 10:00 o'clock appointment with the Attorney General. You can find me there. If you don't bring me cash, then I'll be returning the stolen merchandise to your former employer after I leave Conroe." I hung up on him.

I zipped into the kitchen, grabbed a couple of plastic grocery bags from a cabinet, and headed straight for the master bathroom--I was on a mission to mess him up. I would bundle up all of the toiletries I suspected Seth had stolen in the four weeks that he had worked at the neighborhood grocery store, and if the store manager indicated that his former employee did, indeed, steal all these items, then I would have more damaging evidence against my husband's character, the next time we were in court. I opened up all the bathroom cabinets and searched for unopened toiletries that *I had not brought* into our home. I found a dozen unopened razor packages, a dozen unopened cold medicine boxes, and ten expensive bottles of men's cologne, each still in its wrapped box that I had carted down from the garage rafters. I had hit the jackpot. I estimated he had stolen at least $600 worth of merchandise. I walked into the kitchen and showed my father the full bags. "He's a thief!" I declared. "And he belongs in jail! He stole all this merchandise from his former employer, and I'm taking it back to the store. I hope the store manager presses charges!"

My father puffed on his pipe and nodded in agreement while I grabbed up the bills and the cash for Doren's earache prescription. "I'll be gone for a while, Dad. I'm going to Conroe and apply for food stamps at the welfare agency, and talk to them about getting me some child support, too. I just now told Seth on the phone that I was going to get food stamps today. I told him the court would see him as a man who abandoned his family, and that I had to collect welfare so that the kids and I could eat."

"I heard all that, and he did abandon his family," my father asserted. "That man's irresponsible!"

"Seth never considers anyone but himself!"

"He doesn't consider how he will suffer while living his life out of God's grace," my father added.

"I worry about the hurt Seth causes his children. How will their father's devastation play out on their lives in the long run? Harper stopped believing his father cared about him when Seth left on his big game day. That parade and game was the biggest event in Harper's life. Harper had been talking about being a baseball player for months before he donned that Cubs uniform; and now, Dad, my son has no heart for the game anymore, or for school, really. Not since Seth left," I said while shaking my head in heartbreak and wiping away a tear. "I wear my baby's hurt. Seth is ruining everybody's life."

After mailing my bills that my precious father paid, and after picking up my baby's antibiotics for his most recent ear infection, I found myself parking my father's car at the welfare office in Conroe, Texas. A clerk at the food stamp office told me over the phone to come in and fill out paperwork. I knew the routine because Seth and I had applied for food stamps at this same government office, before we collected the $300,000 out-of-court settlement for the false imprisonment in Florida, and before Seth closed his one-and-only deal with *Bike World* and *Inroad Investment and Securities* and collected $100,000 a year commission for three years. I turned off the ignition and locked my father's car. I walked across the parking lot, crossed the street, and stepped up to a sidewalk that led to the front doors of the welfare office. An oversized Italian male stood in my path. We made eye contact, and I shot him a pleasant smile after seeing him first smile at me. As I walked up near to pass him on the sidewalk, he spoke to me. "Do you accept Jesus Christ as your personal savior?"

I stopped and turned. His words sounded goofy to me, but I replied, "I do! Jesus is cool."

He chuckled at my response while reaching into his hind jean's pocket and pulling out his wallet. I watched him dig out a small glossy card. "Take this," he said while he handed me what looked like a religious tract.

I took the card and read it aloud to him: "*And he had called the people unto him with his disciples also, and he said unto them, 'Whosoever will come after me, let him deny himself, and take up his cross, and follow me. For whosoever will save his life shall lose it, but whosoever shall lose his life for my sake and the gospel's, the same shall save it.*" I looked up at the tall stranger with a black beard. "Amen bro!" I handed him back his card.

"It's yours," he waved off me giving him back his glossy card. "I got more of them tracts at home."

"Thank you," I said as I dropped the card into my open purse.

"Are you going in there to get them food stamps, too, for yours?"

I hesitated to tell him my business, but then assumed that everyone that '*went in there*' was looking for a handout. "Yep," I answered while feeling guarded.

"I hope I'm not bein' too forward by askin' you about your life. I apologize if I seemed rude just then."

"Oh, no, no apology necessary," I cleared for his understanding. "Anybody going into that building is down on their luck, right?"

He chuckled, "I guess you're right about that. I've been waitin' hours in there, guess I'm just looking for a nice conversation. You're just a real pretty woman, if you don't mind me saying so."

I smiled at the country boy. "Thank you."

"I just stepped out to smoke a cigarette. You care for one?" He asked while he pulled out a pack of Marlboro's out of his shirt pocket and offered me one.

"No, thank you. I have to get in there and get my place in line."

"Oh, of course you do, and I don't want to get in your way," he said while he put his cigarettes back into his pocket without taking one for himself. My name is Paolo," he said while extending his hand.

"I shook his hand and introduced myself, "Nice to meet you, Paolo. I'm Jean."

"Jean, huh? I tell you what, Jean. When you get your paperwork filled out, and you find out you have to wait, maybe we can continue to talk, if you don't mind."

I smiled. "Why not? If you're still here when I finish filling out forms, I'll be happy to talk to you. You can pass time with me."

"I be looking forward to it. I'll be in there keepin' an eye on you—you're so pretty, it's hard to not look at you," he chuckled. "There I go again."

"That's alright. Thank you."

"I'm just telling the truth on me," he chuckled. "I'm trying to get food stamps for my brother. He's having a heart transplant soon, we hope. He's had all his teeth pulled out, too, for the operation. I'm just trying to help him."

"You sound like a nice guy."

"I guess I'm being a brother. You gotta do what you gotta do for family."

"What do you do for work, Paolo?"

"Oh, I'm not working right now. I got hurt on the last construction job, and I'm trying to collect workman's comp, and with my brother's medical issues, it's hard for me right now to hold down a job."

I wondered if the man was truly a *nice* person. "I understand how holding down a job can be difficult. I don't hold down a job, right now, either." I began to walk away. "I'll talk to you later, Paolo," I said with a goodbye wave. I headed toward the front doors and entered into a lobby packed with people waiting for the next clerk to call their number. I found the food stamp window and got in a long line. I looked over my shoulder and saw Paolo sitting down and 'keepin' an eye on me,' as he said he would do. I smiled back at the flirt.

An hour passed, and I finally got all the forms filled out and submitted to the Office of the Attorney General personnel. I filled out information about children and myself for AFDC and Medicaid, and perhaps I could get public assistance money for Doren's surgery if the doctor elected to put tubes into his ears to drain the fluid. The soonest I could get an interview was the following morning, and I agreed to show up then, but had no clue how I would get there since I had no car. The office had me give them information about the absent parent and told me that they would go after Seth for child support. I did not know Seth's home address or telephone number, but, instead, gave them *Legal Stop's* address and telephone number. I felt discouraged, and angry, with Seth putting me into a helpless position as I walked out the lobby door. Paolo was waiting for me outside when I exited in a huff.

He smiled. "So how long is your wait now, Jean?"

"I don't have a wait," I said while trying to appear happy. "I have an appointment to come back in the morning."

"Oh," he said as if surprised. "I'm a bit disappointed because I was hoping you and I would have some time to get to know each other."

"Oh, I'm sorry," I said while not caring one way, or the other, if I got to know the cowboy. "My father is watching my kids right now. I need to go relieve him. I have his car."

"How many kids do you have?"

"Four, but three live with me."

"You don't look like a woman who has four children. You sure kept yourself slim and trim."

"Thank you."

"Do you think you would care to have dinner with me tonight?"

"Tonight?" His invite caught me off guard. Paolo was not my type. His placement of the pronoun *them* in front of inanimate objects, made him sound uneducated, but then again, Seth was educated, and we shared no common values.

"Tonight," he reiterated. "Would you do me the honor of having dinner with me?"

I debated whether this over-sized teddy bear could serve some purpose in my life and concluded I needed a friend with a car. "I would like to have dinner with you, but I can't leave my children alone in the evening. Would you like to come to my home tonight for dinner?" I considered inviting a strange man with a Jesus tract to my home no risk at all.

"Your home?" He asked as if surprised.

"Do you have a truck or a car?"

"Yes ma'am—I do."

"I live in The Woodlands."

"I'd very much like to have dinner with you, Jean."

"7:00 p.m.?"

"That's fine," he happily smiled.

I smiled back, then reached into my purse for a pad and pen, and gave him my home address and telephone number.

"Will your father be there?"

"No."

Thirty minutes later, I drove into the grocery store parking lot and carried into the store $600 worth of stolen merchandise. I walked up to the closest cashier. "Would you please call the store manager?"

"Certainly!" The woman happily agreed before speaking into the intercom, "Mr. Kroder, please come to the front. You have a customer here."

A slender man walked up to the cashier who beckoned him up front, and the cashier pointed to me. "This customer here wants a word with you."

He turned his attention to me, "What can I do for you?"

"My husband use to work for you--Seth Zherneboh. He brought home all this merchandise. Do you suspect he stole this stuff, because I do," I asked while I held open the bags of expensive men's colognes and other toiletries for his view.

He looked inside. "We recently did inventory, and there was a severe shortage in the drug department."

"Well, that just happened to be the department Seth worked, right?"

The store manager nodded, "I am aware of where your husband worked."

"I think things might balance out now for all of us," I said as I handed him two full bags of stolen merchandise. "Please prosecute him. He has lots of money these days," I said before I turned and walked away in complete delight, while understanding that Seth was creating the illusion that he was a successful businessman for our next court hearing, and I was stacking up contradicting evidence against him. I had no car or money, but as of this day, I evidenced his character to be that of a thief, and of a man who not only broke his children's hearts repeatedly, but who had abandoned his responsibilities, too.

LATER THAT EVENING. 7:00 p.m., and there was a knock on my door. I flung my door open to find Paolo standing under the porch light. My three children stood in the background behind me gazing at the tall Italian. "Hello, Jean."

"Hi, Paolo. Come in," I said to the cowboy who handed me a bouquet of wild flowers and a bottle of wine as he stepped inside.

"Thank you," I said while I took his gifts and watched him smile at my children. I turned and pointed to each of my offspring, "Bella, Harper, and Doren, this man is Paolo--my new friend."

Bella smiled, and Doren smiled, but Harper did not. I was certain my son did not want another man in our home.

Paolo pointed to each child and called them by their names as if trying to remember. Bella returned his greeting with a hello, Doren giggled, and Harper ran back to his racetrack in the den as if indifferent.

"Come in here," I said to Paolo as I walked into the kitchen. "I'm almost done with dinner. I have to drain my noodles."

"Smells good," he said while he watched me pull out a vase, fill the container with water, and then drop his flowers inside.

I set the vase on the dinner table, and then handed him a bottle opener. "Do me the honor and please open the wine you brought. Red is my favorite."

"I'm happy to hear that; mine too," he said while he unscrewed the cork.

I poured the boiling pasta into a colander that sat in the sink. "Do you like spaghetti?"

"Of course, I'm Italian."

"How could I forget?" We chuckled.

"So tell me about yourself, Paolo. Who are you?"

"I'm a simple man--not like you high-class people with big fancy houses," he said. "You have a pretty home, Jean," he said while he studied the teal color kitchen with tailor-made floral drapes and matching wallpaper.

"Thank you. I've spent quite a bit of time decorating. I'm not rich, Paolo. This is not what it seems."

"I didn't ask you if you were married."

"No, you didn't, Paolo. I am legally married, but he took off."

"He must be stupid to leave you and all this," he said while he peered into the den.

"He's a...well, he's not in love with me. He could never be happy no matter how much God gave him."

"That's a damn shame. Is the fool in love with someone else?"

"I think so," I said and stopped short of explaining to the stranger that my husband had a boyfriend.

"I'd love to have a woman like you to take care of," he finished as he walked up to the kitchen's island and watched me add chopped onions to the red sauce. "The Bible says in the chapter of Peter, it is the husband's responsibility to love, to honor, and to protect his wife, and to see that her physical needs are met. If a husband does not fulfill his responsibilities, the Bible says that his prayers will be hindered."

"Have you ever been married, Paolo?"

"No, but I'd like to get married."

I noticed Paolo wore a leather knife belt off his hip. "What kind of knife is that?" I questioned while suddenly uncomfortable with the presence of a stranger who carried a weapon.

He pulled the cork out of the wine bottle, and then set the bottle down on the counter and pulled out his knife. "This here is a butterfly knife. It's all in the wrist. You just flick it like this, and it opens." I watched the double-handled knife spring open with his quick wrist action.

"Why do you carry that deadly weapon?"

"It's useful. I cut them flowers with this knife right out of a field I spotted while driving over here."

I looked at the cold steel, and its size, and summed it more than what was needed to cut twine or wild flowers. "I guess nobody messes with you."

"They sure don't," he confirmed while he put the knife back into its leather pouch.

"How tall are you?" I asked while I handed him two empty wine stems.

"Six feet five inches," he answered while he poured red wine into the glasses. "I was in the Vietnam War, served on the front line," he said while he handed me a full glass.

I took a swig and considered that if I kept him around here, Seth would stay away. "I like this wine."

"Glad you do," he said while he took a sip. "I fought them gooks."

I nodded while wondering if he hated all Asians.

"Nixon figured that if he put military pressure against North Vietnam, he'd get his way, but it didn't work. Four more years of war in Indochina is what we got, because of Nixon's pressure against North Vietnam. We got a peace settlement that was not honorable, and the peace didn't last. Nixon and Kissinger were confident they could convince Hanoi to accept the terms he consistently rejected. The U.S. thought that the North Vietnamese would eventually figure out they could not boot out the United States from Vietnam by force. And Nixon was sure he could get North Vietnam to agree to a political settlement, and in exchange then, and only then, would

American troops withdraw."

"When did you come home?"

"In 1973—but I went back. I ain't supposed to talk about it. The military recruited me to go back."

"What did you go back for?"

"They needed Special Forces."

"For what?"

"Can't really say, but I will tell you that I took part in the conflict, but I was not a national, or a party to the conflict. I was under the wire, and I was promised by a party of the conflict, material compensation."

"You're a paid sniper?"

"I'm a Mercenary," he corrected.

"Are you still a Mercenary?"

He nodded yes. "The government trained me. They can call me when they need Special Forces."

"Will they do that?"

"Probably not, because I had open heart surgery."

I had been right about Paolo; he *was not* a nice person. He was a trained killer! The man's presence in my home disquieted me.

"I probably scared you now," he gently inquired with a smile.

"Na," I lied. "I like honesty. Did you brother go to Nam, too?"

"He didn't, but he likes them war movies like I do. That's all he looks at these days. I watch them with him. He says them movies make him feel patriotic--especially the music in them movies."

"Well, music is sound, and sound is a vibration that your chakras respond to."

Paolo chuckled, "There you go, talkin' smart. I don't know nothin' about any of that chakra stuff. I just know that my brother is very supportive of his constitutional rights. He's big in the NRA."

"Cheers to the National Rifle Association."

"Yes ma'am, he's pro-militia—me, too. We stand by our Bill of Rights and Constitution. If the world stops valuing human life, then we are dead. If the government can take away our right to own guns, then the government will eventually take away all our rights. We best get ready to defend ourselves in the near future—we don't have any other choice. I go to them militia meetings for him."

"What do you discuss there?"

"Politics, the Illuminati."

"The Illuminati?" I pressed to understand how much he comprehended about a subject matter I had been studying.

"Yeah, the illuminati want to control the world, and they do, too. Two years ago, I was very angry with our president. Clinton sent the wrong signal to every terrorist in the world. The U.S. runs at the first sight of blood. Take the bombing of the World Trade Center this year. Six people were murdered, and the damage exceeded a half billion dollars. Obviously, that incident was an act of war, but Clinton didn't act like a warhead; he acted like a damn attorney. We put a few terrorists on trial, while he continued to meet with Yasser Arafat--the oldest terrorist in the world. The militia knows that if our government continues to negotiate with them terrorists, instead of dropping bombs on them countries when they mess with us, then the U.S. is in trouble. One day, these terrorists will be over here, on our American soil, doing more acts of war on us, and before you know, we'll be run by them damn communists. That's when the militias come up from underground."

"I hate war, Paolo."

"You have to fight evil."

"I suppose." I felt I'd been fighting evil nearly a decade now.

"There's a Colonel, which I ain't at liberty to give any name, but he was in the Air Force, and he worked for the Pentagon for a while, and then, after the Pentagon, he went to Area 51. Have you heard about Area 51?"

"I know of it."

"Well, there's another world, the hollow earth, and there's a whole population of people who live in the interior of the earth. Area 51 is a mega base. Area 51 includes S-2, S-4, Groom Lake—a salt flat in Nevada. Our government spends 28% of its gross national product on building them underground bases, what the government calls the Black Budget, and that money doesn't include the defense budget, or spare parts budget. Every two years, our government spends one trillion dollars on them Black Project programs. Area 51 is one of 131 active, deep underground military bases in America. 18,000 people work in them underground bases around the clock. There are 1,477 underground military bases worldwide."

I took a sip of wine while I considered my dinner guest more intelligent than I first suspected.

He continued, "The Colonel's father was stationed at Roswell, and as part of his son's induction into the military, the Colonel requested they give his son duty in Area 51 in Nevada. They made the son a full-colonel rank, said he had to be full rank before he could serve in S-4."

"S-4?"

"It's like a thirty-story building inside the earth. There is Level 1, Level 2, Level 3, and Level 4, and each level is more sensitive than the previous level. You might remember days in your youth when you would see troops on the highways, moving from Point A to Point B. Now you don't see military on the highways because they do it all underground."

"Is all this really true?" I asked before taking another sip of wine.

"Yes ma'am! They got tunnels stemming from all them underground bases. One shuttle goes to the Edwards Air Force Base in Southern California, and another over to Vanderberg Air Force Base where they test ballistic missiles. Another shuttle runs to a lower subterranean base called Cat, which I suspect is Catalina Island out there off the coast of California. Other shuttles run to Wickiup, Arizona, and to Page, Arizona, and to Salt Lake City, and to various places in Colorado, like Denver and Colorado Springs. There are thousands of miles of underground, high-speed shuttles running to underground bases. Tunnels go to Taos, Los Alamos, Carlsbad, New Mexico, and to Tulsa, Oklahoma, and to the Hutchison Air Force Base in Kansas. And then there's the Grand Canyon, Sedona area."

"Sedona is famous for UFO sightings," I said. "It's famous for its vortexes and their electromagnetic fields."

"Yep, and it's all true. There are reports of an underground city under the Enchantment Resort in Boyton Canyon, where clone-like men in black have been seen."

"Alright, if you say so." I considered Hollywood financiers had access to these tales, too.

"It's true."

"I know there's strange stuff in that part of the country. The vortexes there are created not by wind or water, but from spiraling spiritual energy. Vortex sites supposedly have energy flow that exists on multiple dimensions. I've read that these are power sources for extraterrestrials to come here."

"That makes sense, Jean. Members of the Reptilian Race, from another dimension, work with humans on scientific experiments all underground. Actually there are nine known races of aliens, and some of them species work alongside humans underground. Aliens have given us a lot more elements not mentioned on the periodic table of elements, too. They grow an element so hard that it can scratch diamonds and sapphires, and this substance can withstand 10 million degree Fahrenheit. The aliens grow this stuff underground in crystal systems."

I smiled. "You sound crazy, Paolo!"

"I guess I do," he chuckled. "Some of us here believe we share our planet with aliens."

"Are you certain?"

"I am," he said while he took a sip of wine. "And we believe that there is a creation of a separate government within the U.S. by a secret corporate cabal and extra-terrestrial beings."

I did not doubt him. "I think human arrogance keeps us in the dark."

"Some have seen humanoids in S-4."

"What is a humanoid?"

"I'm not certain, but it's alien, and it's at S-4, near Area 51. I got off track, but I first started telling you about this sentry at S-4 who worked Level Two. He was Navy Intelligence. First, he became a Navy Seal, and then he became a Black Seal and was paid bonus money to assassinate target victims. He made $72,000 a year from the CIA and got a $5,000 bonus for every successful hit. He had Colonel Grade."

"How do you know all this, Paolo?"

"I can't reveal my source."

"That's convenient." I avoided rolling my eyes.

"I could be killed for divulging my sources. The Colonel was given a mission to go to Budapest, Hungry, and murder a Green Beret Sergeant--a Senior Special Services Officer in the Army."

"He killed one of his own?"

Paolo nodded. "Yep, and he knew when he killed that Army officer that he would be killed one day, too. So now he's talking about what he has seen. He doesn't give a damn about his oath to secrecy because he fears for his life."

"I wouldn't, either! It's better to be noisy and tell the world that someone wants to kill you, and why they do, and put the spotlight on the killer. You know, the squeaky wheel gets the grease."

Paolo nodded in agreement. "They'll kill him anyway because he's talking about what he's seen underground. Special Ops get murdered all the time, and family members don't think anything suspicious because they knew their child was in a dangerous position in the first place."

"How do you get selected to be a Special Ops?"

"The military gets impressionistic youths for their special missions. They brainwash them to be so patriotic that they cry when the American flag is raised."

"Wow, that's over the edge."

"All four branches of the military have special operations, and they will take out anybody the government feels is a threat or dangerous, like a dangerous witness that might leak something that should not be leaked."

"And you were recruited to be in Special Forces in the Army?"

He nodded yes.

I stood and realized I had a dangerous man in my home-- another sociopathic personality like Seth. "Did you kill for money?"

"I can't talk about what I did."

I believed every word he spoke for some strange reason. "Were the humanoids that the sentry saw alive or dead?"

"The Navy Seal claimed he identified seven humanoid creatures with grayish skin in tubes in solution. And the military is working alongside live extra-terrestrial, too."

My head spun, and I did not know if he was crazy, or if my own government had duped me.

"You look like you're upset," Paolo asked.

"Not upset," I quipped while I considered that I might be an alien experiment if what he said was true.

"Do you think I'm telling tall tales," he asked?

"I think everything you say is possible. Why else would the military go to such extremes to hide what they hide, inside all those underground facilities? I figure the government wouldn't fund extra-terrestrial research, if they did not know they existed, either."

"There is a geologist and structural engineer who worked in them underground bases—his name is Phil Schneider, and he spent 17 years in Black Budget programs. In 1979 he dropped down into an underground military base and encountered 7' alien grays. He shot two of the grays and one of the aliens shot him back. A blue beam shot out from the gray's torso and burned off Schneider's fingers. Phil Schneider is alive today, and is risking his life to talk about what he has seen, and what is going on in secrecy between those in charge of our government and aliens."

"What's going on?"

"The large grays have been camped here, underground, for 500 years. The alien agenda is to take over this planet. They want to kill off 5/6 or 7/8 of the world's population by 2029, and make slaves out of the remaining human subjects for the benefit of their agenda. This plan is what the New World Order is really about."

"Uh huh," I said doubtfully.

"I don't expect that you digest this very easy. In 1954 during the Eisenhower Era, our government made an agreement with them aliens that live right under our feet. The Black Budget projects sidestep the U.S. Congress, and our Constitution, and us, the people. Those in charge of the Black Budget projects believe we're all a bunch of morons and we don't need to know. The idea of informing the American people on a 'need-to-know basis' about these Black Project programs was made into an executive order during the Eisenhower Era, in 1954, and some believe that informing us on a 'need-to-know basis' is treason."

"If the aliens are so advanced, then why are they hesitant to show their faces here?"

"Not sure. Maybe their immune systems can't handle our diseases."

"Interesting," I nodded. "Maybe some of our new designer diseases, like AIDS or *e coli*, come from the aliens. After all, if 18,000 people work in these underground military bases, perhaps they are transferring alien diseases from alien cadavers to the surface?"

The evening was a continuation of plausible banter. After dinner with the kids, Paolo waited downstairs in front of the TV while I got them all in bed. My guest and I finally had some alone time and he came on strong with his words while we sat on my worn gold sectional sofa in front of my big Sony TV. He told me I was beautiful, and interesting, and he passionately kissed me, and in between his hot breaths, he told me that he wanted to make love to me. His eagerness to get sexually involved with me so quick caught me off guard. He held me as if we were already making love when he made his desires known to me. He pressed me down on the sofa and held me in arms the size of my thighs, and asked me if I desired him? I found myself in a submissive position under a massive body that lay partially on top of me. I breathed in his masculinity and ran my fingers through his long, black, silky hair as if testing the water for temperature. My lusts ruled while I looked into his blue eyes and listened to him persuade me. I had not felt sexually attractive in years, but this night was different. I felt desired by the sexy Italian, and my weakness trumped any greater understanding. Seth had left once a year, for the last three years, and with the passing of each of those years, I had grown less and less attracted to a man, who had never desired me. Paolo was strong, and I had no doubts about his sexual orientation. He desired me, and the thought of sharing intimacy dominated my decision, and by midnight, we were in my king-size bed, making love in a room dimly lit by candlelight. I reasoned I needed this playful outlet and summed that while I was stuck at home, without a car, or job, for the next unnumbered months, while I waited for Seth to crash and burn, or to file the next divorce petition, Paolo would be my distraction. If I were to have a relationship with Paolo, then I would have everything I needed to ride out another storm--a friend, a well-hung lover, a security guard twice the size of my skinflint psycho husband, and a vehicle. I had a father who paid my utilities, gave me cash, and bought me groceries. And I had Jesus, who heard my prayers and gave me strength.

The following morning, Paolo drove my two boys and me to my interview at the welfare office, and later that day, we took Harper to T-ball practice, though he had missed most of the season.

A month passed. Already February 1995, and Paolo came over and spent most days of the week with me and my kids. Bella would go to school every morning, and often times, would say goodbye to me, and Paolo, whom she often found drinking coffee in a robe at the kitchen table. By noon, Doren, Paolo, and I would walk my kindergartener down to the bus stop at the end of the cul-de-sac. After Harper left for afternoon kindergarten, Paolo and I would then sit in the driveway in chaise lounges while Doren rode his four-wheeler and played nearby. I considered whether my relationship with Paolo was adulterous or not. I did not harbor an ounce of guilt. I had no respect for the father of my two youngest children, and could care less if I honored Seth as his wife. I determined love was a matter of the heart, and I no longer had a heart for a man who cared nothing about me or his children. Where the mind goes, the man follows, and what was on my mind was being happy, despite all my challenging circumstances. Paolo told me that he desired me, and God told me that he, my heavenly father, loved me.

One afternoon, Paolo brought over two huge water guns-- Super Soakers that were two-feet in length. Harper and Doren's eyes were wild with excitement. "Let's fill them up, Doren!" Harper ordered.

"Wait a minute!" I said, "Let me show you how. We'll fill them up in the sunken bathtub."

All five of us wandered into the master bathroom and turned on the tub's faucet. I pulled the caps off the reservoirs and filled each toy, and then handed one gun to Bella and the other to Harper. "The war begins! It's the boys against the girls." I declared.

The laughter began when the kids began spraying each other right there in front of the tub.

"Don't spray anybody inside the house," I warned while they all grinned as if I talked foolishly. "I mean it, everyone outside—you, too, Paolo."

"Come on, boys!" Paolo ordered as he led the pack out of the bathroom.

Doren and Harper giggled while following Paolo through the house. Bella held her water gun and looked to me for instruction. "You have to cover me, Bella. If they try to spray me, you spray them first!"

"I have your back, Mom!"

Bella followed her brothers toward the kitchen, and I followed Bella, while we raced through the center of the house. I saw Paolo grinning from behind the kitchen bi-fold doors. A gun came out of hiding, and he shot me with a five-foot stream of water, right there in the den.

I laughed and yelled back, "Not in the house!"

Bella sprayed him back.

"Not in the house, Bella!"

"But, I'm protecting you, Mom!"

Paolo sprayed me again and inserted, "It's just water, Jean. It will dry!"

Harper and Doren were laughing at Paolo's good aim and Mom's squealing when I retaliated. "Bella, get him!"

Bella laughed and aimed at all the boys, while they ran out of the glass kitchen door and hung just on the other side of the threshold. Bella was short on reaching her targets from inside the house, and Harper shot back and stung us girls with water, which sent him into hysterics.

Bella and I ducked behind the kitchen island.

Paolo grabbed the gun from Harper and came up close to

squirt Bella and me. He did not miss his targets and then ran back outside.

"Follow him!" I instructed Bella while I watched her run out the door laughing. I ran to the refrigerator and grabbed eggs out of the door.

Paolo, Doren, and Harper's eyes popped when they saw me run outside with my surprise arsenal. All three boys screamed, "Oh no! Run!"

I giggled while I chased the three boys alongside the house. Harper turned, ran back into the house, and came back out with a squirt bottle of honey. "Here Mom," he yelled while he joined my team.

"Honey! Good idea!" I then grabbed my four-year old, Doren, and put him down on the ground. "Help me, Harper! Squirt your brother with honey!"

Harper ran over giggling, and I handed him the honey bottle and said to my baby that I had pinned to the ground, "Harper is going to turn you into a pancake!"

Doren fought my grasp, leaped up from the ground. He picked up his water gun and went after his older brother.

I caught Doren and held him tight while Harper squeezed honey all over him. Everyone laughed.

I grabbed the gun from Bella, without resistance, and yelled, "Free for all! There are no allegiances!" I squirted Bella, and then Paolo, and then Harper, while Harper chased his brother around the yard with a squirt bottle of honey. Sticky grass covered Doren. I ran back into the kitchen and carried more eggs outside. I passed the ammunition to the boys and to Bella. I ordered, "Throw them at Paolo!"

The next day, I gladly found myself alone with only Doren in the house. The other two children were in school, and Paolo had gone home to care for his ailing brother. I sat at my piano next to Doren, while I practiced reading sheet music, when I heard a very noisy car drive up into my driveway. I turned and looked out the floor-to-ceiling windows and was surprised to see my green Volvo station wagon pulling up into the driveway.

I stepped out onto the front porch and scowled while I watched Seth turn off the ignition and step out of the car. The engine clanged and sounded as if it were about to fall out from under the hood. The stressed and haggard-looking man with big red sores on his face blurted, "I need your help."

"Good luck," I quipped with only one emotion--anger.

"I need this car to do my job. I took it to a mechanic and the turbo quit."

"Not my problem."

"Look, Jean," he angrily yelled. "The turbocharger is a gas compressor, and it's shot."

"Pay to get it fixed."

"The turbocharger increases the density of air entering the engine to create more power."

"And this information is to persuade me to believe what? That I must help you? Or that you're smart about engines?"

"It's going to cost too much to repair, Jean," he said impatiently. "The repair job will cost more than what the car is worth."

"Oh well," I chided with no concern for his problem.

"The car won't roll over ten miles an hour. Both our names are on the title," he continued. "I can't trade this car in, unless you go with me to a notary and sign it over to me."

I smiled. "Let me get my shoes."

He looked relieved.

I laughed and then calmly said, "Not going to help you out ever."

"I knew you would react that way!" He shouted.

"Then you're not as stupid as you look."

"Come on, Jean. I can't help you and the kids, if I can't make my sales calls."

"Oh, then I'll have to tell the court that you don't have a car, and that you can't provide for your kids, and that I'm the better parent." I mumbled, "As if there is a debate!"

"What do you want, Jean?"

"Nothing from you, Seth--not anymore. I'm fine. I don't have any worries. I'm just catching up on my tanning, and reading these days, and spending quality time with my children while I wait for you to crash and burn. We're all just biding time while you get what you've got coming."

"Fuck you, Jean!" He said and then turned around and began walking away. He headed down the street and left my car in the driveway.

"Don't leave this car here, Seth!" I yelled.

"You've got your car back, Jean," he yelled while he walked out of the cul-de-sac.

I looked at my car and knew that if Seth was willing to leave the car in my driveway, that I should call Roy's Wrecker Service, again, and have them haul the junk off. This time they could keep my vehicle, if Seth did not get it out of hawk. I would not be able to get salvage value from the car without Seth's signature either; but, I was more interested in making the vehicle disappear, in case Seth felt repairing the car to be cheaper than purchasing a new car. I knew Seth had unworthy credit and any future car loan would have a 19% or higher interest rate. Suddenly, Seth's agenda became clear. Seth was betting the bank, that if he left my Volvo station wagon in the driveway, my father would repair the vehicle for his daughter and grandchildren, and then Seth would return in the middle of the night, and steal it out of the garage, again.

A week later, I retrieved my mail from the mailbox at the end of the cul-de-sac and found an assortment of envelopes addressed to Seth. I opened up all his mail and studied his bank statements, and other various letters from vendors regarding office products, etc. I also discovered in the mail a copy of his loan docs from an auto dealership confirming Seth had bought a six-year old, 1989 Chrysler LeBaron convertible with a vinyl soft-top roof. I summed he could not have paid too much money for a six-year old car, and the fact that he had financed the car indicated to me that he had no spare cash. Perhaps my father was right when he said Seth would crash and burn.

Later that evening, Linda, my new friend, with blonde hair and blue-eyes, whom I had met in the Landmark Education seminar series I had taken with Sabrina, had come over to visit. I showed Linda the loan doc papers for Seth's new car. We sat in my front room, the music room. "I think we should try to do what he's doing, Linda. He's making a lot of money, and what he is doing isn't anything we can't do."

Linda had recently moved into her deceased grandmother's mobile home that sat on the same property behind her parents' home, not too far from The Woodlands. I knew she was looking for something to generate income, and I piqued her interest with my proposal.

She smiled, "Seth is not that smart. Wouldn't that be funny if we could undercut him and put him out of business?"

"It would be sweet justice," I answered. I stood up and walked around the corner to the wet bar. I picked up all his opened mail that sat next to the phone and caller ID and showed her the bills from the TV stations. "All we have to do is call these same companies and tell them that we want to run ads for less than what he's paying them each month."

She studied the TV stations' breakdown of Seth's airtime and looked up. "Call them up."

"I already did, just after you agreed to come over today." I grinned just as the doorbell rang.

She looked at me as if confused, and I continued to explain as I walked over to answer the front door. "This person is a sales rep from Channel 39," I said as I swung open the door and greeted a clean-cut, twenty-something year old businessman. "Hi," I said to the smiling sharp dresser.

"Hello, ma'am, I'm from Channel 39—I'm Monty Pyles."

"I'm Jean Wynn. Please, come in."

He walked in with his briefcase, and I introduced him to Linda. He shook our hands, and we three sat down in the front room.

"So I understand that you want to run a TV commercial."

"We do," I answered. "I have to tell you that I want to be my husband's competition. He's running his ad on three stations, and I want you to give us cheaper airtime."

Linda smiled, and the man pitched us time slots that would cost thousands of dollars less than what Seth was paying each month.

He came and went, within the hour, and took no payment. After his visit, and with the dollar figures he quoted us, Linda and I then number crunched until 3:00 a.m. that night. We tried to make Seth's business work just as he had set up his business. We plugged in the cost of his lease, and the cost of utilities, and answering service fees, and employee payroll; and no matter how we juggled the expenses, the business model did not fly. Seth was operating in the red. We cut the number of personnel in half, and used contractors that would operate out of our home, and still no deal--the bottom line proved only failure. When we were done, we opened a bottle of wine, and sat and discussed my future after Seth came crawling back home.

"I'm somewhat depressed, Jean, but when I look at your life, I believe I have nothing to be depressed about."

I laughed while feeling crocked. "You've got it pretty good--no kids, a paid-for-home, no husband."

"My last relationship really did a number on me, Jean."

"You'll find someone good, Linda. You're young and pretty; he'll come along."

"What about you? What's going on with this guy you're seeing?"

"Nothing! Paolo is entertainment and adult companionship. I'm not in love with him."

"I think you're jumping out of the frying pan and into the fire--you're not even divorced. You need to take some time out and heal."

"I need a lot of things, Linda--a divorce, a car, a job, some money. I need to sell this house."

"Paolo came on too fast, Jean."

"I agree."

"You're spending all this time with this, this, this...What are you doing with this man if you don't want him in the long term?"

"I know," I groaned. "He helps me with the kids. He drives me to the doctor appointments, to the grocery store. He wants to take me and the kids to church this weekend, too."

"You are leading him on to believe he's got a future with you."

"I know," I groaned while realizing I was wrong. "I like his sex, too—whew! But, I know that's not a reason to string a man along. I have to break up with him, don't I?"

"When are you going to do that?"

"After I get a car," I said while not wanting to find myself alone in the house either. "I'm scared of Seth. I fear not having a car, and not being able to get my kid to the emergency room, if I had to go again. And what if Seth tries to take Harper out of school, and I don't have a car to intercept that act?"

"I'll help you."

"You live too far away—it takes you thirty minutes to drive here."

"I don't like Paolo."

"Irrelevant!"

"My God, Jean, you told me that he was a sniper and belonged to a militia. This isn't somebody that you want around your kids."

"I know, I know, I know--you are exactly right," I groaned again. "I have no other choice right now." My faith faltered.

A few nights later, I lay in bed with the oversized Italian lying next to me. I had crawled into bed that night with a good book to read, and no intention of making love to him. I feared telling him to go away, especially late at night. I wanted to wait and break the bad news to him on the phone, the next time he went back home.

I propped myself up on a stack of pillows and read a library book, while Paolo sat beside me in his blue silky boxers reading the Bible. We had not spoken any words for the last hour, while he stayed glued to his book, and I to the pages of my latest revelation.

I quietly read: *God does not credit any of your sins to your account. You will not find your sins imputed to your account. When Jesus got on the cross, and he paid the debt for your sin, he paid the debt for your sin before you were even born; he paid the debt for your future sin; and he paid the debt for your present sin. Jesus did not die on that cross to just forgive you for your present sin. Jesus' death was an eternal redemption. His death is a finished work; and his redemption for your sin is already done. Why would God not impute your sin to your account? Because He's already imputed your sins to Jesus' account. Jesus paid off your debt. Jesus went to hell in your place after he died on that cross. For you not to accept this truth, and to discount the blood of the lamb, is a slap in the face of God and His Son, Jesus Christ. People who feel guilty are the ones who sin, but as a faithful follower of Jesus Christ, we do not have to carry around a sin consciousness and feel unworthy of God's love.*

I closed my library book and looked over at the man reading the Bible, and considered that God was not angry at me for being in bed with my boyfriend of six weeks. Paolo notice my stare and closed his book, too. He leaned over and kissed me, and his kiss grew more passionate. I was not interested in his sexual overtures, pulled away, and blurted what had been on my mind since my recent conversation with Linda. "We need to talk."

"Okay," he said as he pulled away from me.

I began to explain what I had been composing since dinner. "Paolo, since day one of this relationship, you have known that I have to get a divorce from Seth. I'm not ready for a relationship, and I think we should stop seeing each other. I'm sorry if I've led you on—I didn't mean to, but I told you from the beginning that I was not emotionally ready for a relationship. I don't have much to give, right now."

His facial expression showed me that my words angered him. He yanked my book out of my lap, leaped out of bed on his side, and threw my book across the bed. The library book landed on the floor beside me. I peered down at the floor and saw that the binding was broken. I angrily reacted, "What the hell are you doing?"

"You want to hurt me?" he hollered.

"No, I don't. You moved too fast." I took a breath. I expected he would be angry when I dumped him. I remained calm, hoping that he would calm down. "You need to leave, tonight. This relationship is not going to continue. It's over."

His facial expression changed to something I did not

recognize, and, in that very next second, he lunged across the bed and braised my cheek with his fist.

I jumped up out bed on my side and yelled. "Get the fuck out of here! Get your belongings and get out of my house. No man is ever going to hit me again."

"I didn't hit you. I purposely missed."

"Oh, I see! You want me to fear you? Nope!" I shook my head and blasted, "Not going to happen. Get out of here now, before I call the cops!" I yelled while I watched him grab his nearby jeans and T-shirt and begin to dress.

"I've told you that Seth did this abusive stuff to me; and now, you think you're going to pick up where he left off? Get out of my life!"

He grabbed his duffle bag off the floor at the end of the bed, then quickly picked up his belongings scattered around the room and packed to leave.

I walked around my king size bed toward him while he zipped up his bag and headed out the bedroom. I followed him to the front door, while not willing to listen to another word that came out of the creep's mouth.

"I didn't mean it, Jean."

"You're just one more asshole--all brawn and no brains. Get out of here and never come back. I learned how to communicate in my seminars—or rather, they coached me to understand that you are a repressed buffoon whose anger expresses itself like a blown gasket on a pressure cooker. I don't want anything to do with your kind anymore!" I yelled as I followed him through the living area toward the front door.

He pivoted 180 degrees, and with martial art expertise, he maneuvered, in one swoop, an assault that sent me flying across the Saltillo tile before I knew what hit me. I picked myself up off the floor angrier than ever while ignoring the sting I felt in my hip from hitting the hard tiles. "I'm going to call the police!"

He turned away from me and headed out the door. I raced toward his exit and locked the front door while yelling through the door, "If I see you on my property again, I will call the police, and you will go to jail for assault!"

The following morning, I heard a knock on the door. I saw Paolo through the window beside the front door and did not open the door. He peered back through the window. "Let me talk to you about last night," he said through the glass.

"Go away!" I ordered.

"I'm not going to go away until you hear me out."

"I'll call the police!"

"Don't call the police," he begged. "I need to talk to you about your husband."

He caught my attention. "What about Seth?" I said through the window.

"Open the door, Jean. I can't say what I'm about to say out here."

I turned the deadbolt and angrily flung open the door. "Okay, let's hear it!"

"You need me, Jean. Your husband is dangerous. I know stuff that you don't know about him."

"Stop beating around the bush. Why should I believe anything you say? You will say anything to get back into my life."

"I met your husband. Seth knows me."

"How's that?"

He shrugged, hesitated to speak, but continued. "I saw Seth recently. I saw him and a friend in front of a convenience store."

"So what, you saw Seth. Did you talk to him?

Again, he hesitated to answer.

"Who was his friend?"

"A younger guy with blonde, curly hair, and a sloping forehead—I forget his name."

I considered Seth's sidekick to be the loyal Chad—the boy arrested for moving kilos of cocaine, and the reason for the DEA to chain up Pete's Talent House. "Was his friend's name, Ziggy?" I tried to trip up Paolo.

"No, that ain't the name. I ain't at liberty to say no more than just that I will protect you from that homo."

"And how's that? By throwing me into walls?"

"I'm sorry about last night. I need to be here to protect you. It ain't me that you should fear. I know I was wrong last night. I lost my temper last night because I love you. You were crushing me."

"You better work on that love thing," I snapped.

"I'm trying."

"Why do you say Seth is dangerous?"

"Cause he is. He ain't no good."

"I told you that, Paolo."

"You just got to trust me."

"What did Seth and his friend say to you?" I stood there confused as to whom to trust—the man who threw me across the Saltillo tile the night before because I had tried to break up with him, or the man whom I suspected was poisoning my coffee before he abandoned his family for the third time.

I recalled that morning when I met Paolo. Seth had called me just before I had met Paolo on the front steps of the welfare office. I had told my husband that same morning that my father had come over to watch the kids because I was going to apply for food stamps at the welfare office in Conroe. Did Seth follow me to the welfare office? Had Seth and Chad watched Paolo and me talk in front of the government agency? Did they then follow Paolo to a convenience store and talk to him? Runi's wife, Joyce, warned me that Seth was dangerous; and now, this man told me that Seth was dangerous.

"Did Seth and Chad follow you to a convenience store, after watching you talk to me in front of the welfare office?"

"He doesn't want to go to court again," Paolo answered.

"He doesn't have an option!" I spewed while realizing Paolo was protecting himself for some reason.

"He wants the house and the kids, Jean."

"Oh, I know he does—I told you that, too, Paolo!" I then suddenly understood what Paolo could not say. Had Seth sent Paolo into my life to kill me? Had Seth wanted to know which welfare office I was going to that morning, so that he could send Paolo my way? Was Paolo a hired gun? Was I right? Could it be true that the father of my children would have me killed? Seth was very angry with me for costing him a half-a-mil. He could not pay his mother back her life savings. Could Seth be motivated to kill me? My deductions scared me. "Are you going to kill me, Paolo?"

"No," he adamantly denied. "I love you, Jean. I want to protect you."

Paolo did not think my question strange. I did not want to believe the worse, but what he said made sense to me. Paolo would never admit that he initially came into my life for blood money. He would not incriminate himself.

"I love you, Jean," he tenderly repeated.

"I love you, too, Paolo." I engendered for the sake of my children's lives and mine. I understood that the hired gun had fallen in love with me, or at least I hoped so. Why would Seth take down the *For Sale* sign if he didn't think he could have it all—the house, the kids, and move his mama and boyfriend in too? I needed to take this suspect out of the closet and introduce him to as many people as possible for my safety. How did my life become such a cauldron of uncertainty, tension, and warfare?

"My father will be coming over today. I want him to meet you. Do you have a problem with meeting my father?"

"I would very much like to meet your father."

He passed the test question. I assumed a hired gun would not want to meet anyone close to me if he intended to kill me. I had to keep Paolo on my good side until I could figure out how to handle this dangerous position.

"Does this mean you're giving me another chance?" He sweetly asked as if he did not think for a minute that I considered him a hired gun.

"You hit me again, and you're out of here," I warned while I stepped out of the threshold and waved him inside. "I'll make some coffee," I said. I did not believe that Paolo would kill me, but what if I were wrong? And what if I was allowing a hired gun, back into my home, to finish a job that Seth promised to pay him for? I truly did not know who the bad guy was anymore.

"I'm sorry about last night, Jean," Paolo continued. "You mean the world to me."

"Eck," I sarcastically spewed. "Seth often said the same thing to me and his kids—that we meant the world to him."

"I don't want to be like your husband. I will never hit you again. I promise."

I stood there without comment, and with only one consideration. In a matter of a few minutes, the night before, I became aware that Paolo was abusive and exactly like my husband—a sociopath; and for me to change my opinion about the Italian, and to forget he braised my cheek with his fist, with intent to intimidate me, would never happen. I would not forget that Paolo threw me across the room on his way out my door, or even more chilling, that Seth might have hired him to kill me.

My father came over later that day with groceries, again, and I introduced Paolo as the man with the transportation. I did not tell my father that Paolo had thrown me across the room the night before, or about what he had insinuated about Seth that morning on the front porch. I would not burden the old man, with a dying wife, and two daughters in divorce actions, with any crazy idea that Seth might have hired Paolo to kill me.

When I introduced Paolo to my father, they both lit up like Christmas trees. The two country boys stood in my foyer and shook hands with smiles on their faces and lots of friendly words. Paolo quickly jumped into conversation about religion with my father, after having previously heard from me that my father was a man of God.

"Jean tells me that you have been attending the same Catholic church since she was born?"

"About thirty five years," my father proudly confirmed. "I bought a little house over there in southeast Houston, shortly after her mother and I were married in 1956. I paid it off in five years, and then in 1965, I bought the house that we are still living in today—down the street from that same church that we've been attending since Jean's birth."

"Wow, Paolo chuckled. Who can do that anymore? Everybody these days is so unstable."

I snickered and mumbled under my breath, "That's an

understatement."

My father grinned and looked at me as if waiting on me to explain my comment. I didn't. Dad continued, "I paid $6,000 for that first house and paid it off in five years. Jean Ellen was in first grade when I purchased that second house for $18,000."

I watched Paolo shake his head over my father's biggest accomplishment in life. "My trailer cost more than that, Hank."

My father smiled and obviously did not judge him inbred trailer trash like I did. Dad did not ask Paolo where he hid his trailer, but instead, continued to tell our family stories to the hired killer, and answering any question Paolo asked.

"Jean's mother didn't drive back in those days, and she wanted the four kids to be able to walk to school. We lived right down the street from our Catholic church and their schools. We've been living there at that house now for thirty years, since Jean Ellen was in first grade. I worked in the accounting department for Champion Papers over there in Pasadena on the Ship Channel, and recently retired after forty years with that same company."

I interrupted their exchange. "I'll make you guys some coffee and food."

"That sounds good, Jean Ellen," my father beamed as if delighted to meet the good ol' Texas boy.

"She's a very good cook," Paolo informed my father.

"Oh, I know that!" My father agreed.

I walked into the kitchen and heard Paolo slide the conversation back to religion. I suspected he was going to convince my father that he was a good Christian, just in case I decided to say anything different from a witness stand.

"Jesus is good," Paolo declared.

"He sure is!" My father supported. "Are you a Catholic?"

"I am. I'm a Catholic Italian, but I been taking your daughter and grandkids to a Baptist church nearby. I really like this minister that we listen to every Sunday."

"Well, as long as you go to church, I guess that's alright," my father added.

I stood in the kitchen filling up the coffee basket and

listening to an exchange I considered ridiculous. I recognized that the old man had made some leaps of consciousness since the days when he told his four children, after mass, around the Sunday dinner table, that Mexicans and Baptists were taboo. His favorite ex- son-in-law, Todd, was a Baptist. His prettiest granddaughter, Bella, was half Latino. I suspected that these people had helped him with his evolution. Now, if I could just teach Dad how to break through more paradigms, like him believing all country boys are good. I guessed I would have to tell the man my mother called a country bumpkin the truth eventually, after Dad would express to me his disappointment over me having another failed relationship.

Paolo left after lunch to go check on his ailing brother, and my father appeared impressed with my current boyfriend. "Paolo's a good Christian man, Jean Ellen. Where did he say he was working?"

"He's not working, never known him to hold a job," I answered.

"Oh, I thought he said he was working construction."

"He told me that he got hurt on the last construction job."

"Oh," my father nodded while he puffed on his pipe.

I stopped there and felt no need to express my understanding that Paolo was a man who worked the system. "I think he is trying to collect workman's compensation."

"How did he get hurt?"

"I'm not sure if he is hurt."

Paolo continued to see me as usual, over the next month, and never once concerned himself with getting a job, either. I held to Sun Tzu's philosophy: *Keep your friends close, and your enemies closer*. Paolo remained confident that I cared about him, and I did.

Soon we were floating into early spring of 1995. One night after dinner, we sat on the slider swing outside. He moved the stationary swing from under the covered catwalk that connected the two-story house and detached two-car garage, and placed the bench-style seat under clear dark skies in the backyard. We sat in front of

Seth's twelve-foot Roman column with our coffee mugs in hand, sliding back and forth and chatting.

"Seth erected that column; I think in memory of his boyfriend, Runi."

"Where does Runi live?"

"I'm not sure anymore. He lived in Springfield, Missouri, when he was married; but Joyce, his ex-wife, believes he's now in Arizona on an archeology dig. They split, got a divorce, not too long ago."

"Maybe Seth will move there?"

"I don't know. He's got this *Legal Spot* business up and running. I figured Runi has plans to move into this house one day. Seth tells my children to call his boyfriend Uncle Runi, but I keep reminding my sons, Runi's not our blood."

"Maybe Runi is just a blood sucker homo?" Paolo challenged.

I smiled. I had told Paolo enough about how I felt about Seth and his boyfriend for him to make such an accurate statement. "Runi sucked the life out of my relationship, alright," I confirmed. "Seth wrote his boyfriend a letter a few days before Doren was born, and he described, in his letter, a trip he wanted to share with Runi. Seth painted seductive illusions of them snorkeling in waters off the coast of southern Turkey, and of them pitching their tents and letting their desires graze on the nearby plains, and then inscribing a stone to commemorate another special moment. Seth dreams of floating down the Nile with his so-called *brother*."

"They're just a couple of faggots," Paolo growled with great disapproval before he stood up and kicked the twelve-foot concrete column over. I watched the column fall to the ground in three pieces. "We're not going to have any monument erected in honor of that twisted shit."

I smiled and stared at what now looked like a Roman ruin.

"I'll haul those cylinders away later, if you want me to," he offered.

"Please, that would make me happy."

"I want to make you happy, Jean."

"Thank you," I said. "I'm glad you pushed that column over."

"I'll kill Seth for you if you'd like me to; then you ain't gotta worry about losing your kids to that fag."

My heart stopped. "No, Paolo. Please don't kill Seth."

"Are you sure?" He sincerely asked.

I looked at the trained killer and nodded yes. "Yes, I'm sure. I don't want to go to jail for any murder. No man is worth the risk of me going to jail."

"You're right. You can't take that risk, Jean. If you're going to kill someone, it's got to be risk free."

"Don't kill him, Paolo," I reiterated.

You and your kids would be better off without him."

"We are already without him," I assured Paolo.

"He's got it coming," Paolo angrily warned.

"One day he will reap his karma. God will see to it." I looked up at the dark sky with a full moon and listened to the music trickle from inside. My new boyfriend had turned me on to country music, and Tracy Byrd's *The Keeper of the Stars* began to play on the radio from inside the house and I thought about George. I wondered if he looked at the same stars on this night?

"This is our song, Jean," the cowboy said before he joined the male artist and sang the romantic ballad to me while looking like a man in love. He held my hand while he belted.

♪*It was no accident me finding you*
Someone had a hand in it
Long before we ever knew
Now I just can't believe you're in my life♪
Heaven's smilin' down on me
As I look at you tonight♪

♪*I tip my hat to the keeper of the stars*
He sure knew what he was doin'
When he joined these two hearts♪
I hold everything

When I hold you in my arms
I've got all I'll ever need
Thanks to the keeper of the stars... ♪

When Tracy Byrd's song ended, Paolo wrapped his arm around me and smiled. "You make me happy, Jean." He leaned over to kiss me, and while I kissed him back, I pondered the lyrics, and questioned, *who had a hand in Paolo finding me, if ours was no accident?* God or Seth?

We kissed, but I quickly pulled away and did not return the same words. I didn't feel happy about anything, especially about babysitting an assassin.

"He pulled back from our kiss. You seem distant," he prompted.

"I, uh, have a lot on my mind, Paolo. I have to get a divorce, and I hate the idea of going to court again. You know, big issues concerning my life."

"You gotta trust, Jean--pray." He stood up and pulled me up out of the slider swing. He led me into the house. We walked through the glass kitchen door, through the kitchen, and stepped down into the sunken den. "I want to ask you about something," he said as he walked over to a storage closet under the stairs, in the hallway, off the den. He opened the closet door and pulled out a three-foot tall crucifix that I had bought over the border while in Mexico with Seth and the kids. "This is beautiful."

"It's carved out of a cow bone. I bought it in Laredo, Mexico when Seth and I and the kids went over the border."

"Why didn't you hang it up?"

"I did, but Seth took it down real quick."

Paolo walked over to the fireplace with the crucifix in hand, and above the mantle, he pulled on a nail in the brick where a picture once hung. "Here's the perfect place to hang Jesus," he said while he slipped the crucifix on the nail and then stepped back for a better view.

"That's pretty, Paolo—the bone matches the cream-colored bricks."

"I think it's real nice." He then walked over to the couch, took two blue throw pillows, and placed them on the Saltillo tile in front of the hearth. "Kneel down, Jean," he said while he knelt down on one of the pillows himself.

I knelt down on the pillow beside him and looked at him. "Fold your hands in prayer, Jean," he instructed as he did the same.

I obeyed, and he began to pray. "Dear Jesus, Jean and I come together to ask you for your help. Bless Jean and her children, and me, too. Keep us safe, and from danger and accident. And help Jean get a quick divorce from a man that just ain't right with her and these children. And protect Jean when she walks into that courtroom, when that day finally comes, and keep her safe from the liars and the evil men, and give her custody of her two little boys. And Father God, I ask you, in your son's name, Jesus Christ, to bless this union, that Jean and I share together, because I love this woman. Amen."

"Amen," I added while feeling wrong to have allowed this man to fall in love with me, or to believe that he would kill me. I looked at Paolo with a smile. "Thank you for your prayers."

My boys came down the stairs while Paolo and I were still on our knees. Paolo bellowed, "Get over here Doren, Harper. I want you to come pray for your family."

They grinned while Paolo threw two more throw pillows down on the floor. My babies did as instructed by Paolo. They knelt beside me, and the new man in the house, and folded their hands in prayer. Everyone bowed their heads while Paolo led us in the Lord's Prayer: *"Our Father in heaven, Hallowed be your name, Your kingdom come, Your will be done, on earth as in heaven. Give us today our daily bread. Forgive us our sins as we forgive those who sin against us. Save us from the time of trial, and deliver us from evil. For the kingdom, the power, and the glory are yours now and forever. Amen."*

Seth had been gone since December 1994, and except for that one time when he drove over and left my dead Volvo in the driveway, I had not seen him in three months. I wondered how he truly was doing financially, emotionally, spiritually; and I wondered if Seth cared how his children were doing; and I wondered if he felt guilty about not being there for his kids or me. After Harper's first game and parade, I had no consistent transportation to get him to practices, and my lack of reliable transportation was one reason I eventually withdrew my son from the team. Harper had lost his interest in playing ball after his father left on Opening Day. Seth had not tried to take his son out of his kindergarten class yet, but Paolo informed me that he had seen Seth drive by our house, and for that reason, too, I kept my little baseball player close to home and off the practice field. I kept Paolo and his vehicle here most days of the week. It was just a matter of time before Seth tried to kidnap his kids from me.

     MARCH 1, 1995, and today was my mother's birthday, and maybe her last year on the planet--no one really knew. I could not travel to see my sick mother very often because I had kids in school all week, and though she indicated, through my father, that she wanted to see her grandbabies and me more often, I dared not leave Harper in school for half a day while I visited with my mother thirty-five miles away from The Woodlands, Texas. Paolo had hung out with me the night before, but got up and went home early this particular morning. He had errands to run on this weekend morning for his ailing brother and could not drive me to my parents' home.

    I called my mother and sang happy birthday to her, the traditional way I greeted a family member, or dear friend, over the phone on their special day. While I wanted to avoid the cost of a four-dollar sympathy card and postage stamp, I forced the celebrant to sit through a long-version of a loud tune sung in the mode of a Broadway stage performance. I was actually getting to be a better singer as the years passed.

    Mom chuckled after I sang a comedic version of happy birthday and returned to me a, "I love you, Jean Ellen."

    "I love you, too, Mom. I'm thinking about you all the time these days. How are you?"

    "I'm not doing too well on my sixtieth birthday. My body is breaking down."

"I'm sorry, Mom. What's going on with your body?"

"Well, as you know, the liver normally makes bile, but because I have cirrhosis of the liver caused by this Hepatitis C, the bile isn't released correctly, and toxins have collected in parts of my body where they don't belong. As a result, I'm jaundice. My skin is yellow; my eyes are yellow. I have mild flu-like symptoms."

"What does your doctor say about that?"

"He wants to stick me in the hospital and drain this fluid off."

"Can't you take diuretics?"

"I'm taking diuretics, but my body is resisting them. My cirrhosis has led me to have *portal hypertension* which causes ascites, and usually diuretics and salt restriction is effective with portal hypertension, but not in my case. Portal hypertension is an increase in the pressure within the portal vein, which is the vein that carries blood from the digestive organs to the liver, and this condition causes ascites which is an accumulation of bad fluid in the abdomen."

"What is ascites?"

"It's the presence of excess fluid in the peritoneal cavity; it develops as my liver decomposes."

"What is the peritoneal cavity?"

"The peritoneal cavity is the fluid-filled gap between the wall of the abdomen and the organs contained within the abdomen. So, these ascites that collect in this cavity can carry bacterial infection, tuberculosis, or be a fungal infection. My white cell count is way up which suggests I do have an infection. So, my doctor wants to put a stent in me which will return the ascitic fluids to my body's normal circulatory system."

"Are there risks with this stent device?"

"Yes," she answered. "My doctor says that survival falls off dramatically in patients with severe liver dysfunction."

Tears quietly flowed from my eyes while I concluded my dear mother's fate loomed near.

She continued, "The associated complications with the use of this stent device make this an option for selected patients only. After I have the stint inserted, my doctor says that it should eliminate the ascites, but it could worsen my situation, too, because the procedure will weaken all the organs in my body. Draining off the fluid throws off my electrolytes."

"This is not good news," I said. "It's not fair that you're suffering like this."

She heard my tears and sniffles. "My doctor says I have a while--maybe even five more years."

Or less, I considered, after hearing how fast her health was declining. "Why did this happen to you of all people? You're the most loving person I've ever known. Why do you have to suffer? Why not Seth? Why does God allow this to happen to you?"

"I don't know. We will all carry our cross, sooner or later. I've had a good life."

My mother was being strong for me because I was her child and falling apart.

"How are you doing, Jean Ellen?"

"I'm fine for the most part. I have a boyfriend that's driving me around now." I did not intend to tell my mother the first horrid fact about my life.

"Oh you do?" She said with a smile in her voice.

"His name is Paolo. I don't have a passion for him, but he's helpful. I guess he serves a purpose in my life."

"I'm glad you have someone who cares about you."

"I really do need help with three children. I appreciate everything Dad is doing for me these days, but I really need a car. I have to depend on other people, and I can't get on my feet that way."

"I told your father that he was *not* going to help out Holly and not help you."

"I hated asking him for help."

"Honestly, Jean Ellen, I don't know what it is about your father, and your brother, Henry, that makes them so judgmental toward you. I'm going to be honest with you about them. Just the other night, they were sitting in the living room and tearing you apart."

"Why do they do that?" I asked while feeling hurt.

"I don't know," she said with great disappointment. "I heard them condemning you in the ugliest manner—so mean, and I got mad. I told both of them off for being so nasty—I've heard way too much of that kind of stuff from them for too many years now. I told your father he should be ashamed of how he talks about his firstborn! I don't understand that man, but I told him that he *was not* going to take sides and create camps in this family. And your brother--he's not right with you, either."

"Thank you, Mom, for standing up for me. I'm not surprised to hear that these fear-based personalities sit judgment on me." I refuted while angry over their audacity to shred my character behind my back—"I have not lived in the same state with them for years now, hardly ever see them. How dare either one of them say anything negative about me—they don't walk in my shoes. Henry is thirty-three years old and still lives at home—what does he know about relationships, family, or children?"

"Nothing, Jean Ellen."

My anger over them judging what they did not understand intensified and I struck back. "I suspect they're both jealous. Henry's never been in a long-term relationship with any woman that I know of--I doubt he's ever been laid. He claims he's not gay, either, so I will assume he's just too afraid to take a chance on any level. He has no more ambition than my father ever had a day in his life. Henry's a substitute teacher—he can't commit to anything."

"Of course, he's jealous, Jean Ellen. And your father is a firstborn, so I don't know what you represent to him as his first-born child. I think you threatened him by standing up to him when you were sixteen."

"What, he still thinks I'm that sixteen year old?"

"I'm proud of you, Jean Ellen."

"It took me a while to understand that my father is an abusive personality, and his ways permanently stuck to some members in this family who give respect no relevance either. They've always said whatever they feel about me, no matter how ugly, and then justify their hurtful words as "the truth"; and they do so in the name of their religion. Eck! They disparage me to make themselves feel better about their own pitiful lives."

"I'm sorry Jean Ellen. I was ready to leave your father before

I got sick. I've never been able to be alone with your father because your brother wouldn't leave home like the rest of you kids, and your father enabled him to stay here. I didn't get the opportunity to find the romance with my husband that I wanted to rediscover in our golden years."

"I know, Mom. I think that Dad believed that if all of us kids left home, then you would leave him."

"Probably," she sadly shrugged. "I told him for years before I knew I was sick that if Henry didn't leave, then I would leave."

"I was always too independent for Dad's comfort. He thought early on that I was a bad influence on you, Mom. Dad didn't want me to leave home. After I got out of high school, he took all my money for rent, and then protested my wedding to Todd. You guys had to talk to a priest before you could attend my wedding. It was Dad, not you, that did not want me to marry in that garden. You're not a fanatic about your religion. And when I got divorced from the alcoholic, Dad bashed me to you, and you two sided with the drunkard. I realize you're dependent on him on so many levels. Then Leonardo came around, and you were so impressed with my second husband, and my father knew that, too. Therefore, Dad intensified his argument against me, especially when he realized you wanted to live on the second floor of our Indiana home. He never once came to any of my homes in those five years I was with Leonardo. He spent a lot of energy condemning me to you, and to Henry, and to Holly, making me out to be immoral, or mentally ill, so you wouldn't follow my lead."

"I was ready to come live with you and Leonardo in Indiana. I was talking divorce."

"I'm sorry that plan didn't work out for you."

She sighed in disappointment, "It worked out for the best. Your father is here to care for me now."

"I would have cared for you had my life gone differently."

"I know that," she nodded.

"I keep meeting people who call themselves Christians, and they are the most disturbed people I know, Mom. They are judgmental, and mean people, and as far as them being loving—I don't see it, or feel it, and they want to preach to me?! I am so turned off by these people who call themselves Christians."

"Don't let them prevent you from having a relationship with Jesus Christ and his father. I want to read you something from my Bible."

"Okay," I said while I heard her flipping pages.

"Galatians 6:1: *'Brothers, if anyone is caught in any transgression, you who are spiritual should restore him in a spirit of gentleness. Keep watch on yourself, lest you, too, be tempted. Bear one another's burdens, and so fulfill the law of Christ. For if, anyone thinks he is something, when he is nothing, he deceives himself. But let each one test his own work, and then his reason to boast will be in himself alone and not in his neighbor. For each will have to bear his own load...'*" She stopped reading and added, "Because they are mean-mouthed and hurtful, you will be kind."

"I will try. I don't feel bad about my life--not anymore. My life is hard, right now, but I'm not going to let Seth get me down, or anyone else."

"You're my strongest child, Jean Ellen."

"I don't want to be strong anymore. I give it all to the Lord."

"That's all you can do," she added with a smile. "You've taught me a lot."

"Like what, how to be nuts?" I laughed.

"That, too," she smiled.

"I have jumped into the deep not knowing how to swim, and I was crazy enough to do that before I met Jesus. I still don't know how to swim." I chuckled and continued, "One thing for sure, I don't want to give religion a bad name."

"I want to apologize to you, Jean Ellen."

"You don't need to apologize for them."

"Not for them," she corrected. "I should have been a better role model for you, and shown you what love and respect looks like. I should have shown you what a healthy marriage looks like."

Her admission surprised me. "You owe me no apology."

"I just think had you girls seen differently, you wouldn't be in the messes that you're both trapped in now."

"Like you, Mom, I'm a woman with four children. I know

how difficult it is just to walk out of a marriage. You were a homemaker--you had no career."

"I always had a choice, Jean Ellen, but I let my fear trap me."

Mom and I continued to talk for two hours before we both said goodbye. I hung up the phone feeling selfish to be embroiled in all my drama with Seth, while aware that my mother may be living her last year of life. I walked out of the house and into the cul-de-sac and headed toward the mailbox at the end of the street. I felt sad about losing my mother—she was too young, and my youngest children were too young to lose her. My sons were only four and five years old, and they would probably not remember her. I was furious at Seth for making our family life so chaotic at a time when I needed to give all my attention to my dying mother.

I unlocked the mailbox and pulled out a stack of bills. Seth was still using our marital address, and I noted correspondence from the various TV stations. I ripped open a white legal size envelope addressed to my estranged husband and read what appeared to be another $10,000 bill for another month of 30-second TV spots. I opened a monthly statement from the car dealership where he purchased his new convertible. I was livid that he had an income and could afford to pay TV stations huge amounts of money for advertising costs each month, and that he could afford to pay a monthly note for a new car when I had no car, nor money for food and utilities. The children and I were penniless and depending on my father's help.

I stormed back toward the house with every intention to call Seth's office and stir the pot over there. I had had enough of his games! I picked up the receiver of the phone that sat on the walk-in wet bar in the den and dialed *Legal Spot*. I heard what sounded like a mature woman answer, "Good morning, *Legal Spot*. How may I help you?"

"Good morning," I sweetly responded. "This is Jean Wynn, the owner's wife."

She hesitated and kindly said hello again.

I figured Seth had warned his employees to beware of the big bad witch. I continued in a humble fashion to diffuse any preconceived ideas she may have had about me. "I don't know…," I stopped and regrouped. "Is…Is he there?"

"No."

"Good. I'll just say it like it is." And calmly I began, "Seth has abandoned me and his three children. He's over there collecting money from attorneys and paying employees. He emptied out our bank account and took our only car." I stopped talking to wait for the woman's reaction.

"I'm so sorry for you and your children."

"I'm sure he's probably told you terrible things about me."

"He's said very little other than he was heartbroken over the split."

"Heartbroken, my ass," I grumbled. "He's left us three times now. He comes home when he's broke. He walked out this last time on his son's opening day parade and first baseball game. He had no use for us, after he got *Legal Spot* off the ground."

"I suspected there was more to his story," the woman admitted.

"I don't have enough time in a single day, to tell you how much more there is to this story!"

"I don't have respect for men like Seth," the employee said under her breath. "I was once married to a man like your husband. I raised my two children by myself, and their father did not financially support his kids in any of those years."

"Seth has no concern for how we eat. I went to the welfare office recently so I could get food stamps. I don't have a job, and I can't get a job without a car."

"I'm so sorry," she said. "How can I help you?"

"Keep me apprised. Would you?"

"Sure, I will—I'll have to be discrete."

"Of course! How is his business doing?"

"He had hired this young black girl to act as his secretary. She was extremely obese, and I guess she was grateful to have a job to put up with him for as long as she did."

"What do you mean?"

"He used her car and gas to call on lawyers for a month, before she said no more and quit him."

"That sounds like Seth—he used my girlfriend like that." I was referring to Cheryl, my Florida companion. "He used my best friend's car when I was pregnant with our first child. He would drop my girlfriend off at her office early in the mornings, make sales calls all day long in her car, and leave Cheryl waiting for him to come pick her up, way after her business closed for the day. He would not call her to let her know that he would be late, and when he would finally show up, he would be stoned. He destroyed my friendship with her. She won't talk to me anymore because he burned up her transmission and then didn't want to help repair her car."

"Unbelievable," the woman groaned. "He did the same thing to the big black girl before she quit and he bought himself a car. He has a new secretary now—a pretty, young, gullible thing. He bought her flowers this week and told her that they together were going to expand his business. He says that he will open an office in San Francisco, and he wants her to go with him."

"San Francisco!" I wondered if Runi had agreed to move to the gay capital with them.

"I'm glad you called," she confirmed. "I knew he wasn't what he appeared."

"No, he's not!" I said while still reeling over the flowers and young thing.

"He just walked in. I'll call you later," she whispered.

"Please do," I begged. "What's your name?"

"Barbara. I will stay in touch; I promise."

I hung up feeling satisfied with the press leak. I hoped Barbara would not walk off the job just yet; I needed an insider. I recalled how Gladys, my best seamstress had walked off the job at the worst time, when she discovered that while I was married to Leonardo, I was having an affair with Seth. I regretted I wrecked my relationship with Leonardo. Leonardo's transfer to Indiana forced me to choose between my first-born child, who lived next door to me, and the husband who lived out of state. That debate lasted too long and sent me over the edge, obviously—I bedded with Satan. I had not considered God's laws when I made my choices, and I recognized, a day too late, that there was a life higher than the thoughts and feelings connected to my natural earthly man. There was a way of being outside of the carnal man. My spiritual being provided nourishing energy for any set of circumstances, but I was suffering from spiritual depletion back in those days. A total disconnection from that higher life wrecked my thinking and valuation, and thereby corrupted my entire history of being--down to the most physical of levels.

I spent the days and nights with Paolo and my three young children. Paolo was unemployed and seemed to have no drive to get a job, and, in fact, I overheard him on the phone in my master bedroom trying to collect workers' comp for some injury he claimed he suffered on his last job, which was nothing but a grand invention. I wanted to get rid of this bad feeling I called Paolo, but the weeks meandered around Bella and Harper's school schedule and our church service on Sundays, and nothing urged me to throw Paolo out of our life.

Paolo drove my three children and me to his Baptist church every Sunday morning. We had been attending services for several months now. I liked our Sunday services, and so did my children, and afterward, we would stop at the grocery store and use my food stamps so I could cook the traditional Sunday dinner. If I got rid of Paolo, then we would no longer have a ride to church or to the grocery store. The church minister, along with Paolo's encouragement, offered to baptize my children and me. I entertained the idea, but doubted that such ritual would make any difference in our dysfunctional lives. I did not completely negate baptism for me and my children, but I needed a better understanding as to why, right now, in the midst of our turmoil, this ritual made any difference? Paolo said that baptism was like an insurance policy for the next world. I wanted to know how to live in the heaven here on earth. Paolo quoted the words of Jesus from Mark 16:15: *Go into all the world and preach the gospel to every creature. He who believes, and is baptized, will be saved, but he who does not believe will be condemned.* At three days old, a Catholic priest baptized me. I questioned if that ritual counted enough to get me into heaven? Baptism was a choice made by the individual who desired eternal salvation. My parents were a third party who had me baptized. I figured I needed to eventually buy an insurance policy.

I loved to cook a special dinner for my family after church service too, as my mother had always done after church for her family while I was growing up at home. I would try to convince myself that we were a family, as Paolo insisted we were when he sat at the head of our dinner table. I tried to make our life seem as normal as possible for my three children—I seldom saw Joseph anymore because his father, Todd, was not willing to drive our son across the city to visit his mother, siblings, *and Paolo*--a man he knew to dominate my time. Todd had heard too much about Seth over the past three years from me to trust the situation. Todd found one excuse after another to keep my firstborn busy in baseball events so that Joseph could not come over. I understood his unwillingness to expose our son to this chaotic scene I called my life, and I felt sad over the situation.

My relationship with Paolo was a matter of convenience. I often wrangled with the idea of *when* I would tell him again that we were over. I did not want a volatile Vietnam vet to throw me across the Saltillo tile again, or to feel his fist crack my cheekbone. I also feared getting a call from the elementary school, after I kicked Paolo to the curb, and hearing that Seth was checking our five-year old out of class, and that I would have no transportation to race up there and intercept a kidnapping. Seth had admitted, in our last court hearing, that the school security foiled his attempt to take Harper out of kindergarten.

Paolo seemed to like his new life with us, and after seeing where and how he and his brother lived, I suspected Paolo felt he had hit the mother lode when he met me that day at the welfare office on the front steps. Paolo had taken my kids and me over to his place to meet his brother. They lived in an old singlewide trailer buried in a thicket in Conroe, Texas. The thirty-year old trailer was dark and dingy with chipped particleboard cabinets and stained white Formica counter tops. The gray dirty kitchen floor curled up at the seams, and the indoor/outdoor brown carpet in the TV room was bare. I confirmed then that Paolo had told me the truth about his brother with the white beard—the elderly man was indeed toothless, waiting to have a heart transplant, and living on the welfare system. We found his brother sitting in his tattered recliner in front of a small TV in the dimly lit room. We had not been there ten minutes when Paolo's kind-faced brother pulled out a .45 from under his seat cushion to show my three children. I felt uneasy when I saw Paolo and his brother's impoverished reality for the first time and suspected one of these men, or perhaps both of them, were hiding from the law out there in the woods.

Weeks later, I found myself alone at home without Paolo or my children's company. I was working on the current chapter of my novel when I heard the phone ring. I saw my next-door neighbor's number on the Call I.D. and answered.

"Hi, Marilyn."

"Are you enjoying your alone time?"

"I am! I'm actually working on my novel. I don't feel inspired though, it seems my story is dragging on. I don't know what the point is!" I chuckled.

"It will come to you. Believe you have a story to tell, Jean."

"I wish I had the faith in me, like you have in me."

The woman chuckled. "I was calling to ask you if you would mind if the kids stayed with me overnight. I'll bring them over in the morning. We get up early over here. They will have time to eat breakfast and get ready for school."

"Sure you can keep them!" I said in great delight.

"Okay, then I'll walk them over at 6:00 a.m. I have a Disney movie for them tonight and some green apples. See you in the morning."

"Have fun, give them goodnight kisses for me," I instructed before hanging up the receiver. I had barely set the receiver into the cradle on the wet bar when I heard the phone ring and peered at the Caller I.D. It was George!

"Hello," I said with glee. I had not talked to him in nearly a month.

"What's new, Jean?" He asked with a smile in his voice.

"Hey George, how are you?"

"I'm okay," he answered. "Still working on this disaster I call my home. My siblings really did a number here."

"What do you mean?"

"When they lived here, they destroyed the place."

"On purpose?"

"They just did a lot of crazy stuff, like all the cabinet doors are broken. There are holes in the sheetrock, in the bedroom doors. Part of the kitchen countertop is missing."

"Were they doing drugs?"

"I don't know what they were doing—maybe fighting amongst themselves. They didn't work; they didn't pay rent; that's why I kicked them all out when I separated from Elizabeth."

"Who was all living there?"

"All my brothers."

"You have a sister, too, right?"

"Yeah, she lives with her fiancé, Tony."

"When are they getting married?"

"They've been engaged for ten years."

I chuckled. "Guess they need time to get to know each other before jumping into the fire."

George chuckled. "She's crazy, too."

"Where is your mother?"

"My mother lives with her crazy boyfriend up in Maine. He's a jerk."

"Sounds like you don't approve of your family members."

"My mother is truly nuts, and unfortunately, four of the six of us with the exception of me and my sister inherited my mother's genetic coding."

"How's your mother crazy?"

"She's got the IQ of a moron."

I laughed. "Go light on your mom!"

"No, seriously—she's borderline retarded."

I sobered at his reality. "Oh, I'm sorry for you."

"It was hard, Jean, growing up in this house. The town called us *the house of crazies*. I couldn't wait to go off to college and disassociate with all of them."

"Was your mother living on the welfare system?"

"Always, and my four brothers were all in Special Ed classes. I grew up feeling ashamed of where I came from. I went through therapy after my divorce. I remembered having nightmares as a child about being in a cage, and a blue monster trying to grab me through the bars. I came to understand through therapy that it wasn't a monster, but a cop in a blue uniform. I was my mother's firstborn. My father had left my mother after I was born, and then she ran away, too. My mother left me for three days lying in a crib crying—I was her only child at the time. I was hungry, frightened. I don't know how or why the cop found me, but I learned my grandfather got involved. Grandpa found his daughter, my mother, in Hartford, and dragged her back home, right here to this house."

"That's so sad. I'm sorry."

"My mother is truly crazy. She and I got on a bus when I was about seven years old. The bus driver was at the end of his route, and the only people on the bus were my mother, the driver, and me. He pulled over and told me to stay sitting in the front seat. They went in the back of the bus and had sex. I turned around and watched them."

"Wow, and you *seem* so normal, George."

He laughed. "I guess I am normal. I have always wanted to prove to the people of this community that I am normal."

"I guess you have done that, huh? You went to college; you were a youth pastor—that's shining. Did you have a calling to be a pastor?"

"I did have a calling. Early in life I felt I was filled with the Holy Spirit."

"Or maybe you were just crazy and heard voices?"

"Ha ha!" He chuckled.

"I'm just teasing. But, other than you and your wife wanting more money, was there another reason why you walked away from your calling?"

"Actually there was," he somberly admitted. "After I got married, my wife and I met these two, very young, wayward women in the church, and we brought them into our home to help them. One of the girls had an abusive boyfriend, and she came home one night with a bruised face. I was so angry that I went to her boyfriend's place, and I beat him up so severely that I almost killed him. I left him lying there unconscious in a pool of blood. I felt so ashamed of my actions, and I felt unworthy to represent the church any longer."

"Guilt was the culprit again, huh?"

"Yeah, I guess," he said as if bothered by my statement. "I...I, I did not feel that a pastor should be a man like me, a man who could nearly kill another man."

"That's heavy, George." I considered that the blue-eyed, blonde German had a fierce temper that he could not to control at times.

"My wife wanted me to make more money, too, so I resigned as youth pastor when I got the job as a truck driver for the same company that recently fired me as their vice president."

"Why did they fire you?"

"The son of the owner had an issue with me."

"Why?"

"I was making $150,000 a year. He was jealous of the relationship I had with his old man."

"I see."

"I'm enjoying not working right now. I got a good severance package, and I'm going to finish my house renovation before I get another job. The economy isn't very strong up here, either. Enough about me, how are you doing?"

"Seth is still gone, and he's still running his lawyer referral commercials on TV. My father is paying my bills, but he won't buy me a car so that I can get a job."

"Really, how are you managing to care for your children without a car?"

"I'm seeing a guy named Paolo," I admitted. "He drives me around."

"Oh, you are involved with someone." He sounded disappointed.

"It's not what it sounds like." I hoped to soften the blow to his ego. "The longer I'm involved with him, the more I want out."

"Does he know that?"

"I tried to end it once."

"What happened?"

I skipped over the fact that Paolo came across the bed and braised my cheek. "He came knocking on the door the next morning and begged his way back into my life. I need his help. He drives me places. I worry that the school will call me and tell me that Seth is trying to get Harper out of class, and that I won't be able to get there in time because I don't have a vehicle. Paolo has a truck." I hesitated to reveal what Paolo had insinuated about Seth the morning Paolo came begging his way back into my life—that Seth had hired him to kill me.

"That's a tough situation, not having a car."

"Yeah, not having a car is very inconvenient." I wanted to shift the focus off my problems. "Are you seeing someone now?"

"I recently begged Gail to take me back, but she's involved with a drummer now."

"Oh, that explains why I haven't talked to you in a month of Sundays."

"Yeah, I thought I'd give it another run with Gail."

"Gail is your ex-?"

"Yep, my former secretary, the woman I left my wife and kids for," he answered with the sound of remorse.

"I remember."

"I hurt Gail when I broke up with her. She told me so recently. She told me that she had wanted to marry me at one point, but not anymore. She says I was callous with her, and that she doesn't trust me anymore."

"You left your wife and kids for her, and then you broke up with her? That is a bit fickle."

"My best friend, Wells, convinced me that she was a rebound and a gold digger."

"Was she a gold digger?"

"I don't think so—she's marrying a drummer."

"Maybe she's marrying Don Henley, the drummer for the Eagles."

He laughed.

"Did you love her?"

"Yeah, I did, and thought recently, too, that I still loved her. That's why I went and begged her to take me back, but she has moved on. I was scared of how I felt about her, when I let her go the first time—I didn't think I should have felt so deeply in love with a woman before I ever got a divorce. I felt guilty about divorcing my wife, too."

"Guilt seems to be a theme with you, George."

He laughed, and I questioned if George knew who George was? "Maybe you never truly loved your wife?"

"I loved her, but my wife quit paying attention to me." He took a deep breath and sighed. "All I know is I'm feeling very alone these days. I don't want to be alone anymore."

"I understand. Go back to your wife."

"She remarried, and she's happy, so says my daughters."

"Oh, I'm sorry."

"Let's talk about you. What are you going to do with Paolo?"

"I don't know yet—I'm waiting for Seth to go bankrupt."

"If he does," George added. "What if Seth doesn't go bankrupt and crawl back home again?"

"Then...I don't have the answer," I said with great anxiety. "I fear going to court without a car, without a job. I fear breaking off with Paolo simply because if I do, then I won't be able to go the school and intercept Seth kidnapping Harper."

"Would he do that?" George asked.

"Are you talking to Seth, George?"

"Yes. He calls me once a week."

"I am uncomfortable telling you so much."

"You have my word that I will not tell Seth anything you tell me."

"I don't know why I trust you, but I do."

"Thank you. I have no regard for Seth's character, Jean. He hasn't changed since college. It's one thing to get a divorce, but he's abandon his responsibility. When I left my wife, I gave her the house, and I ensured that I sent my wife financial support each month to feed our children. Seth's actions rile me, as always. He leaves you and his kids without a car, or money, or any way to pay the bills. He's a low life. He calls me, and I listen to him simply because I've known him since we were eighteen years old. I want to help *you*. Seth is not stupid—he tells me what he wants me to know. He knows we talk, Jean."

I felt George was on my side. "I don't doubt Seth would kidnap my children, if he could—we haven't gone to court yet, and possession is 99% of the law. There is nothing, in writing, that says one parent has custody of the children. All is fair in love and war right now. Paolo begged his way back into my life by telling me that he knew Seth, and that they had talked in front of a convenience store. He said Seth was dangerous, and that I should fear my husband."

"What?" George asked as if completely confused.

"I think Seth sent Paolo into my life to kill me."

"What? No. Are you kidding?"

"No, I'm dead serious."

"What did he talk to Seth about?"

"He was not willing to disclose too much—a bit mysterious. I think Seth put Paolo into my life. Seth took down the *For Sale* sign because he has no intention of ever going to court again."

"Jean, your suspicion is not that farfetched."

"It's not, is it, George? He lost twice in court. Both times, I got the house and the kids. The court ordered Seth to pay me child support. He owes his mother her life savings, and I cost him his arbitration. He has a boyfriend, Runi, and I think he wants to move his boyfriend *and* mother into this house."

"Wow, Jean."

"My hand went numb about the same time Runi's wife, Joyce, began having seizures. We both stopped having neurological dysfunction after Seth and Runi physically removed themselves from our lives."

"Wow," he groaned while absorbing what I was saying about his old college roommate.

"Seth acts like he's on drugs. He doesn't care how we get along. He's greedy and all about himself, George. I think he and Runi got scared and quit poisoning their wives."

"How do you think Seth was poisoning you?"

"I don't know, George. He made the coffee all day long, and I drank it. I ask you, why would Seth take down the *For Sale* sign, and not sell the house, and not split the proceeds with me? By not selling the house and splitting the equity 50/50 with me, as we agreed we would do, when he came back the last time, Seth risks the court giving me custody of the children and the house again. He's broke! Why doesn't he want $50,000 of the equity?—It's a sure deal."

"Oh, Jean," he groaned again while getting my reality. "He talks like he's doing well with *Legal Spot*. Maybe he thinks the court will give him the house and the kids, next time, because you still don't have a car or a job?"

"Does he say that to you, George?"

"No, because he assumes that you and I are talking."

"He's in the red, George. My girlfriend, Linda, and I crunched numbers, one night recently, trying to see if we could compete with Seth in the same business. We had a sales rep from the TV station give us a quote, and even when we got cheaper air time, we could not make his lawyer referral business viable."

"Wow, he is such a bullshit artist."

"He sure is, and yeah, I think Seth *would* kill me," I reiterated. "And *I don't doubt*, for a second, he wouldn't kidnap my kids and disappear with them either."

"You've got to get a protection order, Jean."

"I know, but I have *not* a dime to afford a lawyer, and my father is playing hardball. He wants Seth to crawl back home for the third time, and for us to sell this house. It's why my father won't buy me a car—he's making me depend on that scenario happening."

"Tell him what you suspect, Jean."

"I can't."

"Tell your father that Seth hired Paolo to kill you."

"He won't believe me, and I don't want to worry him or Mom, especially Mom. Dad has too much on his plate with Holly's divorce and with my mother's illness—his wife of forty years is dying. And my father thinks Paolo is a good Christian man, to boot!"

"I have to tell you, Jean, that I'm disappointed you are involved with someone."

"George, I'm *not* involved with Paolo!"

"You're not?"

I would not admit to George that I had sex with this man, who initially came on to me with an agenda to kill me. "No, I'm not *emotionally* involved with Paolo."

"Well, he is dangerous, if your suspicions are true and Seth did send him into the picture." He paused as if waiting for a comment.

"I am going to end it with Paolo."

"I was hoping you and I would have an opportunity to date."

"I want that, too, George."

"I would like to see you get a divorce before we date, Jean."

"That would make perfect sense to me. I'm going to dump Paolo, George, and then get Seth to come back home so that we can sell the house, and then divorce the snake. We are going to sell this house, and I'll have money for a lawyer and a car."

"You've got to move on and get rid of Seth, once and for all."

"I want to do that, George." But at that moment, I had no idea how I was going to implement my wishes. I suddenly heard the front door open and saw Paolo walk into view. I smiled at the large Italian force, but the intensity on his face alarmed me. He stood there trying to figure out whom I was talking to, and looked disturbed. I continued my conversation with George, while I waved the one-minute finger in front of Paolo. I felt nervous talking to George in front of Paolo. "I'll talk to you later," I said to George. "I have company."

"Paolo is there?"

"Yes," I answered. I knew George understood.

"Be careful," he warned. "I'll call you later."

"Bye," I said while sure that Paolo never heard me mention the name George. I sat the phone into the receiver.

"Who was that?" Paolo asked.

"That was George, a friend of Seth's. He lives in Connecticut. George was looking for his former college roommate."

"What does he want?" He asked sourly.

Me, I thought, but replied, "He's concerned about all of us."

"Did you tell him you have a boyfriend now?"

"I did tell him about you, Paolo."

"Good. I don't take much to my girlfriend talking to other men."

"Jealousy is a sign of insecurity, Paolo."

"I wouldn't care, if I didn't feel jealous of other men."

"Actually, that's not a healthy reaction, so says the Women's Center." I had been attending a counseling session for abused women in The Woodlands, by recommendation of my neighbor, who headed up the Women's Center. I figured when I told a judge, in the near future, that I had been getting counseling, then I'd get his sympathy and custody of my kids, too.

"I told you those whack jobs are wrong. Jealousy is healthy—it keeps everything in perspective. When I lived up there in the Texas Panhandle, one night, I watched a dude flirt with my girlfriend, and she flirted back. I got angry, I felt jealous. I took care of business that night."

"How's that?" I asked while I got he was warning me not to make him jealous.

"We were out at a night club that night, and this cocky son-ov'a-bitch comes up and starts showin' me he can take my girl. I wasn't going to sit back and take his crap or hers." He angrily admitted.

"What did you do?"

"Well, I don't even want to go there. I will say, though, I got in the last word and taught a lesson or two."

"Did you become violent?"

"He got what he deserved."

"Did you go to jail?"

"It didn't go down well for anybody. Next time, I will take care of that kind of situation out of the public's eye."

I assumed from his answer he went to jail. "You can't let your feelings make you do stupid things. You can't go around beating up people because *you feel like it*, Paolo."

"I know all that—but, they egged it on. It was her fault. She deserved what she got too."

I felt disdain toward him and avoided shaking my head in disapproval. He blamed others for his stupidity. I had experienced his violence in our relationship, and now, he admitted to having been violent with a woman in the Texas Panhandle. "Did your girlfriend leave you, anyway?"

"She left me that night. I over-reacted."

I stopped asking questions—I knew the answer. He assaulted her. "Did you have to leave town?"

"Her brothers had it out for me. I left Lubbock, all that happened years ago." He knew, by my expression, that I disliked his violent nature. "I need to make a trip up there, too. I had a good friend living up there—he recently died. We did a couple of tours together in Nam. I saved his life, and he was always grateful to me. I recently got a letter from his lawyer informing me that he passed, and that he left me some money."

"How much money?"

"Not sure, maybe $50,000, maybe more."

"Wow, $50,000 is a lot of money."

"I need that money, too, but don't want to show my face up there though."

"Where?"

"In Lubbock, due to the fact that I got enemies—her brothers will kill me if they see me."

"Whose brothers?"

"My ex-girlfriend, the one that made me mad that night in the club."

"I would like you to go with me to pick up the money."

"Can't they mail the money to you?" I assumed the police arrested Paolo on assault charges that night in the club, and then he jumped bail, and now the police had a warrant out for the man who lived in the deep woods in Conroe, Texas, if any of what he said was true.

"No, I need to go to a lawyer's office and sign some papers."

"Oh," I said while I thought his story suspicious. Perhaps he was plotting to take me out to the west Texas desert and kill me, and then collect $50,000 from Seth? Did Seth promise to give Paolo half of the equity of our house, if he killed me? We had at least $100,000 of equity in our paid-in-full home. "I'll be happy to go with you, Paolo. I just can't make that trip anytime soon. Maybe when school is out, in a couple of months, I can get my father to come here and watch the kids while we drive up to Lubbock."

"I need to go sooner," he replied.

I agreed; he needed to go sooner than later. My children and I were in trouble because Seth's business did not operate in the black any longer. Seth's boat was sinking fast, and he needed 100% ownership of our marital home. Perhaps Seth had given Paolo a deadline?

"It's a full moon tonight! I feel restless," he admitted with a smile.

I cringed at the idea that the dark man might want to make love to me. "I'm not restless at all, Paolo. I was actually making some headway on my novel until the phone rang."

"Where are the kids?" He asked.

"Next door at Marilyn's house."

"It's a beautiful night. Let's just drive around and enjoy the cool night air and the full moon."

"Okay," I said while resenting his unannounced presence and feeling pressured to take a drive with the restless man in order to keep him out of my bed!

We climbed into his truck and, once inside the cab, he looked at his brow in the rearview mirror. He then looked at me while moving his black silky bangs off his forehead and pointed with the other hand, "You see them marks there?"

I leaned over to take a closer look, "Yeah."

"That's where them damn rats ate me. I hung there upside down in that pit for hours, until mid-morning, when I finally got myself untied and ran from that gook trap." He shook his head and fumed over the memory.

"You must find peace, Paolo. Forgive them."

"I hate them gooks."

"War is horrible, Paolo, but for whatever reason you still feel angry, just pray. Ask for forgiveness, too. You only need to ask God once to forgive you, and then forgive yourself and start new. You don't have to wear guilt for the rest of your life for killing anyone in a war; nor do you have to feel angry about what they did to you." I had finally gotten that concept and put my guilt to rest regarding the abortion I had years earlier.

Paolo stared at me without any expression. "Me, forgive them?"

I nodded, "Yes, do yourself a favor and forgive them. Jesus said that if we don't forgive our brother for his trespasses against us, then our Heavenly Father won't forgive us. I know that's a tough one, Paolo. I would rather kill Seth than forgive him."

He drove without a response and appeared angry over his days on the front line of war.

I believed that a change of scenery would be good for the crazed man, while he headed toward the perimeter of The Woodlands and toward Seth's *Legal Spot* office suite. I grew suspicious that Paolo had an agenda for this late night drive. "Why are we driving to Seth's office?"

"I just want to see if he's there on Sunday night."

"I doubt it. Seth has an aversion to working," I replied while now aware Paolo knew where Seth spent his days.

Paolo drove slowly down a dark wooded street, lit only by an occasional fluorescent street light. The street curved, and we came upon Seth's office building. His office suite was center door between three other businesses, and all the interior lights were out in the entire building. "See, Paolo...I told you. Nobody is working Sunday night."

Paolo did not say a word, but, instead, turned off the radio. He drove slowly past the building and around a bend in the street of nothing more than pine trees on both sides. The street looped around with a wooded esplanade in the center. He drove the circle and came back around to the front of Seth's office building once again—the only building on the loop. Seth's suite sat situated in the midst of piney woods with a dense forest behind his office building and on both sides of his office building. A thick clump of trees and brush grew on the esplanade across the street. Once again, we drove the paved loop and stopped on the far side of the thicket that grew across the street from Seth's office. There were no buildings on this side of the esplanade, just dense woods. Paolo pulled up to the curb of the esplanade and turned off the engine. "Get out," he calmly ordered while he, too, stepped out of his truck.

"Why?"

"I want to look closer at Seth's business."

"You already did when you drove by twice, Paolo."

"I want to snoop, follow me." He kindly answered with a grin.

"Follow you where?" He wasn't making sense.

"Just follow me," he insisted as he led the way into the thicket of trees that grew on the esplanade across the street from Seth's office suite.

I felt annoyed by his order to follow him, while clearly aware that there was no one in the entire building on the other side of the trees. "There are no cars in the parking lot, Paolo. It's completely dark over there. What do you expect to find at this time of night?"

He did not answer, but waited for me to catch up to him. He stood at the edge of the trees that grew in the center of the esplanade. "Come on," he coached while I stood still on the curb questioning his motive. He waited for me to lead the way into the thicket. "I've got your back," he said as he pointed for me to walk in front of him. "Be brave."

"Where are we going?" I asked with great irritation while noting that a nearby streetlight shone on the woods that we were entering.

"We're just cutting through the trees. I don't want to leave my truck in front of Seth's office, in case someone is over there, or pulls up—like a security guard or cleaning crew."

"There are no lights on!"

"I want to snoop, look through his office windows," he said as he took my hand and positioned me to lead the way into the woods. He waited for me to walk so that he could follow me.

I slowly walked into the dark woods when, suddenly, I became aware that Paolo planned to hurt me. I heard a voice tell me that worse would happen if I continued to walk deeper into the woods, that he would kill me in these woods. I panicked on the inside, but refrained from showing fear while remembering the butterfly knife he always wore on his hip belt. The memory of our first night together flashed before my mind's eyes, and I saw how he, with the flick of the wrist, demonstrated the expedient way to kill someone with his deadly weapon. I instantly turned to walk out of the woods. "The mosquitoes are eating me up alive," I said while I brushed past Paolo, and hurried back toward the paved street. I slapped at my arms and legs, in pretense, and remained calm.

"Where are you going?" He impatiently asked.

"Back to the truck. Mosquitoes are biting me. I want to go back home before we get in trouble!" I angrily demanded. "I don't want to walk through the woods at dark! Are you crazy, Paolo?"

He stood still on the edge of the woods, unwilling to follow me back to the curb as if he were contemplating what to do next.

"I want to go home," I reiterated without negotiation or eye contact. I stood by the truck lit up by a green fluorescent street lamp. I waited at the passenger door while I summed that there was no other escape or rescue anywhere near. I looked over the cab of the small truck and watched the large man walk up to his vehicle without any show of emotion. I did not know what he was feeling. I was certain my guardian angel had whispered in my ears, "Don't go any further into the woods with him. Turn around, get out of there quickly." My heart raced while I stood at the door of the passenger side of his truck watching his every move. I never took my eyes off him while he got into his truck. I remained cool and acted as if I had no fear while I got back into the truck. "Look at the full moon, Paolo?" I calmly asked of him while forcing a smile. Paolo glanced at me and then at the moon through the front window. He did not answer, but started up his truck.

"When the moon is full, people will party; dogs will bite; robbers will steal; and murderers will kill. Do you believe that is true, Paolo?"

He glared at me without an answer.

"Probably a myth. Tonight is probably no more significant

than any other night. Let's go home and make love."
He said nothing while he drove us out of the thicket. He appeared annoyed, and I felt I had to play on his tender side. "I just want to go home, Paolo," I said sweetly. "I don't feel right."
"Okay," he said as if still lost in thought.

We walked into my home fifteen minutes later. I sat on the couch upset about the incident in the woods. Was Paolo going to kill me? Why would he want to traipse through the woods at dark except to kill me? There was not a single light on at Seth's office building, and there was nothing to see! If Paolo were going to kill me, why would he do it across the street from Seth's office? Was he angry with Seth, or trying to frame up Seth?

Paolo went into the kitchen to get something to eat after we walked into the house. I sat on the couch in the sunken den not sure how to say what I wanted to say to him. I waited for Paolo to speak first, but he had only indicated that he was hungry since he had driven away from the woods. I looked over my shoulder at the man in the kitchen. He was standing at the island preparing a ham and cheese sandwich. He saw me looking over my shoulder at him. "Are you hungry?"

"No, I'm upset."

"About what?" He said as if lost in his task of layering the food.

I remained cool and continued to flip through the pages of a women's magazine. I continued to explain my feelings. "We've got to end us tonight. I can't do this relationship anymore," I blurted while I casually flipped through the magazine wondering how he was going to react to me wanting out again. "I told you before, Paolo, I'm not in a place emotionally to get involved with you or anyone. I'm not happy right now—it's not you, it's this situation. I'm not happy because I'm *not* concentrating on getting a divorce from Seth. I feel frustrated, and I don't have anything left of me to give you. I don't want a relationship right now because I have *not* resolved the rest of my life." Suddenly, I felt cold steel against the front of my neck. Paolo had crept up behind me while I pretended to be looking at a magazine. He stood behind the sofa that I sat on and held his deadly weapon against my neck.

He growled, "Just try to leave me again. I can't take the pain, Jean."

I was terrified, but I remained calm. I took my right hand and slowly slid it up between my neck and the sharp blade and forced the knife away while I replied as if we were just playing a silly game. "Oh, stop the dramatics!" I chuckled while I slowly stood up and turned to face him. I smiled and realized that my pretense to not fear him disempowered his intent. He seemed a bit mystified by my action and lowered the knife to his side. "Put that up, goof ball. Honestly, you should take those good looks and dramatics and go to Hollywood."

He smiled while relieved I was not on the attack. "You think so?"

"Yeah!" I knew the vet was on the front line the moment he snuck up on me.

"I've heard that a couple of times in my life—I guess I missed my calling. I was just joking with the knife, but you knew that, Jean."

"Of course I did."

"I understand you are stressed out right now, Jean. I don't want you to break up with me. I love you."

"I don't think, for a moment, you would want to hurt me—the woman you love. I've seen you down on your knees praying to this crucifix with me and my kids," I said before looking up at the three foot Jesus that hung over the mantle. "We must always act as if your eternal salvation is on the line."

Paolo turned his attention to the Christian artifact. "I don't want you to break up with me. I ought to just kill Seth, then you don't have the stress of a divorce."

"I don't want to break up with you, not really. I love you, Paolo. I feel I caught between a rock and a hard place."

"I know you feel stuck, Jean, and I forgive you for hurting me. That's what Jesus would do, too."

Paolo was off the chain. Killing was second nature for the

war machine, and like tonight, when he appeared behind me with a knife at my neck, sometimes the psycho did not understand that I was not a gook. As far as I could tell, Paolo was schizophrenic, and a psychopath, or a sociopath--a man who, at times, did not differentiate between right and wrong. Obviously, the long war had eroded his code of moral behavior. No matter what or who was the root of his criminal behavior, I concluded in that moment of terror, that I would be going to bed with Paolo that night...if I wanted to live. I had to keep Paolo calm and myself safe until I could figure out another alternative. I was sure that the man could and would kill me...eventually, especially if Seth was yanking his chain.

15
THE ESCAPE

The following day, I lay in the center of my king-size bed thinking about the current situation. Paolo had gone back to his trailer to check on his ailing brother who needed a heart transplant. Seth needed to speed up the plot he created with Paolo. He couldn't return home if Paolo was still in the picture. Paolo had to make a choice— he would keep me as his lover, or he would kill me and receive payment from Seth for service rendered. If Paolo did not think I wanted him, then he might choose the money. Suddenly, Pete popped into my mind. I recalled my friend, Seth's former boss from the Talent House, warning me about Seth that summer night in 1992, when Seth and I, and our friends, Pete, Karen, Chad, and Jenn, drove down to the lake in Clear Lake City to party on the floating barge. We had all drank too much that night, and before that terrorizing ride home in Pete's convertible Mustang, when he drove over 100 MPH down the freeway, Pete had tried to tell me something after we disembarked the floating barge. I replayed that night in my head:

***

  Pete inhaled the reefer while I continued talking under my breath while avoiding the other parties hearing me. "It's no good anymore," I said and then nodded over to Seth. "Drugs and alcohol have been the demise of us, and nobody's home anymore." I considered my words had no impact on my friend because I got high, too. "Seth doesn't have any sense of urgency to grow his business network. He's abusive—has been for a long while. He's not in love with me, never has been—and now, well…I'm--"
  I hesitated to tell Seth's best friend that I was not in love with my husband, either. I had never felt more alone or unfulfilled than I had with Seth. "I'll just stop there."
  Pete choked out the smoke from his lungs and then grabbed hold of his composure. "Just watch your back, Jean," he warned me before walking toward the driver's door. I stood still repeating his words in my head while I watched him pull open the driver's door and sit down behind the steering wheel. I knew he had more to say to me, but tonight was not the night--too many ears.

***

  I recalled another time, in recent days, when Pete had tried to warn me about Seth. One morning, I had cooked my father breakfast and had made him coffee after he woke up in my guest room. My brother, Henry, had plans that day, and my father had to return home as soon as possible to care for my mother. I was loading up the dishwasher with breakfast dishes just after my father departed when I heard the doorbell. I walked to the front room and peered out the window. Pete stood there with a smile. I smiled back, but my guard went up instantly…

***

  I swung the door open. "What are you doing here, friend?"
  "Checking on you, Jean. Are you alright?"
  "I'm okay--my father just left."
  "Can I come in?"
  "Certainly." I stepped out of the threshold and walked toward the kitchen. "How about a cup of coffee?"

"I would love a mug," he said as he followed me through the sitting room and into the gourmet kitchen.

"Seth moved in with me," he stated without any emotion.

I was startled by the revelation and confused because I knew the wrecker service had confiscated my Volvo from his Clear Lake City apartment on the other side of Houston. "Why is he living with you?"

"He needs a place to stay until he can get financially ahead."

"Oh," I quipped while feeling uncomfortable Seth was now living within walking distance from me. I suspected that without a car, job, or half-a-mil, Seth couldn't fulfill his Clear Lake City lease and moved out just after he moved in. "Where's all his furniture?"

"I think he put his stuff in his sister's garage."

I considered that my word processor and novel was being stored at Demelza's house in League City, Texas, fifty-five miles away from my home. "What's he driving?"

"He isn't driving anything--that's partly why he's living with me. I'm driving him when he needs to go somewhere."

Pete had bought a smaller one-story home in The Woodlands shortly after Seth and I had purchased our two-story in October 1991. I realized Seth would be conveniently close now to commit his crimes on me. "He took my car, Pete! He doesn't have any concerns about how I feed my children without money, or how I could get a job without a car."

"I'm worried about you, Jean. I told Seth that you were my friend. He wants me to go to court and testify against you. I won't do it."

"What lies does he want you to tell the court about me? That I demanded that you guys not do your drugs in my home? That I'm the irresponsible parent?"

"I told Seth you were a good mother. I'm not taking sides here."

"Thank you, Pete," I said while I tried to calm down.

"You need to watch your back, Jean."

"What do you mean?"

"I mean, don't go parachute jumping with Seth, and don't go snorkeling. You know what I mean."

"No, I don't! Elaborate!"

"He's pissed you financially ruined him."

"Oh, boo hoo," I retorted. "He's abandoned me and my children. He doesn't care whether we eat or die! Doren had an accident the other day, and I had to race him to the emergency room, but I didn't have money or a car. I had to knock on the neighbor's door, Pete! And thank God she was home!"

"I don't agree with anything he has done. He's gone off the deep end, Jean."

"I won't lie down! If Seth wants to take me on, then I will put him under."

"This war is getting out of hand, Jean."

***

I snapped to a new realization and knew Seth had been plotting for a while to get me out of the picture, one way, or the other. I supported my theory that Seth wanted to kill me when I considered that when he had left this last time, he took nothing but the clothes out of his closet. The other two times, when he left, he looted the house. Why was the greedy bastard so confident that he would get the house, all the furnishings, and custody of our children? Surely, he knew that the court would see his irresponsibility as despicable?

I considered what lay on my plate this early weekday morning and began to pray aloud with my hands folded. "Dear God, protect me and my children from Satan and his emissaries! Shield us each from danger, disease, and accident, and wrap your arms around us and set us down in your perfect place."

I thought about those particular words I had prayed every morning for years since 1993, when Seth made his first departure from our home via patrol car; and now, it was already 1995, and three abandonments later, and I still prayed these same words with more fervency than ever before. My arduous past urged me to beg God and his angels for protection for my children and myself. I understood clearly that Seth's veracity to win custody at any cost increased with each new court experience. His spirit felt demonic, and my need to ask greater forces, of other dimensions, for protection was not optional. Other dimensions existed, and I knew God our Almighty father, and his son, Jesus Christ, would intercede on my behalf, if I asked. So I prayed in faith believing my life was in good hands, and any self-doubts that often sprinkled my days, I recognized as fear and dismissed to be only that of my lower mind's acceptance of nothing greater than a third-dimension mentality, and that of my doubting carnal man.

My phone rang and I picked up. "Hello."

"Jean, this is Barbara from your husband's office."

"Hi," I said while now aware I had a friend on the inside.

"I've got some interesting information, and I think you should know about it." The woman sounded genuinely concerned to me.

"Okay."

"I got a call from the Montgomery County Sheriff's Department this morning. I thought the call was strange...at first. The sheriff said a former employee here at *Legal Spot* filed a grievance against your husband for non-payment. Seems Seth wrote a bad payroll—my check bounced, too. Then the officer mentioned some other problems." She paused and then began to whisper. "Seth just walked in. Call Betsy."

"Betsy?"

"Write this number down."

"Okay." I sat up in my bed and reached over for a pad and pen off the lamp table. "I'm ready."

Barbara whispered to me the number, and I said thank you for what I expected to be the portal of clarity.

"I'll call you later, Jean." She then hung up.

I immediately dialed the phone number for Betsy, and listened to the telephone ring. A young-sounding female picked up. "Hello."

I hesitated while not certain about my objective. "Hi, is this Betsy?"

"Yes."

"You don't know me, but I'm Seth's soon-to-be ex-wife. I got your number from Barbara at *Legal Spot*."

There was a lull, and then the woman cautiously replied, "Yes, what can I do for you?"

"I'm scared he's going to take my children away from me."

The woman retorted, "He's a bad man."

"You think so?" I prompted.

"Yes," the woman answered. "I filed a police report against Seth."

"Why?"

The woman hesitated, "I guess you ought to know...And if you're a spy for him, you can tell that son-o'va-bitch that I know he was the one behind that call."

"I don't understand," I offered. "I'm not a spy."

"Wait a minute!" the woman suddenly sounded irritated. "What's your name?"

"I'm Jean Wynn."

"Okay, Jean, first of all, I feel sorry for you, and you need to watch your back."

There it was again—I needed to watch my back. Pete had told me the same thing a couple of times.

"Seth called me last week, about seven o'clock in the evening. He knew my husband worked the night shift, and assumed I would be alone. I got this call; my husband was running late for work...so he wasn't gone when Seth called me. Seth called from an unknown number, and he tried to disguise his voice, but I knew it was him."

I found what the woman said mysterious. "What did Seth say to you?"

"First of all, I'm seven months pregnant. This is our first child, and your husband told me that night on the phone that if I talked to a single person about what I heard in the office, that my baby would not be born."

"That's horrible!"

"I was so scared. He's dangerous, and I told my husband about his threat. We called the police and filed a report."

"With the Montgomery County Sheriff's Department?"

"Yes. I don't know what will become of my complaint because I can't prove it was Seth on the phone. The cop says it's just a threatening phone call from an anonymous caller and they can't prosecute anybody."

"I'm so sorry," I said while stunned by Seth's behavior.

"I just don't want anything more to do with Seth, or his sick life."

"I certainly understand—I don't want anything to do with him, either. I'm trying to get a divorce."

"Good. And if you want to tell Seth that my husband will kill him if he gets an opportunity, you may pass on that message."

"I...I...I don't think I will be talking to Seth for a long while. At least not until we go to court," I informed her.

"You better get a protective order; he's dangerous."

"What does he fear you will repeat?" I asked the young girl.

The woman did not answer, and there was a lull in the conversation. "I have to go. Please, I don't work there anymore. Please don't call here again," she said before hanging up.

My head spun while I hung up the receiver—I knew well what would make Seth threaten a pregnant woman. I could not believe Seth was this crazy. I recalled the drive to the woods with Paolo, the other night, and how he wanted me to walk into the thicket with him, and how later, he held a knife against my neck when we went back to my place. Betsy had overheard Seth and Paolo talking! I bet Seth had reneged on a money deal he made with Paolo, and Paolo was angry and wanted to frame Seth up for my murder.

MOTHER'S DAY 1995 and I walked around the grocery store after church with my three young children and Paolo, looking for something to take over to my parents' home later that afternoon. I needed to buy wine for the meal, dessert, a Mother's Day card, and a flowering plant. Paolo had the money for wine, gift, and card—and the transportation. I had the food stamps for the dessert.

Only a few weeks had passed since the woods incident, the same night Paolo had put a knife to my throat when I tried to break up with him for the second time. My thoughts about the dark fortress that walked beside my grocery cart were betwixt and caught between two extremes, good and evil. On one hand, I was certain the hired gun had not killed me because he was crazy enough to have fallen in love with his hit. I often deliberated over Paolo's words, the morning after I threw him out of my home for assaulting me. He insinuated that morning that Seth wanted me dead. He told me that Seth was dangerous. Paolo said that I should not fear him, but, instead, I should fear my husband. Paolo admitted to having met Seth and one of his friend's at a convenience store—I suspected the friend was Seth's former co-worker, the young Chad, who I knew to idolize Seth. Chad, Seth, and the owner of the Talent House, Pete, had run the talent business together, before the IRS put chains on Pete's front door for tax evasion, the same day the DEA arrested Chad for moving kilos from the Mexican food restaurant, next door, and over to Pete's business.

The Mercenary had persuaded me that morning, after his act of intimidation the night before, to overlook the fact that he braised my cheek, and to let him back into my life. He told me that I needed him to protect me. I agreed, and as a result, I kept Paolo around to protect me from Seth and his deviousness. I considered for a while that Paolo might be lying about Seth's intentions, but regardless of whether the vagabond was telling me the truth or not, about my husband's intentions, I knew Seth was a bad guy in my life. Now, after talking to Seth's terrified employee, I felt certain that Paolo was the other bad guy in my life.

Paolo had told me about some war vet who had died and left him money. Supposedly, he had save the man's life in Nam and an inheritance check for fifty thousand dollars waited for him in Lubbock, Texas. Maybe Paolo thought he would kill me outside of Houston, and dump my body somewhere out in the West Texas desert, in the pretense of us going to Lubbock to get that inheritance? I had legitimate concern to believe that a man who would put a knife to my neck would truly kill me. My circumstances seemed to spin out of control. Paolo made love to me! How could he kill what he claimed to love? Even more interesting, how could I make love to a man who put a knife against my neck and threatened to kill me? Worse, how could a man kill the mother of his two children? And even more bizarre, than all of those considerations, Paolo had urged me to get baptized at the Baptist church we attended every Sunday! Perhaps he believed I was about to die.

I took a breath, remained calm in appearance, and gave the man walking beside me in the grocery store aisle a forced smile. I felt as crazy as I knew Seth and Paolo both to be.

Paolo smiled back as we headed toward the bakery to find the perfect dessert for my mother on Mother's Day. My insane boyfriend seemed lost in thought, too.

I perceived my world through my filter of experience. Without a doubt, Paolo would lose his temper again and hurt me, if not kill me, if I tried to break up with him for the third time. My dubious situation had been on my mind for weeks. Then suddenly, an idea sprang forth while I picked up a boxed cake with *Happy Mother's Day* scrawled in red icing on top white frosting.

The words *Lubbock, Texas* surfaced to mind as if the angels were showing me something. I was learning how to listen these days. I called this particular voice the loving spirit—perhaps I heard the Holy Spirit or one of God's angels. I clung to everything I thought these days while discerning some thoughts as instructions from heaven, and some intended for the demise of my well-being. No longer was I quick to dismiss road signs. Fear was nothing more than amnesia, a momentary collapse when I forgot I was the essence of God. The negative voice I called the voice of darkness, what I deemed part of my human machinery. The voice of doubt seldom ceased and had always been an ongoing conversation. The voice of doubt was intrinsically part of my wiring—a depleting voice that told me to doubt myself; to not trust others, or myself; to believe it's too good to be true; or that I should have known better than to believe in such foolishness as *happily ever after*.

Why was *Lubbock, Texas* important to look at? I recalled how Paolo had mentioned another woman in Lubbock, one that he had supposedly loved when he lived in Lubbock. He had claimed to have lost his temper with her, said he got too jealous one night. I knew Paolo was insanely insecure, and I feared him now, after seeing how he reacted both times when I tried to break it off with him. No doubt, he had a history of treating women as he had treated me over the past months. What if he had done his knife-to-the-neck routine on the woman in Lubbock and had actually slit her throat? That would explain if, indeed, he did have a check waiting for him at some law office in Lubbock, why he did not want to show his face in that town. I suspected he had a warrant out for his arrest, and that he and his brother were living in the dense woods in Conroe, Texas for good reason.

We were having a special Mother's Day dinner that afternoon at my parents' home. Paolo had made plans for us to stop at his mother's gravesite first, before we went to celebrate my mother on what could be her last Mother's Day. I was certain my mother would never understand her daughter's attraction to the uneducated Italian cowboy, who did not understand proper pronoun usage; and I was certain, too, that my mother would question why I was allowing this man to be in my life. I would skirt around my mother's inquisition if it came up, and not render to the terminal woman any grueling details. I was firm in my conviction to not give Mom anything but laughs on this special day, or on any day to follow in her short life.

Instantly, I felt annoyed with my father and blamed him for my dire straits. He had continued to pay all my bills over the last several months, but had refused to relinquish his staunch position on affording me a lawyer or buying me a car. He bought Holly her 5,000 square foot house with cash off the county auction block, but would not buy me a car. He wanted me to take Seth back, and to sell the house, and then file for the third divorce action with the proceeds from the equity of the house. He argued he had already bought two lawyers, for two separate hearings, and that the court gave me the house, the kids, and child support each time, and both times, I took the slime bag back and dropped the divorce action. Dad refused to play that court game one more time. My father was dealing with a terminal wife, whom he had been married to for nearly forty years, along with daily interruptions from my neurotic sister who cried the blues over the phone about the dastardly deeds done to her by her second husband and his lawyer. Holly also claimed to be having a nervous breakdown. I, on the other hand, did not want to alarm my father with worries over my life and death situation. I was the strong daughter. As it was, Daddy was shelling out hundreds of thousands of dollars for Mom's hospital bills, visiting nurses, and his daughters' lawyers, utilities bills, and food, not to mention Holly's private investigator. Months had passed since Seth had departed our home. I had not spoken a word to my husband since that morning before I headed over to the welfare office to get on the food stamp program, and before I went to Seth's former employer to turn in $600 worth of stolen merchandise Seth stole from the drug department at the grocery store. Today, I felt I needed to pull Seth back into the scene again. I reasoned he could protect me from Paolo when I finally told Paolo goodbye. I had seen Seth's number on the caller ID every day for the past month, and although I had not picked up the phone, but that one time, just before I headed to the welfare office, Seth persisted to call me every day since that day. I initially thought his persistence to call me every day was driven because his *Legal Spot* business was financially crashing and that he wanted to come back home; but, now, I speculated as to whether he wanted to come back home so that he could prevent Paolo from killing me. Maybe he had a change of heart? On second thought, he probably feared my death would come back on him.

  Paolo had told me that he had seen Seth driving past my home recently, and my current boyfriend felt the worm deserved to die. "Just say the word," Paolo often reminded. He seemed to hate Seth as much as he hated the gooks in Vietnam. I thought that if anyone could put Seth six feet under, Paolo would be the man; but, whenever those murderous thoughts surfaced, I pushed them back down. Strangely, Seth was the answer for my precarious position. The last thing I wanted on my hands was a murder case wherein I was suspect.

  I walked through the grocery store pushing my basket with Paolo and my three children close. Bella, Harper, and Doren enjoyed filling up my basket with their favorite junk food. I never allowed my kids out of my sight at any time, and figured that if Seth was driving by my house, then he was probably trying to kidnap his sons before we went to court for the third and last time. Months of steady fear had been the reason for why I had allowed Paolo to sleep in my home every night, and the fact that Paolo kept his switchblade either on his hip, or on the nightstand, gave me a sense of security, too, until recently. Ironically, the 6'5" two-hundred and fifty pound Italian force, whose arms were as big as my thighs, was now Seth's problem, too.

I guarded my children with my life and the entire task of getting Harper to and from school each day, without Seth's interception, was where my challenge remained during the last weeks of the school year. Seth had recently attempted to go to the elementary school with our friend, Pete, and get Harper out of class, but the school security foiled Seth's attempt to kidnap my child, and once again, I became aware that my children were at risk. My mother's friend, Mrs. Fox, the elementary school secretary, called and warned me that Seth gave the school notice that he would be back that afternoon when Harper's half-day of kindergarten started. Harper didn't go to school that day, and I was glad that four-year old Doren had not started school yet, and that Bella was of no interest to Seth.

I was disgusted with my life. I felt like a prisoner in my own home. I wanted my freedom, and I wanted to be able to breathe and know that my kids would not disappear. I wanted out of this nightmare marriage.

I walked down the grocery aisle thinking about my plans that afternoon and said to Paolo, "When we go to my mother's home today, I've got to take my sister a graduation gift, too."

"That's a nice gesture. I know you must be proud of her," Paolo said.

"I am. She finally got her degree at the age of thirty-five. Do you know what her husband gave her on her graduation day?"

"What?"

"My sister's husband served her a petition for a divorce. Classy, huh?"

Paolo shook his head in disagreement. "I'd be proud of you, if you got your degree. I don't know what's wrong with these men in your family."

I silently disagreed with Paolo. Not for a second, did I think the insecure man could ever handle me going to college, any more than Seth could handle it. I continued, "My sister's husband was short ten hours of college credits, and he never got his degree. He found out she was pregnant in his senior year in college, and they got married; and then he went to work to support his family. He couldn't stand that she finished her degree recently. He's much like Seth, a prick from hell."

"It does seem you two girls married the same kind of man."

"Yep, both control freaks—abusive, dysfunctional, and emotionally retarded. My sister was upset when she graduated. She walked in cap and gown in tears. She really loved her husband, too, when he took off with another woman." I looked over at the man who listened intently. "My sister and Don were married for ten years. He spent the first part of those years chugging Jack Daniels every night, then he quit being an alcoholic and became a Bible thumping fanatic, and then he threw away the Good Book and had an affair with some woman at his office. He then secretly plotted to divorce my sister. He set her up to lose—he intentionally caused her to fight with him every night for a year, sent her into rage, and secretly tape recorded all their fights. And he and his hotshot attorney are trying to win custody of their two children with all this hard evidence, proving she's the nutcase and not stable enough to raise their two children. And my sister *is* a basket case now. She calls my poor daddy every week crying. I refuse to do that to that poor man."

"That's what I like about you...You're strong."

"Did I ever have a choice?" I huffed while I considered this insecure control freak, who had threatened me with a knife to the neck, was no different from Seth. "My mother is dying, and my daddy has two daughters who are going through divorces, and who are both asking him to pay for all these court proceedings. And my sister lost her new job because she can't keep it together emotionally. I had better keep it together! And on top of all that, my sister's house went into foreclosure, and because my father did not want to see his daughter and grandkids on the street...or living with him, he had to buy her house off the auction block!"

"Your daddy must have a lot of money."

"Not really." How much money my daddy had was not Paolo's business.

"I look forward to meeting your entire family when we go over there today."

"You'll get to meet my crazy sister. She is very detached emotionally, talks non-stop because she doesn't listen. I don't really blame my brother-in-law for leaving her, but it's just how he's done her, throughout their marriage, that's wrong. She won't even drink a beer on the lake with me because she's afraid her husband has her followed."

"Does he?"

"So what if someone sees her drinking a beer?"

"I don't see drinking a beer a problem," Paolo stated.

"But she does! And speaking of beer, let's take some beer to Dad. He needs to let loose."

"Okay."

LATER THAT DAY, I spent some one-on-one alone time with my mother on the patio of their home. Paolo and my children, and the rest of the clan, were inside the house helping my father with lunch.

I whispered, "He's a trained soldier, Mom, and I'm keeping him around because I'm afraid of Seth."

"Your father told me earlier that he thinks Paolo is a good man."

"He told Dad that he loves Jesus, and you know that's all it takes to win Dad over."

"You be careful," she said meekly.

"I am. I fed Paolo information about Seth snooping around our home in the past, and I told Paolo how Seth might be planning to disappear with my children. Paolo acts like a pit bull. Seth isn't going to come around the house with Paolo there."

"I told your father, Jean Ellen, that he wasn't going to help out your sister with a lawyer, and not help you out financially."

"I need another lawyer, Mom."

"You certainly do."

"Thank you," I smiled while quickly not wanting to tell her

the grim facts of my life. "Hey, it's Mother's Day, and I don't want to talk about me, enough about my crappy life. How are you holding up?"

"I'm not responding to the drugs anymore," she admitted. "I have a lot of pain these days."

"I'm sorry," I said while I got up to hug her. I pulled back and saw her eyes well up with tears.

She continued to hold me. "I don't want to die, Jean Ellen. I'm going to miss you all. I don't want to leave you. I will miss my children and their children lives. I want to see how the story ends."

My tears streamed down my face. "I'm going to miss you every day, Mom. I don't want you to leave, either."

"I will meet Jesus upstairs, and I'm ready to talk to him."

I smiled while I gently held her and remained conscious of not causing her swollen body any more pain. "I need you," I said with tears streaming down my cheek. "Who am I going to talk to? Dad doesn't understand anything."

"I, I want you to make me a promise."

"Okay."

"I want you to keep in touch with your father. I know you two haven't ever gotten along. You are both so headstrong, but I want you to continue to write your letters...mail them to him after I'm gone. You're an excellent writer, and he always enjoys reading the letters you send me every week."

"I will write Dad—I promise. And I want you to talk to me, every day, from the other side, Mom. Don't go away. I believe in that kind of stuff, and when you see me going in the wrong direction down here, please pipe in and let me know. I'll be listening for your voice."

"I'll be with you," she said with a gentle smile. "And, don't cry for me when I'm gone." She added as she wiped the tears off my cheeks.

"That's asking way too much, Mom."

"Okay, you can cry—but laugh more often than you cry."

I chuckled, "I'm going to try."

"Life moves on, and I'm going to a better place, and I will lose this constant pain that I have lived with day in and day out for too long. I'm okay with death. I...I'm just not okay with leaving my children, but I know we'll all reunite one day again...in spirit form. We're all going to leave these earthly bodies; it's just a matter of when."

She and I both understood how tentative life could be. I prayed every day for my safety, and for her to have a miraculous cure. The patio door opened and my talkative sister stepped out and interrupted us in her southern twang, "Isn't this a great Mother's Day? I'm having so much fun."

I responded just above a whisper while wiping off my wet face, "A great day indeed. Join us, Holly."

My younger sister had not clued in that Mom and I were having a special moment. My mother's words still echoed in my head while I watched Holly take over the moment with her trite conversation, and my sadness lingered over my awareness of my mother's emotional place on this Mother's Day. What would it be like to be surrounded by eighteen people that I loved, and know that soon I would be leaving all of them for what would seem like forever? And while I dwelled on that sad thought, I watched the clan slowly walk out onto the patio, every one of them oblivious with my mother's real struggle. Each adult member of the family carried a beer out of the house, as was the German way, and a child, or two, or three followed closely behind each adult, as was our Catholic way, too. And before the back door slammed, for the final time, the entire family sat in chairs and encircled our beloved matriarch of the family--our mother and grandmother. We were all talking at once when I decidedly stood up to break out of my lingering sadness and loudly announced, "Let's do a cappella!"

Everyone turned their attention to me and cheered on the opportunity for all to take a turn and sing. Singing had been a tradition of the family for a while—ever since I decided Mom's life was too short for this family to keep bickering. I recalled how we had gathered on Father's Day at a restaurant and took turns behind the mike, including my father who sang *Ol' Man River*, a tune by Jerome Kern and Oscar Hammerstein from a 1927 Broadway musical called *Show Boat*.

♪*Ol' man river, dat ol' man river*
He mus' know sumpin', but don't say nuthin'
He jes' keeps rollin'♪
He keeps on rollin' along

♪*He don' plant taters, he don't plant cotton*
An' dem dat plants' em is soon forgotten
But ol'man river♪
He jes' keeps rollin' along

I snapped out of that memory. My father did not sing well, but that he got up in the crowded restaurant and sang was an act of courage I did not know he possessed—perhaps I had inspired him to be courageous?

"I'll start," I offered and then turned to my mother, "This one's for you, Mom!" And I began to sing my mother's favorite—a 1961 song from *Breakfast at Tiffany's* by Johnny Mercer and Henry Mancini. My mother adored this song and made this thirteen year old learn how to play *Moon River* on the piano. And with all my heart, and without the accompaniment of any music, I sang to my best friend while aware this song might be the last song I ever sang to her.

"♪*Moon River...Wider than a mile...I'm searching for you in style...Some day.* ♪ *Old dream...maker...You heart...breaker. Wherever you're g-o-i-n-g...I'm g-o-i-n-g your way.* ♪*Two d-r-i-f-t-e-r-s...off to see the world.* ♪*There's such a lot of world...to see. We're after the s-a-m-e...rainbow's end...Waitin' around the bend...My Huckleberry friend...Moon River and Me.*♪"

I stopped and my audience applauded, but, most precious, were the words of my mother, "I didn't know you could sing so wonderfully...I love your voice!"

I quipped back, "Thank you. There's a lot you don't know about me, Mom!" I shot her a smile with a wink.

"Don't underestimate the wisdom of an old and sick woman!" She smiled at me as if she saw right through me.

Everyone chuckled while I seared my mother's smile in my

mind's eye, and realized again, that how life occurred could change in a nanosecond. I walked over to Mom and gave her a kiss, and reaffirmed in a whisper to the woman, "*Moon River* will always be yours."

And, one-by-one, including Paolo and his cowboy song about the keeper of the stars, each stood up and sang their favorite song to our beloved mother, grandmother, and friend, crowning her life in honor and dignity on what might be her last Mother's Day.

The following day, Runi's ex-wife, Joyce called me. I had not heard from her in a couple of months, since we had last talked about her mysterious seizures and my numb fingers.

"Happy belated Mother's Day, Joyce."

"You, too, Jean."

"Thank you. Did your kids celebrate you?"

"Oh yeah, they all came over with my grandbabies. They cooked me dinner, bestowed gifts upon me."

"Family is the best," I replied.

"How is your mother?"

"We all spent the day with her yesterday. She's doing the best she can, considering."

"I've been praying for her, Jean."

"Thank you."

"Not to change the subject, but, it's best I tell you what I heard on the TV today. I was watching this investigative show, and this cop was talking about how this woman was really sick and having seizures, and how the police department suspected the husband was poisoning her."

"I guess that show did capture your attention!"

"Exactly, Jean. The hospital never did figure out why I was having seizures either, but the seizures finally stopped after Runi left for good."

"My hand has not gone numb either, since Seth left this last time."

"Well, hold on to your seat because what I'm about to tell you is shocking. On this show today, the investigator couldn't figure how the husband was poisoning his wife for the longest time, and there were no explanations for her seizures. The tests proved nothing, and the mystery remained. I was paying close attention, Jean. Turns out this woman's husband poisoned his wife with arsenic."

"Arsenic?"

"You can buy arsenic at a feed store or plant nursery—it's used to kill rats."

"Oh my God," I murmured. "Seth has made a million trips to the nursery over the last couple of years. He lives in the yard."

"Yes, Jean," Joyce continued, "I'm aware of that fact, and I suspect he and Runi both have bought arsenic. Long-term exposure to smaller amounts of arsenic can increase the risk of developing cancer of the bladder, lungs, skin, liver, kidneys, or prostate. Other health effects may include high blood pressure, narrowing of the blood vessels, nerve damage, anemia, diabetes, stomach upset, and skin change."

"Oh my God," I repeated.

"Hold on, there's more you should know. Arsenic occurs naturally in groundwater, usually in trace amounts; but in some areas of the world, the concentration of arsenic in water is high enough to be toxic in people who drink it over long periods of time."

"So it could be in the water?"

"In Springfield and in Houston?" Joyce questioned.

"Yes, our government doesn't care about us."

"You've got a point there, but our husbands had motivation—they wanted to divorce us and keep everything. Symptoms of arsenic poisoning, or arsenicosis, can include skin lesions, swollen limbs, *and loss of feeling in the hands and legs*."

"Oh my God."

"Don't worry, Jean."

"Don't worry?"

"Keep the faith."

"I'm relieved that Seth is gone."

"Me too. I want to read you something from Mark 16. Jesus said, '*Go into all the world and preach the Good News to everyone. Anyone who believes, and is baptized, will be saved. But anyone who refuses to believe will be condemned. These miraculous signs will accompany those who believe: They will cast out demons in my name, and they will speak in new languages. They will be able to handle snakes with safety, and if they drink anything poisonous, it won't hurt them. They will be able to place their hands on the sick, and they will be healed.'* We believers have God's promises."

"I find peace in His Word," I replied while I considered that God protected me from Paolo, too.

"Amen, sister." Joyce aligned. "There's more. Long-term exposure to arsenic can also lead to cancer, possibly affecting the lungs, bladder, and kidneys. Acute arsenic poisoning causes a metallic taste in the mouth, excessive saliva production, and problems swallowing. The next stage is to suffer vomiting and diarrhea coupled with garlic-like breath, stomach cramps, and excessive sweating. As the poison's effects progress, the patient will suffer seizures.

"Seizures?!!!"

"And seizures" Joyce calmly reiterated.

"Oh my God, Joyce."

"The seizures stopped when Runi left."

"As did the numbness of my hand when Seth left."

Later that day, I walked out to my mailbox and retrieved a stack of correspondence from the gas company, from the electric company, from our tax appraiser about our delinquent taxes, and from an unfamiliar law firm. I tore open the legal envelope and read a hostile letter addressed to Seth. Apparently, some of the lawyers were suing him for taking their money and not running the TV commercial for his lawyer referral business. I instantly knew I could help these lawyers understand Seth's game and fast-forward the demise of my husband's business. I went back inside my home and dialed the telephone number in the letterhead. I would explain the character of my estranged husband, play upon their sympathy, and suggest they shut him down immediately.

A WEEK LATER, I attended another counseling session at the Women's Center. I sat across the counselor's desk and watched the woman take notes, and in the pause found between discoveries made in our private one-on-one discussion, I studied the fiftyish woman's family photos on the credenza behind her desk while desiring to know the cryptic details of an assumed ideal life. Was not an ideal life a well thought out life? I had handed my flaws to her on a silver platter while questioning my own sanity. No man was in any of the frames...just children of various sizes. The psychologist was too old to have elementary school age children like mine. I guessed the young faces were her grandchildren. After my lifelong journey of male abuse, I found it plausible that the majority of women at the Women's Center would be male-bashing lesbians who had good reason to sell out and take extreme positions in the aftermath of abuse. And these women could have grandkids, as I would one day.

Paolo called the women in my Wednesday night group "Lesbos," though he had never met them. I knew he was threatened I would leave him after I attended a few meetings with this group when he refuted I needed no counseling from those "wackos." More name-calling. I did not listen to a single word that came out of my stalker's mouth during the last months of our relationship--stupidity that constantly challenged the flow of my creativity. I wanted him permanently out of my life and never to see him again!

I labeled my boyfriend of four months *a stalker* because I could not get rid of him after having tried many times; but now, after having listened carefully to my latest abuser reveal the details of his past, I waited for the perfect opportunity to execute my plan of permanent removal. Why did I allow myself to get sexually involved with another nutcase control freak?

"You know, Ms. Vicar," I continued, "My favorite show as a kid was *Green Acres*. I related to its premise--some cultures don't mix well." I then blurted out the show's theme song in an unusually deep voice as if trying to imitate Eddie Albert. "♫*G-r-e-e-n Acres is the place to be.* ♫*F-a-r-m living is the life for me. L-a-n-d spreading out, so far and wide. Keep Manhattan, just give me the countryside.*♫ '"

She laughed and I continued to sing. I shifted to that of my normal girlish voice and continued singing the part of the farmer's wife, "♫*New York is where I'd rather stay. I get allergic to smelling hay. I just adore a penthouse view, Darling I love you, but give me Park Avenue!* ♪ "

   The psychologist laughed. "That's great, Jean! That show stayed on TV for a long while."

   "Yeah, I was about six when I first started watching. I liked Gabor's elegant clothes."

   "Me, too. She was a beautiful woman. The show ran from the mid-sixties until 1971."

   "I related to Oliver Wendell Douglas and his wife, Lisa," I said. "I lived in Hooterville, too...And to some degree, the farmer and his neurotic city wife were my parents, except that in the TV show, Eva Gabor did not have children to screw with their heads, nor did my mother have her wardrobe."

   The psychologist chuckled and I continued, "It's been no secret that my mother was never happy about her choice in her mate after the first year of their marriage. She was too Catholic--too wimpy to divorce him, was closer to the truth. Too many children and no job kept her stuck in her lifeless marriage to the walking dead. My interpretation then, as a child, was that Mom couldn't appreciate his country background. My father was college educated, but she called him and his entire family *country bumpkins*. I thought his family was sweet, and I didn't understand her hostility then. My mother calling my daddy a *country bumpkin* was probably a nicer term for what he really was. She was angry with him for being hopeless, for being emotionally withdrawn in their marriage. Whatever he was, he was a victim of his circumstances. His parents, my grandparents, had screwed my daddy up by his eighteen birthday with their marital abuse. My daddy witnessed all the drama that goes with having a father who can't quit drinking, and a mother who won't stop fighting with her husband over his alcoholism. And this scenario was exactly the same thing Seth had experienced while growing up, and I didn't pay any attention to Seth's background before I had kids with him."

   "So you would you agree, you married your father?"

   "Oh God, Seth is far worse! He has the morals of an alley cat. He's irresponsible, too." I paused over those facts and wondered why I had been so blind about Seth from the start. I knew the answer—I had no regard for God's Word, either, when I met Seth. I continued, "My mother had often warned me to take note of a man's home life before I made a partnership with him. She said a man will treat his wife like he treats his own mother." I shook off my dismay while I recalled the name-calling I had heard between Seth and his mother in a fierce argument. "Once, during a summer vacation at my grandparents' home, I saw grandpa nailing grandma against a wall with one hand, and holding a butcher knife to her neck with the other hand. He looked as if he was going to cut her jugular. They were fighting when I walked in on them from outside. I didn't know they ever fought; they made no noise that day. That was the first time I realized they didn't like each other. I knew my mother had never liked them, but I had never understood why not...until then."

"How did you feel that day when you walked in on them fighting?"

"Embarrassed, and like I had been stupid all along to believe they loved each other. I stopped believing anyone was happily married."

"That's insightful."

"My daddy had cut himself off emotionally, before he ever left his childhood home, and that's why my mother resented being married to my father. And I, being the quick study that I am, have managed to marry my daddy over and over. Most of the men in my life have had personality traits like dear ol' Daddy —withdrawn, controlling, and insecure. Out of my three husbands, two of them have been like my father. I left the one who wasn't like dear ol' dad-- Leonardo. Number two was a passionate, generous Italian! He was very confident and supportive of me having my dreams come true. I must have felt uncomfortable being treated well!"

I snickered and shook my head at my insanity. "My need to remain in my comfort zone has blocked me. I recognize that the familiar has drawn me, which is comfortable, but not healthy. I realize that early on in my life, I interpreted my daddy's lack of love for himself, his lack of self-esteem, as something personal between us. I have felt rejection from him all my life, always believing that he didn't love me, instead of just seeing him for who he was. He was not open to individuality. He was, still is, very judgmental, all part of his controlling and insecure personality, which I now understand stems out of his fears. His motto always, 'Don't rock the boat! Don't color outside the lines. Don't make a scene! Blend! Don't take a risk!'" I looked at the counselor, "I'm not any of that."

"No?"

"No, not any more, I answered without any doubt. "I concluded early on in life that I was unworthy of my daddy's love. I summed up that if Daddy did not love me, *then* there could not possibly be anything lovable about me. I wore that conclusion as a red light to stop ALL good coming at me. Obviously, I've thought like that!"

"What age do you think you made that decision?"

"When I was too young to be making such life-altering decisions about things I had no experience or knowledge about!" I spouted while feeling disappointed with my life of so much loss.

The counselor smiled.

"I have picked two husbands to hook up with, who could not love themselves, much less could they love me. And my latest companion, Paolo, is another insecure, control freak—he is a sociopath who loves Jesus. But none of these men believe that they are truly lovable."

"You have that belief in common with all of them, don't you?"

The thought was sobering. "No, I don't share that belief *anymore*. When I allowed Seth to come into my life, I felt unworthy of having love, but the hard lessons have taught me differently. Seth took me to hell, and my eyes are wide open now. I deserve to be loved."

"And now what?"

I shrugged. "I have to undo the mess I've created in my life."

"You are on track, Jean. Stay conscious of your goal. Divorce is never easy, but you must commit to having what you want in life—a partner who respects you."

"A man not like my father."

"Your father loved you to the best of his ability. It was hard for him to show love when no one showed him love. Chronic alcoholism and abuse in a family is not love. Your father and Seth both grew up in alcoholic homes without love."

"Seth did not learn what love was from his parents—they fought his entire life," I confirmed.

"He leaves you because he cannot believe you love him. He feels unworthy of being loved. In his mind, his parents did not love him, therefore, he is unlovable. He may feel unworthy of being loved by you for other reasons, too. He doesn't want to be hurt by you—so he leaves first. He may never learn how to leap over his childhood and be loved."

I nodded, and she continued, "Your father and Seth both decided as kids to withdraw emotionally, and they will have to consciously decide as adults to reverse that decision. Only they can flip on that light switch."

I considered what love was, and questioned how does one have love? "I still desire to find that perfect love."

"You're not going to find it on this planet, Jean. People constantly operate out of their ego, until they become conscious of their spirit man; and still, they will operate out of their ego periodically when they fear being hurt."

"I understand no human is perfect."

"Here is how you discern, Jean. Watch how he treats others."

"Why can't Seth just love us?"

"He has the potential to do that, but it might be years before Seth flips on that light switch. He may never flip on that light switch. He has to be willing to leap over his fear of intimacy. He has to be willing to consciously look back, at his difficult childhood, and feel what that scared ten-year old boy felt, when he made that decision to emotionally withdraw. After Seth sees and feels all that pain again, and becomes conscious of the decision he made at that young age about marriage and family, then Seth must be willing to take the risk of being hurt in order to have intimacy and love. He has to agree that he's been wrong his entire life, about the decision he made when only a young child in pain. That's the hard part, Jean. He might not be able to change until he sees what his decision has cost him, and that loss would be you and his children."

"That's sad."

"It is sad, Jean. And asking a person to admit that he's lived his entire life wrong is asking a lot of that person. Being right about our decisions that we put in place at a very young age to avoid any more pain is what we humans do to survive."

"My father lives according to God's Word—he put his fears behind him and walks in faith while believing God's Word is true. Seth believes he is a god. My husband grew up in a war zone. Seth told me about a night his mother hung the last strip of wallpaper on the dining room wall of their mobile home. Seth's father stumbled through the front door drunk and started bitching about her spending money on wallpaper. His father then took a paint scraper to the new wallpaper. They fought all night, as usual, and Daddy ended up bashing out Mom's teeth with a cast iron skillet. She sprayed hair spray in his eyes. They tore up the house...glass broken everywhere. My husband witnessed this kind of exchange between his parents for years. I guess it made him insane, or at least made him believe there is no loving God."

"And until Seth sees what he lost—you and the kids, and feels the pain over his loss, he will not change. He will have to be angry with himself, and learn to take responsibility for being the cause in the outcome, before he will have a transformation of being. And for you to believe, Jean, that everything could be all right with you two is a myth."

"I don't believe there is any possibility with Seth because we are not equally yoked. He is not held accountable by any code of morality, and he denounces God our heavenly Father and his Son, Jesus Christ."

"Your husband has shown you what he believes about love, family, marriage. He swore as a kid that he'd never get married, and he's standing strong in his decision—a flawed belief, but nevertheless, an act of self-preservation and survival."

"It's all so sad," I admitted. "He's breaking his own heart, and he will wake up one day when it's too late, after I've moved on. One day, he won't have the kids and me anymore. It's a vicious circle.

He can't love me. He can't allow himself to ever be happy in love. He runs away. He swears me off forever; and then, he comes back to me. I take him back; we try to work it out; and then, he stops the intimacy, sabotages the goodness we've developed, and then runs away again."

"Right," the middle-aged counselor nodded. "It's the root of bi-polar disorder. And, on a spiritual level, Satan knows how to bind up a loving spirit. No matter how often you tell Seth that you love him, he will never believe you."

"Because he has no faith, in anything, but the child within."

"Satan makes us think the lies we tell ourselves are truths. This dark spirit makes us think we already know how the future will turn out. Man's logic requires no faith in anything greater, and renders no hope in the unseen. Very little possibility, if any, is seen on this level of human understanding."

"Only in faith is there possibility."

"Now you have Paolo in your life. You know he's another mistake."

"I do know that...I'm working on that problem. He's obsessing over me these days. I am perfectly clear that the thought of losing me threatens Paolo, that he's insecure and controlling. I understand I am with another man like Seth, and this one is especially insane."

"Your husband is a white-collar educated abuser, who can't find his career niche; therefore, your success threatens him. Paolo, on the other hand, is under-educated and blue collar, and he feels inadequate with you. Both these men have low self-esteems, and, although they think they love you, they could never believe you could really ever love them. They have issues of trust with you—and they make their issue your problem. Their control is based on this distrust they have with any woman in their lives, and it doesn't help their confidence level, Jean, that you are what men call a man magnet."

I shook my head in the complexity I saw in human nature.

The therapist continued, "At the beginning of a relationship, an abuser will always say that his jealousy is a sign of love. Jealousy has nothing to do with love. It's a sign of insecurity and possessiveness. He will question the woman about who she talks to, accuse her of flirting, or be jealous of time she spends with family, friends, or children. Many battered women dated, or knew their abuser, for less than six months, before he put an engagement ring on her finger, or insisted they live together. He comes on like a whirlwind. He says things like 'You're the only person I could ever talk to,' or 'I've never felt loved like this by anyone.' He needs someone, desperately, and will pressure the woman to commit to him. He is very dependent on the woman for all of his emotional needs. He expects her to be the perfect wife, mother, lover, and friend. He will say things like 'if you love me,' and 'I'm all you need...You're all I need.' The man tries to cut the woman off from all resources. If she has men friends, she is a 'whore'. If she has women friends, she is a 'lesbian'. If she is close to family, she is 'tied to the apron strings'. He accuses people who are her support system of 'causing trouble;' and, he may want to live in the country without a phone. He may not let her use the car, or he may try to keep her from working or going to school. He's going to isolate her one way or the other. If he is chronically unemployed, someone is always doing him wrong, or out to get him. He may make mistakes; and then, he blames the woman for upsetting him and keeping him from concentrating on doing his job."

"Seth blamed me for his dropping out of law school."

"There you have it. The abuser will tell the woman she is at fault for almost anything that goes wrong in his life. He means to be cruel and hurtful. He degrades her. He curses her, and he runs down many of her accomplishments. The typical batterer works part-time, or not at all. His total income is poverty level. Researchers have found that *status inconsistency* is an important component of the profile of the battering husband. An example of status inconsistency occur when a man's educational background is much higher than his occupational attainment...like your husband, for example, a man with a Master's Degree and no steady job throughout the marriage. The most telling of all attributes of the battering man is that *he feels inadequate* and *sees violence as a culturally acceptable way* to be both dominant and powerful. Battered wives have been found to be aggressive, masculine, and frigid."

I considered the time when I sucked my husband off the toilet and slammed him to the floor—I'd had enough. "You've described my husband and Paolo perfectly."

"And your father?"

"He was emotionally, verbally, and physically abusive, too, and I was too young to run away—I wanted to. When I graduated from high school, my father asked me to sign over a bank account that he had held in my name while I was growing up, money that he had saved for my college education. He said while I was signing that CD back over to him that I was not college material, and that he wasn't going to waste his money on me. He ordered me to get a job immediately. He didn't care what kind of job I got, but he demanded that I start paying him rent money. I had wanted to leave home so badly for years before I graduated from high school and get away from him, and he knew that, but he made it impossible for me to leave by taking most my paycheck each month. His actions had everything to do with me getting married at nineteen to Todd."

"That's called emotional abuse, Jean. They break you down in hopes to make you dependent on them. They will isolate you from others, too. You will have no other friendships in a relationship with an abuser."

"Let me remind you, Jean, or warn you. It is common for a woman like you who gets out of one abusive situation to often repeat her mistake, and partner up again with another abusive personality."

"Okay." I wondered if I knew what healthy looked like in a male form.

"When you make love to Paolo, you are making love to a man who has assaulted you on several occasions."

"I understand that," I said while I squirmed due to the discomfort I felt over my reality.

"And you call him a psychopathic-schizophrenic."

"Yes," I replied with a guilty grin stemming out of embarrassment.

"Do you want to be loved back?"

"I want to be loved by a truly loving man. If one more man

lies to me, or pretends to be something that he is not, so that he can deceive me out of some need of his to control me, he will live to regret his cruel act! That I promise! I will turn off that button that tells me what right and wrong is, as I know so well how to do, and I will give the next man, who comes along and thinks he can abuse me, some of his own medicine. The next abuser will pay for what all the abusers in my life before him caused me to suffer. If my life must include me walking down a path that draws every twisted creep from hell, then perhaps it is my purpose in life to teach a lesson or two to these jerks!"

The counselor chuckled, "Be sure to give fair warning to the next abuser you fall in love with, Jean. It is only fair that he understands what he's dealing with!"

I smiled. "Probably won't. If I get broadsided, then it's only fair he gets the same in return."

She shook her head as if I was heading for trouble. "Keeping Paolo around is hazardous. If this psychotic is in love with you, and I suspect that in his own sick way, he believes he loves you, then when you do try to get rid of him, he might go off the deep end in an effort to prevent you from leaving him."

I refrained from telling the woman that I had already experienced the scenario she described with a knife to my neck.

"These abusive men are about control, Jean. Their control intensifies when they think they are going to lose something they cherish."

"I have to get rid of Paolo," I supported with a nod of approval.

"Yes you do...and carefully. And you've got to divorce your abusive husband once and for all, too." The silver hair woman shook her head and smiled, "I'll give it to you, Jean, you've got some stories...You ought to write a book. I hope you live long enough to do so."

"I began a novel. I hope I live long enough to finish it, too."

The following day I woke up in my bedroom alone without Jeffrey Dahmer, that's what I called the boyfriend. Paolo had not spent the night with me because he had to take his sick brother to the hospital early this morning. The phone rang, and Charles Manson was on the other end. I picked up with a great amount of animosity. "What do you want, Seth?"

"It's about time you answer," he scoffed and then diffused his anger by shifting quickly to a kind-sounding, "How are you?"

"I don't have to talk to you!" I refuted while sounding annoyed, but thrilled he was on the other end by his own initiative. "If you want to see your sons, then get a court order. I'm sure that's why you're calling."

"I recall all Ninja and withdraw all ronin," he said and then chuckled.

I translated his statement to mean he called off the hit. I pretended that I did not understand his words. "What's that mean?"

He growled, "I want to see my sons! I love my sons! I'm their father, and I have the right to see them! I haven't seen them in four months!"

"Oh, boo hoo!" I spewed. "Well, like I said, get a court order, and you will have your rights! Until then, you're not seeing them. I don't trust you! And I suggest we hurry up this divorce process, too. I might be moving away."

"You are?" He sounded surprised. "Where are you moving to?"

"I don't know if you've heard, Seth." I paused while wondering if my friend in Connecticut, dear ol' George, told his former college roommate about my friend, Paolo.

"I haven't heard anything," Seth impatiently retorted.

"I'm engaged to a man who loves me, Seth. Imagine that!" I sarcastically harangued.

Seth remained without comment, and I continued, "His name is Paolo. He wants to move to Colorado, with me and the kids, and build a two-story, log cabin there." I refrained from telling my husband any more lies, until I first got his reaction about the guy, whom I suspected Seth hired to kill me.

"What? I don't understand. You are not going to move away, Jean...I won't let it happen--"

His argument revealed to me that perhaps I surprised him with the turn of events. I cut him off in mid-sentence. "What do you mean, *you won't let me?* As soon as we divorce, Seth, I'm out of here. Paolo has some money coming to him, and we're going to start a new life in beautiful Colorado. I'm going to open up a resale store."

"A resale store?" He sounded surprised.

"You know, Seth, one of those junk stores."

"I can't believe it!"

I assumed that what he could not believe was that his hit man and I were hooking up. "Did you expect something different? I'm moving on. You've left us three times, and I'm not going to play this chaotic game anymore. Paolo is crazy...about me. And I need a divorce, and you need to come out of hiding, face the music, and help me have that divorce happen. If you don't, Paolo might just expedite this divorce matter himself!"

"What does that mean?"

Clearly, he sounded threatened. "It means...Paolo hates your fucking guts, Seth. He's heard enough about you to believe that he'd be doing me, and the world, a big favor by removing you from its surface, once and for all!" I silently took glee in threatening him with the man I suspected was double-crossing him. "He's a former Vietnam vet, and I think if I pushed his buttons, he would kill you for free."

Seth remained silent for a few minutes and then blurted, "Do you want to make us work again, Jean?"

Ha! I was right, again! He was calling to beg me to take him back! Seth had never been subtle, and he had more gall than any person I had ever known in my life; and he had never let his pride be an issue, if he could get what he set out to get, no matter how contemptible. I could actually believe what I was hearing from my estranged husband! It seemed all too easy on this early morning. I was going to move Seth back into our home, and move Paolo out on this same day. I guessed the timing was right, and fate was playing its hand. Obviously, Seth's business had gone bust, just as my father, and

I, and Linda, calculated it would. Now, I could get my husband to sell our home. I thought about Seth's question. Did I want to make us work again? Did I have a choice? I wanted to divorce this creep from hell as fast as possible, but first I had to sell the house, according to the Scripture of Daddy-O. I needed money in the bank and a car.

"Well, the boys sure miss you, Seth. And sometimes I miss you. Sometimes I really need you here."

"That's music to my ears!" He reveled.

"Do you miss me?" I sweetly baited while waiting in my own amusement for the bullshit Seth was about to bestow upon me.

"Oh, I could not begin to tell you!"

I chuckled. I was sure that he could not!

"I made a big mistake, Jean."

I was sure about that, too! I knew Seth regretted not having sold the house before he left the last time! I heard him continue, "I want to come back home. There is nothing more important to me than my family!"

I refrained from laughing. Not this line again! Oh, shit! I then maneuvered on his plea, "We should talk about that, Seth. How about today?"

"You want to talk about me coming back home?" He asked as if surprised, but happy to hear my suggestion.

"Yes. I have to look you in the eyes and see if you are straight up with me. I have to be truthful with you, too. I have been sleeping with Paolo steadily for nearly five months. At first, all we were about was great sex. Our relationship was subtle the first five months, and only recently, I began to feel that I might be in love with Paolo. The guy is hung like a horse. Oops, I'm sorry—didn't need to be so insensitive."

"It can happen," he snapped while I interpreted him to be annoyed.

"Yes, I first fell in lust, and then in love. I was at first just killing time, and Paolo was always there, and we had lots and lots of great sex. He's very tall, and you know how tall men are built, right?"

"Yes," he curtly answered clearly indicating he had no need for further explanation.

IN HELL WITH EYES WIDE OPEN

I continued, "Paolo has a huge member—I think I'm addicted, and maybe not really in love."

"Why are you telling me this, Jean?" He clearly was annoyed with the topic.

"I want to be honest with you about everything. Don't you want the same? I'm sorry, but I was just making you aware of where I am emotionally—I'm a bit confused. Are you angry? Because if you are, I can't deal with your anger anymore. I've had total peace over the last five months while you have been gone, Seth, and I'm not willing to have anything less, ever again."

"No, I'm not angry, Jean," he said while calming back down.

"Good, because I have become addicted to the Italian's sex, and you ought to know that my addiction to his large member is now a problem for us—that's all I'm saying. He's the most amazing lover; and anything smaller will be like expecting a rib eye steak and getting a can of Spam."

"Spam!"

I didn't say you were Spam. You're more like a cocktail wiener. I held back my laughter. I loved cutting the desperate malefactor down to size, and I knew he would not express anything right now but total cooperation. "I love Paolo, but I'm not *in love* with Paolo. Do you understand the difference, Seth? Can our relationship work out with you having all this knowledge?"

"I don't know, Jean."

I knew he was debating whether to go along with my game or not, and I continued to make him suffer. "I feel your hesitation. I must be crazy to consider we could ever be together again."

"No, Jean, I understand that you have been involved with another man. I will be patient."

"Good. Paolo is madly in love with me, and when I break up with him, he might be angry with you—and his anger is not to be taken lightly. However, I'll try to talk Paolo out of killing you. It's just like this—if I could have my rathers, then I would rather have you in my life than him. I want you alive, too. The kids feel the same way. Can you get over this Paolo thing, Seth?"

"Yeah, I will for bigger reasons," Seth offered with restraint.

"Let's meet and talk over lunch."

"Are you buying?"

"Sure," he said with little enthusiasm.

"Okay, then I'll ride my bike to the Stoobie's Burger Place on the bike trail. I'll get Marilyn to watch Doren, after Harper gets on the school bus. I'll meet you there at noon."

"Great!" Seth said with delight. "See you there, Jean. You've made me the happiest man in the world."

"Well, why would I ever want to hurt you, Seth?"

"I wouldn't think you would hurt me," he answered.

"You're lucky to feel that way, Seth. See you at lunch." I hung up.

I replayed our conversation and commended myself for my performance. "That stung," I said to myself and chuckled while I walked through the house to change my clothes for my next act. "I'm only getting started, asshole!" I said while I stepped inside my walk-in closet to change. "And, although I know you don't care one iota about me, Seth, it's the thought that someone else would come to my rescue that bothers you so much!"

I stood contemplating what to wear for a lunch with the greedy bastard. I would be sure to order the most expensive meal on the menu! I evaluated his current situation. Seth's *Legal Spot* business was bust, and he still owed his mother $85,000. There would be no negotiation over burgers this afternoon as far as I was concerned. We would immediately list our house on the market at a lower price than we agreed to the last time, and then split the proceeds 50/50, and at closing, we would each get a check in our own name, hopefully for the minimum of $50,000. We would sell the house in six weeks or less. There was no way I was going to spend even two months living with this asshole! I felt like I was asking Charles Manson to rescue me from Jeffrey Dahmer! My life was ridiculous!

Once dressed in cute bike shorts, a clingy T-shirt and tennis shoes, I walked back into the living area of my home. I prayed aloud while looking at the three-foot crucifix Paolo had hung over the mantel. "Please God protect me and my children through all this!" I then picked up the phone on the wet bar to call Paolo, my psychotic hit man. I assumed he and his brother might be back from the hospital now, and if so, I would tell the crazy Italian that my husband and I were back together, and to not ever come back over here again. I would have Seth to protect me from Paolo now. I questioned whether I needed to buy a gun, but, on second thought, I thought it best to leave it alone, and, hopefully, they would kill each other!

An hour later, I arrived at the restaurant on the bike trail in the woods of our country club community. I left Doren with my next-door neighbor, Marilyn, just after Harper got on the school bus. I parked my transportation in the bike rack on the trail adjacent to the back patio and found Seth waiting for me at a table. He stood up when I walked up; we awkwardly hugged; and then, we both sat down. I told him he looked like he had been hungry too many days, and he said I looked great. We quickly ordered matching burgers and fries. We warmed up with small talk, but even that type of conversation made me feel guarded. I did not trust Seth enough to tell him any details about anyone involved in my life. While I watched Seth talk non-stop with his mouth full of hamburger and fries, I questioned what I ever saw in the slight man. I felt nothing, but disgust for him. I continued, "If I do agree to let you come back into the house, we will sell the house and split the money 50/50."

"Give me all the proceeds."

"I'm not giving you *all* the proceeds, Seth! Are you out of your mind?" I rolled my eyes as I chomped into my sour dough burger. "I should let Paolo kill you."

"What?" He asked as if shocked.

"For some reason, Paolo thinks you deserve to die."

"Why?"

"He thinks you're a greedy bastard."

"Jean—this man is dangerous!"

"I know—I figured that out when he told me that he was a hit man."

"What?" Seth again acted as if shocked.

"He's a Mercenary—worked for the government. I don't want to talk about him anymore—my heart is still bleeding." I could see worry in his face. "About the house, Seth."

"Then split the house 75/25."

"Hell no! I'm going to leave, Seth, and end this meeting if you don't get serious. Paolo is right, you are a greedy bastard!" I slammed. "My apparel business lawsuit bought that house! I don't have to sell the house and split the proceeds with you at all! The court will give me the house and kids. They've done it already twice!"

"I worked that apparel business, too, Jean!" Seth reminded with great patience.

"Yeah, that's like you, Seth!" I angrily spouted. "Leonardo funded my business, and you jump in at the last minute, you get his wife pregnant, and then stick your name on the lawsuit that bought this house!"

"Jean, you don't know that the courts will give you that house, or the kids."

"I'm leaving," I said while I angrily got up out of my chair.

"I'm sorry, Jean. Please sit back down." Seth took a breath and stopped his greedy self from saying another word by taking a bite of his burger.

I slowly sat back down pretending to be impatient with his antics. I could see that Seth could control his temper better than he had in days gone by, and I figured he must have been really hard up, on his luck, to venture down this path.

"Let's not dig up the past," he calmly instructed. "I owe my mother money, in case you forgot."

My anger flashed, "Irrelevant! I never agreed with you gambling her entire life savings in the stock market! And I'm not giving her any of *my money* to pay her back. I'll go 50/50. That's it, Seth. That's pretty generous of me!" I watched Seth do the numbers in his head while looking disturbed.

"So," he continued, "we ask $150,000, maybe $160,000 for the house, and then, we come down three thousand dollars, that leaves roughly $70,000 or $80,000 a piece."

"You owe your mother $80,000 right?"

"$85,000."

"We ask $125,000 tops for the house, Seth. We are going to

sell at that price."

"Too low," he said.

"Too bad, I don't agree," I retorted. "I want to sell our home as fast as possible and get on with life. The housing market is saturated with new homes in the back of this community, and anyone can buy a brand new home for the price you want to sell our fifteen year old house."

"We've put $40,000 into remodeling, Jean."

"That's the loss we suffer for you putting us in the position that you've put us in, as a result of your war games."

"Okay, okay," he acquiesced. "$125,000."

"Deal?" I said while I reached over the table and extended my hand.

"Deal," he said while he shook in agreement.

I was not convinced he would be his word—I knew I was shaking hands with the devil. "Why don't you get your stuff and move in tonight?" I hated the sound of those words, but I did not want to be unprotected from Paolo that evening. I had broken it off with him minutes before meeting with Seth, and Paolo was furious with me. I hung up on Paolo when he began his threats.

Seth looked surprise, and I smiled. "The kids are going to be thrilled when I go home and tell them that Daddy is back for good, again."

Seth chuckled, rocked back in his chair, and clapped his hands in delight. He looked authentically happy, and I sat there looking at my nemesis while understanding he had no clue what hell he had created for his children and me.

Paolo had taken the turn of events hard. I had given him the cold, hard facts when he began telling me what he would do to Seth, if I took my husband back into my life. I gave Paolo no room to believe his threats intimidated me when I hung up on him. He had known for months that I did not want the relationship with him.

"Dinner is early tonight, Seth. Be there at five," I said as I stood up from my chair.

"You got it, wife!" Seth said as he hopped up from his chair, too. "Can I have a kiss?"

I felt I wanted to pick up the fork on the table and stab him in the hand as he had done to his first wife, Deb. I grinned at the thought of driving the utensil into his jugular.

He interpreted my smile as a green light to walk up closer and wrap his arms around my waist while I stood there at the table in disbelief. My skin crawled when the maggot touched me. He had put our children and me through hell, for years, with all his lies and con jobs; and now, he wanted a kiss!

I rudely pushed him away. "I have to take it slow, Seth." I felt contempt, and I hated the phony smile he wore on his face. I thought of the psychotic man that had been living with me, and my three children for the past months, a sociopath Seth had put into our lives. "It will take me some time to adjust to you again." I felt I would never get over the anger I felt toward Seth for hurting our children and me.

"I'm sorry—I understand, Jean."

"Good."

"I'm thrilled you're giving me another chance," he declared while I picked up my house keys off the table and headed to the bike rack nearby. Seth followed and watched me unlocked my bike.

"Ride over to my car," he requested. "It's in the front."

"Okay," I said while he turned to walk through the restaurant and exit out the front door. I met him on the other side of the building at his car.

"Nice car," I said while I stared at a convertible Chrysler LeBaron sports car. "More resentment surfaced while I considered the abuse I had suffered because we did not have a car over the past five months."

"Thank you," he proudly said.

"How can you afford it?"

"I can't—it's a long story."

"I'm sure it's the same story," I impatiently spewed while aware he was returning to his family dead broke again, while wanting to convince his children and me that he loved us.

"Okay I see you're feeling angry," he said while wanting to ensure I didn't change my mind about his re-emergence into our paid-for-in-full home. He rubbed my ass, "Can I get some of this tonight?"

"No, no, no!" I adamantly yelled and stepped away while feeling angry. I took a deep breath, shook my head at his audacity, and stared out into the woods on the edge of the parking lot. I silently asked God to give me the ability to be nice. I turned back and smiled at Seth. "I'm sorry." I understood Seth had a motive to emotionally lock me into his device.

"Only if you want to," he soothed while aware I did not desire him.

"I don't want to, okay?"

"Okay."

"Bye, Seth," I said coldly before pedaling away.

The evening sun turned the Texas sky pink while Seth and I sat with our three children, in our living room, eating popcorn, and watching TV on our 42" Sony big screen. Bella was hostile toward me that evening for allowing Seth to come back into the house, but I reminded my twelve-year old daughter, in private, that it was just about the money, and that as soon as we sold our house, I would divorce Seth.

I sat at the opposite side of the couch from Seth and looked over at my husband, who stroked his firstborn's head in his lap. Harper watched TV and looked content with his father back in his life. I whispered to the worn-looking, forty-year old man, "So are you still running the lawyer referral business?"

"I am...I'm just not running the TV commercials."

"How do you do that? I mean, isn't the business based on people seeing the TV commercials?"

"Yeah, but," he hesitated and then let out a deep breath. "I have troubles with the Texas State Bar. They are about to shut me down. They filed an injunction against me. I might have only a few more days to be in business before they force the injunction. And I...I just don't have enough money to keep it all floating. I have to pay ten thousand dollars to a TV station for the commercials. I don't have employees any longer."

"What about the attorneys who already signed up? Don't

they expect you to give them what they paid for--TV commercials?"

"Yeah, they do. I'm being sued by a few of them right now, who paid me before I figured out I could not come up with the cash for the TV commercials."

I saw how uncomfortable Seth became when having to disclose his financial situation to me. He had no clue that I had a recent telephone conversation with those same lawyers, who thereafter filed a grievance with the Texas State Bar to shut him down.

"Look, it's this simple," he continued. "I can pull together $12,000 in the next couple of days. Trust me. I just have to collect $3,000 from four attorneys, and then I'll be back on my feet."

I shook my head. Trust him? He was out of his mind. "So you're still willing to collect money from attorneys?"

"Yes," he admitted as if not understanding why I was confused.

"And when did you run your last TV commercial?"

"About a month ago."

"So you've been collecting money over the last month from attorneys, but there is no TV commercial currently playing?"

"That's right," Seth confirmed.

"So you're screwing attorneys?"

"I'm doing what I have to do, Jean."

He sounded annoyed with me. His familiar words echoed in my head, *I'm doing what I have to do*. Those same words launched our relationship, after he admitted to me in Key West, that he told Runi that *he had to do what he had to do*.

I considered a passage I read to Paolo, in recent days, when I felt he was seriously considering murdering Seth. Romans 12:19–21: *Beloved, never avenge yourselves, but leave it to the wrath of God, for it is written, "Vengeance is mine, I will repay, says the Lord. To the contrary, if your enemy is hungry, feed him; if he is thirsty, give him something to drink; for by so doing you will heap burning coals on his head. Do not be overcome by evil, but overcome evil with good."*

This story felt ill fated. I hoped Paolo retained God's Word. I shook off my discomfort and continued my inquisition. "Seth, you can't collect money from attorneys when you know there is an injunction filed against you by the Texas State Bar. You just admitted to me that you only have a few more days to do business, before the Texas State Bar forces the injunction. Isn't an injunction an order to stop, cease, and desist from conducting that business? What will they have to do to stop you? Arrest you and give you jail time?"

"You can't imagine how hard it has been for me these last months, Jean. You don't have a clue! You've been living here in dreamland with your daddy paying all your bills!"

"Dreamland!" My anger flashed, but I bit my tongue and refrained from saying another word about his delusions. I reminded myself that all I was doing was putting up with Seth long enough to sell the house and get my money out of the deal. What did I care if a bunch of attorneys sued him, or whether or not the Texas State Bar put him in jail for violating their injunction! Or whether Paolo caught up with him.

I turned my attention back to the TV and refused to engage in his deluded thinking. And while I got the magnitude of his financial crisis and criminal intentions, I would never admit to Seth that my father refused to fund another divorce action and forced me to take this snake back into my life and sell my beautiful home.

The next morning, Seth jumped out of his side of our king-size bed to scurry off to his scheduled *Legal Spot* interviews with gullible attorneys. He no longer had a staff of telemarketers, nor a young thing he called his assistant and bought flowers for. There was no business office answering his phones, while he tried to wrap up four more $3,000 contracts with unsuspecting lawyers for the next couple of days. He intended to collect money for a TV commercial he would never run.

I laid in bed watching my nude husband brush his teeth in the bathroom and thought about the night before. I had sex with him the night before because I wanted him to feel my indifference toward him. He felt my disconnection, too, but refused to acknowledge that his touch repelled me. He expressed no words of concern, nor did any facial expression indicate he was bothered on any level by our severed bond. I was certain he believed sooner, or later, he would break me down, and that I would come back around. I vowed to never have sex with the creature from hell again; and after having sex with Paolo for the last several months, whose feet were five inches bigger that Seth's feet, screwing my husband was like having sex with a rabbit. Everything about the experience was small.

I recalled, while held up as a hostage with Paolo over the last five months, reading *The Art of War* by Sun Tzu, a Chinese warrior-philosopher who had written war strategy over two-thousand years ago. My aim at this point in my life was invincibility, victory without battle, and unassailable strength; and the insights I discovered in the book hopefully would render to me psychological power over my enemies. Sun Tzu wrote that to overcome one's enemy, without fighting, is the best of skills. And to take a rational approach, rather than an emotional approach, to the problem of conflict, showed how understanding conflict can lead, not only to its resolution, but even to its avoidance altogether, because for a human to sense and comprehend *after action,* is not worthy of being called *comprehension.*

Sun Tzu wrote that the range of awareness and efficiency of the Taoist adept is unnoticeable, imperceptible to others, because their critical moments take place before ordinary intelligence has mapped out a description of the situation. And to be able to do something before it exists, sense something before it becomes active, see something before it sprouts, are three abilities that develop interdependently; and if mastered, then nothing is sensed, but is comprehended, nothing is undertaken without response, and nowhere does one go without benefit. I was on the path of mastering all living situations, and interested in the study of formulas for sensitivity and timely responsiveness.

I drifted back to sleep while Seth showered and dressed, but was rudely woken when Seth barged back into the bedroom dressed in his suit and screaming, "That psycho fucked up my car!"

"What?" I sat up in the bed.

"Yeah, your boyfriend shredded my convertible top! Come see it!" He waved me out of bed, and then left the bedroom.

"Oh no!" I sarcastically spouted while I got out bed and slipped on my robe feeling amused by Paolo's act. I was not surprised by the turn of events.

I walked through the kitchen, exited the glass kitchen door, walked under the catwalk, and stepped into the two-car garage to see Seth and his convertible.

"Where does that son-ov'a-bitch live?"

"I don't know, Seth." I was not going to give Seth any information to use. Paolo could be detrimental to my mom and apple pie image in the next divorce hearing I planned to execute. "You don't even know if Paolo did it, Seth."

"I'm calling the cops," he said as he walked up to the phone on the garage wall. He took the receiver out of the cradle.

An obnoxious putrid smell offended my senses. "It smells like urine in here!"

"He pissed all over the Astro turf!" Seth snapped.

"Eck! Now that's going too far!" I said as I covered my nose with my robe.

"Look at my car! Who is this guy?" He asked while holding the receiver in his hand.

I looked at the soft top of the convertible and then at Seth. I knew damn well my husband knew who Paolo was, but I played along. "This guy is a guy that hates your guts, Seth. It's personal between you and him now. He wants to kill you—I held him off a couple of times. And now, I suspect that since you've moved back into the house, and he's out of the picture, that he is going to kill you; and I have no say in the matter...this time."

"This time?!!!" A look of terror came across Seth's face. "That's it! I'm calling the police. I have an appointment this morning with an attorney, and I'm going to be late, too, if I don't get out of here. Get this house listed today, Jean!"

"The *For Sale* sign is up there, Seth." I pointed to the rafters. "Just because you took down the *For Sale* sign did not take the house off the market. It's still listed on the MLS—we have it priced too high."

He did not acknowledge me, but, instead, dialed 911.

I continued, "I will ask our Realtor to lower the price as we discussed yesterday. We need to get out of here in a hurry, don't you think so?"

Seth looked insane while I heard the police dispatch. "911 What's your emergency?"

I stood and considered everything. Paolo's act of terror was perfect! Now Seth was convinced that the man he sent in to kill me was going to kill him. I was certain now that Seth would not renege on his agreement with me to sell the house quickly. Seth needed to find safe refuge as much as he needed fast cash.

LATER THAT MORNING, a Montgomery County police officer came to our home. Seth filed a report for the vandalism made on his convertible's ragtop and for the urination on the Astro turf in our garage. He left me and the cop standing in the driveway, and dashed over to his vandalized car parked in the garage, to leave for a meeting with an unwitting lawyer, who Seth expected would give him $3,000 for a TV commercial he did not ever intend to run on TV. As he slowly backed out of the garage, the sky cracked, and a thunderstorm unleashed gallons of water on top of us. The cop and I rushed to find cover under the front porch. I watched Seth back out of the long driveway with water rushing into the car like a sieve, through the shredded soft top, and right on top of the man in the business suit. I laughed and whispered, "Good one, Paolo." I then invited the cop inside, out of the rain.

I stood in my kitchen, alone with the officer, and listened to him say, "We can't go arrest this guy. We have no proof that he did this crime to your husband's car last night. I'm sure he did, from what you tell me about this guy's personality, but...we have to have witnesses."

"I see," I replied with a nod when the phone suddenly rang. I stepped down into the den and looked at the Caller ID that sat beside the phone on the wet bar. "It's him!" I informed to the cop. "It's Paolo."

"I'll pick it up," the cop said as he walked over to the phone.

I pressed a button on the phone and put Paolo on speakerphone.

"Hello," the officer calmly answered.

"Just know this, you son-ov'a-bitch, you are going to die," Paolo threatened in a low voice.

"And why is that?" The cop calmly asked while we both understood Paolo thought he was speaking to Seth.

"I love her...and we had a thing going on. You treat her like shit, man. But more importantly, you just deserve to fucking die for coming between us, and for fucking with me, and with her."

"Is that so?" The cop baited and remained calm.

"Yeah, that's so," Paolo threatened. "You mother fucker, I know where you work, and I'm coming after you. And when I find you...you ain't going to be anything but maggot food."

The cop patiently responded, "Sir, you have been talking to an officer from the Montgomery County Sheriff's Department, and I warn you that should anything happen to these good people over here, you will be our first suspect. I have your number on this Caller ID--" The phone went dead.

"I'm sure Paolo's shook," I said.

"He was surprised, to say the least, when I informed him I was a police officer."

"This will not stop him," I informed the uniform. "Paolo has no regard for the law. He's psychotic, and you don't talk sense into him when he's tripping and back on the front line of Vietnam."

"I understand, ma'am. This man is dangerous, but I can't arrest him for making a threatening phone call, nor can I arrest him without a witness that would confirm he shredded your husband's rooftop, or urinated in your garage."

I was reminded why Seth's pregnant employee did not have her former boss arrested for his threatening phone call.

"Can you give me any other information that might give me grounds for making an arrest?"

"Yes, I can. He's preoccupied with Lubbock, Texas. He wanted me to go up there with him to pick up some money." I stopped short, and did not tell the officer that I thought the story about the $50,000 inheritance was pure fabrication. I did not reveal to the cop that I felt the psychotic, Vietnam vet needed a good story, in order to get me to drive with him across West Texas, so that he could kill me, and then dump my body out there in the vast desert. I did not tell the cop that Seth had put the Mercenary in my life to do just that. "Paolo use to live up there in the Texas Panhandle, but for some reason, he doesn't want to go into Lubbock by himself. He told me that he lost his temper one night with his girlfriend up there. I think he skipped town and is hiding from the law."

The officer nodded while he wrote down information on his tablet and then looked up at me. "For now, just call us, if you see him hanging around, and we'll come out. He might be in trouble. Let me run a background check on him and see if there are any outstanding warrants on him in Lubbock. I'll get back to you later this evening. Do you know his home address?"

"I don't—I've been to his trailer. He lives in Conroe, in the woods with his brother. I could show you how to get there."

"No, that's alright. We can find him. You said he and his brother are collecting welfare."

"I met him at the welfare office in Conroe. His brother is a heart patient and waits to have a heart transplant. Paolo doesn't hold a job, either. They're living on the dole."

"Okay. I'll take your report down to the station, and if anything else happens, call us."

"Yes, sir." I watched the officer open the front door and exit. I stared down at my coffee table and picked up the paperback I had been reading and flipped open the book and read more of Sun Tzu words:

It is best to thwart people by intelligent planning. Invincibility is a matter of self-defense; vulnerability is simply a matter of having gaps. In battle, confrontation is done directly; victory is gained by surprise.

I felt assured that for me to win this war, I was in a good position. Seth filled in the gap, and I strategized to surprise attack Paolo. If what I suspected about Paolo were true, that he had a history of insanity and criminal activity, then the police would arrest him on some warrant for a crime that he committed in Lubbock, Texas. I would then have but a single victory; the war was not near over.

I understood, too, that in war, a warrior does not leak true information. Seth was dastardly enough to use the hit man that he put in my path, against me in the next custody dispute. I guessed that my husband would tell the court one day, that I kept a psychotic criminal around my children while he was absent. I would never admit to Seth that Paolo was anything, but a loving man who loved Jesus, and who occasionally suffered from the effects of the Vietnam War; and my father would be my witness, and verify my positive testimony about Paolo. Dad had concluded Paolo to be a good Christian man, too.

FIVE MONTHS LATER, 1995. I walked home from night school toward my townhouse located adjacent to the college campus in Deer Park, Texas, a cowboy refinery town where men were men, steers were an investment, and gays were reason to send in the KKK. I had made full circle. My first husband, Todd, and I had lived in this same blue-collar community, in this same townhome complex in 1979, sixteen years earlier when I was only twenty. I had even taken college courses at this same college, sixteen years earlier, before I had my first child. The difference between those days so long ago, and the present day was stark. In my twenties, I believed that one day I would have the American dream. Now, nearly two decades later, I was thirty-six years old, had four kids, a worthless husband, no home, and no career—I had achieved the American dream and lost it all.

I recalled that day, five months earlier, when the buyers and I closed on my beautiful home in The Woodlands, Texas. I had handed them the keys and returned to this old apartment complex with Seth and my three children. Unfortunately, we had moved out of our beautiful home a week before the funds were wired. My anger surfaced when I thought about my present situation. I recalled the day that I unpacked my furnishings into the old rental fifty miles away from The Woodlands, Texas. The townhouse we rented was two stories, with three bedrooms--two upstairs, and one down. I had no washer or dryer connections in the place, and the kitchen was apartment size. I had put so much of my creative energy into the decorating of my former, custom, two-story home, and for what reason? Because I was an idiot, and spit in the face of God's Word, I now had nothing! I had married Satan's emissary.

I would not let life's circumstances bring me down another day. I was going to school now in the evenings. I had $50,000 in the bank, and I had bought myself a car in my brother's name. I was working on getting rid of Seth, too. Life was getting better every day. I was taking one careful step at a time.

Only minutes after my last class ended, I had arrived by foot to the front of my townhouse. I headed up the stairs for my front door. It was late at night, and Seth sat on the porch as he had done for the last five months since we had moved into the unit. He was still not working and still playing games—he was forcing me to spend my $50,000 for the lack of us having an income.

"How was school?" He politely asked while he flipped through his business and world news magazine.

"Class was great," I said wearily. "Did you know that the government does not simply print money?" Seth looked up without comment and I continued to explain, "A bank has to give out a certain number of loans, before the bank can qualify to get more money from the Federal Bank."

Seth sucked his cigarette. "I didn't know that."

"Why would you, Seth. You have a degree in Bible!" I smugly quipped.

He ignored my statement. "I'm going to get into the gold and silver market."

"What?" I noted that he was reading *Business Week*. I really could care less what he did with his life, and in a passive-aggressive manner, I had been protesting his presence by not washing his clothes, or cooking for him, or having sex with him anymore. I left every evening for night school with Seth sitting on the couch with his kids watching stupid sitcoms and eating fast food. He was my babysitter and cook, but because Seth did not cook, my children were living on ninety-nine cent burgers and burritos, which he paid for out of his own account. Seth had not made a dime since collecting $12,000 from unsuspecting lawyers, days just before the Texas State Bar forced an injunction against his lawyer referral business. We sold our home as I expected we would, in less than six weeks, after first pricing it way below fair market value. Seth and I did do what we had agreed to do—we split the equity 50/50, and each put $50,000 in an account without the other's name. The family had been living on my portion of equity for the past five months to pay the utilities, food, the children's school clothes and shoes, school supplies, children's karate lessons, Bella's braces, and everything over and above the rent. Seth paid the rent. My fifty thousand dollars was dwindling fast.

I had splurged on a new ring that I now wore on my right hand as a reminder. The extravagant purchase was a cluster of diamonds and sapphires, set in gold; and the day I bought the ring, I slid the ring onto my wedding band finger, in the middle of Macy's, and said, "From this day forward, I shall treat myself good, and love me," meaning, there would be no more Seths or Paolos in my life. I understood that I had to change my thinking to change my life, and the ring was my reminder that as God's faithful follower, God loved me and heard my prayers. God would bless me.

Seth sat on the front porch with a lit cigarette. My class had just ended at 10:00 p.m., and I was ready to fall into bed. He continued, "Yeah, Jean, I went to a meeting today. I answered an ad in the Houston Chronicle. Trading gold and silver on the international market seems like a profitable thing. I then stopped to see a model home."

"You want to buy a home?" I was surprised.

"This home was beautiful...over there off Memorial, just outside of downtown Houston."

"How much was it?"

"About $400,000."

"What the hell, Seth! Why don't you just get a job that has a guaranteed income? Who do you think you are, John Davison Rockefeller? You're going to trade gold and silver on the international market? We're living off our savings—correction, my savings, and you're talking about buying a half-million dollar home in the ritziest section of Houston? Get real!"

Seth laughed.

"I'm tired, Seth. I'm going to bed. I don't want to hear about how you can make a million dollars trading gold and silver on the international market. You better be out there tomorrow looking for a job." I was warning him that my patience had grown thin. We had fought almost every day since we had moved into the townhouse over his lack of ambition, over everything that had happened over the last four years. For a while, I could not figure out why he was immobilized and sitting on the porch, night and day, but then the light came on, and I got that he was forcing me to spend up my $50,000 before he would leave and file for another divorce.

As I had suspected, my former psychotic boyfriend, Paolo, had a warrant for his arrest out of Lubbock, Texas. He had beaten up his former girlfriend with a baseball bat. And when the Montgomery County Sheriff's Department called me, to confirm my suspicions, they had already arrested him. They told me that Paolo would be doing time for a while, and that I should not leave any forwarding address when I moved away. I didn't. How long Paolo would be in jail was a mystery to me, but in my estimation, Paolo would not be getting out for parole violation any time soon. I still had time to get rid of my husband and move on to greener pastures.

Seth stayed up most nights very late and slept until noon every day. He acted as if he was depressed. I got up every morning, got my sons off to pre-kindergarten and first grade, and my daughter off to middle school. I packed lunches every morning, fixed breakfast, and then went for a morning jog after my children left for the bus stop. And when I returned from my hour-long jog, around 10:00 a.m. each morning, I would do my homework for my evening classes. And around noon every day, I would yell at Seth to get his sorry ass out of bed, and go look for work, but all that he did each day was drink coffee and smoke his cigarettes on the front porch of our townhouse. He would spend the day on the porch, until way past midnight, and then sleep until noon. His presence was depressing me, and I did not like the role model he was for his sons.

The next morning, I came down the stairs with my youngest following behind me. Doren was not feeling well on this school day, so I forfeited my morning run and slept late with my four-year old son beside me. I had woken up earlier that morning, and had gotten my older two children off to school, and then went back to sleep with my baby. Seth had dressed in a dark business suit, white shirt, and red tie and had left that early morning to find employment. I assumed that he had taken his wife's warning the night before seriously.

As I descended the spiral staircase, I heard the phone ring beside the couch and picked up with a hello.

"How's Doren?" Seth asked.

"I think he's got an ear infection, again. What are you doing today, Seth?"

"I'm sitting over here at the coffee shop. I just talked to a very sweet waitress who has been serving me coffee and eggs. I've got an idea that's over the top," he said with enthusiasm.

I did not want to hear about any more of Seth's get rich quick schemes and instantly interrupted, "I thought you were out the door this morning to find a job?"

"I'm working on it." Seth said.

"Where have you been this morning?"

"I'm sitting in a restaurant drinking coffee and planning my day."

"Where's that, Seth?" I did not trust Seth. I suspected he plotted to move out, again, and this time, take our two sons. I suspected my husband had been talking to his mother about our dysfunction, and that she encouraged him to move on with his life now that we had sold our marital home. She blamed me for being the sole cause for why her firstborn lost his arbitration regarding the loss of her life savings in the stock market, and I knew she wanted revenge. Seth and I had been fighting every day for months since we sold our home in The Woodlands; and I figured he was currently trying to lease an apartment; and when the timing was right, he would take his two sons and move away to his secret hideaway. He had plotted this very scheme just after he lost his annual $100,000 commission—he had rented an apartment and moved our furnishings into the place, with intention of coming back to our home to get his sons the next day. I foiled his plans then, when I gave the law firm for the New York stock brokerage reason to throw out the arbitration; but now, Seth had $50,000 in his own name, and I had reason to fear him. He would not continue to sit home and babysit for me while I completed my degree.

He had never disclosed to me if he had given any of his

portion of the equity to his mother in return for losing her life savings. He continued to tell me over the phone, "I'm in a restaurant down here on the corner of Red Bluff and Spencer Highway."

I looked at the clock on the wall. It was nearly noon. "You have spent the entire morning drinking coffee?" I felt he was lying about what he was really up to in life. "I'll tell you what, Seth...Just don't come back home. I don't want you here anymore—you are doing nothing to get a job. It's over—I can't forgive you for what you've done to our life. You lie to me—you never change for the better. You're not welcome here—I don't trust you. I don't want you in my life another day. I'm changing the locks today, don't come back home!"

He said nothing in defense, but I knew the wheels were churning in his head. His lack of argument supported my suspicions he already had a place rented, and that he had been sitting there in that coffee shop just waiting for Harper to get out of school before he disappeared with both our sons that day. "I mean it, don't come back home. You don't live here anymore!"

I slammed the phone down and stared down at the floor frightened that he was about to kidnap my children. My breaths were short, and I acknowledged I was right to believe the worst. My stand against the monster felt timely, and until his dark spirit left our home, and I changed the locks, I would have no peace.

My youngest son's voice suddenly broke through my trembling thoughts, and I turned and looked at the short little fellow who stood in front of me with a toy truck in his hand and a sad look on his face. "Mommy, you told Daddy to not come back home?"

He looked as if he was going to cry. Oh, my God! I was horrified he had witnessed the execution. This moment was an imprint, forever in my son's memory. He loved his daddy, and I would now be the reason he lost his daddy! "Oh, Doren, I'm sorry," I said as I squatted down to hug him.

"I don't want Daddy to go, Mommy."

"I know, I know," I said while I anguished over what I had just done. I had shattered my baby's heart. "Let's go get Daddy, okay?"

Doren nodded, and I grabbed my keys and headed for my car.

My sad-looking pre-kindergartner and I drove down the street toward the restaurant Seth had claimed to be sitting in all morning. I wiped the tears of frustration and anger off my face as I thought about what I would say to my husband in front of my child. I would tell Seth that I did not mean any of what I had said to him earlier on the phone. I felt torn between my child's happiness and my own desire for peace. My frustration was too large to make sense.

Since we had moved out of our home in The Woodlands, and into the two-story townhouse, I had only dreamed of the day Seth would finally leave, once and for all. We had fought daily over the issue of Seth not wanting to leave after we got our house proceeds. Our arguments had been often, and always late at night after the children went to sleep; though, I was certain my children had not missed a word of our very loud exchanges. Bella and my sons had admitted they laid upstairs in their bedrooms listening to our horrible fights, and even once, the neighbors had called the cops to calm down the residence. The cops told Seth to leave that night and not come back until the morning. I had wanted Seth to take his things and move out forever; and always, Seth cited he would never leave his kids again. More correctly, Seth would not leave without his sons.

I had protested his existence since his last return home. The problem occurred, for me, when the closing of the real estate transaction happened five days before the money transferred into our accounts. Our buyers took possession of their new home before funding, and forced Seth and I to move out before we had money in the bank to go our separate ways. Seth and I had to borrow money from my father to move into our Deer Park, Texas rental. The bank eventually handed Seth and me separate checks. I got $50,000, my portion of the equity, and Seth got $50,000, his portion of the equity, but we had already moved into a townhouse together when we got the money. I wanted the worm gone. I had never wanted to make the move to Deer Park with Seth, but I had no choice until I could put some big cash into my bank account and buy a car.

I pulled up into the parking lot of the breakfast joint where

Seth had claimed to be all morning. I did not see his maroon convertible LeBaron. Doren and I jumped out of my white four-door Bonneville and headed toward the glass door of the restaurant. I glanced down at my four-year old son who held my hand and watched him grin in anticipation of seeing his father inside. We stepped into the air-conditioned building and scanned the nearly empty room. A waitress walked up to seat us, and I confirmed whether my husband lied to me. "Have you seen a slight, dark hair man in his forties in here this morning drinking coffee, wearing a gray suit?"

"Oh, yes ma'am. He left a few minutes ago."

"Thank you," I said as I looked down at my son and shrugged, "Daddy's not here."

I hoped Seth went back to the apartment to grab his clothes. I would give him time to get out. "Let's see if we can find his car?" I said to my four-year old while praying Seth did not go to Harper's school and try to pull him out.

Doren smiled and shook his head in agreement while we returned to my white Bonneville in the parking lot. "Maybe he went back to our apartment," I said to the child.

I had bought my white Bonneville with the proceeds from the sale of my beautiful Woodland's home and had put the vehicle in my brother's name. No court could ever give Seth use of my car if he lost his convertible for whatever reason. Seth did not know I had bought the car and put the title in my brother's name, but I figured he had already stopped making the payments on his own car and plotted to come after my vehicle—a car I bought with my portion of the equity. I assumed he plotted to use the same tricks as he did before—break me financially, and then go to court and ask for the use of my car because he needed a car to do his job.

I knew that Seth assumed my car was community property, and he was right to make that assumption. And when Seth would try to handicap me, again, and pay his lawyer to go to court on his behalf, and request that the judge give Seth my white Bonneville, so that he could get to work because his finance company repossessed his convertible for nonpayment, his scheme would backfire in his face. I assumed Seth plotted he would go to court, for the last time, when he was certain I had used up all my money supporting our family. I guessed by then, Seth would get a job. He had immobilized me in previous court hearings, but I was all the wiser now. I would never find myself with three kids to feed and no car again!

I drove past Harper's elementary school—I did not see Seth's convertible. I returned home after twenty minutes. My son was sure we had done our best to find Daddy to tell him not to leave. We walked through our townhouse door, and not to my surprise, Seth had returned to the townhouse and had taken a carload of his belongings including a blue leather chair out of the living room, which confirmed he had a place of his own. Upon seeing that my husband had left for the fourth and final time, I called a locksmith. I got off the phone and saw my youngest sitting in the couch looking sad.

I sat down beside Doren and hugged him. I did not know what to say. "Daddy left us three times already, and he was going to leave us again anyway. Whether I told Daddy to leave or not, Doren, he was going to live somewhere else—he already got an apartment, that's where he took our blue chair."

My son angrily objected. "I don't want Daddy to live somewhere else!"

I hugged him and said, "I'm sorry, Doren. Sometimes parents have to separate and not live together. Your daddy and I are too unhappy together. We fight too much; and we are very unhappy. We need a time out. It's better that Daddy has his own apartment. You and Harper will get to go to Daddy's apartment and visit with him. The judge will tell us when you can go see Daddy."

"Okay," he said as if relieved. "When will the judge tell you when I can go see Daddy?"

"When I pay a lawyer," I answered. How could a four-year old understand that his father was a reprobate with no heart? I found relief that I had money in the bank and a car now. I could file the third, and last divorce action, and be rid of the maggot, once and for all. And since Seth and I had moved from Montgomery County, I would have to file my divorce action in a brand new court—The Harris County, Houston, Texas, Family Law Court. I would no longer be dealing with any small town judge in Conroe, Texas, who did not have the sophistication to understand who the bad person was in this marriage. The Conroe Family Law Court served a 200,000 population to include those who lived in The Woodlands, Texas. The Houston Family Law Court in Harris County, Texas, served a population of 3,000,000. I believed a big city mindset would treat me more fairly.

To be concluded in Volume III, THE PRETENSE...The Closing Argument. Released 2014. www.JeanPauley.com

WE'RE GOING TO HOLLYWOOD! Investors Wanted! Contact www.jeanpauley.com if interested in joining the team to produce the film adaptation of this trilogy, or to make a donation toward the creation of this Christian film. Project heads looking for scriptwriters, talent, crew, director, and executive producers to produce an intelligent and spiritually-driven, Hollywood blockbuster. The politically correct need not apply. We tell the truth!

www.ingramcontent.com/pod-product-compliance
Lightning Source LLC
Chambersburg PA
CBHW071932220426
43662CB00009B/887